WELCOME TO SOUTH FLORIDA

From the resorts of Palm Beach to the humblest gingerbread cottage in the Keys, South Florida has something for everyone—romantic retreats for couples, fun activities for families, and hot spots for singles. Whether you're taking a thrilling airboat ride through the Everglades, visiting a world-class art museum, snorkeling off Key Largo, or dancing the night away in a glitzy Miami club, there is plenty to do. Beautiful beaches beckon, so when you're not dining in a great restaurant or playing a round of golf, grab a towel and relax in the tropical warmth.

TOP REASONS TO GO

★ **Miami:** A vibrant, multicultural metropolis that buzzes both day and night

★ **Palm Beach:** Glamorous and sophisticated, the city offers great dining and shopping.

★ **Beaches:** Sceney in South Beach, buzzing in Fort Lauderdale, quieter in the Keys

★ **The Everglades:** The "river of grass" is home to crocodiles, manatees, and panthers.

★ **Fort Lauderdale:** A glittering and revitalized downtown fronts a gorgeous beach.

★ **Key West:** Quirky, fun, and tacky, it's both family-friendly and decidedly not.

Fodor's SOUTH FLORIDA 2015

Publisher: Amanda D'Acierno, *Senior Vice President*

Editorial: Arabella Bowen, *Editor in Chief*; Linda Cabasin, *Editorial Director*

Design: Fabrizio La Rocca, *Vice President, Creative Director*; Tina Malaney, *Associate Art Director*; Chie Ushio, *Senior Designer*; Ann McBride, *Production Designer*

Photography: Melanie Marin, *Associate Director of Photography*; Jessica Parkhill and Jennifer Romains, *Researchers*

Maps: Rebecca Baer, *Senior Map Editor*; Mark Stroud (Moon Street Cartography), David Lindroth, *Cartographers*

Production: Linda Schmidt, *Managing Editor*; Evangelos Vasilakis, *Associate Managing Editor*; Angela L. McLean, *Senior Production Manager*

Sales: Jacqueline Lebow, *Sales Director*

Marketing & Publicity: Heather Dalton, *Marketing Director*; Katherine Punia, *Senior Publicist*

Business & Operations: Susan Livingston, *Vice President, Strategic Business Planning*; Sue Daulton, *Vice President, Operations*

Fodors.com: Megan Bell, *Executive Director, Revenue & Business Development*; Yasmin Marinaro, *Senior Director, Marketing & Partnerships*

Copyright © 2015 by Fodor's Travel, a division of Random House LLC

Writers: Lynne Helm, Jill Martin, Paul Rubio

Editors: Douglas Stallings, Amanda Theunissen

Production Editor: Elyse Rozelle

ISBN 978-0-8041-4277-9

ISSN 1526–2219

All details in this book are based on information supplied to us at press time. Always confirm information when it matters, especially if you're making a detour to visit a specific place. Fodor's expressly disclaims any liability, loss, or risk, personal or otherwise, that is incurred as a consequence of the use of any of the contents of this book.

SPECIAL SALES

This book is available at special discounts for bulk purchases for sales promotions or premiums. For more information, e-mail specialmarkets@randomhouse.com

PRINTED IN THE UNITED STATES OF AMERICA

10 9 8 7 6 5 4 3 2 1

CONTENTS

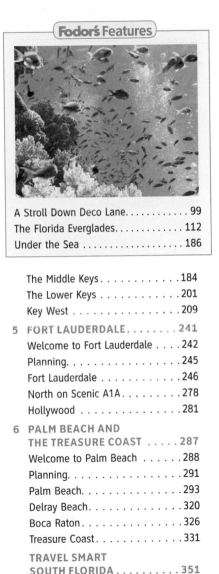

Fodor's Features

CONTENTS

MAPS

ABOUT THIS GUIDE

Fodor's Recommendations
Everything in this guide is worth doing—we don't cover what isn't—but exceptional sights, hotels, and restaurants are recognized with additional accolades. **Fodor'sChoice★** indicates our top recommendations; and **Best Bets** call attention to notable hotels and restaurants in various categories. Care to nominate a new place? Visit Fodors.com/contact-us.

Trip Costs
We list prices wherever possible to help you budget well. Hotel and restaurant price categories from **$** to **$$$$** are noted alongside each recommendation. For hotels, we include the lowest cost of a standard double room in high season. For restaurants, we cite the average price of a main course at dinner or, if dinner isn't served, at lunch. For attractions, we always list adult admission fees; discounts are usually available for children, students, and senior citizens.

Hotels
Our local writers vet every hotel to recommend the best overnights in each price category, from budget to expensive. Unless otherwise specified, you can expect private bath, phone, and TV in your room. *Hotel reviews have been shortened. For full information, visit Fodors.com.*

Top Picks
★ **Fodor's**Choice

Listings
✉ Address
✉ Branch address
☎ Telephone
📠 Fax
🌐 Website
📧 E-mail
🎟 Admission fee
⏲ Open/closed times
[M] Subway
✥ Directions or Map coordinates

Hotels & Restaurants
🏨 Hotel
🛏 Number of rooms
🍽 Meal plans
🍴 Restaurant
✍ Reservations
👔 Dress code
💳 No credit cards
[$] Price

Other
⇨ See also
☞ Take note
🏌 Golf facilities

Restaurants
Unless we state otherwise, restaurants are open for lunch and dinner daily. We mention dress code only when there's a specific requirement and reservations only when they're essential or not accepted. *To make restaurant reservations, visit Fodors.com.*

Credit Cards
The hotels and restaurants in this guide typically accept credit cards. If not, we'll say so.

EXPERIENCE SOUTH FLORIDA

KEEP YOUR BEACH

100J

WHAT'S WHERE

The following numbers refer to chapters.

2 Miami and Miami Beach. Greater Miami is hot—and we're not just talking about the weather. Art Deco buildings and balmy beaches set the scene. Vacations here are as much about lifestyle as locale, so prepare for power shopping, club hopping, and decadent dining.

3 The Everglades. Covering more than 1.5 million acres, the fabled "River of Grass" is the state's greatest natural treasure. Biscayne National Park (95% of which is underwater) runs a close second. It's the largest marine park in the United States.

4 The Florida Keys. This slender necklace of landfalls, strung together by a 113-mile highway, marks the southern edge of the continental United States. It's nirvana for anglers, divers, literature lovers, and Jimmy Buffett wannabes.

5 Fort Lauderdale with Broward County. The town *Where the Boys Are* has grown up. The beaches that first attracted college kids are now complemented by luxe lodgings and upscale entertainment options.

6 Palm Beach with the Treasure Coast. This area scores points for diversity. Palm Beach and environs are famous for their golden sand and glitzy residents, whereas the Treasure Coast has unspoiled natural delights.

GEORGIA

Chattahoochee
Quincy
LAHASSEE
Eastpoint
Apalachicola

Perry

Amelia Island

Jacksonville

Osceola
National
Forest

Lake City

St. Augustine

Gainesville

Ocala
National
Forest

Ocala

Cedar Keys

Daytona Beach

Titusville

Orlando
Walt Disney
World

Kennedy Space Center
Cape Canaveral
Cocoa Beach
Merritt Island

Kissimmee

Tarpon Springs

Clearwater

Tampa

Winter
Haven

Melbourne

Sebastian Inlet
Recreation Area

Vero Beach
Fort Pierce

St. Petersburg

Tampa
Bay

Bradenton
Sarasota

Hutchinson
Island

Venice

Lake
Okeechobee

Singer Island
West Palm
Beach
Palm Beach

Cape Coral
Captiva Island
Sanibel Island

Fort Myers

Big Cypress
National
Preserve

Boca Raton
Fort
Lauderdale

Naples

Miami Beach

Everglades City

Miami
Biscayne
Bay

Florida City

Homestead

Everglades
National
Park

Key Largo

0   50 miles

0   75 kilometers

Cape Sable

Florida Bay

Key West

FLORIDA

KEYS

ATLANTIC OCEAN

Gulf of Mexico

WHEN TO GO

South Florida is a year-round vacation venue, but it divides the calendar into regional tourism seasons. Holidays and school breaks are major factors. However, the clincher is weather, with the milder months being designated as peak periods.

High season starts with the run-up to Christmas and continues through Easter. Snowbirds migrate down then to escape frosty weather back home, and festival-goers flock in because major events are held this time of year to avoid summer's searing heat and high humidity. Winter is also *the* time to visit the Everglades, as temperatures, mosquito activity, and water levels are all lower (making wild-life easier to spot).

Climate

Florida is rightly called the Sunshine State, but it could also be dubbed the "Humid State." From June through September, 90% humidity levels aren't uncommon. Nor are accompanying afternoon thunderstorms; in fact, more than half of the state's rain falls during these months, although these afternoon showers usually pass as quickly as they arrive. Florida's two-sided coastline also makes it a target for tropical storms. Hurricane season officially begins June 1 and ends November 30.

MIAMI EVENTS

HOMERUN HOMETOWN

The eagerly awaited first pitch was thrown at the new **Marlins Park** to start the 2012 baseball season. Catch baseball games and bask in the team's sparkling digs, which made a huge splash with a L.E.E.D.-certified retractable roof, air-conditioning, and glass walls showcasing panoramic views of the Miami skyline. ⊕ *miami.marlins.mlb.com.*

LITTLE HAVANA

Each winter during **Carnaval Miami**, salsa tunes blare and the smell of spicy chorizo fills the air on Calle Ocho, the commercial thoroughfare and heart of Miami's Little Havana. The roaring street festival, which culminates in the world's longest conga line, is the last of 10 events comprising the Latin-spiked Carnaval.

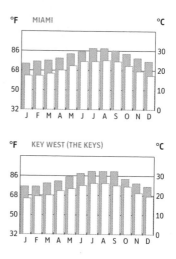

QUINTESSENTIAL SOUTH FLORIDA

Food, Glorious Food

Geography and gastronomy go hand in hand in Florida. Seafood is a staple almost everywhere, yet the way it is prepared changes considerably as you maneuver around the state. In South Florida, menus highlight "Floribbean" cuisine, which marries Floridian, Caribbean, and Latin flavors (think mahimahi with mango salsa), while inland, expect catfish, gator tails, and frogs' legs, all of which are best enjoyed at a Cracker-style fish camp with a side order of hush puppies. A trip to the Miami area is not complete without a taste of Cuban food. The cuisine is heavy, with pork dishes like lechon asado (roast suckling pig) but also arroz con frijoles (the staple side dish of rice and black beans) and arroz con pollo (chicken in sticky yellow rice). Key West is a mecca for lovers of Key lime pie and conch fritters. Stone-crab claws can be savored from October through May.

The Arts

Floridians celebrate the arts year-round. Miami Beach's annual Art Basel festival draws 40,000 art lovers to town in the first week of December. Meanwhile, every April the Palm Beach International Film Festival hosts documentaries, shorts, and feature films. It's easy to catch a bit of bluegrass, country, classical, jazz, blues, or Americana with such festivals as the week-long SunFest in West Palm Beach, or hear some of the nation's best jazz performers at the annual Hollywood Jazz Fest. Miami's ArtCenter South Florida is dedicated to incubating Florida's cultural life with programs for emerging artists of all ages. The oral tradition remains vibrant with the South Florida Storytelling Project, where live readings, storytelling slams, and festivals are free and open to the public through Florida Atlantic University in Boca Raton.

Florida is synonymous with sunshine: every year, more than 80 million visitors revel in it. However, the people who live here—a diverse group that includes Mouseketeers, millionaires, and rocket scientists—know that the state's appeal rests on more than those reliable rays.

1

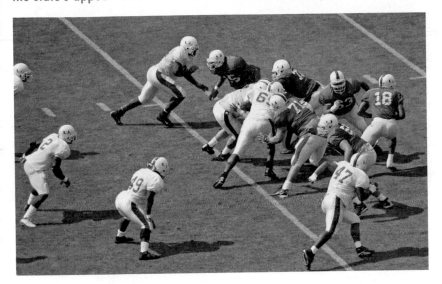

Water, Water Everywhere

Spanish explorer Ponce de León didn't find the Fountain of Youth when he swung through Florida in 1513. But if he'd lingered longer, he could have located 7,700 lakes, 1,700 rivers and creeks, and more than 700 springs. Over the centuries these have attracted American Indians, immigrants, opportunists, and countless outdoor adventurers. Boaters come for inland waterways and a 1,200-mile coast, and anglers are lured by more than 700 species of fish. (Florida claims 4,780 past and present world-record catches, so concocting elaborate "fish tales" may not be necessary.) Snorkelers and divers eager to see what lies beneath can get face time with the marine life that thrives on the world's third-largest coral reef or bone up on maritime history in underwater archaeological preserves (⊕ *www.museumsinthesea. com*). Back on dry land, all those beaches are pretty impressive, too.

Superlative Sports

South Florida is teeming with teams—and residents take the games they play *very* seriously. Baseball fans work themselves into a fever pitch: after all, the state has a pair of Major League franchises (the Miami Marlins christened a new stadium in 2012) and hosts another 13 in spring when the Grapefruit League goes to bat (three alone are in the Palm Beach area). Those who prefer pigskin might cheer for the Miami Dolphins. The state is also home to top-rated college teams, like the Hurricanes. Basketball lovers feel the "Heat" in Miami, especially now that Dwyane Wade, Chris Bosh, and three-time MVP LeBron James are on the roster, and hockey fans stick around to watch the Florida Panthers. The Professional Golfers Association (PGA) is headquartered here as well, and two big annual tennis tournaments serve up fun in Miami and Delray Beach each winter.

SOUTH FLORIDA
TOP ATTRACTIONS

The Florida Keys

(A) Little wonder these 800-plus islands are a prime destination for divers and snorkelers: they boast the world's third-largest reef and aquarium-clear waters that are brimming with sea life. Under the turquoise-blue waters lies a colorful world populated by 60-plus species of coral and more than 500 species of fish, which means you can spot purple sea fans, blue tangs, yellowtail snappers, stoplight parrotfish, and more. Locals debate the premiere place for viewing them, but **John Pennekamp Coral Reef State Park** is high on everyone's list. Underwater excursions organized by park concessionaires let you put your best flipper forward. (⇨ *Chapter 4.*)

South Beach

(B) You can't miss the distinctive forms, vibrant colors, and extravagant flourishes of SoBe's architectural gems. The world's largest concentration of Art Deco edifices

is right here; and the **Art Deco District,** with more than 800 buildings, has earned a spot on the National Register of Historic Places (⇨ *"A Stroll Down Deco Lane"*). The 'hood also has enough "beautiful people" to qualify for the Register of Hippest Places. The glitterati, along with assorted vacationing hedonists, are drawn by trendy shops and a surfeit of celeb-studded clubs. Stellar eateries are the icing—make that the ganache—on South Beach's proverbial cake. (⇨ *Chapter 2.*)

The Everglades

(C) No trip to southern Florida is complete without seeing the Everglades. At its heart is a river—50 miles wide but only 6 inches deep—flowing from Lake Okeechobee into Florida Bay. For an up-close look, speed demons can board an airboat that careens through the marshy waters. Purists, alternately, may placidly canoe or kayak within the boundaries of **Everglades National Park.** Just remember

to keep your hands in the boat. The critters that call this unique ecosystem home (alligators, Florida panthers, and cottonmouth snakes, for starters) can add real bite to your visit! (⇨ *Chapter 3*.)

Palm Beach

(D) If money could talk, you'd hardly be able to hear above the din in Palm Beach. The upper crust started residing there, during the winter months at least, back in the early 1900s. And today it remains a ritzy, glitzy enclave for both old money and the nouveau riche (a coterie led by "The Donald" himself). Simply put, Palm Beach is the sort of place where shopping is a full-time pursuit and people don't just wear Polo—they play it. Oooh and ahhh to your heart's content; then, for more conspicuous consumption, continue south on the aptly named Gold Coast to Boca Raton. (⇨ *Chapter 6*.)

Fort Lauderdale

(E) Mariners should set their compass for Fort Lauderdale (aka the Venice of America), where vessels from around the world moor along some two dozen finger isles between the beach and the mainland. Sailors can cruise Broward County's 300 miles of inland waterways by water taxi and tour boat, or bob around the Atlantic in a chartered yacht. If you're in a buying mood, come during October for the annual Fort Lauderdale International Boat Show. Billed as the world's largest, it has more than a billion dollars' worth of boats in every conceivable size, shape, and price range. (⇨ *Chapter 5*.)

IF YOU LIKE

Animals

The state has more than 1,200 different kinds of critters.

■ **Alligators.** "Gator spotting" in roadside waterways is itself a favorite pastime, but get a good close-up—and even hold a baby one—at **Everglades Gator Park** near Miami (⇨ *Chapter 3*). Farther north, canoeing around the **Arthur R. Marshall Loxahatchee National Wildlife Refuge** or the **Jonathan Dickinson State Park** will almost definitely yield a sighting (⇨ *Chapter 6*).

■ **Birds.** The state draws hundreds of species, from bald eagles and burrowing owls to bubblegum-pink flamingos, and the 2,000-mile **Great Florida Birding Trail** (⊕ *www.floridabirdingtrail.com*) with locations all over the Southeast helps you find them. For a squawkishly good time, feed parrots and budgies at **Lion Country Safari** (⇨ *Chapter 6*).

■ **Manatees.** Florida's official marine mammals are nicknamed sea cows and resemble walruses, and you can scan canals for a telltale glassy "footprint" patch indicating one is swimming below; however, for a surefire viewing, visit the gentle giants who live at the **Miami Seaquarium** (⇨ *Chapter 2*).

■ **Sea Turtles.** Ready for a late-night rendezvous with loggerheads that lumber ashore to lay eggs? Walks are organized throughout South Florida in June and July, but the **Treasure Coast** has a trove of spots (⇨ *Chapter 6*). Elsewhere try the **Museum of Discovery and Science** in Fort Lauderdale (⇨ *Chapter 5*) and **Gumbo Limbo Nature Center** in Boca Raton (⇨ *Chapter 6*).

Beaches

Each of us defines the "perfect" beach differently. But whether you want to swim, surf, lounge, or leer, Florida has one to suit your preference. Best of all, in this skinny state—bounded by the Atlantic *and* Gulf of Mexico—the coast is never more than 60 miles away.

■ **South Beach, Miami.** Over the past 20 years, no American beach has generated as much buzz as the one that hugs Ocean Drive, and it's easy to see why. Fringed with palms, backed by Art Deco architecture, and pulsating with urban energy, South Beach is the place to stretch out or strut (⇨ *Chapter 2*).

■ **Crandon Park Beach, Key Biscayne.** You'll see why this beach is continually ranked among the nation's top ten. After two miles of lagoon-style beach, there's an amusement center and gardens to explore (⇨ *Chapter 2*).

■ **Delray Municipal Beach, Delray Beach.** This super-popular stretch of sand dotted with trademark royal blue umbrellas intersects trendy Atlantic Avenue in the alluring Village by the Sea; delicious nosh and cute boutiques are a short stroll from the waves (⇨ *Chapter 6*).

■ **Matheson Hammock Park Beach, Miami.** Pack a picnic and bring the family to the safe, warm waters of this palm-tree fringed beach. Loll in the balmy breezes as you take in the amazing views or hit up the nature trails, full-service marina, and restaurant built into a historic coral rock building (⇨ *Chapter 2*).

■ **Dry Tortugas National Park, the Florida Keys.** Forget lazily reading a book on these shores. Come here if you're looking for a beach where you can dive in—literally. Set among coral reefs, this cluster of seven islands (accessible only by boat or seaplane) offers outstanding snorkeling and diving (⇨ *Chapter 4*).

Golf

With more than 1,200 courses (and counting), Florida has more greens than any other state in the Union. Palm Beach County alone is home to more than 140 courses. The trend began in 1897, when Florida's first golf course opened in Palm Beach at The Breakers, whose guests included the Rockefellers, Vanderbilts, and Astors. In Southeast Florida there are enough golf courses to allow you to play a new course every week for two years. Even if you're new to the game, you can tee up with a PGA pro for a lesson and soak in the beauty of Florida's tropical flora from one of the country's most exquisitely designed courses. Floridians play golf twelve months out of the year, although the courses are less crowded (and cheaper) between May and October.

■ **Boca Raton Resort & Club.** This scenic course has some of the most exotic terrain, water features, and floral landscapes outside of Hawaii (⇨ *Chapter 6*).

■ **The Breakers, Palm Beach.** The 70-par Ocean Course offers spectacular views of the Atlantic and challenging shots on 140 acres (⇨ *Chapter 6*).

■ **Doral Golf Resort & Spa.** Home of the "Blue Monster": Doral's famous 18th hole has been ranked the best in South Florida. The par-4 hole leaves little room for error with bunkers aplenty and a green that slopes toward water (⇨ *Chapter 2*).

■ **The Club at Emerald Hills.** Test your skills on the course that has been the host site for the U.S. Amateur and U.S. Open Qualifiers since 2003 (⇨ *Chapter 5*).

■ **PGA National Resort & Spa.** Its five championship courses were all done by master designers, plus the pro tour's Honda Classic is held here (⇨ *Chapter 6*).

Scenic Views

Florida is more than its sunsets, from aerial panoramic views to architectural wonders to nature's many surprises. Here are some views we find delightful.

■ **Everglades National Park, from the tower on Shark Valley loop.** This 50-foot observation tower, about 35 miles from downtown Miami, yields a splendid panorama of the wide River of Grass as it sweeps southward toward the Gulf of Mexico. To get to the tower, you can hike or take the tram (⇨ *Chapter 3*).

■ **Ocean Drive in the Art Deco district, Miami Beach.** Feast your eyes on brilliantly restored vintage Art Deco hotels at every turn. The palm-lined beachfront that the hotels are set along hops 24 hours a day. And when you're finished looking at the colorful hotels, you can catch the sea of colorful swimsuits parading by on nearby South Beach (⇨ *"A Stroll Down Deco Lane" in Chapter 2*).

■ **The Mansions of Palm Beach, from South Ocean Boulevard.** Some old, some new. Some ginormous—and the very definition of over-the-top—others a bit more subdued. But all are incredible, particularly the historic Mediterranean-inspired ones built by Addison Mizner and his Gilded Age-peers (⇨ *Chapter 6*).

■ **Sunset scene at Mallory Square, Key West.** Don't be surprised if someone claps for the sunset in Key West. It's that amazing, and those watching can't help but applaud. Along the waterfront the sunset draws street performers, vendors, and thousands of onlookers to the dock at Mallory Square. Fun attractions, like the Key West Aquarium, are nearby (⇨ *Chapter 4*).

GREAT ITINERARIES

2 to 3 Days: Gold Coast and Treasure Coast

The opulent mansions of Palm Beach's Ocean Boulevard give you a glimpse of how the richer half lives. For exclusive boutique shopping, art gallery browsing, and glittery sightseeing, sybarites should wander down "The Avenue" (that's Worth Avenue to non–Palm Beachers). The sporty set will find dozens of places to tee up (hardly surprising given that the PGA is based here), along with tennis courts, polo clubs, and even a croquet center. Those who'd like to see more of the Gold Coast can continue traveling south through Boca Raton to Fort Lauderdale (justifiably known as the "Yachting Capital of the World"). But to balance the highbrow with the low-key, turn northward for a tour of the Treasure Coast. You can also look for the sea turtles that lay their own little treasures in the sands from May through October.

2 to 3 Days: Miami Area

Greater Miami lays claim to the country's most celebrated strand—South Beach—and lingering on it tops most tourist itineraries. (The Ocean Drive section, lined with edgy clubs, boutiques, and eateries, is where the see-and-be-seen crowd gathers.) Once you've checked out the candy-colored Art Deco architecture, park yourself to ogle the parade of stylish people, or join them by browsing Lincoln Road Mall, and admire its latest addition, the gleaming Frank Gehry–designed New World Symphony. Later, merengue over to Calle Ocho, the epicenter of Miami's Cuban community. Elsewhere in the area, Coconut Grove, Coral Gables, and the Miami Design District (an 18-block area crammed with showrooms and galleries) also warrant a visit. Miami is a convenient base for eco-excursions, too. You can take

TIPS

Now that one-way airfares are commonplace, vacationers visiting multiple destinations can fly in to and out of different airports. Rent a car in between, picking it up at your point of arrival and leaving it at your point of departure. If you do these itineraries as an entire vacation, your best bet is to fly in to and out of Miami and rent a car from there.

a day trip to the Everglades or get a spectacular view of the reefs from a glass-bottom boat in Biscayne National Park.

2 to 3 Days: Florida Keys

Some dream of "sailing away to Key Largo," others of "wasting away again in Margaritaville." In any case, almost everybody equates the Florida Keys with relaxation. And they live up to their reputation, thanks to offbeat attractions and that fabled come-as-you-are, do-as-you-please vibe. Key West, alternately known as the Conch Republic, is a good place to get initiated. The Old Town has a funky, laid-back feel. So take a leisurely walk; pay your regards to "Papa" (Hemingway, that is); then rent a moped to tour the rest of the island. Clear waters and abundant marine life make underwater activities another must. After scoping out the parrotfish, you can always head back into town and join local "Parrotheads" in a Jimmy Buffett sing-along. When retracing your route to the mainland, plan a last pit stop at Bahia Honda State Park (it has ranger-led activities plus the Keys' best beach) or John Pennekamp Coral Reef State Park, which offers unparalleled snorkeling and scuba-diving opportunities for beginners and veterans alike.

MIAMI AND
MIAMI BEACH

WELCOME TO MIAMI AND MIAMI BEACH

TOP REASONS TO GO

★ **The beach:** Miami Beach has been rated as one of the 10 best in the world. White sand, warm water, and bronzed bodies everywhere provide just the right mix of relaxation and people-watching.

★ **Dining delights:** Miami's eclectic residents have transformed the city into a museum of epicurean wonders, ranging from Cuban and Argentine fare to fusion haute cuisine.

★ **Wee-hour parties:** A 24-hour liquor license means clubs stay open until 5 am, and after-parties go until noon the following day.

★ **Picture-perfect people:** Miami is a watering hole for the vain and beautiful of South America, Europe, and the Northeast. Watch them—or join them—as they strut their stuff and flaunt their tans on the white beds of renowned art-deco hotels.

★ **Art deco district:** Iconic pastels and neon lights accessorize the architecture that first put South Beach on the map in the 1930s.

1 Downtown. Weave through the glass-and-steel labyrinth of new condo construction to catch a game or a new exhibition.

2 Coconut Grove. Catch dinner and a movie, listen to live music, or cruise the bohemian shops.

3 Coral Gables. Dine and shop on family-friendly Miracle Mile, and take a driving tour of the surrounding neighborhoods.

4 Key Biscayne. Explore the pristine parks and stretches of award-winning beaches by boat, kayak, or foot.

5 Wynwood. Eat, shop, and gawk your way through this trendy, creative neighborhood north of downtown.

6 Midtown. Experience yuppie life in this residential enclave chock full of fabulous restaurants and lounges.

7 Design District. Browse the design showrooms and haute boutiques before dining at Miami's trendiest restaurants.

8 Little Haiti. Practice your Creole and sample Haitian food in this interesting ethnic neighborhood.

2

GETTING ORIENTED

Long considered the gateway to Latin America, Miami is as close to Cuba and the Caribbean as you can get within the United States. The 36-square-mile city is at the southern tip of the Florida peninsula, bordered on the east by Biscayne Bay. Over the bay lies a series of barrier islands, the largest being a thin 18-square-mile strip called Miami Beach. To the east of Miami Beach is the Atlantic Ocean. To the south are the Florida Keys.

9 **Little Havana.** Sip Cuban coffee, roll cigars, and play dominoes in the heart and soul of Cuba's exile community.

10 **South Beach.** People-watch from sidewalk cafés, admire art deco, and party 'til dawn at the nation's hottest clubs.

11 **Mid-Beach.** Experience the booming restaurant scene and trendy hotels just beyond South Beach.

12 **Fisher and Belle Isle.** Be near the pulse of Miami Beach but a man-made island away.

13 **North Beach and Aventura.** Shop and relax in the quieter northern end of Miami Beach.

CUBAN FOOD

If the tropical vibe has you hankering for Cuban food, you've come to the right place. Miami is the top spot in the country to enjoy authentic Cuban cooking.

The flavors and preparations of Cuban cuisine are influenced by the island nation's natural bounty (yuca, sugarcane, guava), as well as its rich immigrant history, from near (Caribbean countries) and far (Spanish and African traditions). Chefs in Miami tend to stick with the classic versions of beloved dishes, though you'll find some variation from restaurant to restaurant, as recipes have often been passed down through generations of home cooks. For a true Cuban experience, try either the popular **Versailles** (⊠ *3555 S.W. 8th St.* ☎ *305/444–0240* ⊕ *www. versaillesrestaurant.com*) or classic **La Carreta** (⊠ *3632 S.W. 8th St.* ☎ *305/444–7501*) in Little Havana, appealing to families seeking a home-cooked, Cuban-style meal. For a modern interpretation of Cuban eats, head to Coral Gable's **Havana Harry's** (⊠ *4612 S. Le Jeune Rd.* ☎ *305/661–2622*). South Beach eatery **Puerto Sagua Restaurant** (⊠ *700 Collins Ave.* ☎ *305/673–1115*) is the beach's favorite Cuban hole-in-the-wall, open daily from 7 am to 2 am.

THE CUBAN SANDWICH

A great *cubano* (Cuban sandwich) requires pillowy Cuban bread layered with ham, garlic-citrus-marinated slow-roasted pork, Swiss cheese, and pickles (plus salami in Tampa, lettuce and tomatoes in Key West), with butter and/or mustard. The sandwich is grilled in a sandwich press until the cheese melts and all the elements are fused together. Try one at **Enriqueta's Sandwich Shop** (⊠ *2830 N.E. 2nd Ave.* ☎ *305/573–4681* ⊙ *Weekdays 6 am–4 pm, Sat. 6 am–2 pm*) in Wynwood, or **Exquisito Restaurant** (⊠ *1510 S.W. 8th St.* ☎ *305/643–0227* ⊙ *Daily 7 am–midnight*) in Little Havana.

KEY CUBAN DISHES

ARROZ CON POLLO
This chicken-and-rice dish is Cuban comfort food. Found throughout Latin America, the Cuban version is typically seasoned with garlic, paprika, and onions, then colored golden or reddish with saffron or *achiote* (a seed paste), and enlivened with a sizable splash of beer near the end of cooking. Green peas and sliced, roasted red peppers are standard toppings.

BISTEC DE PALOMILLA
This thinly sliced sirloin steak is marinated in lime juice and garlic and fried with onions. The steak is often served with *chimichurri* sauce, an olive oil, garlic, and cilantro sauce that sometimes comes with bread (slather bread with butter and dab on the chimichurri). Also try *ropa vieja,* a slow-cooked, shredded flank steak in a garlic-tomato sauce.

DESSERTS
Treat yourself to a slice of *tres leches* cake. The "three milks" come from the sweetened condensed milk, evaporated milk, and heavy cream that are poured over the cake until it's an utterly irresistible gooey mess. Also, don't miss the *pastelitos,* Cuban fruit-filled turnovers. Traditional flavors include plain guava, guava with cream cheese, and cream cheese with coconut. Yum!

DRINKS
Sip *guarapo* (gwa-RA-poh), a fresh sugarcane juice that isn't really as sweet as you might think, or grab a straw and enjoy a frothy *batido* (bah-TEE-doe), a Cuban-style milk shake made with tropical fruits like mango, *piña* (pineapple), or *mamey* (mah-MAY, a tropical fruit with a melon-cherry taste). For a real twist, try the *batido de trigo*—a wheat shake that will remind you of sugarglazed breakfast cereal.

FRITAS
If you're in the mood for an inexpensive, casual Cuban meal, have a *frita*—a hamburger with distinctive Cuban flair. It's made with ground beef that's mixed with ground or finely chopped chorizo, spiced with pepper, paprika, and salt, topped with sautéed onions and shoestring potato fries, and then served on a bun slathered with a special tomato-based ketchuplike sauce.

LECHON ASADO
Fresh ham or an entire suckling pig marinated in *mojo criollo* (parsley, garlic, sour orange, and olive oil) is roasted until fork tender and served with white rice, black beans, and *tostones* (fried plantains) or *yuca* (pronounced YU-kah), a starchy tuber with a mild nut taste that's often sliced into fat sticks and deep-fried like fries.

By Paul Rubio   Three quarters of a century after the art deco movement, Miami remains one of the world's trendiest and flashiest hot spots. Luckily for visitors, South Beach is no longer the only place to stand and pose in Miami. North of downtown Miami's megamakeover, the growing Wynwood and Design districts—along with nearby Midtown—are home to Miami's hipster and fashionista scenes, and the South beach "scene" continues to extend both north and west, with the addition of new venues north of 20th Street, south of 5th Street and along the bay on West Avenue. The reopening of the mammoth Fontainebleau and its enclave of nightclubs and restaurants along Mid-Beach paved the way for a mid-beach renaissance, luring in other globally renowned resorts, lounges, and restaurants into the neighborhood, such as the Soho Beach House and Nobu restaurant.

Visit Miami today and it's hard to believe that 100 years ago it was a mosquito-infested swampland, with an Indian trading post on the Miami River. Then hotel builder Henry Flagler brought his railroad to the outpost known as Fort Dallas. Other visionaries—Carl Fisher, Julia Tuttle, William Brickell, and John Sewell, among others—set out to tame the unruly wilderness. Hotels were erected, bridges were built, the port was dredged, and electricity arrived. The narrow strip of mangrove coast was transformed into Miami Beach—and the tourists started to come. They haven't stopped since!

Greater Miami is many destinations in one. At its best it offers an unparalleled multicultural experience: melodic Latin and Caribbean tongues, international cuisines and cultural events, and an unmistakable joie de vivre—all against a beautiful beach backdrop. In Little Havana the air is tantalizing with the perfume of strong Cuban coffee. In Coconut Grove, Caribbean steel drums ring out during the Miami/Bahamas Goombay Festival. Anytime in colorful Miami Beach, restless crowds wait for entry to the hottest new clubs.

Many visitors don't know that Miami and Miami Beach are really separate cities. Miami, on the mainland, is South Florida's commercial hub. Miami Beach, on 17 islands in Biscayne Bay, is sometimes considered America's Riviera, luring refugees from winter with its warm sunshine; sandy beaches; graceful, shady palms; and tireless nightlife. The natives know well that there's more to Greater Miami than the bustle of South Beach and its Art Deco District. In addition to well-known places such as Ocean Drive and Lincoln Road, the less reported spots—like the burgeoning Design District in Miami, the historic buildings of Coral Gables, and the secluded beaches of Key Biscayne—are great insider destinations.

PLANNING

WHEN TO GO

Miami and Miami Beach are year-round destinations. Most visitors come November through April, when the weather is close to perfect; hotels, restaurants, and attractions are busiest; and each weekend holds a festival or event. The "Season" kicks off in December with Art Basel Miami Beach, and hotel rates don't come down until after the college kids have left after spring break in late March.

It's hot and steamy May through September, but nighttime temperatures are usually pleasant. Also, summer is a good time for the budget traveler. Many hotels lower their rates considerably, and many restaurants offer discounts—especially during **Miami Spice** in August and September, when a slew of top restaurants offer special tasting menus at a steep discount. (Check ⊕ *www.iLoveMiamiSpice.com* for details.)

GETTING HERE AND AROUND

Greater Miami resembles Los Angeles in its urban sprawl and traffic. You'll need a car to visit many attractions and points of interest. If possible, avoid driving during the rush hours of 7–9 am and 5–7 pm—the hour just after and right before the peak times also can be slow going. During rainy weather, be especially cautious of flooding in South Beach and Key Biscayne.

AIR TRAVEL

Miami is serviced by Miami International Airport (MIA), 8 miles northwest of downtown, and Fort Lauderdale–Hollywood International Airport (FLL), 26 miles northeast. Many discount carriers, like Spirit Airlines, Southwest Airlines, and JetBlue, fly into FLL, making it a smart bargain if you're renting a car. Otherwise, look for flights to MIA on American Airlines, Delta, and United. MIA recently underwent an extensive face-lift, improving facilities, common spaces, and the overall aesthetic of the airport.

CAR TRAVEL

Interstate 95 is the major expressway connecting South Florida with points north; State Road 836 is the major east–west expressway and connects to Florida's Turnpike, State Road 826, and Interstate 95. Seven causeways link Miami and Miami Beach, with Interstate 195 and Interstate 395 offering the most convenient routes; the Rickenbacker Causeway extends to Key Biscayne from Interstate 95 and U.S. 1. The high-speed lanes on the left-hand side of I–95 require a prepaid toll gadget called a "Sunpass," available in most drug and grocery stores. It is sometimes included with your rental car (and you are billed for the tolls later). Note, the toll on to Key Biscayne is cash only. Also, remember U.S. 1 (aka Biscayne Boulevard)—you'll hear it often in directions. It starts in Key West, hugs South Florida's coastline, and heads north straight through to Maine.

PUBLIC TRANSPORTATION

Some sights are accessible via the public transportation system, run by the **Metro-Dade Transit Agency,** which maintains 740 Metrobuses on 90 routes; the 23-mile Metrorail elevated rapid-transit system; and the Metromover, an elevated light-rail system. Those planning to use public transportation should get an EASY Card or EASY Ticket available at any Metrorail station and most supermarkets. Fares are discounted, and transfer fees are nominal. The bus stops for the **Metrobus** are marked with blue-and-green signs with a bus logo and route information. The fare is $2.25 (exact change only if paying cash). Cash-paying customers must pay for another ride if transferring. Some express routes carry a surcharge of $0.50. Elevated **Metrorail** trains run from downtown Miami north to Hialeah and south along U.S. 1 to Dadeland. The system operates daily 5 am–midnight. The fare is $2.25; $0.60 transfers to Metrobus are available only for EASY Card and EASY Ticket holders. **Metromover** resembles an airport shuttle and runs on two loops around downtown Miami, linking major hotels, office buildings, and shopping areas. The system spans 4 miles, including the 1-mile Omni Loop and the 1-mile Brickell Loop. There is no fee to ride.

Tri-Rail, South Florida's commuter-train system, stops at 18 stations north of MIA along a 71-mile route. There's a Metrorail transfer station two stops north of MIA. Prices range from $2.50 to $6.90 for a one-way ticket.

Contacts Metro-Dade Transit Agency ☎ 305/891–3131, 3-1-1 ⊕ www. miamidade.gov/transit. **Tri-Rail** ☎ 800/874–7245 ⊕ www.tri-rail.com.

TAXI TRAVEL

Except in South Beach, it's difficult to hail a cab on the street; in most cases you'll need to call a cab company or have a hotel doorman hail one for you. Fares run $2.50 for the first ⅙ of a mile and $2.40 every mile thereafter. Flat-rate fares are also available from the airport to a variety of zones (including Miami Beach) for $32. Expect a $2 surcharge on rides leaving from Miami International Airport or the Port of Miami. For those heading from MIA to downtown, the 15-minute, 7-mile trip costs around $22. Many cabs now accept credit cards; inquire before you get in the car.

Taxi Companies Central Cab ☎ *305/532–5555* ⊕ *www.centralcab.com.*
Tropical Taxi ☎ *305/945–1025* ☞ *Serving Miami Beach only.* **Yellow Cab**
☎ *305/888–8888.*

TRAIN TRAVEL

Amtrak provides service from 500 destinations to the Greater Miami
area. The trains make several stops along the way; north–south service
stops in the major Florida cities of Jacksonville, Orlando, Tampa, West
Palm Beach, and Fort Lauderdale. Note that these stops are often in less
than ideal locations for immediate city access. For extended trips, or if
you want to visit other areas in Florida, you can come via Auto Train
(where you bring your car along) from Lorton, Virginia, just outside
Washington, D.C., to Sanford, Florida, just outside Orlando. From
there it's less than a four-hour drive to Miami. Fares vary, but expect
to pay between around $275 and $350 for a basic sleeper seat and car
passage each way. ■ TIP➜ You must be traveling with an automobile to
purchase a ticket on the Auto Train.

VISITOR INFORMATION

For additional information about Miami and Miami Beach, contact the
city's visitor bureaus. You can also pick up a free Miami Beach INcard
at the Miami Beach Visitors Center 10–4seven days a week, entitling
you to discounts and offers at restaurants, shops, galleries, and more.

Contacts Coconut Grove Chamber of Commerce ✉ *2820 McFarlane
Rd., Coconut Grove* ☎ *305/444–7270* ⊕ *www.coconutgrovechamber.com.*
Coral Gables Chamber of Commerce ✉ *224 Catalonia Ave., Coral Gables*
☎ *305/446–1657* ⊕ *www.coralgableschamber.org.* **Greater Miami Convention & Visitors Bureau** ✉ *701 Brickell Ave., Ste. 2700, Miami* ☎ *305/539–3000,
800/933–8448 in U.S.* ⊕ *www.miamiandbeaches.com.* **Key Biscayne Chamber
of Commerce and Visitors Center** ✉ *88 W. McIntyre St., Ste. 100, Key Biscayne*
☎ *305/361–5207* ⊕ *www.keybiscaynechamber.org.* **Visit Miami Beach—Visitors
Center** ✉ *1901 Convention Center Dr., Hall C* ☎ *786/276–2763, 305/672–1270
for Miami Beach Tourist Hotline* ⊕ *www.miamibeachguest.com.*

EXPLORING MIAMI AND MIAMI BEACH

If you'd arrived here 50 years ago with a guidebook in hand, chances
are you'd be thumbing through listings looking for alligator wrestlers
and you-pick strawberry fields or citrus groves. Things have changed.
While Disney sidetracked families in Orlando, Miami was developing a
unique culture and attitude that's equal parts beach town/big business,
Latino/Caribbean meets European/American—all of which fuels a great
art and food scene, as well as exuberant nightlife and myriad festivals.

To find your way around Greater Miami, learn how the numbering system works (or better yet, use a GPS). Miami is laid out on a grid with
four quadrants—northeast, northwest, southeast, and southwest—that
meet at Miami Avenue and Flagler Street. Miami Avenue separates east
from west, and Flagler Street separates north from south. Avenues and
courts run north–south; streets, terraces, and ways run east–west. Roads
run diagonally, northwest–southeast. But other districts—Miami Beach,
Coral Gables, and Hialeah—may or may not follow this system, and

along the curve of Biscayne Bay the symmetrical grid shifts diagonally. It's best to buy a detailed map, stick to the major roads, and ask directions early and often. However, make sure you're in a safe neighborhood or public place when you seek guidance; cabdrivers and cops are good resources.

DOWNTOWN

Downtown Miami dazzles from a distance. The skyline is fluid, thanks to the sheer number of sparkling glass high-rises between Biscayne Boulevard and the Miami River. Business is the key to downtown Miami's daytime bustle. However, the influx of massive, modern, and affordable condos has lured a young and trendy demographic to the areas in and around downtown, giving Miami much more of a "city" feel come nightfall. In fact, downtown has become a nighttime hot spot in recent years, inciting a cultural revolution that has fostered burgeoning areas north in Wynwood, Midtown, and the Design District, and south along Brickell Avenue. The pedestrian streets here tend to be very restaurant-centric, complemented by lounges and nightclubs.

The free, 23-mile, elevated commuter system known as the Metromover runs inner and outer loops through downtown and to nearby neighborhoods south and north. Many attractions are conveniently located within a few blocks of a station.

TOP ATTRACTIONS

Adrienne Arsht Center. Culture vultures and other artsy types are drawn to this stunning performing arts center, which includes the 2,400-seat Ziff Ballet Opera House, the 2,200-seat Knight Concet Hall, the Carnival Studio black-box theater, and an outdoor Plaza for the Arts. Throughout the year, you'll find top-notch performances by local and national touring groups, including Broadway hits like *Wicked* and *Jersey Boys,* intimate music concerts, and showstopping ballet. Think of it as a sliver of savoir faire to temper Miami's often over-the-top vibe. The massive development was designed by architect César Pelli, and stands as the largest American performing-arts center constructed since the 1980s. Complimentary one-hour tours of the Arsht Center, highlighting the architecture and its public art, are offered every Saturday and Monday at noon. Restaurateur Barton G. presents his pretheater dining extravaganza at the Arsht Center's restaurant, **Prelude by Barton G.,** with a 2-course, $29 prix-fixe menu (☎ *305/357–7900* ⊕ *www.preludebybartong.com*). ✉ *1300 Biscayne Blvd., at N.E. 13th St., Downtown* ☎ *305/949–6722 for box office* ⊕ *www.arshtcenter.org.*

Freedom Tower. In the 1960s this ornate Spanish-baroque structure was the Cuban Refugee Center, processing more than 500,000 Cubans who entered the United States after fleeing Fidel Castro's regime. Built in 1925 for the *Miami Daily News,* it was inspired by the Giralda, an 800-year-old bell tower in Seville, Spain. Preservationists were pleased to see the tower's exterior restored in 1988. Today, it is owned by Miami Dade College (MDC), functioning as a cultural and educational center; it's also home to the MDC Musuem of Art + Design, which showcases a broad collection of contemporary Latin art as well works in the

2

Downtown
Miami

KEY

Ⓜ *Metromover Station*

– – *Metromover*

0 ——————— 1/4 mile

0 ——————— 1/4 km

genres of minimalism and pop art. ■ TIP➔ Admission is free to both the tower and museum. ✉ *600 Biscayne Blvd., at N.E. 6th St., Downtown* ☎ *305/237–7700* ⊕ *www.mdcmoad.org* ⊙ *Wed.–Sun. noon–5.*

HistoryMiami. Discover a treasure trove of colorful stories about the region's history at HistoryMiami, formerly known as the Historical Museum of Southern Florida. Exhibits celebrate the city's multicultural heritage, including an old Miami streetcar and unique items chronicling the migration of Cubans to Miami. ✉ *101 W. Flagler St., between N.W. 1st and 2nd Aves., Downtown* ☎ *305/375–1492* ⊕ *www.historymiami. org* ⊠ *$8* ⊙ *Mon.–Sat. 10–5, Sun. noon–5.*

Fodor's Choice
★

Pérez Art Museum Miami (PAMM). Opened in December 2013, the Pérez Art Museum Miami, known locally as PAMM, shines as the city's first true world-class museum. This über-high-design architectural masterpiece on Biscayne Bay is a sight to behold. Double-story, cylindrical hanging gardens sway from high atop the museum, anchored to stylish wood trusses that help create this gotta-see-it-to-believe-it indoor/outdoor museum. Large sculptures, Asian-inspired gardens, sexy white benches, and steel frames envelop the property. Inside, the 120,000-square-foot space houses multicultural art from the 20th and 21st centuries, some of which were previously on display at the Miami Art Museum (note: downtown's Miami Art Museum no longer exists and the collection has now been incorporated into PAMM). Most of the interior space is devoted to temporary exhibitions, which have included the likes of *Ai Weiwei: According to What?* and *Edouard Duval-Carrié: Imagined Landscapes.* Even if you aren't a "museum type" per se, come check out this magnum opus over lunch at the Verde, the museum's sensational waterfront restaurant and bar. ✉ *1103 Biscayne Blvd., Downtown* ☎ *305/375–3000* ⊕ *www.pamm.org* ⊠ *$12* ⊙ *Tues.–Wed. and Fri.–Sun. 10–6, Thurs. 10–9.*

WORTH NOTING

Bayfront Park. This pedestrian-friendly waterfront park sits on a 32-acre site smack in the heart of downtown Miami on Biscayne Bay; there's a small walking trail and three major event spaces: Bicentennial Park, Tina Hills Pavilion, and Klipsch Amphitheater at Bayfront Park. American sculptor Isamu Noguchi helped redesign the park in the late 1980s, gracing the site with several works, including the white *Challenger* Memorial, commemorating the space shuttle that exploded in 1986. If you want to live like a local, join in the free yoga on the bayfront Monday and Wednesday (at 6 pm) or Saturday (at 9 am). At the park's north end, you'll reach the colossal Bayside Marketplace entertainment, dining, and retail complex, which is particularly popular with cruise passengers as well as visitors from South America. ✉ *301 N. Biscayne Blvd., Downtown* ☎ *305/358–7550* ⊕ *www.bayfrontparkmiami.com.*

FAMILY
Jungle Island. Originally located deep in south Miami and known as Parrot Jungle, South Florida's original tourist attraction opened in 1936 and moved closer to Miami Beach in 2003. Located on Watson Island, a small stretch of land off of I–395 between Downtown Miami and South Beach, Jungle Island is far more than a park where cockatoos ride tricycles; this interactive zoological park is home to just about every

unusual and endangered species you would want to see, including a rare albino alligator, a liger (lion and tiger mix), and myriad exotic birds. The most intriguing offerings are the VIP animal tours, including the Lemur Experience ($79.95), in which the highly social primates make themselves at home on your lap or shoulders. Jungle Island offers complimentary shuttle service to most Downtown Miami and South Beach hotels. ⊠ *Watson Island, 1111 Parrot Jungle Trail, off MacArthur Causeway (I–395), Downtown* ☎ *305/400–7000* ⊕ *www.jungleisland. com* 🖃 *$34.95, plus $8 parking* ☉ *Weekdays 10–5, weekends 10–6.*

FAMILY **Miami Children's Museum.** This Arquitectonica-designed museum, both imaginative and geometric in appearance, is directly across the MacArthur Causeway from Jungle Island. Twelve galleries house hundreds of interactive, bilingual exhibits. Children can scan plastic groceries in the supermarket, scramble through a giant sand castle, climb a rock wall, learn about the Everglades, and combine rhythms in the world-music studio. ⊠ *Watson Island, 980 MacArthur Causeway, off I–395, Downtown* ☎ *305/373–5437* ⊕ *www.miamichildrensmuseum.org* 🖃 *$16, parking $1/hr* ☉ *Daily 10–6.*

COCONUT GROVE

A former haven for writers and artists, Coconut Grove has never quite outgrown its image as a small village. You can still feel the Bohemian roots of this artsy neighborhood, but it has grown increasingly mainstream and residential over the past 20 years. Posh estates mingle with rustic cottages, modest frame homes, and stark modern dwellings, often on the same block. If you're into horticulture, you'll be impressed by the Garden of Eden–like foliage that seems to grow everywhere without care. In truth, residents are determined to keep up the Grove's village-in-a-jungle look, so they lavish attention on exotic plantings even as they battle to protect any remaining native vegetation.

The center of the Grove still attracts its fair share of locals and tourists who enjoy perusing the small boutiques, sidewalk cafés, and cute galleries that remind us of the old Grove. Activities here are family-friendly with easy access to bayside parks, museums, and gardens.

TOP ATTRACTIONS

FAMILY **Patricia and Phillip Frost Museum of Science.** In mid-2015 the Patricia and Phillip Frost Museum of Science will relocate to its much larger, hyper-modern new home in downtown's Museum Park. Until then, this small fun museum in Coconut Grove is chock-full of hands-on sound, gravity, and electricity displays for children and adults alike. For animal lovers, its wildlife center houses native Florida snakes, turtles, tortoises, and birds of prey. Check the museum's schedule for traveling exhibits that appear throughout the year. If you're here the first Friday of the month—called Fabulous First Fridays—stick around for the free star show at 7 pm and then gaze at the planets through two powerful Meade telescopes at the Weintraub Observatory. Also enjoy a laser-light rock-and-roll show nightly at 8, 9, 10, or 11 to the tunes of the Doors, Bob Marley, the Beatles, or Pink Floyd to name a few. ⊠ *3280 S. Miami*

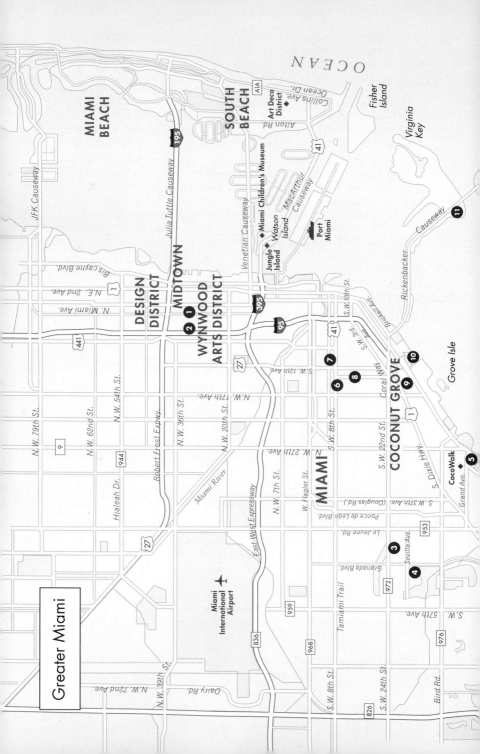

Greater Miami

MIAMI BEACH

SOUTH BEACH

Art Deco District

Collins Ave.
Ocean Dr.

A1A

OCEAN

Fisher Island

Virginia Key

Grove Isle

MacArthur Causeway

Miami Children's Museum

Watson Island

Jungle Island

Port Miami

Venetian Causeway

Rickenbacker Causeway

11

Julia Tuttle Causeway

195

JFK Causeway

Biscayne Blvd.

N.E. 2nd Ave.

N. Miami Ave.

1

441

DESIGN DISTRICT

MIDTOWN

WYNWOOD ARTS DISTRICT

395

95

1

2

27

41

S.W. 13th St.

Brickell Ave.

N.W. 54th St.

N.W. 62nd St.

Robert Frost Expwy.

N.W. 36th St.

N.W. 17th Ave.

N.W. 20th St.

S.W. 12th Ave.

S.W. 3rd

S. Miami Ave.

Coral Way

COCONUT GROVE

7

6

8

9

10

1

MIAMI

N.W. 27th Ave.

N.W. 7th St.

W. Flagler St.

Miami River

East-West Expressway

836

Miami International Airport

N.W. 39th St.

N.W. 22nd Ave.

Dairy Rd.

Hialeah Dr.

N.W. 79th St.

9

944

27

959

968

Ponce de León Blvd.

S.W. 37th Ave. (Douglas Rd.)

Le Jeune Rd.

Granada Blvd.

Tamiami Trail

S.W. 8th St.

S.W. 24th St.

826

S.W. 57th Ave.

976

Bird Rd.

Sevilla Ave.

S. Dixie Hwy.

Grand Ave.

CocoWalk

5

3

4

953

972

S. Le Jeune Rd.

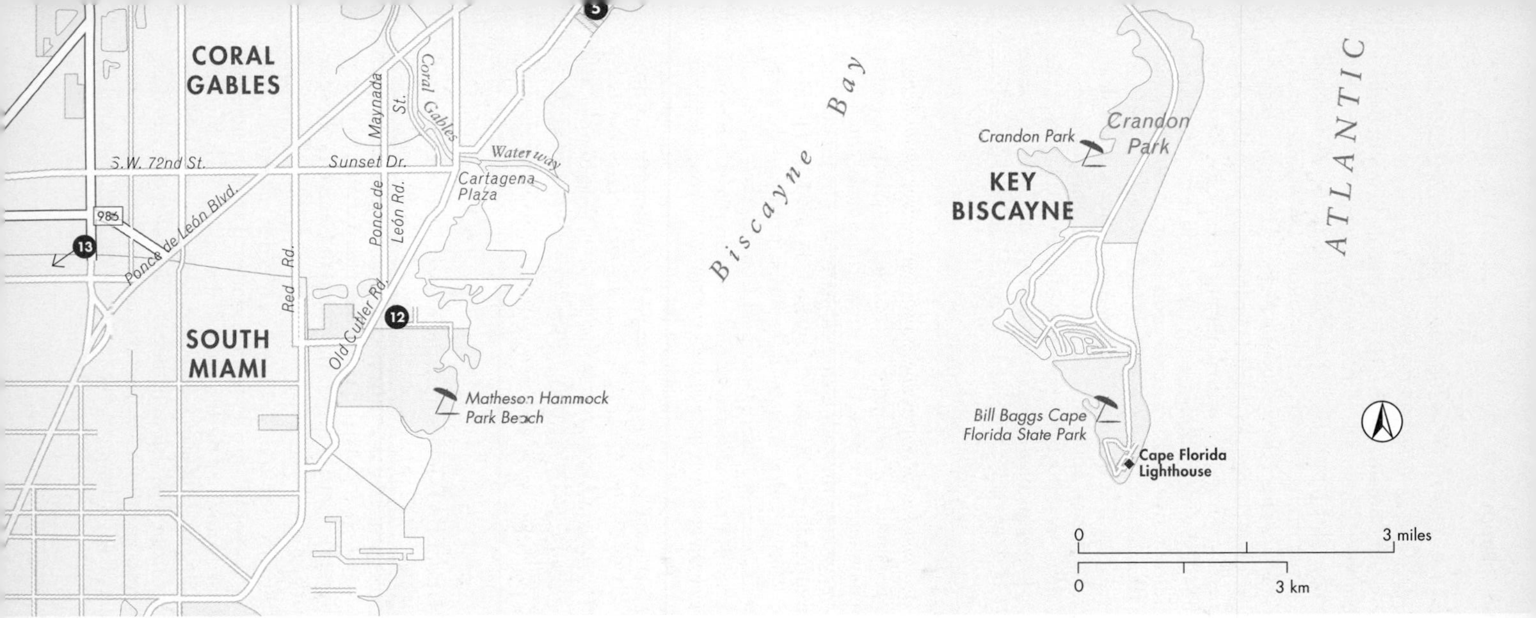
CORAL GABLES
SOUTH MIAMI
KEY BISCAYNE
S.W. 72nd St.
Sunset Dr.
Ponce de León Blvd.
Red Rd.
Maynada St.
Ponce de León Rd.
Old Cutler Rd.
Coral Gables Waterway
Cartagena Plaza
985
Matheson Hammock Park Beach
Biscayne Bay
Crandon Park
Bill Baggs Cape Florida State Park
Cape Florida Lighthouse
ATLANTIC
0
3 miles
3 km

Barnacle Historic State Park 5
Biltmore Hotel 4
Cuban Memorial Boulevard 8
Domino Park 6
El Titan de Bronze 7
Fairchild Tropical Botanic Garden 12
Margulies Collection at the Warehouse 2
Patricia and Phillip Frost Museum of Science 9
Miami Seaquarium 11
Rubell Family Collection 1
Venetian Pool 3
Vizcaya Museum and Gardens 10
Zoo Miami 13

Ave., Coconut Grove ☎ *305/646–4200* ⊕ *www.miamisci.org* ✉ *$14.95* ☉ *Museum daily 10–6; planetarium hrs vary.*

Fodor'sChoice **Vizcaya Museum and Gardens.** Of the 10,000 people living in Miami
★ between 1912 and 1916, about 1,000 of them were gainfully employed
by Chicago industrialist James Deering to build this European-inspired
residence. Once comprising 180 acres, this National Historic Landmark
now occupies a 30-acre tract that includes a rockland hammock (native
forest) and more than 10 acres of formal gardens with fountains overlooking Biscayne Bay. The house, open to the public, contains 70 rooms,
34 of which are filled with paintings, sculpture, antique furniture, and
other fine and decorative arts. The collection spans 2,000 years and
represents the Renaissance, baroque, rococo, and neoclassical periods.
The 90-minute self-guided Discover Vizcaya Audio Tour is available in
multiple languages for an additional $5. Moonlight tours, offered on
evenings that are nearest the full moon, provide a magical look at the
gardens; call for reservations. ⊠ *3251 S. Miami Ave., Coconut Grove*
☎ *305/250–9133* ⊕ *www.vizcayamuseum.org* ✉ *$18* ☉ *Wed.–Mon.
9:30–4:30.*

WORTH NOTING

Barnacle Historic State Park. A pristine bay-front manse sandwiched
between cramped luxury developments, Barnacle is Miami's oldest
house still standing on its original foundation. To get here, you'll hike
along an old buggy trail through a tropical hardwood hammock and
landscaped lawn leading to Biscayne Bay. Built in 1891 by Florida's
first snowbird—New Yorker Commodore Ralph Munroe—the large
home, built of timber that Munroe salvaged from wrecked ships, has
many original furnishings, a broad sloping roof, and deeply recessed
verandas that channel sea breezes into the house. If your timing is
right, you may catch one of the monthly Moonlight Concerts, and the
old-fashioned picnic on July 4 is popular. ⊠ *3485 Main Hwy., Coconut Grove* ☎ *305/442–6866* ⊕ *www.floridastateparks.org/thebarnacle*
✉ *$2 park entry, tours $3, concerts $7* ☉ *Fri.–Mon. 9–5; tours at 10,
11:30, 1, and 2:30. Concerts monthly Sept.–May 6–9 pm; call or check
the website for dates.*

CORAL GABLES

You can easily spot Coral Gables from the window of a Miami-bound
jetliner—just look for the massive orange tower of the Biltmore Hotel
rising from a lush green carpet of trees concealing the city's gracious
homes. The canopy is as much a part of this planned city as its distinctive architecture, all attributed to the vision of George E. Merrick
nearly 100 years ago.

The story of this city began in 1911, when Merrick inherited 1,600
acres of citrus and avocado groves from his father. Through judicious
investment he nearly doubled the tract to 3,000 acres by 1921. Merrick
dreamed of building an American Venice here, complete with canals and
homes. Working from this vision, he began designing a city based on
centuries-old prototypes from Mediterranean countries. Unfortunately
for Merrick, the devastating no-name hurricane of 1926, followed by

the Great Depression, prevented him from fulfilling many of his plans. He died at 54, an employee of the post office. Today Coral Gables has a population of about 47,000. In its bustling downtown more than 150 multinational companies maintain headquarters or regional offices, and the University of Miami campus in the southern part of the Gables brings a youthful vibrancy to the area. A southern branch of the city extends down the shore of Biscayne Bay through neighborhoods threaded with canals.

TOP ATTRACTIONS

Biltmore Hotel. Bouncing back stunningly from its dark days as an army hospital, this hotel has become the jewel of Coral Gables—a dazzling architectural gem with a colorful past. First opened in 1926, it was a hot spot for the rich and glamorous of the Jazz Age until it was converted to an army–air force regional hospital in 1942. Until 1968, the Veterans Administration continued to operate the hospital after World War II. The Biltmore then lay vacant for nearly 20 years before it underwent extensive renovations and reopened as a luxury hotel in 1987. Its 16-story tower, like the Freedom Tower in downtown Miami, is a replica of Seville's Giralda Tower. The magnificent pool is reportedly the largest hotel pool in the continental United States. Because it functions as a full-service hotel, your ticket in—if you aren't staying here—is to patronize one of the hotel's several restaurants or bars. Sunday champagne brunch is a local legend; try to get a table in the courtyard. ⊠ *1200 Anastasia Ave., near De Soto Blvd., Coral Gables* ☎ *855/311–6903* ⊕ *www.biltmorehotel.com.*

FAMILY
Fodor'sChoice
★
Fairchild Tropical Botanic Garden. With 83 acres of lakes, sunken gardens, a 560-foot vine pergola, orchids, bellflowers, coral trees, bougainvillea, rare palms, and flowering trees, Fairchild is the largest tropical botanical garden in the continental United States. The tram tour highlights the best of South Florida's flora; then you can set off exploring on your own. A 2-acre rain-forest exhibit showcases tropical plants from around the world complete with a waterfall and stream. The conservatory, Windows to the Tropics, is home to rare tropical plants, including the Titan Arum (*Amorphophallus titanum*), a fast-growing variety that attracted thousands of visitors when it bloomed in 1998. (It was only the sixth documented bloom in this country in the 20th century.) The Keys Coastal Habitat, created in a marsh and mangrove area in 1995 with assistance from the Tropical Audubon Society, provides food and shelter to resident and migratory birds. Check out the Montgomery Botanical Center, a research facility devoted to palms and cycads. Spicing up Fairchild's calendar are plant sales, afternoon teas, and genuinely special events year-round, such as the International Mango Festival the second weekend in July. The excellent bookstore–gift shop carries books on gardening and horticulture, and the Garden Café serves sandwiches and, seasonally, smoothies made from the garden's own crop of tropical fruits. ⊠ *10901 Old Cutler Rd., Coral Gables* ☎ *305/667–1651* ⊕ *www.fairchildgarden.org* ⌑ *$25* ◔ *Daily 7:30–4:30.*

FAMILY
Venetian Pool. Sculpted from a rock quarry in 1923 and fed by artesian wells, this 820,000-gallon municipal pool had a major face-lift in 2010. It remains quite popular because of its themed architecture—a fantasy

version of a waterfront Italian village—created by Denman Fink. The pool has earned a place on the National Register of Historic Places and showcases a nice collection of vintage photos depicting 1920s beauty pageants and swank soirees held long ago. Paul Whiteman played here, Johnny Weissmuller and Esther Williams swam here, and you should, too (but no kids under 3). A snack bar, lockers, and showers make this must-see user-friendly as well. ✉ *2701 De Soto Blvd., at Toledo St., Coral Gables* ☎ *305/460–5306* ⊕ *www.gablesrecreation.com* ✉ *$11; free parking across De Soto Blvd.* ☉ *Usually Tues.–Sun. 11–4:30, but best to call ahead.*

WORTH NOTING
Miracle Mile. Even with competition from some impressive malls, this half-mile stretch of colorful retail stores continues to thrive because of its intriguing mixture of unique boutiques, bridal shops, art galleries, and charming restaurants. It attracts Latin America's power players, including the overly botoxed women you might see on *The Real Housewives of Miami.* ✉ *Coral Way, between S.W. 37th and S.W. 42nd Aves.* ⊕ *www.shopcoralgables.com.*

OFF THE BEATEN PATH

Zoo Miami. Don't miss a visit to this top-notch zoo, 14 miles southwest of Coral Gables, in the Miami suburbs. The only subtropical zoo in the continental United States, it has 320-plus acres that are home to more than 2,000 animals, including 40 endangered species, which roam on islands surrounded by moats. Amazon & Beyond encompasses 27 acres of simulated tropical rain forests showcasing 600 animals indigenous to the region, such as giant river otters, harpy eagles, anacondas, and jaguars. The Wings of Asia aviary has about 300 exotic birds representing 70 species flying free within the junglelike enclosure. Florida: Mission Everglades showcases the diverse wildlife of native Florida ecosystems. There's also a petting zoo with a meerkat exhibit and interactive opportunities, such as those at Wacky Barn and Dr. Wilde's World and the Ecology Theater, where kids can touch animals like alligators and opossums. An educational and entertaining wildlife show is given three times daily. ✉ *12400 S.W. 152nd St. (1 Zoo Blvd.), Richmond Heights* ☎ *305/251–0400* ⊕ *www.miamimetrozoo.com* ✉ *$15.95; 45-min tram tour $4.95* ☉ *Daily 9:30–5:30, last admission at 4.*

KEY BISCAYNE

Once upon a time, the two barrier islands that make up the village of Key Biscayne (Key Biscayne itself and Virginia Key) were outposts for fishermen and sailors, pirates and salvagers, soldiers and settlers. The 95-foot Cape Florida Lighthouse stood tall during Seminole Indian battles and hurricanes. Coconut plantations covered two-thirds of Key Biscayne, and there were plans as far back as the 1800s to develop the picturesque island as a resort for the wealthy. Fortunately, the state and county governments set much of the land aside for parks, and both keys are now home to top-ranked beaches and golf, tennis, softball, and picnicking facilities. The long and winding bike paths that run through the islands are favorites for in-line skaters and cyclists. Incorporated in 1991, the village of Key Biscayne is a hospitable community of about 12,500, even though Virginia Key remains undeveloped at the moment. These two playground islands are especially family-friendly.

TOP ATTRACTIONS

FAMILY **Miami Seaquarium.** This classic family attraction stages shows with sea lions, dolphins, and Lolita the killer whale. The Crocodile Flats exhibit has 26 Nile crocodiles. Discovery Bay, an endangered mangrove habitat, is home to sea turtles, alligators, herons, egrets, and ibis. You can also visit a shark pool, a tropical reef aquarium, and West Indian and Florida manatees. A popular interactive attraction is the Stingray Touch Tank, where you can touch and feed cow-nose rays and southern stingrays. Another big draw is the Dolphin Interaction program, including the quite intensive Dolphin Odyssey ($199) experience and the lighter shallow-water Dolphin Encounter ($139). Make reservations for either experience. ⊠ *4400 Rickenbacker Causeway, Virginia Key* ☎ *305/361–5705* ⊕ *www.miamiseaquarium.com* ☑ *$41.95, parking $8 (cash only)* ⊗ *Daily 9:30–6, last admission at 4:30.*

SAIL AWAY

If you can sail in Miami, do. Blue skies, calm seas, and a view of the city skyline make for a pleasurable outing—especially at twilight, when the fabled "moon over Miami" casts a soft glow on the water. Key Biscayne's calm waves and strong breezes are perfect for sailing and windsurfing, and although Dinner Key and the Coconut Grove waterfront remain the center of sailing in Greater Miami, sailboat moorings and rentals sit along other parts of the bay and up the Miami River, too.

WYNWOOD

Fodor's Choice ★ Wynwood actually encompasses three trendy, creative neighborhoods 3 to 4 miles north of downtown and has developed an impressive mix of one-of-a-kind shops and galleries, haute couture boutiques, see-and-be-seen bars, and slick restaurants. One thing is still missing from the landscape: a decent hotel. On a positive note, it's kept the vibe in these neighborhoods more local and less touristy. The downside: you'll need a vehicle to get here, and though in close proximity to one another, you'll also need a vehicle to get between these emerging neighborhoods.

Between I–95 and Miami Avenue from 29th to 22nd streets, the funky and edgy **Wynwood Art District** (⊕ *www.wynwoodmiami.com*) is peppered with galleries, art studios, and private collections accessible to the public. Though the neighborhood hasn't completely shed its dodgy past, artist-painted graffiti walls and reinvented urban, industrial buildings have transformed the area from plain old grimy to super trendy. The Wynwood Walls on Northwest 2nd Avenue between Northeast 25th and 26th streets are a cutting-edge enclave of modern urban murals. However, these avant-garde graffiti displays by renowned artists are just the beginning; in fact, almost every street is colored with funky spray-paint art, making the neighborhood a photographer's dream. Wynwood's retail space is a hodgepodge of cheap garment stores, upscale boutiques, and contemporary galleries (some by appointment only). Your best bet is to visit during Wynwood's monthly gallery walk on the second Saturday evening of each month, when studios and galleries are all open at the same time.

TOP ATTRACTIONS

Margulies Collection at the Warehouse. Make sure a visit to Wynwood includes a stop at the Margulies Collection at the Warehouse. Martin Margulies's collection of vintage and contemporary photography, videos, and installation art in a 45,000-square-foot space makes for eye-popping viewing. Admission proceeds go to the Lotus House, a local homeless shelter for women and children. ⊠ *591 N.W. 27th St., between N.W. 5th and 6th Aves., Wynwood* ☎ *305/576–1051* ⊕ *www. margulieswarehouse.com* ⊠ *$10* ☉ *Oct.–Apr., Wed.–Sat. 11–4.*

Fodor's Choice
★

Rubell Family Collection. Fans of edgy art will appreciate the Rubell Family Collection. Mera and Don Rubell have accumulated work by artists from the 1970s to the present, including Jeff Koons, Cindy Sherman, Damien Hirst, and Keith Haring. Admission always includes a complimentary audio tour; however, true art lovers should opt for a complimentary guided tour of the collection, offered Wednesday through Saturday at 11 am and 3 pm. ⊠ *95 N.W. 29th St., between N. Miami and N.W. 1st Aves., Wynwood* ☎ *305/573–6090* ⊕ *www.rfc.museum* ⊠ *$10* ☉ *Tues.–Sat. 10–6.*

MIDTOWN

Northeast of Wynwood, Midtown (⊕ *www.midtownmiami.com*) lies between Northeast 29th and 36th streets, from North Miami Avenue to Northeast 2nd Avenue. This sub-city is anchored by a multitower residential complex with prolific retail space, often housing the latest and greatest in dining and shopping trends.

DESIGN DISTRICT

North of Midtown, from about Northeast 38th to Northeast 42nd streets and across the other side of Interstate 195, the Design District (⊕ *www.miamidesigndistrict.net*) is yet another 18 blocks of clothiers, antiques shops, design stores, and bars and eateries. The real draws here are the interior design and furniture galleries as well as über-high-end shopping that's oh-so Rodeo Drive.

LITTLE HAITI

Miami's Little Haiti is the largest Haitian community outside of Haiti itself, and while people of different ethnic backgrounds have begun to move into the neighborhood, people here are still surprised to see tourists. However, owners of shops and restaurants tend to be welcoming. Creole is commonly spoken, although some people—especially younger folks—also speak English. Once a small farming community, Little Haiti is the heart and soul of Haitian society in the U.S. Its northern and southern boundaries are 85th Street and 42nd Street, respectively, with I–95 to the west and Biscayne Boulevard to the east. The best section to visit is along North Miami Avenue from 54th to 59th streets.

LITTLE HAVANA

Fodor's Choice
★

First settled en masse by Cubans in the early 1960s, after Cuba's Communist revolution, Little Havana is a predominantly working-class area and the core of Miami's Hispanic community. Spanish is the principal language, but don't be surprised if the cadence is less Cuban and more Salvadoran or Nicaraguan: the neighborhood is now home to people from all Latin American countries.

If you come to Little Havana expecting the Latino version of New Orleans's French Quarter, you're apt to be disappointed—it's not about the architecture here. Rather, it's a place to soak in the atmosphere. Little Havana is more about great, inexpensive food (not just Cuban; there's Vietnamese, Mexican, and Argentinean here as well), distinctive affordable Cuban-American art, cigars, and great coffee. It's not a prefab tourist destination—this is real life in Spanish-speaking Miami.

Little Havana's semi-official boundaries are 27th Avenue to 4th Avenue on the west, Miami River to the north, and Southwest 13th Street to the south. Much of the neighborhood is residential; however, you'll quickly discover the area's flavor, both literally and figuratively, along Calle Ocho (Southwest 8th Street), between Southwest 11th and 17th avenues, which is lined with cigar factories, cafés selling guava pastries and rose petal flan, *botanicas* brimming with candles, and Cuban clothes and crafts stores. Your "Welcome to Little Havana" photo op shines on 27th Avenue and 8th Street. Giant hand-painted roosters are found scattered throughout the entire neighborhood, an artistic nod to their real-life counterparts that roam the streets here. You'll need to drive into Little Havana, since public transportation here is limited; but once on Calle Ocho, it's best to experience the neighborhood on foot.

TOP ATTRACTIONS

Cuban Memorial Boulevard. Four blocks in the heart of Little Havana are filled with monuments to Cuba's freedom fighters. South of Calle Ocho (8th Street), S.W. 13th Ave. becomes a ceiba tree–lined parkway known as Cuban Memorial Boulevard, divided at the center by a narrow grassy mall with a walking path through the various memorials. Among them is the *Eternal Torch of the Brigade 2506*, blazing with an endless flame and commemorating those who were killed in the failed Bay of Pigs invasion of 1961. Another is a bas-relief map of Cuba depicting each of its *municipios*. There's also a bronze statue in honor of Nestory (Tony) Izquierdo, who participated in the Bay of Pigs invasion and served in Nicaragua's Somozan forces. ⊠ *S.W. 13th Ave., between S.W. 8th and S.W.12th Sts., Little Havana.*

Domino Park. Watch a slice of old Havana come to life in Miami's Little Havana. At Domino Park, officially known as Maximo Gomez Park, guayabera-clad seniors bask in the sun and play dominoes, while onlookers share neighborhood gossip and political opinions. ■TIP→ There is a little office at the park with a window where you can get information on Little Havana; the office also stores the dominoes for the older gents who play regularly, but it's BYOD ("bring your own dominoes") for everyone else. ⊠ *801 S.W. 15th Ave., Little Havana* ☎ *305/859–2717 for park office.*

NEED A
BREAK?

Las Pinareños Fruteria y Floreria. In the mood for something refreshing or a high-octane jolt? Try Las Pinareños, a *fruteria* (fruit stand) that serves *coco frio* (fresh, cold coconut juice served in a whole coconut), mango juice, and other *jugos* (juices), as well as Cuban coffees and Cuban finger foods. You can order your sweet, hot *cortadito* (coffee with milk) or a *cafecito* (no milk) from the walk-up window and enjoy it at one of the stools in front of the shop or sit at one of the tables inside the fruit and flower market. ⌧ *1334 S.W. 8th St., Little Havana* ☎ *305/285–1135.*

El Titan de Bronze. A peek at the intently focused cigar rollers through the windows doesn't prepare you for the rich, pungent scent that jolts your senses as you step inside the store. Millions of stogies are deftly hand-rolled at this family-owned business every year. Visitors are welcome to watch the rolling action (and of course buy some cigars). ⌧ *1071 S.W. 8th St., Little Havana* ☎ *305/860–1412* ⊕ *www.eltitancigars.com.*

SOUTH BEACH

Fodor's Choice ★ The hub of Miami Beach is South Beach (better known as SoBe), with its energetic Ocean Drive, Collins Avenue, and Washington Avenue. Here life unfolds 24 hours a day. Beautiful people pose in hotel lounges and sidewalk cafés, bronzed cyclists zoom past palm trees, and visitors flock to see the action. On Lincoln Road, café crowds spill onto the sidewalks, weekend markets draw all kinds of visitors and their dogs, and thanks to a few late-night lounges, the scene is just as alive at night. Further north (in Mid-Beach and North Beach), the vibe is decidedly quieter.

TOP ATTRACTIONS

Fodor's Choice ★ **Española Way.** There's a bohemian feel to this street lined with Mediterranean-revival buildings constructed in 1925. Al Capone's gambling syndicate ran its operations upstairs at what is now the Clay Hotel, a youth hostel. At a nightclub here in the 1930s, future bandleader Desi Arnaz strapped on a conga drum and started beating out a rumba rhythm. Visit this quaint avenue on a weekend afternoon, when merchants and craftspeople set up shop to sell everything from handcrafted bongo drums to fresh flowers. Between Washington and Drexel avenues the road has been narrowed to a single lane and Miami Beach's trademark pink sidewalks have been widened to accommodate sidewalk café's and shops selling imaginative clothing, jewelry, and art. ⌧ *Española Way, between 14th and 15th sts. from Washington to Jefferson Aves., South Beach.*

Holocaust Memorial. A bronze sculpture depicts refugees clinging to a giant bronze arm that reaches out of the ground and 42 feet into the air. Enter the surrounding courtyard to see a memorial wall and hear the music that seems to give voice to the 6 million Jews who died at the hands of the Nazis. It's easy to understand why Kenneth Treister's dramatic memorial is in Miami Beach: the city's community of Holocaust survivors was once the second-largest in the country. ⌧ *1933–1945*

Meridian Ave., at Dade Blvd., South Beach ☎ *305/538–1663* ⊕ *www. holocaustmmb.org* ✉ *Free* ☉ *Daily 9–sunset.*

Lincoln Road Mall. This open-air pedestrian mall flaunts some of Miami's best people-watching. The eclectic interiors of myriad fabulous restaurants, colorful boutiques, art galleries, lounges, and cafés are often upstaged by the bustling outdoor scene. It's here among the prolific alfresco dining enclaves that you can pass the hours easily beholding the beautiful people. Indeed, outdoor restaurants and café seating take center stage along this wide pedestrian road adorned with towering date palms, linear pools, and colorful broken-tile mosaics. Some of the shops on Lincoln Road are owner-operated boutiques carrying a smart variety of clothing, furnishings, jewelry, and decorative elements. You'll also find typical chain stores—H&M, American Eagle Outfitters, Forever 21, and so on. Lincoln Road is fun, lively, and friendly for people—old, young, gay, and straight—and their dogs.

Two landmarks worth checking out at the eastern end of Lincoln Road are the massive 1940s keystone building at 420 Lincoln Road, which has a 1945 Leo Birchanky mural in the lobby, and the 1921 Mission-style Miami Beach Community Church, at Drexel Avenue. The Lincoln Theatre (No. 541–545), at Pennsylvania Avenue, is a classical four-story art deco gem with friezes, which now houses H&M. At Euclid Avenue there's a monument to Morris Lapidus, the brains behind Lincoln Road Mall, who in his 90s watched the renaissance of his whimsical South Beach creation. At Lenox Avenue, a black-and-white art deco movie house with a Mediterranean barrel-tile roof is now the Colony Theater (No. 1040), where live theater and experimental films are presented. ✉ *Lincoln Rd., between Washington Ave. and Alton Rd., South Beach* ⊕ *www.lincolnroadmall.com.*

QUICK BITES

Lincoln Road is a great place to cool down with an icy treat while touring South Beach. If you visit on a Sunday, stop at one of the many juice vendors, who'll whip up made-to-order smoothies from mangoes, oranges, and other fresh local fruits.

Frieze Ice Cream Factory. A true South Beach original, this mom-and-pop ice cream shop serves what could very well be the best ice cream in Florida. Delight in mouthwatering homemade ice cream and sorbets including Indian mango, key lime pie, cashew toffee crunch, and chocolate decadence. ✉ *1626 Michigan Ave., just south of Lincoln Rd., South Beach* ☎ *305/538–0207* ⊕ *www.thefrieze.com.*

Gelateria 4D. Authentic Italian gelato is scooped up with plenty of authentic Miami attitude at this sleek glass-and-stainless-steel sweet spot. The gelato is delicious despite the not-so-sweet service and exorbitant price. ✉ *670 Lincoln Rd., between Euclid and Pennsylvania aves., South Beach* ☎ *786/276–9475* ⊕ *www.gelateria4d.com.*

2

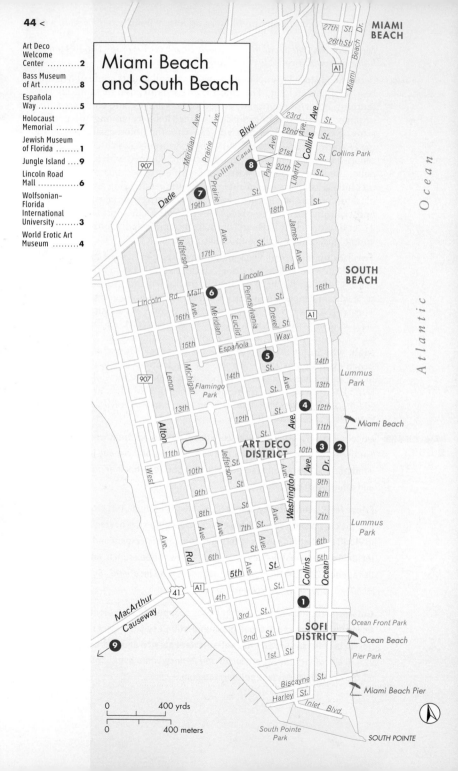

Miami Beach and South Beach

WORTH NOTING

Art Deco Welcome Center. Run by the Miami Design Preservation League, the center provides information about the buildings in the district. An improved gift shop sells 1930s–50s art deco memorabilia, posters, and books on Miami's history. Several tours—covering Lincoln Road, Española Way, North Beach, and the entire Art Deco District, among others—start here. You can choose from a self-guided iPod audio tour or join one of the regular morning walking tours at 10:30 every day. On Thursday a second tour takes place at 6:30 pm. Arrive at the center 15 minutes beforehand and pre-purchase tickets online. All of the options provide detailed histories of the art deco hotels as well as an introduction to the art deco, Mediterranean revival, and Miami Modern (MiMo) styles found within the Miami Beach Architectural Historic District. Don't miss the special boat tours during Art Deco Weekend, in early January. *(⇨ For a map of the Art Deco District and info on some of the sites there, see the "A Stroll Down Deco Lane" in-focus feature.)* ✉ *1001 Ocean Dr., South Beach* ☎ *305/672–2014* ⊕ *www.mdpl.org* 🎟 *Tours $20* ☉ *Daily 9:30–7.*

Bass Museum of Art. Special exhibitions join a diverse collection of European art at this museum whose original building is constructed of keystone and has unique Maya-inspired carvings. An expansion designed by Japanese architect Arata Isozaki houses another wing and an outdoor sculpture garden. Works on permanent display include *The Holy Family,* a painting by Peter Paul Rubens; *The Tournament,* one of several 16th-century Flemish tapestries; and works by Albrecht Dürer and Henri de Toulouse-Lautrec. Docent tours are by appointment but free with entry. ✉ *2100 Collins Ave., South Beach* ☎ *305/673–7530* ⊕ *www. bassmuseum.org* 🎟 *$8* ☉ *Wed.–Sun. noon–5.*

Jewish Museum of Florida—FIU. Listed on the National Register of Historic Places, this former synagogue, built in 1936, contains art deco chandeliers, 80 impressive stained-glass windows, and a permanent exhibit, *MOSAIC: Jewish Life in Florida,* which depicts more than 235 years of the Florida Jewish experience. A partnership with Florida International University, the Jewish Museum also houses a store filled with books, jewelry, and other souvenirs as well as playinh host to traveling exhibits and special events. ✉ *301 Washington Ave., South Beach* ☎ *305/672–5044* ⊕ *www.jmof.fiu.edu* 🎟 *$6* ☉ *Tues.–Sun. 10–5. Museum store closed Sat.*

Wolfsonian–Florida International University. An elegantly renovated 1926 storage facility is now a research center and museum showcasing a 120,000-item collection of modern design and "propaganda arts" amassed by Miami native Mitchell ("Micky") Wolfson Jr., a world traveler and connoisseur. Broad themes of the 19th and 20th centuries—nationalism, political persuasion, industrialization—are addressed in permanent and traveling shows. Included in the museum's eclectic holdings, which represent art deco, art moderne, art nouveau, Arts and Crafts, and other aesthetic movements, are 8,000 matchbooks collected by Egypt's King Farouk. ✉ *1001 Washington Ave., South Beach* ☎ *305/531–1001* ⊕ *www.wolfsonian.org* 🎟 *$7 (free Fri. after 6)* ☉ *Sat.–Tues. and Thurs. noon–6, Fri. noon–9.*

DID YOU KNOW?

From sidewalk cafés, diners enjoy the bohemian ambience of Miami Beach's Española Way.

World Erotic Art Museum (WEAM). The sexy collection of more than 4,000 erotic items, all owned by millionaire Naomi Wilzig, unfolds with unique art of varying quality—fertility statues from around the globe and historic Chinese *shunga* books (erotic art offered as gifts to new brides on the wedding night) share the space with some kitschy knickknacks. If this is your thing, an original phallic prop from Stanley Kubrick's *A Clockwork Orange* and an over-the-top Kama Sutra bed is worth the price of admission, but the real standout is "Miss Naomi," who is usually on hand to answer questions and provide behind-the-scenes anecdotes. Kids 17 and under are not admitted. ✉ *1205 Washington Ave., at 12th St., South Beach* ☎ *305/532–9336* ⊕ *www.weam. com* 🎫 *$15* ⊙ *Mon.–Thurs. 11–10, Fri.–Sun. 11–midnight.*

MID-BEACH

Where does South Beach end and Mid-Beach begin? With the massive amount of money being spent on former 1950s pleasure palaces like the Fontainebleau and Eden Roc, it could be that Mid-Beach will soon just be considered part of South Beach. North of 24th Street, Collins Avenue curves its way to 44th Street, where it takes a sharp left turn after running into the Soho House Miami and then the Fontainebleau resort. The area between these two points—24th Street and 96th Street—is Mid-Beach.

FISHER AND BELLE ISLANDS

A private island community near the southern tip of South Beach, Fisher Island is accessible only by the island's ferry service. The island is predominantly residential with a few hotel rooms on offer at the Resort at Fisher Island Club. Belle Island is a small island connected to both the mainland and Miami Beach by road. It is a mile north of South Beach and just west over the Venetian Causeway.

NORTH BEACH AND AVENTURA

Nearing the 100th Street mark on Collins Avenue, Mid-Beach gives way to North Beach. In particular, at 96th Street, the town of Bal Harbour takes over Collins Avenue from Miami Beach. The town runs a mere 10 blocks to the north before the bridge to Sunny Isles. Bal Harbour is famous for its outdoor high-end shops. If you take your shopping seriously, you'll probably want to stay in this area. At 106th Street, the town of Sunny Isles is an appealing, calm, predominantly upscale choice for families looking for a beautiful beach. There's no nightlife to speak of in Sunny Isles, and yet the half-dozen megaluxurious skyscraper hotels that have sprung up here in the past decade have created a niche-resort town from the demolished ashes of much older, affordable hotels. Farther west are the high-rises of Aventura.

BEACHES

CORAL GABLES

FAMILY **Matheson Hammock Park and Beach.** Kids love the gentle waves and warm water of this beach in Coral Gables suburbia, near Fairchild Tropical Botanic Garden. But the beach is only part of the draw: the park includes a boardwalk trail, a playground, and a golf course. Plus the park is a prime spot for kite-boarding. The man-made lagoon, or "atoll pool," is perfect for inexperienced swimmers, and it's one of the best places in mainland Miami for a picnic. ■TIP➜ However, the water can be a bit murky, and with the emphasis on families, it's not the best place for singles. The park also offers a full-service marina. **Amenities:** parking (fee); toilets. **Best for:** swimming. ⊠ *9610 Old Cutler Rd.* ☎ *305/665–5475* ⊕ *www.miamidade.gov/parks/parks/matheson_beach.asp* 🖃 *$5 per vehicle weekdays, $6 weekends* ☉ *Daily sunrise–sunset.*

KEY BISCAYNE

Fodor's Choice **Bill Baggs Cape Florida State Park.** Thanks to inviting beaches, sunsets, and a tranquil lighthouse, this park at Key Biscayne's southern tip is ★ worth the drive. In fact, the 1-mile stretch of pure beachfront has been named several times in Dr. Beach's revered America's Top 10 Beaches list. It has 18 picnic pavilions available as daily rentals, two cafés that serve light lunches (Lighthouse Café, overlooking the Atlantic Ocean, and the Boater's Grill, on Biscayne Bay), and plenty of space to enjoy the umbrella and chair rentals. A stroll or ride along walking and bicycle paths provides wonderful views of Miami's dramatic skyline. From the southern end of the park you can see a handful of houses rising over the bay on wooden stilts, the remnants of Stiltsville, built in the 1940s and now protected by the Stiltsville Trust. The nonprofit group was established in 2003 to preserve the structures, because they showcase the park's rich history. Bill Baggs has bicycle rentals, a playground, fishing piers, and guided tours of the **Cape Florida Lighthouse,** South Florida's oldest structure. The lighthouse was erected in 1845 to replace an earlier one damaged in an 1836 Seminole attack, in which the keeper's helper was killed. Free tours are offered at the restored cottage and lighthouse at 10 am and 1 pm Thursday to Monday. Be there a half hour beforehand. **Amenities:** food and drink; lifeguards; parking (fee); showers; toilets. **Best for:** solitude; sunsets; walking. ⊠ *1200 S. Crandon Blvd., Key Biscayne* ☎ *305/361–5811* ⊕ *www.floridastateparks.org/capeflorida* 🖃 *$8 per vehicle; $2 per pedestrian* ☉ *Daily 8–sunset.*

FAMILY **Crandon Park Beach.** This relaxing oasis in northern Key Biscayne offers renowned tennis facilities, a great golf course, a family amusement center, and 2 miles of beach dotted with palm trees. The park is divided by Key Biscayne's main road, with tennis and golf on the bayside, the beaches on the oceanside. Families really enjoy the beaches here—the sand is soft, there are no rip tides, there's a great view of the Atlantic, and parking is both inexpensive and plentiful. However, on weekends, be prepared for a long hike from your car to the beach. There are bathrooms, outdoor showers, plenty of picnic tables, and concession stands. The family-friendly park offers abundant options for those who find it challenging simply to sit and build sand castles. Kite-board rentals and lessons are offered from the north water-sports concessions, as are kayak rentals. Eco-tours and nature trails showcase the myriad ecosystems of Key Biscayne including mangroves, coastal hammock, and sea-grass beds. Bird-watching is great at the southern end of the park. The **Crandon Park Amusement Center** at Crandon Park was once the site of a zoo. There are swans, waterfowl, peacocks, and dozens of huge iguanas running loose. Nearby you'll find a restored carousel (it's open weekends and major holidays 10:30–5, and you get three rides for $2), an old-fashioned outdoor roller rink, a dolphin-shape spray fountain, and a playground. **Amenities:** food and drink; lifeguards; parking (fee); showers; toilets; water sports. **Best for:** swimming; walking. ⊠ 6747 *Crandon Blvd., Key Biscayne* 🕾 *305/361–5421* ⊕ *www.miamidade. gov/Parks/Parks/crandon_beach.asp* 🖃 *$5 per vehicle weekdays, $6 weekends* ☉ *Daily sunrise–sunset.*

THE OCEAN DRIVE HUSTLE

As you stroll by the sidewalk restaurants lining Ocean Drive, don't be surprised if you're solicited by a pretty hostess, who'll literally shove a menu in your face to entice you to her café—which is exactly like every other eatery on the strip. Be advised that reputable restaurants refrain from these aggressive tactics. If you're indeed enticed by the fishbowl drinks, use the chance to bargain. A request for free drinks with dinner may very well be accommodated!

SOUTH BEACH

Fodor's Choice ★ **South Beach.** A 10-block stretch of white sandy beach hugging the turquoise waters along Ocean Drive—from 5th to 15th Street—is one of the most popular in America, known for drawing unabashedly modelesque sunbathers and posers. With the influx of new luxe hotels and hotspots from 1st to 5th and 16th to 25th streets, the South Beach stand-and-pose scene is now bigger than ever and stretches yet another dozen-plus blocks. The beaches crowd quickly on the weekends with a blend of European tourists, young hipsters, and sun-drenched locals offering Latin flavor. Separating the sand from the traffic of Ocean Drive is palm-fringed **Lummus Park**, with its volleyball nets and chickee huts (huts made of palmetto thatch over a cypress frame) for shade. The beach at **12th Street** is popular with gays, in a section often marked with rainbow flags. Locals hang out on 3rd Street beach, in an area called **SoFi** (South of Fifth) where they watch fit Brazilians play foot volley, a variation of volleyball that uses everything but the hands. Because much of South Beach leans toward skimpy sunning—women are often in G-strings and casually topless—many families prefer the tamer sections of Mid- and North Beach. Metered parking spots next to the ocean are a rare find. Instead, opt for a public garage a few blocks away and enjoy the people-watching as you walk to find your perfect spot on the sand. **Amenities:** food and drink; lifeguards; parking (fee); showers; toilets.

Best for: partiers; sunrise; swimming; walking. ✉ *Ocean Dr., from 5th to 15th St., then Collins Ave. to 25th St., South Beach.*

NORTH BEACH AND AVENTURA

Haulover Beach Park. This popular clothing-optional beach is embraced by naturists of all ages, shapes, and sizes; there are even sections primarily frequented by families, singles, and gays. However, Haulover has more claims to fame than its casual attitude toward swimwear—it's also the best beach in the area for bodyboarding and surfing, as it gets what pass for impressive swells in these parts. Plus the sand here is fine-grain white, unusual for the Atlantic coast. Once you park in the North Lot, you'll walk through a short tunnel covered with trees and natural habitat until you emerge on the unpretentious beach, where nudity is rarely met by gawkers. There are volleyball nets, and plenty of beach chair and umbrella rentals to protect your birthday suit from too much exposure—to the sun, that is. The sections of beach requiring swimwear are popular, too, given the park's ample parking and relaxed atmosphere. Lifeguards stand watch. More active types might want to check out the kite rentals, or charter-fishing excursions. **Amenities:** food and drink; lifeguards; parking (fee); showers; toilets. **Best for:** nudists; surfing; swimming; walking. ✉ *10800 Collins Ave., north of Bal Harbour, North Beach and Aventura* ☎ *305/944–3040* ⊕ *www.haulouverbeach.org* 💰 *$6 per vehicle if parking in lot* ☉ *Daily 8–sunset.*

FAMILY **Oleta River State Park.** Tucked away in North Miami Beach, this urban park is a ready-made family getaway. Nature lovers will find it easy to embrace the 1,128 acres of subtropical beauty along Biscayne Bay. Swim in the calm bay waters and bicycle, canoe, kayak, and bask among egrets, manatees, bald eagles, and fiddler crabs. Dozens of picnic tables, along with 10 covered pavilions, dot the stunning natural habitat, which was restored with red mangroves to revitalize the ecosystem and draw endangered birds, like the roseate spoonbill. There's a playground for tots, a mangrove island accessible only by boat, 15 miles of mountain-bike trails, a half-mile exercise track, concessions, and outdoor showers. **Amenities:** food and drink; parking (fee); showers; toilets; water sports. **Best for:** solitude; sunrise; sunset; walking. ✉ *3400 N.E. 163rd St., North Beach and Aventura* ☎ *305/919–1846* ⊕ *www.floridastateparks.org/oletariver* 💰 *$6 per vehicle; $2 per pedestrian* ☉ *Daily 8–sunset.*

WHERE TO EAT

Miami's restaurant scene has exploded in the past few years, with dozens of great new restaurants springing up left and right. The melting pot of residents and visitors has brought an array of sophisticated, tasty cuisine. Little Havana is still king for Cuban fare, and Miami Beach is swept up in a trend of fusion cuisine, which combines Asian, French, American, and Latin cooking with sumptuous—and pricey—results. Locals spend the most time in Downtown Miami, Wynwood, Midtown, and the Design District, where the city's ongoing foodie and cocktail revolution is most pronounced. Since Miami dining is a part of the trendy nightlife scene, most dinners don't start until 8 or 9 pm, and may go well into the night. To avoid a long wait among the late-night partiers at hot spots, come before 7 or make reservations. Attire is usually casual-chic, but patrons like to dress to impress. Prices tend to stay high in hot spots like Lincoln Road, but if you venture off the beaten path you can find delicious food for reasonable prices. When you get your bill, check whether a gratuity is already included; most restaurants add between 15% and 20% (ostensibly for the convenience of, and protection from, the many Latin American and European tourists who are used to this practice in their homelands), but supplement it depending on your opinion of the service.

Use the coordinate (✣ C2) at the end of each review to locate a property on the Where to Eat in the Miami Area map.

WHAT IT COSTS

	$	$$	$$$	$$$$
RESTAURANTS	under $15	$16–$20	$21–$30	over $30

Restaurant prices are the average cost of a main course at dinner or, if dinner is not served, at lunch.

DOWNTOWN

$$$$ ECLECTIC ✕ **Azul.** A restaurant known for producing celebrity chefs and delivering dining fantasies of Food Network proportions, Azul is a Miami foodie institution. With its Forbes five-star, award-winning team, Azul offers a haute-cuisine experience on par with a two- or three-Michelin-star restaurant. Chefs fuse disparate ingredients, merging as decadent, gastronomic art. Headliners include Tuna Poke with white soy, scallion, and macadamia nuts and the Basil "Sous-Vide" Salmon with ratatouille and fine herbs. Dine here and you'll undoubtedly experience bold new taste sensations while enjoying one of the finest wine lists in the city and an incomparable skyline view. [$] *Average main: $48* ✉ *Mandarin Oriental, Miami, 500 Brickell Key Dr., Downtown* ☎ *305/913–8358* 🌐 *www.mandarinoriental.com/miami* ✍ *Reservations essential* ✣ *D5.*

$$$$ FRENCH ✕ **db Bistro Moderne Miami.** One of America's most celebrated French chefs, Daniel Boulud brings his renowned cooking to the Miami scene. The menu of Boulud's Miami outpost pays homage to Mediterranean cuisines and the specialties of his homeland. Begin with a cold plate from the fabulous raw bar or the signature house-smoked sturgeon; then feast on *escargots persillade* (wild burgundy snails simmered in parsley, garlic, salted butter with yellow tomatoes and wild mushrooms). For the main course, try the authentic *coq au vin,* which is sure to stir up memories of France through its robust taste and smell. [$] *Average main: $31* ✉ *JW Marriott Marquis Miami, 255 Biscayne Blvd. Way, Downtown* ☎ *305/421–8800* 🌐 *www.dbbistro.com/miami* ✣ *D4.*

$$$ STEAKHOUSE Fodor's Choice ★ ✕ **Edge, Steak & Bar.** It's farm-to-table surf-and-turf at this elegantly understated restaurant in the Four Seasons Hotel Miami, where hefty portions of the finest cuts and freshest seafood headline the menu, prepared by renowned chef Aaron Brooks. The innovative tartares are a

BEST BETS FOR MIAMI DINING

Fodor's writers and editors have selected their favorite restaurants by price, cuisine, and experience in the Best Bets lists below. In the first column, Fodor's Choice designations represent the "best of the best" in every price category. Find specific details about a restaurant in the full reviews, listed alphabetically by neighborhood.

Fodor's Choice ★

Bianca, South Beach, $$$$, p. 61

Bocce Bar, Midtown Miami, $$$, p. 58

De Rodriguez Cuba on Ocean, South Beach, $$$$, p. 62

eating house, Coral Gables, $$$, p. 55

Edge, Steak and Bar, Downtown, $$$, p. 51

Fish Fish, North Beach and Aventura, $$$$, p. 72

Hakkasan, Mid-Beach, $$$$, p. 70

Hy-Vong Vietnamese Cuisine, Little Havana, $$, p. 60

J & G Grill, North Beach and Aventura, $$$$, p. 72

Joe's Stone Crab Restaurant, South Beach, $$$$, p. 63

Juvia, South Beach, $$$$, p. 63

Macchialina Taverna Rustica, South Beach, $$$$, p. 66

Makoto, North Beach and Aventura, $$$$, p. 72

Michael's Genuine Food & Drink, Design District, $$$, p. 59

Oak Tavern, Design District, $$$, p. 59

Pubbelly, South Beach, $$$, p. 67

Rusty Pelican, Key Biscayne, $$$$, p. 57

Sugarcane Raw Bar Grill, Midtown Miami, $$$$, p. 58

SushiSamba Coral Gables, Coral Gables, $$$$, p. 68

Verde at PAMM, Downtown, $, p. 54

Wynwood Kitchen & Bar, Wynwood, $$, p. 58

By Price

$

Verde at PAMM, Downtown, p. 54

$$

Hy-Vong Vietnamese Cuisine, Little Havana, p. 60

$$$

eating house, Coral Gables, p. 55

Oak Tavern, Design District, p. 59

Yardbird, Southern Table & Bar, South Beach, p. 69

$$$$

Hakkasan, Mid-Beach, p. 70

J & G Grill, North Beach and Aventura, p. 72

Juvia, South Beach, p. 63

Sugarcane Raw Bar Grill, Midtown Miami, p. 58

By Cuisine

AMERICAN

Michael's Genuine Food & Drink, Design District, p. 59

ASIAN

Hakkasan, Mid-Beach, p. 70

Makoto, North Beach and Aventura, p. 72

SushiSamba Coral Gables, Coral Gables, p. 58

CUBAN

De Rodriguez Cuba on Ocean, South Beach, p. 62

Versailles, Little Havana, p. 61

ITALIAN

Bianca, South Beach, p. 61

Bocce Bar, Midtown Miami, p. 58

Macchialina Taverna Rustica, South Beach, p. 66

SEAFOOD

Fish Fish, North Beach and Aventura, p. 72

Joe's Stone Crab Restaurant, South Beach, p. 63

STEAKHOUSE

Meat Market, South Beach, p. 66

Prime 112, South Beach, p. 67

2

surefire way to start the night right—try the corvina with baby cucumber, green apple, and a young celery-leaf, yellow-pepper sauce, or the ahi tuna with pickled shallots, watermelon, and mint. For the main event, Edge offers a variety of small, medium, and large cuts from the infrared grill, the most popular being the black Angus filet mignon. For a more casual experience, enjoy your meal and the restaurant's artisan cocktails under the skies in the alfresco terrace, where you can also enjoy complimentary s'mores around the fire pits. Sunday brunch is also excellent with a well-stocked raw bar (including stone crabs in season) and a make-your-own taco station. $ *Average main: $30* ⌗ *Four Seasons Miami, 1435 Brickell Ave, Downtown* ☎ *305/381–3190* ⊕ *www. edgerestaurantmiami.com* ⊕ *D5.*

$$$ ✕ **L'Entrecote de Paris.** Simplicity is just one ingredient to the secret sauce
BISTRO that's made this steak-frites restaurant in downtown Miami so popular. The design and cuisine found in this quiet bistro are as close as you'll get to the City of Light in Miami. The *entrecote* (a sliced flank steak) is the only dish offered here, served with baguette, french fries, and salad, and topped with a secret green sauce of 21 ingredients, which requires 36 hours and four cooking processes to produce. The cocktail and dessert menus are far more extensive, the former including fresh profiteroles with Nutella sauce and tarte tatin, the latter including "Excuse my French" cocktails made with French spirits Chandon and Grey Goose—of course. $ *Average main: $26* ⌗ *1053 S.E. 1st Ave., Downtown* ☎ *305/755–9995* ⊕ *www.lentrecotedeparis.com.br* ⊕ *D5.*

$$$$ ✕ **NAOE.** By virtue of its petite size (eight patrons max) and strict seating
JAPANESE times (twice per night at 6 and 9:30), the Japanese gem, NAOE, will forever remain intimate and original. By virtue of its price ($160 per person), it will forever require deep pockets—but this place is well worth a bit of credit card debt. The all-inclusive menu changes daily, based on the day's best and freshest seafood, but always includes a Bento Box, soup, nigirizushi, and dessert. Every visit ushers in a new exploration of the senses. Chef Kevin Cory prepares the gastronomic adventure a few feet from his patrons, using only the best ingredients and showcasing family treasures, like the renowned products of his centuries' old family *shoyu* (soy sauce) brewery and sake brewery. From start to finish, you'll be transported to Japan through the stellar service, the tastes of bizarre sea creatures and the smoothness of spectacular sakes. $ *Average main: $160* ⌗ *661 Brickell Key Dr., Downtown* ☎ *305/947–6263* ⊕ *www. naoemiami.com* ⚲ *Reservations essential* ⊗ *Closed Sunday* ⊕ *D5.*

$$$ ✕ **Novecento.** This famed Argentine eatery is the Financial District's
ARGENTINE answer to Ocean Drive: the people are still beautiful, but now they're wearing suits or stilettos. Known for its empanadas (tender chicken or spinach and cheese), simple grilled meats (luscious grilled skirt steak with chimichurri sauce), and the innovative Ensalada Novecento (grilled skirt steak, french fries, and mixed baby greens), it's no wonder Novecento is Brickell Avenue's best weekday power-lunch and happy-hour spot (2-for-1 drinks every day 4–7 pm). It's also a really popular place for late-night dining and people-watching. Come for Sunday brunch and enjoy the signature *parillada*, a small grill with an assortment of steaks, sausages, and sweetbreads. You'll also find several pasta

dishes on the menu, a nod to Argentina's strong Italian influence. [$] *Average main: $23* ✉ *1414 Brickell Ave., Downtown* ☎ *305/403–0900* 🌐 *www.novecento.com* ✣ *D5.*

$$ ITALIAN 🍴 **Perricone's Marketplace and Café.** Brickell Avenue south of the Miami River is a haven for Italian restaurants, and this lunch place for local bigwigs is the biggest and most popular among them. It's housed partially outdoors and partially indoors in an 1880s Vermont barn. Recipes were handed down from generation to generation, and the cooking is simple and good. Buy your wine from the on-premises deli, and enjoy it (for a small corkage fee) with homemade minestrone; a generous antipasto; linguine with a sauté of jumbo shrimp, scallops, and calamari; or gnocchi with four cheeses. The homemade tiramisù and cannoli are top-notch. [$] *Average main: $22* ✉ *Mary Brickell Village, 15 S.E. 10th St., Downtown* ☎ *305/374–9449* 🌐 *www.perricones.com* ✣ *D5.*

$ ECLECTIC Fodor's Choice ★ 🍴 **Verde.** As if the new high design Pérez Art Museum Miami (PAMM) weren't cool enough, its waterfront restaurant Verde is also making major waves across Biscayne Bay. The slick, contemporary Stephen Starr restaurant offers seating both indoors and out, with design-savvy décor and accessories true to its "green" name that blend seamlessly with the living walls and hanging gardens strewn across the museum's exterior. The exceptionally affordable, one-page menu features eclectic epicurean lunch plates that include a squash blossoms pizza, bigeye tuna tartare, a house chopped salad (with manchego, garbanzo beans, red peppers, cucumber, baby romaine, and smoked tomato vinaigrette), and gourmet cheeseburgers with applewood-smoked bacon and fries. **■ TIP→ Museum admission is not required to eat here, but the restaurant is open only during museum hours, meaning lunch only, except on Thursdays, when the museum remains open until 9 pm.** [$] *Average main: $14* ✉ *Pérez Art Museum Miami, 1103 Biscayne Blvd., Downtown* ☎ *305/375–3000* 🌐 *www.pamm.org/dining* ⊙ *Closed Monday* ✣ *D4.*

COCONUT GROVE

$$$ PERUVIAN 🍴 **Jaguar Ceviche Spoon Bar & Latam Grill.** A fabulous fusion of Peruvian and Mexican flavors, Jaguar is a gastronomic tour of Latin America in a single restaurant. As the name implies, there is a heavy emphasis on ceviches. The best option for experiencing this delicacy is the spoon sampler, which includes six distinct Peruvian and Mexican ceviches served in oversized spoons. Dishes, such the Mexican Tortilla Lasagna (chicken, poblano peppers, corn, tomato sauce, and cream, topped with melted cheese), are colorful, flavorful, and innovative. [$] *Average main: $23* ✉ *3067 Grand Ave., Coconut Grove* ☎ *305/444–0216* 🌐 *www.jaguarhg.com/jaguarspot* ✣ *C5.*

$$$ FRENCH 🍴 **Le Bouchon du Grove.** This petite French bistro with a supercharged atmosphere is a great spot in the heart of the Grove. Waiters tend to lean on chairs while taking orders, and managers and owners freely mix with the clientele, making Le Bouchon one of the last remaining vestige of the Grove's bohemian days. The result is one big happy family, all enjoying traditional French pâtés, gratins, quiches, chicken fricassee, mussels, duck-leg confit, and steak frites. The lively mood inside is

matched by the throngs that parade outside the French doors. Breakfast is served daily. $ *Average main: $24* ⊠ *3430 Main Hwy., Coconut Grove* ☎ *305/448–6060* ⊕ *www.lebouchondugrove.com* ⊹ *C5*.

$$$
SEAFOOD
FAMILY

✕ **Monty's.** Connected to the Bayshore Landing Marina, Monty's has a Caribbean flair, thanks especially to live calypso and island music on the outdoor terrace. Though it has lost the luster it had back in the '90s, it's still a kid-friendly place where Mom and Dad can kick back early eve and enjoy a beer and the raw bar while the youngsters dance to live music. The extensive menu offers a bit of everything, but the oysters on the half shell and the conch chowder are the best items. $ *Average main: $25* ⊠ *Bayshore Landing Marina, 2550 S. Bayshore Dr., at Aviation Ave., Coconut Grove* ☎ *305/856–3992* ⊹ *C5*.

$$
AMERICAN
FAMILY

✕ **Peacock Garden Café.** Reinstating the artsy and exciting vibe of Coconut Grove circa once-upon-a-time, this lovely spot offers an indoor-outdoor, tea-time setting for light bites. By day, it's one of Miami's most serene lunch spots. The lushly landscaped courtyard is lined with alfresco seating, drawing some of Miami's most fabulous ladies who lunch. Come evening, the café buzzes with a multigenerational crowd, enjoying the South Florida zephyrs and the delicious flatbreads, salads, homemade soups, and entrées. ■ TIP→ Breakfast is also excellent. $ *Average main: $19* ⊠ *2889 McFarlane Rd., Coconut Grove* ☎ *305/774–3332* ⊕ *www.jaguarhg.com/peacockspot* ⊹ *C5*.

CORAL GABLES

$$$
ECLECTIC
Fodor's Choice
★

✕ **eating house.** Check your calorie counter at the door when you enter the hippest eatery in Coral Gables. This microrestaurant sports long wait times, but you'll be talking about your meal here for months to come. The ever-changing small-plates menu teems with extreme culinary innovation and unexpected flavor combinations. Think: first fried cauliflower with lime cream, cotija cheese, and topped with layers of frito dust, followed by chicken "foie-ffles" (fried chicken, foie gras, and waffles smothered with candied bacon, maple syrup, and ranch dressing). Desserts are equally amazing. The famous "dirt cup" indeed resembles a soil-filled flowerpot. However, these roots are made of pretzels, hazelnuts, and *tierra nueva* chocolate ice cream; the "soil" is a mountain of crushed Oreos—and yes, that is a gummy worm, adding a wonderfully campy touch to the dish's creativity. $ *Average main: $23* ⊠ *804 Ponce De Leon Blvd., Coral Gables* ☎ *305/448–6524* ⊕ *www. eatinghousemiami.com* ⊹ *B5*.

$
CUBAN

✕ **El Palacio de los Jugos.** To the northwest of Coral Gables proper, this joint is one of the easiest and truest ways to see Miami's local Latin life in action. It's also one of the best fruit-shake shacks you'll ever come across (ask for a tropical juice of mamey or guanabana). Besides the rows of fresh tropical fruits and vegetables, and the shakes you can make with any of them, this boisterous indoor-outdoor market has numerous food counters where you can get just about any Cuban food—tamales, rice and beans, a *pan con lechón* (roast pork on Cuban bread for $5), fried pork rinds, or a coconut split before you and served with a straw. Order your food at a counter, and eat it along with local families at rows of outdoor picnic-style tables next to the parking lot.

It's disorganized, chaotic, and not for those cutting calories, but it's delicious and undeniably the real thing. $ *Average main: $6* ✉ *5721 W. Flagler St., Flagami* ☎ *305/264–8662* ⊕ *www.elpalaciodelosjugos. com/en* ▭ *No credit cards* ✛ *B4.*

$$
CUBAN

✕ **Havana Harry's.** When Cuban families want an affordable home-cooked meal with a twist but don't want to cook it themselves or go supercheap at the Cuban fast-food joint, Pollo Tropical, they come to this big, unassuming restaurant. In fact, you're likely to see whole families here representing multiple generations. The fare is traditional Cuban: long thin steaks known as *bistec palomilla* (panfried), roast chicken with citrus marinade, and fried pork chunks; contemporary flourishes—mango sauce and guava-painted pork roast—are kept to a minimum. Most dishes come with white rice, black beans, and a choice of ripe or green plantains. The sweet ripe ones offer a good contrast to the savory dishes. Start with the $5.25 *mariquitas* (plantain chips) with mojo. Finish with the acclaimed flan. $ *Average main: $14* ✉ *4612 Le Jeune Rd., Coral Gables* ☎ *305/661–2622* ⊕ *www.havanaharrys. net* ✛ *B5.*

$$$
CARIBBEAN

✕ **Ortanique on the Mile.** Cascading *ortaniques,* a Jamaican hybrid orange, are hand-painted on columns in this warm, welcoming yellow dining room. Food is vibrant in taste and color, as delicious as it is beautiful. Though there is no denying that the strong, full flavors are imbued with island breezes, chef-partner Cindy Hutson's personal "cuisine of the sun" goes beyond Caribbean refinements. The menu centers on fish, since Hutson has a special way with it, and the West Indian Style Bouillabaisse is not to be missed. Ceviches and soups change nightly. The mojitos here—and the cocktails in general—are amazing! Beyond the original Coral Gables location, Ortanique has now spread its island love to the islands themselves, with a location in Grand Cayman and another in Harbour Island, Bahamas. $ *Average main: $32* ✉ *278 Miracle Mile, Coral Gables* ☎ *305/446–7710* ⊕ *www.ortaniquerestaurants. com* ☾ *No lunch weekends* ✛ *B5.*

$$$$
FRENCH

✕ **Pascal's on Ponce.** This French gem amid the Coral Gables restaurant district is always full, thanks to chef-proprietor Pascal Oudin's assured and consistent cuisine. Oudin forgoes the glitz and fussiness often associated with French cuisine, and instead opts for a simple, small, refined dining room that won't overwhelm patrons. The equally sensible menu includes a creamy lobster bisque starter. The main course is a tough choice between oven-roasted duck with poached pears and diver sea scallops with beef short rib. Ask your expert waiter to pair dishes with a selection from Pascal's impressive wine list, and, for dessert, order the bittersweet-chocolate soufflé with chocolate ganache. $ *Average main: $34* ✉ *2611 Ponce de León Blvd., Coral Gables* ☎ *305/444–2024* ⊕ *www.pascalmiami.com* ☾ *Closed Sun. No lunch Sat.* ✛ *B5.*

$$$$
JAPANESE
FUSION
Fodor's Choice
★

✕ **SushiSamba Coral Gables.** A flavor explosion of East-meets-South, SushiSamba beautifully mingles Japanese, Peruvian, and Brazilian cuisines to create an off-the-grid small-plates experience in the heart of Miracle Mile. The sleek 6,500-square-foot restaurant is at once modernist and welcoming. The colorful menu is divided into small hot plates, Samba Rolls, raw dishes, large plates, and skewers from the robata.

Don't miss the divine *chicharrón de calamar,* a deliciously creative incarnation of fried calamari, topped with tamarind sauce. Indulge in the crispy *taquitos,* stuffed with Maine lobster and hearts of palm. Feast on the specialty sushi roll unique to this location, the spicy Samba Coral Gables, which is loaded with steamed lobster, avocado, jalapeno, rice cracker, sweet chili, and key lime mayo. ■TIP➜ Save room for dessert. The Samba Split—a tower of dulce de leche ice cream, caramelized bananas, coconut flan, coconut mochi, and caramel popcorn—is even better than it sounds! $ *Average main: $34* ✉ *The Westin Colonnade Hotel, 180 Aragon Ave., Coral Gables* ☎ *305/448–4990* ⊕ *www. sushisamba.com* ✢ *B5.*

KEY BISCAYNE

$$$
MEXICAN

✕ **Cantina Beach.** Leave it to the Ritz-Carlton Key Biscayne to bring a small, sumptuous piece of coastal Mexico to Florida's fabulous beaches. The pool- and oceanside Cantina Beach showcases authentic and divine Mexican cuisine, including fresh guacamole made tableside. The restaurant also boasts the region's only *tequilier,* mixing and matching 110 high-end tequilas. It's no surprise then that Cantina Beach has phenomenal margaritas. And the best part is that you can enjoy them with your feet in the sand, gazing at the ocean. $ *Average main: $21* ✉ *The Ritz-Carlton Key Biscayne, Miami, 455 Grand Bay Dr., Key Biscayne* ☎ *305/365–4622* ⊕ *www.ritzcarlton.com/keybiscayne* ✢ *D6.*

$$$$
ITALIAN

✕ **Cioppino.** Few visitors think to venture out to the far end of Key Biscayne for dinner, but making the journey to the soothing grounds of this quiet Ritz-Carlton property on the beach is well worth it. Choose your view: the ornate dining room near the exhibition kitchen or the alfresco area with views of landscaped gardens or breeze-brushed beaches. Choosing your dishes may be more difficult, given the many rich, luscious Italian options, including imported cheeses, olive oils, risottos, and fresh fish flown in daily. Items range from the creamy *burrata* mozzarella and authentic pasta dishes to tantalizing risotto with organic spinach and roasted quail, all expertly matched with rare and boutique wines. An after-dinner drink and live music at the old-Havana-style RUMBAR inside the hotel is another treat. $ *Average main: $36* ✉ *The Ritz-Carlton Key Biscayne, Miami, 455 Grand Bay Dr., Key Biscayne* ☎ *305/365–4156* ⊕ *www.ritzcarlton.com/keybiscayne* ✢ *D6.*

$$$$
MODERN
AMERICAN
Fodor'sChoice
★

✕ **Rusty Pelican.** Whether you're visiting Miami for the first or 15th time, a meal at the Rusty Pelican could easily stand out as your most memorable experience. The legendary Key Biscayne restaurant's $7 million reinvention is nothing short of spectacular. Vistas of the bay and Miami skyline are sensational—whether you admire them through the floor-to-ceiling windows or from the expansive outdoor seating area, lined with alluring fire pits. The menu is split between tropically inspired small plates, ideal for sharing, and heartier entrées from land and sea. Standouts include corvina ceviche; baked crab cakes; and the crispy fried, whole local red snapper. $ *Average main: $38* ✉ *3201 Rickenbacker Causeway, Key Biscayne* ☎ *305/361–3818* ⊕ *www.therustypelican.com* ✢ *D5.*

2

WYNWOOD

$$ ITALIAN

🍴 **Joey's.** Veneto-native chef Ivo Mazzon pays homage to fresh ingredients prepared simply in his small, modern Italian café, which carries a full line of flatbread pizzas, including the legendary *dolce e piccante* with figs, Gorgonzola, honey, and hot pepper—it's sweet and spicy goodness through and through. Joey's also serves the full gamut of Italian favorites. One of the first nongallery tenants and the first restaurant in the Wynwood Art District, it's become a favorite in this thriving neighborhood. The wine list is small but carefully chosen. [$] *Average main: $19* ✉ *2506 N.W. 2nd Ave., Wynwood* ☎ *305/438–0488* 🌐 *www.joeyswynwood.com* ✥ *D4.*

$$$ ECLECTIC Fodor's Choice ★

🍴 **Wynwood Kitchen & Bar.** At the center of Miami's artsy gallery-driven neighborhood, Wynwood Kitchen & Bar offers an experience completely different from anything else in the state. While you enjoy Latin-inspired small plates, you can marvel at the powerful, hand-painted murals characterizing the interiors and exteriors, which also spill out onto the captivating Wynwood Walls. Designed for sharing, tapas-style dishes include wood-grilled baby octopus skewers, lemon-pepper calamari, roasted beets, bacon-wrapped dates, and ropa vieja empanadas. It's best to allot a good chunk of time to thoroughly enjoy the creative food, the artist-inspired cocktails, and the coolio crowd, and to venerate the sensational works of art all around you. [$] *Average main: $22* ✉ *2550 N.W. 2nd Ave., Wynwood Art District* ☎ *305/722–8959* 🌐 *www.wynwoodkitchenandbar.com* ✥ *C4.*

MIDTOWN

$$$ MODERN ITALIAN Fodor's Choice ★

🍴 **Bocce Bar.** A splendid slice of the Italian countryside has landed in Miami's trendy Midtown area, and the impressive 3,200 square-foot enclave houses a beautifully appointed rustic Italian restaurant, Miami's first official bocce court, and a throwback-style Italian market. Mosaic-tiled floors, antique mirrors, and exposed wood beams set the scene indoors while towering cypress trees, a traditional bocce court, and alfresco seating aplenty define the front patio. Spectacular design notwithstanding, it's the food that headlines the overall Bocce Bar experience. The small plates sharing menu is a gastronomic tour through Italy with a modern twist. Standouts include the savory salumi and cheese selections; farm-fresh antipasti dishes like the grilled treviso with shaved pecorino or creamy polenta with broccoli rabe and poached egg; the house-made pastas; and the whole branzino over braised fennel. Dishes are beautifully presented, often accented by edible flowers, and never fall below a caliber of blow-your-mind deliciousness. [$] *Average main: $29* ✉ *3252 N.E. 1st Ave., Midtown* ☎ *786/245–6211* 🌐 *www.boccebar.com* ✥ *D4.*

$$$$ JAPANESE FUSION Fodor's Choice ★

🍴 **Sugarcane Raw Bar Grill.** Midtown's most popular restaurant rages seven nights (and days) a week; and it's not hard to see why. The vibrant, supersexy, high-design restaurant perfectly captures Miami's Latin vibe while serving eclectic Latin American tapas and modern Japanese delights from three separate kitchens (robata, raw bar, and hot kitchen). Miami's easy-on-the-eyes crowd often begins the Sugarcane experience in the alfresco lounge, engaging in a fabulous mix of standing, posing, flirting, and sipping on delicious cocktails. Indoors, the trio of kitchens engineers some 60 small bites that include everything from ceviche to sushi to bacon-wrapped dates and grilled maple-glazed sweet potatoes. Sugarcane has its fair share of out-of-the-ordinary dishes (think BBQ-spice pig's-ear and oxtail paella) but it's the specialty sushi rolls (like the Night Crab Roll, filled with snow crab, shrimp tempura, and caper mustard) and the crudos (like the spicy local catch) that are most popular. [$] *Average main: $38* ✉ *3252 N.E. 1st Ave., Midtown* ☎ *786/369–0353* 🌐 *sugarcanerawbargrill.com* ✍ *Reservations essential* ✣ *D4.*

FULL-MOON DINNERS

The Full Moon Dinner Series at Cioppino is fun, romantic, geeky, and one of Miami's most memorable experiences. Held from October to May on the exact night of the full moon, the dinner is a four-course Italian gastronomic extravaganza. Tabletop telescopes serve as centerpieces. The restaurant's Constellation Concierge visits each table to point out key stars and constellations, and then invites guests to look at the moon through the megatelescope. Meanwhile highly attentive staff members serve the divine creations of Chef de Cuisine Ezio Gamba.

DESIGN DISTRICT

$$$ AMERICAN Fodor's Choice ★

🍴 **Michael's Genuine Food & Drink.** Michael's is often cited as Miami's top restaurant, and it's not hard to see why. This indoor-outdoor bistro in Miami's Design District relies on fresh ingredients and a hip but unpretentious vibe to lure diners. Beautifully arranged combinations like crispy, sweet-and-spicy pork belly with kimchi explode with unlikely but satisfying flavor. Owner and chef Michael Schwartz aims for sophisticated American cuisine with an emphasis on local and organic ingredients. He gets it right. Portions are divided into small, medium, and large plates, and the smaller plates are more inventive, so you can order several and explore. Reserve two weeks in advance for weekend tables; also, consider brunch. [$] *Average main: $26* ✉ *130 N.E. 40th St., Design District* ☎ *305/573–5550* 🌐 *www.michaelsgenuine.com* ✍ *Reservations essential* ✣ *D3.*

$$$ MODERN AMERICAN Fodor's Choice ★

🍴 **Oak Tavern.** In the center of Miami's stylish Design District, Oak Tavern delivers perfect modern American cuisine. The personality-driven restaurant, covered in reclaimed wood, and named from the giant oak tree in the alfresco courtyard, is helmed by local celebrity chef David Bracha. Bracha's creative juices flow through his small plates, large plates, and delicacies from the wood oven. Miami A-listers and neighborhood regulars alike return week after week for the *bacalao* croquettes, roasted baby carrots salad, burrata with walnut pesto, artisan pizzas, mushroom-crusted strip steak in truffle butter, and wood-grilled salmon with butternut squash risotto. The crudos and raw oysters are off the charts but not to be outshined by the fire-roasted oysters in chili butter, sizzling out of the wood oven. Excellent mixology is also a highlight of a tavern visit. Spice up your night (or day) with a Frida Kahlo (tequila, crushed tomatoes, fresh rosemary, chilies) or a Green

Mile (gin, cucumber, chili). [$] *Average main: $25* ✉ *35 N.E. 40th St., Design District* ☎ *786/391–1818* 🌐 *www.oaktavernmiami.com* ⏲ *No lunch weekends* ✥ *D3.*

LITTLE HAITI

The east part of Little Haiti is often referred to as the "Upper East Side." Many of the area's newer restaurants are opening here.

$ CARIBBEAN 🍴 **Chez Le Bebe.** Chez Le Bebe offers a short menu of Haitian home cooking—it's been going strong for 30 years and has been featured on shows like the Travel Channel's *Bizarre Foods with Andrew Zimmern* and *The Layover with Anthony Bourdain.* If you want to try stewed goat, this is the place to do it! Other dishes include tender and flavorful chicken, fish, oxtail, and fried pork; each plate comes with rice, beans, plantains, and salad, for around $15. [$] *Average main: $15* ✉ *114 N.E. 54th St., Little Haiti* ☎ *305/751–7639* 💳 *No credit cards* ✥ *D3.*

LITTLE HAVANA

$$$$ SPANISH 🍴 **Casa Juancho.** This meeting place for the movers and shakers of the Cuban *exilio* community is also a haven for lovers of fine Spanish regional cuisine. Strolling balladeers serenade amid brown brick, rough-hewn dark timbers, hanging smoked meats, ceramic plates, and oil still lifes: a bit of old España dropped on Calle Ocho. Try the *dorada a la sal* (sea bream baked in a crust of sea salt), *langostinos al vega Sicilia* (jumbo shrimp sautéed with butter and shallots), or one of the many paellas. The house features one of the largest lists of reserve Spanish wines in the United States. In the evening, there's live Latin music in the dining room and in the lounge. [$] *Average main: $34* ✉ *2436 S.W. 8th St., Little Havana* ☎ *305/642–2452* 🌐 *www.casajuancho.com* ✥ *C4.*

$ CUBAN 🍴 **Exquisito Restaurant.** For a true locals' spot and some substantial Cuban eats in the heart of Little Havana, pop into Exquisito Restaurant, a local institution since the 1970s. The unassuming Cuban café serves up delectable, authentic Cuban favorites, including a great cubano and succulent yuca with garlic sauce. There's a quick-serve café on one side; next door is a full-service restaurant. A Cuban coffee is a whopping $0.75. [$] *Average main: $14* ✉ *1510 S.W. 8th St., Little Havana* ☎ *305/643–0227* 🌐 *www.exquisitorestaurant.com* 💳 *No credit cards* ✥ *C5.*

$$ VIETNAMESE Fodor's Choice ★ 🍴 **Hy-Vong Vietnamese Cuisine.** Florida's best Vietnamese food in the heart of Little Havana? It may sound bizarre, but Hy-Vong will have you rethinking your drive to Calle Ocho for Cuban cuisine. In fact, people are willing to wait on the sidewalk for hours to sample the delights at this tiny restaurant, like *cha gio* (Vietnamese spring rolls), fish panfried with mango or with *nuoc man* (a garlic-lime fish sauce), not to mention the pork *thit kho* (caramelized braised pork) stewed in coconut milk. Beer-savvy proprietors Kathy Manning and Tung Nguyen serve a half-dozen top brews (Double Grimbergen, Peroni, and Spaten among them) to further inoculate the experience from the ordinary—well, as ordinary as a Vietnamese restaurant on Calle Ocho can be. Arrive early to avoid long waits. [$] *Average main: $17* ✉ *3458 S.W. 8th St., Little*

2

Havana ☎ *305/446–3674* ⊕ *www.hyvong.com* ⊘ *No lunch; Closed Mon. and Tues.* ✢ *B5.*

$ ✕ **Las Pinareños Fruteria y Floreria.** In the mood for something refreshing
CUBAN or a high-octane jolt? Try Las Pinareños, a *fruteria* (fruit stand) that
serves *coco frio* (fresh, cold coconut juice served in a whole coconut),
mango juice, and other *jugos* (juices), as well as Cuban coffees and
Cuban finger foods. You can order your sweet, hot *cortadito* (coffee
with milk) or a *cafecito* (no milk) from the walk-up window and enjoy it
at one of the stools in front of the shop or sit at one of the tables inside
the fruit and flower market. Ⓢ *Average main: $7* ✉ *1334 S.W. 8th St.,
Little Havana* ☎ *305/285–1135* ✢ *C5.*

$$ ✕ **Versailles.** ¡*Bienvenido a Miami!* To the area's Cuban population,
CUBAN Miami without Versailles is like rice without black beans. First-timer
Miami visitors looking for that "Cuban food on Calle Ocho" experi-
ence, look no further. The storied eatery, where old émigrés opine daily
about all things Cuban, is a stop on every political candidate's campaign
trail, and it should be a stop for you as well. Order a heaping platter of
lechon asado (roasted pork loin), ropa vieja, or *picadillo* (spicy ground
beef), all served with rice, beans, and fried plantains. Battle the oncom-
ing food coma with a cup of the city's strongest cafecito, which comes in
the tiniest of cups but packs a lot of punch. Versailles operates a bakery
next door as well—take some pastelitos home. Ⓢ *Average main: $15*
✉ *3555 S.W. 8th St., Little Havana* ☎ *305/444–0240* ✢ *C5.*

SOUTH BEACH

$$$$ ✕ **Bianca.** In a hotel where style reigns supreme, this high-profile res-
ITALIAN taurant provides both glamour and solid cuisine. The main attraction
Fodor'sChoice of dining here is to see and be seen, but you may leave talking about
★ the food just as much as the outfits, hairdos, and celebrity appearances.
This Italian restaurant doles out some pretty amazing fare, including a
shaved baby-artichoke salad and truffle tagliatelle—perfection in every
bite. The dessert menu may seem a bit back-to-basics, with tiramisù
and cheesecake among the favorites, but these sweet classics are done
right. For something a bit more casual at the Delano, try sushi from
the Philippe Starck countertop sushi bar, Umi, at the front of the hotel.
Ⓢ *Average main: $50* ✉ *Delano Hotel, 1685 Collins Ave., South Beach*
☎ *305/674–5752* ⊕ *www.delano-hotel.com* ⚑ *Reservations essential*
✢ *H2.*

$$ ✕ **Big Pink.** The décor in this innovative, superpopular diner may remind
AMERICAN you of a roller-skating rink—everything is pink Lucite, stainless steel,
and campy (think sports lockers as decorative touches)—and the menu
is 3 feet tall, complete with a table of contents. Food is solidly all-American, with dozens of tasty sandwiches, pizzas, turkey or beef burgers, and
side dishes, each and every one composed with gourmet flair. Big Pink
also makes a great spot for brunch. Ⓢ *Average main: $14* ✉ *157 Col-
lins Ave., South Beach* ☎ *305/532–4700* ⊕ *www.mylesrestaurantgroup.
com* ✢ *G5.*

$$$$ ✕ **BLT Steak.** This Ocean Drive favorite, renowned for seriously divine
STEAKHOUSE Gruyère cheese popovers and succulent steak and fish dishes, illuminates the vibrant, open lobby of the snazzy Betsy Hotel. It has the

distinction among all of Miami's steakhouses of serving breakfast daily and consistently impressing even the most finicky eaters. You can count on the highest-quality cuts of USDA Prime-certified Black Angus, and American Wagyu beef, in addition to blackboard specials, and sushi and raw-bar selections. Though the name may say steak, the fresh fish is arguably the highlight of the entire menu—the sautéed Dover sole with soy-caper brown butter is legendary. [$] *Average main: $42* ✉ *The Betsy Hotel, 1440 Ocean Dr., South Beach* ☎ *305/673–0044* 🌐 *www.bltrestaurants.com* ✣ *G2.*

$$$$ CUBAN Fodor's Choice ★ 🍴 **De Rodriguez Cuba on Ocean.** If you're seeking a classy, personality-driven joint in which to experience a superlative Miami incarnation of old-world Havana, look no further than this fabulous eatery run by James Beard Award–winning chef Douglas Rodriguez. It captures the essence of circa-1950s Cuba—from the décor to the music to the incredible mojitos. Although you'll find some Cuban classics here, chef Rodriguez truly showcases his creativity and gastronomic prowess across the menu. His sensational ceviches and innovative tapas and appetizers include tuna-watermelon ceviche, Cuban shrimp and sweet-corn grits, smoked marlin tacos, and crispy shrimp *chicharrón*. Larger plates such as the Sugarcane Tuna (thick, fresh, sushi-grade tuna skewered with sugarcanes) served alongside quinoa and Catalan spinach and with squid ink sauce are off-the-charts delicious. Make sure you start your evening here with a Cojito, a coconut mojito made with fresh coconut, coconut rum, lime, and mint. [$] *Average main: $36* ✉ *Hilton Bentley Hotel, 101 Ocean Dr., South Beach* ☎ *305/672–6624* 🌐 *www.drodriguezcuba.com* ✣ *G5.*

$$$ MODERN ITALIAN 🍴 **Dolce Italian.** In the center of the South Beach action, Dolce Italian doles out an irresistible menage à trois: great food, great ambience, and an easy-on-the-eyes crowd. Tucked into the first floors of the renovated Gale South Beach hotel, Miami's "it" crowd clamors for a table to see and be seen feasting on Dolce's spaghetti al pomodoro, Tartufata pizza (with speck, spicy salami, and truffle oil), housemade mozzarella, roasted branzino, and meats from the Tuscan grill. Indeed, Italian-born chef Paolo Dorigato's menu is packed with modern incarnations of Italian classics that would make *nonna* proud. After dinner, stop in the adjacent Regent Cocktail Bar for a classic cocktail in a speakeasy setting or head into the basement to party the night away in the '70s-inspired Rec Room. [$] *Average main: $24* ✉ *1690 Collins Ave., South Beach* ☎ *786/975–2550* 🌐 *www.galehotel.com/dine* ✣ *G2.*

$$$ AMERICAN 🍴 **Florida Cookery.** Originally the brainchild of award-winning Miami chef Kris Wessel (of *Chopped* fame), the Florida Cookery redefined Florida cuisine when it opened. Now that Wessel is gone, it lacks the wow factor it once had but it still delivers taste sensations crafted from just about all things Florida—local fish, stone crabs, and spiny lobster to alligator, Indian River County grapefruit, hearts of palm, and kumquats. Start with the empanadas trio (curry chicken, ropa vieja, and alligator) or the *corvina tiradito*. Splurge on the Miami Paella for your main—a massive skillet of Florida fresh seafood, chorizo, and yellow rice. [$] *Average main: $26* ✉ *The James Royal Palm, 1545 Collins Ave., South Beach* ☎ *786/276–0333* 🌐 *www.florida-cookery.com* ✣ *H2.*

$$$$ SEAFOOD Fodor'sChoice ★

🍴 **Joe's Stone Crab Restaurant.** In South Beach's decidedly new-money scene, the stately Joe's Stone Crab is an old-school testament to good food and good service. South Beach's most storied restaurant started as a turn-of-the-century eating house when Joseph Weiss discovered succulent stone crabs off the Florida coast. A century later, the restaurant stretches a city block and serves 2,000 dinners a day to local politicians and moneyed patriarchs. Stone crabs, served with legendary mustard sauce, crispy hash browns, and creamed spinach, remain the staple. Though stone-crab season runs from October 15 to May 15, Joe's remains open year-round (albeit with a limited schedule) serving other phenomenal seafood dishes. Finish your meal with tart key lime pie, baked fresh daily. ■ **TIP→ Joe's famously refuses reservations, and weekend waits can be three hours long—yes, you read that correctly—so come early or order from Joe's Take Away next door.** [$] *Average main: $45* ✉ *11 Washington Ave., South Beach* ☎ *305/673–0365, 305/673–4611 for takeout* 🌐 *www.joesstonecrab.com* ✍ *Reservations not accepted* ⏲ *No lunch Sun. and Mon. and mid-May–mid-Oct.* ✥ *G5.*

$$$$ JAPANESE FUSION Fodor'sChoice ★

🍴 **Juvia.** High atop South Beach's design-driven parking garage, Juvia commingles urban sophistication with South Beach seduction. Towering over the beach's art deco district, the restaurant rises as a bold amalgamation of steel, glass, hanging gardens, and purple accents—a true work of art high in the sky. Three renowned chefs unite to deliver an amazing eating experience that screams Japanese, Peruvian, and French all in the same breath, focusing largely on raw fish and seafood dishes. The see-and-be-seen crowd can't get enough; neither can we! [$] *Average main: $42* ✉ *1111 Lincoln Rd., South Beach* ☎ *305/763–8272* 🌐 *www.juviamiami.com* ✍ *Reservations essential* ✥ *F2.*

$$$ ASIAN

🍴 **Khong River House.** A James Beard Foundation semifinalist as America's Best New Restaurant 2013, Khong River House brings the exotic flavors of rural Thailand to Miami's storied Lincoln Road. Unlike your typical American Thai restaurant, Khong doles out hefty portions of lesser-known dishes common to the Mekong River and Golden Triangle region, where Myanmar, Thailand, Laos, and Vietnam converge. Ambush your senses with *Kuay Teaw Reau Phama* (Burmese noodle wraps stuffed with chilies, roasted peanuts, palm sugar, and cilantro), *Gang Pah Gai* (northeastern-style jungle stew with chicken, baby corn, and Thai eggplant), or *Ped Pad Cha* (Thai-style crispy duck). The restaurant is also a visual feast for the senses with seductive hardwood walls and furnishings, tastefully placed Buddhist statues, as well as a clandestine, second-floor dining room. [$] *Average main: $26* ✉ *1661 Meridian Ave., South Beach* ☎ *305/763–8147* 🌐 *www.khongriver.com* ✍ *Reservations essential* ✥ *G2.*

$$$ MODERN FRENCH

🍴 **La Gloutonnerie.** Far removed from South Beach's mass-market deco drive strip, this intimate "vintage kitchen" brings the best of French old-school cuisine to the beach's more refined SoFi (South of Fifth) neighborhood. Executive Chef Christian Testa presents everything you'd desire from a renowned French kitchen from *escargots Bourgogne* to *chateubriand* while adding new-world flavors and fusions to the mix with dishes such as the tuna carpaccio and an assortment of fresh pasta entrees. Within the restaurant, a retro mini-market offers cheese, cold

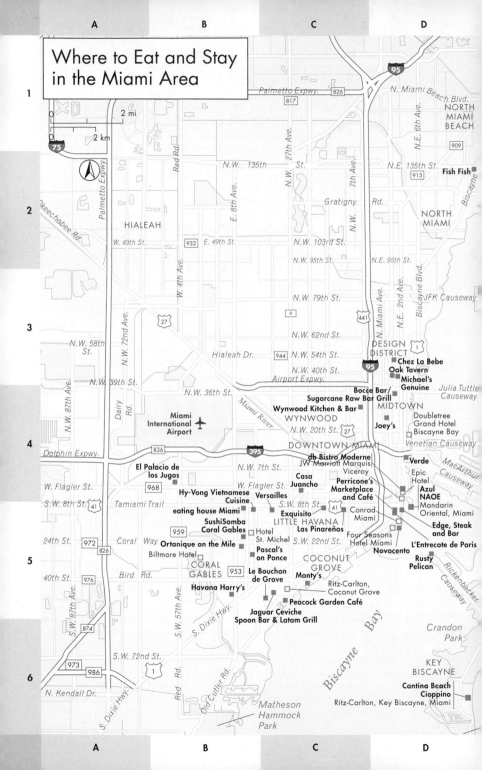

Where to Eat and Stay in the Miami Area

0 2 mi
0 2 km

NORTH MIAMI BEACH
N. Miami Beach Blvd.
Palmetto Expwy.
N.W. 135th St.
Gratigny Rd.
N.E. 135th St.
Fish Fish
HIALEAH
W. 49th St.
E. 49th St.
N.W. 103rd St.
NORTH MIAMI
N.W. 95th St.
N.E. 95th St.
Okeechobee Rd.
N.W. 79th St.
JFK Causeway
Biscayne Blvd.
N.W. 58th St.
N.W. 62nd St.
DESIGN DISTRICT
Chez La Bebe
Oak Tavern
Michael's Genuine
Hialeah Dr.
N.W. 54th St.
N.W. 40th St.
Airport Expwy.
Julia Tuttle Causeway
N.W. 39th St.
N.W. 36th St.
Bocce Bar/
Sugarcane Raw Bar Grill
MIDTOWN
Miami International Airport
Miami River
Wynwood Kitchen & Bar
WYNWOOD
N.W. 20th St.
Joey's
Doubletree Grand Hotel Biscayne Bay
Venetian Causeway
Dolphin Expwy.
DOWNTOWN MIAMI
db Bistro Moderne
Verde
MacArthur Causeway
El Palacio de los Jugos
N.W. 7th St.
JW Marriott Marquis
Viceroy
Epic Hotel
Azul
W. Flagler St.
Casa Juancho
Perricone's Marketplace and Café
NAOE
Mandarin Oriental, Miami
Hy-Vong Vietnamese Cuisine
Versailles
Tamiami Trail
W. Flagler St.
Conrad Miami
eating house Miami
S.W. 8th St.
Exquisito
LITTLE HAVANA
Edge, Steak and Bar
SushiSamba Coral Gables
Las Pinareños
Four Seasons Hotel Miami
L'Entrecote de Paris
Coral Way
Hotel St. Michel
S.W. 22nd St.
Novocento
Ortanique on the Mile
Biltmore Hotel
Pascal's on Ponce
COCONUT GROVE
Rusty Pelican
CORAL GABLES
Bird Rd.
Le Bouchon de Grove
Monty's
Havana Harry's
Ritz-Carlton, Coconut Grove
Peacock Garden Café
Jaguar Ceviche Spoon Bar & Latam Grill
Biscayne Bay
Crandon Park
KEY BISCAYNE
S.W. 72nd St.
N. Kendall Dr.
Matheson Hammock Park
Cantina Beach
Cioppino
Ritz-Carlton, Key Biscayne, Miami

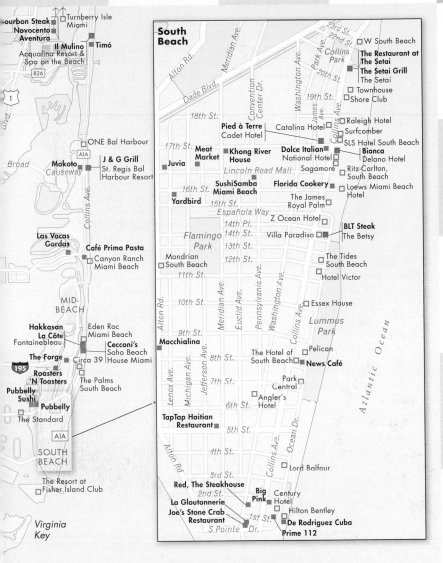

South Beach

Grid labels: E, F, G, H (columns); 1, 2, 3, 4, 5, 6 (rows)

ourbon Steak
Novecento
Aventura
Turnberry Isle Miami
Il Mulino
Timó
Acqualina Resort & Spa on the Beach
826

1

W South Beach
The Restaurant at The Setai
The Setai Grill
The Setai
Townhouse
Shore Club

ONE Bal Harbour
Makoto
Causeway
J & G Grill
St. Regis Bal Harbour Resort
Broad

Collins Park
23rd St.
22nd St.
Park Ave.
20th St.
19th St.
Meridian Ave.
Alton Rd.
Dade Blvd.
Convention Center Dr.
Washington Ave.
James Ave.
Collins Ave.

18th St.
Pied à Terre
Cadet Hotel
17th St.
Meat Market
Khong River House
Juvia
Lincoln Road Mall
16th St.
SushiSamba Miami Beach
Yardbird
15th St.
Española Way
14th Pl.
Flamingo Park
14th St.
13th St.
12th St.
Mondrian South Beach
11th St.

Catalina Hotel
Dolce Italian
National Hotel
Sagamore
Florida Cookery
The James Royal Palm
Z Ocean Hotel
Villa Paradiso

Raleigh Hotel
Surfcomber
SLS Hotel South Beach
Bianca
Delano Hotel
Ritz-Carlton, South Beach
Loews Miami Beach Hotel

BLT Steak
The Betsy

The Tides South Beach
Hotel Victor

MID-BEACH
Hakkasan
La Côte
Fontainebleau
The Forge
195
Roasters 'N Toasters
Pubbelly Sushi
Pubbelly
The Standard
SOUTH BEACH

Eden Roc Miami Beach
Cecconi's Soho Beach House Miami
Circa 39
The Palms South Beach

10th St.
9th St.
Macchialina
8th St.
7th St.
6th St.
TapTap Haitian Restaurant
5th St.
4th St.
3rd St.
Red, The Steakhouse
2nd St.
La Gloutonnerie
Joe's Stone Crab Restaurant
1st St.
S Pointe Dr.

Alton Rd.
Meridian Ave.
Euclid Ave.
Pennsylvania Ave.
Washington Ave.
Lenox Ave.
Michigan Ave.
Jefferson Ave.
Collins Ave.
Ocean Dr.

Essex House
Lummus Park
Pelican
The Hotel of South Beach
News Café
Park Central
Angler's Hotel

Lord Balfour
Big Pink
Century Hotel
Hilton Bentley
De Rodriguez Cuba
Prime 112

Atlantic Ocean

The Resort at Fisher Island Club

Virginia Key

A T L A N T I C   O C E A N

Bill Baggs Cape Florida State Recreation Area

KEY
- □ Hotels
- ■ Restaurants
- ■ Restaurants in Hotels
- ↕ following reviews indicates a map-grid coordinate

cuts, and imported French products. Add stylish black-and-white décor, stellar service, and a hip crowd, and you have the perfect recipe for keeping history in style. [$] *Average main: $28* ✉ *81 Washington Ave., South Beach* ☎ *305/503–3811* 🌐 *www.lagloutonnerie.com* ✥ *G5.*

$$$$ ITALIAN Fodor's Choice ★ 🍴 **Macchialina Taverna Rustica.** Framed by exposed brick walls, decorated with daily specials chalkboards, and packed with gregarious patrons, this local foodie hangout feels like a cozy, neighborhoody, New England tavern. And with a gorgeous menu showcasing the prowess of chef Federico Fellini, Macchialina Taverna Rustica nails the concept of modern Italian cuisine. Combining such great ambience and amazing eats, expect one helluva night. Start with some Italian-imported salumi, local burrata, or creamy polenta with sausage ragù and cipollini onions. Then, move on to the house-made pastas, perhaps the beet-filled *mezzaluna,* the *tagliolini al funghi,* or the spaghetti *con vongole,* before feasting on a lavish chicken or fish entrée (local hog snapper, anyone?). Save room for the house *panna cotta,* smothered in candied pistachios and balsamic-reduced strawberries. [$] *Average main: $34* ✉ *820 Alton Rd., South Beach* ☎ *305/534–2124* 🌐 *www.macchialina.com* ✥ *F3.*

$$$$ STEAKHOUSE 🍴 **Meat Market.** On Lincoln Road, where most of the restaurants emphasize people-watching over good food, this is one spot where you can find the best of both. Indeed, this is a meat market in every sense of the phrase, with great cuts of meat and plenty of sexy people passing by in skimpy clothes and enjoying fruity libations at the bar. Hard-core carnivores go wild over the 14-ounce center-cut prime New York steak as well as the "mixed-grill special," a creative trio of meats and seafood that changes nightly. The tuna tartare is exceptional here, lightly tossed in ginger and soy with mashed avocados and mango mole. Also consider the wood-grilled blackened local snapper cooked to perfection and topped with a light sun-dried-tomato pesto and dollops of black-garlic sauce. The broccolini side makes a nice complement to any meal. [$] *Average main: $39* ✉ *915 Lincoln Rd., South Beach* ☎ *305/532–0088* 🌐 *www.meatmarketmiami.com* ✥ *F2.*

$$ AMERICAN 🍴 **News Café.** No trip to Miami is complete without a stop at this Ocean Drive landmark, though the food is nothing special. The 24-hour café attracts a crowd with snacks, light meals, drinks, periodicals, and the people-parade on the sidewalk out front. Most prefer sitting outside, where they can feel the salt breeze and gawk at the human scenery. Seagrape trees shade a patio where you can watch from a quiet distance. Offering a little of this and a little of that—bagels, pâtés, chocolate fondue, sandwiches, and a terrific wine list—this joint has something for everyone. Although service can be indifferent to the point of laissez-faire and the food is mediocre at best, News Café is just one of those places visitors love. [$] *Average main: $16* ✉ *800 Ocean Dr., South Beach* ☎ *305/538–6397* 🌐 *www.newscafe.com* ✍ *Reservations not accepted* ✥ *G4.*

$$$$ MODERN FRENCH 🍴 **Pied à Terre.** This cozy, 36-seat French Contemporary restaurant with Mediterranean influence resides in the heart of South Beach, but it's everything the beach is not. Quiet, classic, and elegant, this hidden gastro-sanctuary within the historic Cadet Hotel forgoes glitz and gimmicks for taste and sophistication. The restaurant recalls the ambience

CHEAP EATS ON SOUTH BEACH

Miami Beach is notorious for overpriced eateries, but locals know better. **Pizza Rustica** (✉ *8th St. and Washington Ave. and 667 Lincoln Rd.*) serves up humongous slices overflowing with mozzarella, steak, olives, and barbecue chicken until 4 am. **La Sandwicherie** (✉ *14th St. between Collins and Washington aves.*) is a South Beach classic that's been here since 1988, serving gourmet French sandwiches, a delicious prosciutto salad, and healthful smoothies from a walk-up bar. **Lime Fresh Mexican Grill** (✉ *1439 Alton Rd., at 14th St.*) serves fresh and tangy fish tacos and homemade guacamole.

2

of a bona fide, intimate Parisian eatery—the kind you'd randomly discover on a side street in the City of Light's 5th or 6th arrondissement—and doles out succulent French contemporary cuisine enhanced by an excellent and reasonably priced wine list. [$] *Average main: $42* ✉ *Cadet Hotel, 1701 James Ave., South Beach* ☎ *305/531–4533* 🌐 *www.cadethotel.com* ✍ *Reservations essential* ⏲ *Closed Mon. No lunch* ✥ *G2.*

$$$$ STEAKHOUSE 🍴 **Prime 112.** This wildly busy steakhouse is particularly renowned for its well-marbled Prime beef, creamed corn, truffle macaroni and cheese, and buzzing scene: while you stand at the bar awaiting your table (everyone has to wait—at least a little bit), you'll clamor for a drink with all facets of Miami's high society, from the city's top real estate developers and philanthropists to striking models and celebrities (Lenny Kravitz, Jay-Z, and Matt Damon are among a big list of celebrity regulars). [$] *Average main: $42* ✉ *112 Ocean Dr., South Beach* ☎ *305/532–8112* 🌐 *www.mylesrestaurantgroup.com* ✍ *Reservations not accepted* ⏲ *No lunch weekends* ✥ *G5.*

$$$ ECLECTIC Fodor's Choice ★ 🍴 **Pubbelly.** Five years after opening, South Beach's favorite neighborhood gastropub still packs the house nightly. The petite eatery, located on a residential street in SoBe's western reaches, attracts the "who's who" of beach socialites, hipsters, and the occasional tourist coming to chow down on inventive Asian-Latin small plates, dumplings, charcuterie, and seasonal large plates by executive chef/owner Jose Mendin. From bay scallops Bourguignon to short-rib tartare to *huitlacoche* (corn truffle) dumplings in squid ink black butter, Pubbelly constantly pushes the envelope on inventive cuisine, and locals simply can't get enough. Expect deservedly long wait times, especially on weekends. But not to worry: after a few rounds of craft beers, sake cocktails, and eclectic wines from the awesome drink menu, your table will be ready in no time! [$] *Average main: $28* ✉ *1418 20th St., South Beach* ☎ *305/532–7555* 🌐 *www.pubbelly.com* ✥ *E4.*

$$$$ JAPANESE 🍴 **Pubbelly Sushi.** The team behind South Beach's wildly popular Pubbelly gastropub has teamed up with sushi chef Yuki Ieto to create the Pubbelly Sushi, a 40-seat canteen doling out contemporary, Japanese-inspired sharing plates. Of course you go light with the grade-A sashimi

or meats from the *robata* (Japanese charcoal) grill, but the real fun lies in the flavor-rich Snacks, Pubbelly Rolls, and New England Style Rolls. Start with Rock Shrimp Tempura "Buffalo Style" and graduate to the Bigeye Tuna Roll (spicy tuna over squares of crispy rice) and Navarro (salmon, crab, melted mozzarella, and fried onions). Feast on the Fried Clams New England Roll—five buttermilk-soaked clams smothered with coleslaw on a brioche bun. Wash it all down with the house Vodkasake cocktails. They're all deliciously addicting, but the Basil Berry (basil, strawberries, yuzu, sake) and Spicy Pina (jalapeno, pineapple, sake) go best with a steamy Miami evening. $\boxed{\$}$ *Average main: $38* ⊠ *1424 20th St., South Beach* ☎ *305/531–9282* ⊕ *www.pubbellysushi.com* ✛ *E4.*

$$$$
STEAKHOUSE
✕ **Red, the Steakhouse.** The carnivore glamour den seduces with its red and black dominatrix color scheme and overloads the senses with the divine smells and tastes of the extensive menu. Red boasts an equal number of seafood and traditional carnivorous offerings, each delicately prepared, meticulously presented, and gleefully consumed. Start with the tuna tartare, the mussels *diavolo,* or crisp chili calamari and then continue with fresh lobster or the many variations of Angus Beef Prime. And don't forget about the dozen or so sides, often the most exciting part of any steak house experience. $\boxed{\$}$ *Average main: $50* ⊠ *119 Washington Ave., South Beach* ☎ *305/534–3688* ⊕ *www.redthesteakhouse. com* ⚠ *Reservations essential* ✛ *G5.*

$$$$
ASIAN
✕ **The Restaurant at The Setai.** East meets West in the open-theater kitchen helmed by chef Mathias Gervais, where dishes reflect the divine and disparate flavors of Asia—from Thailand and India to China and Malaysia. Indeed, dining here is a culinary tour of Asia. With its harmonious courtyard reflecting pool and polished-stone interiors, the setting of the Setai is so dramatically beautiful that a less-than-heavenly dining experience would be a blow. Even so, the restaurant exceeds all expectations. Dishes—such as steamed yellowtail snapper with ginger soy, sweet soy, and green onions; perfectly cooked dim sum; and curries—come family-style in native crockery. The leather-bound wine list is 45 pages long. $\boxed{\$}$ *Average main: $50* ⊠ *The Setai Hotel, 2001 Collins Ave., South Beach* ☎ *305/520–6400* ⊕ *www.thesetaihotel.com/dining/ therestaurant* ⚠ *Reservations essential* ✛ *H1.*

$$$$
STEAKHOUSE
✕ **The Setai Grill.** If there's such a thing as an haute steakhouse, the Setai Grill is it. Executive Chef Mathias Gervais reinterprets American classics using the Rolls Royces of the food industry (think Pat LaFrieda beef, Cinco Jotas's Jamón Ibérico, and Marky's caviar) and adding a French, contemporary twist. While the LaFrieda prime cuts and the braised meats exemplify tradition perfected, Gervais goes more avante-garde than his "Butcher's Cuts" with the bites, small plates and medium plates. The Crispy Duck salad, for example, is a sensational taste explosion, as the flavors of duck confit, watercress, fried shallots, lychess, and sweet onion vinaigrette unite. $\boxed{\$}$ *Average main: $77* ⊠ *The Setai Hotel, 101 20th St., South Beach* ☎ *305/520–6800* ⊕ *www.thesetaihotel.com* ⚠ *Reservations essential* ⊗ *Closed Mon. and Tues.* ✛ *H1.*

$$$$
JAPANESE
Fodor's Choice
★
✕ **SushiSamba Miami Beach.** Though SushiSamba branched out from NYC to Miami Beach back in 2001, this place is as trendy as ever, with long wait times to prove it. Like its six sister locations, SushiSamba Miami Beach doles out flavor explosions of East-meets-South, fusing

Japanese, Peruvian, and Brazilian cuisines to create an off-the-grid small-plates experience, this time in the heart of pedestrian-friendly Lincoln Road. The results are succulent and superb: skewers of miso-marinated sea bass over roasted corn, crunchy hamachi *taquitos* (yellowtail tartare with spicy aji panca sauce), *mocqueca mista* (Brazilian seafood stew), and South Beach–inspired sushi rolls, including the signature Samba Dromo, filled with lobster, mango, and peanut curry. Always packed with customers, both indoors and out, the blaring beats, great eats, and amazing cocktails are a fabulous rare find of timeless trendiness on South Beach. $ *Average main: $34* ⊠ *600 Lincoln Rd., South Beach* ☎ *305/673–5337* ⊕ *www.sushisamba.com* ✚ *G2.*

$ × **Tap Tap Haitian Restaurant.** Tap Tap is anything but SoBe glitz and
CARIBBEAN glam, but this Haitian restaurant will instantly immerse you in Haiti's cuisine and culture. An extensive collection of Haitian folk art is displayed throughout this house turned restaurant so much so that every wall, table, and chair doubles as a piece of colorful art. Menu highlights include *soup joumou* (pumpkin soup), *spagheti kreyol* (pasta, shrimp or herring, and a creole tomato sauce), *kabrit nan sos* (Bolinas goat stew in a mildly spicy tomato-based sauce), and grilled conch (when available). They also have an extensive vegetarian menu, including several vegan dishes. $ *Average main: $14* ⊠ *819 5th St., South Beach* ☎ *305/672–2898* ✚ *F4.*

$$$ × **Yardbird Southern Table & Bar.** There's a helluva lot of Southern lovin'
SOUTHERN from the Lowcountry at this lively and funky South Beach spot. Miami's A-list puts calorie-counting aside for decadent nights filled with comfort foods and innovative drinks. The family-style menu is divided between "small plates," "the bird," "plates," and "fixins," but have no doubt the "the bird" takes center stage (or plate) here. You'll rave about Mama's chicken biscuits, the chicken 'n' watermelon 'n' waffles, and Llewellyn's fine fried chicken, which requires a 27-hour marination and slow-cooking process. Oh, and then there are the sides, like house-cut fries with a buttermilk dipping sauce and bacon salt or the super-creamy macaroni and cheese. Don't plan on hitting the beach in a bikini the next day. $ *Average main: $28* ⊠ *1600 Lenox Ave., South Beach* ☎ *305/538–5220* ⊕ *www.runchickenrun.com* ✚ *F2.*

MID-BEACH

$$$ × **Cecconi's.** The wait for a table at this outpost of the iconic Italian res-
ITALIAN taurant is just as long as its West Hollywood counterpart, and the dining experience just as fabulous. Eating here is a real scene of "who's who" and "who's eating what." Without a doubt, the truffle pizza, which servers shave huge hunks of black or white truffle onto tableside, is the restaurant's most talked about dish. The fish carpaccios are light and succulent while the classically hearty pastas and risottos provide authentic Italian fare. $ *Average main: $28* ⊠ *Soho Beach House, 4385 Collins Ave., Mid-Beach* ☎ *786/507–7900* ⊕ *www.cecconismiamibeach. com* ⌖ *Reservations essential* ✚ *E3.*

$$$$ STEAKHOUSE 🍴 **The Forge.** Legendary for its opulence, this restaurant has been wowing patrons since 1968. After a renovation, the Forge reemerged in 2010 more decadent than ever—and it hasn't looked back since. It is a steakhouse, but a steakhouse the likes of which you haven't seen before. Antiques, gilt-framed paintings, a chandelier from the Paris Opera House, and Tiffany stained-glass windows from New York's Trinity Church are the fitting background for some of Miami's best cuts. The tried-and-true menu also includes prime rib, bone-in filet, lobster *thermidor,* chocolate soufflé, and sinful side dishes like creamed spinach and roasted-garlic mashed potatoes. For its walk-in humidor alone, the over-the-top Forge is worth visiting. Automated wine machines span the perimeter of the restaurant and allow you to pick your own pour and sample several wines throughout your meal. [$] *Average main: $38* ✉ *432 Arthur Godfrey Rd., Mid-Beach* ☎ *305/538–8533* 🌐 *www.theforge.com* 🕓 *No lunch* ✥ *E4.*

$$$$ CANTONESE Fodor's Choice ★ 🍴 **Hakkasan Miami.** This stateside sibling of the Michelin-star London restaurant brings the haute-Chinese-food movement to South Florida, adding Pan-Asian flair to even quite simple and authentic Cantonese recipes, and producing an entire menu that can be classified as blow-your-mind delicious. Seafood and vegetarian dishes outnumber meat options, with the scallop-and-shrimp dim sum, Szechuan-style braised eggplant, and charcoal-grilled silver cod with champagne and Chinese honey reaching new heights of excellence. ■ **TIP→ It's dinner only here, except on weekends when the restaurant hosts a dim sum lunch.** Superb eats notwithstanding, another reason to experience Hakkasan is that it's arguably the sexiest, best-looking restaurant on Miami Beach. Intricately carved, lacquered-black-wood Chinois panels divide seating sections, creating a deceptively cozy dining experience for such a large restaurant. Dress to impress. [$] *Average main: $42* ✉ *Fontainebleau Hotel, 4441 Collins Ave., 4th fl., Mid-Beach* ☎ *786/276–1388 after 4 pm, 877/326–7412 before 4 pm* 🌐 *www.hakkasan.com/miami* ✍ *Reservations essential* 🕓 *No lunch weekdays* ✥ *E3.*

$$ FRENCH 🍴 **La Côte.** With clean white lines, colorful bursts of aqua-blue cushions, and elegant umbrellas, La Côte at the Fontainebleau whisks you away to the coast of southern France. The two-level, predominantly al fresco restaurant snuggled between the beach and the Fontainebleau's pools opens its arms in a generous embrace while flirting with your taste buds, and maybe your man: the female waitstaff wear bikinis and flip-flops. Depending on your tastes, this may or may not foster a relaxed atmosphere that complements the simple elegant menu. Try the popular fruits de mer, or order a variety of oysters on the half shell. The vegetable pissaladière is a great vegetarian option for the table. Eating lunch here is an inexpensive way to get a good peek at the Fontainebleau while having a nice meal. [$] *Average main: $18* ✉ *Fontainebleau Hotel, 4441 Collins Ave., Mid-Beach* ☎ *305/674–4710* 🌐 *www.fontainebleau.com* 🕓 *No dinner Sun.–Wed.* ✥ *E3.*

$$$$ ARGENTINE 🍴 **Las Vacas Gordas.** Since 1996 this Argentine steak house has welcomed the who's who of Latin high society, fulfilling their wildest carnivore cravings. Recently expanded and reinvented as a glamorous enclave where the Pampas meets contemporary Miami, Vacas's grill sizzles day

and nights to the troves of patrons who patiently wait to feast on mounds of fresh meat from the Argentine lowlands. The reasonably priced house malbecs complement the high-end selections showcased in the floor-to-ceiling, glass-enclosed wine cellar. Those less enthused about massive meat slabs can opt for the *Berecava* (eggplant with tomato sauce and cheese), homemade pastas, grilled peppers, fish and shrimp, or fill up on homemade rolls with spicy chimichurri. $ Average main: $35 ⊠ 933 Normandy Dr., Mid-Beach ☎ 305/867–1717 ⊕ www. lasvacasgordas.com ☾ No lunch weekdays ⊹ E3.

$ ✗ **Roasters 'N Toasters.** Formerly the longtime family establishment Arnie
DELI and Richie's, Roasters 'N Toasters Miami Beach has preserved an inti-
FAMILY mate, Jewish deli feel that would make Arnie and Richie proud. The prices are slightly higher than back in the day, but the faithful still come for the onion rolls and smoked whitefish salad, as well as the new "Famous Zaftig Sandwich," a deliciously juicy skirt steak served on twin challah rolls with a side of apple sauce and mini potato pancakes. Service can be brusque, but it sure is quick. $ Average main: $14 ⊠ 525 Arthur Goddrey Rd., Mid-Beach ☎ 305/531–7691 ⊕ www. roastersntoasters.com ☾ Daily 6 am–3:30 pm ☾ No dinner ⊹ E4.

NORTH BEACH AND AVENTURA

$$$$ ✗ **Bourbon Steak.** Michael Mina's long-standing South Florida steak-
STEAKHOUSE house has never gone out of style. The restaurant design is seductive, the clientele sophisticated, the wine list outstanding, the service phenomenal, and the food exceptional. Dinner begins with a skillet of fresh potato focaccia and chive butter. Mina then presents a bonus starter—his trio of famous fries (fried in duck fat) with three robust sauces. Appetizers are mainly seafood. The raw bar impresses and classic appetizers like the ahi tuna tartare are delightful and super fresh. Entrees like the Maine lobster pot pie and any of the dozen varieties of butter-poached, wood-grilled steaks (from prime cuts to American wagyu) are cooked to perfection. $ Average main: $38 ⊠ Turnberry Isle Miami, 19999 W. Country Club Dr., Aventura ☎ 786/279–6600 ⊕ www.michaelmina.net ⌦ Reservations essential ⊹ E1.

$$ ✗ **Café Prima Pasta.** If Tony Soprano lived in Miami, this is where you'd
ITALIAN find him. This famous, bustling Italian eatery is infused with the energy of the Argentine Cea family, whose clan cooks, serves, and operates this place, while somehow finding the time to pose for photos with the hundreds of celebrities who have eaten here over the years (see them in the photos on the walls). It's on a busy street, yet the low light, soothing music, and intimate seating on this restaurant's outdoor veranda can make Café Prima Pasta a romantic spot. Everything is made in-house—from the fragrant rosemary butter to the pasta, which tastes best as crab-stuffed raviolotti or as homemade squid-ink linguine, served with seafood in a lobster sauce. $ Average main: $20 ⊠ 414 71st St., North Beach and Aventura ☎ 305/867–0106 ⊕ www.primapasta.com ☾ No lunch ⊹ E3.

$$$$
SEAFOOD
Fodor's Choice
★

✕**Fish Fish.** This small seafood eatery in North Miami is one of the city's last remaining insider secrets. Tucked away in a small strip mall, the colorful restaurant showcases Florida's superlative fruits of the sea alongside other ocean-to-table favorites from across the United States. The assortment of fresh regional catch on display makes its way straight to the pan for the restaurant's most popular entrée—the family-style "Whole Fish," prepared either crispy or grilled. But beyond this simple yet delicious "Fish Done Right," the small plates, salads, and specialties run a bit more complex. Stellar flavor explosions include a deconstructed grilled Caesar salad, lobster-truffled mac and cheese, and steamed mussels fra diavolo style. The restaurant also incorporates fish and seafood into its house-made pasta and risotto dishes. What's more? The under-the-sea-themed cocktail menu delivers mixology at its finest. Innovative drinks affectionately carry names like the Starfish (pear, ginger, and lime martini) and the Walrus (watermelon and cucumber gin martini). $ *Average main: $34* ⊠ *13488 Biscayne Blvd., North Beach and Aventura* ☎ *786/732–3124* ⊕ *www.fishfishmiami.com* ✛ *D2.*

$$$$
ITALIAN

✕**Il Mulino New York.** For more than two decades, Il Mulino New York has ranked among the top Italian restaurants in Gotham, so it's no surprise that the Miami outpost is similarly venerable. Even before the antipasti arrive, you may find yourself in a phenomenal carb coma from the fresh breads and the bruschetta. Everything that touches your palate is prepared to perfection, from simply prepared fried calamari and gnocchi pomodoro to the more complex scampi oregenata and ever-changing risottos. The restaurant is seductive, quiet, and intimate, and a favorite hangout of A-list celebs seeking a refined spot where crowds won't gawk over their presence. $ *Average main: $52* ⊠ *Acqualina Resort, 17875 Collins Ave., Sunny Isles* ☎ *305/466–9191* ⊕ *www. acqualinaresort.com* ⇗ *Reservations essential* ✛ *E1.*

$$$$
MODERN FRENCH
Fodor's Choice
★

✕**J & G Grill.** Set in the ultraglamorous St. Regis Bal Harbour, celebrity chef Jean-Gorges Vongerichten brings haute French fusion cuisine to the stunning Miami waterfront. The restaurant interiors flaunt a design sophistication that blends seamlessly with its host hotel. From beginning to end, a meal here is a true gastronomic tour de force, where dishes like the lobster bisque with butternut squash espuma and the porcini risotto with truffle brioche nary fall below the level of mind-blowing. While menu items change seasonally, there are always a number of can't-miss J & G signatures such as the Crispy Poached Egg Caviar with vodka crème fraîche. Save room for the decadent desserts from pastry chef Antonio Bachour; his French-inspired delights are pure foodie fantasia. $ *Average main: $46* ⊠ *St. Regis Bal Harbour, 9703 Collins Ave., North Beach and Aventura* ☎ *305/993–3300* ⊕ *www.jggrillmiami.com* ✛ *E2.*

$$$$
JAPANESE
Fodor's Choice
★

✕**Makoto.** Stephen Starr's Japanese headliner is one of the most popular restaurants in the swanky and prestigious Bal Harbor Shops. The ambience, service, and food all impress; and given its location in haute-couture central, the patrons definitely dress to impress. There are two menus, one devoted solely to sushi, sashimi, and maki; the other to Japanese hot dishes like tempuras, meats, and vegetables grilled over Japanese charcoal (robata), rice and noodle dishes, and steaks and fish inspired by the Land of the Rising Sun. [$] *Average main: $34* ✉ *Bal Harbour Shops, 9700 Collins Ave., North Beach and Aventura, Bal Harbour* ☎ *305/864–8600* 🌐 *www.makoto-restaurant.com* ⊕ *E2.*

$$$ MODERN ARGENTINE 🍴 **Novecento Aventura.** Miami can't get enough of this lively Argentine bistro, where empanadas, *picadas* (sharing platters of small bites), sizzling steaks (including a grilled beef tenderloin in a malbec demi-glace), and homemade pastas (a nod to Argentina's Italian heritage) headline the menu. Following Novecento's long-term success in Downtown Miami, NYC, and of course Buenos Aires, the restaurant has recently expanded across Miami and into Mexico and Uruguay, upping its outposts to a lucky 13. Like all Novecentos, the Aventura is a scene of "who's who" in Miami's Latin American society. The dim lighting, seductive ambience, and early-19th-century black-and-white imagery recall a bona fide Buenos Aires bistro, helping patrons forget that they are, in fact, in suburban Aventura. Besides the hearty eats, the wine list is excellent and surprisingly affordable. [$] *Average main: $24* ✉ *Town Center Aventura, 18831 N. Biscayne Blvd., North Beach and Aventura* ☎ *305/466–0900* 🌐 *www.novecento.com* ⊕ *E1.*

$$$ ITALIAN 🍴 **Timó.** In a glorified strip mall 5 miles north of South Beach, Timó (Italian for "thyme") is worth the trip from anywhere in South Florida. It's a kind of locals' secret. The handsome bistro, owned and operated by chef Tim Andriola, has dark-wood walls, Chicago brick, and a stone-encased wood-burning stove. Andriola has an affinity for robust Mediterranean flavors: sweetbreads with bacon, honey, and aged balsamic vinegar; inexpensive, artisanal pizzas; and homemade pastas. Wood-roasted meats and Parmesan dumplings in a truffle broth are not to be missed. Every bite of every dish attests to the care given, and the service is terrific. [$] *Average main: $27* ✉ *17624 Collins Ave., Sunny Isles* ☎ *305/936–1008* 🌐 *www.timorestaurant.com* 🕑 *No lunch weekends* ⊕ *E1.*

WHERE TO STAY

Room rates in Miami tend to swing wildly. In high season, which is January through May, expect to pay at least $200 per night, even at low-budget hotels. With a rebounding local economy and increased tourism, prices skyrocketed in 2013, increasing up to 70% in some cases. Numerous hotels, previously affordable, have moved to our highest price category. In fact, it's common nowadays for rates to begin around $500 at Miami's top hotels. In summer, however, prices can be as much as 50% lower than the dizzying winter rates. You can also find great deals between Easter and Memorial Day, which is actually a delightful time in Miami. Business travelers tend to stay in downtown Miami, and most vacationers stay on Miami Beach, as close as possible to the water. South Beach is no longer the only "in" place to stay. Mid-Beach and downtown have taken the hotel scene by storm in the past few years and become home to some of the region's most avant-garde and luxurious properties to date. If money is no object, stay in one of the glamorous hotels lining Collins Avenue between 15th and 23rd streets. Otherwise, stay on the quiet beaches farther north, or in one of the small boutique hotels on Ocean Drive, Collins, or Washington avenues between 10th and 15th streets. Two important considerations that affect price are balcony and view. If you're willing to have a room without an ocean view, you can sometimes get a much lower price than the standard rate.

Hotel reviews have been shortened. For full information, visit Fodors. com.

Use the coordinate (⊕ C2) at the end of each review to locate a property on the Where to Stay in the Miami Area map.

WHAT IT COSTS				
	$	$$	$$$	$$$$
HOTELS	under $200	$201–$300	$301–$400	over $400

Hotel prices are the lowest cost of a standard double room in high season.

DOWNTOWN

Miami's skyline continues to grow by leaps and bounds. With downtown experiencing a renaissance of sorts, the hotel scene here isn't just for business anymore. In fact hotels that once relied solely on their Monday–Thursday traffic are now bustling on weekends, with a larger focus on cocktails around the rooftop pool and less a focus on the business center. These hotels offer proximate access to downtown's burgeoning food and cocktail scene, historic sights, and are a short cab ride away from Miami's beaches.

$$$ **Conrad Miami.** Occupying floors 16 to 26 of a 36-story skyscraper in
HOTEL Miami's Financial District, this chic hotel mixes business with pleasure, offering easy access to the best of Downtown Miami. **Pros:** central downtown location; excellent service. **Cons:** poor views from some rooms; expensive parking. [$] *Rooms from: $309* ⊠ *Espirito Santo Plaza, 1395 Brickell Ave., Downtown* 🕾 *305/503–6500* ⊕ *www.conradhotels. com* ➶ *189 rooms, 14 suites* ❑ *No meals* ⊕ *D5.*

$ **Doubletree Grand Hotel Biscayne Bay.** Near the Port of Miami at the
HOTEL north end of Downtown, this waterfront hotel offers relatively basic, spacious rooms and convenient access to and from the cruise ships and Downtown, making it a good crash pad for budget-conscious cruise passengers. **Pros:** marina; proximity to port. **Cons:** still need a cab to get around; dark lobby and neighboring arcade of shops; worn rooms. [$] *Rooms from: $185* ⊠ *1717 N. Bayshore Dr., Downtown* 🕾 *305/372– 0313, 800/222–8733* ⊕ *www.doubletree.com* ➶ *152 rooms, 56 suites* ❑ *No meals* ⊕ *D4.*

$$$ **Epic Hotel.** In the heart of Downtown, Kimpton's pet-friendly, freebie-
HOTEL heavy Epic Hotel has 411 guest rooms, each with a spacious balcony
Fodor'sChoice (many of them overlook Biscayne Bay) and fabulous modern ameni-
★ ties—Frette linens, iPod docks, spa-inspired luxury bath products—that match the modern grandeur of the trendy common areas, which include a supersexy rooftop pool. **Pros:** sprawling rooftop pool deck; balcony in every room; complimentary wine hour, coffee, and Wi-Fi. **Cons:**

BEST BETS FOR MIAMI LODGING

2

Fodor's offers a selective listing of high-quality lodging experiences in every price range, from the city's best budget beds to its most sophisticated luxury hotels. Here, we've compiled our top recommendations by price and experience. The very best properties are designated in the listings with the Fodor's Choice logo. Find specific details about a hotel in the full reviews, listed alphabetically by neighborhood.

Viceroy Miami, Downtown, p. 76

BEST SERVICE

Acqualina Resort & Spa on the Beach, North Beach and Aventura, p. 84

The Ritz-Carlton Key Biscayne, Key Biscayne, p. 77

St. Regis Bal Harbour Resort, North Beach and Aventura, p. 85

BEST VIEWS

Epic Hotel, Downtown, p. 74

St. Regis Bal Harbour Resort, North Beach and Aventura, p. 85

W South Beach, South Beach, p. 82

HIPSTER HOTELS

Catalina Hotel & Beach Club, South Beach, p. 78

Shore Club, South Beach, p. 81

Soho Beach House, Mid-Beach, p. 84

Fodor's Choice ★

Acqualina Resort & Spa on the Beach, North Beach and Aventura, $$$$, p. 84

Delano Hotel, South Beach, $$$$, p. 79

Epic Hotel, Downtown, $$$, p. 74

The James Royal Palm, South Beach, $$$, p. 79

The Lord Balfour, South Beach, $, p. 80

Mandarin Oriental, Miami, Downtown, $$$$, p. 76

Ritz-Carlton, South Beach, $$$$, p. 81

SLS Hotel South Beach, South Beach, $$$$, p. 81

St. Regis Bal Harbour Resort, North Beach and Aventura, $$$$, p. 85

Surfcomber Miami, South Beach, $$, p. 82

W South Beach, South Beach, $$$$, p. 82

By Price

$

The Lord Balfour, South Beach, p. 80

$$

Surfcomber Miami, South Beach, p. 82

$$$

Epic Hotel, Downtown, p. 74

The James Royal Palm, South Beach, p. 79

$$$$

Delano Hotel, South Beach, p. 79

Mandarin Oriental, Miami, Downtown, p. 76

St. Regis Bal Harbour Resort, North Beach and Aventura, p. 85

W South Beach, South Beach, p. 82

By Experience

BEST HOTEL BAR

National Hotel, South Beach, p. 80

Viceroy Miami (rooftop bar), Downtown, p. 76

BEST-KEPT SECRET

The Lord Balfour, South Beach, p. 80

Soho Beach House, Mid-Beach, p. 84

BEST LOCATION

The Betsy Hotel, South Beach, p. 78

Surfcomber Miami, South Beach, p. 82

BEST POOL

Biltmore Hotel, Coral Gables, p. 77

Delano Hotel, South Beach, p. 79

Raleigh Hotel, South Beach, p. 81

some rooms have inferior views; congested valet area. *$ Rooms from: $399 ✉ 270 Biscayne Blvd. Way, Downtown ☎ 305/424–5226 🌐 www.epichotel.com ⇨ 411 rooms 🍴 No meals ✣ D4.*

$$$$ HOTEL **Four Seasons Hotel Miami.** A favorite of business travelers visiting downtown's busy, business-centric Brickell Avenue, this plush sanctuary offers a respite from the nine-to-five mayhem—a soothing water wall greets you, the understated rooms impress you, and the seventh-floor, 2-acre-pool terrace relaxes you. **Pros:** rooms renovated in 2011; sensational service; amazing gym and pool deck. **Cons:** no balconies; caters mostly to business travelers; not near beach. *$ Rooms from: $499 ✉ 1435 Brickell Ave., Downtown ☎ 305/358–3535 🌐 www.fourseasons.com/miami ⇨ 182 rooms, 39 suites 🍴 No meals ✣ D5.*

$$$$ HOTEL **JW Marriott Marquis Miami.** The marriage of Marriott's JW and Marquis brands has created a truly tech-savvy, contemporary, and stylish business-minded hotel—you may never have seen a Marriott quite like this one. **Pros:** entertainment center; amazing technology; pristine rooms. **Cons:** swimming pool receives limited sunshine; lots of conventioneers on weekdays. *$ Rooms from: $419 ✉ 255 Biscayne Blvd. Way, Downtown ☎ 305/421–8600 🌐 www.jwmarriottmarquismiami.com ⇨ 257 rooms, 56 suites 🍴 No meals ✣ D4.*

$$$$ HOTEL Fodor's Choice ★ **Mandarin Oriental, Miami.** Clandestinely situated at the tip of prestigious Brickell Key in Biscayne Bay, the Mandarin Oriental feels as exclusive as it does glamorous, with luxurious rooms, exalted restaurants, and the city's top spa, all of which marry the brand's signature Asian style with Miami's bold tropical elegance. **Pros:** impressive lobby; intimate vibe; ultraluxurious. **Cons:** man-made beach; small infinity pool; few beach cabanas. *$ Rooms from: $519 ✉ 500 Brickell Key Dr., Downtown ☎ 305/913–8288, 866/888–6780 🌐 www.mandarinoriental.com ⇨ 326 rooms, 31 suites 🍴 No meals ✣ D5.*

$$$$ HOTEL **Viceroy Miami.** This hotel cultivates a brash, supersophisticated Miami attitude, likely stemming from its flawless guest rooms decked out with dramatic Kelly Wearstler, Asian-inspired interiors and larger-than-life common areas designed by Philippe Starck. **Pros:** amazing design elements; exceptional pool deck and spa; sleek rooms. **Cons:** poor views from rooms; tiny lobby; some amenities shared with ICON Miami residents. *$ Rooms from: $429 ✉ 485 Brickell Ave., Downtown ☎ 305/503–4400, 866/781–9923 🌐 www.viceroymiami.com ⇨ 150 rooms, 18 suites 🍴 No meals ✣ D4.*

COCONUT GROVE

Although this area certainly can't replace the draw of Miami Beach or the business convenience of downtown, about 20 minutes away, it's an exciting bohemian-chic neighborhood with a gorgeous waterfront.

$$ HOTEL **The Ritz-Carlton Coconut Grove, Miami.** Overlooking Biscayne Bay, this business-centric Ritz-Carlton hotel in the heart of Coconut Grove received a face-lift in 2012 that gave its lobby and lounge a refreshed, livelier look that complements its sophisticated guest rooms—all with marble baths and private balconies. **Pros:** elevated pool deck; near Coconut Grove and Coral Gables shopping; excellent service. **Cons:**

near residential area; more business- than leisure-oriented. $ *Rooms from: $299* ✉ *3300 S.W. 27th Ave., Coconut Grove* ☎ *305/644–4680, 800/241–3333* ⊕ *www.ritzcarlton.com* ⤴ *88 rooms, 27 suites* ⦿ *No meals* ✛ *C5.*

2

CORAL GABLES

Beautiful Coral Gables is set around its beacon, the national landmark Biltmore Hotel. It also has a couple of big business hotels and one smaller boutique property. The University of Miami is nearby.

$$$
HOTEL
Biltmore Hotel. Built in 1926, this landmark hotel has had several incarnations over the years—including a stint as a hospital during World War II—but through it all, this grande dame has remained an opulent reminder of yesteryear, with its palatial lobby and grounds, enormous pool (largest in the lower 48), and distinctive 315-foot tower, which rises above the canopy of trees shading Coral Gables. **Pros:** historic property; gorgeous pool; great tennis and golf. **Cons:** in the suburbs; a car is necessary to get around. $ *Rooms from: $343* ✉ *1200 Anastasia Ave., Coral Gables* ☎ *855/311–6903* ⊕ *www.biltmorehotel. com* ⤴ *241 rooms, 39 suites* ⦿ *No meals* ✛ *B5.*

$
B&B/INN
Hotel St. Michel. This quiet and charming European bed-and-breakfast–inspired hotel dates to 1926—original elevator and all—and is right off the Miracle Mile in Coral Gables. **Pros:** coolest elevator in Florida; historical vibe; totally unexpected in South Florida. **Cons:** small rooms; old, individual in-room a/c units; breakfast no longer included at this B&B. $ *Rooms from: $179* ✉ *162 Alcazar Ave., Coral Gables* ☎ *305/444–1666, 800/848–4683* ⊕ *www.hotelstmichel.com* ⤴ *25 rooms, 3 suites* ⦿ *No meals* ✛ *B5.*

KEY BISCAYNE

There's probably no other place in Miami where slowness is lifted to a fine art. On Key Biscayne there are no pressures, there's no nightlife outside of the Ritz-Carlton's great live Latin music weekends, and the dining choices are essentially limited to the hotel (which has four dining options, including the languorous, Havana-style RUMBAR).

$$$
RESORT
FAMILY
The Ritz-Carlton Key Biscayne, Miami. In this ultra-laid-back Key Biscayne setting, it's natural to appreciate the Ritz brand of pampering with luxurious rooms, attentive service, four on-property dining options, and ample recreational activities for the whole family. **Pros:** on the beach; quiet; luxurious family retreat. **Cons:** far from South Beach and downtown; beach sometimes seaweed-strewn; rental car almost a necessity. $ *Rooms from: $499* ✉ *455 Grand Bay Dr., Key Biscayne* ☎ *305/365–4500, 800/241–3333* ⊕ *www.ritzcarlton.com/keybiscayne* ⤴ *365 rooms, 37 suites* ⦿ *No meals* ✛ *D6.*

SOUTH BEACH

If you are looking to experience the postcard image of Miami, look no further than South Beach. Most of the hotels along Ocean Drive, Collins Avenue, and Washington Avenue are housed in history-steeped art deco buildings, each one cooler than the next. From boutique hotels to high-rise structures, all South Beach hotels are in close distance to the beach and never far from the action. Most hotels here cost a pretty penny, and for good reason. They are more of an experience than a place to crash (think designer lobbies, some of the world's best pool scenes, and unparalleled people-watching).

$$$ **Angler's Hotel.** Miami's newest addition to the Kimpton portfolio has HOTEL an air of serenity and privacy that pervades this discreet little oasis of personality-driven villas (built in 1930 by architect Henry Maloney) and modern tower units, together capturing the feel of a sophisticated private Mediterranean villa community. **Pros:** gardened private retreat; excellent service; daily complimentary wine hour. **Cons:** on busy Washington Avenue; not directly on beach. $ *Rooms from: $339* ⊠ *660 Washington Ave., South Beach* ☎ *305/534–9600* ⊕ *www.anglershotelmiami.com* ⌁ *24 rooms, 20 suites* ¦◯¦ *No meals* ✢ *G4.*

$$$ **The Betsy Hotel.** An art deco treasure elegantly refurbished and totally HOTEL retro-chic, The Betsy sits directly on world-famous Ocean Drive and delivers the full-throttle South Beach experience with style, pizzazz and cultural twist—the Betsy offers cultural programs year-round such as poetry readings, live jazz, and art shows. **Pros:** unbeatable location; super-fashionable; great beach club. **Cons:** some small rooms; service can be hit or miss; no pool scene (but there's a rooftop scene). $ *Rooms from: $389* ⊠ *1440 Ocean Dr., South Beach* ☎ *305/531–6100* ⊕ *www. thebetsyhotel.com* ⌁ *41 rooms, 20 suites* ¦◯¦ *No meals* ✢ *G2.*

$$ **Cadet Hotel.** A former home to World War II air force cadets, this gem HOTEL has been reimagined as an oasis in South Beach, offering the antithesis of the sometimes maddening jet-set scene with 34 distinctive rooms exuding understated luxury. **Pros:** excellent service; lovely garden and spa pool; originality. **Cons:** tiny swimming pool; limited appeal for the party crowd. $ *Rooms from: $279* ⊠ *1701 James Ave., South Beach* ☎ *305/672–6688, 800/432–2338* ⊕ *www.cadethotel.com* ⌁ *32 rooms, 3 suites* ¦◯¦ *Breakfast* ✢ *G2.*

$$ **Catalina Hotel & Beach Club.** The Catalina is the budget party spot in HOTEL the heart of South Beach's hottest block and attracts plenty of twenty-somethings with its free nightly drink hour, airport shuttles, bike rentals, two fun pools, and beach chairs. **Pros:** free drinks; free bikes; free airport shuttle; good people-watching. **Cons:** service not a high priority; loud; rooms not well maintained. $ *Rooms from: $295* ⊠ *1720–1756 Collins Ave., South Beach* ☎ *305/674–1160* ⊕ *www.catalinahotel.com* ⌁ *200 rooms* ¦◯¦ *No meals* ✢ *G2.*

$ **Century Hotel Miami Beach.** If you're looking for a clean place in the HOTEL emerging SoFi (South of 5th) area to rest your head for the evening, this very basic and cheap (but tidy) hotel gives you a chance to discover a more residential side of bustling South Beach while staying in a 1939 two-story art deco masterpiece by Henry Hohauser. **Pros:** good location; complimentary breakfast; pet-friendly. **Cons:** no pool; simple rooms; must call to book. $ *Rooms from: $120* ⊠ *140 Ocean Dr., South Beach* ☎ *305/674–8855* ⊕ *www.centurymiamibeach.com* ⌁ *26 rooms* ¦◯¦ *Breakfast* ✢ *G5.*

$$$$ HOTEL Fodor'sChoice ★ **Delano Hotel.** The hotel that single-handedly made South Beach cool again in the nineties is still making major waves across the beach as this Philippe Starck powerhouse continues to define the paradigm of South Beach décor and glamour. **Pros:** electrifying design; lounging among the beautiful and famous. **Cons:** crowded; sceney; entry level rooms are on small side. [$] *Rooms from: $439* ✉ *1685 Collins Ave., South Beach* ☎ *305/672–2000, 800/555–5001* 🌐 *www.delano-hotel.com* 🛏 *184 rooms, 24 suites* 🍴 *No meals* ✥ *H2.*

$$ HOTEL **Essex House.** This restored art deco gem is a favorite with Europeans desiring good location and a somewhat no-frills practical base—expect average-size rooms with midcentury-style red furniture and marble tubs. **Pros:** a social, heated pool; complimentary beer and wine hour Monday–Friday; in-house sushi restaurant Zen Sai. **Cons:** small pool; not on the beach. [$] *Rooms from: $229* ✉ *1001 Collins Ave., South Beach* ☎ *305/534–2700* 🌐 *www.essexhotel.com* 🛏 *61 rooms, 15 suites* 🍴 *No meals* ✥ *G3.*

$$$ HOTEL FAMILY **Hilton Bentley Miami/South Beach.** One of the area's only kid-friendly boutique hotels, this contemporary, design-driven, and artsy Hilton in the emerging and trendy SoFi (South of 5th) district offers families just the right mix of South Beach flavor and wholesome fun while still providing couples a romantic base without any party madness. **Pros:** quiet location; style and grace; family-friendly. **Cons:** small pool; small lobby. [$] *Rooms from: $360* ✉ *101 Ocean Dr., South Beach* ☎ *305/938–4600* 🌐 *www.hilton.com* 🛏 *104 rooms, 5 suites* 🍴 *No meals* ✥ *G5.*

$$$ HOTEL **The Hotel of South Beach.** Fashion designer Todd Oldham preserved the art-deco roots of The Hotel, which inhabits the historic Tiffany building on Collins Avenue, and has expanded the property with 20 new deluxe oceanfront rooms and suites along fabulous Ocean Drive. **Pros:** great service; coolest roof-deck bar in town; good for couples. **Cons:** pool is tiny; rooms from original building lack good views. [$] *Rooms from: $329* ✉ *801 Collins Ave., South Beach* ☎ *305/531–2222* 🌐 *www.thehotelofsouthbeach.com* 🛏 *68 rooms, 5 suites* 🍴 *No meals* ✥ *G4.*

$$ HOTEL **Hotel Victor.** Fresh from a facelift in late 2013, the sleek Hotel Victor, created by the Parisian designer Jacques Garcia, has replaced the dated jellyfish motif with a newer incarnation of bold modernism. **Pros:** views from pool deck; high hip factor; good service. **Cons:** small rooms; street noise from some rooms; lots of rusty handles. [$] *Rooms from: $297* ✉ *1144 Ocean Dr., South Beach* ☎ *305/779–8700* 🌐 *www.hotelvictorsouthbeach.com* 🛏 *91 rooms* 🍴 *No meals* ✥ *G3.*

$$$ RESORT Fodor'sChoice ★ **The James Royal Palm.** The James Royal Palm is a daily celebration of art deco, Art Basel, modernity, and design detail that also dutifully embodies the mantra of the James brand: "luxury liberated." **Pros:** design blending contemporary style with South Beach identity; impressive spa; multiple pools; unbeatable location; two noteworthy restaurants. **Cons:** occasional noise from in-house nightclub; small driveway for entering. [$] *Rooms from: $359* ✉ *1545 Collins Ave., South Beach* ☎ *786/276–0100* 🌐 *www.jameshotels.com/miami* 🛏 *234 studios, 159 suites* 🍴 *No meals* ✥ *G2.*

$$$ HOTEL FAMILY **Loews Miami Beach Hotel.** A two-tower 800-room megahotel with top-tier amenities, a massive spa, a great pool, and direct beachfront access, the Loews Miami Beach is good for families, businesspeople, groups, and pet-lovers. **Pros:** top-notch amenities; immense spa; pets welcome. **Cons:** insanely large; constantly crowded; pets desperate to go will need to wait several minutes to make it to the grass. [$] *Rooms from: $399* ✉ *1601 Collins Ave., South Beach* ☎ *305/604–1601, 800/235–6397* 🌐 *www.loewshotels.com/miamibeach* 🛏 *733 rooms, 57 suites* 🍴 *No meals* ⊕ *H2.*

$ HOTEL Fodor's Choice ★ **The Lord Balfour.** Quickly making a name for itself in South Beach's emerging SoFi (South of 5th) neighborhood, the luxurious, boutique, and retro-chic Lord Balfour hotel proves that style, sophistication, and the full-throttle, present-day Miami Beach experience need not require the deepest of deep pockets. **Pros:** handcrafted tea-infused cocktails in the lobby bar; whimsical interior design; excellent service. **Cons:** no pool yet (under construction); rooms on smaller side; occasional street noise from some rooms. [$] *Rooms from: $199* ✉ *350 Ocean Dr., South Beach* ☎ *800/949–4075* 🌐 *www.lordbalfourmiami.com* 🛏 *64 rooms* 🍴 *No meals* ⊕ *G4.*

$$$ HOTEL **Mondrian South Beach.** The Mondrian South Beach infuses life into the beach's lesser-known western perimeter and rises as a poster child of SoBe design glam—head to toe, the hotel is a living and functioning work of art, an ingenious vision of provocateur Marcel Wanders. **Pros:** trendy; perfect sunsets; party vibe. **Cons:** busy lobby; doses of South Beach attitude; no direct beach access. [$] *Rooms from: $339* ✉ *1100 West Ave., South Beach* ☎ *305/514–1500* 🌐 *www.mondrian-miami.com* 🛏 *233 rooms, 102 suites* 🍴 *No meals* ⊕ *F3.*

$$$$ HOTEL **National Hotel.** The National Hotel has maintained its distinct art deco heritage (the chocolate- and ebony-hued pieces in the lobby date back to the 1930s, and the baby grand piano headlines the throwback Blues Bar) while also keeping up with SoBe's glossy newcomers with its renovated cabana wing and art deco tower. **Pros:** stunning pool; perfect location. **Cons:** street noise on the weekends; rooms don't have the finesse of neighbors. [$] *Rooms from: $405* ✉ *1677 Collins Ave., South Beach* ☎ *305/532–2311, 800/327–8370* 🌐 *www.nationalhotel.com* 🛏 *143 rooms, 9 suites* 🍴 *No meals* ⊕ *H2.*

$$ HOTEL **Park Central.** This seven-story, oft-photographed 1937 archetypal art deco building on Ocean Drive offers a wide range of somewhat dated, Old Florida–style rooms complete with wicker chairs and black-and-white photos of old beach scenes. **Pros:** spacious rooftop sundeck; comfy beds; good location. **Cons:** dated furnishings; small bathrooms; most rooms have limited views. [$] *Rooms from: $289* ✉ *640 Ocean Dr., South Beach* ☎ *305/538–1611* 🌐 *www.theparkcentral.com* 🛏 *113 rooms, 12 suites* 🍴 *No meals* ⊕ *G4.*

$$$ HOTEL **Pelican Miami Beach.** Each awesome room of this Ocean Drive boutique hotel is completely different, fashioned from a mix of antique and garage-sale furnishings selected by the designer of Diesel's clothing-display windows. **Pros:** unique, over the top design; central Ocean Drive location. **Cons:** rooms are so tiny that the quirky charm wears off quickly; not smoke-free. [$] *Rooms from: $339* ✉ *826 Ocean Dr.,*

South Beach ☎ 305/673–3373 🌐 www.pelicanhotel.com 🛏 28 rooms, 4 suites 🍴 No meals ✣ G4.

$$$ HOTEL **Raleigh Hotel.** This classy art-deco gem, now part of the sbe hotel group, balances the perfect amount of style, comfort, and South Beach sultriness, highlighted by the beach's sexiest pool, which was created for champion swimmer Esther Williams. **Pros:** amazing historic swimming pool; elegance. **Cons:** lobby is a bit dark; not as social as other South Beach hotels. [$] *Rooms from: $315 ✉ 1775 Collins Ave., South Beach ☎ 305/534–6300 🌐 www.raleighhotel.com 🛏 95 rooms, 10 suites 🍴 No meals ✣ H2.*

$$$$ HOTEL FAMILY Fodor's Choice ★ **The Ritz-Carlton, South Beach.** Completely revamped and renovated in 2013, the smoking-hot, art-deco Ritz-Carlton, South Beach is a surprisingly trendy, beachfront bombshell, with a dynamite staff, a snazzy Club Lounge, a "tanning butler," and a long pool deck that leads right out to the beach. **Pros:** luxurious renovated rooms; great service; pool with VIP cabanas; great location. **Cons:** not as small and intimate as other properties. [$] *Rooms from: $629 ✉ 1 Lincoln Rd., South Beach ☎ 786/276–4000, 800/241–3333 🌐 www.ritzcarlton.com/southbeach 🛏 375 rooms 🍴 No meals ✣ H2.*

$$$$ HOTEL **Sagamore, the Art Hotel.** This supersleek, all-white, all-suite hotel in the middle of the action looks and feels like an edgy art gallery, filled with brilliant contemporary works, the perfect complement to the posh, gargantuan, 500-square-foot crash pads. **Pros:** sensational pool; great location; good rate specials. **Cons:** can be quiet on weekdays; patchy Wi-Fi. [$] *Rooms from: $429 ✉ 1671 Collins Ave., South Beach ☎ 305/535–8088 🌐 www.sagamorehotel.com 🛏 93 suites 🍴 No meals ✣ H2.*

$$$$ RESORT **The Setai.** This opulent, all-suite hotel feels like an Asian museum, serene and beautiful, with heavy granite furniture lifted by orange accents, warm candlelight, and the soft bubble of seemingly endless ponds complemented by three oceanfront infinity pools (heated to 75, 85, and 95 degrees) that further spill onto the beach's velvety sands. **Pros:** quiet and classy; beautiful grounds. **Cons:** TVs are far from the beds; high price point. [$] *Rooms from: $833 ✉ 101 20th St., South Beach ☎ 305/520–6000 🌐 www.thesetaihotel.com 🛏 121 suites 🍴 No meals ✣ H1.*

$$$ HOTEL **Shore Club.** In terms of lounging, people-watching, partying, and poolside glitz, the Shore Club still ranks among the ultimate South Beach adult playgrounds; guests generally hang out in the minimalist lobby or by one of the two stylish pools, where a peek behind the cascading white curtains or palm trees can yield a celebrity, a scandal, or a make-out session. **Pros:** hip crowd; good restaurants and bars; nightlife in your backyard. **Cons:** spartan rooms; late-night music. [$] *Rooms from: $379 ✉ 1901 Collins Ave., South Beach ☎ 305/695–3100, 877/640–9500 🌐 www.shoreclub.com 🛏 309 rooms, 79 suites 🍴 No meals ✣ H1.*

$$$$ RESORT Fodor's Choice ★ **SLS Hotel South Beach.** Smack in the center of South Beach, the SLS Hotel marks designer Philippe Starck's triumphant large-scale return to South Beach; but this time he's teamed up with friends Sam Nazarian, chefs José Andrés and Katsuya Uech, and Lenny Kravitz for the whimsical trip down the rabbit hole, creating the latest and greatest in the evolution of Miami's happening hotel/food/pool/beach scene. **Pros:** great

in-house restaurants; masterful design; fun pool scene. **Cons:** sometimes small rooms; no lobby per se; congested valet area. [$] *Rooms from: $415* ✉ *1701 Collins Ave., South Beach* ☎ *305/674–1701* 🌐 *www.slshotels.com/southbeach* 🛏 *127 rooms, 13 suites* 🍴 *No meals* ✥ *H2.*

$$ HOTEL Fodor's Choice ★ **Surfcomber Miami, South Beach.** In 2012 the legendary Surfcomber joined the hip Kimpton Hotel group, spawning a fantastic nip-and-tuck that's rejuvenated the rooms and common spaces to reflect vintage luxe and oceanside freshness, and offering a price point that packs the place with a young, sophisticated yet unpretentious crowd. **Pros:** stylish but not pretentious; pet-friendly; on the beach. **Cons:** small bathrooms; front desk often busy. [$] *Rooms from: $299* ✉ *1717 Collins Ave., South Beach* ☎ *305/532–7715* 🌐 *www.surfcomber.com* 🛏 *182 rooms, 4 suites* 🍴 *No meals* ✥ *H2.*

$$$ HOTEL **The Tides South Beach.** Formerly the crown jewel of the Viceroy Hotel Group, the Tides South Beach is an exclusive Ocean Drive art deco hotel of just 45 ocean-facing suites adorned with soft pinks and corals, gilded accents, and marine-inspired decor. **Pros:** superior service; great beach location; ocean views from all suites plus the terrace restaurant. **Cons:** tiny elevators; mediocre restaurant. [$] *Rooms from: $396* ✉ *1220 Ocean Dr., South Beach* ☎ *305/604–5070* 🌐 *www.tidessouthbeach.com* 🛏 *45 suites* 🍴 *No meals* ✥ *G3.*

$ HOTEL **Townhouse Hotel.** Though sandwiched between the Setai and the Shore Club—two of the coolest hotels on the planet—the Townhouse doesn't try to act all dolled up: it's comfortable being the shabby-chic, lighthearted, relaxed fun hotel on South Beach (and rates include a Parisian-style breakfast). **Pros:** a great budget buy for the style-hungry; direct beach access; hot rooftop lounge. **Cons:** no pool; small rooms not designed for long stays. [$] *Rooms from: $195* ✉ *150 20th St., east of Collins Ave., South Beach* ☎ *305/534–3800* 🌐 *www.townhousehotel.com* 🛏 *69 rooms, 2 suites* 🍴 *Breakfast* ✥ *H1.*

$ B&B/INN **Villa Paradiso.** One of South Beach's best deals for budget travelers, Paradiso has huge rooms with kitchens and a charming tropical courtyard with benches for hanging out at all hours. **Pros:** great hangout spot in courtyard; good value; great location. **Cons:** no pool; no restaurant; not trendy. [$] *Rooms from: $174* ✉ *1415 Collins Ave., South Beach* ☎ *305/532–0616* 🌐 *www.villaparadisohotel.com* 🛏 *17 studios* 🍴 *No meals* ✥ *G2.*

$$$$ HOTEL Fodor's Choice ★ **W South Beach.** Fun, fresh, and funky, the W South Beach is also the flagship for the brand's evolution towards young sophistication, which means less club music in the lobby, more lighting, and more attention to the multimillion-dollar art collection lining the lobby's expansive walls. **Pros:** pool scene; masterful design; ocean-view balconies in each room. **Cons:** not a classic art deco building; hit-or-miss service. [$] *Rooms from: $1379* ✉ *2201 Collins Ave., South Beach* ☎ *305/938–3000* 🌐 *www.whotels.com/southbeach* 🛏 *213 studios, 135 suites* 🍴 *No meals* ✥ *H1.*

$$$ HOTEL **Z Ocean Hotel South Beach.** The lauded firm of Arquitectonica designed the rooms and suites at this glossy and bold hideaway, including 27 rooftop suites endowed with terraces, each complete with Jacuzzi, plush chaise lounges, and a view of the South Beach skyline. **Pros:** incredible balconies; huge rooms; space-maximizing closets. **Cons:** gym is tiny

and basic; not much privacy on rooftop suite decks. [$] *Rooms from: $399* ✉ *1437 Collins Ave., South Beach* ☎ *305/672–4554* 🌐 *www.zoceanhotelsouthbeach.com* 🛏 *79 suites* 🍴 *No meals* ✥ *G2.*

MID-BEACH

The stretch of Miami Beach called "Mid-Beach" is undergoing a renaissance, as formerly run-down hotels are renovated and new hotels and condos are built.

$$$$ RESORT **Canyon Ranch Miami Beach.** Physical and mental well-being top the agenda at this 150-suite beachfront hotel, defined by its 70,000-square-foot wellness spa, including a rock-climbing wall, 54 treatment rooms, and 30 exercise classes daily. **Pros:** directly on the beach; spacious suites (minimum 720 square feet); spa treatments exclusive to hotel guests. **Cons:** far from nightlife; not a very gregarious clientele. [$] *Rooms from: $480* ✉ *6801 Collins Ave., Mid-Beach* ☎ *305/514–7000* 🌐 *www.canyonranch.com* 🛏 *150 suites* 🍴 *No meals* ✥ *E3.*

$ HOTEL **Circa 39 Hotel.** Located in the heart of Mid-Beach, this stylish yet affordable 100-guest room boutique hotel pays attention to every detail and gets them all right, with amenities that include a swimming pool and sundeck complete with cabanas and umbrella-shaded chaises that invite all-day lounging. **Pros:** affordable; chic; intimate; beach chairs provided; art deco fireplace. **Cons:** not on the beach side of Collins Avenue. [$] *Rooms from: $187* ✉ *3900 Collins Ave., Mid-Beach* ☎ *305/538–4900, 877/824–7223* 🌐 *www.circa39.com* 🛏 *96 rooms* 🍴 *No meals* ✥ *E4.*

$$$$ RESORT **Eden Roc Miami Beach.** This grand 1950s hotel designed by Morris Lapidus retains its old glamour even after $230 million in renovations and expansions added sparkle to the rooms and grounds, renewing the allure and swagger of a stay at the Eden Roc. **Pros:** modern rooms; great pools; revival of Golden Age glamour. **Cons:** expensive parking; taxi needed to reach South Beach. [$] *Rooms from: $469* ✉ *4525 Collins Ave., Mid-Beach* ☎ *305/531–0000, 800/327–8337* 🌐 *www.edenrocmiami.com* 🛏 *535 rooms, 92 suites* 🍴 *No meals* ✥ *E3.*

$$$$ RESORT FAMILY **Fontainebleau Miami Beach.** Vegas meets art deco at this colossal classic, deemed Miami's biggest hotel after its $1 billion reinvention, which spawned more than 1,500 rooms (split among 658 suites in two new all-suite towers and 846 rooms in the two original buildings), 12 renowned restaurants and lounges, LIV nightclub, several sumptuous pools with cabana islands, a state-of-the-art fitness center, and a 40,000-square-foot spa. **Pros:** excellent restaurants; historic design mixed with all-new facilities; fabulous pools. **Cons:** away from the South Beach pedestrian scene; massive size; bizarre mix of guests. [$] *Rooms from: $489* ✉ *4441 Collins Ave., Mid-Beach* ☎ *305/538–2000, 800/548–8886* 🌐 *www.fontainebleau.com* 🛏 *846 rooms, 658 suites* 🍴 *No meals* ✥ *E3.*

$$$ HOTEL **The Palms Hotel & Spa.** If you're seeking an elegant, relaxed property away from the noise but still near South Beach, the Palms has an exceptional beach, an easy pace, and beautiful gardens with soaring palm trees and inviting hammocks; the rooms look as fabulous as the grounds, which include a 5,000-square-foot Aveda spa and a signature

farm-to-table restaurant, Essensia. **Pros:** tropical garden; relaxed and quiet. **Cons:** standard rooms do not have balconies (but suites do). [$] *Rooms from: $359* ✉ *3025 Collins Ave., Mid-Beach* ☎ *305/534–0505, 800/550–0505* 🌐 *www.thepalmshotel.com* 🛏 *220 rooms, 22 suites* 🍴 *No meals* ✥ *E4.*

$$$$ HOTEL 🏨 **Soho Beach House.** The Soho Beach House is a throwback to swanky vibes of bygone decades, bedazzled in faded color palates, maritime ambience, and circa-1930s avant-garde furnishings, luring A-listers and wannabes to indulge in the amenity-clad, retro-chic rooms as long as they follow stringent "house rules" (no photos, no mobile phones, no suits, and 1 guest only). **Pros:** trendy; two pools; fabulous restaurant; full spa. **Cons:** members have priority for rooms; lots of pretentious patrons; house rules are a bit much. [$] *Rooms from: $495* ✉ *4385 Collins Ave., Mid-Beach* ☎ *786/507–7900* 🌐 *www.sohobeachhouse.com* 🛏 *55 rooms* 🍴 *No meals* ✥ *E3.*

FISHER AND BELLE ISLANDS

$$$$ RESORT 🏨 **The Resort at Fisher Island Club.** An exclusive private island, just south of Miami Beach but accessible only by ferry, Fisher Island houses an upscale residential community that includes a small inventory of overnight accommodations, including opulent cottages, villas, and junior suites, which surround the island's original 1920s-era Vanderbilt mansion. **Pros:** great private beaches; never crowded; varied on-island dining choices. **Cons:** ferry ride to get on and off island; limited cell service. [$] *Rooms from: $1037* ✉ *1 Fisher Island Dr., Fisher Island* ☎ *305/535–6000, 800/537–3708* 🌐 *www.fisherislandclub.com* 🛏 *50 condo units, 7 villas, 3 cottages* 🍴 *No meals* ✥ *E5.*

$$ RESORT 🏨 **The Standard Miami Beach.** An extension of André Balazs's trendy and hip yet budget-conscious hotel chain, the shabby-chic Standard is a mile from South Beach on an island just over the Venetian Causeway and boasts one of South Florida's most renowned spas and hottest pool scenes. **Pros:** free bike and kayak rentals; swank pool scene; great spa; inexpensive. **Cons:** slight trek to South Beach; small rooms with no views. [$] *Rooms from: $299* ✉ *40 Island Ave., Belle Isle* ☎ *305/673–1717* 🌐 *www.standardhotel.com* 🛏 *104 rooms, 1 suite* 🍴 *No meals* ✥ *E4.*

NORTH BEACH AND AVENTURA

$$$$ RESORT FAMILY Fodor's Choice ★ 🏨 **Acqualina Resort & Spa on the Beach.** Acqualina raises the bar on Miami beachfront luxury, delivering a fantasy of Mediterranean opulence, with oceanfront lawns and pools that evoke Vizcaya. **Pros:** excellent beach; in-room check-in; luxury amenities; huge spa. **Cons:** no nightlife near hotel; hotel's towering height shades the beach by early afternoon. [$] *Rooms from: $625* ✉ *17875 Collins Ave., Sunny Isles* ☎ *305/918–8000* 🌐 *www.acqualinaresort.com* 🛏 *54 rooms, 43 suites* 🍴 *No meals* ✥ *E1.*

$$$$ RESORT 🏨 **ONE Bal Harbour.** In one of South Florida's poshest neighborhoods, ONE Bal Harbour exudes contemporary beachfront luxury design with decadent mahogany-floor guest rooms featuring large terraces with

panoramic views of the water and city, over-the-top bathrooms with 10-foot floor-to-ceiling windows, and LCD TVs built into the bathroom mirrors. **Pros:** proximity to Bal Harbour Shops; beachfront; great contemporary-art collection. **Cons:** narrow beach is a bit disappointing; far from nightlife. [$] *Rooms from: $759* ✉ *10295 Collins Ave., North Beach and Aventura, Bal Harbour* ☎ *305/455–5400* 🌐 *www.onebalharbourresort.com* 🛏 *124 rooms, 63 suites* 🍴 *No meals* ✥ *E2.*

2

$$$$ RESORT Fodor's Choice ★ 🏨 **St. Regis Bal Harbour Resort.** When this $1 billion–plus resort opened in 2012, Miami's North Beach entered a new era of glamour and haute living, with A-list big spenders rushing to stay in this 27-story, 243-room, triple-glass-tower masterpiece. **Pros:** beachfront; beyond glamorous; large rooms. **Cons:** limited lounge space around main pool; limited privacy on balconies. [$] *Rooms from: $679* ✉ *9703 Collins Ave., North Beach and Aventura, Bal Harbour* ☎ *305/993–3300* 🌐 *www.stregisbalharbour.com* 🛏 *190 rooms, 53 suites* 🍴 *No meals* ✥ *E2.*

$$$$ RESORT FAMILY 🏨 **Turnberry Isle Miami.** Golfers and families favor this service-oriented, 300-acre tropical resort with jumbo-size rooms and world-class amenities, including a majestic lagoon pool (winding waterslide and lazy river included), an acclaimed three-story spa and fitness center, and celeb chef Michael Mina's Bourbon Steak restaurant. **Pros:** great golf, pools, and restaurants; free shuttle to Aventura Mall; situated between Miami and Fort Lauderdale. **Cons:** not on the beach; no nightlife. [$] *Rooms from: $459* ✉ *19999 W. Country Club Dr., North Beach and Aventura* ☎ *305/932–6200, 866/612–7739* 🌐 *www.turnberryislemiami.com* 🛏 *408 rooms, 29 suites* 🍴 *No meals* ✥ *E1.*

NIGHTLIFE

One of Greater Miami's most popular pursuits is bar hopping. Bars range from intimate enclaves to showy see-and-be-seen lounges to loud, raucous frat parties. There's a New York–style flair to some of the newer lounges, which are increasingly catering to the Manhattan party crowd who escape to South Beach for long weekends. No doubt, Miami's pulse pounds with nonstop nightlife that reflects the area's potent cultural mix. On sultry, humid nights with the huge full moon rising out of the ocean and fragrant night-blooming jasmine intoxicating the senses, who can resist Cuban salsa with some disco and hip-hop thrown in for good measure? When this place throws a party, hips shake, fingers snap, bodies touch. It's no wonder many clubs are still rocking at 5 am. If you're looking for a relatively nonfrenetic evening, your best bet is one of the chic hotel bars on Collins Avenue.

The *Miami Herald* (🌐 *www.miamiherald.com*) is a good source for information on what to do in town. The Weekend section of the newspaper, included in the Friday edition, has an annotated guide to everything from plays and galleries to concerts and nightclubs. The "Ticket" column details the week's entertainment highlights. Or you can pick up the *Miami New Times* (🌐 *www.miaminewtimes.com*), the city's largest free alternative newspaper, published each Thursday. It lists nightclubs, concerts, and special events; reviews plays and movies; and provides in-depth coverage of the local music scene. *MIAMI* (🌐 *www.*

modernluxury.com/miami) and *Ocean Drive* (⊕ *www.oceandrive.*
com), Miami's model-strewn, upscale fashion and lifestyle magazines,
squeeze club, bar, restaurant, and events listings in with fashion spreads,
reviews, and personality profiles. Paparazzi photos of local party people
and celebrities give you a taste of Greater Miami nightlife before you
even dress up to paint the town.

The Spanish-language *El Nuevo Herald* (⊕ *www.elnuevoherald.com*),
published by the *Miami Herald*, has extensive information on Spanish-
language arts and entertainment, including dining reviews, concert pre-
views, and nightclub highlights.

DOWNTOWN

BARS AND LOUNGES

Fodor's Choice   **Blackbird Ordinary.** This local watering hole has been around since 2011,
★   but it's now trendier than ever. With a vibe that's a bit speakeasy, a
bit dive bar, a bit hipster hangout, and a bit Miami sophisticate, it's
hands-down one of the coolest places in the city and clearly appeals to
a wide range of demographics. Mixology is a huge part of the Blackbird experience—so be prepared for some awesome artisanal cocktails.
There's something going on every night of the week, and the stylish outdoor space is great for cocktails under the stars, movie screenings, and
live music. ⊠ *729 S.W. 1st Ave., Downtown* ☎ *305/671–3307* ⊕ *www.*
blackbirdordinary.com.

Hyde AAA. The Miami outpost of the wildly popular Hyde Lounge
is situated within the AmericanAirlines Arena (AAA) for use before/
during/after Miami Heat games and arena concerts. The 250-person
venue debuted during the Heat's 2012–13 season and quickly became
a Miami institution. Located court-level on the south end of the arena,
Hyde AAA provides a full-blown, big pimpin' dining, lounge, and
nightlife experience that's often better than the event happening in the
arena itself. ⊠ *AmericanAirlines Arena, 601 Biscayne Blvd., Downtown*
☎ *855/777–4933* ⊕ *www.hydeaaarena.com.*

Fodor's Choice   **Tobacco Road.** Opened in 1912, this classic holds Miami's oldest liquor
★   license: No. 0001. Upstairs, in a space that was occupied by a speakeasy during Prohibition, local and national blues bands perform nightly.
There is excellent bar food, a dinner menu, and a selection of single-malt
scotches, bourbons, and cigars. This is the hangout of grizzled journal-
ists, bohemians en route to or from nowhere, and club kids seeking a
way station before the real parties begin. Live blues, R&B, and jazz
bands are on tap, along with food and drink, seven days a week. If
you like your food and drink the way you like your blues—gritty, honest, and unassuming—then this vintage joint will quickly earn your
respect. ⊠ *626 S. Miami Ave., Downtown* ☎ *305/374–1198* ⊕ *www.*
tobacco-road.com.

DANCE CLUBS

Club Space. Want 24-hour partying? Here's the place. Space revolution-
ized the Miami party scene over a decade ago and still gets accolades
as one of the country's best dance clubs. But depending on the month,

Cars whizz by Avalon hotel and other art deco architecture on Ocean Drive, Miami South Beach.

Space wavers between trendy and empty, so make sure you get the up-to-date scoop from your hotel concierge. Created from four downtown warehouses, it has two levels (one blasts house music; the other reverberates with hip-hop), an outdoor patio, a New York–style industrial look, and a 24-hour liquor license. It's open on weekends only, and you'll need to look good to be allowed past the velvet ropes. Note that the crowd can sometimes be sketchy, and take caution walking around the surrounding neighborhood. ⊠ *34 N.E. 11th St., Downtown* ☎ *305/375–0001* ⊕ *www.clubspace.com.*

WYNWOOD

BARS AND LOUNGES

Fodor's Choice
★
Cafeina Wynwood Lounge. This awesome Wynwood watering hole takes center stage during the highly social Gallery Night and Artwalk through the Wynwood Art District, the second Saturday of every month, which showcases the cool and hip art galleries between Northwest 20th and Northwest 36 streets west of North Miami Avenue. For those in the know, the evening either begins or ends at Cafeina, a seductive, design-driven lounge with a gorgeous patio and plenty of art on display. Other weekends, this is still a great place to hang out and get a true feel for Miami's cultural revolution. Open only Thursday–Saturday. ⊠ *297 N.W. 23rd St., Wynwood* ☎ *305/438–0792* ⊕ *www.cafeinamiami.com; www.wynwoodartwalk.com.*

SOUTH BEACH

BARS AND LOUNGES

Blues Bar at National Hotel. Dedicate at least one night of your Miami vacation to an art deco pub crawl, patronizing the hotel bars and lounges of South Beach's most iconic buildings, including the National Hotel. Though it's a low-key affair, the nifty wooden Blues Bar here is well worth a stop. The bar is one of many elements original to the 1939 building that give it such a sense of its era that you'd expect to see Ginger Rogers and Fred Astaire hoofing it along the polished terrazzo floor. The adjoining Martini Room has a great collection of cigars, old airline stickers, and vintage Bacardi ads on the walls, but it's only available for private events. ⊠ *National Hotel, 1677 Collins Ave., South Beach* ☎ *305/532–2311* ⊕ *www.nationalhotel.com.*

Fodor's Choice **FDR at the Delano.** The Delano's famous Florida Room was reinvented
★ and reopened in spring 2012 as FDR, an überexclusive subterranean lounge, developed by Las Vegas's Light Group. The world's hottest DJs are on tap for a stylish see-and-be-seen crowd. Seductive lighting illuminates the two-room, 200 person watering hole, decked out in dark and sexy décor. Bottle service is available for high rollers. ⊠ *1685 Collins Ave., South Beach* ☎ *305/672–2000* ⊕ *www.delano-hotel.com.*

Lost Weekend. Slumming celebs and locals often patronize this pool hall–resto–dive bar on quaint Española Way. The hardcore locals are serious about their pastime, so it can be challenging to get a table on weekends. However, everyone can enjoy the pinball machines, the grub, and the full bar, which has 150 kinds of beer (a dozen of which are on tap). Each night, Lost Weekend draws an eclectic crowd, from yuppies to drag queens to celebs on the down-low. So South Beach! ⊠ *218 Española Way, South Beach* ☎ *305/672–1707.*

MOVA. Formerly known as Halo Lounge, this gay bar and lounge off of Lincoln Road is where most LGBT South Beach nights begin (and some end), with ample eye candy to whet the palate for a scintillating night of drinking and partying. The minimalist lounge gives off an undeniably sexy vibe, augmented by the handsome bartenders muddling fresh fruits for the ever-changing avant-garde drink menu. The place gets packed on Friday and Saturday; other nights are hit-or-miss. ⊠ *1625 Michigan Ave., South Beach* ☎ *305/534–8181* ⊕ *www.movalounge.com.*

Mynt Lounge. This is the quintessential celeb-studded, super-VIP, South Beach party where you may or may not be let in, depending on what you wear or who you know. It's the kind of place where back in the day LiLo would act out, Brit-Brit would chill out, and Paris Hilton would zone out, namely because of the club's "no paparazzi" policy. Admittedly, owner Romain Zago says that "Mynt is for the famous and fabulous." Every summer the lounge undergoes renovations to stay at the top of its game, revealing a slightly different look. ⊠ *1921 Collins Ave., South Beach* ☎ *305/532–0727* ⊕ *www.myntlounge.com.*

The Regent Cocktail Club. This classic cocktail bar recalls an intimate gentleman's club (and not the stripper kind) with strong masculine cocktails, dark furnishings, bartenders dressed to the nines, and the sounds

THE VELVET ROPES

How to get past the velvet ropes at the hottest South Beach nightspots? First, if you're staying at a hotel, use the concierge. Decide which clubs you want to check out (consult *Ocean Drive* magazine celebrity pages if you want to be among the glitterati), and the concierge will email, fax, or call in your names to the clubs so you'll be on the guest list when you arrive. This means much easier access and usually no cover charge (which can be upward of $20) if you arrive before midnight. Guest list or no guest list, follow these pointers: Make sure there are more women than men in your group. Dress up: casual chic is the dress code. For men this means no sneakers, no shorts, no sleeveless vests, and no shirts unbuttoned past the top button. For women, provocative and seductive is fine; overly revealing is not. Black is always right. At the door: don't name-drop—no one takes it seriously. Don't be pushy while trying to get the doorman's attention. Wait until you make eye contact, then be cool and easygoing. If you decide to tip him (which most bouncers don't expect), be discreet and pleasant, not big-bucks obnoxious—a $10 or $20 bill quietly passed will be appreciated, however. With the right dress and the right attitude, you'll be on the dance floor rubbing shoulders with South Beach's finest clubbers in no time.

of jazz legends in the background. The intimate space exudes elegance and timelessness. It's a welcome respite from South Beach's predictable nightlife scene. Cocktails—each with bespoke ice cubes—change daily and are posted on the house blackboard. ⊠ *Gale South Beach, 1690 Collins Ave., South Beach* ☎ *305/673–0199* ⊕ *www.galehotel.com/nightlife.*

Rose Bar at the Delano. Tucked away inside the chic Delano hotel, the Rose Bar is a South Beach mainstay and an essential stop on any South Beach bar crawl. Now managed by Las Vegas's The Light Group, the Rose Bar mixes classic art deco architecture with the best in mixology (and a bit of Vegas bling). The bar pushes the envelope on creative cocktails. ⊠ *Delano Hotel, 1685 Collins Ave., South Beach* ☎ *305/672–2000* ⊕ *www.delano-hotel.com.*

Fodor'sChoice
★ **Skybar at the Shore Club.** An entire enclave dedicated to alcohol-induced fun for grown-ups, the Skybar is actually a collection of adjoining lounges at the Shore Club, including a chic outdoor lounge, the indoor Red Room, and the areas in between, which teem with party-hungry visitors. Splendor-in-the-garden is the theme in the outdoor lounge, accessorized with daybeds and glowing Moroccan lanterns. Groove to dance music in the Red Room or have a cocktail (or five) stargazing on the daybeds with your new best friends. ⊠ *Shore Club Hotel, 1901 Collins Ave., South Beach* ☎ *305/695–3100* ⊕ *www.shoreclub.com.*

DANCE CLUBS

Cameo. One of Miami's longest-running dance clubs, Cameo is constantly reinventing itself, but the result always seems to be the same—long lines filled with everyone claiming to be on the guest list, hoochie mamas wearing far too little clothing, and some unsuspecting tourists trying to see what all the fuss is about. The combination makes for some insane partying, especially if the night is headlined by an all-star DJ. You'll find both plentiful dance space and plush VIP lounges. If you can brave the velvet rope, the thuggish crowd, and the nonsense described above, Saturday-night parties are the best. ✉ *1445 Washington Ave., South Beach* ☎ *786/235–5800* ⊕ *www.cameomiami.com.*

Nikki Beach Club. Smack-dab on the beach, the full-service Nikki Beach Club was once upon a time a favorite of SoBe's pretty people and celebrities. Nowadays, it's filled with more suburbanites than the "in" crowd. Nikki's late-night parties are reserved for Sundays only. Other days, the Beach Club is open from 11 to 11 (except Monday and Tuesday when it closes at 6). Visitors can eat at the Nikki Beach Restaurant, and get their food and drink on in the tepees, hammocks, and beach beds (expect rental fees). Sunday brunch at the club's restaurant is pretty spectacular. ✉ *1 Ocean Dr., South Beach* ☎ *305/538–1111* ⊕ *www. nikkibeach.com/miami.*

Fodor's Choice
★

The Rec Room. Entering The Rec Room is like stumbling upon an awesome basement party that just happens to be packed with the hottest people ever. This underground space of the Gale Hotel pays homage to everything 1977 (memorabilia included) and features a collection of over 3,000 vinyl records at the disposal of resident DJs. The vibe is totally speakeasy meets modern day. The easy-on-the-eyes crowd lets loose, free of inhibitions, jamming out to old-school hip-hop and eighties and nineties throwbacks. ✉ *Gale South Beach, 1690 Collins Ave., South Beach* ☎ *305/673–0199* ⊕ *www.galehotel.com/nightlife.*

Score. Since the nineties, Score has been the see-and-be-seen HQ of Miami's gay community, with plenty of global hotties coming from near and far to show off their designer threads and six-pack abs. After moving in 2013 to Washington Avenue from its long-time Lincoln Road location, this South Beach powerhouse shows no signs of slowing down. DJs spin five nights a week, but Planeta Macho Latin Tuesday is exceptionally popular, as are the weekend dance-offs—Filthy Gorgeous Fridays and Bigger Saturdays. Dress to impress (and then be ready to go shirtless). ✉ *1437 Washington Ave., South Beach* ☎ *305/535–1111* ⊕ *www.scorebar.net* ☉ *Closed Mon. and Wed.*

Twist. Twist is a gay institution in South Beach, having been the late-night go-to place for decades, filling to capacity around 2 am after the beach's fly-by-night bars and more established lounges begin to die down (though it's in fact open daily from 1 pm to 5 am). There's never a cover here—not even on holidays or during gay pride events. The dark club has several rooms spread over two levels and patios, pumping out different tunes and attracting completely disparate groups. It's not uncommon to have young college boys partying to Top 40 in one room and strippers showing off their stuff to the straight girls in another area, while an all-out hip-hop throwdown is taking place upstairs. ✉ *1057 Washington Ave., South Beach* ☎ *305/538–9478* ⊕ *www.twistsobe. com.*

LIVE MUSIC

Jazid. If you're looking for an unpretentious alternative to the velvet-rope nightclubs, this unassuming, live-music hot spot is a standout on the SoBe strip. Eight-piece bands play danceable Latin rhythms, as well as reggae, hip-hop, and fusion sounds. Each night caters to a different genre. Get ready for a late night though, as bands are just getting started at 11 pm. Call ahead to reserve a table. ⊠ *1342 Washington Ave., South Beach* ☎ *305/673–9372* ⊕ *www.jazid.net.*

MID-BEACH

DANCE CLUBS

Fodor'sChoice
★ **LIV Nightclub.** Since its 2009 opening, the Fontainebleau's LIV Nightclub has garnered plenty of global attention. It's not hard to see why—if you can get in, that is (LIV is notorious for lengthy lines, so don't arrive fashionably late). Past the velvet ropes, the dance palladium impresses with its lavish décor, well-dressed international crowd, sensational light-and-sound system, and seductive bilevel club experience. Sometimes the lobby bar, filled with LIV's overflow (and rejects), is just as fun as the club itself. ■ **TIP→ Men beware: Groups of guys entering LIV are often coerced into insanely priced bottle service.** ⊠ *Fontainebleau Miami Beach, 4441 Collins Ave., Mid-Beach* ☎ *305/674–4680* ⊕ *www. livnightclub.com.*

SHOPPING

Beyond its fun-in-the-sun offerings, Miami has evolved into a world-class shopping destination. People fly to Miami from all over the world just to shop. The city teems with sophisticated shopping malls—from multistory, indoor climate-controlled temples of consumerism to sun-kissed, open-air retail enclaves—and bustling avenues and streets, lined at once with affordable chain stores, haute couture boutiques, and one-off, "only in Miami"–type shops.

Miami's shopping centers are record breakers. Several chain stores in the massive Aventura Mall bank as the best-selling outposts in the country, while Bal Harbour Shops flaunt the most lucrative square footage of any shopping arena in the country, with its sales reaching up to $2,555 per square foot.

Following the incredible success of the Bal Harbour Shops in the highest of the high-end market (think Chanel, Alexander McQueen, ETRO, and Hermès), the Design District has followed suit. Beyond fabulous designer furniture showrooms, the district's tenants now include Dior Homme, Rolex, and Prada. In addition, an entire LVMH mall is currently under construction to create more upscale retail space.

If you're from a region ripe with the climate-controlled slickness of shopping malls and food-court "meals," you'll love the choices in Miami. Head out into the sunshine and shop the city streets, where you'll find big-name retailers and local boutiques alike. Take a break at a sidewalk café to power up on some Cuban coffee or fresh-squeezed OJ and enjoy the tropical breezes.

Beyond clothiers and big-name retailers, Greater Miami has all manner of merchandise to tempt even the casual browser. For consumers on a mission to find certain items—art-deco antiques or cigars, for instance—the city streets burst with a rewarding collection of specialty shops.

Stroll through Spanish-speaking neighborhoods where shops sell clothing, cigars, and other goods from all over Latin America or even head to Little Haiti for rare vinyl records.

COCONUT GROVE

MALLS

CocoWalk. This three-story indoor-outdoor mall has three floors of nearly 40 shops that stay open almost as late as its popular restaurants. Typically 1990s chain stores like Victoria's Secret and Gap blend with a few specialty shops like Guayabera World; the space mixes the bustle of a mall with the breathability of an open-air market. Touristy kiosks with cigars, beads, incense, herbs, and other small items are scattered around the ground level, and commercial restaurants and nightlife (Cheesecake Factory, Fat Tuesday, and Paragon Grove 13—a multiscreen, state-of-the-art movie theater with a wine bar and lounge) line the upstairs perimeter. Hanging out and people-watching is something of a pastime here for Miami suburbanites. ⊠ *3015 Grand Ave., Coconut Grove* ☎ *305/444–0777* ⊕ *www.cocowalk.net.*

OUTDOOR MARKETS

Coconut Grove Organic Farmers' Market. This pricey, outdoor organic market is a Saturday ritual for Coconut Grove locals. It specializes in a mouthwatering array of local produce as well as such ready-to-eat, raw vegan goodies as cashew butter, homemade salad dressings, and fruit pies. If you are looking for a downright granola crowd and experience, pack your Birkenstocks, because this is it. It's open Saturday from 10 to 7, rain or shine. ⊠ *3300 Grand Ave., Coconut Grove* ☎ *305/238–7747* ⊕ *www.glaserorganicfarms.com.*

ANTIQUES

Worth Galleries. Find an enormous selection of fine European antiques as well as large and eclectic items—railroad crossing signs, statues, English roadsters. This gallery possesses South Florida's largest collection of antique books and antique chandeliers. There's also vintage furniture, modern art, oil paintings, and silverware, all in a cluttered setting that makes shopping an adventure. ⊠ *2520 S.W. 28th La., Coconut Grove* ☎ *305/285–1330* ⊕ *www.worthgalleries.com.*

CORAL GABLES

MALLS

Village of Merrick Park. At this Mediterranean-style, trilevel, shopping-and-dining venue, Neiman Marcus and Nordstrom anchor 115 specialty shops. Designers such as ETRO, Jimmy Choo, Tiffany & Co., Burberry, CH Carolina Herrera, and Gucci fulfill most high-fashion needs, and haute-décor shopping options include Brazilian contemporary-furniture designer Artefacto. International food favorite C'est

Bon and pampering specialist Elemis Day-Spa offer further indulgences. ✉ *358 San Lorenzo Ave., Coral Gables* ☎ *305/529–0200* ⊕ *www. villageofmerrickpark.com.*

SHOPPING DISTRICTS

Miracle Mile. The centerpiece of the downtown Coral Gables shopping district, lined with trees and busy with strolling shoppers, is home to men's and women's boutiques, jewelry and home-furnishings stores, and a host of exclusive couturiers and bridal shops. Running from Douglas Road to LeJeune Road and Aragon Avenue to Andalusia Avenue, more than two dozen first-rate restaurants offer everything from French to Japanese-fusion cuisine, and art galleries and the Actors' Playhouse at the Miracle Theater give the area a cultural flair. ■ TIP➔ If debating Miracle Mile versus Bal Harbour or Lincoln Road or the Design District, check out the others first. ✉ *Miracle Mile (Coral Way), Douglas Rd. to LeJeune Rd., and Aragon Ave. to Andalusia Ave., Coral Gables* ⊕ *www. shopcoralgables.com.*

ANTIQUES

Alhambra Antiques. The collection of high-quality antique French furniture and decorative pieces are acquired on annual jaunts to France. Expect a wide range of classic chandeliers, clocks, chairs, daybeds, tables, and mirrors. While the showroom offers regular hours (Monday–Saturday noon–6), it's usually best to call ahead as many high-end Coral Gables shops prefer to open their stores by appointment only, rather than maintaining an open-door policy during their operating hours. ✉ *2850 Salzedo St., Coral Gables* ☎ *305/446–1688* ⊕ *www. alhambraantiques.com.*

BOOKS

FAMILY
Fodor'sChoice
★

Books & Books, Inc. Long live the classic book store! Greater Miami's only independent, English-language bookshop, Books & Books, specializes in contemporary and classical literature as well as in books on the arts, architecture, Florida, and Cuba. The Coral Gables store is the largest of its three South Florida locations. Here, you can sip 'n' read in the courtyard lounge or dine at the old-fashioned in-store café while browsing the photography gallery. Multiple rooms are filled with myriad genres, making for a fabulous afternoon of book shopping— plus there's an entire area dedicated to kids. There are book signings, literary events, poetry, and other readings too. Two smaller locations on Lincoln Road in South Beach and at the Bal Harbour Shops also carry great reads. ✉ *265 Aragon Ave., Coral Gables* ☎ *305/442–4408* ⊕ *www.booksandbooks.com* ☾ *Sun.–Thurs. 9 am–11 pm, Fri.–Sat. 9 am–midnight.*

CLOTHING

Koko & Palenki. Shoe shopaholics come here for the well-edited selection of trendy footwear by Alexandre Birman, Giuseppe Zanotti, Emilia Castillo, Rachel Zoe, Rebecca Minkoff, and others. Handbags and belts add to the selection. Clothing hails from designers like Catherine Malandrino, Issa, J Brand, and Citizens of Humanity. Koko & Palenki also has a store in Aventura Mall. ✉ *Village of Merrick Park, 342*

San Lorenzo Ave., Ste. 1090, Coral Gables ☎*305/444–0626* ⊕*www. kokopalenki.com.*

Silvia Tcherassi. The Colombian designer's signature boutique in the Village of Merrick Park features ready-to-wear, feminine, and frilly dresses and separates accented with chiffon, tuille, and sequins. A neighboring atelier at 4101 Ponce de Leon Boulevard showcases the designer's bridal collection. ⊠ *Village of Merrick Park, 350 San Lorenzo Ave., No. 2140, Coral Gables* ☎*305/461–0009* ⊕*www.silviatcherassi.com.*

JEWELRY

Beverlee Kagan. Specializing in vintage and antique jewelry, this jeweler showcases over 30,000 eclectic items, including art deco–era bangles, bracelets, and cuff links. ⊠ *5831 Sunset Dr., Coral Gables* ☎*305/663– 1937* ⊕*www.kaganjewelry.com.*

ONLY IN MIAMI

La Casa de las Guayaberas. This clothing shop sells custom-made Ramon Puig guayaberas, the natty four-pocket dress shirts favored by older Cuban men and hipsters alike. Ramon Puig is known as "the King of Guayaberas," and his shirts are top of the line as far as guayaberas go. Hundreds are available off the rack. There are styles for women, too. ⊠ *5840 S.W. 8th St., Coral Gables* ☎*305/266–9683* ⊕*www. ramonpuig.com.*

WYNWOOD

SHOPPING NEIGHBORHOODS

Miami Design District. Miami is synonymous with good design, and this visitor-friendly shopping district—from Northeast 38th to Northeast 42nd Street, between North Miami Avenue and Northeast 2nd Avenue—is an unprecedented melding of public space and the exclusive world of design. There are more than 200 showrooms and galleries, including Baltus, Animadomus, Kartell, Ann Sacks, Poliform USA, and Luminaire Lab. Upscale retail outlets also grace the district. Cartier, En Avance, Louis Vuitton, Prada, Rolex and Scotch & Soda now neighbor the design showrooms. Meanwhile, restaurants like Michael's Genuine Food & Drink also make this trendy neighborhood a hip place to dine. Unlike most showrooms, which are typically the beat of decorators alone, the Miami Design District's showrooms are open to the public and occupy windowed, street-level spaces. Although in some cases you'll need a decorator to secure your purchases, browsers are encouraged to consider for themselves the array of rather exclusive furnishings, decorative objects, antiques, and art. ⊠ *N.E. 2nd Ave. and N.E. 40th St., Miami Design District* ⊕ *www.miamidesigndistrict.net.*

CLOTHING

Fly Boutique. After 13 years on South Beach, Fly Boutique has found its new home in Miami's up and coming MIMO district, north of the Design District. This resale boutique is where Miami hipsters flock for the latest arrival of used clothing. Eighties glam designer pieces fly out at a premium price, but vintage camisoles and Levi's corduroys are still a resale deal. You'll find supercool art, furniture, luggage, and collectibles throughout the boutique. And be sure to look up—the eclectic lanterns are also for sale. ✉ *7235 Biscayne Blvd., Design District* ☏ *305/604–8508* ⊕ *www.flyboutiquevintage.com.*

ONLY IN MIAMI

ABC Costume Shop. ABC Costume Shop is a major costume source for TV, movie, and theatrical performances. Open to the public, it has over 30,000 costumes in stock—outfits range from Venetian kings and queens to Tarzan and Jane. Hundreds of these costumes and accessories, such as wigs, masks, gloves, tights, and makeup, are available to buy off the rack; others are available to rent. ✉ *575 N.W. 24th St., Wynwood* ☏ *305/573–5657* ⊕ *www.abccostumeshop.com* ⊘ *Closed Sat. in July and Aug.*

FAMILY **Genius Jones.** This is a modern design store for kids and parents. It's the best—and one of the few—places to buy unique children's gifts in Miami. Pick up furniture, strollers, clothing, home accessories, and playthings, including classic wooden toys, vintage-rock T-shirts by Claude and Trunk, and toys designed by Takashi Murakami and Keith Haring. ✉ *2800 NE 2nd Ave., Wynwood* ☏ *305/571–2000* ⊕ *www. geniusjones.com.*

LITTLE HAITI

MUSIC

Sweat Records. Though Little Haiti's shopping "scene" is mostly botanicas and voodoo supply shops, one of its most popular residents is Sweat Records, a record store with Miami's biggest selection of new LPs; there's also a vegan, organic coffee shop. Sweat sells a wide range of music—rock, pop, punk, electronic, hip-hop, and Latino—as well as turntables and vinyl accessories. ✉ *5505 N.E. 2nd Ave., Little Haiti* ☏ *786/693–9309* ⊕ *www.sweatrecordsmiami.com.*

LITTLE HAVANA

ONLY IN MIAMI

FAMILY **La Casa de los Trucos (The House of Costumes).** This popular costume store first opened in Cuba in the 1920s; the exiled owners reopened it here in the 1970s. They have cartoon costumes, rockstar costumes, pet costumes, couples costumes, you name it. If you come any time near Halloween, expect to stand in line just to enter the tiny store. Wooden, life-size costume cut-outs in the parking lot make for great photo ops. ✉ *1343 S.W. 8th St., Little Havana* ☏ *305/858–5029* ⊕ *www. crazyforcostumes.com.*

Lily's Records. The last of a dying breed, Lily's Records sells old-fashioned CDs and records, specializing in hard-to-get beats from across Latin America. The store is divided into sounds from various countries/regions, including (but not limited to) Puerto Rico, Mexico, Argentina, and Dominican Republic. ✉ *1419 S.W. 8th St., Little Havana* ☏ *305/856–0536* ⊕ *www.lilysrecords.com.*

CIGARS

Sosa Family Cigars. Sosa offers a wide selection of premium and house cigars from around the world. It's one of the only cigar shops in Little Havana where you can sit and play dominoes while smoking stogies. There's a selection of wines for purchase, too. Humidors and other accessories are also available. ⊠ *3475 S.W. 8th St., Little Havana* ☎ *305/446–2606.*

SOUTH BEACH

SHOPPING DISTRICTS

★
Collins Avenue. Give your plastic a workout in South Beach shopping at the many high-profile tenants on this densely packed stretch of Collins between 5th and 10th streets, with stores like Steve Madden, Club Monaco, MAC Cosmetics, Ralph Lauren, Kenneth Cole, and Intermix. Sprinkled among the upscale vendors are hair salons, spas, cafés, and such familiar stores as the Gap and Urban Outfitters. Be sure to head over one street east to Ocean Drive or west to Washington Avenue for a drink or a light bite, or go for more retail therapy on Lincoln Road. ⊠ *Collins Ave. between 5th and 10th Sts., South Beach* ⊕ *www.lincolnroadmall.com/shopping/collins-avenue.*

Lincoln Road Mall. The eight-block-long pedestrian mall is the trendiest place on Miami Beach. Home to more than 150 shops, 20-plus art galleries and nightclubs, about 50 restaurants and cafés, and the renovated Colony Theatre, Lincoln Road, between Alton Road and Washington Avenue, is like the larger, more sophisticated cousin of Ocean Drive. The see-and-be-seen theme is furthered by outdoor seating at every restaurant, where tourists and locals lounge and discuss the people (and pet) parade passing by. An 18-screen movie theater anchors the west end of the street, which is where most of the worthwhile shops are; the far east end is mostly discount and electronics shops. Due to higher rents, you are more likely to see big corporate stores like American Eagles Outfitters, H&M, and Victoria's Secret than original boutiques. However, a few emporiums and stores with unique personalities, like Chroma, Base, and Books & Books, remain. ⊠ *Lincoln Rd. between Alton Rd. and Washington Ave., South Beach* ⊕ *www.lincolnroadmall.com.*

CLOTHING

Base. This is the quintessential South Beach fun-and-funky boutique experience. Stop here for men's eclectic clothing, shoes, jewelry, and accessories that mix Japanese design with Caribbean-inspired materials. Constantly evolving, this shop features an intriguing magazine section, a record section, groovy home accessories, and the latest in men's swimwear and sunglasses. The often-present house-label designer may help select your wardrobe's newest addition. The boutique has small outposts in the Delano Hotel and the Mondrian South Beach, as well as an haute vending machine in the latter. ⊠ *939 Lincoln Rd., South Beach* ☎ *305/531–4982* ⊕ *www.baseworld.com.*

Intermix. This modern New York–based boutique has the variety of a department store. You'll find fancy dresses, stylish shoes, slinky accessories, and trendy looks by sassy and somewhat pricey designers like

Chloé, Stella McCartney, Marc Jacobs, Moschino, and Diane von Furstenberg. There is a branch at the Bal Harbour Shops at 9700 Collins Avenue in North Beach and Aventura. ⊠ *634 Collins Ave., South Beach* ☎ *305/531–5950* ⊕ *www.intermixonline.com.*

2

ONLY IN MIAMI

Fodor'sChoice ★ **Dog Bar.** Just north of Lincoln Road's main drag, this over-the-top pet boutique caters to enthusiastic animal owners with a variety of unique items for the super-pampered pet. From luxurious pet sofas imported from Italy to bling-bling-studded collars to chic poopy-bag holders, Miami's "original pet boutique" carries pretty much every pet accessory imaginable. They also have plenty of gourmet food and treats as well as a wide variety of fancy toys for dogs, large and small. ⊠ *1684 Jefferson Ave., South Beach* ☎ *305/532–5654* ⊕ *www.dogbar.com.*

Fodor'sChoice ★ **The Webster Miami.** Occupying an entire circa-1939 art deco building, the Webster is a trilevel, 20,000-square-foot, one-stop shop for fashionistas. This retail sanctuary carries ready-to-wear fashions by more than 100 top designers, plus in-store exclusive shirts, candles, books, and random trendy items you might need for your South Beach experience—a kind of haute Urban Outfitters for grown-ups. Too many choices? Sit down for a café au lait and pastry at the first U.S. outpost of Paris-based patisserie-chocolatier Hugo & Victor, located inside the store. ⊠ *1220 Collins Ave., South Beach* ☎ *305/674–7899* ⊕ *www.thewebstermiami.com.*

OUTDOOR MARKETS

Lincoln Road Farmers' Market. With all the familiar trappings of a farmers market (except for farmers—most of the people selling veggies appear to be resellers), this is a weekly South Beach Sunday (9–6:30) ritual. It brings local produce and bakery vendors to Lincoln Road and often features plant workshops, art sales, and children's activities. This is a good place to pick up live orchids, too. ⊠ *Lincoln Rd. between Meridian and Washington Aves., South Beach* ☎ *305/531–0038* ⊕ *www. themarketcompany.org.*

VINTAGE CLOTHING

Consign of the Times. Come to this shop for vintage and consignment items by top designers at pre-owned prices, including Chanel suits, Fendi bags, and Celine and Prada treasures. ⊠ *1635 Jefferson Ave., South Beach* ☎ *305/535–0811* ⊕ *www.consignofthetimes.com.*

NORTH BEACH AND AVENTURA

MALLS

Fodor'sChoice ★ **Aventura Mall.** This three-story megamall offers the ultimate in South Florida retail therapy. Aventura houses many global top performers such as the most lucrative Abercrombie & Fitch in the United States, a supersize Nordstrom and Bloomingdale's, and 300 other shops like Façonnable, Dior, and Braccialini, which together create the fifth-largest mall in the United States. This is the one-stop, shop-'til-you-drop retail Mecca for locals, out-of-towners, and—frequently—celebrities. ⊠ *19501 Biscayne Blvd., North Beach and Aventura* ☎ *305/935–1110* ⊕ *www.aventuramall.com.*

Fodor's Choice **Bal Harbour Shops.** Beverly Hills meets the South Florida sun at this
★ swank collection of 100 high-end shops, boutiques, and department
stores, which include such names as Alexander McQueen, Gucci, Hermès, Salvatore Ferragamo, Tiffany & Co., and Valentino. Many European designers open their first North American signature store at this
outdoor, pedestrian-friendly mall, and many American designers open
their first boutique outside of New York here. Restaurants and cafés, in
tropical garden settings, overflow with style-conscious diners. People-
watching on the terrace of the Japenese restaurant Makoto is the best
in town. The ambience is oh-so Rodeo Drive. ⊠ *9700 Collins Ave.,
Bal Harbour, North Beach and Aventura* ☎ *305/866–0311* ⊕ *www.
balharbourshops.com.*

JEWELRY

MIA Jewels. This jewelry and accessories boutique is known for its colorful, gem- and bead-laden, gold and silver earrings, necklaces, bracelets,
and brooches by lines such as Cousin Claudine, Amrita, and Alexis
Bittar. This is a shoo-in store for everyone: you'll find things for trend
lovers (gold-studded chunky Lucite bangles), classicists (long, colorful,
wraparound beaded necklaces), and ice lovers (long Swarovski crystal
cabin necklaces) alike. ⊠ *Aventura Mall, 19575 Biscayne Blvd., North
Beach and Aventura* ☎ *305/931–2000.*

SPORTS AND THE OUTDOORS

Sun, sand, and crystal-clear water mixed with an almost nonexistent
winter and a cosmopolitan clientele make Miami and Miami Beach
ideal for year-round sunbathing and outdoor activities. Whether the
priority is showing off a toned body, jumping on a Jet Ski, or relaxing
in a tranquil natural environment, there's a beach tailor-made to please.
But tanning and water sports are only part of this sun-drenched picture.
Greater Miami has championship golf courses and tennis courts, miles
of bike trails along placid canals and through subtropical forests, and
skater-friendly concrete paths amidst the urban jungle. For those who
like their sports of the spectator variety, the city offers up a bonanza
of pro teams for every season. There's even a crazy ball-flinging game
called jai alai that's billed as the fastest sport on earth.

In addition to contacting venues directly, get tickets to major events
from **Ticketmaster** (☎ *800/745–3000* ⊕ *www.ticketmaster.com*).

BASEBALL

FAMILY **Miami Marlins.** Miami's baseball team, formerly known as the Florida
Marlins, moved into a new home in 2012: Marlins Park—a 37,442-
seat retractable-roof, air-conditioned baseball stadium on the grounds
of Miami's famous Orange Bowl. Go see the team that came out of
nowhere to beat the New York Yankees and win the 2003 World Series.
Home games are April through early October. ⊠ *Marlins Park, 501
N.W. 16 Ave., Little Havana* ☎ *305/480–1300, 877/627–5467 for tickets* ⊕ *www.miami.marlins.mlb.com* ⌦ *$10–$395; parking from $20
and should be pre-purchased online.*

Continued on page 104

A STROLL DOWN

DECO LANE

by Susan MacCallum Whitcomb

"It was an age of miracles, it was an age of art,
it was an age of excess, and it was an age of satire."

—F. Scott Fitzgerald, *Echoes of the Jazz Age*

The 1920s and '30s brought us flappers and gangsters, plunging stock prices and soaring skyscrapers, and plenty of headline-worthy news from the arts scene, from talking pictures and the jazz craze to fashions where pearls piled on and sequins dazzled. These decades between the two world wars also gave us an art style reflective of the changing times: art deco.

Distinguished by geometrical shapes and the use of industrial motifs that fused the decorative arts with modern technology, art deco became the architectural style of choice for train stations and big buildings across the country (think New york's Radio City Music Hall and Empire State Building).

Using a steel-and-concrete box as the foundation, architects dipped into art deco's grab bag of accessories, initially decorating facades with spheres, cylinders, and cubes. They later borrowed increasingly from industrial design, stripping elements used in ocean liners and automobiles to their streamlined essentials.

The style was also used in jewelry, furniture, textiles, and advertising. The fact that it employed inexpensive materials, such as stucco or terrazzo, helped art deco thrive during the Great Depression.

MIAMI BEACH'S ART DECO DISTRICT

With its warm beaches and tropical surroundings, Miami Beach in the early 20th century was establishing itself as America's winter playground. During the roaring '20s luxurious hostelries resembling Venetian palaces, Spanish villages, and French châteaux sprouted up. In the 1930s, middle-class tourists started coming, and more hotels had to be built. Designers like Henry Hohauser chose art deco for its affordable yet distinctive design.

An antidote to the gloom of the Great Depression, the look was cheerful and tidy. And with the whimsical additions of portholes, colorful racing bands, and images of rolling ocean waves painted or etched on the walls, these South Beach properties created an oceanfront fantasy world for travelers.

Many of the candy-colored hotels have survived and been meticulously restored. They are among the more than 800 buildings of historical significance in South Beach's art deco district. Composing much of South Beach, the 1-square-mi district is bounded by Dade Boulevard on the north, the Atlantic Ocean on the east, 6th Street on the south, and Alton Road on the west.

Because the district as a whole was developed so rapidly and designed by like-minded architects—**Henry Hohauser, L. Murray Dixon, Albert Anis,** and their colleagues—it has amazing stylistic

unity. Nevertheless, on this single street you can trace the evolution of period form from angular, vertically emphatic early deco to aerodynamically rounded Streamline Moderne. The relatively severe Cavalier and more curvaceous Cardozo are fine examples of the former and latter, respectively.

To explore the district, begin by loading up on literature in the **Art Deco Welcome Center** (✉ *1001 Ocean Dr.* ☎ *305/763–8026* ⊕ *www.mdpl.org*). If you want to view these historic properties on your own, just start walking. A four-block stroll north on Ocean Drive gets you up close to camera-ready classics: the **Clevelander** (1020), the **Tides** (1220), the **Leslie** (1244), the **Carlyle** (1250), the **Cardozo** (1300), the **Cavalier** (1320), and the **Winterhaven** (1400).

ART DECO TOURS

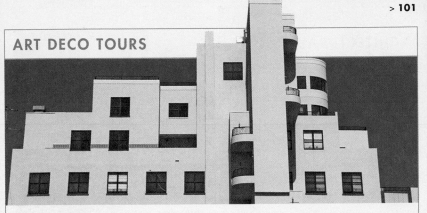

See the bold looks of classic Art Deco architecture along Ocean Drive.

SELF-GUIDED AUDIO TOURS

Expert insight on the architecture and the area's history is yours on the Miami Design Preservation League's (MDPL) 90-minute self-guided walks that use an iPod or iphone and include a companion map. You can pick up the iPod version and companion map at the Art Deco Welcome Center from 9:30 AM to 5 PM daily; the cost is $15.

WALKING TOURS

The tour offers a primer in the three predominate styles found in the Art Deco District: Art Deco, Meditteranean Revival, and Miami Modern (MiMo).

The MDPL's 90-minute "Ocean Drive and Beyond" group walking tour gives you a guided look at area icons, inside and out. (A number of interiors are on the itinerary, so it's a good chance to peek inside spots that might otherwise seem off-limits.) Morning tours depart daily at 10:30 AM from the Art Deco Welcome Center Gift Shop. An additional evening tour departs at 6:30 PM on Thursdays. Buy tickets in advance at ⊕ *mdpl.org*, or arrive 15–20 minutes early to buy tickets ($20).

BIKE TOURS

Rather ride than walk? Half-day cycling tours of the city's art deco history are organized daily for groups (5 or more) by **South Beach Bike Tours** (☎ *305/673–2002* ⊕ *www.southbeachbiketours. com*). The $59 cost includes equipment, snacks, and water.

ART DECO WEEKEND

Tours, lectures, film screenings, and dozens of other '30s-themed events are on tap in mid-January, during the annual **Art Deco Weekend** (☎ *305/672-2014*, ⊕ *www. ArtDecoWeekend.com*). Festivities—many of them free—kick off with a Saturday morning parade and culminate in a street fair. More than a quarter of a million people join in the action, which centers on Ocean Drive between 5th and 15th streets.

Celebrate the 1930s during Art Deco Weekend.

ARCHITECTURAL HIGHLIGHTS

FRIEZE DETAIL, CAVALIER HOTEL

The decorative stucco friezes outside the Cavalier Hotel at 1320 Ocean Drive are significant for more than aesthetic reasons. Roy France used them to add symmetry (adhering to the "Rule of Three") and accentuate the hotel's verticality by drawing the eye upward. The pattern he chose also reflected a fascination with ancient civilizations engendered by the recent rediscovery of King Tut's tomb and the Chichén Itzá temples.

Cavalier Hotel

LOBBY FLOOR, PARK CENTRAL HOTEL

Terrazzo—a compound of cement and stone chips that could be poured, then polished—is a hallmark of deco design. Terrazzo floors typically had a geometric pattern, like this one in the Park Central Hotel, a 1937 building by Henry Hohauser at 640 Ocean Drive.

Park Central Hotel

CORNER FACADE, ESSEX HOUSE HOTEL

Essex House Hotel, a 1938 gem that appears permanently anchored at 1001 Collins Avenue, is a stunning example of Maritime deco (also known as Nautical Moderne). Designed by Henry Hohauser to evoke an ocean liner, the hotel is rife with marine elements, from the rows of porthole-style windows and natty racing stripes to the towering smokestack-like sign. With a prow angled proudly into the street corner, it seems ready to steam out to sea.

Essex House Hotel

NEON SPIRE, THE HOTEL

The name spelled vertically in eye-popping neon on the venue's iconic aluminum spire—Tiffany—bears evidence of the hotel's earlier incarnation. When the L. Murray Dixon–designed Tiffany Hotel was erected at 801 Collins Avenue in 1939, neon was still a novelty. Its use, coupled with the spire's rocket-like shape, combined to create a futuristic look influenced by the sci-fi themes then pervasive in popular culture.

The Hotel

ENTRANCE, JERRY'S FAMOUS DELI

Inspired by everything from car fenders to airplane noses, proponents of art deco's Streamline Moderne look began to soften buildings' hitherto boxy edges. But when Henry Hohauser designed Hoffman's Cafeteria in 1940 he took moderne to the max. The landmark at 1450 Collins Avenue (now Jerry's Famous Deli) has a sleek, splendidly curved facade. The restored interior echoes it through semicircular booths and rounded chair backs.

Jerry's Famous Deli

ARCHITECTURAL TERMS

The Rule of Three: Early deco designers often used architectural elements in multiples of three, creating tripartite facades with triple sets of windows, eyebrows, or banding.

Eyebrows: Small shelf-like ledges that protruded over exterior windows were used to simultaneously provide much-needed shade and serve as a counterpoint to a building's strong vertical lines.

Tropical Motifs: In keeping with the setting, premises were plastered, painted, or etched with seaside images. Palm trees, sunbursts, waves, flamingoes, and the like were particularly common.

Banding: Enhancing the illusion that these immobile structures were rapidly speeding objects, colorful horizontal bands (also called "racing stripes") were painted on exteriors or applied with tile.

Stripped Classic: The most austere version of art deco (sometimes dubbed Depression Moderne) was used for buildings commissioned by the Public Works Administration.

(top) Hotel Marlin; (left) Sherbrooke Hotel; (right) U.S. Post Office in Miami Beach.

Miami Beach residential buildings tower over the sand.

BICYCLING

Perfect weather and flat terrain make Miami–Dade County a popular place for cyclists; however, biking here can also be quite dangerous. Be very vigilant when biking on Miami Beach, or better yet, steer clear and bike the beautiful paths of Key Biscayne instead.

Key Cycling. On an island where biking is a way of life, this Key Biscayne bike shop carries a wide range of amazing bikes in its showroom, as well as any kind of bike accessory imaginable. Out-of-towners can rent mountain or hybrid bikes for $15 for two hours, $24 for the day, and $80 for the week. ⊠ *Galleria Shopping Center, 328 Crandon Blvd., Ste. 121, Key Biscayne* ☎ *305/361–0061* ⊕ *www.keycycling.com.*

Miami Beach Bicycle Center. The easiest and most economical place for a bike rental on Miami Beach is this shop near Ocean Drive. Rent a bike for $5 per hour, $18 per day, or $80 for the week. All bike rentals include locks, helmets, and baskets. ⊠ *601 5th St., South Beach* ☎ *305/674–0150* ⊕ *www.bikemiamibeach.com.*

BOATING AND SAILING

Boating, whether on sailboats, powerboats, luxury yachts, WaveRunners, or windsurfers, is a passion in Greater Miami. The Intracoastal Waterway, wide and sheltered Biscayne Bay, and the Atlantic Ocean provide ample opportunities for fun aboard all types of watercraft.

The best windsurfing spots are on the north side of the Rickenbacker Causeway at Virginia Key Beach or to the south at, go figure, Windsurfer Beach. Kite surfing adds another level to the water-sports craze.

OUTFITTERS AND EXPEDITIONS

Playtime Watersports. A regularly scheduled evening sunset cruise through Biscayne Bay on the 50-foot sailing "Great White Catamaran" departs nightly at 6:30 pm from Marbella Marina in downtown; however, Playtime also offers all-inclusive, fully crewed private charters on its catamaran. ⊠ *Marbella Marina, 801 Brickell Ave., Downtown* ☎ *305/216–6967* ⊕ *www.playtimewatersport.com.*

Fodor'sChoice
★ **Sailboards Miami.** Rent paddle boards and kayaks or learn how to windsurf from this permanent, roadside adventure outfitter, directly off Rickenbacker Causeway. These friendly folks say they teach more windsurfers each year than anyone in the United States and promise to teach you to windsurf within two hours—for $79. ⊠ *Mile 6.5 on Rickenbacker Causeway (go right before bridge), Key Biscayne* ☎ *305/892–8992* ⊕ *www.sailboardsmiami.com* ⊙ *Fri.–Tues. 10–6.*

GOLF

Greater Miami has more than 30 private and public courses. Costs at most courses are higher on weekends and in season, but you can save by playing on weekdays and after 1 or 3 pm, depending on the course. Call ahead to find out when afternoon-twilight rates go into effect. For information on most courses in Miami and throughout Florida, you can visit ⊕ *www.floridagolferguide.com.*

Biltmore Golf Course. On the grounds of the historic circa 1926 Biltmore hotel, the Biltmore Golf Course provides a golf experience primarily for in-house guests, local residents, and those visiting the Coral Gables area. The 6,800-yard, 18-hole, par-71, championship golf course was designed in 1925 by Scotsman Donald Ross, the "it" golf designer of the Roaring Twenties. Today, the lush, well-maintained course is easily accessible thanks to its advanced online booking system, where you can easily reserve your tee time and decide between pricing, depending on the time of day and year. There's a pro-shop on site, and golf instruction is available through the Biltmore Golf Academy or the more extensive, on-site Total Performance Golf programs. ⊠ *The Biltmore Hotel, 1210 Anastasia Ave., Coral Gables* ☎ *855/311–6903* ⊕ *www. biltmorehotel.com/golf* 🏌 *$113 for 9 holes, $195 for 18 holes* 🏌. *18 holes. 6800 yards. par 71.*

Fodor'sChoice
★ **Crandon Golf at Key Biscayne.** On the serene island of Key Biscayne, overlooking Biscayne Bay, this top-rated, championship municipal golf course is considered one of the state's most challenging par-72 courses. Enveloped by tropical foliage, mangroves, saltwater lakes, and bayside waters, the course also happens to be the only one in North America with a subtropical lagoon. The Devlin/Von Hagge–designed course has a USGA rating of 75.4 and a slope rating of 129 and has received national awards from both *Golfweek* and *Golf Digest*. The course is located on the south side of Crandon Park. Nonresidents should expect to pay $180 (Monday–Thursday) to $225 (Friday–Sunday) for a round during peak hours in peak season (December 15–April) and roughly half that off season. Deeply discounted twilight rates of $40 apply after 3:30 pm. Tee times can be booked online. ⊠ *Crandon Park, 6700*

Crandon Blvd., Key Biscayne ☎ *305/361–9129* ⊕ *www.golfcrandon. com* ⌨ *$180 for 18 holes* 🏌. *18 holes. 7400 yards. par 72.*

Fodor'sChoice **Trump National Doral Miami.** Just west of Miami proper, Trump National
★ Doral Miami is best known for the par-72 Blue Monster course (renovated in 2013) and the World Golf Championships–Cadillac Championship. The week of festivities planned around this March tournament, which offers $8.5 million in prize money, brings hordes of pro-golf aficionados to South Florida. But there's far more to the Trump golf grounds than the Dick Wilson–designed Blue Monster and the Cadillac Championship. There are four other renowned golf courses—the Greg Norman–designed Great White Course, the Raymon Floyd–redesigned Gold Course, the Jim McClean Signature Course, and the Red Course (under renovation at press time)—and numerous other tournaments throughout the year. Hence, golf enthusiasts flock here year-round. ✉ *4400 N.W. 87th Ave., 36th St. exit off Rte. 826, Doral* ☎ *800/713–6725* ⊕ *www.trumphotelcollection.com/miami* ⌨ *$450 for Blue Monster Course, $250 for Great White Course, $190 for Gold Course* 🏌. *Blue Monster Course: 18 holes. 7300 yards. par 72. Great White Course: 18 holes. 7200 yards. par 72. Gold Course: 18 holes. 6600 yards. par 70.*

The Senator Course at Shula's Golf Club. Deep in the suburbs of west Miami, the Senator Course at Shula's Golf Club boasts the longest championship course in the area (7,055 yards, par 72), a lighted par-3 course, and a golf school. The championship, classic-style Senator Course was originally designed in 1962 by Bill Watts, updated by Kipp Schulties in 1998, and completely refreshed in late 2013, with improvements that included sparkling new Champion Bermuda greens and new Celebration Bermuda tees. The club hosts dozens of tournaments yearly. Because of its remote location, greens fees tend to be on the lower side. They run from $40 to $130, depending on the season and time. You'll pay in the lower range on weekdays, more on weekends, and $40 after 2 pm. Golf carts are included. For true golf enthusiasts, there's the on-site Don Shula hotel—a comfortable base to eat, live, and breathe golf. ✉ *7601 Miami Lakes Dr., 154th St. Exit off Rte. 826, Miami Lakes* ☎ *305/820–8088* ⊕ *www.shulasgolfclub.com* ⌨ *$130 for 18 holes* 🏌. *18 holes. 7055 yards. par 70.*

GUIDED TOURS

BOAT TOURS

Duck Tours Miami. Like the campy duck tours that originated in Boston and are now commonplace in several cities across the U.S., ducked-themed amphibious WWII vehicles make daily 90-minute tours of Miami that combine land and sea views. Comedy, quacks, and cheese are part of the mix. ✉ *1661 James Ave., South Beach* ☎ *305/673–2217* ⊕ *www.ducktourssouthbeach.com* ⌨ *$32.*

Island Queen Cruises. Tours on Island Queen Cruises run the gamut—sunset cruises, dance cruises, fishing cruises, speedboat rides and their signature, tours of Millionaire's Row, Miami's waterfront homes of the rich and famous. *The Island Queen, Island Lady,* and *Miami Lady* are three double-decker, 140-passenger tour boats docked at Bayside Marketplace that set sail daily for 90-minute narrated tours of the Port of Miami and Millionaires' Row. For the same tour with a lot more speed, take the tour on the high-speed Bayside Blaster. ⊠ *401 Biscayne Blvd., Downtown* ☎ *305/379–5119* ⊕ *www.islandqueencruises.com* ⊠ *$28.*

WALKING TOURS

Art Deco District Tour. Operated by the Miami Design Preservation League, this is a 90-minute guided walking tour that departs from the league's welcome center at Ocean Drive and 10th Street. It starts at 10:30 am daily, with an extra tour at 6:30 pm Thursday. Alternatively, you can go at your own pace with the league's self-guided iPod audio tour, which also takes roughly an hour and a half. ⊠ *1001 Ocean Dr., South Beach* ☎ *305/763–8026* ⊕ *www.mdpl.org* ⊠ *$20 guided tour, $15 audio tour.*

Little Havana Cuban Cuisine and Culture Walk. HistoryMiami runs culinary and cultural tours of Little Havana. Enjoy the unique architecture of this ethnic enclave and community history by visiting botanicas, cigar factories, and sipping Cuban coffee. The two-hour tour is offered monthly and leaves from Los Pinareños Fruteria at 10 am. Tours aren't available every month, so check the website ahead of time to book. ⊠ *1334 S.W. 8th St., Little Havana* ☎ *305/375–1621* ⊕ *www.historymiami. org* ⊠ *$30.*

SCUBA DIVING AND SNORKELING

Diving and snorkeling on the offshore coral wrecks and reefs on a calm day can be very rewarding. Chances are excellent that you'll come face-to-face with a flood of tropical fish. One option is to find Fowey, Triumph, Long, and Emerald reefs in 10- to 15-foot dives that are perfect for snorkelers and beginning divers. On the edge of the continental shelf a little more than 3 miles out, these reefs are just a ¼ mile away from depths greater than 100 feet. Another option is to paddle around the tangled prop roots of the mangrove trees that line the coast, peering at the fish, crabs, and other creatures hiding there. ⇨ *For the best snorkeling in Miami–Dade, head to Biscayne National Park. See the Everglades chapter for more information.*

Artificial Reefs. Perhaps the area's most unusual diving options are its artificial reefs. Since 1981, Miami–Dade County's Department of Environmental Resources Management has sunk tons of limestone boulders and a water tower, army tanks, and almost 200 boats of all descriptions to create a "wreckreational" habitat where divers can swim with yellow tang, barracudas, nurse sharks, snapper, eels, and grouper. The website offers an interactive map of wreck locations. Dive outfitters are familiar with most of these artificial reefs and can take you to the best ones. ⊠ *Miami Beach* ⊕ *www.miamidade.gov/environment/reefs-artificial.asp.*

OUTFITTERS

Divers Paradise of Key Biscayne. This complete dive shop and diving-charter service next to the Crandon Park Marina, includes equipment rental and scuba instruction with PADI and NAUI affiliation. Four-hour dive trips are offered Tuesday through Friday at 10:30, weekends at 8:30 and 1:30. The trip is $60. Night dives are offered Saturdays at 5:30. ⊠ *Crandon Park Marina, 4000 Crandon Blvd., Key Biscayne* ☎ *305/361–3483* ⊕ *www.keydivers.com* ☾ *Closed Mon.*

Fodor'sChoice **South Beach Dive and Surf.** Dedicated to all things ocean, this PADI 5-Star
★ Dive Shop offers multiple diving and snorkeling trips weekly as well as surfboard, paddleboard, and skateboard sales, rentals and lessons. The Discover Scuba course (for noncertified divers) trains newcomers every Monday, Tuesday, Thursday, and Saturday at 8 am which includes two dives in Key Largo's John Pennekamp Marine Sanctuary that same day. Night dives take place each Wednesday at 5, and wreck and reef dives weekends at 7:30 am and noon. The center also runs dives in Key Largo's Spiegel Grove, the second-largest wreck ever to be sunk for the intention of recreational diving, and in the Neptune Memorial Reef, inspired by the city of Atlantis and created in part using the ashes of cremated bodies. The dive shop itself is located in the heart of South Beach, but boats depart from marinas in Miami Beach and Key Largo, in the Florida Keys. ⊠ *850 Washington Ave., South Beach* ☎ *305/531–6110* ⊕ *www.southbeachdivers.com.*

THE EVERGLADES

WELCOME TO THE EVERGLADES

TOP REASONS TO GO

★ **Fun fishing:** Cast for some of the world's fightingest game fish—600 species of fish in all—in the Everglades' backwaters.

★ **Abundant birdlife:** Check hundreds of birds off your life list, including—if you're lucky—the rare Everglades snail kite.

★ **Cool kayaking:** Do a half-day trip in Big Cypress National Preserve or reach for the ultimate—the 99-mile Wilderness Trail.

★ **Swamp cuisine:** Hankering for alligator tail and frogs' legs? Or how about swamp cabbage, made from hearts of palm? Better yet, try stone-crab claws fresh from the traps.

★ **Gator-spotting:** This is ground zero for alligator viewing in the United States, and there's a good bet you'll leave having spotted your quota.

1 Everglades National Park. Alligators, Florida panthers, black bears, manatees, dolphins, bald eagles, and roseate spoonbills call this vast habitat home.

2 Biscayne National Park. Mostly under water, this is where the string of coral reefs and islands that form the Florida Keys begins.

Hialeah

95

Miccosukee
Indian Village

Everglades
Gator Park

Tamiami Trail

41

Shark
Valley

Everglades
Safari Park

836

Miami

826

Coral
Gables

Kendall

Observation
Tower

1

997

1

2

Biscayne
National Park

Homestead

Florida City

9336

Convoy
Point

Biscayne
Bay

Boca Chita
Key

Elliott Key

Adams Key

Barnes
Sound

ATLANTIC
OCEAN

_nake
Bight_

Joe Kemp
Key

_Florida
Bay_

Florida
Keys

GETTING ORIENTED

3

The southern third of the Florida peninsula is largely taken up by protected government land that includes Everglades National Park, Big Cypress National Preserve, and Biscayne National Park. Miami lies to the northeast, and Naples and Marco Island are northwest. Land access to Everglades National Park is primarily by two roads. The park's main road traverses the southern Everglades from the gateway towns of Homestead and Florida City to the outpost of Flamingo, on Florida Bay. To the north, Tamiami Trail (U.S. 41) cuts through the Everglades from the Greater Miami area on the east coast or from Naples on the west coast to the western park entrance in Everglades City at Route 29.

3 Big Cypress National Preserve. Neighbor to Everglades National Park, it's an outdoor-lover's paradise.

THE FLORIDA
EVERGLADES

by Lynne Helm

Alternately described as elixir of life or swampland muck, the Florida Everglades is one of a kind—a 50-mi-wide "river of grass" that spreads across hundreds of thousands of acres. It moves at varying speeds depending on rainfall and other variables, sloping south from the Kissimmee River and Lake Okeechobee to estuaries of Biscayne Bay, Florida Bay, and the Ten Thousand Islands.

Today, apart from sheltering some 70 species on America's endangered list, the Everglades also embraces more than 7 million residents, 50 million annual tourists, 400,000 acres of sugarcane, and the world's largest concentration of golf courses.

Demands on the land threaten the Everglades' finely balanced ecosystem. Irrigation canals for agriculture and roadways disrupt natural water flow. Drainage for development leaves wildlife scurrying for new territory. Water runoff, laced with fertilizers, promotes unnatural growth of swamp vegetation. What remains is a miracle of sorts, given decades of these destructive forces.

Creation of the Everglades required unique conditions. South Florida's geology, linked with its warm, wet subtropical climate, is the perfect mix for a marshland ecosystem. Layers of porous, permeable limestone create water-bearing rock,

soil, and aquifers, which in turn affects climate, weather, and hydrology.

This rock beneath the Everglades reflects Florida's geologic history—its crust was once part of the African region. Some scientists theorize that continental shifting merged North America with Africa, and then continental rifting later pulled North America away from the African continent but took part of northwest Africa with it—the part that is today's Florida. The Earth's tectonic plates continued to migrate, eventually placing Florida at its current location as a land mass jutting out into the ocean, with the Everglades at its tip.

EXPERIENCING THE ECOSYSTEMS

Eight distinct habitats exist within Everglades National Park, Big Cypress National Preserve, and Biscayne National Park.

Carnestown ○ Ochopee
29 41
Gulf Coast Visitor Center ● Everglades City
Chokoloskee

TEN THOUSAND ISLANDS

ECOSYSTEMS	EASY WAY	MORE ACTIVE WAY
COASTAL PRAIRIE: An arid region of salt-tolerant vegetation lies between the tidal mud flats of Florida Bay and dry land. **Best place to see it: The Coastal Prairie Trail**	Take a guided boat tour of Florida Bay, leaving from Flamingo Marina.	Hike the Coastal Prairie Trail from Eco Pond to Clubhouse Beach.
CYPRESS: Capable of surviving in standing water, cypress trees often form dense clusters called "cypress domes" in natural water-filled depressions. **Best place to see it: Big Cypress National Preserve**	Drive U.S. 41 (also known as Tamiami Trail—pronounced Tammy-Amee), which cuts across Southern Florida, from Naples to Miami.	Hike (or drive) the scenic Loop Road, which begins off Tamiami Trail, running from the Loop Road Education Center to Monroe Station.
FRESH WATER MARL PRAIRIE: Bordering deeper sloughs are large prairies with marl (clay and calcium carbonate) sediments on limestone. Gators like to use their toothy snouts to dig holes in prairie mud. **Best place to see it: Pahayokee Overlook**	Drive there from the Ernest F. Coe Visitor Center.	Take a guided tour, either through the park service or from permitted, licensed guides. You also can set up camp at Long Pine Key.
FRESH WATER SLOUGH AND HARDWOOD HAMMOCK: Shark River Slough and Taylor Slough are the Everglades' two sloughs, or marshy rivers. Due to slight elevation amid sloughs, dense stands of hardwood trees appear as teardrop-shaped islands. **Best place to see it: The Observation Tower**	Take a two-hour guided tram tour from the Shark Valley Visitor Center to the tower and back.	Walk or bike (rentals available) the route to the tower via the tram road and (walkers only) Bobcat Boardwalk trail and Otter Cave Hammock Trail.
MANGROVE: Spread over South Florida's coastal channels and waterways, mangrove thrives where Everglades fresh water mixes with salt water. **Best place to see it: The Wilderness Waterway**	Picnic at the area near Long Pine Key, which is surrounded by mangrove, or take a water tour at Biscayne National Park.	Boat your way along the 99-mi Wilderness Waterway. It's six hours by motorized boat, seven days by canoe.
MARINE AND ESTUARINE: Corals, sponges, mollusks, seagrass, and algae thrive in the Florida Bay, where the fresh waters of the Everglades meet the salty seas. **Best place to see it: Florida Bay**	Take a boat tour from the Flamingo Visitor Center marina.	Canoe or kayak on White Water Bay along the Wilderness Waterway Canoe Trail.
PINELAND: A dominant plant in dry, rugged terrain, the Everglades' diverse pinelands consist of slash pine forest, saw palmettos, and more than 200 tropical plant varieties. **Best place to see it: Long Pine Key trails**	Drive to Long Pine Key, about 6 mi off the main road from Ernest F. Coe Visitor Center.	Hike or bike the 28 mi of Long Pine Key trails.

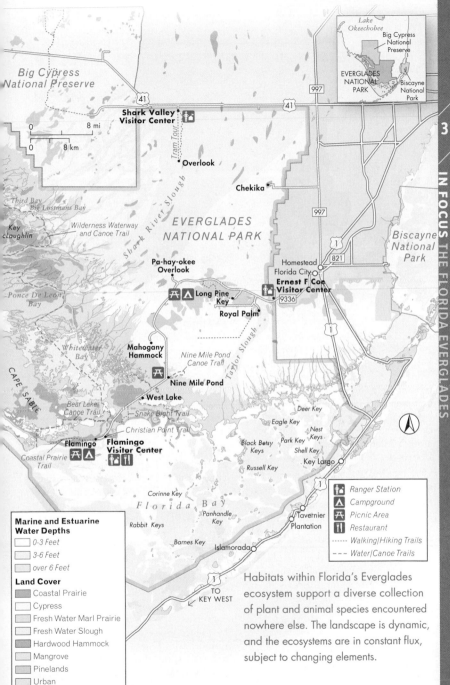

Big Cypress
National Preserve

Lake
Okeechobee

Big Cypress
National
Preserve

EVERGLADES
NATIONAL
PARK

Biscayne
National
Park

997

Shark Valley
Visitor Center

0   8 mi
0   8 km

Tram Tour

Overlook

Chekika

Third Bay
Big Lostmans Bay

Key
cLaughlin

Wilderness Waterway
and Canoe Trail

Shark River Slough

EVERGLADES
NATIONAL PARK

997

Biscayne
National
Park

Ponce De Leon
Bay

Pa-hay-okee
Overlook

Long Pine
Key

Homestead
Florida City
Ernest F Coe
Visitor Center
9336

821

Royal Palm

Whitewater
Bay

Mahogany
Hammock

Nine Mile Pond
Canoe Trail

Taylor Slough

CAPE SABLE

Nine Mile Pond

West Lake

Bear Lake
Canoe Trail

Snake Bight Trail

Christian Point Trail

Deer Key

Eagle Key

Nest
Keys

Flamingo

Flamingo
Visitor Center

Black Betsy
Keys

Park Key

Shell Key

Key Largo

Coastal Prairie
Trail

Russell Key

Corinne Key

Florida Bay

Panhandle
Key

Rabbit Keys

Tavernier

Plantation

Barnes Key

Islamorada

**Marine and Estuarine
Water Depths**
0-3 Feet
3-6 Feet
over 6 Feet

Land Cover
Coastal Prairie
Cypress
Fresh Water Marl Prairie
Fresh Water Slough
Hardwood Hammock
Mangrove
Pinelands
Urban

Ranger Station
Campground
Picnic Area
Restaurant
------ Walking/Hiking Trails
--- Water/Canoe Trails

TO
KEY WEST

Habitats within Florida's Everglades
ecosystem support a diverse collection
of plant and animal species encountered
nowhere else. The landscape is dynamic,
and the ecosystems are in constant flux,
subject to changing elements.

FLORA

❶ Cabbage Palm

It's virtually impossible to visit the Everglades and not see a cabbage palm, Florida's official state tree. The cabbage palm (or sabal palm), graces assorted ecosystems and grows well in swamps.
Best place to see them: At Loxahatchee National Wildlife Refuge (embracing the northern part of the Everglades, along Alligator Alley), throughout Everglades National Park, and at Big Cypress National Preserve.

❷ Sawgrass

With spiny, serrated leaf blades resembling saws, sawgrass inspired the term "river of grass" for the Everglades.
Best place to see them: Both Shark Valley and Pahayokee Overlook provide terrific vantage points for gazing over sawgrass prairie; you also can get an eyeful of sawgrass when crossing Alligator Alley, even when doing so at top speeds.

❸ Mahogany

Hardwood hammocks of the Everglades live in areas that rarely flood because of the slight elevation of the sloughs, where they're typically found.
Best place to see them: Everglades National Park's Mahogany Hammock Trail (which has a boardwalk leading to the nation's largest living mahogany tree).

❹ Mangrove

Mangrove forest ecosystems provide both food and protected nursery areas for fish, shellfish, and crustaceans.
Best place to see them: Along Biscayne National Park shoreline, at Big Cypress National Preserve, and within Everglades National Park, especially around the Caple Sable area.

❺ Gumbo Limbo

Sometimes called "tourist trees" because of peeling reddish bark (not unlike sunburns).
Best place to see them: Everglades National Park's Gumbo Limbo Trail and assorted spots throughout the expansive Everglades.

FAUNA

❶ American Alligator
In all likelihood, on your visit to the Everglades you'll see at least a gator or two. These carnivorous creatures can be found throughout the Everglades swampy wetlands.
Best place to see them: Loxahatchee National Wildlife Refuge (also sheltering the endangered Everglades snail kite) and within Everglades National Park at Shark Valley or Anhinga Trail. Sometimes (logically enough) gators hang out along Alligator Alley, basking in early morning or late-afternoon sun along four-lane I–75.

❷ American Crocodile
Crocs gravitate to fresh or brackish water, subsisting on birds, fish, snails, frogs, and small mammals.
Best place to see them: Within Everglades National Park, Big Cypress National Preserve, and protected grounds in or around Billie Swamp Safari.

❸ Eastern Coral Snake
This venomous snake burrows in underbrush, preying on lizards, frogs, and smaller snakes.
Best place to see them: Snakes typically shy away from people, but try Snake Bight or Eco Pond near Flamingo, where birds are also prevalent.

❹ Florida Panther
Struggling for survival amid loss of habitat, these shy, tan-colored cats now number around 100, up from lows of near 30.
Best place to see them: Protected grounds of Billie Swamp Safari sometimes provide sightings during tours. Signage on roadway linking Tamiami Trail and Alligator Alley warns of panther crossings, but sightings are rare.

❺ Green Tree Frog
Typically bright green with white or yellow stripes, these nocturnal creatures thrive in swamps and brackish water.
Best place to see them: Within Everglades National Park, especially in or near water.

● =Extremely Common ● =Very Common ● =Somewhat Common ● =Rare

BIRDS

❶ Anhinga

The lack of oil glands for waterproofing feathers helps this bird to dive as well as chase and spear fish with its pointed beak. The Anhinga is also often called a "water turkey" because of its long tail, or a "snake bird" because of its long neck.

Best place to see them: The Anhinga Trail, which also is known for attracting other wildlife to drink during especially dry winters.

❷ Blue-Winged Teal

Although it's predominantly brown and gray, this bird's powder-blue wing patch becomes visible in flight. Next to the mallard, the blue-winged teal is North America's second most abundant duck, and thrives particularly well in the Everglades.

Best place to see them: Near ponds and marshy areas of Everglades National Park or Big Cypress National Preserve.

❸ Great Blue Heron

This bird has a varied palate and enjoys feasting on everything from frogs, snakes, and mice to shrimp, aquatic insects, and sometimes even other birds! The all-white version, which at one time was considered a separate species, is quite common to the Everglades.

Best place to see them: Loxahatchee National Wildlife Refuge or Shark Valley in Everglades National Park.

❹ Great Egret

Once decimated by plume hunters, these monogamous, long-legged white birds with S-shaped necks feed in wetlands, nest in trees, and hang out in colonies that often include heron or other egret species.

Best place to see them: Throughout Everglades National Park, along Alligator Alley, and sometimes even on the fringes of Greater Fort Lauderdale.

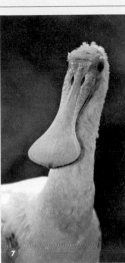

❺ Greater Flamingo

Flocking together and using long legs and webbed feet to stir shallow waters and mud flats, color comes a couple of years after hatching from ingesting shrimplike crustaceans along with fish, fly larvae, and plankton.

Best place to see them: Try Snake Bight or Eco Pond, near Flamingo Marina.

❻ Osprey

Making a big comeback from chemical pollutant endangerment, ospreys (sometimes confused with bald eagles) are distinguished by black eyestripes down their faces. Gripping pads on feet with curved claws help them pluck fish from water.

Best place to see them: Look near water, where they're fishing for lunch in the shallow areas. Try the coasts, bays, and ponds of Everglades National Park. They also gravitate to trees You can usually spot them from the Gulf Coast Visitor Center, or you can observe them via boating in the Ten Thousand Islands.

❼ Roseate Spoonbill

These gregarious pink-and-white birds gravitate toward mangroves, feeding on fish, insects, amphibians, and some plants. They have long, spoon-like bills, and their feathers can have a touch of red and yellow. These birds appear in the Everglades year-round.

Best place to see them: Sandy Key, southwest of Flamingo, is a spoonbill nocturnal roosting spot, but at sunrise these colorful birds head out over Eco Pond to favored day hangouts throughout Everglades National Park.

❽ Wood Stork

Recognizable by featherless heads and prominent bills, these birds submerge in water to scoop up hapless fish. They are most common in the early spring and often easiest to spot in the morning.

Best place to see them: Amid the Ten Thousand Island areas, Nine Mile Pond, Mrazek Pond, and in the mangroves at Paurotis Pond.

● =*Extremely Common* ● =*Very Common* ● =*Somewhat Common* ● =*Rare*

3

IN FOCUS THE FLORIDA EVERGLADES

THE BEST EVERGLADES ACTIVITIES

HIKING

Top experiences: At Big Cypress National Preserve, you can hike along designated trails or push through unmarked acreage. (Conditions vary seasonally, which means you could be tramping through waist-deep waters.) Trailheads for the Florida National Scenic Trail are at Loop Road off U.S. 41 and Alligator Alley at mile marker 63.

What will I see? Dwarf cypress, hardwood hammocks, prairies, birds, and other wildlife.

For a short visit: A 6.5-mi section from Loop Road to U.S. 41 crosses Robert's Lake Strand, providing a satisfying sense of being out in the middle nowhere.

With more time: A 28-mile stretch from U.S. 41 to I–75 (Alligator Alley) reveals assorted habitats, including hardwood hammocks, pinelands, prairie, and cypress.

Want a tour? Big Cypress ranger-led exploration starts from the Oasis Visitor Center, late November through mid-April.

WALKING

Top experiences: Everglades National Park magnets: wheelchair accessible walkways at Anhinga Trail, Gumbo Limbo Trail, Pahayokee Overlook, Mahogany Hammock, and West Lake Trail.

What will I see? Birds and alligators at Anhinga; tropical hardwood hammock at Gumbo Limbo; an overlook of the River of Grass from Pahayokee's tower; a subtropical tree island with massive mahogany growth along Mahogany Hammock; and a forest of mangrove trees on West Lake Trail.

For a short visit: Flamingo's Eco Pond provides for waterside wildlife viewing.

With more time: Shark Valley lets you combine the quarter-mile Bobcat Boardwalk (looping through sawgrass prairie and a bayhead) with the 1-mi-long round-trip Otter Cave, allowing you to steep in subtropical hardwood hammock.

Want a tour? Pahayokee and Flamingo feature informative ranger-led walks.

The Anhinga Trail near the Royal Palm Visitor Center at Everglades National Park

BOATING

Top experiences: Launch a boat from the Gulf Coast Visitors Center or Flamingo Marina. Bring your own watercraft or rent canoes or skiffs at either location.

What will I see? Birds from bald eagles to roseate spoonbills, plus plenty of mangrove and wildlife—and maybe even some baby alligators with yellow stripes.

For a short visit: Canoe adventurers often head for Hells Bay, a 3-mile stretch about 9 mi north of Flamingo. Or put in at the Turner River alongside the Tamiami Trail in the Big Cypress National Preserve and paddle all the way (about eight hours) to Chocoloskee Bay at Everglades City.

With more time: Head out amid the Ten Thousand Islands and lose yourself in territory once exclusively the domain of only the hardiest pioneers and American Indians. If you've got a week or more for paddling, the 99-mile Wilderness Waterway stretches from Flamingo to Everglades City.

Want a tour? Sign on for narrated boat tours at the Gulf Coast or Flamingo visitor center.

BIRD WATCHING

Top experiences: Anhinga Trail, passing over Taylor Slough.

What will I see? Anhinga and heron sightings are a nearly sure thing, especially in early morning or late afternoon. Also, alligators can be seen from the boardwalk.

For a short visit: Even if you're traveling coast to coast at higher speeds via Alligator Alley, chances are you'll spot winged wonders like egrets, osprey, and heron.

With more time: Since bird-watching at Flamingo can be a special treat early in the morning or late in the afternoon, try camping overnight even if you're not one for roughing it. Reservations are recommended. (Flamingo Lodge remains closed after 2005 hurricane damage.)

Want a tour? Ranger-led walks at Pahayokee and from Everglades National Park visitor centers provide solid birding background for novices.

(top left) Tourists cruise the Everglades by airboat; (bottom left) Green Heron; (right) Eastern Meadowlark

THE BEST EVERGLADES ACTIVITIES

BIKING

Top experiences: Shark Valley (where bicycling is allowed on the tram road) is great for taking in the quiet beauty of the Everglades. Near Ernest F. Coe Visitor Center, Long Pine Key's 14-mile nature trail also can be a way to bike happily away from folks on foot.

What will I see? At Shark Valley, wading birds, turtles, and, probably alligators. At Long Pine Key, shady pinewood with subtropical plants and exposed limestone bedrock.

For a short visit: Bike on Shark Valley tram road but turn around to fit time schedule.

With more time: Go the entire 15-mi tram road route, which has no shortcuts. Or try the 22-mile route of Old Ingraham Highway near the Royal Palm Visitor Center, featuring mangrove, sawgrass, and birds (including hawks).

Want a tour? In Big Cypress National Preserve, Bear Island Bike Rides (8 mile round-trip over four to five hours) happen on certain Saturdays.

SNORKELING

Top experiences: Biscayne National Park, where clear waters incorporate the northernmost islands of the Florida Keys.

What will I see? Dense mangrove swamp covering the park shoreline, and, in shallow waters, a living coral reef and tropical fish in assorted colors.

For a short visit: Pick a sunny day to optimize your snorkeling fun, and be sure to use sunscreen.

With more time: Advanced snorkel tours head out from the park on weekends to the bay, finger channels, and around shorelines of the barrier islands. Biscayne National Park also has canoe and kayak rentals, picnic facilities, walking trails, fishing, and camping.

Want a tour? You can swim and snorkel or stay dry and picnic aboard tour boats that depart from Biscayne National Park's visitor center.

(top left) Biking near the Shark Valley Visitor Area. (top right) Snorkeling on the surface in the Atlantic Ocean.

DID YOU KNOW?

You can tell you're looking at a crocodile if you can see its lower teeth protruding when its jaws are shut, whereas an alligator shows no teeth when his mouth is closed. Gators are much darker in color—a grayish black—compared with the lighter tan color of crocodiles. Alligators' snouts are also much broader than their long, thin crocodilian counterparts.

THE STORY OF THE EVERGLADES

Dreams of draining southern Florida took hold in the early 1800s, expanding in the early 1900s to convert large tracts from wetlands to agricultural acreage. By the 1920s, towns like Fort Lauderdale and Miami boomed, and the sugar industry—which came to be known as "Big Sugar"—established its first sugar mills. In 1947 Everglades National Park opened as a refuge for wildlife.

KEY

Extent of the Everglades

1900
1999

Meanwhile, the sugar industry grew. In its infancy, about 175,000 tons of raw sugar per year was produced from fields totaling about 50,000 acres. But once the U.S. embargo stopped sugar imports from Cuba in 1960 and laws restricting acreage were lifted, Big Sugar took off. Less than five years later, the industry produced 572,000 tons of sugar and occupied nearly a quarter of a million acres.

Fast-forward to 2008, to what was hailed as the biggest conservation deal in U.S. history since the creation of the national parks. A trailblazing restoration strategy hinged on creating a water flow-way between Lake Okeechobee and the Everglades by buying up and flooding 187,000 acres of land. The country's largest producers of cane sugar agreed to sell the necessary 187,000 acres to the state of Florida for $1.75 billion. Environmentalists cheered.

But within months, news broke of a scaled-back land acquisition plan: $1.34 billion to buy 180,000 acres. By spring 2009, the restoration plan had shrunk to $536,000 to buy 73,000 acres. With the purchase still in limbo, critics claim the state might overpay for acreage appraised at pre-recession values and proponents fear dwindling revenues may derail the plan altogether.

The Big Sugar land deal is part of a larger effort to preserve the Everglades. In 2010, two separate lawsuits charged the state, along with the United States Environmental Protection Agency, with stalling Everglades cleanup that was supposed to begin in 2006. "Glacial delay" is how one judge put it. The state must reduce phosphorus levels in water that flows to the Everglades or face fines and sanctions for violating the federal Clean Water Act. The fate of the Everglades remains in the balance.

3

Updated by
Lynne Helm

More than 1.5 million acres of South Florida's 4.3 million acres of subtropical, watery wilderness were given national-park status and protection in 1947 with the creation of Everglades National Park. It's one of the country's largest national parks and is recognized by the world community as a Wetland of International Importance, an International Biosphere Reserve, and a World Heritage Site. Come here if you want to spend the day biking, hiking, or boating in deep, raw wilderness with lots of wildlife.

To the east of Everglades National Park, Biscayne National Park brings forth a pristine, magical, subtropical Florida. It's the nation's largest marine park and the largest national park within the continental United States boasting living coral reefs. A small portion of the park's 172,000 acres consists of mainland coast and outlying islands, but 95% remains under water. Of particular interest are the mangroves and their tangled masses of stiltlike roots that thicken the shorelines. These "walking trees," as some locals call them, have curved prop roots, which arch down from the trunk, and aerial roots that drop from branches. The trees draw fresh water from salt water and create a coastal nursery that sustains myriad types of marine life. You can see Miami's high-rise buildings from many of Biscayne's 44 islands, but the park is virtually undeveloped and large enough for escaping everything that Miami and the Upper Keys have become. To truly escape, don scuba-diving or snorkeling gear and lose yourself in the wonders of the coral reefs.

On the northern edge of Everglades National Park is Big Cypress National Preserve, one of South Florida's least developed watersheds. Established by Congress in 1974 to protect the Everglades, it comprises extensive tracts of prairie, marsh, pinelands, forested swamps, and sloughs. Hunting is allowed, as is off-road-vehicle use. Come here if you like alligators. Stop at the Oasis Visitor Center's boardwalk with alligators lounging underneath, and then drive Loop Road for a backwoods experience. If time permits, kayak the Turner River.

Surrounding the parks and preserve are several communities where you'll find useful outfitters: Everglades City, Florida City, and Homestead.

PLANNING

WHEN TO GO

Winter is the best, and busiest, time to visit the Everglades. Temperatures and mosquito activity are more tolerable, low water levels concentrate the resident wildlife, and migratory birds swell the avian population. In late spring the weather turns hot and rainy, and tours and facilities are less crowded. Migratory birds depart, and you must look harder to see wildlife. Summer brings intense sun and afternoon rainstorms. Water levels rise and mosquitoes descend, making outdoor activity virtually unbearable, unless you swath yourself in netting. Mosquito repellent is a necessity any time of year.

GETTING HERE AND AROUND

Miami International Airport (MIA) is 34 miles from Homestead and 47 miles from the eastern access to Everglades National Park. ⇨ *For MIA airline carrier information, refer to the Miami chapter.* Shuttles run between MIA and Homestead. Southwest Florida International Airport (RSW), in Fort Myers, a little over an hour's drive from Everglades City, is the closest major airport to the Everglades' western entrance. On-demand taxi transportation from the airport to Everglades City is available from MBA Airport Transportation and costs $150 for up to three passengers ($10 each for additional passengers).

Contacts MBA Airport Transportation. MBA is the taxi concessionaire for Southwest Florida International Airport, providing transportation to Everglades City. Call for rates. ☎ *239/225–0428* ⊕ *www.mbaairport.com.*

HOTELS

Accommodations near the parks range from inexpensive to moderate and offer off-season rates in summer, when rampant mosquito populations discourage spending time outdoors, especially at dusk. If you're devoting several days to exploring the east coast Everglades, stay in park campgrounds; 11 miles away in Homestead–Florida City, where there are reasonably priced chain motels and RV parks; in the Florida Keys; or in the Greater Miami–Fort Lauderdale area. Lodgings and campgrounds are also plentiful on the Gulf Coast (in Everglades City, Marco Island, and Naples, the latter of which has the most upscale area accommodations).

Hotel reviews have been shortened. For full information, visit Fodors. com.

RESTAURANTS

Dining in the Everglades area centers on mom-and-pop places serving hearty homestyle food, and small eateries specializing in fresh local fare: alligator, fish, stone crab, frogs' legs, and Florida lobster from the Keys. American Indian restaurants serve local favorites as well as catfish,

Indian fry bread (a flour-and-water flatbread), and pumpkin bread. A growing Hispanic population around Homestead means plenty of authentic, inexpensive Latin cuisine, with an emphasis on Cuban and Mexican dishes. Restaurants in Everglades City, especially those along the river, have fresh seafood including particularly succulent, sustainable stone crab. These places are casual to the point of rustic, and are often closed in late summer or fall. For finer dining, go to Marco Island or Naples.

WHAT IT COSTS				
	$	$$	$$$	$$$$
RESTAURANTS	under $16	$16–$20	$21–$30	over $30
HOTELS	under $201	$201–$300	$301–$400	over $400

Restaurant prices are the average cost of a main course at dinner or, if dinner is not served, at lunch. Hotel prices are the lowest cost of a standard double room in high season.

ABOUT ACTIVITIES
⇨ *While outfitters are listed with the parks and preserve, see our What's Nearby section later in this chapter for information about each town.*

EVERGLADES NATIONAL PARK

45 miles southwest of Miami International Airport.

If you're heading across South Florida on U.S. 41 from Miami to Naples, you'll breeze right through the Everglades. Also known as Tamiami Trail, this mostly two-lane road skirts the edge of Everglades National Park and cuts across the Big Cypress National Preserve. You'll also be near the park if you're en route from Miami to the Florida Keys on U.S. 1, which cuts through Homestead and Florida City—communities east of the main park entrance. Basically, if you're in South Florida, you can't escape at least fringes of the Everglades. With tourist strongholds like Miami, Naples, and the Florida Keys so close, travelers from all over the world typically make day trips to the park.

Everglades National Park has three main entry points: the park headquarters at Ernest F. Coe Visitor Center, southwest of Homestead and Florida City; the Shark Valley area, accessed by Tamiami Trail (U.S. 41); and the Gulf Coast Visitor Center, south of Everglades City to the west and closest to Naples.

Explore on your own or participate in free ranger-led hikes, bicycle or bird-watching tours, and canoe trips. The variety of these excursions is greatest from mid-December through Easter, and some adventures (canoe trips, for instance) typically aren't offered in sweltering summer. Among the more popular are the Anhinga Amble, a 50-minute walk around the Taylor Slough (departs from the Royal Palm Visitor Center), and the Early Bird Special, a 90-minute walk centered on birdlife (departs from Flamingo Visitor Center). Check with the visitor centers for details.

War on Pythons

CLOSE UP

In 2013, Florida launched its first Python Challenge™ to put the kibosh on Burmese pythons, those deadly snakes literally squeezing the life out of Everglades wonders, from colorful birds to full-grown deer to gators.

The state-sponsored winter competition was a trailblazer, attracting amateurs and professionals alike from 38 states and Canada to help decimate this growing environmental threat. Sadly, only 68 pythons were captured out of the thousands estimated to live in the Everglades.

Even experienced 'Gladesmen with special permits to regularly stalk these predators had trouble finding them—partly because tan, splotchy skin provides natural camouflage for slithering about and causing mayhem within the ecosystem. Unseasonably warm winter weather also left the pythons, which grow up to 26 feet long, without incentive to boldly sun themselves.

In 2012, the U.S. Department of the Interior—hailing a milestone in Everglades protection—announced a nationwide ban on the import of Burmese pythons and other nonnative, large constrictor snakes, including both northern and southern African pythons and the yellow anaconda.

No matter what the future of the state's Python Challenge™, its war against invasive species and the efforts to protect Everglades wildlife continue unabated.

—By Lynne Helm

PARK ESSENTIALS

Admission Fees The fee is $10 per vehicle; and $5 per pedestrian, bicycle, or motorcycle. Payable at gates, the admission is good for seven consecutive days at all park entrances. Annual passes are $25.

Admission Hours The park is open daily, year-round. Both the main entrance near Florida City and Homestead, and the Gulf Coast entrance are open 24 hours. The Shark Valley entrance is open 8:30 am to 6 pm.

COE VISITOR CENTER TO FLAMINGO

About 30 miles from Miami.

The most popular access to Everglades National Park is via the park headquarters entrance southwest of Homestead and Florida City. If you're coming to the Everglades from Miami, take Route 836 West to Route 826/874 South to the Homestead Extension of Florida's Turnpike, U.S. 1, and Krome Avenue (Route 997/old U.S. 27). To reach the Ernest F. Coe Visitor Center from Homestead, go right (west) from U.S. 1 or Krome Avenue onto Route 9336 (Florida's only four-digit route) in Florida City and follow signage to the park entrance.

EXPLORING

To explore this section of the park, follow Route 9336 from the park entrance to Flamingo; you'll find many opportunities to stop along the way, and an assortment of activities to pursue in the Flamingo area.

Ernest F. Coe Visitor Center. Get your park map here, but don't just grab and go; this visitor center's numerous interactive exhibits and films are well worth your time. The 15-minute film *River of Life*, updated frequently, provides a succinct park overview. A movie on hurricanes and a 35-minute wildlife film for children are available upon request. A bank of telephones offers differing viewpoints on the Great Water Debate, detailing how last century's gung ho draining of swampland for residential and agricultural development also cut off water-supply routes for precious wetlands in the Everglades ecosystem. You'll also find a schedule of daily ranger-led activities, mainly walks and talks; information on the popular Nike missile site tour (harking back to the Cuban missile crisis era); and details about canoe rentals and boat tours at Flamingo. The Everglades Discovery Shop stocks books, kids' stuff, and jewelry including bird-oriented earrings, plus insect repellent, sunscreen, and water. Coe Visitor Center, which has restrooms, is outside park gates, so you can stop in without paying park admission. ✉ *40001 Rte. 9336, 11 miles southwest of Homestead* ☎ *305/242–7700* ◷ *Daily 9–5, subject to change.*

> **WORD OF MOUTH**
>
> "Sign up at the Ernest Coe Visitor Center or call the Flamingo Visitor Center for the free ranger-led canoe tour.... No experience necessary—maneuvering the long canoe through the twists and turns of the mangroves was a challenge, but very fun."   —JC98

Main road to Flamingo. Route 9336 travels 38 miles from the Ernest F. Coe Visitor Center southwest to the Florida Bay at Flamingo. It crosses a section of the park's eight distinct ecosystems: hardwood hammock, freshwater prairie, pinelands, freshwater slough, cypress, coastal prairie, mangrove, and marine-estuarine. Route highlights include a dwarf cypress forest, the transition zone between sawgrass and mangrove forest, and a wealth of wading birds at Mrazek and Coot Bay ponds—where in early morning or late afternoon you can observe them feeding. Be forewarned, however, that flamingo sightings are extremely rare. Boardwalks, looped trails, several short spurs, and observation platforms help you stay dry. You may want to stop along the way to walk several short trails (each takes about 30 minutes): the wheelchair-accessible **Anhinga Trail,** which cuts through sawgrass marsh and allows you to see lots of wildlife (be on the lookout for alligators and the trail's namesake water birds: anhingas); the junglelike—yet, also wheelchair-accessible—**Gumbo-Limbo Trail;** the **Pinelands Trail,** where you can see the park's limestone bedrock; the **Pahayokee Overlook Trail,** ending at an observation tower; and the **Mahogany Hammock Trail** with its dense growth. ■**TIP**→ Before heading out on the trails, inquire about insect and weather conditions to plan accordingly, stocking up on bug repellent, sunscreen, and water as necessary. Even on seemingly sunny days, it's smart to bring rain gear.

Royal Palm Visitor Center. Ideal for when there's limited time to experience the Everglades, this small center with a bookstore and vending machines permits access to the **Anhinga Trail boardwalk,** where in winter spotting alligators congregating in watering holes is almost guaranteed.

The neighboring **Gumbo-Limbo Trail** takes you through a hardwood hammock. Combining these short strolls (½ mile or so) allows you to experience two Everglades ecosystems. Rangers conduct daily Anhinga Ambles in season (call ahead for times). A Glades Glimpse program takes place afternoons daily in season, as do starlight walks and bike tours. If you have a mind for history, ask about narrated Nike missile site tours, stemming from the '60s-era Cuban missile crisis. ⊠ *Rte. 9336, 4 miles west of Ernest F. Coe Visitor Center* ☎ *305/242–7700* ⊙ *Daily 8–4:15.*

┌ **NEED A**
│ **BREAK?**

Good spots to pull over for a picnic lunch are **Paurotis Pond**, about 10 miles north of Florida Bay, or **Nine Mile Pond**, less than 30 miles from the main visitor center. Another option is along **Bear Lake**, 2 miles north of the Flamingo Visitor Center.

Flamingo. At the far end of the main road to the Flamingo community along Florida Bay, you'll find a marina with a gift shop, visitor center, and campground, with nearby hiking and nature trails. Despite the name, what you are unlikely to find here are flamingos. To improve your luck for glimpsing these flamboyant pink birds with toothpick legs, check out Snake Bight Trail, starting about five miles from the Flamingo outpost. Before hurricanes Katrina and Wilma washed them away in 2005, a lodge, cabins, and restaurant facilities in Flamingo provided Everglades National Park's only accommodations. Rebuilding of Flamingo Lodge, long projected, has yet to materialize. For now, you can still pitch tents or bring RVs to the campground, where improvements include solar-heated showers and electricity for RV sites. A houseboat rental concession offers a pair of 35-footers each sleeping six and equipped with shower, toilet, bedding, kitchenware, stereo, and depth finder. The houseboats (thankfully air-conditioned) have 60-horsepower outboards and rent for $350 per night, plus a $200 fuel deposit.

Flamingo Marina Store—Everglades National Park Boat Tours 2. Next to the Flamingo Visitor Center, the only general store within Everglades National Park stocks limited groceries, snacks, souvenirs, bait, tackle, firewood, tents, and camping supplies, as well as fuel for boats and vehicles. It's a sister operation to Everglades National Park Boat Tours in Everglades City. ⊠ *Flamingo* ☎ *239/695–3101* ⊙ *Daily 7–7.*

Flamingo Visitor Center. Check the schedule here for ranger-led activities, such as naturalist discussions, trail hikes, and evening programs in the 100-seat campground amphitheater, replacing the old gathering spot destroyed by 2005 hurricanes. If you're starving, the center's Buttonwood Cafe serves sandwiches, salads, and pizza. You'll find natural history exhibits and pamphlets on canoe, hiking, and biking trails in the 2nd-floor Florida Bay Flamingo Museum, accessible only by stairway and a steep ramp. ⊠ *1 Flamingo Lodge Hwy., Flamingo* ☎ *239/695–2945, 239/695–3101 for marina* ⊙ *Exhibits always open, staffed mid-Nov.–mid-Apr., daily 8–4:30.*

SPORTS AND THE OUTDOORS
BIRD-WATCHING
Some of the park's best birding is in the Flamingo area.

BOATING

The 99-mile inland **Wilderness Trail** between Flamingo and Everglades City is open to motorboats as well as canoes, although, depending on the water level, powerboats may have trouble navigating above Whitewater Bay. Flat-water canoeing and kayaking are best in winter, when temperatures are moderate, rainfall diminishes, and mosquitoes back off—a little, anyway. You don't need a permit for day trips, although there's a seven-day, $5 launch fee for all motorized boats brought into the park. The Flamingo area has well-marked canoe trails, but be sure to tell someone where you're going and when you expect to return. Getting lost is easy, and spending the night without proper gear can be unpleasant, if not dangerous.

GOOD READS

■ *The Everglades: River of Grass.* This circa-1947 classic by pioneering conservationist Marjory Stoneman Douglas (1890–1998) is a must-read.

■ *Everglades Wildguide.* Jean Craighead George gives an informative account of the park's natural history in this official National Park Service handbook.

■ *Everglades: The Park Story.* Wildlife biologist William B. Robertson Jr. presents the park's flora, fauna, and history.

Flamingo Lodge, Marina, and Everglades National Park Tours. Everglades National Park's official concessionaire operates a marina, runs tours, and rents canoes, kayaks, and skiffs, secured by credit cards. A one-hour, 45-minute backcountry cruise aboard the 50-passenger *Pelican* ($32.50) winds under a heavy canopy of mangroves, revealing abundant wildlife—from alligators, crocodiles, and turtles to herons, hawks, and egrets. Renting a 17-foot, 40-hp skiff from 7 am runs $195 per day (eight hours, if returned by 4 pm), $150 per half day, or $80 for two hours; there is a $100 credit card deposit required. Canoes for up to three paddlers rent for $16 for two hours (minimum), $22 for four hours, $32 for eight hours, and $40 overnight. Family canoes for up to four go for $20 for two hours, $30 for four hours, $40 for eight hours, and $50 for 24 hours. The concessionaire also rents bikes, binoculars, rods, reels, and other equipment by the half or full day. Feeling sticky after a day in the 'Glades? Hot showers are $3. (Flamingo Lodge, a victim of massive hurricane damage in 2005, remains closed pending a fresh start.) ■TIP→ An experimental Eco Tent of canvas and wood, unveiled in winter 2012–13, was immediately booked solid for the season. Built by University of Miami architecture students, Eco Tent sleeps four, has a table and chairs, and wins rave reviews from designers, park officials, and campers. It's a prototype for up to 40 more units, once funding is secured. ⊠ *1 Flamingo Lodge Hwy., on Buttonwood Canal, Flamingo* ☎ *239/695–3101, 239/695–0124 for Eco Tent reservations* ⊕ *www.evergladesnationalparkboattoursflamingo.com.*

GULF COAST ENTRANCE

To reach the park's western gateway, take U.S. 41 west from Miami for 77 miles, turn left (south) onto Route 29, and travel another 3 miles through Everglades City to the Gulf Coast Ranger Station. From Naples

Much skill is required to navigate boats through the shallow, muddy waters of the Everglades.

on the Gulf Coast, take U.S. 41 east for 35 miles, and then turn right onto Route 29.

Gulf Coast Visitor Center. The best place to bone up on Everglades National Park's watery western side is at this center just south of Everglades City (5 miles south of Tamiami Trail) where rangers can give you the park lowdown and address your questions. In winter, backcountry campers purchase permits here and canoeists check in for trips to the Ten Thousand Islands and 99-mile Wilderness Waterway Trail. Nature lovers view interpretive exhibits on local flora and fauna while waiting for naturalist-led boat trips. In season (Christmas through Easter), rangers lead bike tours and canoe trips. A selection of about 30 nature presentations and orientation films are available by request for view on a big screen. Admission is free only to this section, and no direct roads from here link to other parts of the park. ⊠ *815 Oyster Bar La., off Rte. 29, Everglades City* ☎ *239/695–3311* ☉ *Mid-Nov.–mid-Apr., daily 8–4:30; mid-Apr.–mid-Nov., daily 9–4:30.*

SPORTS AND THE OUTDOORS
BOATING AND KAYAKING
Everglades National Park Boat Tours. In conjunction with boat tours at Flamingo, this operation runs 1½-hour trips ($32) through the Ten Thousand Islands National Wildlife Refuge. Adventure-seekers often see dolphins, manatees, bald eagles, and roseate spoonbills. In peak season (November–April), 49-passenger boats run on the hour and half-hour daily. Mangrove wilderness tours ($40) on smaller boats are for up to six passengers. These one-hour, 45-minute trips are the best option to see alligators. The outfitter also rents canoes ($24 per day) and kayaks

(from $45 per day). Taxes are additional. ✉ *Gulf Coast Visitor Center, 815 Oyster Bar La.*, *Everglades City* ☎ *239/695–2591, 866/628–7275* ⊕ *www.evergladesnationalparkboattoursgulfcoast.com/index.php.*

Fodor'sChoice **Everglades Rentals & Eco Adventures.** Ivey House Inn houses this estab-
★ lished, year-round source for guided Everglades paddling tours and
rentals. Canoes cost $35 the first day, $27 daily thereafter. Day-long
kayak rentals are from $45. Shuttles deliver you to major launching
areas such as Turner River ($25.60 to $32, one-way for up to two
people). Highlights include bird and gator sightings, mangrove forests, no-man's-land beaches, and spectacular sunsets. Longer adventures include equipment rental, guide, and meals. ✉ *Ivey House, 107
Camellia St., Everglades City* ☎ *877/567–0679, 239/695–3299* ⊕ *www.
evergladesadventures.com.*

SHARK VALLEY

*23½ miles west of Florida's Turnpike, off Tamiami Trail. Approxi-
mately 45 mins west of Miami.*

You won't see sharks at Shark Valley. The name comes from the Shark
River, also called the River of Grass, flowing through the area. Several
species of shark swim up this river from the coast (about 45 miles
south of Shark Valley) to give birth, though not at this particular spot.
Young sharks (called pups), vulnerable to being eaten by adult sharks
and other predators, gain strength in waters of the slough before heading out to sea.

EXPLORING

Although Shark Valley is the national park's north entrance, no roads
here lead directly to other parts of the park. However, it's still worth
stopping to take the two-hour narrated tram tour (reservations recommended; ⇨ *see listing below*). Stop at the halfway point and ascend to
the top of the observation tower via a ramp.

Prefer to do the trail on foot? It takes nerve to walk the paved 15-mile
loop in Shark Valley, because in the winter months alligators lie alongside the road, basking in the sun—most, however, do move quickly
out of the way.

You also can ride a bicycle (the outfitter here rents one-speed, well-used
bikes daily 8:30–4 for $8.50 per hour). Behind the bike-rental area a
short boardwalk trail meanders through sawgrass, and another passes
through a tropical hardwood hammock. An underwater live camera
in the canal behind the center (viewed from the gift shop) lets visitors
sporadically see the alligators and otters.

Observation Tower. At the Shark Valley trail's end (really, the halfway
point of the 15-mile loop), you can pause to navigate this tower, first
built in 1984, spiraling 50 feet upward. Once on top, you'll find the
River of Grass gloriously spreads out as far as you can see. Observe
water birds as well as alligators, and maybe even river otters crossing the road. The tower has a wheelchair-accessible ramp to the top.
✉ *Shark Valley Loop Rd.*

Shark Valley Visitor Center. This small center has rotating exhibits, an underwater camera, a bookstore (run by the Everglades Association) with hats, postcards, and other souvenirs, plus park rangers ready for your questions. ✉ *36000 S. W. 8th St., Miami* ✛ *23½ miles west of Florida's Turnpike, off Tamiami Trail* ☎ *305/221–8776* ☉ *Daily 9:15–5:15.*

SPORTS AND THE OUTDOORS

BOATING

Many Everglades-area tours operate only in season, roughly November through April.

Buffalo Tiger's Airboat Tours. A former chief of Florida's Miccosukee tribe founded this Shark Valley area tour operation, although at 94 years and counting, the chief no longer skippers the boat. Savvy guides narrate the trip to an old Indian camp on the north side of Tamiami Trail from the American Indian perspective. Don't worry about airboat noise, since engines are shut down during informative talks. The 45-minute tours run 10–5 Saturday through Thursday at $27.50 per person. Look online for discount coupons. Reservations are not required, and credit cards are now accepted at this once cash-only outpost. ✉ *29708 S. W. 8th St., 5 miles east of Shark Valley, 25 miles west of Florida's Turnpike* ☎ *305/559–5250* ⊕ *www.buffalotigersairboattours.com.*

GUIDED TOURS

Shark Valley Tram Tours. Starting at the Shark Valley visitor center, these popular two-hour, narrated tours ($22) on bio-diesel trams follow a 15-mile loop road—great for viewing gators—into the interior, stopping at a 50-foot observation tower. Bring your own water. Reservations are strongly recommended December through April. ✉ *Shark Valley Visitor Center, Shark Valley Loop Rd.* ☎ *305/221–8455* ⊕ *www. sharkvalleytramtours.com* ☉ *Tours Dec.–Apr., hrly 9–4; May–Nov., hrly 9–3.*

BIG CYPRESS NATIONAL PRESERVE

Through the early 1960s the world's largest cypress-logging industry prospered in Big Cypress Swamp until nearly all the trees were cut down. With the death of the industry, government entities began buying parcels. Now more than 729,000 acres, or nearly half of the swamp, form this national preserve. "Big" refers not to the new-growth trees but to the swamp, jutting into the north edge of Everglades National Park like a jigsaw-puzzle piece. Size and strategic location make Big Cypress an important link in the region's hydrological system, where rainwater first flows through the preserve, then south into the park, and eventually into Florida Bay. Its variegated pattern of wet prairies, ponds, marshes,

---

THE EVERGLADES WITH KIDS

Although kids of all ages can enjoy the park, those six and older will get the most out of the experience. Consider how much you as a supervising adult will enjoy keeping tabs on tiny ones around so much water and so many teeth. Some children are frightened by sheer wilderness.

sloughs, and strands provides a wildlife sanctuary, and thanks to a policy of balanced land use— "use without abuse"—the watery wilderness is devoted to recreation as well as to research and preservation. Bald cypress trees that may look dead are actually dormant, with green needles springing to life in spring. The preserve allows— in limited areas—hiking, hunting, and off-road vehicle use (airboat, swamp buggy, four-wheel drive) by permit. Compared with Everglades National Park, the preserve is less

> **WORD OF MOUTH**
>
> "We drove from Ft. Lauderdale to the Everglades and rented bikes to do the loop at Shark Valley. Lots of wildlife to see! It took us the morning. I think you get better views of the wildlife on the bikes than the tram and of course since you can stop anytime you want, better pics. It's a very easy ride since it's flat and paved."
>
> —klam_chowder

developed and hosts fewer visitors. That makes it ideal for naturalists, birders, and hikers preferring to see more wildlife than people.

Several scenic drives link from Tamiami Trail, some requiring four-wheel-drive vehicles, especially in wet summer months. A few lead to camping areas and roadside picnic spots. Apart from the Oasis Visitor Center, popular as a springboard for viewing alligators, the newer Big Cypress Swamp Welcome Center features a platform for watching manatees. Both centers, along Tamiami Trail between Miami and Naples, feature a top-notch 25-minute film on Big Cypress.

PARK ESSENTIALS

Admission Fees There's no admission fee to visit the preserve.

Admission Hours The park is open 24 hours daily, year-round. Accessible only by boat, Adams Key is for day use only.

Contacts Big Cypress National Preserve ☎ 239/695–1201 ⊕ www.nps.gov/bicy.

EXPLORING

Big Cypress Swamp Welcome Center. As a sister to the Oasis Visitor Center, the newer Big Cypress Swamp Welcome Center on the preserve's western side has lots of information, as well as restrooms, picnic facilities, and a 70-seat auditorium. An outdoor breezeway showcases an interactive Big Cypress watershed exhibit, illustrating Florida water flow. ■TIP➔ **Love manatees? Here you'll find a platform for viewing these intriguing mammals that are attracted to warm water. (They were possibly once mistaken for mermaids by thirsty or love-starved ancient sailors.)** ⊠ *33000 Tamiami Trail E, 5 miles east of SR29, Ochopee* ☎ *239/695–4758* ⊕ *www.nps.gov/bicy/planyourvisit/visitorcenters.htm* 🎟 *Free* ☉ *Daily 9–4:30.*

Clyde Butcher's Big Cypress Gallery. For taking home swamp memories in stark black and white, you can't do better than picking up a postcard, calendar, or more serious piece of artwork by photographer Clyde Butcher at his namesake trailside gallery. Butcher, a big guy with an even bigger beard, is an affable personality renowned for his knowledge of the 'Glades and his ability to capture its magnetism through a large format lens. Even if you can't afford his big stuff, you're warmly invited to gaze. Out back, Butcher and his wife Niki also rent a bungalow ($225 per night, October–April) and a cottage ($275 per night, year-round). **■ TIP→ Ask about Clyde's muck-abouts or Saturday Swamp Walks ($50), September through March. You'll need a hat, long pants, old sneakers, and—because you*will*get wet—a spare set of dry clothing.** ✉ *52388 Tamiami Trail, at mile marker 54.5, Ochopee* ☎ *239/695–2428* 🌐 *www.clydebutchersbigcypressgallery.com* 🕒 *Daily 10–5.*

Oasis Visitor Center. The big attraction at Oasis Visitor Center, on the east side of Big Cypress Preserve, is the observation deck for viewing fish, birds, and other wildlife. A small butterfly garden's native plants seasonally attract winged wonders. Inside, you'll find an exhibit area, bookshop, and a theater showing an informative 25-minute film on Big Cypress Preserve swamplands. Leashed pets allowed, but not on boardwalk deck. **■ TIP→ Get your gator watch on at the center's observation deck where big alligators congregate.** ✉ *52105 Tamiami Trail, Ochopee* ✣ *24 miles east of Everglades City, 50 miles west of Miami, 20 miles west of Shark Valley* ☎ *239/695–1201* 🌐 *www.nps.gov/bicy/planyourvisit/visitorcenters* 🎟 *Free* 🕒 *Daily 9–4:30.*

FAMILY **Ochopee Post Office.** North America's smallest post office is a former irrigation pipe shed on the Tamiami Trail's south side. Blink and you'll risk missing it. To support this picturesque outpost during an era of postal service closures and layoffs, why not buy a postcard of this one-room shack for mailing to whoever would appreciate it? You can mail packages or buy money orders here, too. ✉ *38000 Tamiami Trail E, 4 miles east of Rte. 29, Ochopee* ☎ *239/695–2099* 🕒 *Weekdays 8–10 and noon–4, Sat. 10–11:30.*

WHERE TO EAT

$ SEAFOOD 🍴 **Joanie's Blue Crab Cafe.** West of the nation's tiniest post office by a quarter mile or so, you'll find this red barn of a place dishing out catfish, frogs' legs, gator, grouper, burgers, salads, and (no surprise here) an abundance of soft-shell crabs, crab cakes, and she-crab soup. Entrées run from $12.95 to market price. Grab an icy beer from the cooler and eat out front or on the back patio—keep an eye out for Gertrude, a neighborhood gator on the loose. Joanie's doors are open from 11 am to 5 pm, so don't be late for supper, and don't be surprised if there's some live entertainment. [$] *Average main: $13* ✉ *39395 Tamiami Trail, Ochopee* ✣ *About 3½ miles east of Rte. 29, less than a mile west of Ochopee post office* ☎ *239/695–2682* 🌐 *www.joaniesbluecrabcafe.com* 🕒 *Closed Mon. (varies seasonally; call to confirm).*

SPORTS AND THE OUTDOORS

There are three types of trails—walking (including part of the extensive Florida National Scenic Trail), canoeing, and bicycling. All three trail types are easily accessed from the Tamiami Trail near the preserve visitor center, and one boardwalk trail departs from the center. Canoe and bike equipment can be rented from outfitters in Everglades City, 24 miles west, and Naples, 40 miles west.

Hikers can tackle the Florida National Scenic Trail, which begins in the preserve and is divided into segments 6.5 to 28 miles each. Two 5-mile trails, Concho Billy and Fire Prairie, can be accessed off Turner River Road, a few miles east. Turner River Road and Birdon Road form a 17-mile gravel loop drive that's excellent for birding. Bear Island has about 32 miles of scenic, flat, looped trails that are ideal for bicycling. Most trails are hard-packed lime rock, but a few miles are gravel. Cyclists share the road with off-road vehicles, most plentiful from mid-November through December.

To see the best variety of wildlife from your car, follow 26-mile Loop Road, south of U.S. 41 and west of Shark Valley, where alligators, raccoons, and soft-shell turtles crawl around beside the gravel road, often swooped upon by swallowtail kites and brown-shouldered hawks. Stop at H. P. Williams Roadside Park, west of the Oasis, and walk along the boardwalk to spy gators, turtles, and garfish in the river waters.

RANGER PROGRAMS

From the Oasis Visitor Center you can get in on the seasonal ranger-led or self-guided activities, such as campfire and wildlife talks, hikes, slough slogs, and canoe excursions. The 8-mile Turner River Canoe Trail begins nearby and crosses through Everglades National Park before ending in Chokoloskee Bay, near Everglades City. Rangers lead four-hour canoe trips and two-hour swamp walks in season; call for days and times. Bring shoes and long pants for the swamp walks and be prepared to wade at least knee-deep in water. Ranger program reservations are accepted up to 14 days in advance.

BISCAYNE NATIONAL PARK

Occupying 172,000 acres along the southern portion of Biscayne Bay, south of Miami and north of the Florida Keys, Biscayne National Park is 95% submerged, its terrain ranging from 4 feet above sea level to 60 feet below. Contained within are four distinct zones: Biscayne Bay, undeveloped upper Florida Keys, coral reefs, and coastal mangrove forest. Mangroves line the mainland shore much as they do elsewhere along South Florida's protected waters. Biscayne Bay serves as a lobster sanctuary and a nursery for fish, sponges, crabs, and other sea life. Manatees and sea turtles frequent its warm, shallow waters. The park hosts legions of boaters and landlubbers gazing in awe over the bay.

GETTING HERE

To reach Biscayne National Park from Homestead, take Krome Avenue to Route 9336 (Palm Drive) and turn east. Follow Palm Drive about 8 miles until it becomes S.W. 344th Street, and follow signs to park headquarters in Convoy Point. The entry is 9 miles east of Homestead and 9 miles south and east of Exit 6 (Speedway Boulevard/S.W. 137th Avenue) off Florida's Turnpike.

PARK ESSENTIALS

Admission Fees There's no fee to enter Biscayne National Park, and you don't pay a fee to access the islands, but there's a $20 overnight camping fee that includes a $5 dock charge to berth vessels at some island docks. The park concession charges for trips to the coral reefs and islands.

Admission Hours The park is open daily, year-round.

Contacs Biscayne National Park ✉ *Dante Fascell Visitor Center, 9700 S.W. 328th St., Homestead* ☎ *305/230-7275* ⊕ *www.nps.gov/bisc.*

EXPLORING

Biscayne is a magnet for diving, snorkeling, canoeing, birding, and, to some extent (if you have a private boat), camping. Elliott Key is the best place to hike (⇨ *see The Islands*).

THE CORAL REEF

Biscayne's corals range from soft, flagellant fans, plumes, and whips found chiefly in shallow patch reefs to the hard brain corals, elkhorn, and staghorn forms that can withstand depths and heavier shoreline wave action.

THE ISLANDS

To the east, about 8 miles off the coast, 44 tiny keys stretch 18 nautical miles north to south, and are reached only by boat. No mainland commercial transportation operates to the islands, and only a handful are accessible: Elliott, Boca Chita, Adams, and Sands keys, lying between Elliott and Boca Chita. The rest are wildlife refuges or have rocky shores or waters too shallow for boats. December through April, when the mosquito population is less aggressive, is the best time to explore. Bring repellent, sunscreen, and water.

Adams Key. A stone's throw from the western tip of Elliott Key and 9 miles southeast of Convoy Point, the island is open for day use. It was the onetime site of the Cocolobo Club, a yachting retreat famous for hosting presidents Harding, Hoover, Johnson, and Nixon as well as other luminaries. Hurricane Andrew blew away what remained of club facilities in 1992. Adams Key has picnic areas with grills, restrooms, dockage, and a short trail running along the shore and through a hardwood hammock. Rangers live on-island. Access is by private boat, with no pets or overnight docking allowed. ⊕ *www.nps.gov/bisc/planyourvisit/adamskey.*

Boca Chita Key. Ten miles northeast of Convoy Point and about 12 miles south of the Cape Florida Lighthouse on Key Biscayne, this key once was owned by the late Mark C. Honeywell, former president of Honeywell Company, and is on the National Register of Historic Places for its 10 historic structures. A ½-mile hiking trail curves around the island's south side. Climb the 65-foot-high ornamental lighthouse (by ranger tour only) for a panoramic view of Miami or check out the cannon from the HMS *Fowey*. There's no fresh water, access is by private boat only, and no pets are allowed. Only portable toilets are on site, with no sinks or showers. A $20 fee for overnight docking (6 pm to 6 am) covers a campsite; pay at the harbor's automated kiosk.

BISCAYNE IN ONE DAY

Most visitors come to snorkel or dive. Divers should plan to spend the morning on the water and the afternoon exploring the visitor center. The opposite is true for snorkelers, as snorkel trips (and one-tank shallow-dive trips) depart in the afternoon. If you want to hike as well, turn to the trails at Elliott Key—just be sure to apply insect repellent (and sunscreen, too, no matter what time of year).

Elliott Key. The largest of the islands, 9 miles east of Convoy Point, Elliott Key has a mile-long loop trail on the bay side at the north end of the campground. Boaters may dock at any of 36 slips (call ahead; Hurricane Sandy forced closure of the boardwalk and harbor in 2012, and at press time docks remained closed). Head out on your own to hike the 6-mile trail along so-called Spite Highway, a 225-foot-wide swath of green that developers mowed down in hopes of linking this key to the mainland. Luckily the federal government stepped in, and now it's a hiking trail through tropical hardwood hammock. Facilities include restrooms, picnic tables, fresh drinking water, cold (occasionally lukewarm) showers, grills, and a campground. Leashed pets are allowed in developed areas only, not on trails. A 30-foot-wide sandy shoreline about a mile north of the harbor on the west (bay) side of the key is the only one in the national park, and boaters like to anchor off here to swim. The beach, fun for families, is for day use only; it has picnic areas and a short trail that cuts through the hammock.

VISITOR CENTER

FAMILY **Dante Fascell Visitor Center.** Go outside on the wide veranda to soak up views across mangroves and Biscayne Bay at this Convoy Point visitor center. Inside the museum, artistic vignettes and on-request videos including the 11-minute *Spectrum of Life* explore the park's four ecosystems, while the Touch Table gives both kids and adults a feel for bones, feathers, and coral. Facilities include the park's canoe and tour concession, restrooms with showers, a ranger information area, gift shop with books, and vending machines. Various ranger programs take place daily during busy fall and winter seasons. On the second Sunday monthly (December through April), the free Family Fun Fest offers hands-on activities. Rangers also give informal tours on Boca Chita key; arrange in advance. A short trail and boardwalk lead to a jetty, and there are picnic tables and grills. This is the only area of the park accessible without a boat. ⊠ *9700 S.W. 328th St., Homestead* ☎ *305/230–7275* ⊕ *www.nps.gov/bisc* ⊠ *Free* ☉ *Daily 9–5.*

SPORTS AND THE OUTDOORS

BIRD-WATCHING

More than 170 species of birds have been identified around the park. Expect to see flocks of brown pelicans patrolling the bay—suddenly rising, then plunging beak first to capture prey in their baggy pouches. White ibis probe exposed mudflats for small fish and crustaceans. Although all the keys are excellent for birding, Jones Lagoon (south of Adams Key, between Old Rhodes Key and Totten Key) is outstanding. It's approachable only by nonmotorized craft.

DIVING AND SNORKELING

Diving is great year-around but best in summer, when calmer winds and smaller seas result in clearer waters. Ocean waters, 3 miles east of the keys, showcase the park's main attraction—the northernmost section of Florida's living tropical coral reefs. Some are the size of an office desk, others as large as a football field. Glass-bottom-boat rides, when operating, showcase this underwater wonderland, but you really should snorkel or scuba dive to fully appreciate it.

A diverse population of colorful fish—angelfish, gobies, grunts, parrotfish, pork fish, wrasses, and many more—flits through the reefs. Shipwrecks from the 18th century are evidence of the area's international maritime heritage, and a Maritime Heritage Trail is being developed to link six of the major shipwreck and underwater cultural sites. Thus far, three sites, including a 19th-century wooden sailing vessel, have been plotted with GPS coordinates and marked with mooring buoys. Plastic dive cards are being developed that will contain navigational and background information.

WHAT'S NEARBY

EVERGLADES CITY

35 miles southeast of Naples and 83 miles west of Miami.

Aside from a chain gas station or two, Everglades City is perfect Old Florida. No high-rises (other than an observation tower) mar the landscape at this western gateway to Everglades National Park, just off the Tamiami Trail. It was developed in the late 19th century by Barron Collier, a wealthy advertising entrepreneur, who built it as a company town to house workers for his numerous projects, including construction of the Tamiami Trail. It grew and prospered until the Depression and World War II. Today this ramshackle town draws adventure seekers heading to the park for canoeing, fishing, and bird-watching excursions. Airboat tours, though popular, are banned within the preserve and park because of the environmental damage they cause to the mangroves. The Everglades Seafood Festival, going strong for about 40 years and held the first full weekend of February, draws crowds of more than 50,000 for delights from the sea, music, and craft displays. At quieter times, dining choices are limited to a handful of basic eateries. The town is small, fishing-oriented, and unhurried, making it excellent for boating,

Native plants along the Turner River Canoe Trail hem paddlers in on both sides, and alligators lurk nearby.

bicycling, or just strolling around. You can pedal along the waterfront on a 2-mile strand out to Chokoloskee Island.

Contacts Everglades Area Chamber of Commerce Welcome Center. Pick up brochures and pamphlets for area lodging, restaurants, and attractions, and ask for additional information from friendly staffers. ✉ *32016 Tamiami Trail E, at Rte. 29* ☎ *239/695–3941* ⊕ *www.evergladeschamber.net.*

EXPLORING

Fakahatchee Strand Preserve State Park. The ½-mile Big Cypress Bend boardwalk through this linear swamp forest provides opportunity to see rare plants, nesting eagles, and Florida's largest stand of native royal palms co-existing—unique to Fakahatchee Strand—with bald cypress under the forest canopy. Fakahatchee Strand, about 20 miles long and 5 miles wide, is also the orchid and bromeliad capital of the continent with 44 native orchids and 14 native bromeliads, many blooming most extravagantly in hotter months. It's particularly famous for its ghost orchids (as featured in Susan Orlean's novel *The Orchid Thief*), visible on guided hikes. In your quest for ghost orchids, keep alert for white-tailed deer, black bears, bobcats, and the Florida panther. For park nature on parade, take the 12-mile-long (one-way) W. J. Janes Memorial Scenic Drive ($3 payable at the honor box; have exact change). Hike its spur trails if you have time. Rangers lead swamp walks and canoe trips November through April. ✉ *Boardwalk on north side of Tamiami Trail, 7 miles west of Rte. 29; W. J. Janes Memorial Scenic Dr., ¾ mile north of Tamiami Trail on Rte. 29; ranger station at 137 Coastline Dr., Copeland* ☎ *239/695–4593* ⊕ *www.floridastateparks. org/fakahatcheestrand* ✉ *Free* ☉ *Daily 8 am–sunset.*

Collier-Seminole State Park. The opportunity to try biking, hiking, camping, and canoeing into Everglades territory make this park a prime introduction to this often forbidding land. Of historical interest, a Seminole War blockhouse has been re-created to hold the interpretative center, and one of the "walking dredges"—a towering black machine invented to carve the Tamiami Trail out of the muck—stands silent on grounds amid tropical hardwood forest. Campsites (plans to re-open in 2015) include electricity, water, and picnic tables. Restrooms have hot water showers, and one has a couple of washers and dryers outside. ⊠ *20200 Tamiami Trail E, Naples* ☎ *239/394–3397* ⊕ *www.floridastateparks.org/collier-seminole* ⊠ *$5 per car, $4 with lone driver, $2 for pedestrians or bikers* ⊙ *Daily 8–sunset.*

Florida Panther National Wildlife Refuge. When this refuge opened in 1989, it was off-limits to the public to protect endangered cougar subspecies. In 2005, responding to public demand, the 26,400-acre refuge opened two short loop trails in a region lightly traveled by panthers so visitors could get tastes of wet prairies, tropical hammocks, and pine uplands where panthers roam and wild orchids thrive. The 1.3-mile trail is rugged and often thigh-high under water during summer and fall; it's closed when completely flooded. The shorter 0.3-mile Leslie M. Duncan Memorial Trail is wheelchair-accessible and open year-round. For either, bring drinking water and insect repellent. Although sightings are rare, you may spot deer, black bears, and the occasional panther—or their tracks. Annual events include the Save the Panther Week in March, with an open house, plant walks, and tours. ⊠ *Off Rte. 29, between U.S. 41 and I–75* ☎ *239/353–8442* ⊕ *www.fws.gov/floridapanther* ⊠ *Free* ⊙ *Daily dawn–dusk; trails may be closed July–Nov. because of rain.*

Museum of the Everglades. Through artifacts and photographs you can meet American Indians, pioneers, entrepreneurs, and anglers who played roles in southwest Florida development. Exhibits and a short film chronicle the tremendous feat of building the Tamiami Trail across mosquito-ridden, gator-infested Everglades wetlands. Permanent displays and monthly exhibits rotate works of local artists. The museum is housed in the Laundry Building, completed in 1927 and once used for washing linens from the Rod and Gun Club and Everglades Inn. ⊠ *105 W. Broadway* ☎ *239/695–0008* ⊠ *Free* ⊙ *Tues.–Sat. 9–4.*

WHERE TO EAT

$
SEAFOOD

✕ **City Seafood.** Owner Richard Wahrenberger serves up gems from the sea delivered fresh from his own boats. Even better, you can chow down on his delectable, sustainable stone crabs—medium, large, jumbo, and colossal based on weight—with clear conscience. After removal of meaty claws, crabs are returned to waters where they grow new ones. Enjoy breakfast, lunch, or dinner inside this rustic haven, or sit outdoors to watch pelicans, gulls, tarpon, manatee, and the occasional gator play off the dock in the Barron River. Relax with a beer or wine by the glass. Appetizers run from deep-fried corn to conch, and sandwiches from hot dogs to pulled pork. Big draws, however, remain stone crabs and baskets of smoked mullet, grouper, shrimp, oysters, blue crab, gator, or frogs' legs. Got a cooler? City Seafood wraps for the road, and also ships. A gift shop sells cutesy crabby-style tanks, boxers, and tees. [$] *Average main: $15* ✉ *702 Begonia St.* ☎ *239/695–4700* 🌐 *www.cityseafood1.com.*

$$ SEAFOOD 🍴 **Everglades Seafood Depot.** Count on tasty, affordable meals in a scenic setting at this storied 1928 Spanish-style stucco structure fronting Lake Placid. Beginning life as the original Everglades train depot, the building later was deeded to the University of Miami for marine research, and appeared in the 1958 film *Winds across the Everglades* (starring Christopher Plummer, Peter Falk, Gypsy Rose Lee, and Burl Ives). Seafood is the star here now including lobster, frogs' legs, crab, and alligator. Steak, seafood, and combo entrées include salad or soup, or an extra-charge option for a salad bar with steamed shrimp. All-you-can-eat specials—fried chicken, a taco bar, or a seafood buffet—are staged on selected nights. Save room for "secret family recipe" coconut guava cake. If you'd like a view, ask for a back porch table or a lakeside window seat. [$] *Average main: $20* ✉ *102 Collier Ave.* ☎ *239/695–0075* 🌐 *www.evergladesseafooddepot.com.*

$ CUBAN 🍴 **Havana Cafe.** Cuban specialties are a tasty change from the seafood houses of Everglades City. This cheery eatery with a dozen or so tables inside, has more seating on the porch. Service is order-at-the-counter for breakfast and lunch (7 am–3 pm), with dinner in season on Friday and Saturday nights. Jump-start your day with café con leche and a pressed-egg sandwich, or try a Havana omelet. For lunch, you'll find the ubiquitous Cuban sandwich, burgers, shrimp, grouper, steak, and pork plates with rice and beans and yucca. [$] *Average main: $15* ✉ *191 Smallwood Dr., Chocoloskee* ☎ *239/695–2214* 🌐 *www.myhavanacafe.com* 💳 *No credit cards* ⏲ *No dinner Apr.–Oct. or Sun.–Thurs. Nov.–Mar.*

$$ SEAFOOD FAMILY 🍴 **Oyster House Restaurant.** One of the town's oldest fish houses, Oyster House serves all the local staples—shrimp, gator tail, frogs' legs, oysters, stone crab, and grouper—in a lodgelike setting with mounted wild game on walls and rafters. Deep-frying remains an art in these parts, so if you're going to indulge, do it here where you can create your own fried platter for under $25. Try to dine at sunset for golden rays with your watery view. Outside, a 75-foot observation tower affords a terrific overview of the Ten Thousand Islands. [$] *Average main: $20* ✉ *901 South Copeland Ave.* ☎ *239/695–2073* 🌐 *www.oysterhouserestaurant.com.*

$$$ SEAFOOD 🍴 **Rod and Gun Club.** Striking, polished pecky-cypress woodwork in this historic building dates from the 1920s, when wealthy hunters, anglers, and yachting parties arrived for the winter season. Presidents Hoover, Roosevelt, Truman, Eisenhower, and Nixon stopped by here, as did Ernest Hemingway, Burt Reynolds, and Mick Jagger. The main dining room holds overflow from the expansive screened porch overlooking the river. Like life in general here, friendly servers move slowly and upkeep is minimal. Fresh seafood dominates, from stone crab in season (October 15–May 15) to a surf-and-turf combo of steak and grouper or a swamp-and-turf duet of frogs' legs and steak (each $26.95), or pasta pairings, from $19.95. For $14.95 you can have your own catch fried, broiled, or blackened, served with salad, veggies, and potato. Pie choices are key lime and chocolate–peanut butter. Separate checks are discouraged at this cash-only venue, and there's a $5 plate-sharing charge.

Yesteryear's main lobby is well worth a look—even if you're eating elsewhere. Arrive by boat or land. [$] *Average main: $25* ✉ *200 Riverside Dr.* ☎ *239/695–2101* 🌐 *www.evergladesrodandgun.com* 💳 *No credit cards* ⏲ *Sometimes shuts down in summer; call ahead.*

$ SEAFOOD 🍴 **Triad Seafood.** Along the Barron River, seafood houses, fishing boats, and crab traps populate one shoreline; mangroves the other. Selling fresh off the boat, some seafood houses added picnic tables and eventually grew into restaurants. Family-owned Triad Seafood Market & Cafe is one, with a screened dining area, and additional outdoor seating under a breezeway and on a deck (heated in winter) overhanging the river. Here you can savor fresh seafood at its finest, or have it shipped. Nothing fancy (although smoked fish and oyster caesar salad are on the menu), but you'd be hard-pressed to find a better grouper sandwich. An all-you-can-eat fresh stone crab feast with butter or mustard sauce (October 15 to May 15; market prices fluctuate wildly) can thin your wallet, especially for the jumbos. Lunch starts at 11 am with fried shrimp, oyster, crab cake, and soft-shell blue crab baskets, plus reubens, Philly cheesesteaks, burgers, and kids' meals under $5 [$] *Average main: $15* ✉ *401 School Dr.* ☎ *239/695–0722* 🌐 *www.triadseafoodmarketcafe.com* ⏲ *Closed May 16–Oct. 15.*

WHERE TO STAY

$ HOTEL 🏨 **Glades Haven Cozy Cabins.** Bob Miller wanted to build a Holiday Inn next to his Oyster House Restaurant on marina-channel shores, but when that didn't fly, he sent for cabin kits and set up mobile-home-size units around a pool on his property as part of "Miller's World." **Pros:** great nearby food options; convenient to ENP boating; free docking; marina. **Cons:** trailer-park-crowded feel with a noisy bar nearby; no phones, no pets. [$] *Rooms from: $95* ✉ *801 Copeland Ave.* ☎ *239/695–2746, 888/956–6251* 🌐 *www.gladeshaven.com* 🛏 *24 cabins, 2 3-bedroom houses* 🍽 *No meals.*

$ B&B/INN Fodor's Choice ★ 🏨 **Ivey House.** A remodeled 1928 boardinghouse originally built for crews working on the Tamiami Trail, Ivey House (originally operated by Mr. and Mrs. Ivey) now fits adventurers on assorted budgets. **Pros:** historic; pleasant; affordable. **Cons:** not on water; some small rooms. [$] *Rooms from: $169* ✉ *107 Camellia St.* ☎ *877/567–0679, 239/695–3299* 🌐 *www.iveyhouse.com* 🛏 *30 rooms, 18 with bath; 1 2-bedroom cottage* 🍽 *Breakfast.*

SPORTS AND THE OUTDOORS

AIR TOURS

Wings Ten Thousand Islands Aero Tours. These 20-minute to nearly 2-hour scenic flightseeing tours of the Ten Thousand Islands National Wildlife Refuge, Big Cypress National Preserve, Everglades National Park, and Gulf of Mexico operate November through April. Aboard an Alaskan Bush plane, you can see sawgrass prairies, American Indian shell mounds, alligators, and wading birds. Rates start at $46 and go up to $224 for a two-hour Everglades tour (per person with groups of three or four). Flights can be booked to the Florida Keys, connecting to the Dry Tortugas. ✉ *Everglades City Airpark, 650 Everglades City Airpark Rd.* ☎ *239/695–3296.*

BOATING AND CANOEING

On the Gulf Coast explore the nooks, crannies, and mangrove islands of Chokoloskee Bay and Ten Thousand Islands National Wildlife Refuge, as well as the many rivers near Everglades City. The Turner River Canoe Trail, a pleasant day trip with almost guaranteed bird and alligator sightings, passes through the mangrove, dwarf cypress, coastal prairie, and freshwater slough ecosystems of Everglades National Park and Big Cypress National Preserve.

> ### SHUTTLES FROM MIAMI
>
> **Super Shuttle.** This 24-hour service runs air-conditioned vans between MIA and the Homestead–Florida City area; pickup is outside baggage claim and costs around $61 per person depending on your destination. For a return to MIA, reserve 24 hours in advance and know your pickup zip code for a price quote. ☎ 305/871–2000 ⊕ www.supershuttle.com.

Glades Haven Marina. Get out on Ten Thousand Islands waters in a 19-foot Sundance or a 17-foot Flicker fishing boat. Rates start at $200 a day, plus fuel, with half-day and hourly options. The outfitter also rents kayaks and canoes and has a 24-hour boat ramp and dockage for up to 24-ft. vessels. Launch your own boat for $15, a canoe or kayak for $5. ⊠ 801 Copeland Ave. S ☎ 239/695–2628 ⊕ www.gladeshaven.com.

FLORIDA CITY

3 miles southwest of Homestead on U.S. 1.

Florida's Turnpike ends in Florida City, the southernmost town on the peninsula, spilling thousands of vehicles onto U.S. 1 and eventually west to Everglades National Park, east to Biscayne National Park, or south to the Florida Keys. Florida City and Homestead run into each other, but the difference couldn't be more noticeable. As the last outpost before 18 miles of mangroves and water, this stretch of U.S. 1 is lined with fast-food eateries, service stations, hotels, bars, dive shops, and restaurants. Hotel rates increase significantly during NASCAR races at the nearby Homestead-Miami Speedway. Like Homestead, Florida City is rooted in agriculture, with expanses of farmland west of Krome Avenue and a huge farmers' market that ships produce nationwide.

EXPLORING

Tropical Everglades Visitor Center. Run by the nonprofit Tropical Everglades Visitor Association, this pastel pink center with teal signage offers abundant printed material plus tips from volunteer experts on exploring south Dade County, Homestead, Florida City, and the Florida Keys. ⊠ 160 U.S. 1 ☎ 305/245–9180, 800/388–9669 ⊕ www. tropicaleverglades.com.

WHERE TO EAT

$$
ITALIAN
✕ **Capri Restaurant.** This friendly family-owned enterprise has been a magnet for affordable Italian-American classics since 1958. Dine amid red brick walls at round tables, or at sunny courtyard tables with umbrellas. Options range from the all you care to eat pasta on Tuesdays ($8) to crunchy crust pizza or paninis, or steak, prime rib, and a multitude of seafood-pasta combos. Tuesday is also lobster night. Daily

early-birds (4:30–6:30) include soup or salad and potato or spaghetti. Specialty martinis and fruity cocktails supplement an extensive wine list. $ *Average main: $16* ⊠ *935 N. Krome Ave.* ☎ *305/247–1542* ⊕ *www. dinecapri.com* ☉ *No lunch Sun.*

$ ✗ **Farmers' Market Restaurant.** Although this eatery is within the farm-
SEAFOOD ers' market on the edge of town and is big on serving fresh vegetables, seafood figures prominently on the menu. A family of anglers runs the place, so fish and shellfish are only hours from the sea, and there's a fish fry on Friday nights. Catering to farmers, the restaurant opens at 5:30 am, serving pancakes, jumbo eggs, and fluffy omelets with home fries or grits in a pleasant dining room with red and green checked tablecloths. For lunch or dinner, choose among fried shrimp or conch, seafood pasta, country-fried steak, and roast turkey, as well as salads, burgers and sandwiches. $ *Average main: $13* ⊠ *300 N. Krome Ave.* ☎ *305/242–0008.*

$$ ✗ **Mutineer Wharf Restaurant.** Families and older couples flock to this
SEAFOOD kitschy roadside outpost with a fish-and-duck pond. Built in 1980 to look like a ship—back when Florida City barely got on maps—etched glass divides bilevel dining rooms, with velvet-upholstered chairs, an aquarium, and nautical antiques. Florida lobster tails, stuffed grouper, shrimp, and snapper top the menu, along with another half-dozen daily seafood specials. Add to that steaks, ribs, and chicken. Yellowfin tuna wraps and grouper sandwiches are filling items for lunch, especially before a trip into Everglades Park. You also can relax for dinner in the restaurant's Wharf Lounge. Friday and Saturday nights feature live entertainment and dancing. $ *Average main: $18* ⊠ *11 S.E. 1st Ave. (U.S. 1), at Palm Dr.* ☎ *305/245–3377* ⊕ *www.mutineerrestaurant.com.*

WHERE TO STAY

$ 🏨 **Best Western Gateway to the Keys.** For easy access to Everglades and
HOTEL Biscayne national parks as well as the Keys, you'll be well situated at this sprawling, two-story lodging spot two blocks off Florida's Turn-pike. **Pros:** convenient to parks, outlet shopping, and dining; business services; attractive pool area. **Cons:** traffic noise; fills up fast in high season. $ *Rooms from: $135* ⊠ *411 S. Krome Ave.* ☎ *305/246–5100, 888/981–5100* ⊕ *www.bestwestern.com/gatewaytothekeys* ⇱ *114 rooms* ⦿ *Breakfast.*

$ 🏨 **Econo Lodge.** Close to Florida's Turnpike and with access to the
HOTEL Keys, this is a serviceable overnight pullover spot with a complimentary breakfast. **Pros:** laundry facility on property; pool; proximity to mall outlet shopping. **Cons:** urban-ugly location; noisy. $ *Rooms from: $89* ⊠ *553 N.E. 1st Ave.* ☎ *305/248–9300, 800/553–2666* ⊕ *www. econolodge.com* ⇱ *42 rooms* ⦿ *Breakfast.*

$ 🏨 **Fairway Inn.** With a waterfall pool, this two-story motel with exterior
HOTEL room entry has some of the area's lowest chain rates, and it's next to the Chamber of Commerce visitor center so you'll have easy access to reading and planning material. **Pros:** affordable; convenient to restaurants, parks, and raceway. **Cons:** plain, small rooms; no-pet policy. $ *Rooms from: $89* ⊠ *100 S.E. 1st Ave.* ☎ *305/248–4202, 888/340–4734* ⇱ *160 rooms* ⦿ *Breakfast.*

$ ⚏ **Quality Inn.** Amid an asphalt complex of hotels, gas stations, and eat-
HOTEL   eries just off U.S. 1, this two-story Quality Inn (previously a Comfort
Inn) with exterior corridors has a friendly front desk staff offering tips
on Everglades or Keys adventures, or action at the nearby track. **Pros:**
close to restaurants and services. **Cons:** no elevator; noisy location.
§ *Rooms from: $89* ⌧ *333 S.E. 1st Ave.* ☎ *305/248–4009, 888/352–
2489* ⊕ *www.qualityinn.com* ↶ *123 rooms* ¶❶ *Breakfast.*

$ ⚏ **Ramada Inn.** If you're looking for an uptick from other chains, this
HOTEL   pet-friendly property offers more amenities and comfort, such as
32-inch flat-screen TVs, duvet-covered beds, closed closets, and stylish
furnishings. **Pros:** extra room amenities; convenient location. **Cons:**
chain anonymity. § *Rooms from: $99* ⌧ *124 E. Palm Dr.* ☎ *305/247–
8833* ⊕ *www.hotelfloridacity.com* ↶ *123 rooms* ¶❶ *Breakfast.*

SHOPPING

FAMILY   **Robert Is Here.** Want take-home gifts? This remarkable fruit stand sells
more than 100 types of jams, jellies, honeys, and salad dressings along
with its vegetables, juices, fresh-fruit milk shakes (try the key lime),
and some 30 kinds of tropical fruits, including (in season) carambola,
lychee, egg fruit, monstera, sapodilla, dragonfruit, genipa, sugar apple,
and tamarind. Back in 1960, the stand got started when seven-year-old
Robert sat at this spot hawking his father's bumper cucumber crop.
Now Robert (still on the scene daily with his wife and kids), ships
nationwide and donates seconds to needy area families. An assortment
of animals out back—goats to iguanas and emus, along with a splash
pool—creates entertainment value for kids. Picnic tables, benches, and
a waterfall with a koi pond add serenity. On the way to Everglades
National Park, Robert opens at 8 am, operating until at least 7, and
shutting down from Labor Day until November. ⌧ *19200 S.W. 344th
St.* ☎ *305/246–1592.*

HOMESTEAD

30 miles southwest of Miami.

Since recovering from Hurricane Andrew in 1992, Homestead has
redefined itself as a destination for tropical agro- and ecotourism. At
a crossroads between Miami and the Keys as well as Everglades and
Biscayne national parks, the area has the added dimension of shopping centers, residential development, hotel chains, and the Homestead-
Miami Speedway—when car races are scheduled, hotels hike up their
rates and require minimum stays. The historic downtown has become a
preservation-driven Main Street. Krome Avenue, where it cuts through
the city's heart, is lined with restaurants, an arts complex, antiques
shops, and low-budget, sometimes undesirable, accommodations. West
of north–south Krome Avenue, miles of fields grow fresh fruits and
vegetables. Some are harvested commercially, and others beckon with
"U-pick" signs. Stands selling farm-fresh produce and nurseries that
grow and sell orchids and tropical plants abound. In addition to its
agricultural legacy, the town has an eclectic flavor, attributable to its
population mix: descendants of pioneer Crackers, Hispanic growers and

farm workers, professionals escaping the Miami hubbub, and latter-day northern retirees.

EXPLORING

Fruit & Spice Park. Because it officially qualifies for tropical status, this 37-acre park in Homestead's Redland historic agricultural district is the only public botanical garden of its type in the United States. More than 500 varieties of fruit, nuts, and spices typically grow here, and there are 75 varieties of banana alone, plus 160 of mango. Tram tours (included in admission) run three times daily, and you can sample fresh fruit at the gift shop, which also stocks canned and dried fruits plus cookbooks. The Mango Café, open daily, serves mango salsa, smoothies, and shakes along with salads, wraps, sandwiches, and a yummy Mango Passion Cheesecake. Picnic in the garden at provided tables or on your own blankets. Annual park events include January's Redland Heritage Festival and June's Summer Fruit Festival. ✉ *24801 S.W. 187th Ave.* ☎ *305/247–5727* 🌐 *www.fruitandspicepark.org* 🎟 *$8* 🕒 *Daily 9–5; guided tram tours at 11, 1:30, and 3.*

3

Schnebly Redland's Winery. Enjoy Homestead's fruity bounty in liquid form at this winery that began producing wines of lychee, mango, guava, and other fruits as a way to avoid waste from family groves each year—bounty not perfect enough for shipping. Over the years, the winery (now with a brewery, too) has expanded with an indoor reception/tasting area serving snacks and a lush plaza area landscaped in coral rock, tropical plants, and waterfalls—topped with an Indian thatched chickee roof. Tours and tastings are offered daily. The Ultimate Tasting ($9.95) includes five wines, and an etched Schnebly glass you can keep. ✉ *30205 S.W. 217th Ave.* ☎ *305/242–1224, 888/717–9463 (WINE)* 🌐 *www.schneblywinery.com* 🕒 *Weekdays 10–5, Sat. 10–6, Sun. noon–5.*

WHERE TO EAT

$ MEXICAN 🍴 **NicaMex.** Among the local Latin population this 68-seat eatery is a low-budget favorite for Nicaraguan and Mexican flavors. It helps if you know Spanish, but the menu is bilingual and some staffers speak English. Although they term it *comidas rapidas* (fast food), the cuisine is not Americanized. Try authentic huevos rancheros or *chilaquiles* (corn tortillas cooked in red-pepper sauce) for breakfast. Specialties include *chicharron en salsa verde* (fried pork skin in hot-green-tomato sauce). Hearty beef soups are top sellers. If you want (or dare), Mexican plates from tacos to tostadas can be made with beef tongue. Choose among domestic or imported beers, and escape south of the border. [$] *Average main: $10* ✉ *32 N.W. 1st St., across from Krome Ave. bandstand* ☎ *305/247–0727.*

WHERE TO STAY

$ HOTEL 🏨 **Hotel Redland.** Of downtown Homestead's smattering of mom-and-pop lodging options, this historic inn is by far the most desirable with its Victorian-style rooms done up in pastels and reproduction antique furniture. **Pros:** historic character; convenient to downtown and near antique shops; well maintained; smoke-free. **Cons:** traffic noise; some

Are baby alligators more to your liking than their daddies? You can pet one at Gator Park.

small rooms. [$] *Rooms from: $100* ✉ *5 S. Flagler Ave.* ☎ *305/246–1904, 800/595–1904* 🌐 *www.hotelredland.com* 🛏 *13 rooms* 🍴 *No meals.*

SPORTS AND THE OUTDOORS

AUTO RACING

Homestead-Miami Speedway. The speedway buzzes more than 280 days each year with racing, manufacturer testing, car-club events, driving schools, and ride-along programs. The facility has 65,000 grandstand seats, club seating eight stories above racing action, and two tracks—a 2.21-mile continuous road course and a 1.5-mile oval. A packed schedule includes GRAND-AM and NASCAR events. Two tunnels on the grounds are below sea level. ✉ *One Speedway Blvd.* ☎ *866/409–7223* 🌐 *www.homesteadmiamispeedway.com.*

WATER SPORTS

Homestead Bayfront Park. Boaters, anglers, and beachgoers give high ratings to facilities at this recreational area adjacent to Biscayne National Park. The 174-slip marina, accommodating vessels up to 50 feet, has a ramp, dock, bait-and-tackle shop, fuel station, ice, and dry storage. The park also has a snack bar, tidal swimming area, a beach with lifeguards, playground, ramps for people with disabilities, and a picnic pavilion with grills, showers, and restrooms. ✉ *9698 S.W. 328th St.* ☎ *305/230–3033* 🎟 *$6 per passenger vehicle; $12 per vehicle with boat Mon.–Thurs., $15 Fri.–Sun.; $15 per RV or bus* 🕒 *Daily sunrise–sunset.*

TAMIAMI TRAIL

U.S. 41, between Naples and Miami

An 80-mile stretch of U.S. 41 (known as the Tamiami Trail) traverses the Everglades, Big Cypress National Preserve, and Fakahatchee Strand Preserve State Park. The road was conceived in 1915 to link Miami to Fort Myers and Tampa. When it finally became a reality in 1928, it cut through the Everglades and altered the natural flow of water as well as the lives of the Miccosukee Indians, who were trying to eke out a living fishing, hunting, farming, and frogging here. The landscape is surprisingly varied, changing from hardwood hammocks to pinelands, then abruptly to tall cypress trees dripping with Spanish moss and back to sawgrass marsh. Slow down to take in the scenery and you'll likely be rewarded with glimpses of alligators sunning themselves along the banks of roadside canals and hundreds of waterbirds, especially in the dry winter season. The man-made landscape includes Native American villages, chickee huts, and airboats parked at roadside enterprises. Between Miami and Naples the road goes by several names, including Tamiami Trail, U.S. 41, 9th Street in Naples, and, at the Miami end, S.W. 8th Street. ■TIP→ Businesses along the trail give their addresses based on either their distance from Krome Avenue, Florida's Turnpike, or Miami on the east coast or Naples on the west coast.

EXPLORING

Everglades Safari Park. A perennial favorite with tour-bus operators, this family-run park has an arena, seating up to 300 for shows with alligator wrestling. Before and after, get a closer look at both alligators and crocodiles on Gator Island, follow a jungle trail, walk through a small wildlife museum, or climb aboard an airboat for a 40-minute ride on the River of Grass (included in admission). There's also a restaurant, gift shop, and an observation platform looking out over the Glades. Smaller, private airboats can be chartered for tours lasting 40 minutes to 2 hours. Check online for coupons. ⊠ *26700 S.W. 8th St., 15 miles west of Florida's Turnpike* ☎ *305/226–6923, 305/223–3804* ⊕ *www.evergladessafaripark.com* ☑ *$23* ⊗ *Daily 9–5, last tour at 3:30.*

FAMILY **Gator Park.** Here you can get face-to-face with and even touch an alligator—albeit a baby one—during the park's Wildlife Show. You also can squirm in a "reptilium" of venomous and nonpoisonous native snakes or learn about American Indians of the Everglades through a reproduction of a Miccosukee village. The park, open rain or shine, also has 35-minute airboat tours as well as a gift shop and restaurant serving fare from burgers to gator tail. ⊠ *24050 Tamiami Trail, 12 miles west of Florida's Turnpike* ☎ *305/559–2255, 800/559–2205* ⊕ *www.gatorpark.com* ☑ *Tours, wildlife show, and airboat ride $22.99* ⊗ *Daily 9–5.*

FAMILY **Miccosukee Indian Village and Gift Shop.** Showcasing the skills and lifestyle of the Miccosukee Tribe of Florida, this cultural center offers craft demonstrations and insight into interaction with alligators. Narrated 30-minute airboat rides take you into the wilderness where natives hid after the Seminole Wars and Indian Removal Act of the mid-1800s. In modern times, many of the Miccosukee have relocated to this village along Tamiami Trail, but most still maintain their hammock farming and hunting camps. The museum shows a film and displays chickee structures and artifacts. Guided tours run throughout the day, and a gift shop stocks dolls, apparel, silver jewelry, beadwork, and other handcrafts. The Miccosukee Everglades Music and Craft Festival falls on a July weekend, and the 10-day Miccosukee Indian Arts Festival is in late December. ⊠ *U.S. 41, just west of Shark Valley entrance, 25 miles west of Florida's Turnpike at MM 70* ☎ *305/552–8365* ⊕ *www. miccosukee.com* ⊠ *Village $8, airboat rides $10* ⊗ *Daily 9–5.*

CROCS OR GATORS?

You can tell you're looking at a crocodile, not an alligator, if you can see its lower teeth protruding when its jaws are shut. Gators are much darker in color—a grayish black—compared with the lighter tan color of crocodiles. Alligator snouts—sort of U-shape—are also much broader than their long, thin A-shape crocodilian counterparts. South Florida is the world's only place where the two coexist. Alligators are primarily found in freshwater habitats, whereas crocodiles (better at expelling salt from water) are typically in coastal estuaries.

WHERE TO EAT

$ ✕ **Coopertown Restaurant.** Make
AMERICAN this a pit stop for local color and cuisine fished straight from the swamp. Started a half century ago as a sandwich stand, this eatery inside an airboat concession storefront has long attracted the famous and the humbly hungry. Besides catfish and shrimp, house specialties are frogs' legs and alligator tail breaded in cornmeal and deep-fried, served with lemon wedges and Tabasco. Sandwich options include burgers, hot dogs, and grilled cheese. $ *Average main: $12* ⊠ *22700 S.W. 8th St., 11 miles west of Florida's Turnpike* ☎ *305/226–6048* ⊕ *www.coopertownairboats.com* ⊗ *No dinner.*

$ ✕ **Miccosukee Restaurant.** For breakfast or lunch (or dinner until 9 pm,
SOUTHWESTERN November–April), this roadside cafeteria a quarter mile from the Miccosukee Indian Village provides the best menu variety along Tamiami Trail in Everglades territory. Atmosphere comes from the view overlooking the River of Grass, servers wearing traditional Miccosukee patchwork vests, and a mural depicting American Indian women cooking while men powwow. Catfish and frogs' legs are breaded and deep-fried. Besides pumpkin and Indian fry bread, you'll also find burgers, salads, and south-of-the-border dishes. The Miccosukee Platter (around $25) offers a sampling of local favorites, including gator bites. $ *Average main: $15* ⊠ *U.S. 41, 18 miles west of Miccosukee Resort & Gaming; 25 miles west of Florida's Turnpike* ☎ *305/894–2374* ⊗ *No dinner May–Oct.*

$ ✕ **Pit Bar-B-Q.** This old-fashioned roadside eatery along Tamiami Trail
BARBECUE near Krome Avenue was launched in 1965 by the late Tommy Little,
FAMILY who wanted to provide easy access to cold drinks and rib-sticking fare for folks heading into or out of the Everglades. This recently spiffed up backwood heritage vision remains a popular, affordable family option. Order at the counter, grab your food, and eat at picnic tables on the screened porch or outdoors. Specialties include barbecued chicken and ribs with a tangy sauce, fries, coleslaw, and a fried biscuit, plus burgers and fish sandwiches. The whopping double-decker beef or

pork sandwich with slaw requires multiple napkins. Latin specialties include deep-fried pork and fried green plantains. Beer is by the bottle or pitcher. Locals flock here with kids on weekends for pony rides. [$] *Average main: $12* ✉ *16400 S.W. 8th St., 5 miles west of Florida's Turnpike* ☎ *305/226–2272* 🌐 *www.thepitbarbq.com.*

WHERE TO STAY

$ RESORT 🏨 **Miccosukee Resort & Gaming.** Like an oasis on the horizon of endless sawgrass, this nine-story resort at the southeastern edge of the Everglades can't help but attract attention, even if you're not on the lookout for 24-hour gaming action. **Pros:** casino; most modern resort in these parts; golf. **Cons:** smoky lobby; hotel guests find parking lot fills with gamblers; feels incompatible with the Everglades. [$] *Rooms from: $149* ✉ *500 S.W. 177th Ave., 6 miles west of Florida's Turnpike* ☎ *305/925–2555, 877/242–6464* 🌐 *www.miccosukee.com* 🛏 *256 rooms, 46 suites* 🍴 *No meals.*

SPORTS AND THE OUTDOORS

BOAT TOURS

Many Everglades-area tours operate only in season, roughly November through April.

Coopertown Airboats. In business since 1945, the oldest airboat operator in the Everglades offers 35- to 40-minute tours ($23) that take you 9 miles to hammocks and alligator holes. You also can book private charters of up to two hours. ✉ *22700 S.W. 8th St., 11 miles west of Florida's Turnpike* ☎ *305/226–6048* 🌐 *www.coopertownairboats.com.*

Everglades Alligator Farm. Open daily near the entrance to Everglades National Park, this working farm—home of the 14-foot "Grandpa" gator—runs a 4-mile, 30-minute airboat tour with departures 25 minutes after the hour. The tour ($23) includes free hourly alligator, snake, and wildlife shows, or see only the gator farm and show ($15.50). Alligator feedings are at noon and 3 pm. Look for online coupons. ✉ *40351 S.W. 192nd Ave., Homestead* ☎ *305/247–2628* 🌐 *www.everglades.com.*

Everglades Safari Park. A 30-minute eco-adventure airboat ride costs $23, while longer, smaller, private airboat adventures, like the eco-adventure and sunset tours, cost more. All prices include the alligator show and access to walking trails and exhibits. Look for online discounts. ✉ *26700 S.W. 8th St., 15 miles west of Florida's Turnpike* ☎ *305/226–6923, 305/223–3804* 🌐 *www.evergladessafaripark.com.*

Gator Park Airboat Tours. Open daily rain or shine, Gator Park conducts 45-minute narrated airboat tours ($22.99), including a park tour and wildlife show. Look for significant online discounts. ✉ *24050 S.W. 8th St., 12 miles west of Florida's Turnpike* ☎ *305/559–2255, 800/559–2205* 🌐 *www.gatorpark.com.*

FAMILY **Wooten's Everglades Airboat Tours.** This classic Florida roadside attraction runs airboat tours (starting at $28 per person) through the Everglades for up to 18 people and swamp-buggy rides ($24 per person) through the Big Cypress Swamp for up to 25 passengers. Each lasts approximately 30 minutes. (Swamp-buggies are giant tractorlike vehicles with huge rubber wheels.) More personalized airboat tours on smaller boats, seating six to eight, last about an hour. An on-site animal sanctuary with a live gator show ($8) shelters the typical Everglades array of alligators, snakes, and other creatures. Ask about packages that include an airboat ride, swamp-buggy adventure, and sanctuary access. Rates change frequently, but check out the website for combo packages. ✉ *32330 Tamiami Trail E, 1½ miles east of Rte. 29, Ochopee* ☎ *239/695–2781, 800/282–2781* ⊕ *www.wootenseverglades.com* ☉ *Daily 8:30–5; last ride departs at 4:30.*

THE FLORIDA KEYS

WELCOME TO THE FLORIDA KEYS

TOP REASONS TO GO

★ **John Pennekamp Coral Reef State Park:** A perfect introduction to the Florida Keys, this nature reserve offers snorkeling, diving, camping, and kayaking. An underwater highlight is the massive *Christ of the Deep* statue.

★ **Under the sea:** Whether you scuba dive, snorkel, or ride a glass-bottom boat, don't miss gazing at the coral reef and its colorful denizens.

★ **Sunset at Mallory Square:** Sure, it's touristy, but just once while you're here, you've got to witness the circuslike atmosphere of this nightly celebration.

★ **Duval crawl:** Shop, eat, drink, repeat. Key West's Duval Street and the nearby streets make a good day's worth of window-shopping and people-watching.

★ **Get on the water:** From angling for trophy-size fish to zipping out to the Dry Tortugas, a boat trip is in your future. It's really the whole point of the Keys.

1 The Upper Keys. As the doorstep to the islands' coral reefs and blithe spirit, the Upper Keys introduce all that's sporting and sea-oriented about the Keys. They stretch from Key Largo to the Long Key Channel (MM 105–65).

2 The Middle Keys. Centered on the town of Marathon, the Middle Keys hold most of the chain's historic and natural attractions outside of Key West. They go from Conch (pronounced *konk*) Key through Marathon to the south side of the Seven Mile Bridge, including Pigeon Key (MM 65–40).

3 The Lower Keys. Pressure drops another notch in this laid-back part of the region, where key-deer viewing and fishing reign supreme. The Lower Keys go from Little Duck Key west through Big Coppitt Key (MM 40–9).

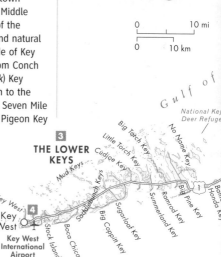

4 Key West. The ultimate in Florida Keys craziness, this party town isn't for the closed-minded or those seeking a quiet retreat. The Key West area encompasses MM 9–0.

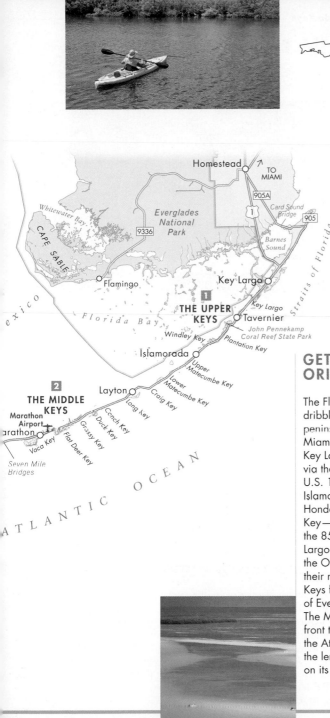

4

Homestead
TO MIAMI
905A
1
Card Sound Bridge
905

Everglades National Park
9336

Whitewater Bay

CAPE SABLE

Barnes Sound

Flamingo

Key Largo

1
THE UPPER KEYS

Key Largo

Gulf of Mexico

Florida Bay

Tavernier
Straits of Florida
John Pennekamp Coral Reef State Park
Plantation Key

Windley Key

Islamorada
Upper Matecumbe Key

2
THE MIDDLE KEYS

Layton
Lower Matecumbe Key

Long Key

Craig Key

Marathon Airport
arathon

Conch Key
Duck Key
Grassy Key
Vaca Key
Flat Deer Key

Seven Mile Bridges

ATLANTIC OCEAN

GETTING ORIENTED

The Florida Keys are the dribble of islands off the peninsula's southern tip. From Miami International Airport, Key Largo is a 56-mile drive via the Florida Turnpike and U.S. 1. The rest of the keys— Islamorada, Marathon, Bahia Honda Key, and Big Pine Key—fall in succession for the 85 miles between Key Largo and Key West along the Overseas Highway. At their north end, the Florida Keys front Florida Bay, part of Everglades National Park. The Middle and Lower Keys front the Gulf of Mexico; the Atlantic Ocean borders the length of the chain on its eastern shores.

SEAFOOD IN THE FLORIDA KEYS

Fish. It's what's for dinner in the Florida Keys. The Keys' runway between the Gulf of Mexico or Florida Bay and Atlantic warm waters means fish of many fin. Restaurants take full advantage by serving it fresh, whether you caught it or a local fisherman did.

Menus at a number of colorful waterfront shacks such as **Snapper's** (⊠ *139 Seaside Ave., Key Largo* ☎ *305/852–5956*) in Key Largo and **Half Shell Raw Bar** (⊠ *231 Margaret St., Key West* ☎ *305/294–7496*) range from basic raw, steamed, broiled, grilled, or blackened fish to some Bahamian and New Orleans–style interpretations. Other seafood houses dress up their fish in creative haute cuisine styles, such as **Pierre's** (⊠ *MM 81.5 BS, Islamorada* ☎ *305/664–3225* ⊕ *www.pierres-restaurant.com*) hogfish meunière, or yellowtail snapper with pear-ricotta pasta purses with caponata and red pepper coulis at **Café Marquesa** (⊠ *600 Fleming St., Key West* ☎ *305/292–1244* ⊕ *www.marquesa.com*). Try a Keys-style breakfast of "grits and grunts"—fried fish and grits—at the **Stuffed Pig** (⊠ *3520 Overseas Hwy., Marathon* ☎ *305/743–4059*).

BUILT-IN FISH

You know it's fresh when you see a fish market as soon as you open the door to the restaurant where you're dining. It happens frequently in the Keys. You can even peruse the seafood showcases and pick the fish fillet or lobster tail you want.

Many of the Keys' best restaurants are found in marina complexes, where the commercial fishermen bring their catches straight from the sea. Those in **Stock Island** (one island north of Key West) and at **Keys Fisheries Market & Marina** (⊠ *MM 49 BS, end of 35th St., Marathon* ☎ *305/743-4353, 866/743-4353*) take some finding.

CONCH

One of the tastiest legacies of the Keys' Bahamian heritage (and most mispronounced), conch (pronounced *konk*) shows up on nearly every menu in some shape or form. It's so prevalent in local diets that natives refer to themselves as Conchs. Conch fritters are the most popular culinary manifestations, followed by cracked (pounded, breaded, and fried) conch, and conch salad, a ceviche-style refresher. Since the harvesting of queen conch is now illegal, most of the islands' conch comes from the Bahamas.

FLORIDA LOBSTER

Where are the claws? Stop looking for them: Florida spiny lobsters don't have 'em, never did. The sweet tail meat, however, makes up for the loss. Commercial and sport divers harvest these glorious crustaceans from late July through March. Check with local dive shops on restrictions, and then get ready for a fresh feast. Restaurants serve them broiled with drawn butter or in creative dishes such as lobster Benedict, lobster spring rolls, lobster Reuben, and lobster tacos.

GROUPER

Once central to Florida's trademark seafood dish—fried grouper sandwich—its populations have been overfished in recent years, meaning that the state has exerted more control over

bag regulations and occasionally closes grouper fishing on a temporary basis during the winter season. Some restaurants have gone antigrouper to try to bring back the abundance, but most grab it when they can. Black grouper is the most highly prized of the several varieties.

STONE CRAB

In season October 15 through May 15, it gets its name from its rock-hard shell. Fishermen take only one claw, which can regenerate in a sustainable manner. Connoisseurs prefer them chilled with tangy mustard sauce. Some restaurants give you a choice of hot claws and drawn butter, but this means the meat will be cooked twice, because it's usually boiled or steamed as soon as it's taken from its crab trap.

YELLOWTAIL SNAPPER

The preferred species of snappers, it's more plentiful in the Keys than in any other Florida waters. As pretty as it is tasty, it's a favorite of divers and snorkelers. Mild, sweet, and delicate, its meat lends itself to any number of preparations. It's available pretty much year-round, and many restaurants will give you a choice of broiled, baked, fried, or blackened. Chefs top it with everything from key lime beurre blanc to mango chutney. **Ballyhoo's** in Key Largo (⊠ *MM 97.8, in median* ☎ *305/852–0822*) serves it 10 different ways.

Updated by Jill Martin Your Keys experience begins on your 18-mile drive south on "The Stretch," a portion of U.S. 1 with a specially colored blue median that takes you from Florida City to Key Largo. The real magic begins at mile marker 113, where the Florida Keys Scenic Highway begins. As the only All-American Road in Florida, it is a destination unto itself, one that crosses 42 bridges over water, including the Seven Mile Bridge—with its stunning vistas—and ends in Key West. Look for crocodiles, alligators, and bald eagles along the way.

Key West has a Mardi Gras mood with Fantasy Festival, a Hemingway look-alike contest, and the occasional threat to secede from the Union. It's an island whose eclectic natives, known as "Conchs," mingle well with visitors (of the spring break variety as well as those seeking to escape reality for a while) on this scenic, sometimes raucous 4x2-mile island paradise.

Although life elsewhere in the island chain isn't near as offbeat, it is as diverse. Overflowing bursts of bougainvillea, shimmering waters, and mangrove-lined islands can be admired throughout. The one thing most visitors don't admire much in the Keys are their beaches. They're not many, and they're not what you'd expect. The reason? The coral reef. It breaks up the waves and prevents sand from being dumped on the shores. That's why the beaches are mostly rough sand, as it's crushed coral. Think of it as a trade-off: the Keys have the only living coral reef in the U.S., but that reef prevents miles of shimmering sands from ever arriving.

In season, a river of traffic gushes southwest on this highway. But that doesn't mean you can't enjoy the ride as you cruise along the islands. Gaze over the silvery blue-and-green Atlantic and its living coral reef, with Florida Bay, the Gulf of Mexico, and the backcountry on your right (the Keys extend southwest from the mainland). At a few points the ocean and gulf are as much as 10 miles apart; in most places, however, they're from 1 to 4 miles apart, and on the narrowest landfill islands they're separated only by the road. While the views can be mesmerizing, to appreciate the Keys you need to get off the highway, especially in more developed regions like Key Largo, Islamorada, and Marathon. Once you do, rent a boat, anchor, and then fish, swim, or marvel at the sun, sea, and sky. Or visit one of the many sandbars, which are popular places to float the day away. Oceanside, dive or snorkel spectacular coral reefs or pursue grouper, blue marlin, mahimahi, and other deepwater game fish. Along Florida Bay's coastline, kayak to secluded islands through mangrove forests, or seek out the bonefish, snapper, snook, and tarpon that lurk in the shallow grass flats and mangrove roots of the backcountry.

4

PLANNING

WHEN TO GO

High season in the Keys falls between Christmas and Easter. November to mid-December crowds are thinner, the weather is wonderful, and hotels and shops drastically reduce their prices. Summer, which is hot and humid, is becoming a second high season, especially among Floridians, families, and European travelers. If you plan to attend the wild Fantasy Fest in October, book your room at least six months in advance. Accommodations are also scarce during the last consecutive Wednesday and Thursday in July (lobster sport season) and starting the first weekend in August, when the commercial lobster season begins.

Winter is typically 10°F warmer than on the mainland; summer is usually a few degrees cooler. The Keys also get substantially less rain, around 40 inches annually, compared with an average 55–60 inches in Miami and the Everglades. In the summertime, "thunder boomers" (quick-moving thunder storms) pass through most afternoons, although tropical storms can dump rain for two or more days. Winter cold fronts occasionally stall over the Keys, dragging overnight temperatures down to the low 50s.

GETTING HERE AND AROUND

AIR TRAVEL

About 450,000 passengers use the **Key West International Airport (EYW)** each year; its most recent renovation includes a beach where travelers can catch their last blast of rays after clearing security. Because flights are few, many prefer flying into Miami International Airport (MIA) and driving the 110-mile Overseas Highway (aka U.S. 1).

Contact Key West International Airport (*EYW*). ⊠ *3491 S. Roosevelt Blvd., Key West* ☎ *305/296–5439* ⊕ *www.keywestinternationalairport.com.*

BOAT AND FERRY TRAVEL

Key West can be reached by high-speed catamaran ferry from Fort Myers and Marco Island through Key West Express.

Boaters can travel to and along the Keys either along the Intracoastal Waterway through Card, Barnes, and Blackwater sounds and into Florida Bay or along the deeper Atlantic Ocean route through Hawk

Channel. The Keys are full of marinas that welcome transient visitors, but there aren't enough slips for all the boats heading to these waters. Make reservations far in advance and ask about channel and dockage depth—many marinas are quite shallow.

Contact Key West Express ✉ *100 Grinnell St., Key West* ☎ *888/539–2628* ⊕ *www.seakeywestexpress.com.*

BUS TRAVEL

Those unwilling to tackle the route's 42 bridges and peak-time traffic can take **Greyhound's** Keys Shuttle, which has multiple daily departures from Miami International Airport.

Contacts Greyhound ☎ *800/231–2222* ⊕ *www.greyhound.com.* **Keys Shuttle** ✉ *1333 Overseas Hwy., Marathon* ☎ *888/765–9997* ⊕ *www.keysshuttle.com.*

CAR TRAVEL

By car, from Miami International Airport, follow signs to Coral Gables and Key West, which puts you on LeJeune Road, then Route 836 west. Take the Homestead Extension of Florida's Turnpike south (toll road), which ends at Florida City and connects to the Overseas Highway (U.S. 1). Tolls from the airport run approximately $3. Payment is collected via SunPass, a prepaid toll program, or with Toll-By-Plate, a system that photographs each vehicle's license plate and mails a monthly bill for tolls, plus a $2.50 administrative fee, to the vehicle's registered owner.

Vacationers traveling in their own cars can obtain a mini-SunPass sticker via mail before their trip for $4.99 and receive the cost back in toll credits and discounts. The pass also is available at many major Florida retailers and turnpike service plazas. It works on all Florida toll roads and many bridges. For details on purchasing a mini-SunPass, call or visit the website.

For visitors renting cars in Florida, most major rental companies have programs allowing customers to use the Toll-By-Plate system. Tolls, plus varying service fees, are automatically charged to the credit card used to rent the vehicle (along with a hefty service charge in most cases). For details, including pricing options at participating rental-car agencies, check the program website. Under no circumstances should motorists attempt to stop in high-speed electronic tolling lanes. Travelers can contact Florida's Turnpike Enterprise for more information about the all-electronic tolling on Florida's Turnpike.

The alternative from Florida City is Card Sound Road (Route 905A), which has a (cash-only) bridge toll of $1. SunPass isn't accepted. Continue to the only stop sign and turn right on Route 905, which rejoins the Overseas Highway 31 miles south of Florida City. The best Keys road map, published by the Homestead–Florida City Chamber of Commerce, can be obtained for $5.50 from the Tropical Everglades Visitor Center.

Contacts Florida's Turnpike Enterprise ☎ *800/749–7453* ⊕ *www. floridasturnpike.com.* **SunPass** ☎ *888/865–5352* ⊕ *www.sunpass.com.*

THE MILE MARKER SYSTEM

Getting lost in the Keys is almost impossible once you understand the unique address system. **Many addresses are simply given as a mile marker (MM) number.** The markers are small, green, rectangular signs along the side of the Overseas Highway (U.S. 1). They begin with MM 126, 1 mile south of Florida City, and end with MM 0, in Key West. **Keys residents use the abbreviation BS for the bayside of Overseas Highway and OS for the oceanside.** From Marathon to Key West, residents may refer to the bayside as the gulfside.

HOTELS

Throughout the Keys, the types of accommodations are remarkably varied, from 1950s-style motels to cozy inns to luxurious resorts. Most are on or near the ocean, so water sports are popular. Key West's lodging portfolio includes historic cottages, restored Conch houses, and large resorts. Some larger properties throughout the Keys charge a mandatory daily resort fee of $15 or more, which can cover equipment rental, fitness-center use, and other services. You can expect another 12.5% (or more) in state and county taxes. Some guesthouses and inns don't welcome children, and many don't permit smoking.

Hotel reviews have been shortened. For full information, visit Fodors.com.

RESTAURANTS

Seafood rules in the Keys, which is full of chef-owned restaurants with not-too-fancy food. Many restaurants serve cuisine that reflects the proximity of the Bahamas and Caribbean (you'll see the term "Floribbean" on many menus). Tropical fruits figure prominently—especially on the beverage side of the menu. Florida spiny lobster should be local and fresh from August to March, and stone crabs from mid-October to mid-May. And don't dare leave the islands without sampling conch, be it in a fritter or in ceviche. Keep an eye out for authentic key lime pie—yellow custard in a graham-cracker crust. If it's green, just say "no." Note: Particularly in Key West and particularly during spring break, the more affordable and casual restaurants can get loud and downright rowdy, with young visitors often more interested in drinking than eating. Live music contributes to the decibel levels. If you're more of the quiet, intimate-dining type, avoid such overly exuberant scenes by eating early or choosing a restaurant where the bar isn't the main focus.

WHAT IT COSTS				
	$	$$	$$$	$$$$
RESTAURANTS	under $16	$16–$20	$21–$30	over $30
HOTELS	under $201	$201–$300	$301–$400	over $400

Restaurant prices are the average cost of a main course at dinner or, if dinner is not served, at lunch. Hotel prices are the lowest cost of a standard double room in high season.

THE UPPER KEYS

Diving and snorkeling are the primary draws in the Upper Keys, thanks to the tropical coral reef that runs a few miles off the seaward coast. Divers of all skill levels benefit from accessible dive sites and an established tourism infrastructure. Fishing is another huge draw, especially around Islamorada, known for its sportfishing in both deep offshore waters and in the backcountry. Offshore islands accessible only by boat are popular destinations for kayakers. In short, if you don't like the water, you might get bored here.

Other nature lovers won't feel shortchanged. Within 1½ miles of the bay coast lie the mangrove trees and sandy shores of Everglades National Park, where naturalists lead tours of one of the world's few saltwater forests. Here you'll see endangered manatees, curious dolphins, and other underwater creatures. Although the number of birds has dwindled since John James Audubon captured their beauty on canvas, the rare Everglades snail kite, bald eagles, ospreys, and a colorful array of egrets and herons delight bird-watchers. At sunset, flocks take to the skies as they gather to find their night's roost, adding a swirl of activity to an otherwise quiet time of day.

The Upper Keys are full of low-key eateries where the owner is also the chef and the food is tasty and never too fussy. The one exception is Islamorada, where you'll find more upscale restaurants. Places to eat may close for a two- to four-week vacation during the slow season between mid-September and late October.

In the Upper Keys the accommodations are as varied as they are plentiful. The majority of lodgings are in small waterfront complexes with furnished one- or two-bedroom units. These places offer dockage and often arrange boating, diving, and fishing excursions. There are also larger resorts with every type of activity imaginable and smaller boutique hotels where the attraction is personalized service.

Depending on which way the wind blows and how close the property is to the highway, there may be some noise from Overseas Highway. If this is an annoyance for you, ask for a room as far from the traffic as possible. Some properties require two- or three-day minimum stays during holiday and high-season weekends. Conversely, discounts may apply for midweek, weekly, and monthly stays.

GETTING HERE AND AROUND

Airporter operates scheduled van and bus pickup service from all Miami International Airport (MIA) baggage areas to wherever you want to go in Key Largo ($50) and Islamorada ($55). Groups of three or more passengers receive discounts. There are three departures daily; reservations are required 48 hours in advance. The SuperShuttle charges about $165 for two passengers for trips from Miami International Airport to the Upper Keys; reservations are required. For a trip to the airport, place your request 24 hours in advance.

Contacts Airporter ☎ *305/852–3413, 800/830–3413.* **SuperShuttle** ☎ *305/871–2000* ⊕ *www.supershuttle.com.*

KEY LARGO

56 miles (90 km) south of Miami International Airport.
The first of the Upper Keys reachable by car, 30-mile-long Key Largo is also the largest island in the chain. Key Largo—named Cayo Largo ("Long Key") by the Spanish—makes a great introduction to the region. The history of Largo is similar to that of the rest of the Keys, with its succession of native people, pirates, wreckers, and developers. The first settlement on Key Largo was named Planter, back in the days of pineapple, and later, key lime plantations. For a time it was a convenient shipping port, but when the railroad arrived, Planter died on the vine. Today three communities—North Key Largo, Key Largo, and Tavernier—make up the whole of Key Largo.

If you've never tried diving, Key Largo is the perfect place to learn. Dozens of companies will be more than happy to show you the ropes. Nobody comes to Key Largo without visiting John Pennekamp Coral Reef State Park, one of the jewels of the state-park system. Also popular is the adjacent Key Largo National Marine Sanctuary, which encompasses about 190 square miles of coral reefs, seagrass beds, and mangrove estuaries. Both are good for underwater exploration.

Fishing is the other big draw, and world records are broken regularly. There are plenty of charter operations to help you find the big ones and teach you how to hook the elusive (but inedible) bonefish, sometimes known as the ghost fish. On land, restaurants will cook your catch or dish up their own offerings with inimitable style.

Key Largo offers all the conveniences of a major resort town, with most businesses lined up along Overseas Highway (U.S. 1), the four-lane highway that runs down the middle of the island. Cars whiz past at all hours—something to remember when you're booking a room. Most lodgings are on the highway, so you'll want to be as far from the road as possible.

GETTING HERE AND AROUND
Key Largo is 56 miles south of Miami International Airport, with the mile markers going from 105 to 91. The island runs northeast–southwest, with Overseas Highway running down the center. If the highway is your only glimpse of the island, you're likely to feel barraged by its tacky commercial side. Make a point of driving Route 905 in North Key Largo and down side streets to the marinas to get a better feel for it.

VISITOR INFORMATION
Contact **Key Largo Chamber of Commerce.** Stop in for brochures, directions, recommendations, or some colorful Key Largo T-shirts and gifts. ⊠ *MM 106 BS, 10600 Overseas Hwy.* ☎ *305/451–4747, 800/822–1088* ⊕ *www. keylargochamber.org.*

EXPLORING
Dagny Johnson Key Largo Hammock Botanical State Park. American crocodiles, mangrove cuckoos, white-crowned pigeons, Schaus swallowtail butterflies, mahogany mistletoe, wild cotton, and 100 other rare critters and plants inhabit these 2,400 acres, sandwiched between Crocodile

Lake National Wildlife Refuge and Pennekamp Coral Reef State Park. The park is also a user-friendly place to explore the largest remaining stand of the vast West Indian tropical hardwood hammock and mangrove wetland that once covered most of the Keys' upland areas. Interpretive signs describe many of the tropical tree species along a wide 1-mile paved road (2-mile round trip) that invites walking and biking. There are also more than 6 miles of nature trails accessible to bikes and wheelchairs. Pets are welcome if on a leash no longer than 6 feet. You'll also find restrooms, information kiosks, and picnic tables. ■ TIP➔ Rangers recommend not visiting when it's raining as the trees can drip poisonous sap. ✉ *Rte. 905 OS, 0.5 mile north of Overseas Hwy., North Key Largo* ☎ *305/451–1202* ⊕ *www.floridastateparks. org/keylargohammock* ⛁ *$2.50 (exact change needed)* ⊙ *Daily 8–sundown.*

FAMILY **Dolphin Cove.** This educational program begins at the facility's bayside lagoon with a get-acquainted session from a platform. After that, you slip into the water for some frolicking with your new dolphin pals. Options range from a sea lion swim (new at this location), to a shallow-water swim with a dolphin, to a hands-on structured swim with a dolphin. You can also spend the day shadowing a trainer for a hefty $670 fee. ✉ *MM 101.9 BS, 101900 Overseas Hwy.* ☎ *305/451–4060, 877/365–2683* ⊕ *www.dolphinscove.com* ⛁ *$10 admission only; interactive programs from $140* ⊙ *Daily 8–5.*

FAMILY **Dolphins Plus.** A sister property to Dolphin Cove, Dolphins Plus offers some of the same programs and the age requirement is lower. The cheapest option, a Natural Swim program, begins with a one-hour briefing; then you enter the water to become totally immersed in the dolphins' world. In this visual orientation, participants snorkel but are not allowed to touch the dolphins. For tactile interaction (kissing, fin tows, etc.), sign up for the Structured Swim program, which is more expensive. ✉ *MM 99, 31 Corrine Pl.* ☎ *305/451–1993, 866/860–7946* ⊕ *www.dolphinsplus.com* ⛁ *Programs from $165* ⊙ *Daily 8–5.*

FAMILY **Jacobs Aquatic Center.** Take the plunge at one of three swimming pools: an 8-lane, 25-meter lap pool with two diving boards; a 3- to 4-foot-deep pool accessible to people with mobility challenges; and an interactive children's play pool with a waterslide, pirate ship, waterfall, and sloping zero entry instead of steps. Because so few of the motels in Key Largo have pools, it remains a popular destination for visiting families. ✉ *Key Largo Community Park, 320 Laguna Ave., at St. Croix Pl.* ☎ *305/453–7946* ⊕ *www.jacobsaquaticcenter.org* ⛁ *$12 ($2 discount weekdays)* ⊙ *Daily 10–6 (10–7 in summer).*

BEACHES

FAMILY **John Pennekamp Coral Reef State Park.** This state park is on everyone's
Fodor's Choice list for easy access to the best diving and snorkeling in Florida. The
★ underwater treasure encompasses 78 square miles of coral reefs and sea-grass beds. It lies adjacent to the Florida Keys National Marine Sanctuary, which contains 40 of the 52 species of coral in the Atlantic Reef System and nearly 600 varieties of fish, from the colorful parrot fish to the demure cocoa damselfish. Whatever you do, get in the

water. Snorkeling and diving trips ($30 and $55, respectively, equipment extra) and glass-bottom-boat rides to the reef ($24) are available, weather permitting. One of the most popular snorkel trips is to see *Christ of the Deep*, the 2-ton underwater statue of Jesus. The park also has nature trails, two man-made beaches, picnic shelters, a snack bar, and a campground. **Amenities:** food and drink; parking (fee); showers; toilets; water sports. **Best for:** snorkeling; swimming. ⊠ *MM 102.5 OS, 102601 Overseas Hwy.* ☎ *305/451–1202 for park, 305/451–6300 for excursions* ⊕ *www.pennekamppark.com, www.floridastateparks.org/ pennekamp* 🖃 *$4.50 for 1 person in vehicle, $8 for 2–8 people, $2 for pedestrians and cyclists or extra people (plus a $0.50 per-person county surcharge)* ⊙ *Daily 8–sunset.*

WHERE TO EAT

$$$
SEAFOOD
Fodor's Choice
★

✕ **Buzzard's Roost Grill and Pub.** The views are nice at this waterfront restaurant but the food is what gets your attention. Burgers, fish tacos, and seafood baskets are lunch faves. Dinner is about seafood and steaks, any way you like them. Try the smoked-fish dip, served with Armenian heart-shaped lavash crackers. Look for the big signs on U.S. 1 that direct you where to turn—it's worth finding. 💲 *Average main: $21* ⊠ *Garden Cove Marina, 21 Garden Cove Dr., Northernmost Key Largo* ☎ *305/453–3746* ⊕ *www.buzzardsroostkeylargo.com.*

$$$
SEAFOOD

✕ **The Fish House.** Restaurants not on the water have to produce the highest quality food to survive in the Keys. That's how the Fish House has succeeded since the 1980s—so much so that it built the Fish House Encore (a fancier version) next door to accommodate fans. The pan-sautéed catch of the day is a long-standing favorite, as is the "Matecumbe-style" preparation—baked with tomatoes, capers, olive oil, and lemon juice, it will make you moan with pleasure. Prefer shellfish? Choose from shrimp, lobster, and (mid-October to mid-May) stone crab. The smoked fish chunks are the best in the Keys. The only thing bland is their side dishes: simple boiled red potatoes, a hunk of corn on the cob, or black beans and rice. For a sweet ending, the homemade key lime pie is award-winning. 💲 *Average main: $21* ⊠ *MM 102.4 OS, 102341 Overseas Hwy.* ☎ *305/451–4665* ⊕ *www.fishhouse.com* ⚞ *Reservations not accepted* ⊙ *Closed Sept.* ⚞ *American Express not accepted.*

$
AMERICAN

✕ **Harriette's Restaurant.** If you're looking for comfort food—like melt-in-your-mouth biscuits the size of a salad plate—try this refreshing throwback. The kitchen makes muffins daily in 13 different flavors like mango, coconut, and key lime. Since the early 1980s, owner Harriette Mattson has been here to personally greet guests who come for the to-die-for omelets and old-fashioned hotcakes with sausage or bacon. For something unique, try the conch burger and eggs. At lunch, Harriette shines in the burger department, and her soups—from garlic tomato to chili—are homemade. 💲 *Average main: $8* ⊠ *MM 95.7 BS, 95710 Overseas Hwy.* ☎ *305/852–8689* ⚞ *Reservations not accepted* ⊙ *No dinner* ⚞ *American Express not accepted.*

$$
SEAFOOD

✕ **JJ's Big Chill.** Owned by former NFL coach, Jimmy Johnson, this waterfront establishment offers three entertaining experiences, and all are big winners. You'll find the best sports bar in the Upper Keys complete with the coach's Super Bowl trophies, a main restaurant with all-glass indoor seating and a waterfront deck, and an enormous outdoor tiki bar with entertainment seven nights a week. There's even a pool and cabana club where (for an entrance fee) you can spend the day sunning. Menu favorites are the Parmesan-crusted snapper and brick-oven roasted chicken wings, but don't miss the tuna nachos—as delicious as they are artfully presented. As the sun sets over the bay, enjoy the views and a slice of white chocolate–macadamia cheesecake. Ⓢ *Average main: $16* ✉ *MM 104 BS, 104000 Overseas Hwy.* ☎ *305/453–9066* ⊕ *www.jjsbigchill.com.*

$ ✕ **Key Largo Conch House.** Tucked into the trees along the Overseas Highway, this Victorian-style home (family-owned since 2004) and its true-to-the-Keys style of cooking is worth seeking out—at least the Food Network and the Travel Channel have thought so in the past. The Old South veranda and patio seating are ideal for winter dining, but indoors the seating is tighter. Raisin pecan French toast and seven varieties of Benedicts, including conch, are reason enough to rise early to get your fresh coffee fix. Lunch and dinner menus cover all bases, from a conch chowder bread bowl and vegetarian wraps to lobster and conch ceviche. Lionfish is proudly served when available, as is local yellowtail snapper. Interesting fact: the restaurant's "loo" was voted "Best of" for local restaurants. Ⓢ *Average main: $15* ✉ *MM 100.2, 100211 Overseas Hwy.* ☎ *305/453–4844* ⊕ *www.keylargoconchhouse.com* ⌦ *Reservations essential.*

AMERICAN

$ ✕ **Mrs. Mac's Kitchen.** Townies pack the counters and booths at this tiny eatery, where license plates are stuck on the walls and made into chandeliers, for everything from blackened prime rib to crab cakes. Every night is themed including Meatloaf Mondays, Italian Wednesdays, and Seafood Sensation (offered Friday and Saturday). There's also a champagne breakfast (at this original location) and an assortment of tasty Angus beef burgers, sandwiches, a famous chili, and key lime freeze (a tangy concoction somewhere between a shake and a float). In season, ask about the hogfish special du jour. A second location, Mrs. Mac's Kitchen 2, is located half a mile south (✉ *MM 99 Center, 99020 Overseas Hwy.*), also in Key Largo. The newer location offers a similar menu, a full bar, and double the seating space. It's also kid-friendly. Ⓢ *Average main: $15* ✉ *MM 99.4 BS, 99336 Overseas Hwy.* ☎ *305/451–3722, 305/451–6227* ⊕ *www.mrsmacskitchen.com* ⊙ *Closed Sun.*

SEAFOOD

$$$ ✕ **Sundowners.** The name doesn't lie. If it's a clear night and you can snag a reservation, this restaurant will treat you to a sherbet-hue sunset over Florida Bay. If you're here in mild weather—anytime other than the dog days of summer or the rare winter cold snap—the best seats are on the patio. The food is excellent: try the key lime seafood, a happy combo of sautéed shrimp, lobster, and lump crabmeat swimming in a tangy sauce spiked with Tabasco served over penne or rice. Wednesday and Saturday are all about prime rib, and Friday draws the crowds with an all-you-can-eat fish fry. Vegetarian and gluten-free options are available. To beat the crowds, stop in for lunch, which offers the same great food, minus the hassle. Ⓢ *Average main: $22* ✉ *MM 104 BS, 103900 Overseas Hwy.* ☎ *305/451–4502* ⊕ *sundownerskeylargo.com* ⌦ *Reservations essential.*

AMERICAN

4

WHERE TO STAY

$$ B&B/INN 🏨 **Azul del Mar.** The dock points the way to many beautiful sunsets at this no-smoking, adults-only boutique hotel, which Karol Marsden (an ad exec) and her husband Dominic (a travel photographer) have transformed from a run-down mom-and-pop place into a waterfront gem. **Pros:** great garden; good location; sophisticated design. **Cons:** small beach; high-priced; minimum stays during holidays. [$] *Rooms from: $279* ✉ *MM 104.3 BS, 104300 Overseas Hwy.* ☎ *305/451–0337, 888/253–2985* 🌐 *www.azulkeylargo.com* 🛏 *2 studios, 3 1-bedroom suites, 1 2-bedroom suite* 🍴 *No meals.*

$ RESORT 🏨 **Coconut Bay Resort & Bay Harbor Lodge.** Some 200 feet of waterfront is the main attraction at these side-by-side sister properties that offer a choice between smaller rooms and larger separate cottages. **Pros:** bay front; neatly kept gardens; walking distance to restaurants; complimentary kayak and paddleboat use. **Cons:** a bit dated; small sea-walled sand beach. [$] *Rooms from: $175* ✉ *MM 97.7 BS, 97702 Overseas Hwy.* ☎ *305/852–1625, 800/385–0986* 🌐 *www.coconutbaykeylargo.com* 🛏 *7 rooms, 5 efficiencies, 2 suites, 1 2-bedroom villa, 6 1-bedroom cottages* 🍴 *No meals.*

$$ B&B/INN 🏨 **Coconut Palm Inn.** You'd never find this waterfront haven unless someone told you it was there, as it's tucked into a residential neighborhood beneath towering palms and native gumbo limbos. **Pros:** secluded; quiet; sophisticated feel. **Cons:** Front desk closes early each evening; no access to ice machine when staff leaves; breakfast is ho-hum. [$] *Rooms from: $279* ✉ *MM 92 BS, 198 Harborview Dr., via Jo-Jean Way off Overseas Hwy., Tavernier* ☎ *305/852–3017* 🌐 *www.coconutpalminn.com* 🛏 *13 rooms, 7 suites* 🍴 *Breakfast.*

$$ B&B/INN 🏨 **Dove Creek Lodge.** With its sherbet-hued rooms and plantation-style furnishings, these tropical-style units (19 in all) range in size from simple lodge rooms to luxury two-bedroom suites. **Pros:** luxurious rooms; walk to Snapper's restaurant; complimentary kayaks and Wi-Fi. **Cons:** no beach; some find the music from next door bothersome. [$] *Rooms from: $229* ✉ *MM 94.5 OS, 147 Seaside Ave.* ☎ *305/852–6200, 800/401–0057* 🌐 *www.dovecreeklodge.com* 🛏 *4 room, 10 suites* 🍴 *Breakfast.*

$$ RESORT Fodor's Choice ★ 🏨 **Hilton Key Largo Resort.** Nestled within a hardwood hammock (localese for uplands habitat where hardwood trees such as live oak grow) near the southern border of Everglades National Park, this sprawling resort had a $12-million renovation in 2012 and offers a full slate of amenities in a woodsy setting. **Pros:** nice nature trail on bay side; pretty pools with waterfalls; awesome trees; bicycles available for rent. **Cons:** some rooms overlook the parking lot; pools near the highway; expensive per-night resort fee. [$] *Rooms from: $219* ✉ *MM 97 BS, 97000 Overseas Hwy.* ☎ *305/852–5553, 888/871–3437* 🌐 *www.keylargoresort.com* 🛏 *190 rooms, 10 suites* 🍴 *No meals.*

$$ RENTAL 🏨 **Island Bay Resort.** When Mike and Carol Shipley took over this off-the-beaten-path resort in 2000, they revamped the 10 bayside cottages, improved the landscaping, and added touches such as hammocks and Adirondack chairs that make you feel like this is your own personal tropical playground. **Pros:** on the water; sunset views. **Cons:** most units are small; no pool; lacks on-site amenities. [$] *Rooms from: $209*

✉ *92530 Overseas Hwy.* ☎ *305/852–4087* 🌐 *www.islandbayresort.com* 🛏 *10 units* 🍴 *No meals.*

$$ RESORT Fodor's Choice ★ **Kona Kai Resort, Gallery & Botanic Gardens.** Brilliantly colored bougainvillea, coconut palm, and guava trees—and a botanical garden of other rare species—make this 2-acre adult hideaway one of the prettiest places to stay in the Keys. **Pros:** free custom tours of botanical gardens for guests; free use of sports equipment; knowledgeable staff. **Cons:** expensive; some rooms are very close together. [$] *Rooms from: $289* ✉ *MM 97.8 BS, 97802 Overseas Hwy.* ☎ *305/852–7200, 800/365–7829* 🌐 *www.konakairesort.com* 🛏 *8 suites, 3 rooms* ⏲ *Closed Sept.* 🍴 *No meals.*

$ RESORT FAMILY **Marriott's Key Largo Bay Beach Resort.** This 17-acre bayside resort has plenty of diversions, from diving to parasailing to a day spa. **Pros:** lots of activities; free covered parking; dive shop on property; free Wi-Fi. **Cons:** rooms facing highway can be noisy; thin walls. [$] *Rooms from: $139* ✉ *MM 103.8 BS, 103800 Overseas Hwy.* ☎ *305/453–0000, 866/849–3753* 🌐 *www.marriottkeylargo.com* 🛏 *132 rooms, 20 2-bedroom suites, 1 penthouse suite* 🍴 *No meals.*

$ HOTEL **The Pelican.** This 1950s throwback is reminiscent of the days when parents packed the kids into the station wagon and headed to no-frills seaside motels, complete with an old-timer fishing off the dock. **Pros:** free use of kayaks and a canoe; well-maintained dock; reasonable rates. **Cons:** some small rooms; basic accommodations and amenities. [$] *Rooms from: $110* ✉ *MM 99.3, 99340 Overseas Hwy.* ☎ *305/451–3576, 877/451–3576* 🌐 *www.hungrypelican.com* 🛏 *13 rooms, 4 efficiencies, 4 suites, 2 trailers* 🍴 *Breakfast.*

NIGHTLIFE

The semiweekly *Keynoter* (Wednesday and Saturday), weekly *Reporter* (Thursday), and Friday through Sunday editions of the *Miami Herald* are the best sources of information on entertainment and nightlife.

Breezers Tiki Bar & Grille. Mingle with locals over cocktails and sunsets at Marriott's Key Largo Bay Beach Resort. ✉ *Marriott Key Largo Bay Beach Resort, 103800 Overseas Hwy.* ☎ *305/453–0000.*

Caribbean Club. Walls plastered with Bogart memorabilia remind customers that the classic 1948 Bogart–Bacall flick *Key Largo* has a connection with this worn watering hole. Although no food is served and the floors are bare concrete, this landmark draws boaters, curious visitors, and local barflies to its humble bar stools and pool tables. But the real magic is around back, where you can grab a seat on the deck and catch a postcard-perfect sunset. Live music draws revelers Thursday through Sunday. ✉ *MM 104 BS, 10404 Overseas Hwy.* ☎ *305/451–4466.*

SHOPPING

For the most part, shopping is sporadic in Key Largo, with a couple of shopping centers and fewer galleries than you find on the other big islands. If you're looking to buy scuba or snorkeling equipment, you'll have plenty of places from which to choose.

Bluewater Potters. Bluewater Potters creates functional and decorative ceramics ranging from signature vases and kitchenware to one-of-a-kind pieces where the owners' creative talent at the wheel blazes. In addition to their main gallery location in Key Largo, find them in the new Morada Way Arts and Culture District in Islamorada at MM 81.5. ⊠ *MM 102.9 OS, 102991 Overseas Hwy.* ☎ *305/453–1920* ⊕ *www. bluewaterpotters.com.*

Fodor's Choice **Key Largo Chocolates.** Specializing in key lime truffles made with quality
★ Belgian chocolate, this is the only chocolate factory in the entire Florida Keys. But you'll find much more than just the finest white, milk, and dark chocolate truffles; try their cupcakes, ice cream, and famous "chocodiles." Another fan favorite is the salted turtles, which are worth every calorie. Chocolate classes are also available for kids and adults, and a small gift area showcases local art, jewelry, hot sauces, and other goodies. Look for the bright green and pink building. ⊠ *MM 100 BS, 100471 Overseas Hwy.* ☎ *305/453–6613* ⊕ *www.keylargochocolates.com.*

Randy's Florida Keys Gift Co. Since 1989, Randy's has been "the" place for unique gifts. Owner Randy and his wife Lisa aren't only fantastic at stocking the store with a plethora of items, they're well respected in the community for their generosity and dedication. Stop in and say hello then browse the tight aisles and loaded shelves filled with key lime candles, books, wood carvings, jewelry, clothing, T-shirts, and eclectic, tropical decor items. This friendly shop prides itself on carrying wares from local craftsmen and there's something for every budget. ⊠ *1102421 Overseas Hwy.* ✢ *Right on U.S. 1, next to the Sandal Factory Outlet* ☎ *305/453–9229* ⊕ *www.keysmermaid.com.*

SPORTS AND THE OUTDOORS

BOATING

Everglades Eco-Tours. Captain Sterling operates Everglades and Florida Bay ecology tours and more expensive sunset cruises. You can see dolphins, manatees, and birds from the casual comfort of his pontoon boat, equipped with PVC chairs. Bring your own food and drinks. ⊠ *Sundowners Restaurant, MM 104 BS, 103900 Overseas Hwy.* ☎ *305/853– 5161, 888/224–6044* ⊕ *www.captainsterling.com* ⊠ *From $50.*

M.V. Key Largo Princess. Two-hour glass-bottom-boat trips and sunset cruises on a luxury 70-foot motor yacht with a 280-square-foot glass viewing area depart from the Holiday Inn docks three times a day. ⊠ *Holiday Inn, MM 100 OS,99701 Overseas Hwy.* ☎ *305/451–4655, 877/648–8129* ⊕ *www.keylargoprincess.com* ⊠ *$30.*

CANOEING AND KAYAKING

Sea kayaking continues to gain popularity in the Keys. You can paddle for a few hours or the whole day, on your own or with a guide. Some outfitters even offer overnight trips. The **Florida Keys Overseas Paddling Trail,** part of a statewide system, runs from Key Largo to Key West. You can paddle the entire distance, 110 miles on the Atlantic side, which takes 9–10 days. The trail also runs the chain's length on the bayside, which is a longer route.

Coral Reef Park Co. At John Pennekamp Coral Reef State Park, this operator has a fleet of canoes and kayaks for gliding around the 2½-mile mangrove trail or along the coast. Powerboat rentals also available. ⊠ *MM 102.5 OS, 102601 Overseas Hwy.* ☎ *305/451–6300* ⊕ *www. pennekamppark.com* ⊠ *Rentals from $12 per hr.*

Florida Bay Outfitters. Rent canoes or sea kayaks from this company, which sets up self-guided trips on the Florida Keys Overseas Paddling Trail, helps with trip planning, and matches equipment to your skill level. It also runs myriad guided tours around Key Largo. Take a full-moon paddle or a one- to seven-day canoe or kayak tour to the Everglades, Lignumvitae Key, or Indian Key. ✉ *MM 104 BS, 104050 Overseas Hwy.* ☎ *305/451–3018* ⊕ *www.kayakfloridakeys.com* ✇ *From $25.*

FISHING

Private charters and big head boats (so named because they charge "by the head") are great for anglers who don't have their own vessel.

Sailors Choice. Fishing excursions depart twice daily (half-day trips are cash-only), but the company also does private charters. The 65-foot boat leaves from the Holiday Inn docks. Rods, bait, and license are included. ✉ *Holiday Inn Resort & Marina, MM 100 OS, 99701 Overseas Hwy.* ☎ *305/451–1802, 305/451–0041* ⊕ *www.sailorschoicefishingboat.com* ✇ *From $40.*

SCUBA DIVING AND SNORKELING

Much of what makes the Upper Keys a singular dive destination is variety. Places like Molasses Reef, which begins 3 feet below the surface and descends to 55 feet, have something for everyone, from novice snorkelers to experienced divers. The *Spiegel Grove,* a 510-foot vessel, lies in 130 feet of water, but its upper regions are only 60 feet below the surface. On rough days, Key Largo Undersea Park's Emerald Lagoon is a popular spot. Expect to pay about $80 for a two-tank, two-site dive trip with tanks and weights, or $35–$40 for a two-site snorkel outing. Get big discounts by booking multiple trips.

Amy Slate's Amoray Dive Resort. This outfit makes diving easy. Stroll down to the full-service dive shop (NAUI, PADI, TDI, and BSAC certified), then onto a 45-foot catamaran. ✉ *MM 104.2 BS, 104250 Overseas Hwy.* ☎ *305/451–3595, 800/426–6729* ⊕ *www.amoray.com* ✇ *From $85.*

Conch Republic Divers. Book diving instruction as well as scuba and snorkeling tours of all the wrecks and reefs of the Upper Keys. Two-location dives are the standard, and you'll pay an extra $20 for tank and weights. ✉ *MM 90.8 BS, 90800 Overseas Hwy.* ☎ *305/852–1655, 800/274–3483* ⊕ *www.conchrepublicdivers.com* ✇ *From $65.*

Coral Reef Park Co. At John Pennekamp Coral Reef State Park, this company gives 3½-hour scuba and 2½-hour snorkeling tours of the park. In addition to the great location and the dependability it's also suited for water adventurers of all levels. ✉ *MM 102.5 OS, 102601 Overseas Hwy.* ☎ *305/451–6300* ⊕ *www.pennekamppark.com* ✇ *From $30.*

Ocean Divers. The PADI five-star facility has been around since 1975 and offers day and night dives, a range of courses, and dive-lodging packages. Two-tank reef dives include tank and weight rental. There are also organized snorkeling trips with equipment. ✉ *MM 100 OS, 522 Caribbean Dr.* ☎ *305/451–1113, 800/451–1113* ⊕ *www.oceandivers.com* ✇ *Snorkel trips from $35, diving from $85.*

Fodor'sChoice **Quiescence Diving Services.** This operator sets itself apart in two ways: it
★ limits groups to six to ensure personal attention and offers both two-
dive day and night dives, as well as twilight dives when sea creatures
are most active. There are also organized snorkeling excursions. ⊠ *MM
103.5 BS, 103680 Overseas Hwy.* ☎ *305/451–2440* ⊕ *www.quiescence.
com* ✉ *Snorkel trips $49, diving from $75.*

ISLAMORADA

Islamorada is between mile markers 90.5 and 70.

Early settlers named this key after their schooner, *Island Home,* but
to make it sound more romantic they translated it into Spanish: *Isla
Morada.* The chamber of commerce prefers to use its literal transla-
tion "Purple Island," which refers either to a purple-shelled snail that
once inhabited these shores or to the brilliantly colored orchids and
bougainvilleas.

Early maps show Islamorada as encompassing only Upper Matecumbe
Key. But the incorporated "Village of Islands" is made up of a string of
islands that the Overseas Highway crosses, including Plantation Key,
Windley Key, Upper Matecumbe Key, Lower Matecumbe Key, Craig
Key, and Fiesta Key. In addition, two state-park islands accessible only
by boat—Indian Key and Lignumvitae Key—belong to the group.

Islamorada (locals pronounce it *eye*-la-mor-*ah*-da) is one of the world's
top sportfishing destinations. For nearly 100 years, seasoned anglers
have fished these clear, warm waters teeming with trophy-worthy fish.
There are numerous options for those in search of the big ones, including chartering a boat with its own crew or heading out on a vessel
rented from one of the plethora of marinas along this 20-mile stretch
of the Overseas Highway.

ESSENTIALS

Visitor Information Islamorada Chamber of Commerce & Visitors Center
⊠ *MM 87.1 BS, 87100 Overseas Hwy.* ☎ *305/664–4503, 800/322–5397* ⊕ *www.
islamoradachamber.com.*

EXPLORING

Florida Keys Memorial / Hurricane Monument. On Monday, September 2,
1935, more than 400 people perished when the most intense hurricane
to make landfall in the U.S. swept through this area of the Keys. Two
years later, the Florida Keys Memorial was dedicated in their honor.
Native coral rock, known as keystone, covers the 18-foot obelisk monument that marks the remains of over 300 storm victims. A sculpted
plaque of bending palms and waves graces the front (although many
are bothered that the palms are bending in the wrong direction). In
1995, the memorial was placed on the National Register of Historic
Places. ⊠ *MM 81.5, OS, 81000 Overseas Hwy., Upper Matecumbe
Key* ✉ *Free.*

History of Diving Museum. Adding to the region's reputation for world-
class diving, this museum plunges into the history of man's thirst for
undersea exploration. Among its 13 galleries of interactive and other
interesting displays are a submarine and helmet re-created from the film

Islamorada's warm waters attract large fish and the anglers and charter captains who want to catch them.

20,000 Leagues Under the Sea. Vintage U.S. Navy equipment, diving helmets from around the world, and early scuba gear explore 4,000 years of diving history. For the grand finale, spend $3 for a mouthpiece and sing your favorite tune at the helium bar. There are extended hours (until 7 pm) on the third Wednesday of every month. ✉ *MM 83 BS, 82990 Overseas Hwy., Upper Matecumbe Key* ☎ *305/664–9737* ⊕ *www.divingmuseum.org* ✉ *$12* ☉ *Daily 10–5.*

Islamorada Founder's Park. This public park is the gem of Islamorada and boasts a palm-shaded beach, swimming pool, marina, skate park, tennis, and plenty of other facilities. If you want to rent a boat or learn to sail, businesses here can help you. If you're staying in Islamorada, admission is free. Those staying elsewhere pay $8 to enter the park. Either way, you pay an additional $3 to use the Olympic-size pool. A spiffy amphitheater hosts concerts, plays, and shows. The shallow water beach is ideal for swimming and families with little ones. Showers and bathrooms beachside. ✉ *MM 87 BS, 87000 Overseas Hwy., Plantation Key* ☎ *305/853–1685.*

FAMILY **Robbie's Marina.** Huge, prehistoric-looking denizens of the not-so-deep, silver-sided tarpon congregate around the docks at this marina on Lower Matecumbe Key. Children—and lots of adults—pay $3 for a bucket of sardines to feed them and $1 each for dock admission. Spend some time hanging out at this authentic Keys community, where you can grab a bite to eat indoors or out, shop at a slew of artisans' booths, or charter a boat, kayak, or other water craft. ✉ *MM 77.5 BS, 77522 Overseas Hwy., Lower Matecumbe Key* ☎ *305/664–9814, 877/664–8498* ⊕ *www.robbies.com* ✉ *Dock access $1* ☉ *Daily sunrise–sunset.*

FAMILY **Theater of the Sea.** The second-oldest marine-mammal center in the world doesn't attempt to compete with more modern, more expensive parks. Even so, it's among the better attractions north of Key West, especially if you have kids in tow. In addition to marine life exhibits and shows, you can make reservations for up-close-and-personal encounters like a swim with a dolphin or sea lion, or stingray and turtle feedings (which include general admission; reservations required). These are popular, so reserve in advance. Ride a "bottomless" boat to see what's below the waves and take a guided tour of the marine-life exhibits. Nonstop animal shows highlight conservation issues. You can stop for lunch at the grill, shop in the extensive gift shop, or sunbathe and swim at their private beach. This easily could be an all-day attraction. ⊠ *MM 84.5 OS, 84721 Overseas Hwy., Windley Key* ☏ *305/664–2431* ⊕ *www.theaterofthesea. com* ✉ *$31.95; interaction programs $35–$185* ⊙ *Daily 9:30–5 (last ticket sold at 3:30).*

Upper Matecumbe Key. This was one of the first of the Upper Keys to be permanently settled. Early homesteaders were so successful at growing pineapples in the rocky soil that at one time the island yielded the country's largest annual crop. However, foreign competition and the hurricane of 1935 killed the industry. Today, life centers on fishing and tourism, and the island is filled with everything from bait shops and charter boats to eclectic galleries and fusion restaurants. ⊠ *MM 84–79.*

OFF THE BEATEN PATH **Indian Key Historic State Park.** Mystery surrounds 10-acre Indian Key, on the ocean side of the Matecumbe islands. Before it became one of the first European settlements outside of Key West, it was inhabited by American Indians for several thousand years. The islet served as a base for 19th-century shipwreck salvagers until an Indian attack wiped out the settlement in 1840. Dr. Henry Perrine, a noted botanist, was killed in the raid. Today his plants grow in the town's ruins. Most people kayak or canoe here from Indian Key Fill or take a boat from Robbie's Marina to tour the nature trails and the town ruins or to snorkel. There are no restrooms or picnic facilities on Indian Key. ☏ *305/664–2540 for park* ⊕ *www.floridastateparks.org/indiankey* ✉ *Free* ⊙ *Daily 8–5.*

OFF THE BEATEN PATH **Lignumvitae Key Botanical State Park.** On the National Register of Historic Places, this 280-acre bay-side island is the site of a virgin hardwood forest and the 1919 home of chemical magnate William Matheson. His caretaker's cottage serves as the park's visitor center. Access is by boat—your own, a rented vessel, or a tour operated from Robbie's Marina. The tour leaves at 8:30 am Friday through Sunday and takes in both Lignumvitae and Indian keys (reservations required). Paddling here from Indian Key Fill, at MM 78.5, is a popular pastime. The only way to do the trails is by a guided ranger walk, offered at 10 am and 2 pm Friday to Sunday. Wear long sleeves and pants, and bring mosquito repellent. On the first Saturday in December is the Lignumvitae Christmas Celebration, when the historic home is decorated 1930s-style. ☏ *305/664–2540 for park, 305/664–8070 for boat tours* ⊕ *www.floridastateparks.org/lignumvitaekey* ✉ *$1 for ranger tours, $35 for boat tours* ⊙ *Park Thurs.–Mon. 8–5, house tours Fri.–Sun. at 10 and 2.*

Windley Key Fossil Reef Geological State Park. The fossilized-coral reef, dating back about 125,000 years, demonstrates that the Florida Keys were once beneath the ocean. Excavation of Windley Key's limestone bed by the Florida East Coast Railway exposed the petrified reef, full of beautifully fossilized brain coral and sea ferns. Visitors can see the fossils along a 300-foot quarry wall when hiking the park's three trails. There are guided (Friday, Saturday, and Sunday only) and self-guided tours along the trails, which lead to the railway's old quarrying equipment and cutting pits, where you can make rubbings of the quarry walls. The **Alison Fahrer Environmental Education Center** holds historic, biological, and geological displays about the area, including videos. The first Saturday in March is Windley Key Day, when the park sells native plants and hosts environmental exhibits. ✉ *MM 84.9 BS, Windley Key* ☎ *305/664–2540* 🌐 *www.floridastateparks.org/windleykey* 🎟 *$2.50, plus $2 for guided tours* 🕒 *Education center Fri.–Sun. 9–5 (tours at 10 and 2).*

BEACHES

Anne's Beach Park. On Lower Matecumbe Key this popular village park is named for a local environmental activist. Its "beach" (really a typical Keys-style sand flat with a gentle slope) is best enjoyed at low tide. The nicest feature here is an elevated, wooden half-mile boardwalk that meanders through a natural wetland hammock. Covered picnic areas along the way give you places to linger and enjoy the view. Restrooms are at the north end. Weekends are packed with Miami day-trippers as it's the only public beach until you reach Marathon. **Amenities:** parking (no fee); toilets. **Best for:** partiers; snorkeling; swimming; windsurfing. ✉ *MM 73.5 OS, Lower Matecumbe Key* ☎ *305/853–1685.*

WHERE TO EAT

$$$ SEAFOOD Fodor's Choice ★

✕ **Chef Michael's.** Peace. Love. Hogfish. That's the motto of this local favorite that's been making big waves since its opening in 2011 with Chef Michael Ledwith at the helm. Sit outdoors on the covered wood deck and tap your toes to the live music, or dine inside amid dark wood floors and white linens. Seafood is selected fresh daily, then elegantly prepared with a splash of tropical flair. Try hogfish with mango sauce, or the catch "Juliette" with shrimp, scallops, chardonnay butter, and toasted almonds. Carnivores can feast on prime-grade beef, carved in-house—that kind of marbling just melts in your mouth. Chef Michael even grows his own herbs, right out the kitchen door. How about a watermelon mint sangria? Just say yes. Gluten-free and vegetarian dishes are available. $ *Average main: $29* ✉ *MM 81.7, 81671 Overseas Hwy., Upper Matecumbe Key* ☎ *305/664–0640* 🌐 *www.foodtotalkabout.com* ✍ *Reservations essential* 🕒 *No lunch Mon.–Sat.*

$$ SEAFOOD

✕ **Hungry Tarpon.** As part of the colorful, bustling Old Florida scene at Robbie's Marina, you know that the seafood here is fresh and top quality. The extensive menu seems as if it's bigger than the dining space, which consists of a few tables and counter seating indoors, plus tables out back under the mangrove trees, close to where tourists pay to feed the tarpon in the marina. While tarpon are snacking on sardines, diners enjoy quite the impressive smattering of dishes for breakfast, lunch, and dinner. Specialties include biscuits and gravy, grilled ahi tuna nachos, a Matecumbe fish sandwich with provolone and bacon on grilled sourdough, and a shrimp burrito. $ *Average main: $19* ✉ *MM 77.5 BS, 77522 Overseas Hwy., Lower Matecumbe Key* ☎ *305/664–0535* ⊕ *www.hungrytarpon.com* ⚓ *Reservations not accepted.*

$ ✕ **Islamorada Fish Company.** When a restaurant is owned by Bass Pro
SEAFOOD Shops, you know the seafood should be as fresh as you can get it. The
FAMILY fun begins in the parking lot with painted white fish marking the parking spaces. The restaurant is housed in an open-air, oversized tiki hut right on Florida Bay, making this the quintessential Keys experience. There's a small, low-key tiki bar area if you prefer a stool to a table. Menu highlights include cracked conch beaten 'til tender and fried crispy, and Grouper Portofino, which will keep you coming back for more. Each afternoon, the staff feed the fish in the bay. Jump out of your seat and walk over for a close-up view of snapper, large tarpon, and even sharks. $ *Average main: $15* ✉ *MM 81.5 BS, 81532 Overseas Hwy., Windley Key* ☎ *305/664–9271* ⊕ *restaurants.basspro.com/ fishcompany/Islamorada* ☾ *Daily 11–10.*

$ ✕ **Island Grill.** Don't be fooled by appearances; this shack on the water-
SEAFOOD front takes island breakfast, lunch, and dinner up a notch. The eclectic menu tempts you with such dishes as its famed "original tuna nachos," lobster rolls, and a nice selection of seafood and sandwiches. Southern-style shrimp and andouille sausage with grits join island-style specialties such as grilled ribs with guava barbecue sauce on the list of entrées. There's an air-conditioned dining room and bar as well as open seating under a vaulted porch ceiling. The outdoor bar hosts live entertainment Wednesday to Sunday. Don't be in a hurry; service is usually slow. $ *Average main: $12* ✉ *MM 85.5 OS, 85501 Overseas Hwy., Windley Key* ☎ *305/664–8400* ⊕ *www.keysislandgrill.com* ⚓ *Reservations not accepted.*

$$$ ✕ **Marker 88.** A few yards from Florida Bay, this seafood restaurant
SEAFOOD has been popular since the late '60s. Large picture windows offer great sunset views, but the bay is lovely no matter what time of day you visit. Outdoor dining is popular, too. Chef Bobby Stoky serves such irresistible entrées as onion-crusted mahimahi, crispy yellowtail snapper, and mangrove-honey-and-chipotle-glazed ribeye. In addition, there are a half-dozen burgers and sandwiches, and you can't miss the restaurant's famous key lime baked Alaska dessert. The extensive wine list is an oenophile's delight. $ *Average main: $28* ✉ *MM 88 BS, 88000 Overseas Hwy., Plantation Key* ☎ *305/852–9315* ⊕ *www.marker88. info* ⚓ *Reservations essential.*

$$$ ✕ **Morada Bay Beach Café.** This bayfront restaurant wins high marks for
ECLECTIC its surprisingly stellar cuisine, tables planted in the sand, and tiki torches
FAMILY that bathe the evening in romance. Entrées feature alluring combinations like fresh fish of the day sautéed with Meyer lemon butter and whole fried snapper with coconut rice. Seafood takes center stage, but you can always get roasted organic chicken or prime rib. Tapas and raw bar menus cater to smaller appetites or those who can't decide with offerings like fried calamari, conch fritters, and Wagyu beef sliders. Lunch adds interesting sandwiches to the mix. Sit in a dining room outfitted with surfboards, or outdoors on a beach, where the sunset puts on a mighty show and kids (and your feet) play in the sand. $ *Average*

main: $27 ✉ *MM 81 BS, 81600 Overseas Hwy., Upper Matecumbe Key* ☎ *305/664–0604* 🌐 *www.moradabay-restaurant.com.*

$$$$ FRENCH Fodor's Choice ★ 🍴 **Pierre's.** One of the Keys' most elegant restaurants, Pierre's marries colonial style with modern food trends. Full of interesting architectural artifacts, the place oozes style, especially the wicker chair–strewn veranda overlooking the bay. Save your best "tropical chic" duds for dinner here, so you don't stand out from your surroundings. The food, drawn from French and Floridian influences, is multilayered and beautifully presented. Among the seasonally changing appetizer choices, you might find smoked hogfish chowder and foie gras sliders with a butternut squash milk shake. A changing list of entrées might include hogfish meunière and scallops with pork belly tortellini. The downstairs bar is a perfect spot for catching sunsets, sipping martinis, and enjoying light eats. [$] *Average main: $35* ✉ *MM 81.5 BS, 81600 Overseas Hwy., Upper Matecumbe Key* ☎ *305/664–3225* 🌐 *www.moradabay.com* ✍ *Reservations essential* ⏲ *No lunch.*

4

WHERE TO STAY

$$ B&B/INN Fodor's Choice ★ 🏨 **Casa Morada.** This relic from the 1950s has been restyled into a suave, design-forward, all-suites property with outdoor showers and Jacuzzis in some of the suites. **Pros:** cool design; complimentary snacks and bottled water; complimentary use of bikes, kayaks, and snorkel gear. **Cons:** trailer park across the street; beach is small and inconsequential. [$] *Rooms from: $299* ✉ *MM 82 BS, 136 Madeira Rd., Upper Matecumbe Key* ☎ *305/664–0044, 888/881–3030* 🌐 *www.casamorada.com* 🛏 *16 suites* 🍽 *Breakfast.*

$$ RESORT Fodor's Choice ★ 🏨 **Cheeca Lodge & Spa.** At 27 acres, this may be the largest resort in the Keys, and it's also big on included amenities. **Pros:** beautifully landscaped grounds; new designer rooms; water-sports center on property. **Cons:** expensive rates; expensive resort fee; very busy. [$] *Rooms from: $299* ✉ *MM 82 OS, Box 527, Upper Matecumbe Key* ☎ *305/664–4651, 800/327–2888* 🌐 *www.cheeca.com* 🛏 *60 1-bedroom suites, 64 junior suites* 🍽 *No meals.*

$ HOTEL 🏨 **Drop Anchor Resort and Marina.** Immaculately maintained, this place has the feel of an old friend's beach house. **Pros:** bright and colorful; attention to detail; laid-back charm. **Cons:** noise from the highway; beach is better for fishing than swimming. [$] *Rooms from: $149* ✉ *MM 85 OS, 84959 Overseas Hwy., Windley Key* ☎ *305/664–4863, 888/664–4863* 🌐 *www.dropanchorresort.com* 🛏 *18 suites* 🍽 *No meals.*

$$ RESORT 🏨 **The Islander, A Guy Harvey Outpost Resort.** Guests here get to choose between a self-sufficient townhouse on the bay with room for a boat, or an oceanfront resort with on-site restaurants and oodles of amenities. **Pros:** spacious rooms; nice kitchens; eye-popping views. **Cons:** pricey for what you get; beach has rough sand. [$] *Rooms from: $249* ✉ *MM 82.1 OS, 82200 Overseas Hwy., Upper Matecumbe Key* ☎ *305/664–2031, 800/753–6002* 🌐 *www.guyharveyoutpostislamorada.com* 🛏 *114 rooms, 12 suites, 25 townhouses* 🍽 *Breakfast.*

$$$ HOTEL Fodor's Choice ★ 🏨 **The Moorings Village.** This tropical retreat is everything you imagine when you think of the Keys—from hammocks swaying between towering trees to sugar-white sand (arguably the Keys' best resort beach) lapped by aqua-green waves. **Pros:** romantic setting; good

dining options with room-charging privileges; beautiful beach. **Cons:** no room service; extra fee for housekeeping; daily resort fee for activities. *Rooms from: $375 MM 81.6 OS, 123 Beach Rd., Upper Matecumbe Key 305/664–4708 www.themooringsvillage.com 6 cottages, 12 houses No meals.*

$$ HOTEL Fodor's Choice ★ **Ocean House.** Islamorada's newest adult boutique hotel is situated right on the Atlantic, yet it's hidden from passersby amidst lush gardens. **Pros:** complimentary use of kayaks, snorkel equipment and bicycles; luxurious facilities and amenities. **Cons:** limited number of units means they're often booked solid; luxury comes at a price. *Rooms from: $299 MM 82 OS, 82885 Old Hwy., Windley Key 866/540–5520 www.oceanhousefloridakeys.com 8 suites Some meals.*

$$ RESORT **Postcard Inn Beach Resort & Marina at Holiday Isle.** After an $11-million renovation that encompassed updating everything from the rooms to the public spaces, this iconic property (formerly known as the Holiday Isle Beach Resort) has found new life. **Pros:** large private beach; heated pools; on-site restaurants including Shula's 2. **Cons:** rooms near Tiki bar are noisy; minimum stay required during peak times; bathrooms need updating. *Rooms from: $215 MM 84 OS, 84001 Overseas Hwy., Plantation Key 305/664–2321 www.holidayisle.com/Islamorada-beachclub 143 rooms No meals.*

$ HOTEL FAMILY **Ragged Edge Resort.** Nicely tucked away in a residential area at the ocean's edge, this family-owned hotel draws returning guests who'd rather fish off the dock and grill up dinner than loll around in Egyptian cotton sheets. **Pros:** oceanfront; boat docks and ramp; cheap rates. **Cons:** dated décor; off the beaten path. *Rooms from: $110 MM 86.5 OS, 243 Treasure Harbor Rd., Plantation Key 305/852–5389, 800/436–2023 www.ragged-edge.com 6 studios, 1 efficiency, 3 2-bedroom suites No meals.*

SHOPPING

Art galleries, upscale gift shops, and the mammoth World Wide Sportsman (if you want to look the part of a local fisherman, you must wear a shirt from here) make up the variety and superior style of Islamorada shopping.

Banyan Tree. A sharp-eyed husband-and-wife team successfully combines antiques and contemporary gifts for the home and garden with plants, pots, and trellises in a stylishly sophisticated indoor–outdoor setting. *MM 81.2 OS, 81197 Overseas Hwy., Upper Matecumbe Key 305/664–3433 www.banyantreegarden.com.*

Casa Mar Village. Change is good, and in this case, it's fantastic. What was once a row of worn-down buildings is now a merry blend of gift shops and galleries with the added bonus of a place selling fresh-roasted coffee. By day, these colorful shops glisten at their canalfront location; by nightfall, they're lit up like a lovely Christmastown. The offerings include the Jolly Pelican, Jewels by Vivi, the Little White Gallery, Olive Morada (upscale oils and vinegars), and the Fresh Press Cafe. *MM 90 OS, 90775 Old Hwy., Upper Matecumbe Key 305/522-0330.*

Gallery Morada. This gallery is a go-to destination for one-of-a-kind gifts, beautifully displayed blown glass, original sculptures, paintings, lithographs, and jewelry by 200 artists. Its location, front and center, makes it the gateway to the Morada Way Arts & Cultural District, an area with artist galleries, shops, potters, gardens, and culinary classes. ✉ *MM 81.6 OS, 81611 Old Hwy., Upper Matecumbe Key* ☎ *305/664–3650* ⊕ *www.gallerymorada.com.*

Rain Barrel Artisan Village. This is a natural and unhurried shopping showplace. Set in a tropical garden of shady trees, native shrubs, and orchids, the crafts village has shops selling the work of local and national artists as well as resident artists who sell work from their own studios. Have your photo taken with "Betsy," the giant Florida lobster, roadside. ✉ *MM 86.7 BS, 86700 Overseas Hwy., Plantation Key* ☎ *305/852–3084* ⊕ *www.seefloridaonline.com/rainbarrel/index.html.*

Redbone Gallery. One of the largest sportfishing–art galleries in Florida stocks hand-stitched clothing and giftware, in addition to work by wood and bronze sculptors such as Kendall van Sant; watercolorist C. D. Clarke; and painters Daniel Caldwell, David Hall, Steven Left, and Stacie Krupa. Proceeds benefit cystic fibrosis research. Find them in the Morada Way Arts & Cultural District. ✉ *MM 81.5 OS, 200 Morada Way, Upper Matecumbe Key* ☎ *305/664–2002* ⊕ *www.redbone.org.*

World Wide Sportsman. This two-level retail center sells upscale and everyday fishing equipment, resort clothing, sportfishing art, and other gifts. When you're tired of shopping, relax at the Zane Grey Long Key Lounge, located above the store—but not before you step up and into *Pilar,* a replica of Hemingway's boat. ✉ *MM 81.5 BS, 81576 Overseas Hwy., Upper Matecumbe Key* ☎ *305/664–4615, 800/327–2880.*

SPORTS AND THE OUTDOORS
BOATING
Marinas pop up every mile or so in the Islamorada area, so finding a rental or tour is no problem. Robbie's Marina is a prime example of a salty spot where you can find it all—from fishing charters and kayaking rentals to lunch and tarpon feeding.

Bump & Jump. You can rent both fishing and deck boats here (from 15 to 29 feet) by the day or the week. There's free local delivery for those without trailers. ✉ *MM 81.2 OS, 81197 Overseas Hwy., Upper Matecumbe Key* ☎ *305/664–9404, 877/453–9463* ⊕ *www.keysboatrental.com* 🖃 *Rentals from $145 per day.*

Houseboat Vacations of the Florida Keys. See the islands from the comfort of your own boat (captain's cap optional). The company maintains a fleet of 44- to 55-foot boats that accommodate up to 10 people and come outfitted with everything you need besides food. (You may provision yourself at a nearby grocery store.) There's a three-day minimum; weekly rates are available. Kayaks and paddleboards suitable for bayside use are also available. ✉ *MM 85.9 BS, 85944 Overseas Hwy.* ☎ *305/664–4009* ⊕ *www.baysidetikiboats.com* 🖃 *From $1,150.*

Robbie's Boat Rentals & Charters. This full-service company will even give you a crash course on how not to crash your boat. The rental fleet includes an 18-foot skiff with a 90-horsepower outboard to a 21-foot deck boat with a 130-horsepower engine. Robbie's also rents snorkeling gear (there's good snorkeling nearby) and sells bait, drinks and snacks. Want to hire a guide who knows the local waters and where

Kayak ready to be used on the beach in the Florida Keys

the fish lurk? Robbie's offers offshore-fishing trips, patch-reef trips, and party-boat fishing. Backcountry flats trips are a specialty. ⊠ *MM 77.5 BS, 77522 Overseas Hwy., Lower Matecumbe Key* ☎ *305/664–9814, 877/664–8498* ⊕ *www.robbies.com* 🖃 *From $185 per day.*

Treasure Harbor Marine. The Anderson family will provide everything you need for a bareboat sailing vacation at sea. They also give excellent advice on where to find the best anchorages, snorkeling spots, or lobstering sites. Vessels range from a 23.5-foot Hunter to a 41-foot Morgan Out Island. Boats can be rented by the day or week. Marina facilities include water, electric, ice machine, laundry, picnic tables, and restrooms with showers. Transient and longterm dockage available. A store sells snacks, beverages, and sundries. ⊠ *MM 86.5 OS, 200 Treasure Harbor Dr., Plantation Key* ☎ *305/852–2458, 800/352–2628* ⊕ *www.treasureharbor.com* 🖃 *From $160 per day.*

FISHING

Here in the self-proclaimed "sportfishing capital of the world," sailfish is the prime catch in the winter and dolphinfish (mahimahi) in the summer. Buchanan Bank just south of Islamorada is a good spot to try for tarpon in the spring. Blackfin tuna and amberjack are generally plentiful in the area, too. ■TIP→ **The Hump at Islamorada ranks highest among anglers' favorite fishing spots in Florida because of the incredible offshore marine life.**

Captain Ted Wilson. Go into the backcountry for bonefish, tarpon, redfish, snook, and shark aboard a 17-foot boat that accommodates up to three anglers. Two people can choose half- or full-day trips, two hour sunset bonefishing excursions, or evening fishing excursions. There's an extra

$100 charge for each additional person. ⊠ *MM 79.9 OS, 79851 Overseas Hwy., Upper Matecumbe Key* ☎ *305/942–5224, 305/664–9463* ⊕ *www.captaintedwilson.com* ✉ *Bonefishing from $250, half-day trips from $400.*

Florida Keys Fly Fish. Like other top fly-fishing and light-tackle guides, Captain Geoff Colmes helps his clients land trophy fish in the waters around the Keys. ⊠ *105 Palm La., Upper Matecumbe Key* ☎ *305/853–0741* ⊕ *www.floridakeysflyfish.com* ✉ *From $400.*

Florida Keys Outfitters. Long before fly-fishing became popular, Sandy Moret was fishing the Keys for bonefish, tarpon, and redfish. Now he attracts anglers from around the world on a quest for the big catch. His weekend fly-fishing classes include classroom instruction, equipment, and daily lunch. Guided fishing trips can be done for a half day or full day. Packages combining fishing and accommodations at Islander Resort are available. ⊠ *Green Turtle, MM 81.2, 81219 Overseas Hwy., Upper Matecumbe Key* ☎ *305/664–5423* ⊕ *www.floridakeysoutfitters. com* ✉ *Half-day trips from $496.*

Hubba Hubba Charters. Captain Ken Knudsen has fished the Keys waters since the 1970s. A licensed backcountry guide, he's ranked among Florida's top 10 by national fishing magazines. He offers four-hour sunset trips for tarpon and two-hour sunset trips for bonefish, as well as half- and full-day outings. Prices are for one or two anglers, and tackle and bait are included. ⊠ *MM 79.8 OS, Upper Matecumbe Key* ☎ *305/664–9281* ✉ *From $200.*

SCUBA DIVING AND SNORKELING

Florida Keys Dive Center. Dive from John Pennekamp Coral Reef State Park to Alligator Light with this outfitter. The center has two 46-foot Coast Guard–approved dive boats, offers scuba training, and is one of the few Keys dive centers to offer Nitrox and Trimix (mixed gas) diving. ⊠ *MM 90.5 OS, 90451 Overseas Hwy., Plantation Key* ☎ *305/852–4599, 800/433–8946* ⊕ *www.floridakeysdivectr.com* ✉ *Snorkeling from $38, diving from $65.*

Islamorada Dive Center. This one-stop dive shop has a resort, pool, restaurant, lessons, and twice-daily dive and snorkel trips. You can take a day trip with a two-tank dive or a one-tank night trip without equipment. Snorkel trips are also available. ⊠ *MM 84 OS, 84001 Overseas Hwy., Windley Key* ☎ *305/664–3483, 800/327–7070* ⊕ *www. islamoradadivecenter.com* ✉ *Snorkel trips from $45, diving from $80.*

WATER SPORTS

The Kayak Shack. You can rent kayaks for trips to Indian (about 20 minutes one way) and Lignumvitae (about 45 minutes one way) keys, two favorite destinations for paddlers. Kayaks can be rented for a half day—and you'll need plenty of time to explore those mangrove canopies. Pedal kayaks are also available and are a bit more expensive. The company also offers guided three-hour tours, including a snorkel trip to Indian Key. It also rents stand-up paddleboards, including instruction, and canoes. ⊠ *Robbie's Marina, MM 77.5 BS, 77522 Overseas Hwy., Lower Matecumbe Key* ☎ *305/664–4878* ⊕ *www.kayakthefloridakeys. com* ✉ *From $40 for single, $55 for double; guided trips from $45.*

EN ROUTE **Long Key Viaduct.** As you cross Long Key Channel, look beside you at the old viaduct. The second-longest bridge on the former rail line, this 2-mile-long structure has 222 reinforced-concrete arches. The old bridge is popular with cyclists and anglers, who fish off the sides day and night.

THE MIDDLE KEYS

Most of the activity in this part of the Florida Keys centers on the town of Marathon—the region's third-largest metropolitan area. On either end of it, smaller keys hold resorts, wildlife research and rehab facilities, a historic village, and a state park. The Middle Keys make a fitting transition from the Upper Keys to the Lower Keys not only geographically but mentally. Crossing Seven Mile Bridge prepares you for the slow pace and don't-give-a-damn attitude you'll find a little farther down the highway. Fishing is one of the main attractions—in fact, the region's commercial-fishing industry was founded here in the early 1800s. Diving is another popular pastime. There are many natural areas to enjoy in the Middle Keys, where mainland stress becomes an ever more distant memory.

If you get bridge fever—the heebie-jeebies when driving over long stretches of water—you may need a pair of blinders (or a couple of tranquilizers) before tackling the Middle Keys. Stretching from Conch Key to the far side of the Seven Mile Bridge, this zone is home to the region's two longest bridges: Long Key Viaduct and Seven Mile Bridge, both historic landmarks.

DUCK KEY

Duck Key is at mile marker 61.

Duck Key holds one of the region's nicest marina resorts, Hawks Cay, plus a boating-oriented residential community.

EXPLORING

Dolphin Connection. Hawk's Cay Resort's Dolphin Connection offers three programs, including Dockside Dolphins, a 30-minute encounter from the dry training docks; Dolphin Discovery, an in-water program that lasts about 45 minutes and lets you kiss, touch, and feed the dolphins; and Trainer for a Day, a three-hour session with the animal training team. ✉ *Hawk's Cay Resort, MM 61 OS,61 Hawks Cay Blvd.* ☎ *305/743–7000* 🌐 *www.dolphinconnection.com* 🎟 *From $60.*

WHERE TO EAT AND STAY

$$$ LATIN AMERICAN 🍴 **Alma.** A refreshing escape from the Middle Keys' same-old menus, Alma serves expertly prepared Florida and Latin-Caribbean dishes in an elegant setting. Nightly changing menus might include a trio of ceviche, ahi tuna with a wonderful garbanzo bean–tomato sauce, gnocchi and exotic mushroom ragout, or pan-seared Wagyu steak. Finish your meal with the silky, smooth, passion fruit crème brûlée, which has just the right amount of tartness to balance the delicate caramelized crust. [$] *Average main: $28* ✉ *Hawks Cay Resort, MM 61 OS, 61*

Hawks Cay Blvd. ☎ *305/743–7000, 888/432–2242* ⊕ *www.hawkscay. com* ⊘ *No lunch.*

$$ 🏨 **Hawks Cay Resort.** The 60-acre, Caribbean-style retreat with a full-
RESORT   service spa and restaurants has plenty to keep the kids occupied (and
FAMILY   adults happy). **Pros:** huge rooms; restful spa; full-service marina and dive
Fodor'sChoice   shop. **Cons:** no real beach; far from Marathon's attractions. 💲 *Rooms*
★   *from: $240* ✉ *MM 61 OS, 61 Hawks Cay Blvd.* ☎ *305/743–7000,
888/432–2242* ⊕ *www.hawkscay.com* ⚓ *161 rooms, 16 suites, 225
2- and 3-bedroom villas* 🍴 *No meals.*

GRASSY KEY

Grassy Key is between mile markers 60 and 57.

Local lore has it that this sleepy little key was named not for its veg-
etation—mostly native trees and shrubs—but for an early settler by
the name of Grassy. The key is inhabited primarily by a few families
operating small fishing camps and roadside motels. There's no marked
definition between it and Marathon, so it feels sort of like a suburb of
its much larger neighbor to the south. Grassy Key's sights tend toward
the natural, including a worthwhile dolphin attraction and a small
state park.

GETTING HERE AND AROUND
Most visitors arriving by air drive to this destination either from Miami
International Airport or Key West International Airport. Rental cars are
readily available at both, and in the long run, are the most convenient
means of transportation for getting here and touring around the Keys.

EXPLORING
Curry Hammock State Park. Looking for a slice of the Keys that's far
removed from tiki bars? On the ocean and bay sides of Overseas High-
way are 260 acres of upland hammock, wetlands, and mangroves.
On the bay side, there's a trail through thick hardwoods to a rocky
shoreline. The ocean side is more developed, with a sandy beach, a
clean bathhouse, picnic tables, a playground, grills, and a 28-site camp-
ground. Locals consider the paddling trails under canopies of arching
mangroves one of the best kayaking spots in the Keys. Manatees fre-
quent the area, and it's a great spot for bird-watching. Herons, egrets,
ibis, plovers, and sanderlings are commonly spotted. Raptors are often
seen in the park, especially during migration periods. ✉ *MM 57 OS,
56200 Overseas Hwy., Little Crawl Key* ☎ *305/289–2690* ⊕ *www.
floridastateparks.org/curryhammock* 💲 *$4.50 for 1 person, $6 for 2,
$0.50 per additional person* ⊘ *Daily 8–sunset.*

FAMILY   **Dolphin Research Center.** The 1963 movie *Flipper* popularized the notion
of humans interacting with dolphins, and Milton Santini, the film's cre-
ator, also opened this center, which is home to a colony of dolphins and
sea lions. The nonprofit center has educational sessions and programs
that allow you to greet the dolphins from dry land or play with them in
their watery habitat. You can even paint a T-shirt with a dolphin; you
pick the paint, the dolphin "designs" your shirt. The center also offers
five-day programs for children and adults with disabilities. ✉ *MM 59*

Continued on page 195

UNDER THE SEA
SNORKELING AND DIVING
IN THE FLORIDA KEYS by Lynne Helm

Up on the shore they work all day...

> While we devotin',
>
> Full time to floatin',
>
> Under the sea...

—"Under the Sea,"
from Disney's *Little Mermaid*

All Floridians—even those long-accustomed to balmy breezes and swaying palms—turn ecstatic at the mere thought of tripping off to the Florida Keys. Add the prospect of underwater adventure, and hot diggity, it's unparalleled bliss.

Perennially laid back, the Keys annually attract nearly 800,000 snorkeling and scuba diving aficionados, and why not? There's arguably no better destination to learn these sports that put you up close to the wonders of life under the sea.

THE BARRIER REEF
The continental United States' only living coral barrier reef stretches 5 mi offshore of the Keys and is a teeming backbone of marine life, ranging from brilliant corals to neon-colored fish from blue-striped grunts to green moray eels. This is the prime reason why the Keys are where you descend upon intricate natural coral formations and encrusted shipwrecks, some historic, others sunk by design to create artificial reefs that attract divers

and provide protection for marine life. Most diving sites have mooring buoys (nautical floats away from shore, sometimes marking specific sites); these let you tie up your boat so you don't need to drop anchor, which could damage the reef. Most of these sites also are near individual keys, where dozens of dive operators can cater to your needs.

Reef areas thrive in waters as shallow as 5 feet and as deep as 50 feet. Shallow reefs attract snorkelers, while deeper reefs suit divers of varying experience levels. The Keys' shallow diving offers two benefits: longer time safely spent on the bottom exploring, and more vibrant colors because of sunlight penetration. Most divers log maximum depths of 20 to 30 feet.

(left) Shallow-water coral reef, (top) Nine Foot Stake is a popular site for underwater photography.

WHERE TO SNORKEL AND DIVE

KEY WEST
Mile Marker 0–4

You can soak up a mesmerizing overview of submerged watery wonders at the **Florida Keys Eco-Discovery Center**, opened in 2007 on Key West's Truman

Nine Foot Stake

Annex waterfront. Both admission and parking are free at the 6,000 square–foot center (🕐 9–4 Tues.–Sat. ☎ 305/809–4750); interactive exhibits here focus on Keys marine life and habitats. Key West's offshore reefs are best accessed via professional charters, but it's easy to snorkel from shore at **Key West Marine Park**. Marked by a lighthouse, **Sand Key Reef** attracts snorkelers and scuba divers. **Joe's Tug**, at 65-foot depths, sets up encounters with Goliath grouper. **Ten-Fathom Ledge**, with coral caves and

dramatic overhangs, shelters lobster. The **Cayman Salvor**, a buoy tender sunk as an artificial reef in 1985, shelters baitfish. Patch reef **Nine Foot Stake**, submerged 10 to 25 feet, has soft corals and juvenile marine life. **Kedge Ledge** features a pair of coral-encrusted anchors from 18th-century sailing vessels. 🚹 *Florida Keys main visitor line at* ☎ *800/FLA-KEYS (352-5397).*

BIG PINE KEY/LOWER KEYS
Mile Marker 4–47

Many devotees feel a Florida dive adventure would not be complete without heading 5 mi from Big Pine Key to **Looe Key National Marine Sanctuary**, an underwater preserve named for the HMS Looe running aground in 1744. If you time your visit for July, you might hit the one-day free underwater music festival for snorkelers

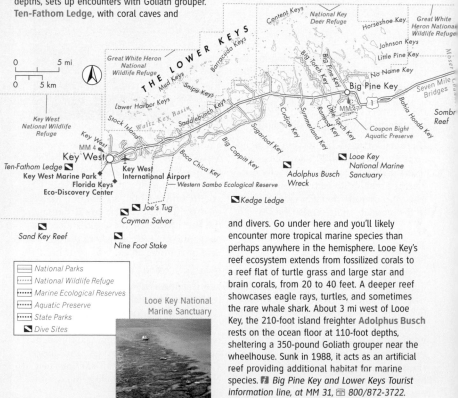

Looe Key National
Marine Sanctuary

and divers. Go under here and you'll likely encounter more tropical marine species than perhaps anywhere in the hemisphere. Looe Key's reef ecosystem extends from fossilized corals to a reef flat of turtle grass and large star and brain corals, from 20 to 40 feet. A deeper reef showcases eagle rays, turtles, and sometimes the rare whale shark. About 3 mi west of Looe Key, the 210-foot island freighter **Adolphus Busch** rests on the ocean floor at 110-foot depths, sheltering a 350-pound Goliath grouper near the wheelhouse. Sunk in 1988, it acts as an artificial reef providing additional habitat for marine species. 🚹 *Big Pine Key and Lower Keys Tourist information line, at MM 31,* ☎ *800/872-3722.*

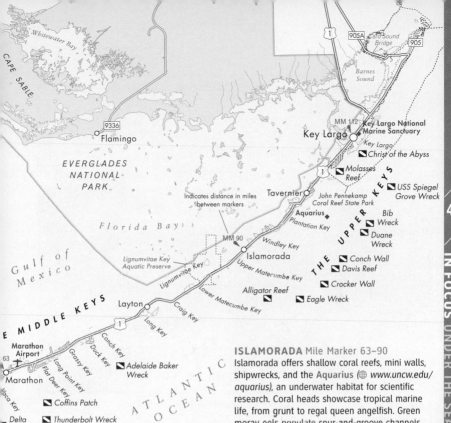

MARATHON/MIDDLE KEYS
Mile Marker 47–63
The Middle Keys yield
a marine wilderness
of a spur-and-groove
coral and patch reefs.
The Adelaide Baker
historic shipwreck
has a pair of stacks
in 25 feet of water.

Sombrero Reef

Popular Sombrero Reef, with coral canyons
and archways, is marked by a 140-foot lighted
tower. Six distinct patch reefs known as
Coffin's Patch have shallow elkhorn forests.
Delta Shoals, a network of coral canyons
fanning seaward from a sandy shoal, attracts
divers to its elkhorn, brain, and star coral
heads. Marathon's Thunderbolt, a 188-foot
ship sunk in 1986, sits upright at 115-foot
depths, coated with sponge, coral, and hydroid,
and attracting angelfish, jacks, and deepwater pelagic creatures. ⚑ Greater Marathon
Chamber and visitors center at MM 53.5,
☎ 800/262-7284.

ISLAMORADA Mile Marker 63–90
Islamorada offers shallow coral reefs, mini walls,
shipwrecks, and the Aquarius (⊕ www.uncw.edu/
aquarius), an underwater habitat for scientific
research. Coral heads showcase tropical marine
life, from grunt to regal queen angelfish. Green
moray eels populate spur-and-groove channels,
and nurse sharks linger around overhangs.
Submerged attractions include the Eagle, a 287-
foot ship in 110 feet of water; Davis Reef, with
gorgonian coral; Alligator Reef, where the USS
Alligator sank while fighting pirates; the sloping
Conch Wall, with barrel sponges and gorgonian;
and Crocker Wall, featuring spur-and-groove and
block corals. ⚑ Islamorada Chamber and visitor
center at MM 83.2, ☎ 800/322-5397.

KEY LARGO Mile Marker 90–112
Key Largo marine conservation got a big leg up
with creation of John Pennekamp Coral Reef
State Park in 1960, the nation's first undersea
preserve, followed by 1975's designation of the
Key Largo National Marine Sanctuary. A popu-
lar underwater attraction is the bronze statue of
Christ of the Abyss between coral formations.
Explorers with a "lust for rust" can dive down to
60 to 90 feet and farther to see the murky cem-
etery for two twin 327-foot U.S. Coast Guard cut-
ters, Duane and Bibb, used during World War II;
USS Spiegel Grove, a 510-foot Navy transport
ship sunk in 2002 to create an artificial reef; and
Molasses Reef, showcasing coral heads. ⚑ Key
Largo Chamber at MM 106, ☎ 800/822-1088.

SCUBA DIVING

A diver explores the coral reef in the Florida Keys National Marine Sanctuary off Key Largo.

Florida offers wonderful opportunities to spend your vacation in the sun and become a certified diver at the same time. In the Keys, count on setting aside three to five days for entry-level or so-called "Open Water" certification offered by many dive shops. Basic certification (covering depths to about 60 feet) involves classroom work and pool training, followed by one or more open-water dives at the reef. After passing a knowledge test and completing the required water training (often starting in a pool), you become a certified recreational scuba diver, eligible to rent dive gear and book dive trips with most operations worldwide. Learning through video or online computer programs can enable you to complete classroom work at home, so you can more efficiently schedule time in the Keys for completing water skills and getting out to the reef for exploration.

Many would-be divers opt to take the classroom instruction and pool training at home at a local dive shop and then spend only two days in the Keys completing four dives. It's not necessarily cheaper, but it can be far more relaxing to commit to only two days of diving.

Questions you should ask: Not all dive shops are created equal, and it may be worthwhile to spend extra money for a better diving experience. Some of the larger dive shops take out large catamarans that can carry as many as 24 to 40 people. Many people prefer the intimacy of a smaller boat.

Good to know: Divers can become certified through PADI *(www.padi.com)*, NAUI *(www.naui.org)*, or SSI *(www.divessi.com)*. The requirements for all three are similar, and if you do the classroom instruction and pool training with a dive shop associated with one organization, the referral for the open water dives will be honored by most dive shops. Note that you are not allowed to fly for at least 24 hours after a dive, because residual nitrogen in the body can pose health risks upon decompression. While there are no rigid rules on diving after flying, make sure you're well-hydrated before hitting the water.

Cost: The four-day cost can range from $300 to $475, but be sure to ask if equipment, instruction manuals, and log books are extra. Some dive shops have relationships with hotels, so check for dive/stay packages. Referral dives (a collaborative effort among training agencies) run from $285 to $300 and discover scuba runs around $175 to $200.

SNUBA

Beyond snorkeling or the requirements of scuba, you also have the option of "Snuba." The word is a trademarked portmanteau or combo of snorkel and scuba. Marketed as easy-to-learn family fun, Snuba lets you breathe underwater via tubes from an air-supplied vessel above, with no prior diving or snorkel experience required.

NOT CERTIFIED?

Not sure if you want to commit the time and money to become certified? Not a problem. Most dive shops and many resorts will offer a discover scuba day-long course. In the morning, the instructor will teach you the basics of scuba diving: how to clear your mask, how to come to the surface in the unlikely event you lose your air supply, etc. In the afternoon, instructors will take you out for a dive in relatively shallow water—less than 30 feet. Be sure to ask where the dive will take place. Jumping into the water off a shallow beach may not be as fun as actually going out to the coral. If you decide that diving is something you want to pursue, the open dive may count toward your certification.

■ TIP→ You can often book the discover dives at the last minute. It may not be worth it to go out on a windy day when the currents are stronger. Also the underwater world looks a whole lot brighter on sunny days.

(top) Scuba divers; (bottom) Diver ascending line.

SNORKELING

Snorkling lets you see the wonders of the sea from a new perspective.

The basics: Sure, you can take a deep breath, hold your nose, squint your eyes, and stick your face in the water in an attempt to view submerged habitats . . . but why not protect your eyes, retain your ability to breathe, and keep your hands free to paddle about when exploring underwater? That's what snorkeling is all about.

Equipment needed: A mask, snorkel (the tube attached to the mask), and fins. In deeper waters (any depth over your head), life jackets are advised.

Steps to success: If you've never snorkeled before, it's natural to feel a bit awkward at first, so don't sweat it. Breathing through a mask and tube, and wearing a pair of fins take getting used to. Like any activity, you build confidence and comfort through practice.

If you're new to snorkeling, begin by submerging your face in shallow water or a swimming pool and breathing calmly through the snorkel while gazing through the mask.

Next you need to learn how to clear water out of your mask and snorkel, an essential skill since splashes can send water into tube openings and masks can leak. Some snorkels have built-in drainage valves, but if a tube clogs, you can force water up and out by exhaling through your mouth. Clearing a mask is similar: lift your head from water while pulling forward on mask to drain. Some masks have built-in purge valves, but those without can be cleared underwater by pressing the top to the forehead and blowing out your nose (charming, isn't it?), allowing air to bubble into the mask, pushing water out the bottom. If it sounds hard, it really isn't. Just try it a few times and you'll soon feel like a pro.

Now your goal is to get friendly with fins—you want them to be snug but not too tight—and learn how to propel yourself with them. Fins won't help you float, but they will give you a leg up, so to speak, on smoothly moving through the water or treading water (even when upright) with less effort.

Flutter stroking is the most efficient underwater kick, and the farther your foot bends forward the more leg power you'll be able to transfer to the water and the farther you'll travel with each stroke. Flutter kicking movements involve alternately separating the legs and then drawing them back together. When your legs separate, the leg surface encounters drag from the water, slowing you down. When your legs are drawn back together, they produce a force pushing you forward. If your kick creates more forward force than it causes drag, you'll move ahead.

Submerge your fins to avoid fatigue rather than having them flailing above the water when you kick, and keep your arms at your side to reduce drag. You are in the water—stretched out, face down, and snorkeling happily away—but that doesn't mean you can't hold your breath and go deeper in the water for a closer look at some fish or whatever catches your attention. Just remember that when you do this, your snorkel will be submerged, too, so you won't be breathing (you'll be holding your breath). You can dive head-first, but going feet-first is easier and less scary for most folks, taking less momentum. Before full immersion, take several long, deep breaths to clear carbon dioxide from your lungs.

If your legs tire, flip onto your back and tread water with inverted fin motions while resting. If your mask fogs, wash condensation from lens and clear water from mask.

TIPS FOR SAFE SNORKELING

■ Snorkel with a buddy and stay together.

■ Plan your entry and exit points prior to getting in the water.

■ Swim into the current on entering and then ride the current back to your exit point.

■ Carry your flippers into the water and then put them on, as it's difficult to walk in them.

■ Make sure your mask fits properly and is not too loose.

■ Pop your head above the water periodically to ensure you aren't drifting too far out, or too close to rocks.

■ Think of the water as someone else's home—don't take anything that doesn't belong to you, or leave any trash behind.

■ Don't touch any sea creatures; they may sting.

■ Wear a T-shirt over your swimsuit to help protect you from being fried by the sun.

■ When in doubt, don't go without a snorkeling professional; try a guided tour.

Cayman Salvor

DID YOU KNOW?

Dolphins in Florida are predominantly of the Atlantic bottlenose variety. These playful and smart creatures love to leap out of the water and synchronize their movements with others. By swimming next to boats, dolphins can conserve energy.

BS, 58901 Overseas Hwy. ☏ *305/289–1121 for info, 305/289–0002 for reservations* ⊕ *www.dolphins.org* ✉ *$20* ⊙ *Daily 9–4:30.*

WHERE TO EAT

$$$ ✕ **Hideaway Café.** The name says it all. Tucked between Grassy Key and
AMERICAN Marathon, it's easy to miss if you're barnstorming through the Middle Keys. When you find it (upstairs at Rainbow Bend Resort), you'll discover a favorite of locals who appreciate a well-planned menu, lovely ocean view, and quiet evening away from the crowds—fancy with white tablecloths, but homey with worn carpeting. For starters, dig into escargots à la Edison (sautéed with vegetables, pepper, cognac, and cream). Then feast on several specialties, such as a rarely found chateaubriand for one, a whole roasted duck, or the seafood medley combining the catch of the day with scallops and shrimp in a savory sauce. $ *Average main: $30* ⊠ *Rainbow Bend Resort, MM 58 OS, 57784 Overseas Hwy.* ☏ *305/289–1554* ⊕ *www.hideawaycafe.com* ⊙ *No lunch.*

MARATHON

Marathon is between mile markers 53 and 47.5.

Marathon is a bustling town, at least compared with other Keys communities. If you get off the main drag, you'll find the few oceanfront hotels, but there are a number of good dining options right on Overseas Highway, so you'll definitely want to stop for a bite even if you're just passing through on the way to Key West.

If you stop a while, you'll find Marathon has the most historic attractions outside of Key West, and the well-worth-visiting Sombrero Beach—though fishing, diving, and boating are the main events here. The town throws tarpon tournaments in April and May, more fishing tournaments in June and September, a seafood festival in March, and lighted boat parades around the winter holidays.

New Englanders founded this former fishing village in the early 1800s. The community on Vaca Key subsequently served as a base for pirates, salvagers (also known as "wreckers"), spongers, and, later, Bahamian farmers who eked out a living growing cotton and other crops. More Bahamians arrived in hopes of finding work building the railroad. According to local lore, Marathon was renamed when a worker commented that it was a marathon task to position the tracks across the 6-mile-long island. During the building of the railroad, Marathon developed a reputation for lawlessness that rivaled that of the Old West. It's said that to keep the rowdy workers from descending on Key West for their off-hours endeavors, residents would send boatloads of liquor up to Marathon. Needless to say, things have quieted down considerably since then. Grassy Key segues into Marathon with little more than a slight increase in traffic and higher concentration of commercial establishments. Marathon's roots are anchored to fishing and boating, so look for marinas to find local color, fishing charters, and good restaurants. At its north end, Key Colony Beach is an old-fashioned island neighborhood worth a visit for its shops and restaurants. Just be warned the police are plentiful and love to catch speeders. Nature lovers shouldn't miss the attractions on Crane Point. Other good places to leave the main road are at Sombrero Beach Road (MM 50), which leads to the beach, and 35th Street (MM 49), which takes you to a funky little marina and restaurant. Overseas Highway hightails through Hog Key and Knight Key before the big leap over Florida Bay and Hawk's Channel via the Seven Mile Bridge.

GETTING HERE AND AROUND

The SuperShuttle charges $102 per passenger for trips from Miami International Airport to the Upper Keys. To go farther into the Keys, you must book an entire 11-person van, which costs about $250 to Marathon. For a trip to or from the airport, place your request 24 hours in advance.

Miami Dade Transit provides daily bus service from MM 50 in Marathon to the Florida City Walmart Supercenter on the mainland. The bus stops at major shopping centers as well as on-demand anywhere along the route during daily round trips on the hour from 6 am to 10 pm. The cost is $2 one-way, exact change required. The Lower Keys Shuttle bus runs from Marathon to Key West ($4 one way), with scheduled stops along the way.

ESSENTIALS

Transportation Contacts Lower Keys Shuttle ☎ *305/809–3910* ⊕ *www. kwtransit.com.* **Miami Dade Transit** ☎ *305/770–3131* ⊕ *www.miamidade.gov/ transit.* **SuperShuttle** ☎ *305/871–2000, 800/258–3826* ⊕ *www.supershuttle.com.*

Visitor Information Greater Marathon Chamber of Commerce and Visitor Center ⊠ *MM 53.5 BS, 12222 Overseas Hwy.* ☎ *305/743–5417, 800/262–7284* ⊕ *www.floridakeysmarathon.com.*

EXPLORING

FAMILY **Crane Point Museum, Nature Center, and Historic Site.** Tucked away from the highway behind a stand of trees, Crane Point—part of a 63-acre tract that contains the last-known undisturbed thatch-palm hammock—is delightfully undeveloped. This multiuse facility includes the **Museum of Natural History of the Florida Keys,** which has displays about local wildlife, a seashell exhibit, and a marine-life display that makes you feel you're at the bottom of the sea. Kids love the replica 17th-century galleon and pirate dress-up room where they can play, and the re-created **Cracker House** filled with insects, sea-turtle exhibits, and children's activities. On the 1-mile indigenous loop trail, visit the **Laura Quinn Wild Bird Center** and the remnants of a Bahamian village, site of the restored **George Adderly House.** It is the oldest surviving example of Bahamian tabby (a concretelike material created from sand and seashells) construction outside of Key West. A boardwalk crosses wetlands, rivers, and mangroves before ending at Adderly Village. From November to Easter, docent-led tours are available; bring good walking shoes and bug repellent during warm weather. ⊠ *MM 50.5 BS, 5550 Overseas Hwy.* ☎ *305/743–9100* ⊕ *www.cranepoint.net* ⁂ *$12.50* ☉ *Mon.–Sat. 9–5, Sun. noon–5; call to arrange trail tours.*

Pigeon Key. There's much to like about this 5-acre island under the Old Seven Mile Bridge. You might even recognize it from one season finale of the TV show *The Amazing Race*. You can reach it via a ferry that departs from behind the visitors center (look for the old red railroad car on Knight's Key, MM 47 OS). Once there, tour the island on your own or join a guided tour to explore the buildings that formed the early-20th-century work camp for the Overseas Railroad that linked the mainland to Key West in 1912. Later the island became a fish camp, a state park, and then government-administration headquarters. Exhibits in a small museum recall the history of the Keys, the railroad, and railroad baron Henry M. Flagler. The ferry ride with tour lasts two hours; visitors can self-tour and catch the ferry back in a half hour. ⊠ *MM 45 OS, 1 Knights Key Blvd., Pigeon Key* 🕿 *305/743–5999* ⊕ *www.pigeonkey.net* 💲 *$12* ⏱ *Daily 9:30–2:30; ferry departures at 10, 12 and 2.*

Seven Mile Bridge. This is one of the most photographed images in the Keys. Actually measuring slightly less than 7 miles, it connects the Middle and Lower Keys and is believed to be the world's longest segmental bridge. It has 39 expansion joints separating its various concrete sections. Each April runners gather in Marathon for the annual Seven Mile Bridge Run. The expanse running parallel to Seven Mile Bridge is what remains of the **Old Seven Mile Bridge,** an engineering and architectural marvel in its day that's now on the National Register of Historic Places. Once proclaimed the Eighth Wonder of the World, it rested on a record 546 concrete piers. No cars are allowed on the old bridge today.

FAMILY **The Turtle Hospital.** More than 100 injured sea turtles check in here every year. The 90-minute guided tours take you into recovery and surgical areas at the world's only state-certified veterinary hospital for sea turtles. In the "hospital bed" tanks, you can see recovering patients and others that are permanent residents due to their injuries. After the tour, you can feed some of the "residents." Call ahead—space is limted and tours are sometimes cancelled due to medical emergencies. The turtle ambulance out front makes for a memorable souvenir photo. ⊠ *MM 48.5 BS, 2396 Overseas Hwy.* 🕿 *305/743–2552* ⊕ *www.turtlehospital. org* 💲 *$18* ⏱ *Daily 9–5.*

BEACHES

FAMILY **Sombrero Beach.** No doubt one of the best beaches in the Keys, here you'll find pleasant, shaded picnic areas that overlook a coconut palm–lined grassy stretch and the Atlantic Ocean. Roped-off areas allow swimmers, boaters, and windsurfers to share the narrow cove. Facilities include barbecue grills, a large playground, a pier, a volleyball court, and a paved, lighted bike path off Overseas Highway. Sunday afternoons draw lots of local families toting coolers. The park is accessible for those with disabilities and allows leashed pets. Turn east at the traffic light in Marathon and follow signs to the end. **Amenities:** showers; toilets. **Best for:** families; swimming; windsurfing. ⊠ *MM 50 OS, Sombrero Beach Rd.* 🕿 *305/743–0033* 💲 *Free* ⏱ *Daily 8–sunset.*

WHERE TO EAT

$ ✕ **Fish Tales Market and Eatery.** This roadside eatery with its own seafood
SEAFOOD market serves signature dishes such as snapper on grilled rye with coleslaw and melted Muenster cheese and a fried fish burrito. You also can slurp luscious lobster bisque or tomato-based conch chowder. There

are burgers, chicken, and dogs for those who don't do seafood. Plan to dine early; it's only open until 6:30 pm (4 pm on Saturdays).This is a no-frills kind of place with a loyal local following, unfussy ambiance, a couple of outside picnic tables, and friendly service. [$] *Average main: $9* ✉ *MM 52.5 OS, 11711 Overseas Hwy.* ☎ *305/743–9196, 888/662–4822* 🌐 *www.floridalobster.com* ✍ *Reservations not accepted* 🕒 *Closed Sun. No dinner Sat.*

$$ ITALIAN 🍴 **Key Colony Inn.** The inviting aroma of an Italian kitchen pervades this family-owned favorite with a supper-club atmosphere. As you'd expect, the service is friendly and attentive. For lunch there are fish and steak entrées served with fries, salad, and bread in addition to Italian specialties. At dinner you can't miss with traditional dishes like veal Oscar and New York strip, or such specialties as seafood *Italiano,* a dish of scallops and shrimp sautéed in garlic butter and served with marinara sauce over a bed of linguine. The place is renowned for its Sunday brunch, served from November to April. [$] *Average main: $19* ✉ *MM 54 OS, 700 W. Ocean Dr., Key Colony Beach* ☎ *305/743–0100* 🌐 *www.kcinn.com.*

$$ SEAFOOD FAMILY 🍴 **Keys Fisheries Market & Marina.** From the parking lot, you can't miss the enormous tiki bar on stilts, but the walk-up window on the ground floor is the heart of this warehouse-turned restaurant. Order at the window, pick up your food, then dine at one of the waterfront tables outfitted with rolls of paper towels. The menu comprises fresh seafood and a token hamburger and chicken sandwich. A huge lobster reuben ($14.95) served on thick slices of toasted bread is the signature dish. Other delights include the shrimp burger, very rich whiskey-peppercorn snapper, and the Keys Kombo (grilled lobster, shrimp, scallops, and mahimahi for $29). The adults-only upstairs tiki bar offers a sushi and raw bar for eat-in only. Bring quarters for fish food—you can feed the tarpon while you wait for your food. [$] *Average main: $16* ✉ *MM 49 BS, 3390 Gulfview Ave., at the end of 35th St. (turn right on 35th St. off Gulfview Ave.)* ☎ *305/743–4353, 866/743–4353* 🌐 *www.keysfisheries.com* ✍ *Reservations not accepted.*

$$$ SEAFOOD Fodor's Choice ★ 🍴 **Lazy Days South.** Tucked into Marathon Marina a half mile north of the Seven Mile Bridge, this restaurant offers views just as spectacular as its highly lauded food. A spin-off of an Islamorada favorite, here you'll find a wide range of daily offerings from fried- or sautéed conch and a coconut-fried fish du jour sandwich to seafood pastas and beef tips over rice. Choose a table on the outdoor deck, or inside underneath paddle fans and surrounded by local art. [$] *Average main: $22* ✉ *MM 47.3 OS, 725 11th St.* ☎ *305/289–0839* 🌐 *www.keysdining.com/lazydays.*

$ DINER 🍴 **The Stuffed Pig.** With only nine tables and a counter inside, this breakfast-and-lunch place is always hopping. When the weather's right, grab a table out back. The kitchen whips up daily lunch specials like burgers, seafood platters, or pulled pork with hand-cut fries, but a quick glance around the room reveals that the all-day breakfast is the main draw. You can get the usual breakfast plates, but most newcomers opt for oddities like the lobster omelet, alligator tail and eggs, or "grits and grunts" (that's fish, to the rest of us). [$] *Average main: $9* ✉ *MM 49*

BS, 3520 Overseas Hwy. ☎ *305/743–4059* 🌐 *www.thestuffedpig.com* ✍ *Reservations not accepted* 💳 *No credit cards* ⏲ *No dinner.*

WHERE TO STAY

$$ RENTAL 🏨 **Glunz Ocean Beach Hotel & Resort.** The Glunz family got it right when they purchased this former timeshare property and put a whole lot of love into renovating it to its full oceanfront potential. **Pros:** oceanfront; convenient amenities; excellent free Wi-Fi. **Cons:** neighbor noise; small elevator; no interior corridors; not cheap. [$] *Rooms from: $260* ✉ *MM 53.5 OS, 351 E. Ocean Dr., Key Colony Beach* ☎ *305/289–0525* 🌐 *www.GlunzOceanBeachHotel.com* 🛏 *22 rooms, 16 suites* 🍴 *No meals.*

$$$ RESORT FAMILY Fodor's Choice ★ 🏨 **Tranquility Bay.** Ralph Lauren could have designed the rooms at this stylish, luxurious resort on a nice beach. **Pros:** secluded setting; gorgeous design; lovely crescent beach. **Cons:** a bit sterile; no real Keys atmosphere; cramped building layout. [$] *Rooms from: $399* ✉ *MM 48.5 BS, 2600 Overseas Hwy.* ☎ *305/289–0888, 866/643–5397* 🌐 *www.tranquilitybay.com* 🛏 *16 guestrooms, 45 2-bedroom suites, 41 3-bedroom suites* 🍴 *No meals.*

SPORTS AND THE OUTDOORS

BIKING

Bike Marathon Bike Rentals. "Have bikes, will deliver" could be the motto of this company, which gets beach cruisers to your hotel door, including a helmet and basket. They also rent kayaks. Note that there's no physical location, but services are available Monday through Saturday 9–4 and Sunday 9–2. ☎ *305/743–3204* 🌐 *www.bikemarathonbikerentals.com* 🎟 *$35 per wk.*

Overseas Outfitters. Aluminum cruisers and hybrid bikes are available for rent at this outfitter. It's open weekdays 9–5:30 and Saturday 9–3. All rentals include a helmet and lock. ✉ *MM 48 BS, 1700 Overseas Hwy.* ☎ *305/289–1670* 🌐 *www.overseasoutfitters.com* 🎟 *Rentals from $15 per day.*

BOATING

Sail, motor, or paddle—whatever your choice of modes, boating is what the Keys are all about. Brave the Atlantic waves and reefs or explore the backcountry islands on the calmer gulfside. If you don't have a lot of boating and chart-reading experience, it's a good idea to tap into local knowledge on a charter.

Captain Pip's. This operator rents 20- to 24-foot outboards as well as tackle and snorkeling gear. Fishing charters are also available with a captain and a mate (full-day charters are also available). Ask about multiday deals, or try one of their accommodation packages and walk right from your bayfront room to your boat. ✉ *MM 47.5 BS, 1410 Overseas Hwy.* ☎ *305/743–4403, 800/707–1692* 🌐 *www.captainpips.com* 🎟 *Rentals from $195 per day; half-day charters from $650.*

Fish 'n Fun. Get out on the water on 19- to 26-foot powerboats. Rentals can be for a half or full day. The company also offers free delivery in the Middle Keys. ✉ *Banana Bay Resort & Marina, MM 49.5 OS, 4590 Overseas Hwy.* ☎ *305/743–2275, 800/471–3440* 🌐 *www.fishnfunrentals.com* 🎟 *From $175.*

FISHING

For recreational anglers, the deepwater fishing is superb in the ocean. Marathon West Hump, one good spot, has depths ranging from 500 to more than 1,000 feet. Locals fish from a half dozen bridges, including Long Key Bridge, the Old Seven Mile Bridge, and both ends of Tom's Harbor. Barracuda, bonefish, mahimahi, and tarpon all frequent local waters. Party boats and private charters are available.

Marathon Lady. Morning, afternoon, and night, fish for mahimahi, grouper, and other tasty catch aboard this 73-footer, which departs on half-day excursions from the Vaca Cut Bridge (MM 53), north of Marathon. Join the crew for night fishing ($55) from 6:30 to midnight from Memorial Day to Labor Day; it's especially beautiful on a full-moon night. ⊠ *MM 53 OS, at 117th St., 11711 Overseas Hwy.* ☏ *305/743–5580* ⊕ *www.marathonlady.net* ⊠ *From $50.*

Sea Dog Charters. Captain Jim Purcell, a deep-sea specialist for ESPN's *The American Outdoorsman*, provides one of the best values in Keys fishing. Next to the Seven Mile Grill, his company offers half- and full-day offshore, reef and wreck, and backcountry fishing trips, as well as fishing and snorkeling trips aboard 30- to 37-foot boats. The per-person for a half-day trip is the same regardless of whether your group fills the boat, and includes bait, light tackle, ice, coolers, and fishing licenses. If you prefer an all-day private charter on a 37-foot boat, he offers those, too, for up to six people. A fuel surcharge may apply. ⊠ *MM 47.5 BS, 1248 Overseas Hwy.* ☏ *305/743–8255* ⊕ *www. seadogcharters.net* ⊠ *From $60.*

SCUBA DIVING AND SNORKELING

Local dive operations take you to Sombrero Reef and Lighthouse, the most popular down-under destination in these parts. For a shallow dive and some lobster nabbing, Coffins Patch, off Key Colony Beach, is a good choice. A number of wrecks such as *Thunderbolt* serve as artificial reefs. Many operations out of this area will also take you to Looe Key Reef.

Hall's Diving Center & Career Institute. The institute has been training divers for more than 40 years. Along with conventional twice-a-day snorkel and two-tank dive trips to the reefs at Sombrero Lighthouse and wrecks like the *Thunderbolt*, the company has more unusual offerings like rebreather, photography and nitrox courses. ⊠ *MM 48.5 BS, 1994 Overseas Hwy.* ☏ *305/743–5929, 800/331–4255* ⊕ *www.hallsdiving. com* ⊠ *From $40.*

Spirit Snorkeling. Join regularly scheduled snorkeling excursions to Sombrero Reef and Lighthouse Reef on this company's comfortable catamaran. They also offer sunset cruises, private charters, and new-age yoga cruises. ⊠ *MM 47.5 BS, 1410 Overseas Hwy., Slip No. 1* ☏ *305/289–0614* ⊕ *www.spiritsnorkeling.net* ⊠ *From $30.*

THE LOWER KEYS

Beginning at Bahia Honda Key, the islands of the Florida Keys become smaller, more clustered, and more numerous—a result of ancient tidal water flowing between the Florida Straits and the gulf. Here you're likely to see more birds and mangroves than other tourists, and more refuges, beaches, and campgrounds than museums, restaurants, and hotels. The islands are made up of two types of limestone, both denser than the highly permeable Key Largo limestone of the Upper Keys. As a result, freshwater forms in pools rather than percolating through the rock, creating watering holes that support alligators, snakes, deer, rabbits, raccoons, and migratory ducks. Many of these animals can be seen in the National Key Deer Refuge on Big Pine Key. Nature was generous with her beauty in the Lower Keys, which have both Looe Key Reef, arguably the Keys' most beautiful tract of coral, and Bahia Honda State Park, considered one of the best beaches in the world for its fine-sand dunes, clear warm waters, and panoramic vista of a historic bridge, hammocks, and azure sky and sea. Big Pine Key is fishing headquarters for a laid-back community that swells with retirees in the winter. South of it, the dribble of islands can flash by in a blink of an eye if you don't take the time to stop at a roadside eatery or check out tours and charters at the little marinas.

GETTING HERE AND AROUND

The Lower Keys in this section include the keys between MM 37 and MM 9. The Seven Mile Bridge drops you into the lap of this homey, quiet part of the Keys.

Heed speed limits in these parts. They may seem incredibly strict given that the traffic is lightest of anywhere in the Keys, but the purpose is to protect the resident key deer population, and officers of the law pay strict attention and will readily issue speeding tickets.

BAHIA HONDA KEY

Bahia Honda Key is between mile markers 38 and 36.

All of Bahia Honda Key is devoted to its eponymous state park, which keeps it in a pristine state. Besides the park's outdoor activities, it offers an up-close look at the original railroad bridge.

EXPLORING

FAMILY

Fodor's Choice

★

Bahia Honda State Park. Most first-time visitors to the region are dismayed by the lack of beaches—but then they discover Bahia Honda Key. The 524-acre park sprawls across both sides of the highway, giving it 2½ miles of fabulous sandy coastline. The snorkeling isn't bad, either; there's underwater life (soft coral, queen conchs, random little fish) just a few hundred feet offshore. Although swimming, kayaking, fishing, and boating are the main reasons to visit, you shouldn't miss biking along the 2½ miles of flat roads or hiking the Silver Palm Trail, with rare West Indian plants and several species found nowhere else in the nation. Along the way you'll be treated to a variety of butterflies. Seasonal ranger-led nature programs take place at or depart from the Sand and Sea Nature Center. There are rental cabins, a campground, snack bar,

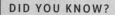

DID YOU KNOW?

An old railroad bridge connected Bahia Honda Key with Key West until a hurricane destroyed it in 1935. The bridge is no longer in operation, yet it's standing, barely. Falling debris prevents snorkeling below or exploring, but it makes for pretty photos, especially at sunrise and sunset.

gift shop, 19-slip marina, nature center, and facilities for renting kayaks and arranging snorkeling tours. Get a panoramic view of the island from what's left of the railroad—the Bahia Honda Bridge. ✉ *MM 37 OS, 36850 Overseas Hwy.* ☎ *305/872–2353* 🌐 *www.floridastateparks.org/bahiahonda* 🎟 *$4.50 for single-occupant vehicle, $9 for vehicle with 2–8 people* 🕑 *Daily 8–sunset.*

BEACHES

Sandspur Beach. Bahia Honda Key State Beach contains three beaches in all—on both the Atlantic Ocean and the Gulf of Mexico. Sandspur Beach, the largest, is regularly declared the best beach in the Florida Keys, and you'll be hard-pressed to argue. The sand is baby-powder soft, and the aqua water is warm, clear, and shallow. With their mild currents, the beaches are great for swimming, even with small fry. **Amenities:** food and drink; showers; toilets; water sports. **Best for:** snorkeling; swimming. ✉ *MM 37 OS, 36850 Overseas Hwy.* ☎ *305/872–2353* 🌐 *www.floridastateparks.org/bahiahonda* 🎟 *$4.50 for single-occupant vehicle, $9 for vehicle with 2–8 people* 🕑 *Daily 8–sunset.*

4

WHERE TO STAY

$$$ RENTAL 🏨 **Bahia Honda State Park Cabins.** Elsewhere you'd pay big bucks for the wonderful water views available at these cabins on Florida Bay. **Pros:** great bayfront views; beachfront camping; affordable rates. **Cons:** books up fast; area can be buggy. [$] *Rooms from: $183* ✉ *MM 37 OS, 36850 Overseas Hwy.* ☎ *305/872–2353, 800/326–3521* 🌐 *www.reserveamerica.com* 🛏 *6 cabins* 🍴 *No meals.*

SPORTS AND THE OUTDOORS

SCUBA DIVING AND SNORKELING

Bahia Honda Dive Shop. The concessionaire at Bahia Honda State Park manages a 19-slip marina; rents wet suits, snorkel equipment, and corrective masks; and operates twice-a-day offshore-reef snorkel trips. Park visitors looking for other fun can rent kayaks and beach chairs. ✉ *MM 37 OS, 36850 Overseas Hwy.* ☎ *305/872–3210* 🌐 *www.bahiahondapark.com* 🕑 *Kayak rentals from $10 per hr.; snorkel tours from $30.*

BIG PINE KEY

Big Pine Key runs from mile marker 32 to 30.

Welcome to the Keys' most natural holdout, where wildlife refuges protect rare and endangered animals. Here you've left behind the commercialism of the Upper Keys for an authentic backcountry atmosphere.

How could things get more casual than Key Largo? Find out by exiting Overseas Highway to explore the habitat of the charmingly diminutive Key deer or cast a line from No Name Bridge. Tours explore the expansive waters of National Key Deer Refuge and Great White Heron National Wildlife Refuge, one of the first such refuges in the country. Along with Key West National Wildlife Refuge, it encompasses more than 200,000 acres of water and more than 8,000 acres of land on 49 small islands. Besides its namesake bird, the Great White Heron National Wildlife Refuge provides habitat for uncounted species of birds and three species of sea turtles. It's the only U.S. breeding site for the endangered hawksbill turtle.

ESSENTIALS

Visitor Information Big Pine and the Lower Keys Chamber of Commerce
☎ *305/872–2411, 800/872–3722* ⊕ *www.lowerkeyschamber.com.*

EXPLORING

National Key Deer Refuge. This 84,824-acre refuge was established in 1957 to protect the dwindling population of the Key deer, one of more than 22 animals and plants federally classified as endangered or threatened, including five that are found nowhere else on earth. The Key deer, which stands about 30 inches at the shoulders and is a subspecies of the Virginia white-tailed deer, once roamed throughout the Lower and Middle Keys, but hunting, destruction of their habitat, and a growing human population caused their numbers to decline to 27 by 1957. The deer have made a comeback, increasing their numbers to approximately 750. The best place to see Key deer in the refuge is at the end of Key Deer Boulevard and on No Name Key, a sparsely populated island just east of Big Pine Key. Mornings and evenings are the best time to spot them. Deer may turn up along the road at any time of day, so drive slowly. They wander into nearby yards to nibble tender grass and bougainvillea blossom, but locals do not appreciate tourists driving into their neighborhoods after them. Feeding them is against the law and puts them in danger.

A quarry left over from railroad days, the **Blue Hole** is the largest body of freshwater in the Keys. From the observation platform and nearby walking trail, you might see the resident alligator, turtles, and other wildlife. There are two well-marked trails, recently revamped: the Jack Watson Nature Trail (0.6 mile), named after an environmentalist and the refuge's first warden; and the Fred Mannillo Nature Trail, one of the most wheelchair-accessible places to see an unspoiled pine-rockland forest and wetlands. The visitor center has exhibits on Keys biology and ecology. The refuge also provides information on the Key West National Wildlife Refuge and the Great White Heron National Wildlife Refuge. Accessible only by water, both are popular with kayak outfitters. ⊠ *Visitor Center–Headquarters, Big Pine Shopping Center, MM 30.5 BS, 28950 Watson Blvd.* ☎ *305/872–2239* ⊕ *www.fws.gov/nationalkeydeer* 🎫 *Free* ☉ *Daily sunrise–sunset; headquarters weekdays 8–5.*

WHERE TO EAT

$ ✕**Good Food Conspiracy.** Like good wine, this small natural-foods eatery and market, surrenders its pleasures a little at a time. Step inside to the aroma of brewing coffee, and then pick up the scent of fresh strawberries or carrots blending into a smoothie, the green aroma of wheatgrass juice, followed by the earthy odor of hummus. Order raw or cooked vegetarian and vegan dishes, organic soups and salads, and organic coffees and teas. Bountiful sandwiches include the popular tuna melt or hummus and avocado. Sit at the counter or in the back garden and mingle with the locals as folks have been doing since the early 1980s. Then stock up on healthful snacks like dried fruits, raw nuts, and carob-covered almonds. Gluten-free items, too. 💲 *Average*

VEGETARIAN

main: $10 ✉ MM 30.2 OS, 30150 Overseas Hwy. ☎ 305/872–3945 🌐 www.goodfoodconspiracy.com ✍ Reservations not accepted ⏱ No dinner Sun.

$ AMERICAN 🍴 **No Name Pub.** This no-frills honky-tonk has been around since 1936, delighting inveterate locals and intrepid vacationers who come for the excellent pizza, cold beer, and *interesting* companionship. The décor, such as it is, amounts to the autographed dollar bills that cover every inch of the place. The full menu printed on place mats includes a tasty conch chowder, a half-pound fried-grouper sandwich, spaghetti and meatballs, and seafood baskets. The lighting is poor, the furnishings are rough, and the music is oldies. This former brothel and bait shop is just before the No Name Key Bridge in the midst of a residential neighborhood. It's a bit hard to find, but worth the trouble if you want a singular Keys experience. [$] *Average main: $15 ✉ MM 30 BS, 30813 Watson Blvd. ✣ From U.S. 1, turn west on Wilder Rd., left on South St., right on Ave. B, right on Watson Blvd. ☎ 305/872–9115 🌐 www.nonamepub.com ✍ Reservations not accepted.*

WHERE TO STAY

$ HOTEL 🏨 **Big Pine Key Fishing Lodge.** There's a congenial atmosphere at this lively family-owned lodge-campground-marina—a happy mix of tent campers (who have the fabulous waterfront real estate), RVers (who look pretty permanent), and motel dwellers who like to mingle at the rooftop pool and challenge each other to a game of poker. **Pros:** local fishing crowd; nice pool; great price. **Cons:** RV park is too close to motel; deer will eat your food if you're camping. [$] *Rooms from: $114 ✉ MM 33 OS, 33000 Overseas Hwy. ☎ 305/872–2351 🌐 www.big-pine-key.com/fishinglodge.php 🛏 16 efficiencies 🍽 No meals.*

$$ B&B/INN 🏨 **Deer Run Bed & Breakfast.** Innkeepers Jen DeMaria and Harry Appel were way ahead of the green-lodging game when they opened in 2004, and guests love how Key deer wander the grounds of this beachfront B&B on a residential street lined with mangroves. **Pros:** quiet location; vegan, organic breakfasts; complimentary bikes, kayaks, and state park passes. **Cons:** price is a bit high; hard to find. [$] *Rooms from: $255 ✉ MM 33 OS, 1997 Long Beach Dr. ☎ 305/872–2015 🌐 www.deerrunfloridabb.com 🛏 4 rooms 🍽 Breakfast.*

SPORTS AND THE OUTDOORS

BIKING

A good 10 miles of paved roads run from MM 30.3 BS, along Wilder Road, across the bridge to No Name Key, and along Key Deer Boulevard into the National Key Deer Refuge. Along the way you might see some Key deer. Stay off the trails that lead into wetlands, where fat tires can do damage to the environment.

Big Pine Bicycle Center. Owner Marty Baird is an avid cyclist and enjoys sharing his knowledge of great places to ride. He's also skilled at selecting the right bike for the journey, and he knows his repairs, too. His old-fashioned single-speed, fat-tire cruisers rentby the half or full day. Helmets, baskets, and locks are included. *✉ MM 30.9 BS, 31 County Rd. ☎ 305/872–0130 🌐 www.bigpinebikes.com 🎟 From $8.*

BOATING AND FISHING EXCURSIONS

Those looking to fish can cast from No Name Key Bridge or hire a charter to take them into backcountry or deep waters for fishing year-round. If you're looking for a good snorkeling spot, stay close to Looe Key Reef, which is prime scuba and snorkeling territory. One resort caters to divers with dive boats that depart from their own dock. Others can make arrangements for you.

Strike Zone Charters. Glass-bottom-boat excursions venture into the backcountry and Atlantic Ocean. The five-hour Island Excursion emphasizes nature and Keys history; besides close encounters with birds, sea life, and vegetation, there's a fish cookout on an island. Snorkel and fishing equipment, food, and drinks are included. This is one of the few nature outings in the Keys with wheelchair access. Deep-sea charter rates for up to six people can be arranged for a half- or full day. It also offers flats fishing in the Gulf of Mexico. Dive excursions head to the wreck of the 110-foot *Adolphus Busch,* and scuba and snorkel trips to Looe Key Reef, prime scuba and snorkeling territory, aboard glass-bottom boats. ⊠ *MM 29.6 BS, 29675 Overseas Hwy.* ☎ *305/872–9863, 800/654–9560* ⊕ *www.strikezonecharter.com* ✆ *From $38.*

KAYAKING

There's nothing like the vast expanse of pristine waters and mangrove islands preserved by national refuges from here to Key West. The maze-like terrain can be confusing, so it's wise to hire a guide at least the first time out.

Big Pine Kayak Adventures. There's no excuse to skip a water adventure with this convenient kayak rental service, which delivers them to your lodging or anywhere between Seven Mile Bridge and Stock Island. The company, headed by *The Florida Keys Paddling Guide* author Bill Keogh, will rent you a kayak and then ferry you—called taxi-yakking—to remote islands with clear instructions on how to paddle back on your own. Rentals are by the half day or full day. Three-hour group kayak tours are the cheapest option and explore the mangrove forests of Great White Heron and Key Deer National Wildlife Refuges. More expensive four-hour custom tours transport you to exquisite backcountry areas teeming with wildlife. Kayak fishing charters are also popular. ⊠ *Old Wooden Bridge Fishing Camp* ✛ *From MM 30, turn right at traffic light, continue on Wilder Rd. toward No Name Key; the fishing camp is just before the bridge with a big yellow kayak on the sign out front* ☎ *305/872–7474* ⊕ *www.keyskayaktours.com* ✆ *From $50.*

LITTLE TORCH KEY

Little Torch Key is between mile markers 29 and 10.

Little Torch Key and its neighbor islands, Ramrod Key and Summerland Key, are good jumping-off points for divers headed for Looe Key Reef. The islands also serve as a refuge for those who want to make forays into Key West but not stay in the thick of things.

The undeveloped backcountry at your door makes Little Torch Key an ideal location for fishing and kayaking. Nearby Ramrod Key, which also caters to divers bound for Looe Key, derives its name from a ship that wrecked on nearby reefs in the early 1800s.

NEED A BREAK?

Baby's Coffee. The aroma of rich roasting coffee beans arrests you at the door of "the Southernmost Coffee Roaster." Buy it by the pound or by the cup along with sandwiches and sweets. ✉ *MM 15 OS, 3178 Overseas Hwy.* ☎ *305/744–9866, 800/523–2326* 🌐 *www.babyscoffee.com.*

WHERE TO EAT

$$ AMERICAN

🍴 **Geiger Key Smokehouse Bar & Grill.** There's a strong hint of the Old Keys at this oceanside marina restaurant, which came under new management in 2010 by the same folks who own Hogfish Grill on Stock Island. "On the backside of paradise," as the sign says, its tiki structures overlook quiet mangroves at an RV park marina. Locals usually outnumber tourists. The all-day menu spans an ambitious array of sandwiches, tacos, and seafood. Local fishermen stop here for breakfast before heading out in search of the big one. Don't miss the Sunday BBQ from 4–9. [$] *Average main: $16* ✉ *MM 10, 5 Geiger Key Rd., off Boca Chica Rd., Bay Point, Geiger Key* ☎ *305/296–3553, 305/294–1230* 🌐 *www.geigerkeymarina.com.*

$$ SEAFOOD

🍴 **Mangrove Mama's Restaurant.** This could be the prototype for a Keys restaurant, given its shanty appearance, lattice trim, and roving sort of indoor-outdoor floor plan. Then there's the seafood, from the ubiquitous fish sandwich (fried, grilled, broiled, or blackened) to lobster reubens, crab cakes, and coconut shrimp. Burgers, steaks, and ribs round out the menu. Hidden in a grove of banana and palm trees, the place opens for lunch, Sunday brunch, and dinner. [$] *Average main: $20* ✉ *MM 20 BS, Sugarloaf Key* ☎ *305/745–3030* 🌐 *www.mangrovemamasrestaurant.com* 🕐 *Closed Sept.*

$$$ SEAFOOD Fodor's Choice ★

🍴 **Square Grouper.** In an unassuming warehouse-looking building right off U.S. 1, chef and owner Lynn Bell is creating seafood magic. Just ask the locals, who wait in line for a table along with visitors in the know. But don't let the exterior fool you: the dining room is surprisingly suave, with butcher paper–lined tables, mandarin-colored walls, and textural components throughout. While the restaurant earns rave reviews, its name still earns snickers. (A "square grouper" is slang for bales of marijuana dropped into the ocean during the drug-running 1970s.) The dishes here not only taste close-your-eyes-and-grin good, their presentation is lovely. For starters, try the flash-fried conch with wasabi drizzle or home-smoked fish dip. Then perhaps order the seafood pasta with key lime butter sauce. It's okay to drool. Upstairs, Chef Lynn has just opened a beatnik-style tapas bar. [$] *Average main: $25* ✉ *MM 22.5 OS, Cudjoe Key* ☎ *305/745–8880* 🌐 *www.squaregrouperbarandgrill.com* 🕐 *Closed Sun., Sept., and several wks in summer.*

WHERE TO STAY

$$$$ RESORT Fodor's Choice ★

🏨 **Little Palm Island Resort & Spa.** *Haute tropicale* best describes this luxury retreat, and "second mortgage" might explain how some can afford the extravagant prices. **Pros:** secluded setting; heavenly spa; easy wildlife viewing. **Cons:** expensive; might be too quiet for some; only accessible by boat or seaplane. [$] *Rooms from: $1590* ✉ *MM 28.5*

OS, 28500 Overseas Hwy. ☎ *305/872–2524, 800/343–8567* 🌐 *www.littlepalmisland.com* 🛏 *30 suites* 🍴 *Some meals.*

$ HOTEL 🏨 **Looe Key Reef Resort & Center.** If your Keys vacation is all about diving, you'll be well served at this scuba-obsessed operation—the closest place to stay to the stellar reef (and affordable to boot). **Pros:** guests get discounts on dive and snorkel trips; fun bar. **Cons:** small rooms; unheated pool; close to road. [$] *Rooms from: $89* ✉ *MM 27.5 OS, 27340 Overseas Hwy., Ramrod Key* ☎ *305/872–2215, 877/816–3483* 🌐 *www.diveflakeys.com* 🛏 *23 rooms, 1 suite* 🍴 *No meals.*

$ HOTEL 🏨 **Parmer's Resort.** Almost every room at this budget-friendly option has a view of South Pine Channel, with the lovely curl of Big Pine Key in the foreground. **Pros:** bright rooms; pretty setting; good value. **Cons:** a bit out of the way; housekeeping costs extra; little shade around the pool. [$] *Rooms from: $159* ✉ *MM 28.7 BS, 565 Barry Ave.* ☎ *305/872–2157* 🌐 *www.parmersresort.com* 🛏 *18 rooms, 12 efficiencies, 15 apartments, 1 penthouse, 1 2-bedroom cottage* 🍴 *Breakfast.*

SPORTS AND THE OUTDOORS

BOATING AND KAYAKING

Dolphin Marina. Dolphin Marina rents 19- and 22-foot boats with 150 horsepower for up to eight people by the half day and full day. ✉ *28530 Overseas Hwy.* ☎ *305/872–2685* 🌐 *www.dolphinmarina.net* 🎟 *From $200 half-day, from $250 full-day.*

Sugarloaf Marina. Rates for one-person kayaks are based on an hourly or daily rental; two-person kayaks are also available. Delivery is free for rentals of three days or more. The folks at the marina can also hook you up with an outfitter for a day of offshore or backcountry fishing. There's also a well-stocked ship store. ✉ *MM 17 BS, 17015 Overseas Hwy., Sugarloaf Key* ☎ *305/745–3135* 🌐 *www.sugarloafkeymarina.com* 🎟 *From $15 per hr.*

SCUBA DIVING AND SNORKELING

In 1744 the HMS *Looe,* a British warship, ran aground and sank on one of the most beautiful coral reefs in the Keys, 5 nautical miles off the coast of Little Torch Key. Today the key owes its name to the ill-fated ship. The 5.3-square-nautical-mile reef, part of the Florida Keys National Marine Sanctuary, has strands of elkhorn coral on its eastern margin, purple sea fans, and abundant sponges and sea urchins. On its seaward side, it drops almost vertically 50 to 90 feet. In its midst, Shipwreck Trail plots the location of nine historic wreck sites in 14 to 120 feet of water. Buoys mark the sites, and underwater signs tell the history of each site and what marine life to expect. Snorkelers and divers will find the sanctuary a quiet place to observe reef life—except in July, when the annual Underwater Music Festival pays homage to Looe Key's beauty and promotes reef awareness with six hours of music broadcast via underwater speakers. Dive shops, charters, and private boats transport about 500 divers and snorkelers to hear the spectacle, which includes classical, jazz, new age, and Caribbean music, as well as a little Jimmy Buffett. There are even underwater Elvis impersonators.

Looe Key Reef Resort & Dive Center. This center, the closest dive shop to Looe Key Reef, offers two affordable trips daily, 7:30 am or 12:15 pm (for divers, snorkelers, or bubble watchers). The maximum depth is 30 feet, so snorkelers and divers go on the same boat. On Wednesday and Sunday, it runs a trip for advanced divers that visits a wreck and a reef in the area. The dive boat, a 45-foot catamaran, is docked at the full-service Looe Key Reef Resort. ⊠ *Looe Key Reef Resort, MM 27.5 OS, 27340 Overseas Hwy., Ramrod Key* ☎ *305/872–2215, 877/816–3483* ⊕ *www.diveflakeys.com* ⌑ *From $39.*

EN
ROUTE

The huge object that looks like a white whale floating over Cudjoe Key (MM 23–21) isn't a figment of your imagination. It's Fat Albert, a radar balloon that monitors local air and water traffic.

KEY WEST

4

Situated 150 miles from Miami, 90 miles from Havana, and an immeasurable distance from sanity, this end-of-the-line community has never been like anywhere else. Even after it was connected to the rest of the country—by the railroad in 1912 and by the highway in 1938—it maintained a strong sense of detachment.

Key West reflects a diverse population: Conchs (natives, many of whom trace their ancestry to the Bahamas), freshwater Conchs (longtime residents who migrated from somewhere else years ago), Hispanics (primarily descendants of Cuban immigrants), recent refugees from the urban sprawl of mainland Florida, military personnel, and an assortment of vagabonds, drifters, and dropouts in search of refuge. The island was once a gay vacation hot spot, and it remains a decidedly gay-friendly destination. Some of the most renowned gay guesthouses, however, no longer cater to an exclusively gay clientele. Key Westers pride themselves on their tolerance of all peoples, all sexual orientations, and even all animals. Most restaurants allow pets, and it's not surprising to see stray cats, dogs, and chickens roaming freely through the dining rooms. The chicken issue is one that government officials periodically try to bring to an end, but the colorful iconic fowl continue to strut and crow, particularly in the vicinity of Old Town's Bahamian Village.

Although the rest of the Keys are known for outdoor activities, Key West has something of a city feel. Few open spaces remain, as promoters continue to churn out restaurants, galleries, shops, and museums to interpret the city's intriguing past. As a tourist destination, Key West has a lot to sell—an average temperature of 79°F, 19th-century architecture, and a laid-back lifestyle. Yet much has been lost to those eager for a buck. Duval Street looks like a miniature Las Vegas lined with garish signs for T-shirt shops and tour-company offices. Cruise ships dwarf the town's skyline and fill the streets with day-trippers gawking at the hippies with dogs in their bike baskets, gay couples walking down the street holding hands, and the oddball lot of locals, some of whom bark louder than the dogs.

KEY WEST'S COLORFUL HISTORY

The United States acquired Key West from Spain in 1821, along with the rest of Florida. The Spanish had named the island Cayo Hueso, or Bone Key, after the Native American skeletons they found on its shores. In 1823 President James Monroe sent Commodore David S. Porter to chase pirates away. For three decades the primary industry in Key West was wrecking—rescuing people and salvaging cargo from ships that foundered on the nearby reefs. According to some reports, when pickings were lean, the wreckers hung out lights to lure ships aground. Their business declined after 1849, when the federal government began building lighthouses.

In 1845 the army began construction on Fort Taylor, which kept Key West on the Union side during the Civil War, even though most of Florida seceded. After the fighting ended, an influx of Cubans unhappy with Spain's rule brought the cigar industry here. Fishing, shrimping, and sponge gathering became important industries, as did pineapple canning. Through much of the 19th century and into the 20th, Key West was Florida's wealthiest city in per-capita terms. But in 1929 the local economy began to unravel. Cigar making moved to Tampa, Hawaii dominated the pineapple industry, and the sponges succumbed to blight. Then the Depression hit, and within a few years half the population was on relief.

Tourism began to revive Key West, but that came to a halt when a hurricane knocked out the railroad bridge in 1935. To help the tourism industry recover from that crushing blow, the government offered incentives for islanders to turn their charming homes—many of them built by shipwrights—into guesthouses and inns. The wise foresight has left the town with more than 100 such lodgings, a hallmark of Key West vacationing today. In the 1950s the discovery of "pink gold" in the Dry Tortugas boosted the economy of the entire region. Harvesting Key West shrimp required a fleet of up to 500 boats and flooded local restaurants with sweet, luscious shrimp. The town's artistic community found inspiration in the colorful fishing boats.

GETTING HERE AND AROUND
CAR TRAVEL
Between mile markers 4 and 0, Key West is the one place in the Keys where you could conceivably do without a car, especially if you plan on staying around Old Town. If you've driven the 106 miles down the chain, you're probably ready to abandon your car in the hotel parking lot anyway. Trolleys, buses, bikes, scooters, and feet are more suitable alternatives. To explore the beaches, New Town, and Stock Island, you'll probably need a car.

Old Town Key West is the only place in the Keys where parking is a problem. There are public parking lots that charge by the hour or day (some hotels and bed-and-breakfasts provide parking or discounts at municipal lots). If you arrive early, you can sometimes find a spot on side streets off Duval and Whitehead, where you can park for free—just be sure it's not marked for residential parking only. Your best bet is to bike or take the trolley around town if you don't want to walk. You can disembark and reboard the trolley at will.

BUS TRAVEL

Greyhound Lines runs a special Keys shuttle two times a day (depending on the day of the week) from Miami International Airport (departing from Concourse E, lower level) and stops throughout the Keys. Fares run about $45 for Key West (✉ 3535 S. Roosevelt, Key West International Airport). Keys Shuttle runs scheduled service six times a day in 15-passenger vans between Miami Airport and Key West with stops throughout the Keys for $70 to $90 per person.

The City of Key West Department of Transportation has six color-coded bus routes traversing the island from 6:30 am to 11:30 pm. Stops have signs with the international bus symbol. Schedules are available on buses and at hotels, visitor centers, and shops. The fare is $2 one way. The Lower Keys Shuttle bus runs from Marathon to Key West ($4 one way), with scheduled stops along the way.

Contacts **City of Key West Department of Transportation** ☎ 305/809-3910 ⊕ www.kwtransit.com. **Greyhound Lines** ☎ 800/410–5397 for local info, 800/231–2222 ⊕ www.greyhound.com. **Keys Shuttle** ☎ 305/289–9997, 888/765–9997 ⊕ www.keysshuttle.com. **SuperShuttle** ☎ 305/871–2000, 800/258–3826 ⊕ www.supershuttle.com.

BOAT TRAVEL

Key West Express operates air-conditioned ferries between the Key West Terminal (Caroline and Grinnell streets) and Marco Island and Fort Myers Beach. The trip from Fort Myers Beach takes at least four hours each way and costs $86 one-way, $146 round-trip. Ferries depart from Fort Myers Beach at 8:30 am and from Key West at 6 pm. The Marco Island ferry costs $86 one-way and $146 round-trip, and departs at 8:30 am (the return trip leaves Key West at 5 pm). A photo ID is required for each passenger. Advance reservations are recommended. The SuperShuttle charges $102 per passenger for trips from Miami International Airport to the Upper Keys. To go farther into the Keys, you must book an entire 11-person van, which costs about $350 to Key West. You need to place your request for transportation back to the airport 24 hours in advance.

Contact **Key West Express** ✉ 100 Grinnell St. ☎ 888/539–2628 ⊕ www.seakeywestexpress.com.

VISITOR INFORMATION

Contact **Greater Key West Chamber of Commerce** ☎ 305/294–2587, 800/527–8539 ⊕ www.keywestchamber.org.

EXPLORING

OLD TOWN

The heart of Key West, the historic Old Town area runs from White Street to the waterfront. Beginning in 1822, wharves, warehouses, chandleries, ship-repair facilities, and eventually, in 1891, the U.S. Custom House sprang up around the deep harbor to accommodate the navy's large ships and other sailing vessels. Wreckers, merchants, and sea captains built lavish houses near the bustling waterfront. A remarkable number of these fine Victorian and pre-Victorian structures have been restored to their original grandeur and now serve as homes, guesthouses, shops, restaurants, and museums. These, along with the dwellings of famous writers, artists, and politicians who've come to Key West over the past 175 years, are among the area's approximately 3,000 historic structures. Old Town also has the city's finest restaurants and hotels, lively street life, and popular night spots.

TOP ATTRACTIONS

Audubon House and Tropical Gardens. If you've ever seen an engraving by ornithologist John James Audubon, you'll understand why his name is synonymous with birds. See his works in this three-story house, which was built in the 1840s for Captain John Geiger and filled with period furniture. It now commemorates Audubon's 1832 stop in Key West while he was traveling through Florida to study birds. After an introduction by a docent, you can do a self-guided tour of the house and gardens (or just the gardens). An art gallery sells lithographs of the artist's famed portraits. ⊠ *205 Whitehead St.* ☏ *305/294–2116, 877/294–2470* ⊕ *www.audubonhouse.com* ✉ *$7.50 gardens only; $12 house and gardens* ⊙ *Daily 9:30–5 (last tour at 4:15).*

Fodor'sChoice   **Ernest Hemingway Home and Museum.** Amusing anecdotes spice up the
★   guided tours of Ernest Hemingway's home, built in 1801 by the town's most successful wrecker. While living here between 1931 and 1942, Hemingway wrote about 70% of his life's work, including classics like *For Whom the Bell Tolls.* Few of his belongings remain aside from some books, and there's little about his actual work, but photographs help you visualize his day-to-day life. The famous six-toed descendants of Hemingway's cats—many named for actors, artists, authors, and even a hurricane—have free rein of the property. Tours begin every 10 minutes and take 30 minutes; then you're free to explore on your own. Be sure to find out why there is a urinal in the garden! ⊠ *907 Whitehead St.* ☏ *305/294–1136* ⊕ *www.hemingwayhome.com* ✉ *$13* ⊙ *Daily 9–5.*

Fort Zachary Taylor Historic State Park. Construction of the fort began in 1845 but was halted during the Civil War. Even though Florida seceded from the Union, Yankee forces used the fort as a base to block Confederate shipping. More than 1,500 Confederate vessels were detained in Key West's harbor. The fort, finally completed in 1866, was also used in the Spanish-American War. Take a 30-minute guided walking tour of the redbrick fort, a National Historic Landmark, at noon and 2, or self-tour anytime between 8 and 5. In February a celebration called Civil War Heritage Days includes costumed reenactments and demonstrations. From mid-January to mid-April the park serves as an open-air gallery for pieces created for Sculpture Key West. One of its most popular features is its man-made beach, a rest stop for migrating birds in the spring and fall; there are also picnic areas, hiking and biking trails, and a kayak launch. ⊠ *Southard St., at the end of the street, through Truman Annex* ☏ *305/292–6713* ⊕ *www.floridastateparks. org/forttaylor* ✉ *$4 for single-occupant vehicle, $6 for 2–8 people in a vehicle, plus a $0.50 per person county surcharge.* ⊙ *Daily 8–sunset.*

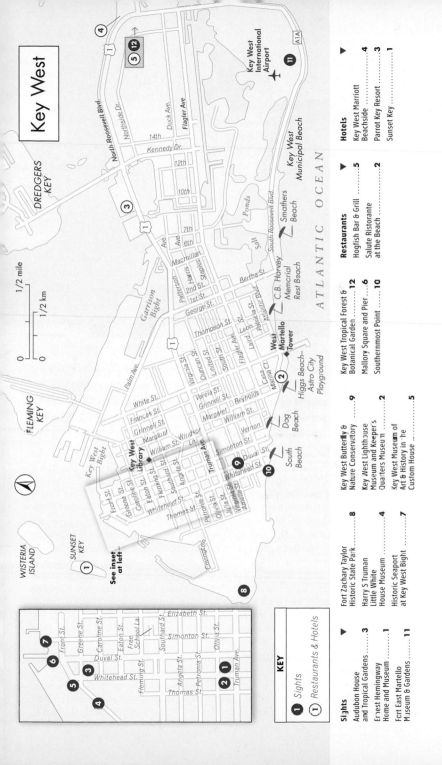

See the typewriter Hemingway used at his home office in Key West. He lived here from 1931 to 1942.

NEED A BREAK? **Key West Library.** Check out the pretty palm garden next to the Key West Library at 700 Fleming Street, just off Duval. This leafy, outdoor reading area, with shaded benches, is the perfect place to escape the frenzy and crowds of downtown Key West. There's free Internet access in the library, too. ⊠ *700 Fleming St.* ☎ *305/292–3595.*

Harry S Truman Little White House Museum. Renovations to this circa-1890 landmark have restored the home and gardens to the Truman era, down to the wallpaper pattern. A free photographic review of visiting dignitaries and presidents—John F. Kennedy, Jimmy Carter, and Bill Clinton are among the chief executives who passed through here—is on display in the back of the gift shop. Engaging 45-minute tours begin every 20 minutes until 4:30. They start with an excellent 10-minute video on the history of the property and Truman's visits. On the grounds of **Truman Annex,** a 103-acre former military parade grounds and barracks, the home served as a winter White House for presidents Truman, Eisenhower, and Kennedy. ■ TIP➜ The house tour does require climbing steps. Visitors can do a free self-guided botanical tour of the grounds with a brochure from the museum store. ⊠ *111 Front St.* ☎ *305/294–9911* ⊕ *www.trumanlittlewhitehouse.com* ⊠ *$16.13* ⊗ *House daily 9–5, grounds daily 7–6.*

Historic Seaport at Key West Bight. What was once a funky—in some places even seedy—part of town is now an 8½-acre historic restoration of 100 businesses, including waterfront restaurants, open-air bars, museums, clothing stores, bait shops, dive shops, docks, a marina, and water-sports concessions. It's all linked by the 2-mile waterfront **Harborwalk,**

CLOSE UP

4

Hemingway Was Here

In a town where Pulitzer Prize–winning writers are almost as common as coconuts, Ernest Hemingway stands out. Bars and restaurants around the island claim that he ate or drank there (except Bagatelle, where a sign in the bar reads, "Hemingway never liked this place").

Hemingway came to Key West in 1928 at the urging of writer John dos Passos and rented a house with wife number two, Pauline Pfeiffer. They spent winters in the Keys and summers in Europe and Wyoming, occasionally taking African safaris. Along the way they had two sons, Patrick and Gregory. In 1931 Pauline's wealthy uncle Gus gave the couple the house at 907 Whitehead Street. Now known as the Ernest Hemingway Home & Museum, it's Key West's number-one tourist attraction. Renovations included the addition of a pool and a tropical garden.

In 1935, when the visitor bureau included the house in a tourist brochure, Hemingway promptly built the brick wall that surrounds it today. He wrote of the visitor bureau's offense in a 1935 essay for *Esquire,* saying, "The house at present occupied by your correspondent is listed as number eighteen in a compilation of the forty-eight things for a tourist to see in Key West. So there will be no difficulty in a tourist finding it or any other of the sights of the city, a map has been prepared by the local F.E.R.A. authorities to be presented to each arriving visitor. This is all very flattering to the easily bloated ego of your correspondent but very hard on production."

During his time in Key West, Hemingway penned some of his most important works, including *A Farewell to Arms, To Have and Have Not, Green Hills of Africa,* and *Death in the Afternoon.* His rigorous schedule consisted of writing almost every morning in his second-story studio above the pool, and then promptly descending the stairs at midday. By afternoon and evening he was ready for drinking, fishing, swimming, boxing, and hanging around with the boys.

One close friend was Joe Russell, a craggy fisherman and owner of the rugged bar Sloppy Joe's, originally at 428 Greene Street but now at 201 Duval Street. Russell was the only one in town who would cash Hemingway's $1,000 royalty check. Russell and Charles Thompson introduced Hemingway to deep-sea fishing, which became fodder for his writing. Another of Hemingway's loves was boxing. He set up a ring in his yard and paid local fighters to box with him, and he refereed matches at Blue Heaven, then a saloon at 729 Thomas Street.

Hemingway honed his macho image, dressed in cutoffs and old shirts, and took on the name Papa. In turn, he gave his friends new names and used them as characters in his stories. Joe Russell became Freddy, captain of the *Queen Conch* charter boat in *To Have and Have Not.*

Hemingway stayed in Key West for 11 years before leaving Pauline for wife number three. Pauline and the boys stayed on in the house, which sold in 1951 for $80,000, 10 times its original cost.

—Jim and Cynthia Tunstall

which runs between Front and Grinnell streets, passing big ships, schooners, sunset cruises, fishing charters, and glass-bottom boats. ⊠ *100 Grinnell St.* ☎ *305/293–8309* ⊕ *www.keywestseaport.com.*

NEED A BREAK?

Coffee Plantation. Get your morning (or afternoon) buzz, and hook up to the Internet in the comfort of a homelike setting in a circa-1890 Conch house. Munch on sandwiches, wraps, and pastries, and sip a hot or cold espresso beverage. ⊠ *713 Caroline St.* ☎ *305/295–9808* ⊕ *www. coffeeplantationkeywest.com.*

FAMILY **Key West Butterfly & Nature Conservatory.** This air-conditioned refuge for butterflies, birds, and the human spirit gladdens the soul with hundreds of colorful wings—more than 45 species of butterflies alone—in a lovely glass-encased bubble. Waterfalls, artistic benches, paved pathways, birds, and lush, flowering vegetation elevate this above most butterfly attractions. The gift shop and gallery are worth a visit on their own. ⊠ *1316 Duval St.* ☎ *305/296–2988, 800/839–4647* ⊕ *www. keywestbutterfly.com* ☒ *$12* ☉ *Daily 9–5 (gallery and shop until 5:30).*

Key West Lighthouse Museum & Keeper's Quarters Museum. For the best view in town, climb the 88 steps to the top of this 1847 lighthouse. The 92-foot structure has a Fresnel lens, which was installed in the 1860s at a cost of $1 million. The keeper lived in the adjacent 1887 clapboard house, which now exhibits vintage photographs, ship models, nautical charts, and lighthouse artifacts from all along the Key reefs. A kids' room is stocked with books and toys. ⊠ *938 Whitehead St.* ☎ *305/295–6616* ⊕ *www.kwahs.com* ☒ *$10* ☉ *Daily 9:30–4:30.*

Fodor'sChoice ★ **Key West Museum of Art & History in the Custom House.** When Key West was designated a U.S. port of entry in the early 1820s, a customs house was established. Salvaged cargoes from ships wrecked on the reefs were brought here, setting the stage for Key West to become—for a time—the richest city in Florida. The imposing redbrick-and-terra-cotta Richardsonian Romanesque–style building reopened as a museum and art gallery in 1999. Smaller galleries have long-term and changing exhibits about the history of Key West, including a Hemingway room and a fine collection of folk artist Mario Sanchez's wood paintings. In 2011, to commemorate the 100th anniversary of the railroad's arrival to Key West in 1912, a new permanent Flagler exhibit opened. ⊠ *281 Front St.* ☎ *305/295–6616* ⊕ *www.kwahs.com* ☒ *$9* ☉ *Daily 9:30–4:30.*

Mallory Square and Pier. For cruise-ship passengers, this is the disembarkation point for an attack on Key West. For practically every visitor, it's the requisite venue for a nightly sunset celebration that includes street performers—human statues, sword swallowers, tightrope walkers, musicians, and more—plus craft vendors, conch fritter fryers, and other regulars who defy classification. (Wanna picture with my pet iguana?) With all the activity, don't forget to watch the main show: a dazzling tropical sunset.

The Southernmost Point. Possibly the most photographed site in Key West (even though the actual geographic southernmost point in the continental United States lies across the bay on a naval base, where you see a satellite dish), this is a must-see. Who wouldn't want his picture taken

Divers examine the intentionally scuttled 327-foot former U.S. Coast Guard cutter *Duane* in 120 feet of water off Key Largo.

next to the big striped buoy that marks the southernmost point in the continental United States? A plaque next to it honors Cubans who lost their lives trying to escape to America and other signs tell Key West history. ✉ *Whitehead and South sts.*

NEW TOWN

The Overseas Highway splits as it enters Key West, the two forks rejoining to encircle New Town, the area east of White Street to Cow Key Channel. The southern fork runs along the shore as South Roosevelt Boulevard (Route A1A), skirting Key West International Airport. Along the north shore, North Roosevelt Boulevard (U.S. 1) leads to Old Town. Part of New Town was created with dredged fill. The island would have continued growing this way had the Army Corps of Engineers not determined in the early 1970s that it was detrimental to the nearby reef.

Fort East Martello Museum & Gardens. This redbrick Civil War fort never saw a lick of action during the war. Today it serves as a museum, with historical exhibits about the 19th and 20th centuries. Among the latter are relics of the USS *Maine*, cigar factory and shipwrecking exhibits, and the citadel tower you can climb to the top. The museum, operated by the Key West Art and Historical Society, also has a collection of Stanley Papio's "junk art" sculptures inside and out, and a gallery of Cuban folk artist Mario Sanchez's chiseled and painted wooden carvings of historic Key West street scenes. ✉ *3501 S. Roosevelt Blvd.* ☎ *305/296–3913* ⊕ *www.kwahs.com* 🎫 *$9* ⊙ *Daily 9:30–4:30.*

Key West Tropical Forest & Botanical Garden. Established in 1935, this unique habitat is the only frost-free botanical garden in the continental United States. You won't see fancy topiaries and exotic plants, but you'll

THE CONCH REPUBLIC

Beginning in the 1970s, pot smuggling became a source of income for islanders who knew how to dodge detection in the maze of waterways in the Keys. In 1982 the U.S. Border Patrol threw a roadblock across the Overseas Highway just south of Florida City to catch drug runners and undocumented aliens. Traffic backed up for miles as Border Patrol agents searched vehicles and demanded that the occupants prove U.S. citizenship. Officials in Key West, outraged at being treated like foreigners by the federal government, staged a protest and formed their own "nation": the so-called Conch Republic. They hoisted a flag and distributed mock border passes, visas, and Conch currency. The embarrassed Border Patrol dismantled its roadblock, and now an annual festival recalls the city's victory. You can even "apply" for a Conch Republic passport (for entertainment purposes, not travel!). It'll set you back $100, but those who hold one think it's priceless. Begin your journey online at ⊕ www.conchrepublic.com.

see a unique ecosystem that naturally occurs in this area and the Caribbean. There are paved walkways that take you past butterfly gardens, mangroves, Cuban palms, lots of birds like herons and ibis, and ponds where you can spy turtles and fish. It's a nice respite from the sidewalks and shops, and offers a natural slice of Keys paradise. ⊠ 5210 College Rd. ☎ 305/296–1504 ⊕ www.kwbgs.org ⊠ $7 ⊙ Daily 10–4.

BEACHES

OLD TOWN

Dog Beach. Next to Louie's Backyard, this tiny beach—the only one in Key West where dogs are allowed unleashed—has a shore that's a mix of sand and rocks. **Amenities:** none. **Best for:** walking. ⊠ Vernon and Waddell sts. ⊠ Free ⊙ Daily sunrise–sunset.

FAMILY **Fort Zachary Taylor Beach.** The park's beach is the best and safest place to swim in Key West. There's an adjoining picnic area with barbecue grills and shade trees, a snack bar, and rental equipment, including snorkeling gear. A café serves sandwiches and other munchies. **Amenities:** food and drink; showers, toilets; water sports. **Best for:** swimming; snorkeling. ⊠ Southard St., at the end of the street, through Truman Annex ☎ 305/292–6713 ⊕ www.floridastateparks.org/forttaylor ⊠ $4 for single-occupant vehicle, $6 for 2–8 people in a vehicle, plus $0.50 per person county surcharge ⊙ Daily 8–sunset; tours at noon and 2.

FAMILY **Higgs Beach–Astro City Playground.** This Monroe County park with its groomed pebbly sand is a popular sunbathing spot. A nearby grove of Australian pines provides shade, and the West Martello Tower provides shelter should a storm suddenly sweep in. Kayak and beach-chair rentals are available, as is a volleyball net. The beach also has a marker and cultural exhibit commemorating the gravesite of 295 enslaved Africans who died after being rescued from three South America–bound slave ships in 1860. Across the street, **Astro City Playground** is popular with

young children. **Amenities:** parking (free); toilets; water sports. **Best for:** swimming; snorkeling. ✉ *Atlantic Blvd., between White and Reynolds sts.* 🎟 *Free* 🕒 *Daily 6 am–11 pm.*

NEW TOWN

C. B. Harvey Memorial Rest Beach. This beach and park were named after Cornelius Bradford Harvey, former Key West mayor and commissioner. Adjacent to Higgs Beach, it has half a dozen picnic areas across the street, dunes, a pier, and a wheelchair and bike path. **Amenities:** none. **Best for:** walking. ✉ *Atlantic Blvd., east side of White St. Pier* 🎟 *Free* 🕒 *Daily 6 am–11 pm.*

Smathers Beach. This wide beach has nearly 1 mile of nice white sand, plus beautiful coconut palms, picnic areas, and volleyball courts, all of which make it popular with the spring-break crowd. Trucks along the road rent rafts, windsurfers, and other beach "toys." **Amenities:** parking (free); toilets; water sports. **Best for:** partiers. ✉ *S. Roosevelt Blvd.* 🎟 *Free* 🕒 *Daily 7 am–11 pm.*

WHERE TO EAT

Bring your appetite, a sense of daring, and a lack of preconceived notions about propriety. A meal in Key West can mean overlooking the crazies along Duval Street, watching roosters and pigeons battle for a scrap of food that may have escaped your fork, relishing the finest in what used to be the dining room of some 19th-century Victorian home, or gazing out at boats jockeying for position in the marina. And that's just the diversity of the setting. Seafood dominates local menus, but the treatment afforded that fish or crustacean can range from Cuban and American to Asian and Continental.

$$ JAPANESE

🍴 **Ambrosia.** Ask any savvy local where to get the best sushi on the island and you'll undoubtedly be pointed to this bright and airy dining room with modern indoor waterfall literally steps from the Atlantic. Grab a seat at the sleek bar, where the back wall glows from purple to blue, or sit at the sushi bar and watch owner and head sushi chef Masa (albeit not the famous chef of the eponymous restaurants in New York and Las Vegas) prepare an impressive array of super fresh sashimi delicacies. Sushi lovers can't go wrong with the Ambrosia special: miso soup served with a sampler of 15 kinds of sashimi, seven pieces of sushi, and sushi rolls. There's an assortment of lightly fried tempura and teriyaki dishes and a killer bento box at lunch. Enjoy it all with a glass of premium sake or a cold glass of Sapporo beer. [$] *Average main: $20* ✉ *Santa Maria Resort, 1401 Simonton St.* ☎ *305/293–0304* 🌐 *www.keywestambrosia.com* 🕒 *Closed 2 wks after Labor Day. No lunch weekends.*

$$$ ECLECTIC

🍴 **Azur Restaurant.** Fuel up on the finest fare at this former gas station, now part of the Eden House complex. In a contemporary setting with indoor and outdoor seating, welcoming staff serves breakfast, lunch, and dinner that stand out from the hordes of Key West restaurants by virtue of originality. For instance, key lime–stuffed French toast and yellowtail snapper Benedict make breakfast a pleasant wake-up call. The crab cake BLT, duck Cubano with fontina cheese, and charred marinated octopus command notice on the lunch menu. Four varieties of homemade gnocchi are a dinner-time specialty, along with tasting plates, "almost entrees" like braised lamb ribs over Moroccan-spiced chickpeas, and main courses that include seafood risotto with chorizo and grilled sea bass. Sunday brunch served. $ Average main: $26 ⊠ 425 Grinnell St. ☎ 305/292–2987 ⊕ www.azurkeywest.com ⌕ Reservations essential.

$ ✕ **B.O.'s Fish Wagon.** What started out as a fish house on wheels appears

SEAFOOD to have broken down on the corner of Caroline and William streets and is today the cornerstone for one of Key West's junkyard-chic dining institutions. Step up to the wood-plank counter window and order the specialty: a grouper sandwich fried or grilled and topped with key lime sauce. Other choices include fish nuts (don't be scared, they're just fried nuggets), hot dogs, cracked conch sandwich, and shrimp or softshell-crab sandwich. Talk sass with your host and find a picnic table or take a seat at the plank. Grab some paper towels off one of the rolls hanging around and busy yourself reading graffiti, license plates, and irreverent signs. It's a must-do Key West experience. $ Average main: $12 ⊠ 801 Caroline St. ☎ 305/294–9272 ⊕ www.bosfishwagon.com ▭ No credit cards.

$$$ ✕ **Blue Heaven.** The outdoor dining area here is often referred to as

CARIBBEAN "the quintessential Keys experience," and it's hard to argue. There's much to like about this historic restaurant where Hemingway refereed boxing matches and customers cheered for cockfights. Although these events are no more, the free-roaming chickens and cats add that "what-a-hoot" factor. Nightly specials include black bean soup, Caribbean BBQ shrimp, bison strip steak with blackberry salad, and jerk chicken. Desserts and breads are baked on the premises. The banana bread and shrimp and grits are hits during breakfast, but the signature meal here is the lobster Benedict with key lime hollandaise. Bring patience as there is always a wait. $ Average main: $24 ⊠ 729 Thomas St. ☎ 305/296–8666 ⊕ www.blueheavenkw.com ⌕ Reservations not accepted ⊘ Closed after Labor Day for 6 wks.

$ ✕ **The Café.** You don't have to be a vegetarian to love this new-age café

VEGETARIAN decorated with bright artwork and a corrugated tin–fronted counter. Local favorites include homemade soup, veggie sandwiches and burgers (order them with a side of sweet potato fries), grilled portobello mushroom salad, seafood, vegan specialties, stir-fry dinners, and grilled Gorgonzola pizza. There's also a nice selection of draft beer and wines by the glass, plus daily desserts (including vegan selections). $ Average main: $11 ⊠ 509 Southard St. ☎ 305/296–5515 ⊕ www.thecafekw.com ⌕ Reservations not accepted ⊘ Closed Sun.

$$$ ✕ **Café Marquesa.** Chef Susan Ferry presents seven or more inspired

EUROPEAN entrées on her changing menu each night; delicious dishes can include

Fodor's Choice yellowtail snapper with pear, ricotta pasta purses with caponata, and

★ Australian rack of lamb crusted with goat cheese and a port-fig sauce. End your meal on a sweet note with key lime napoleon with tropical fruits and berries. There's also a fine selection of wines and custom martinis such as the key limetini and the Irish martini. Adjoining the intimate Marquesa Hotel, the dining room is equally relaxed and elegant.

$ Average main: $29 ✉ 600 Fleming St. ☎ 305/292–1244 🌐 www.marquesa.com ✍ Reservations essential ⏲ No lunch.

$$$ FRENCH 🍴 **Café Solé.** This little corner of France hides behind a high wall in a residential neighborhood. Inside, French training intertwines with local ingredients, creating delicious takes on classics, including a must-try conch Carpaccio, yellowtail snapper with mango salsa, and some of the best bouillabaisse that you'll find outside of Marseilles. Hog snapper (aka hogfish) is a house specialty here, prepared several ways by Chef John Correa, including with beurre blanc or red pepper–custard sauce. From the land, there is filet mignon with a wild-mushroom demi-glaze. Lunch is served from 11 to 2, dinner from 5 to 10. *$ Average main: $27 ✉ 1029 Southard St. ☎ 305/294–0230 🌐 www.cafesole.com ✍ Reservations essential.*

$$$ MODERN AMERICAN 🍴 **Camille's Restaurant.** Break out the stretchy pants because everything on the menu at this affordable hot spot not only sounds scrumptious, it is. Start your day with a shrimp, lobster, or crab-cake Benedict—the latter was voted best in the Florida Keys. Lunch brings dishes like hand-pulled chicken salad or a mahimahi wrap. Evenings will have you swooning for the famous grilled stone-crab cakes with an addictive Captain Morgan spiced rum–mango sauce. Locals have tried to keep this place a secret for over 20 years, but the word is out. Line up beneath the bright pink awning and happily wait for your seat. Be sure to ask your server about the Barbie dolls—they have a most unique collection, many with a Key West flair. *$ Average main: $21 ✉ 1202 Simonton St., at Catherine St. ☎ 305/296-4811 🌐 www.camilleskeywest.com ✍ Reservations essential.*

$$$ MODERN AMERICAN 🍴 **Deuce's Off the Hook Grill.** It's a tight fit with only six tables (and six counter seats), but if you don't mind sitting close to fellow diners, you will be rewarded with a made-from-scratch meal almost any time of day. Battered chicken tenders with waffles and huevos rancheros will rev up your morning. Coconut-crusted mahimahi with mango salsa is the signature lunch dish, but the lobster pie (pizza with poached lobster, goat cheese, arugula, and shaved fig) is a close second. Dinners run the gamut with the likes of "The Gobbler" (freshly roasted turkey with bacon smashed potatoes on a sage-stuffed waffle) to grouper in bouillabaisse with fennel. A specials board lists plenty of tempting options too, but be sure to ask the price since seafood risotto might *sound* great, but when the reality hits your bill, your wallet won't be happy. *$ Average main: $21 ✉ 728 Simonton St. ☎ 305/414–8428 ✍ Reservations essential.*

$$ CUBAN 🍴 **El Meson de Pepe.** If you want to get a taste of the island's Cuban heritage, this is the place. Perfect for after watching a Mallory Square sunset, you can dine alfresco or in the dining room on refined versions of Cuban classics. Begin with a megasize mojito while you enjoy the basket of bread and savory sauces. The expansive menu offers *tostones rellenos* (green plantains with different traditional fillings), ceviche, and more. Choose from Cuban specialties such as roasted pork in a cumin mojo sauce and *ropa vieja* (shredded beef stew). At lunch, the local Cuban population and cruise-ship passengers enjoy Cuban sandwiches and smaller versions of dinner's most popular entrées. A Latin band performs outside at the bar during sunset celebration. *$ Average main: $19*

✉ *410 Wall St., Mallory Sq.* ☎ *305/295–2620* 🌐 *www.elmesondepepe.com.*

$ CUBAN 🍴 **El Siboney.** Dining at this family-style restaurant is like going to Mom's for Sunday dinner—if your mother is Cuban. The dining room is noisy, and the food is traditional *cubano*. There are well-seasoned black beans, a memorable paella, traditional ropa vieja, and local seafood served grilled, stuffed, and breaded. Dishes come with plantains and beans and rice or salad and fries. To make a good thing even better, the prices are very reasonable. [$] *Average main: $10* ✉ *900 Catherine St.* ☎ *305/296–4184* 🌐 *www.elsiboneyrestaurant.com* ✍ *Reservations not accepted.*

$$ SEAFOOD FAMILY 🍴 **Half Shell Raw Bar.** Smack-dab on the docks, this legendary institution gets its name from the oysters, clams, and peel-and-eat shrimp that are a departure point for its seafood-based diet. It's not clever recipes or fine dining (or even air-conditioning) that packs 'em in; it's fried fish, po'boy sandwiches, and seafood combos. For a break from the deep fryer, try the fresh and light conch ceviche "cooked" with lime juice. The potato salad is flavored with dill, and the "PamaRita" is a new twist in Margaritaville. [$] *Average main: $16* ✉ *Lands End Village at Historic Seaport, 231 Margaret St.* ☎ *305/294–7496* 🌐 *www.halfshellrawbar.com* ✍ *Reservations not accepted.*

$ SEAFOOD 🍴 **Hogfish Bar & Grill.** It's worth a drive to Stock Island, just outside of Key West, to sit along one of Florida's last surviving working waterfronts, watch the shrimpers and fishermen unloading their catch, and indulge in the freshness you're witnessing at this down-to-earth spot. Hogfish is of course the specialty. The "Killer Hogfish Sandwich" comes on Cuban Bread (you can also have it as a breakfast Benedict); sprinkle it with one of the house hot sauces. Other favorites include lobster BLT, pulled pork sandwich, hogfish tacos, gator bites, lobster potpie, and barbeque ribs. [$] *Average main: $13* ✉ *6810 Front St., Stock Island* ☎ *305/293–4041* 🌐 *www.hogfishbar.com.*

$ AMERICAN FAMILY 🍴 **Lobo's Mixed Grill.** Famous for its selection of wrap sandwiches, Lobo's has a reputation among locals for its 8-ounce, charcoal-grilled ground chuck burger—thick and juicy and served with lettuce, tomato, and pickle on a toasted bun. Mix it up with toppings like Brie, blue cheese, or portobello mushroom. The menu of 30 wraps includes ribeye, oyster, grouper, Cuban, and chicken Caesar. The menu includes salads and quesadillas, as well as a fried-shrimp-and-oyster combo. Beer and wine are served. This courtyard food stand closes around 5, so eat early. Most of Lobo's business is takeout (it has a half-dozen outdoor picnic tables), and it offers free delivery within Old Town. [$] *Average main: $9* ✉ *5 Key Lime Sq., east of intersection of Southard and Duval sts.* ☎ *305/296–5303* 🌐 *www.lobosmixedgrill.com* ✍ *Reservations not accepted* ⏲ *Closed Sun. Apr.–early Dec.*

$$$$ ECLECTIC 🍴 **Louie's Backyard.** Feast your eyes on a steal-your-breath-away view and beautifully presented dishes prepared by executive chef Doug Shook. Once you get over sticker shock on the seasonally changing menu, settle in on the outside deck and enjoy dishes like grilled scallops with portobello relish, grilled king salmon with fried risotto, and mint-rubbed pork chop with salsa verde. A more affordable option upstairs is the Upper Deck, which serves tapas such as flaming ouzo shrimp, roasted

Where to Eat and Stay in Old Town

ATLANTIC OCEAN

0 — 1/2 mile
0 — 1/2 km

olives with onion and feta, and Gruyère and duck confit pizza. If you come for lunch, the menu is less expensive but the view is just as fantastic. For night owls, the tin-roofed Afterdeck Bar serves cocktails on the water until the wee hours. $ *Average main: $36* ✉ *700 Waddell Ave.* ☎ *305/294–1061* ⊕ *www.louiesbackyard.com* ✍ *Reservations essential* ☺ *Closed Labor Day to mid-Sept. Upper Deck closed Sun. and Mon. No lunch on Upper Deck.*

$$
ITALIAN

✕ **Mangia Mangia.** This longtime favorite serves large portions of home-made pastas that can be matched with any of their homemade sauces. Tables are arranged in a brick garden hung with twinkling lights and in a cozy, casual dining room in an old house. Everything out of the open kitchen is outstanding, including the *bollito misto di mare* (fresh seafood sautéed with garlic, shallots, white wine, and pasta) or the memorable spaghettini "schmappellini," homemade pasta with asparagus, tomatoes, pine nuts, and Parmesan. The wine list—with more than 350 offerings—includes old and rare vintages, and also has a good by-the-glass selection. $ *Average main: $16* ✉ *900 Southard St.* ☎ *305/294–2469* ⊕ *www.mangia-mangia.com* ✍ *Reservations not accepted* ☺ *No lunch.*

$$$
AMERICAN

✕ **Michaels Restaurant.** White tablecloths, subdued lighting, and romantic music give Michaels the feel of an urban eatery. Garden seating reminds you that you are in the Keys. Chef-owner Michael Wilson flies in prime rib, cowboy steaks, and ribeyes from Allen Brothers in Chicago, which has supplied top-ranked steakhouses for more than a century. Also on the menu is a melt-in-your-mouth grouper stuffed with jumbo lump crab, Kobe and tenderloin meat loaf, veal saltimbocca, and a variety of made-to-order fondue dishes (try the pesto pot, spiked with hot pepper and basil). To lighten up, smaller portions of many of the favorites are available until 7:30 Sunday through Thursday. The Hemingway (mojito-style) and the Third Degree (raspberry vodka and white crème de cacao) top the cocktail menu. $ *Average main: $25* ✉ *532 Margaret St.* ☎ *305/295–1300* ⊕ *www.michaelskeywest.com* ✍ *Reservations essential* ☺ *No lunch.*

$$$
ECLECTIC

✕ **Nine One Five.** Twinkling lights draped along the lower- and upper-level outdoor porches of a 100-year-old Victorian mansion set an elegant—though unstuffy—stage here. If you like to sample and sip, you'll appreciate the variety of smaller plate selections and wines by the glass. Starters include a cheese platter, crispy duck confit, a tapas platter, and the signature "tuna dome" with fresh crab, lemon-miso dressing, and an ahi tuna–sashimi wrapping. There are also larger plates if you're craving something like seafood soup or steak au poivre frites. Dine outdoors and people-watch along upper Duval, or sit at a table inside while listening to light jazz. $ *Average main: $28* ✉ *915 Duval St.* ☎ *305/296–0669* ⊕ *www.915duval.com* ✍ *Reservations essential* ☺ *No lunch.*

$$$$
EUROPEAN

✕ **Pisces.** In a circa-1892 former store and home, chef William Arnel and staff create a contemporary setting with a stylish granite bar, Andy Warhol originals, and glass oil lamps. Favorites include "lobster tango mango," flambéed in cognac and served with saffron butter sauce and sliced mangoes; filet mignon with bordelaise sauce; and yellowtail Atocha with lemon brown butter, shrimp, and scallops. [$] *Average main: $35* ✉ *1007 Simonton St.* ☎ *305/294–7100* 🌐 *www.pisceskeywest.com* ✍ *Reservations essential* ⏲ *No lunch.*

$$ ITALIAN 🍴 **Salute Ristorante at the Beach.** Sister restaurant to Blue Heaven, this colorful establishment sits on Higgs Beach, giving it one of the island's best lunch views—and a bit of sand and salt spray on a windy day. The intriguing menu is Italian with a Caribbean flair and will not disappoint. For dinner, popular dishes include linguine with mussels, lasagna, and white bean soup. At lunch the gazpacho refreshes with great flavor and texture, and the calamari marinara, antipasti sandwich, and yellowtail sandwich will having you singing "Amore." [$] *Average main: $20* ✉ *1000 Atlantic Blvd., Higgs Beach* ☎ *305/292–1117* 🌐 *www.saluteonthebeach.com* ✍ *Reservations not accepted.*

$ TAPAS Fodor's Choice ★ 🍴 **Santiago's Bodega.** If you've ever wondered where chefs go for a great meal in the lower Keys, this is their secret spot. Picky palates will be satisfied at this funky, dark, and sensuous corner house, which is well off the main drag. Dine on the front porch surrounded by fuchsia bougainvillea or inside amid eclectic paintings and mismatched chandeliers. Waiters recommend choosing three of the small plates per person, then sharing. That number works. Cold tapas include dishes like yellowfin tuna ceviche with large hunks of avocado and mango, and shaved beef carpaccio with smoked sea salt and truffle oil. Favorite hot tapas are filet mignon with creamy Gorgonzola butter and cherry-hoisin-glazed beef shortribs. Dessert? The bread pudding is legendary. Reward yourself for finding this place with a fruit-filled glass of homemade red or white sangria. All bets say you'll eat here over and over again. [$] *Average main: $13* ✉ *Bahama Village, 207 Petronia St.* ☎ *305/296–7691* 🌐 *www.santiagosbodega.com* ✍ *Reservations essential.*

$$$ SEAFOOD 🍴 **Seven Fish.** A local hot spot, this intimate, off-the-beaten-track eatery is good for an eclectic mix of dishes like tropical shrimp salsa, wild-mushroom quesadilla, seafood marinara, and old-fashioned meat loaf with real mashed potatoes. For dessert, the sweet potato pie provides an added measure of down-home comfort. Those in the know reserve for dinner early to snag one of the 20 or so tables clustered in the bare-bones dining room. [$] *Average main: $26* ✉ *632 Olivia St.* ☎ *305/296–2777* 🌐 *www.7fish.com* ✍ *Reservations essential* ⏲ *Closed Tues. No lunch.*

$$ SEAFOOD FAMILY 🍴 **Turtle Kraals.** Named for the *kraals,* or corrals, where sea turtles were once kept until they went to the cannery, this place calls to mind the island's history. The lunch-dinner menu offers an assortment of marine cuisine that includes seafood enchiladas, mesquite-grilled fish of the day, and mango crab cakes. The slow-cook wood smoker results in wonderfully tender ribs, brisket, mesquite-grilled oysters with Parmesan and cilantro, and mesquite-grilled chicken sandwich. The open restaurant overlooks the marina at the Historic Seaport. Turtle races entertain during happy hour on Monday and Friday at 6 pm. [$] *Average main: $16* ✉ *231 Margaret St.* ☎ *305/294–2640* 🌐 *www.turtlekraals.com.*

WHERE TO STAY

Historic cottages, restored century-old Conch houses, and large resorts are among the offerings in Key West, the majority charging from $100 to $300 a night. In high season, Christmas through Easter, you'll be hard-pressed to find a decent room for less than $200, and most places raise prices considerably during holidays and festivals. Many guesthouses and inns don't welcome children under 16, and most don't permit smoking indoors. Rates often include an expanded continental breakfast and afternoon wine or snack.

$$$
B&B/INN

Ambrosia Key West. If you desire personal attention, a casual atmosphere, and a dollop of style, stay at these twin inns spread out on nearly 2 acres. **Pros:** spacious rooms; poolside breakfast; friendly staff. **Cons:** on-street parking can be tough to come by; a little too spread out. $ *Rooms from: $319* ⊠ *615, 618, 622 Fleming St.* ☎ *305/296–9838, 800/535–9838* ⊕ *www.ambrosiakeywest.com* ➷ *6 rooms, 3 town houses, 1 cottage, 10 suites* ⏐◯⏐ *Breakfast.*

$
B&B/INN

Angelina Guest House. In the heart of Old Town, this home away from home offers simple, clean, attractively priced accommodations. **Pros:** good value; nice garden; friendly staff. **Cons:** thin walls; basic rooms; shared balcony. $ *Rooms from: $109* ⊠ *302 Angela St.* ☎ *305/294–4480, 888/303–4480* ⊕ *www.angelinaguesthouse.com* ➷ *13 rooms* ⏐◯⏐ *Breakfast.*

$$
B&B/INN

Azul Key West. The ultramodern—nearly minimalistic—redo of this classic circa-1903 Queen Anne mansion is a break from the sensory overload of Key West's other abundant Victorian guesthouses. **Pros:** lovely building; marble-floored baths; luxurious linens. **Cons:** on a busy street. $ *Rooms from: $249* ⊠ *907 Truman Ave.* ☎ *305/296–5152, 888/253–2985* ⊕ *www.azulhotels.us* ➷ *10 rooms, 1 suite* ⏐◯⏐ *Breakfast.*

$$$
RESORT
FAMILY

Casa Marina Resort & Beach Club. At any moment, you expect the landed gentry to walk across the oceanfront lawn of this luxurious resort, just as they did when this 13-acre resort was built back in the 1920s. **Pros:** nice beach; historic setting; away from the crowds. **Cons:** long walk to central Old Town; expensive resort fee. $ *Rooms from: $359* ⊠ *1500 Reynolds St.* ☎ *305/296–3535, 866/203–6392* ⊕ *www.casamarinaresort.com* ➷ *241 rooms, 70 suites* ⏐◯⏐ *No meals.*

$$
B&B/INN

Courtney's Place. If you like kids, cats, and dogs, you'll feel right at home in this collection of accommodations ranging from cigar-maker cottages to shotgun houses. **Pros:** near Duval Street; fairly priced. **Cons:** small parking lot; small pool; minimum-stay requirements. $ *Rooms from: $249* ⊠ *720 Whitmarsh La., off Petronia St.* ☎ *305/294–3480, 800/869–4639* ⊕ *www.courtneysplacekeywest.com* ➷ *6 rooms, 2 suites, 2 efficiencies, 8 cottages* ⏐◯⏐ *Breakfast.*

$
HOTEL

Crowne Plaza Key West–La Concha. History and franchises can mix, as this 1920s-vintage hotel proves with its handsome faux-palm atrium lobby and sleep-conducive rooms. **Pros:** restaurant and Starbucks in house; close to downtown attractions; free Wi-Fi. **Cons:** high-traffic area; confusing layout; expensive valet-only parking. $ *Rooms from: $199* ⊠ *430 Duval St.* ☎ *305/296–2991* ⊕ *www.laconchakeywest.com* ➷ *160 rooms, 8 rooms with balconies, 10 suites* ⏐◯⏐ *No meals.*

4

$ 🏨 **Eden House.** From the vintage metal rockers on the street-side porch
HOTEL   to the old neon hotel sign in the lobby, this 1920s rambling Key West
mainstay hotel is high on character, low on gloss. **Pros:** free parking;
hot tub is actually hot; daily happy hour around the pool; discount at
excellent Azur restaurant. **Cons:** pricey; a bit of a musty smell in some
rooms; no TV in some rooms. $ *Rooms from: $200* ⊠ *1015 Fleming St.*
☎ *305/296–6868, 800/533–5397* ⊕ *www.edenhouse.com* ⌇ *36 rooms,
8 suites* ⦿ *No meals.*

$$$ 🏨 **The Gardens Hotel.** Built in 1875, this gloriously shaded, award-win-
HOTEL   ning property was a labor of love from the get-go, and it covers a third
Fodor'sChoice   of a city block in Old Town. **Pros:** luxurious bathrooms; secluded gar-
★   den seating; free domestic phone calls and Wi-Fi. **Cons:** hard to get
reservations; expensive; nightly secure-parking fee. $ *Rooms from:
$385* ⊠ *526 Angela St.* ☎ *305/294–2661, 800/526–2664* ⊕ *www.
gardenshotel.com* ⌇ *17 rooms* ⦿ *Breakfast.*

$$ 🏨 **Hyatt Key West Resort and Spa.** With its own man-made beach, the
RESORT   Hyatt Key West is one of few resorts where you can dig your toes in
FAMILY   the sand, then walk a short distance away to the streets of Old Town.
Pros: a little bit away from the bustle of Old Town; plenty of activities.
Cons: beach is small; cramped-feeling property. $ *Rooms from: $290*
⊠ *601 Front St.* ☎ *305/809–1234* ⊕ *www.keywest.hyatt.com* ⌇ *118
rooms* ⦿ *No meals.*

$ 🏨 **Key Lime Inn.** This 1854 Grand Bahama–style house on the National
B&B/INN   Register of Historic Places succeeds by offering amiable service, a
great location, and simple rooms with natural-wood furnishings. **Pros:**
free parking; some rooms have private outdoor spaces. **Cons:** standard rooms are pricey; pool faces a busy street; mulch-covered paths.
$ *Rooms from: $179* ⊠ *725 Truman Ave.* ☎ *305/294–5229, 800/549–
4430* ⊕ *www.keylimeinn.com* ⌇ *37 rooms* ⦿ *Breakfast.*

$ 🏨 **Key West Bed and Breakfast/The Popular House.** There are accommo-
B&B/INN   dations for every budget, but the owners reason that budget travelers
deserve as pleasant an experience (and lavish a tropical Continental
breakfast) as their well-heeled counterparts. **Pros:** lots of art; tiled outdoor shower; hot tub and sauna area is a welcome hangout. **Cons:** some
rooms are small. $ *Rooms from: $99* ⊠ *415 William St.* ☎ *305/296–
7274, 800/438–6155* ⊕ *www.keywestbandb.com* ⌇ *10 rooms, 6 with
private bath* ⦿ *Breakfast.*

$$$ 🏨 **Key West Marriott Beachside Hotel.** This hotel vies for convention busi-
HOTEL   ness with the biggest ballroom in Key West, but it also appeals to fam-
ilies with its spacious condo units decorated with impeccable taste.
Pros: private beach; poolside cabanas. **Cons:** small beach; long walk
to Old Town; cookie-cutter facade. $ *Rooms from: $340* ⊠ *3841 N.
Roosevelt Blvd., New Town* ☎ *305/296–8100, 800/546–0885* ⊕ *www.
keywestmarriottbeachside.com* ⌇ *93 rooms, 93 1-bedroom suites, 10
2-bedroom suites, 26 3-bedroom suites* ⦿ *No meals.*

$$$ 🏨 **Marquesa Hotel.** In a town that prides itself on its laid-back luxury,
HOTEL   this complex of four restored 1884 houses stands out. **Pros:** elegant set-
Fodor'sChoice   ting; romantic atmosphere; turndown service. **Cons:** street-facing rooms
★   can be noisy; expensive rates. $ *Rooms from: $345* ⊠ *600 Fleming St.*

☎ *305/292–1919, 800/869–4631* 🌐 *www.marquesa.com* 🛏 *27 rooms* 🍴 *No meals.*

$$ B&B/INN 🏨 **Merlin Guesthouse.** Key West guesthouses don't usually welcome families, but this laid-back jumble of rooms and suites is an exception. **Pros:** good location near Duval Street; good rates. **Cons:** neighbor noise; street parking. [$] *Rooms from: $279* ✉ *811 Simonton St.* ☎ *305/296–3336, 800/642–4753* 🌐 *www.merlinguesthouse.com* 🛏 *10 rooms, 6 suites, 4 cottages* 🍴 *Breakfast.*

$$ B&B/INN 🏨 **Mermaid & the Alligator.** An enchanting combination of flora and fauna makes this 1904 Victorian house a welcoming retreat. **Pros:** hot plunge pool; massage pavilion; island-getaway feel. **Cons:** minimum stay required (length depends on season); dark public areas; plastic lawn chairs. [$] *Rooms from: $268* ✉ *729 Truman Ave.* ☎ *305/294–1894, 800/773–1894* 🌐 *www.kwmermaid.com* 🛏 *9 rooms* 🍴 *Breakfast.*

4

$$$$ RESORT Fodor's Choice ★ 🏨 **Ocean Key Resort & Spa.** A pool and lively open-air bar and restaurant sit on Sunset Pier, a popular place to watch the sun sink into the horizon. **Pros:** well-trained staff; lively pool scene; best spa on the island. **Cons:** $20 per night valet parking; too bustling for some; pricey. [$] *Rooms from: $450* ✉ *Zero Duval St.* ☎ *305/296–7701, 800/328–9815* 🌐 *www.oceankey.com* 🛏 *64 rooms, 36 suites* 🍴 *No meals.*

$$$ HOTEL 🏨 **Parrot Key Resort.** This revamped destination resort feels like an old-fashioned beach community with picket fences and rocking-chair porches. **Pros:** four pools; finely appointed units; access to marina and other facilities at three sister properties in Marathon. **Cons:** outside of walking distance to Old Town; no transportation provided; hefty resort fee. [$] *Rooms from: $329* ✉ *2801 N. Roosevelt Blvd.* ☎ *305/809–2200* 🌐 *www.parrotkeyresort.com* 🛏 *74 rooms, 74 suites, 74 3-bedroom villas* 🍴 *No meals.*

$$$$ RESORT 🏨 **Pier House Resort and Caribbean Spa.** The location—on a quiet stretch of beach at the foot of Duval—is ideal as a buffer from and gateway to the action. **Pros:** beautiful beach; good location; nice spa. **Cons:** lots of conventions; poolside rooms are small; not really suitable for children under 16. [$] *Rooms from: $460* ✉ *1 Duval St.* ☎ *305/296–4600, 800/327–8340* 🌐 *www.pierhouse.com* 🛏 *116 rooms, 26 suites* 🍴 *No meals.*

$$ RESORT 🏨 **The Reach Resort.** Embracing Key West's only natural beach, this full-service, luxury resort offers sleek rooms with modern amenities as well as shared access to its sister Casa Marina resort nearby. **Pros:** removed from Duval hubbub; great sunrise views; pullout sofas in most rooms. **Cons:** expensive resort fee; high rates. [$] *Rooms from: $300* ✉ *1435 Simonton St.* ☎ *305/296–5000, 888/318–4316* 🌐 *www.reachresort.com* 🛏 *72 rooms, 78 suites* 🍴 *No meals.*

$$$ RENTAL Fodor's Choice ★ 🏨 **Santa Maria Suites.** It's odd to call this a "hidden gem" when it sits on a prominent corner just one block off Duval, but you'd never know the luxury that awaits behind its concrete facade. **Pros:** amenities galore; front desk concierge services; private parking lot. **Cons:** daily resort fee; beds low to the ground. [$] *Rooms from: $350* ✉ *1401 Simonton St.* ☎ *866/726–8259, 305/296–5678* 🌐 *www.santamariasuites.com* 🛏 *34 suites* 🍴 *No meals.*

Sunset Key cottages are right on the water's edge, far away from the action of Old Town.

$$
B&B/INN

🏨 **Simonton Court.** A small world all its own, this adult lodging makes you feel deliciously sequestered from Key West's crasser side, but close enough to get there on foot. **Pros:** lots of privacy; well-appointed accommodations; friendly staff. **Cons:** minimum stays required in high season. [$] *Rooms from: $275* ✉ *320 Simonton St.* ☎ *305/294–6386, 800/944–2687* ⊕ *www.simontoncourt.com* 🛏 *17 rooms, 6 suites, 6 cottages* ꊡ *Breakfast.*

$$$
HOTEL

🏨 **Southernmost Hotel.** This hotel's location on the quiet end of Duval means you don't have to deal with the hustle and bustle of downtown unless you want to—it's within a 20-minute walk (but around sunset, this end of town gets its share of car and foot traffic). **Pros:** pool attracts a lively crowd; access to nearby properties and beach; free parking and Wi-Fi. **Cons:** can get crowded around the pool and public areas; expensive nightly resort fee. [$] *Rooms from: $359* ✉ *1319 Duval St.* ☎ *305/296–6577, 800/354–4455* ⊕ *www.southernmostresorts.com* 🛏 *124 rooms* ꊡ *No meals.*

$
B&B/INN

🏨 **Speakeasy Inn.** During Prohibition, Raul Vasquez made this place popular by smuggling in rum from Cuba; today its reputation is for having reasonably priced rooms within walking distance of the beach. **Pros:** good location; reasonable rates; kitchenettes. **Cons:** no pool; on busy Duval. [$] *Rooms from: $169* ✉ *1117 Duval St.* ☎ *305/296–2680* ⊕ *www.speakeasyinn.com* 🛏 *4 suites* ꊡ *Breakfast.*

$$$$
RESORT
Fodor's Choice
★

🏨 **Sunset Key.** This private island retreat with its own sandy beach feels completely cut off from the world, yet you're just minutes away from the action. **Pros:** peace and quiet; roomy verandas; free 24-hour shuttle; free Wi-Fi. **Cons:** luxury doesn't come cheap. [$] *Rooms from:*

$695 ✉ *245 Front St.* ☎ *305/292–5300, 888/477–7786* ⊕ *www.
westinsunsetkeycottages.com* ⤴ *40 cottages* ✵*Breakfast.*

NIGHTLIFE

Rest up: Much of what happens in Key West does so after dark. Open
your mind and have a stroll. Scruffy street performers strum next to
dogs in sunglasses. Brawls tumble out the doors of Sloppy Joe's. Drag
queens strut across stages in Joan Rivers garb. Tattooed men lick
whipped cream off women's body parts. And margaritas flow like a
Jimmy Buffett tune.

BARS AND LOUNGES

Capt. Tony's Saloon. When it was the original Sloppy Joe's in the mid-
1930s, Hemingway was a regular. Later, a young Jimmy Buffett sang
here and made this watering hole famous in his song "Last Mango
in Paris." Captain Tony was even voted mayor of Key West. Yes, this
place is a beloved landmark. Stop in and take a look at the "hanging
tree" that grows through the roof, listen to live music seven nights a
week, and play some pool. ✉ *428 Greene St.* ☎ *305/294–1838* ⊕ *www.
capttonyssaloon.com.*

Durty Harry's. This megasize entertainment complex is home to eight different bars and clubs, both indoor and outdoor. Their motto is, "Eight
Famous Bars, One Awesome Night," and they're right. You'll find pizza,
dancing, live music, a martini bar, and the infamous Red Garter strip
club. ✉ *208 Duval St.* ☎ *305/296–5513.*

Green Parrot Bar. Pause for a libation in the open air and breathe in the
spirit of Key West. Built in 1890 as a grocery store, this property has
been many things to many people over the years It's touted as the oldest
bar in Key West and the sometimes-rowdy saloon has locals outnumber-
ing out-of-towners, especially on nights when bands play. ✉ *601 Whitehead St., at Southard St.* ☎ *305/294–6133* ⊕ *www.greenparrot.com.*

Hog's Breath Saloon. Belly up to the bar for a cold mug of the signature
Hog's Breath Lager at this infamous joint, a must-stop on the Key West
bar crawl. Live bands play daily 1 pm–2 am (except when the game's on
TV). You never know who'll stop by and perhaps even jump on stage
for an impromptu concert. ✉ *400 Front St.* ☎ *305/296–4222* ⊕ *www.
hogsbreath.com.*

Margaritaville Café. A youngish, touristy crowd mixes with aging Parrot Heads. It's owned by former Key West resident and recording star
Jimmy Buffett, who has been known to perform here. The drink of
choice is, of course, a margarita, made with Jimmy's own brand of
Margaritaville tequila. There's live music nightly, as well as lunch and
dinner. ✉ *500 Duval St.* ☎ *305/292–1435* ⊕ *www.margaritaville.com.*

Pier House. The party here begins with a steel-drum band to celebrate
the sunset on the beach (on select Thursdays and Fridays), then moves
indoors to the Wine Galley piano bar for live jazz. ✉ *1 Duval St.*
☎ *305/296–4600, 800/327–8340* ⊕ *www.pierhouse.com.*

Schooner Wharf Bar. This open-air waterfront bar and grill in the historic seaport district retains its funky Key West charm and hosts live

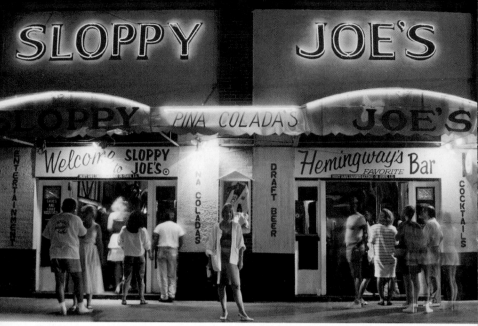

Sloppy Joe's is one must-stop on most Key West visitors' bar-hop stroll, also known as the Duval Crawl.

entertainment daily. Its margaritas rank among Key West's best, as does the bar itself, voted Best Local's Bar six years in a row. For great views, head up to the second floor and be sure to order up some fresh seafood and fritters and Dark and Stormy cocktails. ⊠ *202 William St.* ☎ *305/292–3302* ⊕ *www.schoonerwharf.com.*

Sloppy Joe's. There's history and good times at the successor to a famous 1937 speakeasy named for its founder, Captain Joe Russell. Decorated with Hemingway memorabilia and marine flags, the bar is popular with travelers and is full and noisy all the time. A Sloppy Joe's T-shirt is a de rigueur Key West souvenir, and the gift shop sells them like crazy. Grab a seat (if you can) and be entertained by the bands and by the parade of people in constant motion. ⊠ *201 Duval St.* ☎ *305/294–5717* ⊕ *www.sloppyjoes.com.*

The Top. On the seventh floor of the Crowne Plaza Key West La Concha, this is one of the best places in town to view the sunset and enjoy live entertainment on Friday and Saturday nights. ⊠ *430 Duval St.* ☎ *305/296–2991* ⊕ *www.laconchakeywest.com.*

Virgilio's Martini Bar. In the best traditions of a 1950s cocktail lounge, this bar serves chilled martinis to the soothing tempo of live jazz and blues. Locals love the late night dancing and $5 Martini Mondays. ⊠ *524 Duval St.* ☎ *305/296–8118* ⊕ *www.virgilioskeywest.com.*

SHOPPING

On these streets you'll find colorful local art of widely varying quality, key limes made into everything imaginable, and the raunchiest T-shirts in the civilized world.

MALLS AND SHOPPING CENTERS

Bahama Village. Where to start your shopping adventure? This cluster of spruced-up shops, restaurants, and vendors is responsible for the restoration of the colorful historic district where Bahamians settled in the 19th century. The village lies roughly between Whitehead and Fort streets and Angela and Catherine streets. Hemingway frequented the bars, restaurants, and boxing rings in this part of town. ⊠ *Between Whitehead and Fort sts. and Angela and Catherine sts..*

ARTS AND CRAFTS

Alan S. Maltz Gallery. The owner, declared the state's official wildlife photographer by the Wildlife Foundation of Florida, captures the state's nature and character in stunning portraits. Spend four figures for large-format images on canvas or save on small prints and closeouts. ⊠ *1210 Duval St.* ☎ *305/294–0005* ⊕ *www.alanmaltz.com.*

Art@830. This inviting gallery carries a little bit of everything, from pottery to paintings and jewelry to sculptures. Most outstanding is its selection of glass art, particularly the jellyfish lamps. Take time to admire all that is here. ⊠ *830 Caroline St., Historic Seaport* ☎ *305/295–9595* ⊕ *www.art830.com.*

Gallery on Greene. This is the largest gallery–exhibition space in Key West and it showcases 37 museum-quality artists. They pride themselves on being the leader in the field of representational fine art, painting, sculptures, and reproductions from the Florida Keys and Key West. You can immediately see the love from gallery curator Nancy Frank, who aims to please everyone, from the casual buyer to the established collector. ⊠ *606 Greene St.* ☎ *305/294–1669* ⊕ *www.galleryongreene.com.*

Gingerbread Square Gallery. The oldest private art gallery in Key West represents local and internationally acclaimed artists on an annually changing basis, in mediums ranging from graphics to art glass. ⊠ *1207 Duval St.* ☎ *305/296–8900* ⊕ *www.gingerbreadsquaregallery.com.*

Glass Reunions. Find a collection of wild and impressive fine-art glass here. It's worth a stop in just to see the imaginative and over-the-top glass chandeliers, jewelry, dishes, and platters. ⊠ *825 Duval St.* ☎ *305/294–1720* ⊕ *www.glassreunions.com.*

Key West Pottery. You won't find any painted coconuts here, but you will find a collection of contemporary tropical ceramics. Wife and husband owners Kelly Lever and Adam Russell take real pride in this working studio that, in addition to their own creations, features artists from around the country. This is one of the island's only specialty galleries. ⊠ *929 Truman Ave.* ☎ *305/900–8303* ⊕ *www.keywestpottery.com.*

KW Light Gallery at Island Arts. Historian, photographer, and painter Sharon Wells opened this gallery to showcase her own fine-art photography, painted tiles and canvases. She also offers private tours of Key West. ⊠ *1128 Duval St.* ☎ *305/923–5133* ⊕ *www.keywesttiles.com.*

Nightlife, shops, and some interesting street art can all be found on Key West's Duval Street.

Lucky Street Gallery. High-end contemporary paintings are the focus at this gallery with over 30 years of experience and a passionate staff. There are also a few pieces of jewelry by internationally recognized Key West–based artists. Changing exhibits, artist receptions, and special events make this a lively venue. ✉ *1130 Duval St.* ☎ *305/294–3973* ⊕ *www.luckystreetgallery.com.*

Pelican Poop Shoppe. Caribbean art sells in a historic building (with Hemingway connections, of course). For $2 admission or a $10 purchase, you can stroll the tropical courtyard garden. The owners buy directly from the artisans every year, so the prices are very attractive. ✉ *314 Simonton St.* ☎ *305/292–9955.*

BOOKS

Key West Island Bookstore. This home away from home for the large Key West writers' community carries new, used, and rare titles. It specializes in Hemingway, Tennessee Williams, and South Florida mystery writers. ✉ *513 Fleming St.* ☎ *305/294–2904* ⊕ *www.keywestislandbooks.com.*

CLOTHING AND FABRICS

Fairvilla Megastore. Don't leave town without a browse through the legendary shop, where you'll find an astonishing array of fantasy wear, outlandish costumes (check out the pirate section), and other "adult" toys. ✉ *520 Front St.* ☎ *305/292–0448* ⊕ *www.fairvilla.com.*

Kino Sandals. A pair of Kino Sandals was once a public declaration that you'd been to Key West. The attraction? You can watch these inexpensive items being made. The factory has been churning out several styles since 1966. Walk up to the counter, grab a pair, try them on, and lay down some cash. It's that simple. ⊠ *107 Fitzpatrick St.* ☎ *305/294– 5044* ⊕ *www.kinosandalfactory.com* ⊙ *Closed Sun. in off-season.*

FOOD AND DRINK

Fausto's Food Palace. Since 1926 Fausto's has been the spot to catch up on the week's gossip and to chill out in summer—it has groceries, organic foods, marvelous wines, a sushi chef on duty 8 am–3 pm, and box lunches to go. There are two locations you can shop in Key West (the other is at 1105 White Street), plus a recently opened online store. ⊠ *522 Fleming St.* ☎ *305/296–5663* ⊕ *www.faustos.com.*

Fodor'sChoice **Kermit's Key West Lime Shoppe.** You'll see Kermit himself standing on the
★   corner every time a trolley passes, pie in hand. Besides pie, his shop carries a multitude of key lime products from barbecue sauce to jelly-beans. His prefrozen pies, dressed with a special long-lasting whipped cream instead of meringue, travels well. This is a must-stop shop while in Key West. The key lime pie is the best on the island; once you try it frozen on a stick, dipped in chocolate, you may consider quitting your job and moving here. Savor every bite on their outdoor patio/garden area. Heaven. ⊠ *200 Elizabeth St., Historic Seaport* ☎ *305/296–0806, 800/376–0806* ⊕ *www.keylimeshop.com.*

GIFTS AND SOUVENIRS

Cayo Hueso y Habana. Part museum, part shopping center, this circa-1879 warehouse includes a hand-rolled cigar shop, one-of-a-kind souvenirs, a Cuban restaurant, and exhibits that tell of the island's Cuban heritage. Outside, a memorial garden pays homage to the island's Cuban ances-tors. ⊠ *410 Wall St., Mallory Sq.* ☎ *305/293–7260.*

Cocktails! Key West. Could there possibly be a better location to cel-ebrate the art of the drink than Key West? This celebratory shop car-ries everything you need for cocktails including beautiful hand-painted stemware, highball, martini, and shot glasses, mugs, accessories, and art that blends perfectly. Most of the designs are made on the island. ⊠ *808 Duval St.* ☎ *305/292–1190* ⊕ *www.cocktailskeywest.com.*

Montage. For that unique (but slightly overpriced) souvenir of your trip to Key West head here, where you'll discover hundreds of handcrafted signs of popular Key West guesthouses, inns, hotels, restaurants, bars, and streets. If you can't find what you're looking for, they'll make it for you. ⊠ *291 Front St.* ☎ *305/395–9101, 877/396–4278* ⊕ *www. montagekeywest.com.*

SPORTS AND THE OUTDOORS

Unlike the rest of the region, Key West isn't known primarily for out-door pursuits. But everyone should devote at least half a day to relaxing on a boat tour, heading out on a fishing expedition, or pursuing some other adventure at sea. The ultimate excursion is a boat trip to Dry Tor-tugas National Park for snorkeling and exploring Fort Jefferson. Other excursions cater to nature lovers, scuba divers and snorkelers, anglers, and those who would just like to get out in the water and enjoy the scenery and sunset. For those who prefer their recreation land-based, biking is the way to go.

BIKING

Key West was practically made for bicycles, but don't let that lull you into a false sense of security. Narrow and one-way streets along with car traffic result in several bike accidents a year. Some hotels rent or lend bikes to guests; others will refer you to a nearby shop and reserve a bike for you. Rentals usually start at about $10 a day, but some places also rent by the half day. ∎ TIP→ Lock up! Bikes—and porch chairs!—are favorite targets for local thieves.

A&M Rentals. Rent beach cruisers with large baskets or scooters. Look for the huge American flag on the roof, or call for free airport, ferry, or cruise ship pick-up. ⊠ 523 Truman Ave. ☎ 305/294–0399 ⊕ www. amscooterskeywest.com ⊠ Bicycles from $15, scooters from $35.

Eaton Bikes. Tandem, three-wheel, and children's bikes are available in addition to the standard beach cruisers and hybrid bikes. Delivery is free for all Key West rentals. ⊠ 830 Eaton St. ☎ 305/294–8188 ⊕ www. eatonbikes.com ⊠ From $18 per day.

Lloyd's Original Tropical Bike Tour. Explore the natural, noncommercial side of Key West at a leisurely pace, stopping on backstreets and in backyards of private homes to sample native fruits and view indigenous plants and trees with a 30-year Key West veteran. The behind-the-scenes tours run two hours and include a bike rental. ⊠ Truman Ave. and Simonton St. ☎ 305/304–4700, 305/294–1882 ⊕ www. lloydstropicalbiketour.com ⊠ $39.

Moped Hospital. This outfit supplies balloon-tire bikes with yellow safety baskets for adults and kids, as well as scooters and even double-seater scooters. ⊠ 601 Truman Ave. ☎ 305/296–3344, 866/296–1625 ⊕ www. mopedhospital.com ⊠ Bicycles from $12 per day, scooters from $35 per day.

BOAT TOURS

Dancing Dolphin Spirit Charters. Victoria Impallomeni, a wilderness guide and environmental marine science expert, invites up to six nature lovers—especially children—aboard the *Imp II*, a 25-foot Aquasport, for four-hour and seven-hour ecotours that frequently include encounters with wild dolphins. While island-hopping, you visit underwater gardens, natural shoreline, and mangrove habitats. For her Dolphin Day for Humans tour, Impallomeni pulls you through the water, equipped with mask and snorkel, on a specially designed "dolphin water massage board" that simulates dolphin swimming motions. Sometimes dolphins follow the boat and swim among participants. All equipment is supplied. ⊠ Murray's Marina, MM 5 OS, 5710 Overseas Hwy. ☎ 305/304–7562, 888/822–7366 ⊕ www.captainvictoria.com ⊠ From $500.

White Knuckle Thrill Boat Ride. For something with an adrenaline boost, book with this specially designed jet boat. It holds up to 10 people and does amazing maneuvers like 360s, fishtails, and other water stunts. The cost includes a pickup shuttle from your hotel. ⊠ Sunset Marina, 555 College Rd. ☎ 305/797–0459 ⊕ www.whiteknucklethrillboatride. com ⊠ $59.

BUS AND TROLLEY TOURS

City View Trolley Tours. In 2010, City View Trolley Tours began service, offering a little competition to the Conch Train and Old Town Trolley, which are owned by the same company. Purchase your tickets online or with your smartphone, but you pay double if you pay in person. Tours depart every 30 minutes 9:30–4:30. Passengers can board and disembark at any of nine stops, and can reboard at will. ☎ *305/294–0644* ⊕ *www.cityviewtrolleys.com* ✉ *From $19.*

Conch Tour Train. The Conch Tour Train is a 90-minute narrated tour of Key West, traveling 14 miles through Old Town and around the island. Board at Mallory Square or Angela Street and Duval Street depot every half hour (9–4:30 from Mallory Square). Discount tickets are available online. ☎ *305/294–5161, 888/916–8687* ⊕ *www.conchtourtrain.com* ✉ *$30.45.*

Gay & Lesbian Trolley Tour. Decorated with a rainbow, the Gay and Lesbian Trolley Tour rumbles around the town beginning at 4 pm every Saturday afternoon. The 70-minute tour highlights Key West's gay history. ✉ *513 Truman Ave.* ☎ *305/294–4603* ⊕ *www.gaykeywestfl.com* ✉ *$25.*

Old Town Trolley. Old Town Trolley operates trolley-style buses, departing from the Mallory Square every 30 minutes 9–4:30, for 90-minute narrated tours of Key West. The smaller trolleys go places the larger Conch Tour Train won't fit and you can ride a second consecutive day for free. You may disembark at any of 12 stops and reboard a later trolley. You can save $3 by booking online. It also offers package deals with Old Town attractions. ✉ *201 Front St.* ☎ *305/296–6688, 888/910–8687* ⊕ *www.trolleytours.com* ✉ *$30.*

FISHING

Key West Bait & Tackle. Prepare to catch a big one with the live bait, frozen bait, and fishing equipment provided here. They even offer rod and reel rentals (starting at $15 for 24 hours). Stop by their onsite Live Bait Lounge where you can sip ice-cold beer while telling fish tales. ✉ *241 Margaret St.* ☎ *305/292–1961* ⊕ *www.keywestbaitandtackle.com.*

Key West Pro Guides. This outfitter offers only private charters, and you pay by the half day. Trips include flats and backcountry fishing and reef and offshore fishing. ✉ *G-31 Miriam St.* ☎ *866/259–4205* ⊕ *www. keywestproguides.com* ✉ *From $400.*

GOLF

Key West Golf Club. Key West isn't a major golf destination, but there is one course on Stock Island designed by Rees Jones that will downright surprise you with its water challenges and tropical beauty. It's also the only "Caribbean" golf course in the United States, boasting 200 acres of unique Florida foliage and wildlife. Hole 8 is the famous "Mangrove Hole," which will give you stories to tell. It's a 143-yard par 3 that is played completely over a mass of mangroves with their gnarly roots and branches completely intertwined. Bring extra balls and book your tee time early in season. Nike rental clubs available. ✉ *6450 E. College Rd.* ☎ *305/294–5232* ⊕ *www.keywestgolf.com* ✉ *$52–$97* ⛳ *18 holes. 6500 yards. Par 70.*

KAYAKING

Key West Eco-Tours. Key West is surrounded by marinas, so it's easy to find a water-based activity or tour, whether it's sailing with dolphins or paddling in the mangroves. These sail-kayak-snorkel excursions take you into backcountry flats and mangrove forests without the crowds. The 4½-hour trip includes lunch. Private sunset sails and private charters are also available. ⊠ *Historic Seaport, 100 Grinnell St.* ☎ *305/294–7245* ⊕ *www.keywesteco tours.com* ☜ *From $115.*

Lazy Dog Kayak Guides. Take a two- or four-hour guided sea kayak–snorkel tour around the mangrove islands just east of Key West. Costs include transportation, bottled water, a snack, and supplies, including snorkeling gear. Paddleboard tours are also available, as are rentals for self-touring. ⊠ *5114 Overseas Hwy.* ☎ *305/295–9898* ⊕ *www.lazydog.com* ☜ *From $40.*

SUP Key West. This ancient sport from Hawaii involves a surfboard and a paddle and has quickly become a favorite Florida water sport known as SUP (stand-up paddleboarding). SUP Key West gives lessons and tours of the estuaries. What's more, your tour guides are experts (one's even a PhD) in marine biology and ecology. Call ahead to make arrangements. ⊠ *110 Grinnell St.* ☎ *305/240–1426* ⊕ *www.supkeywest.com* ☜ *From $45.*

SCUBA DIVING AND SNORKELING

The Florida Keys National Marine Sanctuary extends along Key West and beyond to the Dry Tortugas. Key West National Wildlife Refuge further protects the pristine waters. Most divers don't make it this far out in the Keys, but if you're looking for a day of diving as a break from the nonstop party in Old Town, expect to pay about $65 and upward for a two-tank dive. Serious divers can book dive trips to the Dry Tortugas.

Captain's Corner. This PADI-certified dive shop has classes in several languages and twice-daily snorkel and dive trips to reefs and wrecks aboard the 60-foot dive boat *Sea Eagle.* Use of weights, belts, masks, and fins is included. ⊠ *125 Ann St.* ☎ *305/296–8865* ⊕ *www.captainscorner.com* ☜ *From $40.*

Dive Key West. Operating over 40 years, Dive Key West is a full-service dive center that has charters, instruction, gear rental, sales, and repair. You can take either snorkel excursions and regular scuba trips. ⊠ *3128 N. Roosevelt Blvd.* ☎ *305/296–3823* ⊕ *www.divekeywest.com* ☜ *Snorkeling from $59, scuba from $75.*

Snuba of Key West. Safely dive the coral reefs without getting a scuba certification. Ride out to the reef on a catamaran, then follow your guide underwater for a one-hour tour of the coral reefs. You wear a regulator with a breathing hose that is attached to a floating air tank on the surface. No prior diving or snorkeling experience is necessary, but you must know how to swim. The price includes beverages. ⊠ *Garrison Bight Marina, Palm Ave. between Eaton St. and N. Roosevelt Blvd.* ☎ *305/292–4616* ⊕ *www.snubakeywest.com* ☜ *From $99.*

WALKING TOURS

West Martello Tower. Among the arches and ruins of this redbrick Civil War–era fort, the Key West Garden Club maintains lovely gardens of native and tropical plants, fountains, and sculptures. It also holds art, orchid, and flower shows February through April and leads private garden tours one weekend in March. ⊠ *Atlantic Blvd. and White St.* ☎ *305/294–3210* ⊕ *www.keywestgardenclub.com* ✉ *Donations welcome* ☉ *Daily 9:30–5.*

DRY TORTUGAS NATIONAL PARK

70 miles southwest of Key West.

History buffs might remember long-deactivated Fort Jefferson as the prison that held Dr. Samuel Mudd for his role in the Lincoln assassination. But today's "guests" are much more captivated by this sanctuary's thousands of birds and marine life.

GETTING HERE AND AROUND

At this writing, the ferryboat *Yankee Freedom II* departs from a marina in Old Town and does day trips to Garden Key. Key West Seaplane Adventures has half- and full-day trips to the Dry Tortugas, where you can explore Fort Jefferson, built in 1846, and snorkel on the beautiful protected reef. Departing from the Key West airport, the flights include soft drinks and snorkeling equipment for $280 (half day) and $495 (full day), plus there's a $5 (cash only) park fee. If you want to explore the park's other keys, look into renting a boat or hiring a private charter. ⇨ *For more information on the two ferries and the seaplane, see Exploring.*

ESSENTIALS

Visitor Information Dry Tortuqas National Park ☎ *305/242-7700* ⊕ *www. nps.gov/drto.*

EXPLORING

Dry Tortugas National Park. This park, 70 miles off the shores of Key West, consists of seven small islands. Tour the fort, then lay out your blanket on the sunny beach for a picnic before you head out to snorkel on the protected reef. Many people like to camp here ($3 per person per night, eight sites plus group site and overflow area; first come, first served), but note that there's no freshwater supply and you must carry off whatever you bring onto the island.

The typical visitor from Key West, however, makes it no farther than the waters of Garden Key. Home to 19th-century Fort Jefferson, it is the destination for seaplane and fast ferry tours out of Key West. With 2½ to 6½ hours to spend on the island, visitors have time to tour the mammoth fort-cum-prison and then cool off with mask and snorkel along the fort's moat wall.

History buffs might remember long-deactivated Fort Jefferson, the largest brick building in the western hemisphere, as the prison that held Dr. Samuel Mudd, who unwittingly set John Wilkes Booth's leg after the assassination of Abraham Lincoln. Three other men were also held there for complicity in the assassination. Original construction on the fort began in 1846 and continued for 30 years, but was never completed because the invention of the rifled cannon made it obsolete. That's when it became a Civil War prison and later a wildlife refuge. In 1935 President Franklin Roosevelt declared it a national monument for its historic and natural value.

The brick fort acts as a gigantic, almost 16-acre reef. Around its moat walls, coral grows and schools of snapper, grouper, and wrasses hang out. To reach the offshore coral heads requires about 15 minutes of swimming over sea-grass beds. The reef formations blaze with the color and majesty of brain coral, swaying sea fans, and flitting tropical fish. It takes a bit of energy to swim the distance, but the water depth pretty much measures under 7 feet all the way, allowing for sandy spots to stop and rest. (Standing in sea-grass meadows and on coral is detrimental to marine life.)

Serious snorkelers and divers head out farther offshore to epic formations, including Palmata Patch, one of the few surviving concentrations of elkhorn coral in the Keys. Day-trippers congregate on the sandy beach to relax in the sun and enjoy picnics. Overnight tent campers have use of restroom facilities and achieve a total getaway from noise, lights, and civilization in general. Remember that no matter how you get here, the park's $5 admission fee must be paid in cash.

Birders in the know bring binoculars to watch some 100,000 nesting sooty terns at their only U.S. nesting site, Bush Key, adjacent to Garden Key. Noddy terns also nest in the spring. During winter migrations, birds fill the airspace so thickly they literally fall from the sky to make their pit stops, birders say. Nearly 300 species have been spotted in the park's seven islands, including frigatebirds, boobies, cormorants, and broad-winged hawks. Bush Key is closed to foot traffic during nesting season, January through September. ⊕ *www.nps.gov/drto* ✉ *$5.*

Yankee Freedom III. The fast, sleek, 110-foot catamaran *Yankee Freedom III* travels to the Dry Tortugas in 2¼ hours. The time passes quickly on the roomy vessel equipped with four restrooms, three warm freshwater showers, and two bars. Stretch out on two decks that are both air-conditioned, with cushioned seating. There is also an open sundeck with sunny and shaded seating. Continental breakfast and lunch are included. On arrival, a naturalist leads a 45-minute guided tour, which is followed by lunch and a free afternoon for swimming, snorkeling (gear included), and exploring. The vessel is ADA-certified for visitors using wheelchairs. ■ TIP→ The Dry Tortugas lies in the Central time zone. ✉ *Lands End Marina, 240 Margaret St., Key West* ☎ *305/294–7009, 800/634–0939* ⊕ *www.yankeefreedom.com* ✉ *$170, parking $5* ☉ *Trips daily at 8 am (check in 7:15 am).*

5

FORT LAUDERDALE

With Broward County

Visit Fodors.com for advice, updates, and bookings

WELCOME TO FORT LAUDERDALE

TOP REASONS TO GO

★ **Blue waves:** Sparkling Lauderdale beaches spanning Broward County's entire coast were Florida's first to capture Blue Wave Beach status from the Clean Beaches Council.

★ **Inland waterways:** More than 300 miles of inland waterways, including downtown Fort Lauderdale's historic New River, create what's known as the Venice of America.

★ **Everglades access:** Just minutes from luxury hotels and golf courses, the rugged Everglades tantalize with alligators, colorful birds, and other wildlife.

★ **Vegas-style gaming:** Since slots and blackjack tables hit Hollywood's glittering Seminole Hard Rock Hotel & Casino in 2008, smaller competitors have followed this lucrative trend on every square inch of Indian Territory.

★ **Cruise gateway:** Port Everglades—home port for *Allure* and *Oasis of the Seas,* the world's largest cruise vessels—hosts ships from major cruise lines.

1 Fort Lauderdale. Anchored by the fast-flowing New River and its attractive Riverwalk, Fort Lauderdale embraces high-rise condos along with single-family homes, museums, parks, and attractions. Las Olas Boulevard, lined with boutiques, sidewalk cafés, and restaurants, links downtown with 20 miles of sparkling beaches.

2 North on Scenic A1A. Stretching north on Route A1A, old-school seaside charm abounds, from high-rise Galt Ocean Mile to quiet, low-rise resort communities farther north.

3 Hollywood. From its beachside Broadwalk to historic Young Circle (the latter transformed into an Arts Park) to South Broward's main destination provides grit, glitter, and diversity in attractions.

441
91
811
1
Deerfield
Beach
A1A

Coconut
Creek
811
Hillsboro
Beach

Sample Rd.
834
Hillsboro
Lighthouse

7 **Butterfly ◆**
World

Margate

Coconut Cr.
Pkwy.

North
Lauderdale
Atlantic Blvd.
Pompano
Beach

95
1

Cypress Creek Rd.

Commercial Blvd.
Lauderdale-
by-the-Sea
2

Oakland Park Blvd.
A1A

Lauderdale
Lakes

441

Sunrise Blvd.
Fort
Lauderdale

Broward Blvd.
1
Las Olas
Blvd.

Davie Blvd.

Melrose
Park
84
S.E. 17th St.
Causeway

7

Port Everglades

595
Fort Lauderdale-Hollywood
International Airport

Griffin Rd.
1

Stirling Rd.
Dania Beach
Blvd.

Dania
Beach
A1A

Sheridan St.
822

95

Hollywood Blvd.
Hollywood
3

Pembroke Rd.

Hallandale Blvd.
Hallandale

ATLANTIC OCEAN

0   3 mi
0   3 km

GETTING ORIENTED

Along the southeast's Gold Coast, Fort Lauderdale and Broward County anchor a delightfully chic middle ground between the posh and elite Palm Beaches and the international hubbub of Miami. From downtown Fort Lauderdale, it's about a four-hour drive to either Orlando or Key West, but there's plenty to keep you in Broward. All told, Broward boasts 31 communities from Deerfield Beach to Hallandale Beach along the coast, and from Coral Springs to Southwest Ranches closer to the Everglades. Big—in fact, huge—shopping options await in the western suburbs, home of Sawgrass Mills, the upscale Colonnade Outlets at Sawgrass, and IKEA Sunrise.

5

By Paul Rubio   Collegians of the 1960s returning to Fort Lauderdale would be hard-pressed to recognize the onetime "Sun and Suds Spring Break Capital of the Universe." Back then, Fort Lauderdale's beachfront was lined with T-shirt shops, and downtown consisted of a lone office tower and dilapidated buildings waiting to be razed. Not anymore!

The beach and downtown have since exploded with upscale shops, restaurants, and luxury resort hotels equipped with enough high-octane amenities to light up skies all the way to western Broward's Alligator Alley. At risk of losing small-town 45-rpm magic in iPod times—when hotel parking fees alone eclipse room rates of old—Greater Fort Lauderdale somehow seems to meld disparate eras into nouveau nirvana, seasoned with a lot of Gold Coast sand.

The city was named for Major William Lauderdale, who built a fort at the river's mouth in 1838 during the Seminole Indian wars. It wasn't until 1911 that the city was incorporated, with only 175 residents, but it grew quickly during the Florida boom of the 1920s. Today's population hovers around 165,000, and suburbs keep growing—1.75 million live in Broward County's 31 municipalities and unincorporated areas.

As elsewhere, many speculators busily flipping property here got caught when the sun-drenched real-estate bubble burst, leaving Broward's foreclosure rate to skyrocket. But the worst is far behind us. By the time the city began celebrating its centennial in 2011, it had resumed the renaissance that began before the economic crisis. The 20-mile shoreline—with wide ribbons of golden sand for beachcombing and sunbathing—remains the anchor draw for Fort Lauderdale and Broward County, but amazing beaches are now complemented by show-stopping hotels, an exploding foodie scene, and burgeoning cultural scene. In a little more than 100 years, Fort Lauderdale has grown into Fort Fabulous.

PLANNING

WHEN TO GO

Peak season runs Thanksgiving through April, when concert, art, and entertainment seasons go full-throttle. Expect heat and humidity and some rain in summer. Hurricane winds come most notably in August and September. Golfing tee-time waits are longer on weekends year-round. Regardless of season, remember that Fort Lauderdale sunshine can burn even in cloudy weather.

GETTING HERE AND AROUND

AIR TRAVEL

Serving more than 23 million travelers a year, **Fort Lauderdale–Hollywood International Airport** is 3 miles south of downtown Fort Lauderdale, just off U.S. 1 between Fort Lauderdale and Hollywood, and near Port Everglades and Fort Lauderdale Beach. Other options include **Miami International Airport,** about 32 miles to the southwest, and the far less chaotic **Palm Beach International Airport,** about 50 miles to the north. All three airports link to **Tri-Rail,** a commuter train operating seven days through Palm Beach, Broward, and Miami-Dade counties.

Airport Information Fort Lauderdale–Hollywood International Airport *(FLL).* ⊠ *Ft. Lauderdale* ☎ *866/435–9355* ⊕ *www.broward.org/airport.* **Miami International Airport** *(MIA).* ⊠ *Miami* ☎ *305/876–7000* ⊕ *www.miami-airport. com.* **Palm Beach International Airport** *(PBI).* ⊠ *Palm Beach* ☎ *561/471–7420* ⊕ *www.pbia.org.* **Tri-Rail** ☎ *800/874–7245* ⊕ *www.tri-rail.com.*

BUS TRAVEL

Broward County Transit operates bus route No. 1 between the airport and its main terminal at Broward Boulevard and Northwest 1st Avenue, near downtown Fort Lauderdale. Service from the airport is every 20 minutes and begins at 5:22 am on weekdays, 5:37 am Saturday, and 8:41 am Sunday; the last bus leaves the airport at 11:38 pm Monday–Saturday and 9:41 pm Sunday. The fare is $1.75 (coins only). ⚠ The Northwest 1st Avenue stop is in a crime-prone part of town. Exercise special caution there, day or night. Better yet, take a taxi to and from the airport. Broward County Transit (BCT) also covers the county on 303 fixed routes. The fare is $1.75 (cash only). Service starts around 5 am and continues to 11:30 pm, except on Sunday.

Bus Contact Broward County Transit ☎ *954/357–8400* ⊕ *www.broward.org/ BCT.*

CAR TRAVEL

Renting a car to get around Broward County is highly recommended. Taxis are scarce and costly. Public transportation is rarely used.

By car, access to Broward County from north or south is via Florida's Turnpike, Interstate 95, U.S. 1, or U.S. 441. Interstate 75 (Alligator Alley, requiring a toll despite being part of the nation's interstate-highway system) connects Broward with Florida's west coast and runs parallel to State Road 84 within the county. East–west Interstate 595 runs from westernmost Broward County and links Interstate 75 with Interstate 95 and U.S. 1, providing handy access to the airport and seaport.

Route A1A, designated a Florida Scenic Highway by the state's Department of Transportation, parallels the beach.

TRAIN TRAVEL

Amtrak provides daily service to Fort Lauderdale and stops at Deerfield Beach and Hollywood.

HOTELS

Back-to-back openings of luxury beachfront hotels have created Fort Lauderdale's upscale "hotel row"—with the Atlantic Resort & Spa, the Hilton Beach Resort, the Ritz-Carlton, the W, and the Westin all less than a decade old. More upscale places to hang your hat are on the horizon, whereas smaller family-run lodging spots are disappearing. You can also find chain hotels along the Intracoastal Waterway. If you want to be *on* the beach, be sure to ask specifically when booking your room, since many hotels advertise "waterfront" accommodations that are along inland waterways or overlooking the beach from across Route A1A.

Hotel reviews have been shortened. For full information, visit Fodors. com.

RESTAURANTS

References to "Fort Liquordale" from spring-break days of old have given way to au courant allusions for the decidedly cuisine-oriented "Fork Lauderdale." Greater Fort Lauderdale offers some of the finest, most varied dining of any U.S. city its size, spawned in part by the advent of new luxury hotels and upgrades all around. From among more than 4,000 wining-and-dining establishments in Broward, choose from basic Americana or cuisines of Asia, Europe, or Central and South America, and enjoy more than just food in an atmosphere with subtropical twists.

WHAT IT COSTS				
	$	$$	$$$	$$$$
RESTAURANTS	under $16	$16–$20	$21–$30	over $30
HOTELS	under $201	$201–$300	$301–$400	over $400

Restaurant prices are the average cost of a main course at dinner or, if dinner is not served, at lunch. Hotel prices are the lowest cost of a standard double room in high season.

FORT LAUDERDALE

Like many southeast Florida neighbors, Fort Lauderdale has long been revitalizing. In a state where gaudy tourist zones often stand aloof from workaday downtowns, Fort Lauderdale exhibits consistency at both ends of the 2-mile Las Olas corridor. The sparkling look results from upgrades both downtown and on the beachfront. Matching the downtown's innovative arts district, cafés, and boutiques is an equally inventive beach area, with hotels, cafés, and shops facing an undeveloped shoreline, and new resort-style hotels replacing faded icons of yesteryear. Despite wariness of pretentious overdevelopment, city leaders have allowed a striking number of glittering high-rises. Nostalgic locals and frequent visitors fret over the diminishing vision of sailboats bobbing in waters near downtown; however, Fort Lauderdale remains the yachting capital of the world, and the water toys don't seem to be going anywhere. Sharp demographic changes are also altering the faces of Greater Fort Lauderdale communities, increasingly cosmopolitan with more minorities, including Hispanics and people of Caribbean descent, as well as gays and lesbians. In Fort Lauderdale, especially, a younger populace is growing, whereas longtime residents are heading north, to a point where one former city commissioner likens the change to that of historic New River—moving with the tide and sometimes appearing at a standstill: "The river of our population is at still point, old and new in equipoise, one pushing against the other."

GETTING HERE AND AROUND

The Fort Lauderdale metro area is laid out in a grid system, and only myriad canals and waterways interrupt the mostly straight-line path of streets and roads. Nomenclature is important here. Streets, roads, courts, and drives run east–west. Avenues, terraces, and ways run north–south. Boulevards can (and do) run any which way. For visitors, boutique-lined Las Olas Boulevard is one of the most important east–west thoroughfares from the beach to downtown, whereas Route A1A—referred to as Atlantic Boulevard, Ocean Boulevard, and Fort Lauderdale Beach along some stretches—runs along the north–south oceanfront. These names can confuse visitors, since there are separate streets called Atlantic and Ocean in Hollywood and Pompano Beach. Boulevards, composed of either pavement or water, give Fort Lauderdale its distinct "Venice of America" character.

The city's transportation system, though less congested than elsewhere in South Florida, suffers from traffic overload. I–595 connects the city and suburbs and provides a direct route to the Fort Lauderdale–Hollywood International Airport and Port Everglades, but lanes slow to a crawl during rush hours. The Intracoastal Waterway, paralleling Route A1A, is the nautical equivalent of an interstate highway. It runs north–south between downtown Fort Lauderdale and the beach and provides easy boating access to neighboring beach communities.

Catch an orange-bottomed, yellow-topped Sun Trolley, running every 15 minutes, for as little as $0.50 each way. Sun Trolley's *Convention Connection* runs round-trip from Cordova Road's Harbor Shops near Port Everglades (where you can park free) to past the Convention Center, over the 17th Street Causeway, and north along Route A1A to Beach Place. Sun Trolley's Las Olas Beaches route passes from downtown through Las Olas and then north on A1A. Wave at trolley drivers—yes, they'll stop—for pickups anywhere along the route.

Meters in Yellow Cab taxis run at rates of $4.50 for the first mile and $2.40 for each additional mile; waiting time is $0.40 per minute. There's a $10-fare minimum to or from seaport or airport, and an additional $2 service charge when you are collected from the airport. All Yellow Cab vehicles accept major credit cards.

Transportation Contacts Sun Trolley ☎ *954/761–3543* ⊕ *www.suntrolley. com.* **Yellow Cab** ☎ *954/777–7777* ⊕ *www.yellowcabbroward.com.*

TOURS

Honeycombed with some 300 miles of navigable waterways, Fort Lauderdale is the home port for about 44,000 privately owned vessels, but you don't need to be a boat owner to ply the waters. For a scenic way to really see this canal-laced city, take a relaxing boat tour or simply hop on a Water Taxi, part of Fort Lauderdale's water-transportation system. See why the city is called the "Venice of America."

Carrie B Harbor Tours. Board a 300-passenger day cruiser for a 90-minute tour on the New River and Intracoastal Waterway. Cruises depart at 11, 1, and 3 daily November through May and Thursday–Monday between June and October. The cost is $22.95. ■**TIP**➔ Book ahead online. ⊠ *440 N. New River Dr. E, off Las Olas Blvd.* ☎ *954/642–1601* ⊕ *www.carriebcruises.com.*

FAMILY **Fort Lauderdale Duck Tours.** Quack, quack! The famous 45-passenger amphibious Hydra-Terra tours, which first gained popularity in Boston, have arrived in Fort Lauderdale. Ninety-minute tours include lots of land/water family fun, cruising and driving through Venice of America neighborhoods, historic areas, and the Intracoastal Waterway. Several tours depart daily and cost just under $34. Schedule varies and ducks sometimes don't run in low season, so check ahead of time. ⚠ The website shares its booking engine with the Duck Tours South Beach, so be sure to book for the correct location! ⊠ *17 S. Fort Lauderdale Beach Blvd., at Beach Pl.* ☎ *954/761–4002* ⊕ *www.fortlauderdaleducktours.com.*

Jungle Queen Riverboat. The kitsch *Jungle Queen* riverboat seats more than 550 and cruises up the New River through the heart of Fort Lauderdale, as it has for more than 75 years. It's old-school and totally touristy but that's half the fun! The sightseeing cruises at 9:30 and 1:30 cost $19.95, and the 6 pm all-you-can-eat BBQ dinner cruise costs $42.95. ⊠ *Bahia Mar Beach Resort, 801 Seabreeze Blvd.* ☎ *954/462–5596* ⊕ *www.junglequeen.com.*

FAMILY
Fodor's Choice
★
Water Taxi. A great way to experience the multimillion-dollar homes, hotels, and seafood restaurants along Fort Lauderdale's waterways is via the public Water Taxi, which runs every 30 minutes beginning at 10 am and ending at midnight. There are 14 regularly scheduled pickup stations in Fort Lauderdale, including Las Olas Riverfront, the Shops of Las Olas, Bahia Mar, and Gallery ONE near the Galleria Mall. An unlimited day pass serves as both a tour and a means of transportation between Fort Lauderdale's hotels and hot spots, though Water Taxi is most useful when viewed as a tour. It's possible to cruise all afternoon while taking in the waterfront sights. Captains and helpers indulge guests in fun factoids about Fort Lauderdale, white lies about the city's history, and bizarre tales about the celebrity homes along the Intracoastal. A day pass is $22. Water Taxi also connects Fort Lauderdale to Hollywood, where there are seven scheduled stops. ☎ *954/467–6677* ⊕ *www.watertaxi.com.*

VISITOR INFORMATION
Greater Fort Lauderdale Convention and Visitors Bureau ☎ *954/765–4466*
⊕ *www.sunny.org.*

EXPLORING

DOWNTOWN AND LAS OLAS

The jewel of downtown along New River is the small Arts and Entertainment District, with Broadway shows, ballet, and theater at the riverfront Broward Center for the Performing Arts. Clustered within a five-minute walk are the Museum of Discovery & Science, the expanding Fort Lauderdale Historical Museum, and the Museum of Art—home to stellar touring exhibits. Restaurants, sidewalk cafés, bars, and dance clubs flourish along Las Olas and its downtown extension. Tying these areas together is the Riverwalk, extending 2 miles along the New River's north and south banks. Tropical gardens with benches and interpretive displays fringe the walk on the north, boat landings on the south.

TOP ATTRACTIONS

Fort Lauderdale History Center. Surveying city history from the Seminole era to more recent times, the Fort Lauderdale Historical Society's museum has expanded into several adjacent buildings, including the historic King-Cromartie House (typical early 20th-century-style Fort Lauderdale home), the 1905 New River Inn (Broward's oldest remaining hotel building), and the Hoch Heritage Center, a public research facility archiving original manuscripts, maps, and more than 250,000 photos. Daily docent-led tours run on the hour from 1–3 pm. ⊠ *231 S.W. 2nd Ave., Downtown and Las Olas* ☎ *954/463–4431* ⊕ *www. oldfortlauderdale.org* ⌨ *$10* ⊙ *Tues.–Sun. noon–4.*

Fodor's Choice **Las Olas Boulevard.** What Lincoln Road is to South Beach, Las Olas Bou-
★ levard is to Fort Lauderdale. The terrestrial heart and soul of Broward County, Las Olas is the premier street for restaurants, art galleries, shopping, and people-watching. From west to east the landscape of Las Olas transforms from modern downtown high-rises to original boutiques and ethnic eateries. Beautiful mansions and traditional Floridian homes line the Intracoastal and define Fort Lauderdale. The streets of Las Olas connect to the pedestrian friendly Riverwalk, which continues to the edge of the New River on Avenue of the Arts. ⊠ *E. Las Olas Blvd., Downtown and Las Olas* ⊕ *www.lasolasboulevard.com.*

Museum of Art Fort Lauderdale. Currently in an Edward Larrabee Barnes–designed building that's considered an architectural masterpiece, activists started this museum in a nearby storefront more than 50 years ago. MOAFL, part of Nova Southeastern University, hosts world-class touring exhibits and has an impressive permanent collection of 6,000 works of 20th-century European and American art, including pieces by Picasso, Calder, Dalí, Mapplethorpe, Warhol, and Stella, as well as works by celebrated Ashcan School artist William Glackens. ■**TIP→** The lobby-level store and café combo, Museum Cafe, is a cool local hangout. ⊠ *1 E. Las Olas Blvd., Downtown and Las Olas*

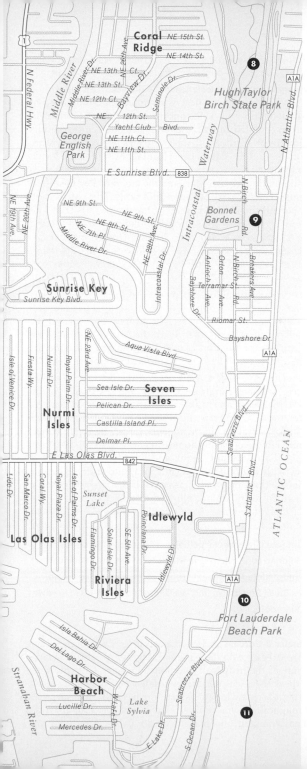

☎ *954/525–5500* ⊕ *www.moafl.org* ✉ *$10* ⊘ *Tues.–Wed. and Fri.–Sat.*
11–5, Thurs.11–7, Sun. noon–5 ⊘ *Closed Mon.*

FAMILY

Fodor's Choice

★

Museum of Discovery & Science/AutoNation IMAX Theater. With more than
200 interactive exhibits, the aim here is to entertain children—*and*
adults—with the wonders of science and the wonders of Florida. In
2012, the museum doubled in size, meaning twice the fun! Exhibits
include the Ecodiscovery Center with an Everglades Airboat Adventure
ride, resident otters, and an interactive Florida storm center. Florida
Ecoscapes has a living coral reef, plus sharks, rays, and eels. Runways to
Rockets offers stimulating trips to Mars and the moon while nine different cockpit simulators let you try out your pilot skills. The AutoNation
IMAX theater, part of the complex, shows films (some in 3-D) on an
80-foot by 60-foot screen with 15,000 watts of digital surround sound
broadcast from 42 speakers. ✉ *401 S.W. 2nd St., Downtown and Las
Olas* ☎ *954/467–6637 for museum, 954/463–4629 for IMAX* ⊕ *www.
mods.org* ✉ *Museum $14 ($19 with one IMAX show)* ⊘ *Mon.–Sat.
10–5, Sun. noon–6.*

Riverwalk. Lovely views prevail on this paved promenade on the New
River's north bank. On the first Sunday of every month a free jazz festival attracts visitors. From west to east, the Riverwalk begins at the
residential New River Sound, passes through the Arts and Science District, then the historic center of Fort Lauderdale, and wraps around the
New River until it meets with Las Olas Boulevard's shopping district.

Stranahan House. The city's oldest residence, on the National Register
of Historic Places, and increasingly dwarfed by high-rise development,
was once home to businessman Frank Stranahan, who arrived in 1892.
With his wife, Ivy, the city's first schoolteacher, he befriended and traded
with Seminole Indians, and taught them "new ways." In 1901 he built
a store that would later become his home after serving as a post office,
a general store, and a restaurant. Frank and Ivy's former residence is
now a museum, with many period furnishings, and tours. The historic home remains Fort Lauderdale's principal link to its brief history.
Note that self-guided tours are not allowed. ✉ *335 S.E. 6th Ave., at
Las Olas Blvd., Downtown and Las Olas* ☎ *954/524–4736* ⊕ *www.
stranahanhouse.org* ✉ *$12* ⊘ *Tours Oct.–Aug., daily at 1, 2, and 3 pm.*

QUICK
BITES

Kilwins Ft. Lauderdale. The sweet smell of waffle cones lures pedestrians to an old-fashioned confectionery in the heart of Las Olas Boulevard
that also sells hand-paddled fudge and scoops of homemade ice cream.
✉ *809 E. Las Olas Blvd., Downtown and Las Olas* ☎ *954/523–8338* ⊕ *www.
kilwins.com/ftlauderdale.*

ALONG THE BEACH

Fodor's Choice

★

Bonnet House Museum & Gardens. A 35-acre oasis in the heart of the beach
area, this subtropical estate on the National Register of Historic Places
stands as a tribute to the history of Old South Florida. This charming
home, built in the 1920s, was the winter residence of the late Frederic
and Evelyn Bartlett, artists whose personal touches and small surprises
are evident throughout. If you're interested in architecture, artwork,
or the natural environment, this place is worth a visit. After admiring

THE GHOSTS OF STRANAHAN HOUSE

These days the historic Stranahan House is as famous for its nighttime ghost tours as it is for its daytime history tour. Originally built as a trading post in 1901 and later expanded into a town hall, a post office, a bank, and the personal residence of Frank Stranahan and his wife, Ivy Cromartie, the historic Stranahan House was more than plagued by a number of tragic events and violent deaths, including Frank's suicide. After financial turmoil, Stranahan tied himself to a concrete sewer grate and jumped into New River, leaving his widow to carry on. Sunday night at 7:30, house staff reveal the multiple tragic tales from the Stranahan crypt during the River House Ghost Tour ($25) and help visitors communicate with "the other side." Using special tools and snapping photos to search for orbs, guests are encouraged to field energy from the supposed five ghosts in the house. Given the high success rate of reaching out to the paranormal, the Stranahan House has become a favorite campground for global ghost hunters and television shows. Advance reservations are required.

the fabulous gardens, be on the lookout for playful monkeys swinging from trees. Interesting fact: The Bonnet House was the final stop in the 2005 season of CBS's Amazing Race hit television show. ⊠ *900 N. Birch Rd., Along the beach* ☎ *954/563–5393* ⊕ *www.bonnethouse.org* 🖃 *$20 for house tours, $10 for gardens only* ⊙ *Tues.–Sun. 9–4; tours hourly from 9:30–3:30.*

Casablanca Café. For respite from the sun, duck in for a nice glass of chardonnay or a light bite. ⊠ *3049 Alhambra St., Along the beach* ☎ 954/764–3500.

Steak 954. Recover from a long day in the sun with a much-deserved, refreshing cocktail. ⊠ *401 N. Fort Lauderdale Beach Blvd., Along the beach* ☎ 954/414–8333.

WESTERN SUBURBS AND BEYOND

West of Fort Lauderdale is ever-growing suburbia, with most of Broward's golf courses, shopping, casinos, and chain restaurants. As you head farther west, the terrain takes on more characteristics of the Everglades, and you'll occasionally see alligators sunning on canal banks. Eventually, you reach the Everglades themselves after hitting the airboat outfitters on the park's periphery. Tourists flock to these airboats, but the best way of seeing the Everglades is to visit the Everglades National Park itself.

FAMILY **Ah-Tah-Thi-Ki Museum.** A couple of miles from Billie Swamp Safari is Ah-Tah-Thi-Ki Museum, whose name means "a place to learn, a place to remember." This museum documents the traditions and culture of the Seminole Tribe of Florida through artifacts, exhibits, and reenactments of rituals and ceremonies. The 60-acre site includes a living-history Seminole village, nature trails, and a wheelchair-accessible boardwalk through a cypress swamp. ■ TIP➔ Guided tours are available daily,

NEED A BREAK?

5

DID YOU KNOW?

Sculptor Peter Wolf Toth fashioned this totem pole for Fort Lauderdale's D. C. Alexander Park on Seabreeze Boulevard near the New River Sound. Toth, who has sculpted works throughout the country, often creates art that represents the lives of early Native Americans.

but call for exact times. Self-guided audio tours are available anytime. There are also children's programs. ⊠ *34725 W. Boundary Rd., Clewiston* ☎ *877/902–1113* ⊕ *www.ahtahthiki.com* ☒ *$9* ⊙ *Daily 9–5.*

FAMILY **Billie Swamp Safari.** At the Billie Swamp Safari, experience the majesty of the Everglades firsthand. Daily tours of wildlife-filled wetlands and hammocks yield sightings of deer, water buffalo, raccoons, wild hogs, hawks, eagles, and alligators. Animal and reptile shows entertain audiences. Ecotours are conducted aboard motorized swamp buggies, and airboat rides are available, too. The on-site Swamp Water Café serves gator nuggets, frogs' legs, catfish, and Indian fry bread with honey. ⊠ *Big Cypress Seminole Indian Reservation, 30000 Gator Tail Trail, Clewiston* ☎ *863/983–6101, 800/949–6101* ⊕ *www.swampsafari.com* ☒ *Swamp Safari Day Package $49.95 (includes ecotour, shows, exhibits, and airboat ride)* ⊙ *Daily 9–6.*

FAMILY
Fodor's Choice
★
Butterfly World. As many as 80 butterfly species from South and Central America, the Philippines, Malaysia, Taiwan, and other Asian nations are typically found within the serene 3-acre site inside Tradewinds Park in the northwest reaches of Broward County. A screened aviary called North American Butterflies is reserved for native species. The Tropical Rain Forest Aviary is a 30-foot-high construction, with observation decks, waterfalls, ponds, and tunnels filled with thousands of colorful butterflies. There are lots of birds, too, and kids love going in the lorikeet aviary, where the colorful birds land on every limb! ⊠ *Tradewinds Park, 3600 W. Sample Rd., Coconut Creek* ☎ *954/977–4400* ⊕ *www. butterflyworld.com* ☒ *$24.95* ⊙ *Mon.–Sat. 9–5, Sun. 11–5.*

FAMILY **Everglades Holiday Park.** This 30-acre park provides a decent glimpse of the Everglades and Florida's wild west circa 1950. Take an hour-long airboat tour, look at an 18th-century-style American Indian village, or catch the alligator wrestling. The airboats tend to be supersized and the experience very commercialized. Most episodes of Animal Planet's *Gator Boys* are filmed here. ⊠ *21940 Griffin Rd., Western Suburbs and Beyond* ☎ *954/434–8111* ⊕ *www.evergladesholidaypark.com* ☒ *Park free, airboat tour $26.50* ⊙ *Daily 9–5.*

FAMILY **Flamingo Gardens.** Gators, crocodiles, river otters, and birds of prey lie in wait at Flamingo Gardens, with a walk-through aviary, plant house, and Everglades museum in the pioneer Wray Home. A half-hour guided tram ride winds through a citrus grove and wetlands area, and the gift shop helps you ship oranges, grapefruit and tangerines home. ⊠ *3750 S. Flamingo Rd., Davie* ☎ *954/473–2955* ⊕ *www.flamingogardens.org* ☒ *$18, tram ride $4* ⊙ *Daily 9:30–5.*

FAMILY **Sawgrass Recreation Park.** A half-hour airboat ride through the Everglades allows you to view a good variety of plants and wildlife, from ospreys and alligators to turtles, snakes, and fish. Besides the ride, your entrance fee covers admission to an Everglades nature exhibit; a native Seminole village; and exhibits on alligators, other reptiles, and birds of prey. Supercool airboat nights tours are offered on Wednesday and Saturday at 8:30 to experience the nocturnal world of the 'glades. Reservations required for night tours. ⊠ *1006 N. U.S. 27, Weston*

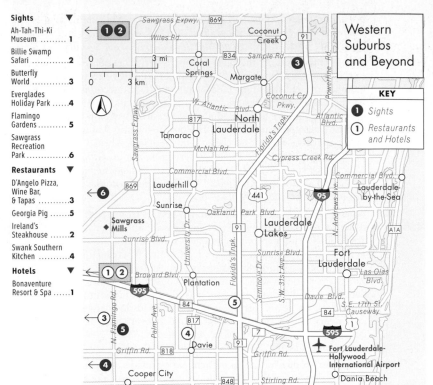

☎ 888/424–7262 ⊕ *www.evergladestours.com* 🎫 *$19.50, night tours* *$40* ⊙ *Airboat rides daily 9–5.*

BEACHES

Fodor'sChoice
★

Fort Lauderdale Beach. The same downy sands that once welcomed America's youth-gone-wild (aka wild spring breakers) now frame a multimile shoreline of beachside sophistication. Alone among Florida's major beachfront communities, Fort Lauderdale's principal beach remains gloriously open and uncluttered. Walkways line both sides of the beach roadway, and traffic has been trimmed to two gently curving northbound lanes. Fort Lauderdale Beach unofficially begins between the Sheraton Fort Lauderdale and Hilton's Bahia Mar Resort, starting with the quiet **South Beach Park**, where picnic tables and palm trees rule. Going north, the younger, barely legal crowd gravitates toward the section of sand at the mouth of Las Olas Boulevard. The beach is actually most crowded between Las Olas and Sunrise Boulevards, directly in front of the major hotels and condominiums, namely in front of **Beach Place**, home to the Marriott time-share building and touristy places like Hooters and Fat Tuesday (and a beach-themed CVS Pharmacy). Gay men and women get their fix of vitamin D along **Sebastian Beach**, on Sebastian Street, just north of The Ritz-Carlton, Fort Lauderdale.

Families with children enjoy hanging out between Seville Street and Vistamar Street, between the Westin Fort Lauderdale Beach and the Atlantic Resort and Spa. **Amenities:** food and drink; lifeguards; parking (fee). **Best for:** sunrise; swimming; walking. ⊠ *Rte. A1A from Holiday Dr. to Sunrise Blvd., Along the beach.*

Harbor Beach. The posh neighborhood of Harbor Beach boasts Fort Lauderdale's most opulent homes along the Intracoastal Waterway. Due east of this community, and just south of Fort Lauderdale's South Beach Park, a stunning swath of beach has adopted the name of its neighborhood—Harbor Beach. This section offers some of the few private beaches in Fort Lauderdale, most of which belong to big hotel names like the Marriott Harbor Beach and the Lago Mar. (Only hotel guests can access these beaches.) Such status permits the hotels to offer full-service amenities and eating and drinking outlets on their bespoke slices of sugarloafed heaven. **Amenities:** water sports. **Best for:** solitude; swimming; walking. ⊠ *S. Ocean La. and southern tip of Holiday Dr., Along the beach.*

Hugh Taylor Birch State Recreation Area. North of Fort Lauderdale's bustling beachfront, past Sunrise Boulevard, the quieter sands of Fort Lauderdale beach run parallel to Hugh Taylor Birch State Recreation Area, a nicely preserved patch of primeval Florida. The 180-acre tropical park sports lush mangrove areas along the Intracoastal waterway, and lovely nature trails. Visit the Birch House Museum, enjoy a picnic, play volleyball, or paddle a rented canoe. Since parking is limited on Route A1A, park here and take a walkway underpass to the beach (which can be accessed daily 9–5). **Amenities:** toilets. **Best for:** solitude; walking. ⊠ *3109 E. Sunrise Blvd., Along the beach* ☎ *954/564–4521* ⊕ *www. floridastateparks.org/HughTaylorBirch* 🎟 *$6 per vehicle, $2 per pedestrian* ☉ *Daily 8–sunset.*

WHERE TO EAT

DOWNTOWN AND LAS OLAS

$$
MODERN
AMERICAN
Fodor's Choice
★

✕ **American Social.** A charming slice of Americana in the heart of Las Olas Boulevard, American Social flaunts a sexy nerd vibe, packing the house nightly with Fort Lauderdale's hottest twenty- and thirtysomethings. The intimate restaurant and bar are adorned with framed *Life* magazine covers and library books, fostering an ambience that is oh-so Boston. The drinks here rock, and the modern American cuisine is equally awesome. Choose from 16 beers on tap or some tantalizing mixology (e.g. the Strawberry Honey Smash—vodka, strawberries, simple syrup, honey liqueur, and fresh lemon juice). Feast on the seafood mac-and-cheese skillet, shrimp pesto flatbread, and the full gamut of gourmet burgers with sides of Parmesan and truffle fries or sweet-potato fries. ■**TIP→** Arrive early on weekends as the restaurant quickly reaches capacity. 💲 *Average main: $20* ⊠ *721 E. Las Olas Blvd., Downtown and Las Olas* ☎ *954/764–7005* ⊕ *www.americansocialbar.com.*

5

$$$
MODERN
AMERICAN
FAMILY
Fodor's Choice
★

✕ **Big City Tavern.** A Las Olas landmark, Big City Tavern is the boulevard's most consistent spot for good food, good spirits, and good times. The diverse menu commingles Asian entrées like pad thai, Italian options like homemade meatballs and cheese ravioli in a toasted garlic marinara, and American dishes like the grilled skirt-steak Cobb salad. Don't forget to ask about the crispy flatbread of the day, and make sure to save room for the homemade desserts. The pistachio brown-butter bundt cake with honey-roasted spiced peaches and pistachio gelato, the caramelized banana sundae in a Mason jar, and the devil's-food-cake ice-cream sandwich are all heaven on earth. ■ TIP➔ Big City is open late into the night for drinks, desserts, and even offers a special late-night menu. $ *Average main: $24* ⊠ *609 E. Las Olas Blvd., Downtown and Las Olas* ☎ *954/727–0307* ⊕ *www.bigtimerestaurants.com.*

$
AMERICAN

✕ **The Floridian.** This classic diner is plastered with photos of Monroe, Nixon, and local notables past and present in a succession of brightly painted rooms with funky chandeliers. The kitchen dishes up typical grease-pit breakfast favorites (no matter the hour), with oversized omelets that come with biscuits, toast, or English muffins, plus a choice of grits or tomatoes. The restaurant also has good hangover eats, but don't expect anything exceptional (besides the location and the rock-bottom prices). It's open 24 hours—even during hurricanes, as long as the power holds out. $ *Average main: $13* ⊠ *1410 E. Las Olas Blvd., Downtown and Las Olas* ☎ *954/463–4041* ▬ *No credit cards.*

$
CAFÉ
Fodor's Choice
★

✕ **Gran Forno Cafe.** The gamble of importing an entire Italian bakery direct from Brescia, Italy definitely paid off. Most days, the sandwiches, fresh baked breads, and pastries sell out even before lunchtime. All products are made fresh daily (except Monday), beginning at 4 am, by a team of bakers who can be seen hard at work through the café's glass windows. Customers line up at the door early in the morning to get their piping-hot artisanal breads, later returning for the scrumptious paninis and decadent desserts. A second branch, five blocks east on Las Olas at No. 704, called Gran Forno Pronto, offers full service and a more extensive menu seven days a week, but it's only open until 7 pm. $ *Average main: $12* ⊠ *1235 E. Las Olas Blvd., Downtown and Las Olas* ☎ *954/467–2244* ⊕ *www.granforno.com* ☽ *Closed Mon.*

$$$
STEAKHOUSE

✕ **Grille 401.** Enveloped in panes of wine bottles, floor-to-ceiling glass windows, and masculine wood panels, seductive Grille 401 is part avant-garde steakhouse, part pan-Asian eatery, part chic lounge—all together 100% fabulous. With a diverse menu that includes Osaka-style pressed sushi, classic filet mignon, crispy crab fritters, wood-grilled lobster, as well as a "light and healthy" menu for the lithe and calorie-conscious, there's something special for just about everyone. For the not-so-calorie-conscious, the homemade desserts, including a white-chocolate brioche bread pudding and, arguably, the world's best carrot cake are must tries. By day, Grille 401 caters to a power-lunch crowd escaping the ordinary in the Las Olas financial district; by night, Grille 401 is all about sophisticated dining and excellent cocktails. $ *Average main: $28* ⊠ *401 E. Las Olas Blvd., Downtown and Las Olas* ☎ *954/767–0222* ⊕ *www.grille401.com.*

$$$$ SEAFOOD Fodor's Choice ★ 🍴 **Lobster Bar Sea Grille.** A spectacular, high-design restaurant at the crossroads of Las Olas's financial and shopping districts, Lobster Bar Sea Grille brings a much-needed infusion of sophisticated dining to the Fort Lauderdale scene. The intricately tiled archways and high ceilings of the restaurant recall New York's Grand Central station while the nautical-inspired décor is meant to evoke an ambience of fine dining on a yacht. Mission accomplished. The seafood and fish selections here are sublime, specializing in simply prepared, fresh whole fish and flash-fried lobster tails. There's also a range of custom-aged prime steaks with the full gamut of sides from Parmesan-baked asparagus to cauliflower gratin. [$] *Average main: $46* ✉ *450 E. Las Olas Blvd., Downtown and Las Olas* ☎ *954/772–2675* 🌐 *www.buckheadrestaurants.com/lobster-bar-sea-grille* ✍ *Reservations essential.*

$$$ MODERN MEXICAN Fodor's Choice ★ 🍴 **Rocco's Tacos & Tequila Bar.** The busiest spot on the Las Olas strip, Rocco's is more of a scene than just a restaurant. With pitchers of margaritas a-flowin', the middle-age crowd is boisterous and fun, recounting (and reliving) the days of spring-break debauchery from their preprofessional years. In fact, Rocco's drink menu is even larger than its sizeable food menu. Guacamole is made tableside, and Mexican dishes such as chimichangas and enchiladas have been reinvented (and made far less spicy) for the American palate. Expect a wild night and lots of fun! [$] *Average main: $23* ✉ *1313 E. Las Olas Blvd., Downtown and Las Olas* ☎ *954/524–9550* 🌐 *www.roccostacos.com.*

$$$ CAJUN Fodor's Choice ★ 🍴 **Royal Pig Pub.** Fort Lauderdale's coolest gastro-pub revels in doling out hefty portions of cajun comfort cuisine and potent, creative libations. As the name implies, this is indeed the place to be a pig and unapologetically pig out on the beer and butter-soaked New Orleans–style BBQ shrimp; grilled fish-of-the-day atop cheese grits and mussel étouffée; sweet-potato fries with honey-cider drizzle; and grilled free-range turkey burgers loaded with exotic condiments. Plenty of folks come here just for the awesome drinks. In fact, it's one of Fort Lauderdale's busiest watering holes. The pub's arched ceilings are lined with flat-screen TVs, and the bar occupies nearly half the restaurant. Rub elbows with Fort Lauderdale's yuppies and hotties over dragon fruit cosmos and spiked, cucumber and mint berry lemonades. [$] *Average main: $22* ✉ *350 E. Las Olas Blvd., Downtown and Las Olas* ☎ *954/617–7447* 🌐 *www.royalpigpub.com.*

$$$$ SEAFOOD 🍴 **Wild Sea Oyster Bar & Grille.** In the heart of tony Las Olas Boulevard, this oyster bar and grille keeps things simple with a small menu focused on a beautiful raw bar and ever-changing preparations of diverse catches from Florida, Hawaiian, and New England waters. With everything filleted and/or shucked in house, the just-caught freshness is evident in each bite. Make sure to try the ahi tuna *poke* (Hawaiian raw fish salad) as well as the fruity West Florida grouper with mango, heirloom tomatoes, and blackberry drizzle. [$] *Average main: $39* ✉ *Riverside Hotel, 620 E. Las Olas Blvd, Downtown and Las Olas* ☎ *954/467–0671* 🌐 *www.wildsealasolas.com* 🕓 *Closed Sun. and Mon. No lunch.*

$$$ AMERICAN 🍴 **YOLO.** The now-overused term YOLO stands for "You Only Live Once," but you will definitely want to eat here more than once. For Fort Lauderdale's bourgeoisie, this is the place to see and be seen and

to show off your hottest wheels in the driveway. For others, it's an upscale restaurant with affordable prices and a great ambience. The restaurant serves the full gamut of new American favorites like tuna sashimi, fried calamari, garden burgers, and short ribs with a sophisticated spin. For example, the Szechuan calamari is flash-fried, and then covered in garlic-chili sauce, chopped peanuts, and sesame seeds; the garden burger is made from bulgur wheat, cremini mushrooms, and cashews and served with thin-cut fries. [$] *Average main: $24* ✉ *333 E. Las Olas Blvd., Downtown and Las Olas* ☎ *954/523–1000* 🌐 *www.yolorestaurant.com.*

ALONG THE BEACH

$$ ECLECTIC 🍴 **Casablanca Cafe.** Located along Route A1A in the heart of Fort Lauderdale's hotel row, Casablanca Cafe offers alfresco and indoor dining with a fabulous ocean view. The historic two-story Moroccan-style villa was built in the 1920s by local architect Francis Abreu. The menu at this piano bar and restaurant showcases a global potpourri of American, Mediterranean, and Asian flavors; however, the recommended "house favorites" focus on eclectic preparations of Florida fish. The food isn't particularly delicious, but the location and ambience are excellent. Prepare for long waits to eat in the outdoor section; it's wildly popular morning, noon, and night with tourists and locals alike. [$] *Average main: $18* ✉ *3049 Alhambra St., Along the beach* ☎ *954/764–3500* 🌐 *www.casablancacafeonline.com.*

$$$ MEXICAN 🍴 **Dos Caminos.** An institution in New York City's Mexican dining scene, Dos Caminos opened its first Florida outpost at the Sheraton Fort Lauderdale Beach Hotel. Rounds of traditional and nontraditional margaritas (like the pineapple–brown sugar margarita) begin the journey south of the border. Chips are served with a trio of authentic salsas, usually followed by fantastic guacamole, made to order. The house specialties, tacos, quesadillas, and enchiladas are a commingling of traditional Mexican and neo-Mexican gastronomy, reinvented with an American flair. [$] *Average main: $21* ✉ *Sheraton Fort Lauderdale Beach Hotel, 1140 Seabreeze Blvd., Along the beach* ☎ *954/727–7090* 🌐 *www.doscaminos.com.*

$$ AMERICAN 🍴 **Oasis Cafe.** On a spit of land near Route A1A, this outdoor-only spot has swing-glide tables covered by green-striped awnings affording plenty of shade. The swinging tables are enticing, but the food you'll get is just okay (except the key lime pie). Drinks are great though! Friendly staffers serve up libations and casual fare from burgers and wraps to salads and steak. Be aware that a gratuity is tacked on no matter what your party size. A free valet assists with cramped parking. [$] *Average main: $18* ✉ *600 Seabreeze Blvd., Along the beach* ☎ *954/463–3130* 🌐 *www.oasiscafefortlauderdalebeach.com.*

$$$$ SEAFOOD Fodor's Choice ★ 🍴 **Ocean 2000.** This waterfront restaurant and lounge at the Pelican Grand Beach Resort is a favorite of locals in the know, renowned for its stunning Atlantic ocean views and excellent fish and seafood (prepared with a Latin flair). Expect succulent and savory dishes that include local fish ceviche, swordfish "sashimi style," and Florida yellowtail snapper *á la plancha* (skillet-grilled). If indulging in the wildly popular Sunday brunch or a casual seaside lunch, make sure to request seating

on the oceanfront patio, arguably the best seats in any house in Fort Lauderdale. Come nightfall, the slick dining room comes to life, illuminated by futuristic chandeliers, ubiquitous candles, and the moonlight over the ocean through oversized windows. $ *Average main: $34* ⊠ *Pelican Grand Beach Resort, 2000 N. Ocean Blvd., Along the beach* ☎ *954/556–7667* ⊕ *www.pelicanbeach.com/ocean2000.*

$$$
SEAFOOD

✕ **S3.** S3 stands for the fabulous trio of sun, surf, and sand, paying homage to its prime beachfront location. Located on the ground floor of the Hilton Fort Lauderdale Beach Resort, S3 flaunts a fun, fresh, sophisticated, beachside swagger. On any given night, you'll have an even mix of locals and tourists loving life, taking Twit-pics of their S3 cocktail sampler—a tray of adorable miniature versions of the signature libations. The menu features a variety of Japanese-inspired raw dishes, sushi rolls, and small plates, all meant for sharing and delivered as soon as they're ready. A few must-tries: the spicy Kamikaze roll, the crunchy mac 'n' cheese with smoked gouda and crispy prosciutto, and the shrimp toast from the wood-fired oven. $ *Average main: $29* ⊠ *Hilton Fort Lauderdale Beach Resort, 505 N. Fort Lauderdale Beach Blvd., Along the beach* ⊕ *www.s3restaurant.com.*

$$$$
SUSHI
Fodor'sChoice
★

✕ **SAIA Sushi.** The superlative locale for getting your sushi fix in Fort Lauderdale, SAIA offers innovative rolls and perfectly executed classics as well as a great selection of hot Thai and Japanese dishes. SAIA's master chef, Subin Chenkosorn, hails from the renowned Blue Sea at the Delano in Miami and has brought his amazing skill set to the Fort Lauderdale shoreline. The stylish restaurant doubles as a gregarious lounge come late evening, perfect for enjoying another round of saketinis, soju-based cocktails, and other specialty drinks like the divine SAIA-rita and Ruby Foo, after a fabulous dinner. $ *Average main: $35* ⊠ *Sonesta Fort Lauderdale, 999 N. Fort Lauderdale Beach Blvd., Along the beach* ☎ *954/302–5252* ⊕ *saiasushi.com.*

$$$$
STEAKHOUSE

✕ **Shula's on the Beach.** For anyone who gets positively misty-eyed at the mere mention of Don Shula's Miami Dolphins 17–0 Perfect Season of 1972, the good news is that this beachfront spot also turns out culinary winners just as handily. Despite dozens of new, trendy steakhouses in Miami and Fort Lauderdale, Shula's on the Beach remains staunch competition. Carnivores rejoice over the aged premium Black Angus beef grilled over a super-hot fire for quick charring. The seafood is excellent, too, and served in generous portions. The jumbo sea scallops and jumbo lump crab cakes are indeed "jumbo" and überdelicious. For a more casual affair, check out the lively bar area adorned with sports memorabilia and large-screen TVs. $ *Average main: $52* ⊠ *The Westin Beach Resort & Spa, Fort Lauderdale, 321 N. Fort Lauderdale Beach Blvd., Along the beach* ☎ *954/355–4000* ⊕ *www.donshula.com/shulas-on-the-beach-ft-lauderdale.*

$$$$
STEAKHOUSE
Fodor'sChoice
★

✕ **Steak 954.** It's not just the steaks that impress at Stephen Starr's superstar restaurant. The lobster and crab-coconut ceviche and the red snapper tiradito are divine; the butter-poached Maine lobster is perfection; the raw bar showcases only the best and freshest seafood on the market; and the ice cream sandwiches are pure foodie fantasia. Located on the 1st floor of the swanky W Fort Lauderdale, Steak 954 offers spectacular

5

Sand can sometimes be forgiving if you fall, and bicyclists also appreciate the ocean views.

views of the ocean for those choosing outdoor seating; inside, there's a sexy, sophisticated ambience for those choosing to dine in the main dining room, with bright tropical colors balanced with dark woods and an enormous jellyfish tank spanning the width of the restaurant. Sunday brunch is very popular, so arrive early for the best views. $ *Average main: $55* ✉ *W Fort Lauderdale, 401 N. Fort Lauderdale Beach Blvd., Along the beach* ☎ *954/414–8333* ⊕ *www.steak954.com.*

$$$$
SEAFOOD
Fodor'sChoice
★

✕ **3030 Ocean.** 3030 Ocean has been the talk of the town for decades. Previously under the direction of celebrity chef Dean Max, Fort Lauderdale's most legendary fish and seafood restaurant is now helmed by another top chef—Paula DaSilva of 1500 Degrees fame (who, interestingly enough, got her start at 3030 more than a decade ago). Constantly evolving with new flavors and fusions, 3030 Ocean gives plenty of great reasons to return time and time again. The ahi tuna poke—a tuna tartare tossed with macadamia nuts, chili sauce, and cucumber—is so fresh, it melts in your mouth. The pan-seared branzino over gnocchi and sautéed Maine scallops over curried corn purée are nothing short of experiential. The martini menu is also heaven sent, advancing mixology with basil-and-passion-fruit martinis, Bellini martinis, and açai-and-sage martinis. $ *Average main: $32* ✉ *Marriott's Harbor Beach Resort & Spa, 3030 Holiday Dr., Along the beach* ☎ *954/765–3030* ⊕ *www.3030ocean.com.*

INTRACOASTAL AND INLAND

$$
PIZZA
FAMILY

✕ **Anthony's Coal Fired Pizza.** Before this legendary "pizza well done" spread to nearly 50 outposts across five states, Anthony's original coal-fired oven was heating up Fort Lauderdale in a big way. The petite first location of the wildly popular pizza joint still packs the house nightly serving a simple menu of coal-fired pizza, chicken wings, and salad. Vegetarians and nonvegetarians alike love the cheeseless Eggplant Marino pizza and the Roasted Cauliflower pizza, with olive oil and whole garlic cloves, bread crumbs, and Romano and mozzarella cheeses. [$] *Average main: $16 ✉ 2203 South Federal Hwy., Intracoastal and Inland ☎ 954/462–5555 🌐 www.anthonyscoalfiredpizza.com.*

$$$$ SOUTHWESTERN 🍴 **Canyon Southwest Cafe.** Southwestern fusion fare helps you escape the ordinary at this small, magical enclave, managed hands-on by executive chef Chris Wilber. Order, for example, bison medallions with scotch bonnets, a tequila-jalapeño smoked salmon tostada, coriander-crusted tuna, or blue-corn fried oysters. Chipotle, wasabi, mango, and red chilies accent fresh seafood and wild game. Cocktail lovers should start off with a signature prickly-pear margarita or choose from a well-rounded wine list or beer selection. **■ TIP→ On every night but Saturday ladies get the special price of $6 margaritas and ½ off small plates.** [$] *Average main: $32 ✉ 1818 E. Sunrise Blvd., Intracoastal and Inland ☎ 954/765–1950 🌐 www.canyonfl.com ⏲ No lunch.*

$$$$ STEAKHOUSE 🍴 **The Capital Grille, Fort Lauderdale.** The Capital Grille is a rare example of a restaurant chain that has managed to uphold the superlative food quality and stellar service on which it was founded, regardless of expansion. Indeed, the Fort Lauderdale outpost of this American darling never fails to impress, every dish cooked being to perfection and meticulously presented. The dining room feels warm and welcoming, buzzing with the constant chatter of patrons raving about the food and ordering another round of "Stoli dolis" (Stoli vodka marinating in a tub of fresh-cut pineapples for two weeks and then served as a smooth martini). Though the steaks and sides are the main draw, the calamari appetizer, shrimp cocktail, sushi-grade tuna steak, and salmon should not be overlooked; they are all phenomenal. [$] *Average main: $34 ✉ Galleria Fort Lauderdale, 2430 E. Sunrise Blvd., Intracoastal and Inland ☎ 954/446–2000 🌐 www.thecapitalgrille.com.*

$$$$ ITALIAN 🍴 **Casa D'Angelo Ristorante.** Casa D'Angelo is packed year-round and for good reason. Owner-chef Angelo Elia has created a gem of a Tuscan-style white-tablecloth restaurant in Fort Lauderdale and the city can't get enough, so expect long waits. Casa D'Angelo's oak oven turns out marvelous seafood and beef dishes. The pappardelle with porcini mushrooms takes pasta to pleasant heights. Another favorite is antipasto "Angelo," an assortment of seasonal grilled vegetables and mozzarella. Ask about the oven-roasted fish of the day at market price. The restaurant's raging popularity has lead to a handful of other outposts by Chef Angelo in the South Florida area. [$] *Average main: $38 ✉ 1201 N. Federal Hwy., #5A, Intracoastal and Inland ☎ 954/564–1234 🌐 www.casa-d-angelo.com ⏲ No lunch.*

$$$ ASIAN Fodor's Choice ★ 🍴 **Coco Asian Bistro & Bar.** The best of Thai and Japanese cuisine unite under one roof at Coco Asian Bistro & Bar, a locally famous gastronomic gem in a jazzy Fort Lauderdale strip mall. Chef Mike Ponluang's expansive menu spans authentic Asian to pan-Asian flavors better-suited to the American palate to downright avant-garde interpretations of Asian cuisine. You'll never go wrong with the traditional pad thai or the

5

variety of classic curries, but there are also dishes like the Emerald Scallops, a decadent marriage of diver scallops, asparagus, and portobello mushrooms in a green curry, as well as the off-the-menu lobster pad thai served in the shell. The oversize sushi rolls are beautifully crafted, often mingling at least five flavors, fostering utter sushitopia. Try, for example, Mike's Roll, a taste explosion of tuna, spinach, avocado, tempura flakes, and kampyo rolled in sweet, black sticky rice and served with sweet chili sauce for dipping. The artisan cocktails are also excellent; don't leave without having a lycheetini or two! $ *Average main: $27* ✉ *1841 Cordova Rd., Intracoastal and Inland* ☎ *954/525–3541* ⊕ *www.cocoasianbistro.com* ⊘ *No lunch weekends.*

$$$
MODERN
AMERICAN

✕ **d.b.a./café.** Expect the unexpected at this small, eclectic, and artsy eatery that serves food with both modern American and modern French accents. With a dozen or so tables in a dimly lit space lined with exposed brick and adorned with family photos, this neighborhood restaurant exudes a true one-of-a-kind flair and serves up some pretty amazing food, too. Entrées are served in either half or full portions, catering either to those who like hearty mains or to those who want to have a variety of small plates. Enjoy simple sensations like pan-seared sea scallops with porcini-mushroom butter and fresh ricotta gnocchi with gorgonzola sauce, or dive into personality-driven dishes like the flavorful onion-crusted Florida grouper with saffron-vanilla beurre blanc, mushroom risotto, and spinach. A full roster of nightly specials and the desserts of the evening are posted on the restaurant's blackboard menu. $ *Average main: $24* ✉ *2364 N. Federal Hwy., Intracoastal and Inland* ☎ *954/565–3392* ⊕ *www.dbacafeandwinebar.com* ⌲ *Reservations essential* ⊘ *Closed Mon. No lunch.*

$$
PIZZA

✕ **Giorgio's 17th Street.** The delicious brick-oven pizza lures customers to this tiny restaurant, but it's really the salads and sandwiches that provide the wow factor. The blackened-chicken Caesar salad and the monstrous grilled-chicken sandwiches (with grilled peppers and fresh mozzarella on freshly baked bread) are both memorable. Nevertheless, the homemade seafood salad is still Giorgio's best seller, a healthy mix of tender squid, shrimp, and scallops in a light vinaigrette. All meals are served with piping hot rolls and homemade hummus. $ *Average main: $18* ✉ *1499 S.E. 17th St., Intracoastal and Inland* ☎ *954/767–8300* ⊕ *www.letseat.at/giorgios* ⊘ *No lunch Sun.*

$$$$
MODERN
AMERICAN
Fodor's Choice
★

✕ **Market 17.** Using only the best ingredients from regional farmers and local fishermen, Market 17 leads the organic farm-to-table revolution in South Florida. The menu at this chic restaurant shifts seasonally, lending to an ever-changing kaleidoscope of mouthwatering creations. The Florida wahoo crudo in citrus marinade and the pan-basted Florida yelloweye snapper with leek puree are two local favorites. The desserts, too, are outstanding and include homemade ice creams in flavors like bananas Foster, chocolate cake batter, and ginger and honey. For something awesome and different with a small group, Market 17 offers "dining in the dark," where dinner is served in a blacked-out room, forcing you to rely on your senses of touch, taste, and smell to figure out what you're eating and drinking. $ *Average main: $36* ✉ *1850 S.E.*

17th St., Ste. 109, Intracoastal and Inland ☎ *954/835–5507* 🌐 *www.market17.net* ✍ *Reservations essential* 🕒 *No lunch.*

$ SEAFOOD Fodor's Choice ★ 🍴 **Pelican Landing.** In this age of globalization and instant information, it's nearly impossible to remain the city's "best-kept secret," but somehow Pelican Landing has managed to do exactly that. Located on a second-story terrace in the Pier Sixty-Six Marina, the serene outdoor restaurant serves mouthwatering beach-shack-style eats surrounded by picturesque panoramas of boats, sea, and sunset. The fish is caught daily, served blackened or grilled, presented with sides, on a salad, or in a burrito. The ceviches and conch fritters are some of the best in South Florida. And matched with frozen drinks and pitchers of mojitos, you'll quickly reach a state of "paradise found!" [$] *Average main: $14* ✉ *Hyatt Regency Pier Sixty Six, 2301 S.E. 17th St. Causeway, at end of main dock, Intracoastal and Inland* ☎ *954/525–6666* 🌐 *www.pier66.hyatt.com.*

$$$$ STEAKHOUSE 🍴 **Ruth's Chris Steak House.** Service at the Fort Lauderdale outpost of the steakhouse juggernaut is outstanding, and waitstaff are eager to guide you through the protein-rich menu. Steaks are served on a sizzling 500-degree plate to keep them piping hot and are dripping with melted butter. Appetizers include the "crabtini," a generous portion of lump crabmeat, lightly dressed in a chilled martini glass, and the sensational lobster bisque. **■ TIP→ Save room for a decadent dessert: the caramelized banana cream pie and chocolate sin cake are off-the-charts delicious.** [$] *Average main: $38* ✉ *2525 N. Federal Hwy., Intracoastal and Inland* ☎ *954/565–2338* 🌐 *www.ruthschris.com.*

$ SEAFOOD 🍴 **Southport Raw Bar.** You can't go wrong at this unpretentious spot where the motto, on bumper stickers for miles around, proclaims, "eat fish, live longer, eat oysters, love longer, eat clams, last longer." Raw or steamed clams, raw oysters, and peel-and-eat shrimp are market price. Sides range from Bimini bread to key lime pie, with conch fritters, beer-battered onion rings, and corn on the cob in between. Order wine by the bottle or glass, and beer by the pitcher, bottle, or can. Eat outside overlooking the Intracoastal, or inside at booths, tables, or in the front or back bars. Limited parking is free, and a grocery-store parking lot is across the street. [$] *Average main: $14* ✉ *1536 Cordova Rd., Intracoastal and Inland* ☎ *954/525–2526* 🌐 *www.southportrawbar.com.*

$$ VEGETARIAN Fodor's Choice ★ 🍴 **Sublime.** Pamela Anderson, Alec Baldwin, Alicia Silverstone and their celebrity pals are not the only vegetarians that love this vegan powerhouse. The vegan sushi, the portobello stack, and innovative pizzas and pastas surprisingly can satisfy even carnivore cravings. All dishes are organic and void of any animal by-products, showing the world how vegan eating does not compromise flavor or taste. Even items like the key lime cheesecake, and chicken scaloppini use alternative ingredients and headline an evening of health-conscious eating. [$] *Average main: $17* ✉ *1431 N. Federal Hwy., Intracoastal and Inland* ☎ *954/539–9000* 🌐 *www.sublimerestaurant.com* 🕒 *Closed Mon.*

$$$ GREEK 🍴 **Thasos Greek Taverna.** A small, heavenly slice of the Greek Isles has floated ashore between Fort Lauderdale's beach and the Intracoastal Waterway. Upon entering Thasos Greek Taverna, you'll immediately think Greek chic, with the white-washed walls, blue trim, streaming

5

images of Greece on the walls, and the easy-on-the-eyes crowd. Plan on eating family-style. Start with a variety of *pikilia* (Greek spreads), which include spicy whipped feta, divine *tzatziki* (a garlicky yogurt-cucumber dip), and melt-in-your-mouth *taramosalata* (whitefish caviar). Then move onto the *mezedes* (hot shared plates) that include shrimp *saganaki* (fried with tomatoes, olives, and feta), stuffed grape leaves, and the oh-so-tender fire-grilled octopus. Finally, expand your waistline with a main course, including specialties like the traditional *moussaka* (soufflé of ground lamb and eggplant). [$] *Average main: $28* ✉ *3330 E. Oakland Park Blvd., between N. Ocean Blvd and N.E. 33rd Ave., Intracoastal and Inland* ☎ *954/200–6006* 🌐 *www.thasostaverna.com* ✍ *Reservations essential.*

$ MEXICAN Fodor's Choice ★ 🍴 **Zona Fresca.** A local favorite on the cheap, Zona Fresca serves healthful, Mexican fast food with the best chips, salsas, burritos, and quesadillas in town. Everything is made fresh on the premises, including the authentic salsas, presented in a grand salsa bar. Zona is busy seven days a week for both lunch and dinner and offers both indoor and outdoor seating. It's likely to be your best (and cheapest) lunch in Fort Lauderdale. [$] *Average main: $8* ✉ *1635 N. Federal Hwy., Intracoastal and Inland* ☎ *954/566–1777* 🌐 *www.zonafresca.com.*

WESTERN SUBURBS

$$ PIZZA FAMILY 🍴 **D' Angelo: Pizza, Wine Bar, and Tapas.** Expanding the D'Angelo restaurant empire, Florida's famous restaurateur and Tuscan chef Angelo Elia has opened an outpost of his casual pizza, tapas, and wine bar in the western suburbs of Fort Lauderdale. D'Angelo serves affordable small plates, salads, ceviches, and pizzas (based with either red or white sauce) and has quickly become a neighborhood favorite. Both kids and adults love the rotating selections of homemade gelatos. Don't miss the zucchini flowers stuffed with mozzerella, the spinach gnocchi with four cheeses and pine nuts, and the Sorrentina pizza with eggplant, mozzarella, fresh tomato, and basil oil. This is superb Italian comfort food! [$] *Average main: $20* ✉ *Country Isle Shopping Center, 1370 Weston Rd., Weston* ☎ *954/306–0037* 🌐 *www.dangelopizza.com.*

$ SOUTHERN 🍴 **Georgia Pig.** When heading out to the area's western reaches, this postage-stamp-size outpost can add down-home zing to your day—if you can find it, that is (signage has been known to disappear), and if you don't mind the somewhat gritty atmosphere. Breakfast, which includes sausage gravy and biscuits, is served 6–11 am, but the big attraction is barbecue beef, pork, or chicken, on platters or in sandwiches for lunch through dinner until about 8 pm. Alternatives include a spicy Brunswick stew and fried jumbo shrimp. There's apple, peach, cherry, and pecan pie, and a small-fry menu. Order takeout or eat at the counter, at wooden tables, or at a half dozen or so booths. [$] *Average main: $12* ✉ *1285 S. State Rd. 7 (U.S. 441) just south of Davie Blvd., Western Suburbs and Beyond* ☎ *954/587–4420* 💳 *No credit cards* 🕒 *Closed Sun. No dinner Sat.*

$$$$ STEAKHOUSE 🍴 **Ireland's Steakhouse.** Don't let the name fool you. Ireland's Steakhouse is not particularly Irish nor is it just a steakhouse. In fact, this restaurant is most popular for its sustainable seafood menu. Promoting a holistic philosophy of green eating, the restaurant meticulously chooses its

ingredients and the purveyors that supply them, while staying true to the international "Seafood Watch" guide. The restaurant is a warm and woodsy enclave in the back corner of the Bonaventure Resort & Spa. In keeping with trends of other steakhouses, hearty mains (like the cherry balsamic yellowfin tuna and the 20-oz. bone-in ribeye) are paired with loads of decadent sides made for sharing (like lobster mac 'n' cheese and lobster fries). $ *Average main: $36* ✉ *Bonaventure Resort & Spa, 250 Racquet Club Rd., Weston* ☎ *800/327–8090* ⊕ *www. bonaventureresortandspa.com* ☾ *Closed Sun. and Mon. No lunch.*

$$
SOUTHERN
✕ **Swank Southern Kitchen.** This hip, personality-driven eatery is the type of joint you'd expect to find in a big city, not in the suburbs. The farmhouse-chic restaurant is all about Southern hospitality, high-cal comfort food, and some darn good cocktails. First-timers are bound to start the night with "Swamp Water," a mason jar filled with a greenish concoction of 100% blue agave tequila, blue curaçao, orange juice, and gummy worms. The eating frenzy often begins with fried green tomatoes and crab hush puppies before moving on to the chicken and waffles or the beer-can chicken (smothered in beer gravy). After a few mason jars, head to the old-fashioned, dress-up photo booth to shoot some incriminating, for-your-eyes-only, photos. $ *Average main: $20* ✉ *4198 S. University Dr., Western Suburbs and Beyond* ☎ *954/727– 5497* ⊕ *www.swanksouthern.com* ☾ *No lunch.*

WILTON MANORS AND OAKLAND PARK

$$$
AMERICAN
✕ **Lips.** The 1990s trend of drag dining is still alive and well in Fort Lauderdale. The hit restaurant and show bar Lips is a favorite for large groups celebrating birthdays, bachelorette parties, and other milestones. Expect some show-stopping entertainment while you eat, peppered with quite a few embarrassing moments as the queens love to drag guests up on stage. ■ TIP→ Locals tend to visit Lips on Sunday for Sunday Gospel Brunch, the only "church" service with unlimited sparkling wine. Besides the meal, there's a show charge that ranges from $5 to $10. $ *Average main: $25* ✉ *1421 E. Oakland Park Blvd., Oakland Park* ☎ *954/567–0987* ⊕ *www.floridalips.com* ☾ *Closed Mon.*

$$$$
SOUTH PACIFIC
FAMILY
✕ **Mai-Kai.** Touristy to some yet exciting to others, the South Pacific meets South Florida at this torch-lit landmark. It's undeniably gimmicky, but droves arrive for the popular Polynesian dance review and fire shows, Peking duck, and umbrella-garnished exotic tropical drinks. The Pacific allure is maintained with freshly planted palms, thatch, and bamboo, and a wood-planked bridge rebuilt to make arriving cars sound like rumbling thunder. An expanded wine list embraces boutique vintages from around the world. Valet parking is available. $ *Average main: $39* ✉ *3599 N. Federal Hwy., Wilton Manors and Oakland Park* ☎ *954/563–3272* ⊕ *www.maikai.com.*

$$$$
SEAFOOD
✕ **Sunfish Grill.** The former Pompano Beach institution migrated south in 2009 and hasn't looked back since. Quickly establishing itself in the Oakland Park area (albeit in a quiet strip mall), Sunfish Grill doles out beautifully presented contemporary American cuisine, namely well-executed, outside-the-box seafood and fish dishes. The spaghetti Bolognese is made with ground tuna instead of beef; the Sunfish Caesar with Maytag Blue Cheese instead of Parmesan; the "not the usual" key lime

pie with coconut sorbet instead of whipped cream. The results of this ingenuity are fantastic. [$] *Average main: $36* ✉ *2775 E. Oakland Park Blvd., Wilton Manors and Oakland Park* ☎ *954/561–2004* 🌐 *www.sunfishgrill.com.*

WHERE TO STAY

DOWNTOWN AND LAS OLAS

$$ B&B/INN 🏨 **Pineapple Point.** Tucked a few blocks behind Las Olas Boulevard in the residential neighborhood of Victoria Park, clothing-optional Pineapple Point is a magnificent maze of posh tropical cottages and dense foliage catering to the gay community and is nationally renowned for its stellar service. **Pros:** superior service; tropical setting. **Cons:** difficult to find at first; need a vehicle for beach jaunts. [$] *Rooms from: $289* ✉ *315 N.E. 16th Terr., Downtown and Las Olas* ☎ *954/527–0094* 🌐 *www.pineapplepoint.com* 🛏 *25 rooms* 🍴 *Breakfast.*

$$ HOTEL 🏨 **Riverside Hotel.** On Las Olas Boulevard, just steps from boutiques, restaurants, and art galleries, Fort Lauderdale's oldest hotel (circa 1936) evokes a time bygone with historical photos gracing hallways, and guest rooms outfitted with antique oak furnishings, ornamental palm trees, and a bold tropical color palate with a Tommy Bahamas throwback flair. **Pros:** historic appeal; in the thick of Las Olas action; nice views. **Cons:** questionable room décor; dated lobby; small bathrooms. [$] *Rooms from: $239* ✉ *620 E. Las Olas Blvd., Downtown and Las Olas* ☎ *954/467–0671, 800/325–3280* 🌐 *www.riversidehotel.com* 🛏 *208 rooms, 6 suites* 🍴 *No meals.*

ALONG THE BEACH

$$$ HOTEL 🏨 **The Atlantic Resort & Spa.** The hotel that catalyzed Fort Lauderdale's luxe revolution circa 2000 continues to be a beautiful and well-run gem, and the skyscraping, oceanfront beauty seems well positioned to stay at the top of her contemporary game for years to come. **Pros:** sophisticated lodging option; en-suite kitchenettes; hotel received full renovation in 2011. **Cons:** no complimentary water bottles in room; expensive parking. [$] *Rooms from: $323* ✉ *601 N. Fort Lauderdale Beach Blvd., Along the beach* ☎ *954/567–8020, 877/567–8020* 🌐 *www.atlantichotelfl.com* 🛏 *61 rooms, 58 suites, 4 penthouses* 🍴 *No meals.*

$ HOTEL 🏨 **Bahia Mar Fort Lauderdale Beach Hotel, A DoubleTree by Hilton.** This nicely situated Fort Lauderdale beachfront classic received a long-overdue nip/tuck in 2011–12 that included cheery, refreshed guestrooms and rebranding as a DoubleTree hotel. **Pros:** crosswalk from hotel to beach; on-site yacht center; easy to navigate Fort Laud with on-site water-taxi stop. **Cons:** dated exteriors; small bathrooms; popcorn ceilings. [$] *Rooms from: $189* ✉ *801 Seabreeze Blvd., Along the beach* ☎ *954/764–2233* 🌐 *www.bahiamarhotel.com* 🛏 *296 rooms* 🍴 *No meals.*

$$ RESORT FAMILY Fodor'sChoice ★ 🏨 **Hilton Fort Lauderdale Beach Resort.** This 26-story oceanfront sparkler features 374 tastefully appointed guest rooms and a fabulous 6th-floor pool deck, colorfully and whimsically decorated. **Pros:** excellent gym; most rooms have balconies; great location. **Cons:** charge for Wi-Fi; no outdoor bar; expensive valet parking. [$] *Rooms from: $279* ✉ *505 N.*

Fort Lauderdale Beach Blvd., Along the beach ☎ *954/760–7177* 🌐 *www.fortlauderdalebeachresort.hilton.com* 🛏 *374 rooms* 🍴 *No meals.*

$$$$ RESORT FAMILY 🏨 **Lago Mar Resort and Club.** The sprawling, kid-friendly Lago Mar, owned by the Banks family since the early 1950s, retains its sparkle and a refreshed old Florida feel thanks to frequent renovations; brilliantly colored bougainvillea edges the swimming lagoon, and you have direct access to a large private beach in an exclusive neighborhood. **Pros:** secluded setting; plenty of activities; on the very private Harbor beach. **Cons:** not easy to find; far from restaurants and beach action. [$] *Rooms from: $425* ✉ *1700 S. Ocean La., Along the beach* ☎ *954/523–6511, 800/524–6627* 🌐 *www.lagomar.com* 🛏 *52 rooms, 160 suites* 🍴 *No meals.*

$$$ RESORT FAMILY Fodor's Choice ★ 🏨 **Marriott Harbor Beach Resort.** Bill Marriott's personal choice for his annual four-week family vacation, the Marriott Harbor Beach Resort sits on a quarter-mile swath of private beach and bursts with the luxe beachfront personality of an upscale Caribbean resort. **Pros:** excellent gym; all rooms have balconies; great eating outlets; no resort fees. **Cons:** Wi-Fi isn't free; expensive parking; interiors are new but feel a little cookie-cutter. [$] *Rooms from: $379* ✉ *3030 Holiday Dr., Along the beach* ☎ *954/525–4000* 🌐 *www.marriottharborbeach.com* 🛏 *650 rooooms, 31 suites* 🍴 *No meals.*

$$ RESORT FAMILY 🏨 **Pelican Grand Beach Resort.** Smack on Fort Lauderdale beach, this yellow spired, Key West–style, Noble House property fuses a heritage of Old Florida seaside charm with understated luxury; there's renovated rooms upstairs, an amazing beachfront, an old-fashioned emporium, and Fort Lauderdale's only lazy river. **Pros:** free popcorn in the Postcard Lounge; directly on the beach; Ocean 2000 restaurant. **Cons:** high tide can swallow most of beach area; small fitness center. [$] *Rooms from: $272* ✉ *2000 N. Atlantic Blvd., Along the beach* ☎ *954/568–9431, 800/525–6232* 🌐 *www.pelicanbeach.com* 🛏 *156 rooms* 🍴 *No meals.*

$$$ B&B/INN 🏨 **The Pillars Hotel.** Once a "small secret" kept by locals in the know, this elegant boutique gem, sandwiched between Fort Lauderdale beach and the Intracoastal Waterway, rarely falls below capacity since it invariably lands on reader's choice lists. **Pros:** attentive staff; lovely décor; idyllic pool area. **Cons:** small rooms; not for families with young kids given proximity to dock and water with no lifeguard on duty. [$] *Rooms from: $309* ✉ *111 N. Birch Rd., Along the beach* ☎ *954/467–9639* 🌐 *www.pillarshotel.com* 🛏 *13 rooms, 5 suites* 🍴 *No meals.*

$$$$ HOTEL Fodor's Choice ★ 🏨 **The Ritz-Carlton, Fort Lauderdale.** Inspired by the design of an opulent luxury liner, 24 dramatically tiered, glass-walled stories rise from the sea, forming a sumptuous Ritz-Carlton hotel with guest rooms that reinvent a golden era of luxury travel, a lavish tropical sundeck and infinity-edge pool peering over the ocean, and a Club Lounge that spans an entire floor. **Pros:** prime beach location; modern seaside elegance deviates dramatically from traditional Ritz-Carlton décor; sensational Club Lounge. **Cons:** no complimentary Wi-Fi; expensive valet parking. [$] *Rooms from: $429* ✉ *1 N. Fort Lauderdale Beach Blvd., Along the beach* ☎ *954/465–2300* 🌐 *www.ritzcarlton.com/FortLauderdale* 🛏 *138 rooms, 54 suites* 🍴 *No meals.*

5

$$
HOTEL

⛱ **Sheraton Fort Lauderdale Beach Hotel.** As part of its global rebranding, Sheraton has reinvented (and renamed) its Fort Lauderdale landmark— once the Sheraton Yankee Clipper Hotel—with updated interiors and public spaces throughout its four towers of rooms and suites. **Pros:** Friday night retro mermaid show in swimming pool; proximity to beach; excellent gym. **Cons:** small rooms; low ceilings in lobby; faded exteriors. $ *Rooms from: $229* ✉ *1140 Seabreeze Blvd., Along the beach* ☎ *954/524–5551* ⊕ *www.sheratonftlauderdalebeach.com* ↪ *486 rooms* ¶◯¶ *No meals.*

$$
RESORT
FAMILY

⛱ **The Westin Beach Resort & Spa, Fort Lauderdale.** Smack-dab in the center of Fort Lauderdale Beach and connected directly to the beach through a private overpass, the hotel once known as the Sheraton Yankee Trader has been transformed into a modern convention-centric Westin. **Pros:** direct beach access; heavenly beds and spa. **Cons:** lengthy walks to get to some rooms; fee for Wi-Fi; a lot of conventioneers. $ *Rooms from: $289* ✉ *321 N. Fort Lauderdale Beach Blvd., Along the beach* ☎ *954/467–1111* ⊕ *www.westin.com/fortlauderdalebeach* ↪ *433 rooms* ¶◯¶ *No meals.*

$$$
HOTEL
Fodor'sChoice
★

⛱ **W Fort Lauderdale.** Fort Lauderdale's trendiest hotel—equipped with a rooftop see-through swimming pool, a wide range of spectacular contemporary rooms and suites, and an easy-on-the-eyes youthful crowd—boasts a vibe highly reminiscent of South Beach. **Pros:** trendy and flashy; tony scene; amazing pool; great spa. **Cons:** party atmosphere not for everyone; impersonal service. $ *Rooms from: $355* ✉ *435 N. Fort Lauderdale Beach Blvd., Along the beach* ☎ *954/462– 1633* ⊕ *www.wfortlauderdalehotel.com* ↪ *346 rooms, 171 condominiums* ¶◯¶ *No meals.*

$
B&B/INN

⛱ **Worthington Guest House.** Located five minutes from gay Sebastian Beach, this hotel is one of Fort Lauderdale Beach's 27 clothing-optional guesthouses for gay men. **Pros:** fresh-squeezed orange juice in the morning; nice pool area; ability to also hang out at sister properties Alcazar and Villa Venice. **Cons:** not on the beach; windows open towards fence or other buildings. $ *Rooms from: $165* ✉ *543 N. Birch Rd., Along the beach* ☎ *954/563–6819* ⊕ *www.theworthington.com* ↪ *14 rooms* ¶◯¶ *Breakfast.*

INTRACOASTAL AND INLAND

$$
HOTEL

⛱ **Gallery ONE by DoubleTree.** A condo hotel favored by vacationers preferring longer stays, the residential-style Gallery ONE rises over the Intracoastal, within short walking distance of both Fort Lauderdale Beach and the city's popular Galleria Mall. **Pros:** walking distance to both beach and supermarket; easy water taxi access; good for longer stays. **Cons:** pool area needs refurbishment; kitchens don't have stoves; no bathtubs. $ *Rooms from: $209* ✉ *2670 E. Sunrise Blvd., Intracoastal and Inland* ☎ *954/565–3800* ⊕ *www.doubletree.com* ↪ *231 rooms* ¶◯¶ *No meals.*

$
RESORT
FAMILY
Fodor'sChoice
★

⛱ **Hilton Fort Lauderdale Marina.** After a $72 million renovation in 2011, the mammoth, 589-room, 20-boat-slip Hilton Fort Lauderdale Marina infused luxury and modernity into its charming Key West style. **Pros:** sexy fire pit; outdoor bar popular with locals; easy water taxi access. **Cons:** no bathtubs in tower rooms; small fitness center. $ *Rooms from:*

Lago Mar Resort and Club in Fort Lauderdale has its own private beach on the Atlantic Ocean.

$189 ✉ 1881 S.E. 17th St., Intracoastal and Inland ☎ 954/463–4000 🌐 www.fortlauderdalemarinahotel.com 🛏 589 rooms 🍴 No meals.

$$ RESORT 🏨 **Hyatt Regency Pier Sixty-Six Resort & Spa.** Don't let the 1970s exterior of the iconic 17-story tower fool you; this lovely 22-acre resort teems with contemporary interior-design sophistication and remains one of Florida's few hotels where a rental car isn't necessary. **Pros:** great views; plenty of activities; free shuttle to beach; easy Water Taxi access. **Cons:** tower rooms are far less stylish than lanai rooms; totally retro rotating rooftop is used exclusively for private events. [$] *Rooms from: $219 ✉ 2301 S.E. 17th St. Causeway, Intracoastal and Inland ☎ 954/525–6666 🌐 www.pier66.hyatt.com 🛏 384 rooms 🍴 No meals.*

$$ HOTEL FAMILY 🏨 **Il Lugano Luxury Suite Hotel.** This all-suite condo hotel on Fort Lauderdale's northern Intracoastal waterway offers all the comforts of home (washer, dryer, kitchenette, fridge, sleeper sofa, huge terraces) with all the glamour of a hyper-modern trendsetting hotel. **Pros:** 800-square-foot rooms; easy water taxi access; good for longer stays. **Cons:** limited sunlight in pool area; need wheels to reach main beach and downtown area. [$] *Rooms from: $289 ✉ 3333 N.E. 32nd Ave., Intracoastal and Inland ☎ 954/564–4400 🌐 www.illugano.com 🛏 28 suites 🍴 No meals.*

WESTERN SUBURBS

$ HOTEL FAMILY 🏨 **Bonaventure Resort & Spa.** This massive suburban enclave—formerly a Hyatt Regency–flagged resort—targets conventioneers and business executives as well as international vacationers who value golf, the Everglades, and shopping over beach proximity. Factor in the allure of the huge and soothing aLaya Spa and the "Choose Your Journey" package that includes a spa treatment with the room, and you'll see why. **Pros:** lush landscaping; pampering spa; great in-house restaurant, Ireland's Steakhouse. **Cons:** difficult to find; in the suburbs; poor views from some rooms. [$] *Rooms from: $169* ✉ *250 Racquet Club Rd., Westin* ☎ *954/389–3300* 🌐 *www.bonaventureresortandspa.com* 🛏 *501 rooms* 🍴 *No meals.*

NIGHTLIFE AND PERFORMING ARTS

For the most complete weekly listing of events, check "Showtime!," the *South Florida Sun-Sentinel*'s tabloid-size entertainment section and events calendar published on Friday. "Weekend," in the Friday Broward edition of the *Herald,* also lists area happenings. The weekly *City Link* and *New Times Broward* are free alternative newspapers, detailing plenty of entertainment and nightlife options. For the latest happenings in GLBT nightlife, visit **Mark's List** (🌐 *www.jumponmarkslist.com*), the online authority of all things GLBT in South Florida or pick up one of the weekly gay rags, *MARK* or *Hot Spots.*

NIGHTLIFE

DOWNTOWN AND LAS OLAS

The majority of Fort Lauderdale nightlife takes place near downtown, beginning on Himmarshee Street (2nd Street) and continuing on to the Riverfront, and then to Las Olas Boulevard. The downtown Riverfront tends to draw a younger demographic somewhere between underage teens and late twenties. On Himmarshee Street, a dozen rowdy bars and clubs, ranging from the seedy to the sophisticated, entice a wide range of partygoers. Toward East Las Olas Boulevard, near the financial towers and boutique shops, bars cater to the yuppie crowd.

Maguire's Hill 16. With the requisite lineup of libations and pub-style food, this classic Irish pub is good for no-frills fun, fried eats, and daily live music. It's famous locally as the oldest award-winning Traditional Irish Pub and Restaurant in Fort Lauderdale. Live music is on tap every Wednesday, Friday, and Saturday night. ✉ *535 N. Andrews Ave., Downtown and Las Olas* ☎ *954/764–4453* 🌐 *www.maguireshill16.com.*

O Lounge. This lounge and two adjacent establishments, **Yolo** and **Vibe,** on Las Olas and under the same ownership, cater to Fort Lauderdale's sexy yuppies, business men, desperate housewives, and hungry cougars letting loose during happy hour and on the weekends. Crowds alternate between Yolo's outdoor fire pit, O Lounge's chilled atmosphere and lounge music, and Vibe's more intense beats. Expect flashy cars in the driveway and a bit of plastic surgery. ✉ *333 E. Las Olas Blvd., Downtown and Las Olas* ☎ *954/523–1000* 🌐 *www.yolorestaurant.com.*

Off the Hookah. After a not-very-visible $21 million renovation in 2012, the downtown space formerly home to Voodoo Lounge returned as Off the Hookah. Totally revamped from top to bottom and filled with VIP areas, Hookah attempts to reinstate the late-night electro and pop parties that made downtown Fort Lauderdale famous circa 2006. The club also regularly hosts local and national talent. The long-running Sunday gay-straight mixer, Life's a Drag, continues on from its Voodoo days. It's a fun-filled night of drag performances and incriminating debauchery.

⊠111 S.W. 2nd Ave., Downtown and Las Olas ☎954/761–8686 ⊕*www.offthehookah.com.*

ROK: BRG. Downtown Fort Lauderdale warmly welcomed this personality-driven burger bar and gastro-pub in early 2011, giving the grown-ups something to enjoy in teenage-infested downtown. The long and narrow venue, adorned with exposed-brick walls and flat-screen TVs is great for watching sports and for mingling on weekends. Locals come here for the great cocktails and beer selection. ⊠*208 S.W. 2nd St., Downtown and Las Olas* ☎954/525–7656 ⊕*www.rokbrgr.com.*

Fodor's Choice ★ **Tap 42 Bar and Kitchen.** With 42 rotating draft beers from around the U.S., 50-plus bourbons, a few dozen original cocktails (including beer cocktails), and 66 bottled craft beers, awesome drinks and good times headline a typical evening at classy cool Tap 42. Although the indoor/outdoor gastro-pub is a bit off the beaten path, it's well worth the detour. The 42 drafts protrude from a stylish wall constructed of pennies, surfacing more like a work of art than a beer-filling station. The venue attracts large crowds of young professionals for nights of heavy drinking and highly caloric new-age bar eats. ⊠*1411 S. Andrews Ave., Downtown and Las Olas* ☎954/463–4900 ⊕*www.tap42.com.*

Fodor's Choice ★ **Tarpon Bend.** This casual two-story restaurant transforms into a jovial resto-bar in the early evening, ideal for enjoying a few beers, mojitos, and some great bar food. It's consistently busy, day, night, and late night with young professionals, couples, and large groups of friends. It's one place that has survived all the ups and downs of downtown Fort Lauderdale. ⊠*200 S.W. 2nd St., Downtown and Las Olas* ☎954/523–3233 ⊕*www.tarponbend.com.*

ALONG THE BEACH
Given its roots as a beachside party town, it's hard to believe that Fort Lauderdale Beach offers very few options in terms of nightlife. A few dive bars are at opposite ends of the main strip, near Sunrise Boulevard and Route A1A, as well as Las Olas Boulevard and A1A. On the main thoroughfare between Las Olas and Sunrise, a few high-end bars at the beach's show-stopping hotels have become popular, namely those at the W Fort Lauderdale.

Elbo Room. You can't go wrong wallowing in the past, lifting a drink, and exercising your elbow at the Elbo, a noisy, suds-drenched hot spot since 1938. It seems like nothing has changed here since Fort Lauderdale's spring-break heyday, and the clientele still includes far too many scantily clad girls that will do anything for booze. At least the bathrooms were redone in 2011. The watering hole phased out food (except for light nibbles) ages ago, but kept a hokey sense of humor: upstairs a sign proclaims, "We don't serve women here. You have to bring your own." ⊠*241 S. Fort Lauderdale Blvd., Along the beach* ☎954/463–4615 ⊕*www.elboroom.com.*

Living Room at the W. The large living-room-like space next to the lobby of the W Fort Lauderdale transforms into a major house-party-style event, mainly on weekends. There are plenty of plush couches, but it's usually standing-room-only early for this South Beach–style throw-down, with great DJs, awesome libations, and an easy-on-the-eyes crowd. A breezy and beautiful outdoor area is idyllic for the overflow, as is the downstairs lounge, Whiskey Blue (which is only open Thursday–Saturday). ⊠ *W Fort Lauderdale, 401 N. Fort Lauderdale Beach Blvd., Along the beach* ☎ *954/414–8300* ⊕ *www.wfortlauderdalehotel. com/living-room.*

Parrot Lounge. An old-school Fort Lauderdale hangout, this dive bar/ sports bar is particularly popular with Philadelphia Eagles fans, those longing to recall *Where the Boys Are,* and folks reminiscing about Fort Lauderdale's big-hair, sprayed-tan, Sun-In-bright 1980s heyday. This place is stuck in the past, but it's got great libations, wings, fingers, poppers, and skins. 'Nuff said. ⊠ *911 Sunrise La., Along the beach* ☎ *954/563–1493* ⊕ *www.parrotlounge.com.*

INTRACOASTAL AND INLAND
Bars and pubs along Fort Lauderdale's Intracoastal cater to the city's large, transient boating community. Heading inland along Sunrise Boulevard, the bars around Galleria Mall target thirty- and fortysomething singles.

Blue Martini Fort Lauderdale. A hot spot for thirtysomething-plus adults gone wild, Blue Martini's menu is filled with tons of innovative martini creations (42 to be exact) and lots of cougars on the prowl, searching for a first, second, or even third husband. And the guys aren't complaining! The drinks are great and the scene is fun for everyone, even those who aren't single and looking to mingle. ⊠ *Galleria Fort Lauderdale, 2432 E. Sunrise Blvd., Intracoastal and Inland* ☎ *954/653–2583* ⊕ *www. bluemartinilounge.com.*

Kim's Alley Bar. Around since 1948, Kim's Alley Bar is the ultimate no-frills South Florida dive bar, a neighborhood spot in a strip mall near the Intracoastal. It has two smoke-filled bar areas, a jukebox, and pool tables that provide endless entertainment (if the patrons aren't providing enough diversion). ⊠ *The Gateway, 1920 E. Sunrise Blvd., Intracoastal and Inland* ☎ *954/763–2143.*

WILTON MANORS AND OAKLAND PARK
Fort Lauderdale's gay nightlife is most prevalent in Wilton Manors, affectionately termed Fort Lauderdale's "gayborhood." Wilton Drive, known as "the Drive," has dozens of bars, clubs, and lounges that cater to all types of GLBT subcultures.

Georgie's Alibi. A Fort Lauderdale GBLT institution, Georgie's Alibi is an anchor for the Wilton Manors gay community. The gargantuan pub fills to capacity for $3, 32-ounce Long Island Iced Tea Thursdays (from 9 pm 'til close). Any night of the week, Alibi stands out as a kind of gay Cheers of Fort Lauderdale—a neighborhood bar with darts, pool, libations, and some eye candy, offering a no-frills, laid-back attitude. ⊠ *2266 Wilton Dr., Wilton Manors and Oakland Park* ☎ *954/565– 2526* ⊕ *www.alibiwiltonmanors.com.*

The Manor. Inspired by The Abbey in West Hollywood, The Manor sought to offer a one-stop gay party shop in the heart of the Wilton Manors gayborhood. It didn't quite work out that way, but the multifaceted two-story enclave is still open Friday for the campy pop night Bubble Gum Fridays and the circuit-party style Epic Saturdays.

✉ *2345 Wilton Dr., Wilton Manors and Oakland Park* ☎ *954/626–0082* ⊕ *www.themanorcomplex.com.*

Fodor'sChoice
★
Rosie's Bar and Grill. Rosie's is consistently lively, pumping out tons of pop tunes and volumes of joyous laughter to surrounding streets. The former Hamburger Mary's has become an institution in South Florida as the go-to gay-friendly place for cheap drinks, decent bar food, and great times. Most of the fun at Rosie's is meeting new friends and engaging in conversation with the person seated next to you. Drink specials change daily. Sunday brunch with alternating DJs is wildly popular. ✉ *2449 Wilton Dr., Wilton Manors and Oakland Park* ☎ *954/563–0123* ⊕ *www.facebook.com/RosiesBarAndGrill.*

Sidelines. One of the most popular and consistently busy joints on "The Drive" is this spacious sports and video bar that taps into the butch side of gay culture. The bar is often locally awarded the "Best Gay Bar in South Florida," and its all-welcoming vibe draws crowds both young and old, men and women. Expect large crowds during major football and basketball games. ✉ *2031-A Wilton Dr., Wilton Manors* ☎ *954/563–8001* ⊕ *www.sidelinessports.com.*

WESTERN SUBURBS AND BEYOND

Florida's cowboy country, Davie, offers country-western fun out in the 'burbs. In addition, South Florida's Native American tribes have long offered gambling on Indian Territory near Broward's western suburbs. With new laws, Broward's casinos offer Vegas-style slot machines and even blackjack. Hollywood's Seminole Hard Rock Hotel & Casino offers the most elegant of Broward's casino experiences. ⇨ *See Nightlife in Hollywood.*

SHOPPING

MALLS

Galleria Fort Lauderdale. Fort Lauderdale's most upscale mall is just west of the Intracoastal Waterway. The split-level emporium entices with Neiman Marcus, Dillard's, Macy's, an Apple Store plus 150 specialty shops for anything from cookware to exquisite jewelry. Chow down at Capital Grille, Truluck's, P. F. Chang's, or Seasons 52, or head for the food court, which will defy expectations with its international food-market feel. The mall itself is open Monday through Saturday 10–9, Sunday noon–6. The standalone restaurants and bars, like Capital Grille and Blue Martini Fort Lauderdale, are open later. ✉ *2414 E. Sunrise Blvd., Intracoastal and Inland* ☎ *954/564–1036* ⊕ *www.galleriamall-fl.com.*

FAMILY
Fodor'sChoice
★
Sawgrass Mills. This alligator-shaped megamall draws 26 million shoppers a year to its collection of 400 outlet stores and name-brand discounters. The mall claims to be the second-largest attraction in Florida—second only to Disney World. Though that claim is probably an exaggeration, you should prepare for insane crowds even during off-peak hours and seasons. ✉ *12801 W. Sunrise Blvd., at Flamingo Rd., Sunrise* ⊕ *www.sawgrassmills.com.*

Swap Shop. For those who grew up in Fort Lauderdale, the Swap Shop's cheesy commercials of yesteryear will forever remain. "Where's the bargains?" "At the Swap Shop!" The South's largest flea market, with 2,000 vendors, is open daily. Thankfully, they've done away with the awful circus after years of protests by animal-rights activists. While exploring this indoor–outdoor entertainment-and-shopping complex, hop on the carousel, try some fresh sugarcane juice, or stick around for movies at the 14-screen Swap Shop drive-in. ⊠ *3291 W. Sunrise Blvd., Western Suburbs and Beyond* ☎ *954/791–7927* ⊕ *www. floridaswapshop.com.*

SHOPPING DISTRICTS

The Gallery at Beach Place. Just north of Las Olas Boulevard on Route A1A, this shopping gallery is attached to the mammoth Marriott Beach Place timeshare. Spaces are occupied by touristy shops that sell everything from sarongs to alligator heads, chain restaurants like Hooter's, bars serving frozen drinks, and a supersize CVS pharmacy, which sells everything you need for the beach. ■TIP→ Beach Place has covered parking, and usually has plenty of spaces, but you can pinch pennies by using a nearby municipal lot that's metered. ⊠ *17 S. Fort Lauderdale Beach Blvd., Along the beach* ⊕ *www.galleryatbeachplace.com.*

Fodor'sChoice **Las Olas Boulevard.** Las Olas Boulevard is the heart and soul of Fort Lau-
★ derdale. Not only are fifty of the city's best boutiques, thirty top restaurants, and a dozen art galleries found along this beautifully landscaped street, but Las Olas links Fort Lauderdale's growing downtown with its superlative beaches. Though you'll find a Cheesecake Factory on the boulevard, the thoroughfare tends to shun chains and welcomes one-of-a-kind clothing boutiques, chocolatiers, and ethnic eateries. Window shopping allowed. ⊠ *East Las Olas Blvd., Downtown and Las Olas* ⊕ *www.lasolasboulevard.com.*

FOOD

Chef Jean-Pierre Cooking School. Catering to locals, seasonal snowbirds, and folks winging in for even shorter stays, Jean-Pierre Brehier (former owner of the Left Bank Restaurant on Las Olas) teaches the basics, from boiling water onward. The enthusiastic Gallic transplant has appeared on NBC's *Today* among other shows. Choose from demonstration classes, hands-on classes, and a full series of cooking classes. Book ahead as classes often fill up. For souvenir hunters, this fun cooking facility also sells nifty pots, pastas, oils, and other great items. ⊠ *1436 N. Federal Hwy., Intracoastal and Inland* ☎ *954/563–2700* ⊕ *www. chefjp.com* ✉ *From $65 per demonstration class, $125 hands-on class; "Cooking 101" and "Cooking 102" series $350 each* ☉ *Store Mon.– Sat. 10–7, class schedules vary.*

SPORTS AND THE OUTDOORS

BIKING

Among the most popular routes are Route A1A and Bayview Drive, especially in early morning before traffic builds, and a 7-mile bike path that parallels State Road 84 and New River and leads to Markham Park, which has mountain-bike trails. ■TIP→ Alligator alert: Do not dangle your legs from seawalls.

Broward B–cycle. The big-city trend of "pay and ride" bicycles has now reached Broward County. With 40 station locations over 20 scenic miles, from as far south as Hallandale to as far north as Pompano Beach and Coconut Creek, bikes can be rented for as little as 30 minutes or as long as a week, and can be picked up and dropped off at any and all stations in Broward County. Most stations are found downtown and along the beach. This is an excellent green and health-conscious way to explore Fort Lauderdale. Please note, however, that helmets are not provided at the kiosks. ⊕ *www.broward.bcycle.com.*

FISHING

Bahia Mar Marina. If you're interested in a saltwater charter, check out the offerings at the marina of the Bahia Mar Fort Lauderdale Beach Hotel, A DoubleTree by Hilton. Sportfishing and drift-fishing bookings can be arranged. Snorkeling and diving outfitter Sea Experience also leaves from here, as does the famous *Jungle Queen* steamboat. In addition, the water taxi makes regular stops here. ⊠ *Bahia Mar Lauderdale Beach Hotel, A DoubleTree by Hilton, 801 Seabreeze Blvd., Along the beach* ☎ *954/627–6309.*

RODEOS

Davie Pro Rodeo. It may sound strange, but South Florida has a rather large cowboy scene, concentrated in the western suburb of Davie. And for over four decades, the Bergeron Rodeo Grounds has surfaced as Davie's biggest tourist attraction. Throughout the year, the Rodeo hosts national tours and festivals as well as the annual Southeaster Circuit Finals. Check the website for the exact dates of these rodeos. ⊠ *Davie Pro Rodeo Arena, 4271 Davie Rd., Davie* ☎ *954/680–8005* ⊕ *www. davieprorodeo.com.*

SCUBA DIVING AND SNORKELING

Lauderdale Diver. A PADI 5-Star Certification Agency, this dive center facilitates daily trips on a variety of dive boats up and down Broward's shoreline (they don't have their own boat but work with a handful of preferred outfitters). A variety of snorkeling, reef diving, and wreck diving trips are offered daily as well as scuba diving lessons. ⊠ *1334 S.E. 17th St., Intracoastal and Inland* ☎ *954/467–2822* ⊕ *www. lauderdalediver.com.*

FAMILY **Sea Experience.** The *Sea Experience I* leaves daily at 10:15 am and 2:15 pm for two-hour glass-bottom-boat and snorkeling combination trips that explore Fort Lauderdale's offshore reefs. The tour costs $28 ($7 more to snorkel, equipment provided). They also offer beginner and more advanced scuba diving experiences. ⊠ *Bahia Mar Fort Lauderdale Beach Hotel, A DoubleTree by Hilton, 801 Seabreeze Blvd., Along the beach* ☎ *954/770–3483* ⊕ *www.seaxp.com.*

SEGWAY TOURS

FAMILY
Fodor's Choice
★
M.Cruz Rentals. M.Cruz Rentals offers Segway tours of Fort Lauderdale Beach four times per day and bicycle rentals by the hour. The rental facility is at the beach entrance of Hugh Taylor Birch State Park, just north of hotel row. The Segway Tours leave from here as well. Staff are exceptionally friendly and accommodating. ⊠ *Hugh Taylor Birch*

State Park, 3109 E. Sunrise Blvd., Along the beach ☎ *954/235–5082* ⊕ *www.mcruzrentals.com.*

TENNIS

Jimmy Evert Tennis Center. With 22 courts (18 lighted clay courts, 3 hard courts, and a low-compression sand "beach" court), this is the crown jewel of Fort Lauderdale's public tennis facilities. Legendary champ Chris Evert learned her two-handed backhand here under the watchful eye of her now-retired father, Jimmy, the center's tennis pro for 37 years. ⊠ *Holiday Park, 701 N.E. 12th Ave., Intracoastal and Inland* ☎ *954/828–5378* ⊕ *www.fortlauderdale.gov/tennis/jetc.htm* ✉ *$18 day pass (for Broward nonresidents)* ⊙ *Weekdays 7:45 am–9 pm, weekends 7:45 am–6 pm.*

NORTH ON SCENIC A1A

North of Fort Lauderdale's Birch Recreation Area, Route A1A edges away from the beach through a stretch known as Galt Ocean Mile, and a succession of oceanside communities line up against the sea. Traffic can line up, too, as it passes through a changing pattern of beach-blocking high-rises and modest family vacation towns and back again. As far as tourism goes, these communities tend to cater to a different demographic than Fort Lauderdale. Europeans and cost-conscious families head to Lauderdale-by-the-Sea, Pompano, and Deerfield for fewer frills and longer stays.

Towns are shown on the Broward County map.

LAUDERDALE-BY-THE-SEA

Lauderdale-by-the-Sea is 5 miles north of Fort Lauderdale.

Just north of Fort Lauderdale's northern boundary, this low-rise family resort town traditionally digs in its heels at the mere mention of high-rises. The result is choice shoreline access that's rapidly disappearing in nearby communities. Without a doubt, Lauderdale-by-the-Sea takes delight in embracing its small beach-town feel and welcoming guests to a different world of years gone by.

GETTING HERE AND AROUND

Lauderdale-by-the-Sea is just north of Fort Lauderdale. If you're driving from Interstate 95, exit east onto Commercial Boulevard and head over the Intracoastal Waterway. From U.S. 1 (aka Federal Highway), turn east on Commercial Boulevard. If coming from A1A, just continue north from Fort Lauderdale Beach.

ESSENTIALS

Visitor Information Lauderdale-by-the-Sea Chamber of Commerce ☎ *954/776–1000* ⊕ *www.lbts.com.*

BEACHES

FAMILY **Lauderdale-by-the-Sea Beach.** Especially popular with divers and snorkelers, this laid-back stretch of sand provides great access to lovely coral reefs. When you're not underwater, look up and you'll likely see

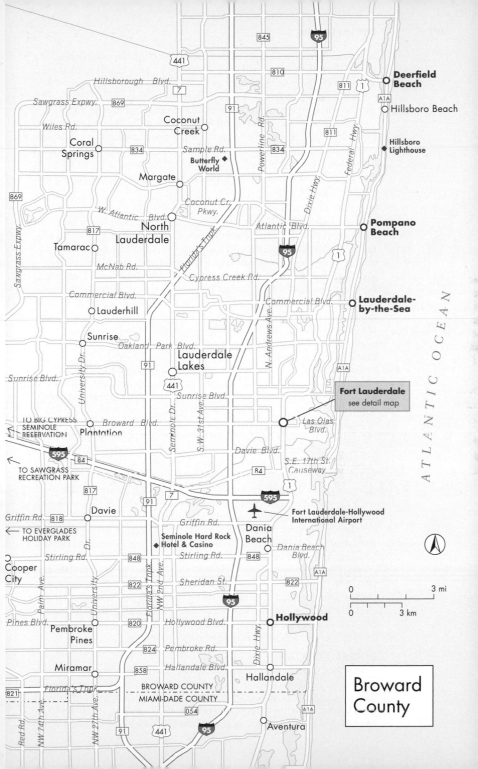

a pelican flying by. Gentle trade winds make this an utterly relaxing retreat from the hubbub of Fort Lauderdale's busier beaches. That said, the southern part of the beach at Commercial Boulevard and A1A is often busy due to a concentrated number of restaurants at the intersection, including the wildly popular Aruba Beach Café. Going north from Commercial Boulevard the beach is lined with no-frills hotels and small inns for families and vacationers visiting Fort Lauderdale for longer periods of time, mainly Europeans. Look for metered parking around Commercial Boulevard and A1A. **Amenities:** food and drink; lifeguards; parking (fee). **Best for:** solitude; snorkeling; swimming. ⊠ *Commercial Blvd. at Rte. A1A.*

WHERE TO EAT

$$ ✕ **Aruba Beach Café.** This casual beachfront eatery is always crowded
CAFÉ and always fun. One of Lauderdale-by-the-Sea's most famous restau-
FAMILY rants, Aruba Beach serves a wide range of American and Caribbean cuisine, including Caribbean conch chowder and conch fritters. There are also fresh tropical salads, sandwiches, and seafood. The café is famous for its divine fresh-baked Bimini bread with Aruba glaze (think challah with donut glaze). A band performs day and night, so head for the back corner with excellent views of the beach if you want conversation while you eat and drink. Sunday breakfast buffet starts at 9 am. $ *Average main: $20* ⊠ *1 Commercial Blvd.* ☎ *954/776–0001* ⊕ *www.arubabeachcafe.com.*

$$$ ✕ **Blue Moon Fish Company.** Most tables have stellar views of the Intra-
SEAFOOD coastal Waterway, but Blue Moon East's true magic comes from the kitchen, where the chefs create moon-and-stars-worthy seafood dishes. It's also the best deal in town with a two-for-one word-of-mouth lunch special Monday through Saturday. Start with whole roasted garlic and bread and continue on to the mussels, the baby spinach and pecan-crusted goat-cheese-fritter salad (with caramelized onions and blackened shrimp), or pan-seared fresh-shucked oysters. For Sunday's champagne brunch book early, even in the off-season. They now also offer Saturday brunch, too, but it's an à la carte menu not like Sunday's grand buffet. $ *Average main: $40* ⊠ *4405 W. Tradewinds Ave.* ☎ *954/267–9888* ⊕ *www.bluemoonfishco.com.*

$ ✕ **LaSpada's Original Hoagies.** The crew at this seaside hole-in-the-wall
AMERICAN puts on quite a show of ingredient-tossing flair while assembling takeout hoagies, subs, and deli sandwiches. Locals rave that they are the best around. LaSpada's popularity has resulted in higher prices and the addition of four other South Florida locations, taking away from the joint's former one-of-a-kind appeal. Fill up on the foot-long "Monster" (ham, cheese, roast beef, and turkey piled high), "Hot Meatballs Marinara," or an assortment of salads. $ *Average main: $12* ⊠ *4346 Seagrape Dr.* ☎ *954/776–7893* ⊕ *www.laspadashoagies.com.*

WHERE TO STAY

$ ☷ **Blue Seas Courtyard.** Husband-and-wife team Cristie and Marc Furth
B&B/INN run this quaint Mexican-themed motel across the street from Lauderdale-by-the-Sea's family-friendly beaches. **Pros:** south-of-the-border vibe; friendly owners; vintage stoves from 1971; memory-foam mattress toppers. **Cons:** rooms lack ocean views; old bathtubs in some rooms.

Ⓢ *Rooms from: $163* ✉ *4525 El Mar Dr.* ☎ *954/772–3336* ⊕ *www. blueseascourtyard.com* ➳ *12 rooms* ❘⊙❘ *Breakfast.*

$$
HOTEL
⛱ **High Noon Beach Resort.** Family-run since 1961, this hotel sits on 300 feet of beautiful beach, with plenty of cozy spots and an old-school homey ambience that keeps repeat visitors coming back for more. **Pros:** smack on the beach; friendly vibe; great staff. **Cons:** early booking required; not on "happening" part of beach. Ⓢ *Rooms from: $201* ✉ *4424 El Mar Dr.* ☎ *954/776–1121, 800/382–1265* ⊕ *www. highnoonresort.com* ➳ *40 rooms* ❘⊙❘ *Breakfast.*

$
HOTEL
⛱ **Sea Lord Hotel & Suites.** This attractive oceanside hotel received major upgrades in 2010, including a new pool deck, restaurant, lobby, sundeck, entranceway, small fitness center, and room enhancements. **Pros:** terrific beach location; void of the moldy smell in nearby older hotels. **Cons:** shaky elevators; limited parking. Ⓢ *Rooms from: $170* ✉ *4140 El Mar Dr.* ☎ *954/776–1505, 800/344–4451* ⊕ *www.sealordhotel.com* ➳ *47 rooms* ❘⊙❘ *Breakfast.*

$$
HOTEL
FAMILY
⛱ **Tropic Seas Resort Motel.** This two-story property has an unbeatable location—directly on the beach, flanking 150 feet of pristine sands and sparkling blues—and is a favorite of annual European vacationers looking for longer stays. **Pros:** family-owned friendliness; great lawn furniture. **Cons:** must reserve far ahead; dated bathrooms. Ⓢ *Rooms from: $205* ✉ *4616 El Mar Dr.* ☎ *954/772–2555, 800/952–9581* ⊕ *www. tropicseasresort.com* ➳ *16 rooms* ❘⊙❘ *Breakfast.*

SPORTS AND THE OUTDOORS

Anglin's Fishing Pier. This longtime favorite for 24-hour fishing has a fresh, renovated appearance after shaking off repeated storm damage that closed the pier at intervals during the past decade. ✉ *2 Commercial Blvd.* ☎ *954/491–9403* ⊕ *www.boatlessfishing.com/anglins.htm.*

HOLLYWOOD

Hollywood has had several face-lifts to shed its old-school image, but there's still something delightfully retro about the city. Young Circle, once down-at-heel, is now Broward's first Arts Park. On Hollywood's western outskirts, the flamboyant Seminole Hard Rock Hotel & Casino has enlivened this previously downtrodden section of the State Road 7/U.S. 441 corridor, drawing local weekenders, architecture buffs, partiers, and gamblers. But Hollywood's redevelopment efforts don't end there: new shops, restaurants, and art galleries open at a persistent clip, and the city has continually spiffed up its boardwalk—a wide pedestrian walkway along the beach—where local joggers are as commonplace as sun-seeking snowbirds from the north. On the coast of Hallandale, the beach is backed by older, towering condominiums. Inland, Hallandale has been trying to get some business from neighboring Aventura and Sunny Isles in Dade County with the development of the high-end Village at Gulfstream Park, a luxury retail arcade anchored by a reinvented casino and race track.

DID YOU KNOW?

Fort Lauderdale's harbor is home to myriad sailboats as well as two of the largest cruise ships in the world, Royal Caribbean's *Allure of the Seas* and *Oasis of the Seas*.

GETTING HERE AND AROUND

From Interstate 95, exit east on Sheridan Street or Hollywood Boulevard for Hollywood or Hallandale Beach Boulevard for either Hollywood or Hallandale.

ESSENTIALS

Visitor Information Hollywood Community Redevelopment Agency
☎ *954/924–2980* ⊕ *www.visithollywoodfl.org.*

EXPLORING

FAMILY **Arts Park at Young Circle.** This 10-acre urban park has completely transformed the run-down traffic circle linking downtown Hollywood with its beaches into a beautiful, lively public space. There's no shortage of things to do here: a huge playground beckons for the little ones, a state-of-the-art amphitheater hosts regular concerts, and educational workshop spaces host regular events, like Friday glassblowing workshops and jewelry-making classes. ⊠ *1 Young Circle, Hollywood Blvd. and U.S. 1* ☎ *954/921–3500* ⊕ *www.visithollywoodfl.org/artspark.aspx.*

Downtown Hollywood Art & Design District. From 21st Avenue to Young Circle on Hollywood Boulevard and Harrison Street, the streets are peppered with boutiques, bistros, sidewalk cafés, and galleries featuring original artwork (eclectic paintings, sculpture, photography, and mixed media).

IGFA Fishing Hall of Fame and Museum. This creation of the International Game Fishing Association is a shrine to the sport. It has an extensive museum and research library where seven galleries feature fantasy fishing and other interactive displays. At the Catch Gallery, you can cast off virtually to reel in a marlin, sailfish, trout, tarpon, or bass. (If you suddenly get an urge to gear up for your own adventures, a Bass Pro Shops Outdoor World is next door.) ⊠ *300 Gulf Stream Way* ☎ *954/922–4212* ⊕ *www.igfa.org* ⊠ *$10* ⊙ *Mon.–Sat. 10–6, Sun. noon–6.*

FAMILY **West Lake Park.** Rent a canoe, kayak, or take the 40-minute boat tour at this park bordering the Intracoastal Waterway. At 1,500 acres, it is one of Florida's largest urban nature facilities. Extensive boardwalks traverse mangrove forests that shelter endangered and threatened species. A 65-foot observation tower showcases the entire park. At the free **Anne Kolb Nature Center,** named after Broward's late environmental advocate, there's a 3,500-gallon aquarium. The center's exhibit hall has 27 interactive displays. ⊠ *1200 Sheridan St.* ☎ *954/357–5161* ⊕ *www. broward.org/parks/WestLakePark* ⊠ *Weekends $1.50, weekdays free* ⊙ *Park daily 9–6:30, Nature Center daily 9–5.*

BEACHES

FAMILY **Hollywood Beach and Broadwalk.** The name might be Hollywood, but
Fodor'sChoice there's nothing hip or chic about **Hollywood North Beach Park**, which
★ sits at the north end of Hollywood (Route A1A and Sheridan Street), before the pedestrian Broadwalk begins. And that's a good thing. It's just a laid-back, old-fashioned place to enjoy the sun, sand, and sea. The film *Marley & Me,* starring Jennifer Aniston and Owen Wilson and

filmed in Greater Fort Lauderdale, spurred a comeback for dog beaches in South Florida, and ever since then, the year-round **Dog Beach of Hollywood** in North Beach Park has allowed dogs to enjoy fun in the sun from 3 to 7 pm Friday–Sunday (4 to 8 pm during Daylight Savings Time). Farther south on Hollywood beach, the 2.5-mile **Broadwalk** is a delightful throwback to the '50s, with mom-and-pop stores, ice cream parlors, elderly couples going for long strolls, and families building sand castles on the beach. Thanks to millions in investment, this popular stretch of beach has spiffy features like a pristine pedestrian walkway, a concrete bike path, a crushed-shell jogging path, an 18-inch decorative wall separating the Broadwalk from the sand, and places to shower off after a dip. Expect to hear French spoken throughout Hollywood, since its beaches have long been a favorite getaway for Quebecois. **Amenities:** food and drink; lifeguards; parking (fee); toilets. **Best for:** sunrise; swimming; walking. ✉ *Rte. A1A from Dania Beach Blvd. to Halladale Beach Blvd.* 🎟 *Parking in public lots is $1.75 per hr.*

John U. Lloyd Beach State Recreation Area. The once pine-dotted natural area was restored to its natural state, thanks to government-driven efforts to pull out all but indigenous plants. Now native sea grape, gumbo-limbo, and other native plants offer shaded ambience. Nature trails and a marina are large draws as is canoeing on Whiskey Creek. The beaches are also excellent, but beware of mosquitos in summer! **Amenities:** parking (fee); toilets. **Best for:** solitude; sunrise. ✉ *6503 N. Ocean Dr.* ☎ *954/923–2833* 🌐 *www.floridastateparks.org/lloydbeach* 🎟 *$6 per vehicle for 2–8 passengers, $4 for lone driver* 🕒 *Daily 8–sunset.*

WHERE TO EAT

$$$ ITALIAN Fodor's Choice ★

🍴 **Café Martorano.** Located within Seminole Hard Rock's adjoining entertainment and restaurant zone, this Italian-American institution pays homage to anything and everything that has to do with the "Godfather" and impresses with humongous family-style portions. Dishes run the full Italian-American gamut, from the classic parmigianas to the lobster and snapper francese. The homemade mozzarella and fried calamari are excellent choices for starters. It's easy to gorge here since each dish is so succulent and savory. The ever-present *Godfather* motif is taken to the extreme—dinner is interrupted hourly with clips from the movie played on the surrounding flat screens. There's an undeniable nightclub vibe to the joint, especially later into the night. [$] *Average main: $27* ✉ *5751 Seminole Way* ☎ *954/584–4450* 🌐 *www.cafemartorano.com* 🕒 *No lunch.*

$$$$ STEAKHOUSE Fodor's Choice ★

🍴 **Hollywood Prime.** Hollywood's superlative choice for fine dining, the intimate 15-table Hollywood Prime is a classic American steakhouse done right. A living slice of golden-age glamour, the restaurant's ambience recalls a bygone era of dress-up dining in South Florida, where decked-out patrons are rightfully treated as VIPs. Perfected steakhouse classics headline the menu: jumbo shrimp cocktail, lobster bisque, onion soup gratinée, Caesar salad, 21-day dry-aged prime steaks including a 28-ounce prime porterhouse and an 18-ounce prime ribeye as well as a 3½-pound Maine lobster (yes, you read correctly!). All this is complemented by a wine list with more than 600 fine wines. It doesn't get much better than this. Oh wait, it does! The key lime pie is a divine intervention of creamy tart pie, buttery crust, fresh whipped cream, and white chocolate. [$] *Average main: $67* ✉ *The Westin Diplomat Resort & Spa, 3555 S. Ocean Dr.* ☎ *954/602–8347* 🌐 *www.hollywoodprime.com* ✍ *Reservations essential* 🕒 *No lunch.*

$ AMERICAN FAMILY Fodor's Choice ★ 🍴 **Jaxson's Ice Cream Parlour & Restaurant.** This 1950s landmark whips up malts, shakes, and jumbo sundaes from ice creams prepared daily on premises, plus sandwiches and salads, amid an antique-license-plate décor. Owner Monroe Udell's trademarked Kitchen Sink—a small sink full of ice cream, topped by sparklers—for parties of four or more goes for $12.75 per person (no sharing). Those wanting a sample before committing to a flavor, think again. The oh-so-popular Jaxson's doesn't give samples! [$] *Average main: $13* ✉ *128 S. Federal Hwy.* ☎ *954/923–4445* 🌐 *www.jaxsonsicecream.com.*

$$ AMERICAN 🍴 **LeTub.** Once a Sunoco gas station, this quirky waterside saloon has an enduring affection for claw-foot bathtubs. Hand-painted porcelain is everywhere—under ficus, sea grape, and palm trees. If a potty doesn't appeal, there's a secluded swing facing the water north of the main dining area. Despite molasses-slow service and an abundance of flies at sundown, this eatery is favored by locals, and management seemed genuinely appalled when hordes of trend-seeking city slickers started jamming bar stools and tables after Oprah declared its thick, juicy Angus burgers the best around. A 13-oz. Sirloin burger and large fries will run you around $16. ⚠ **There's no children's menu and no children allowed after 8 pm.** [$] *Average main: $16* ✉ *1100 N. Ocean Dr.* ☎ *954/921–9425* 🌐 *www.theletub.com.*

$$$ GREEK 🍴 **Taverna Opa.** It's a Greek throwdown every night at this Hollywood institution, chock-full of loud music, belly dancers, napkin throwing, and most importantly, delectable Greek food. Expect a lively night of great eats (including amazing hot and cold meze, wood-fire grilled meats, and seafood), tabletop dancing, and awkward moments (especially when suburban dads with two left feet decide to get in on the act). ■ **TIP→ Best experienced with a large group and plenty of alcohol.** [$] *Average main: $23* ✉ *410 N. Ocean Dr.* ☎ *954/929–4010* 🌐 *www.www.tavernaopa.com/hollywood.*

WHERE TO STAY

$ RENTAL 🏨 **Manta Ray Inn.** Canadians Donna and Dwayne Boucher run this immaculate, affordable circa 1940s, two-story complex of apartment units that sits right on the beach. **Pros:** on the beach; low-key atmosphere. **Cons:** no restaurant; no pool (but access to one next door is included). [$] *Rooms from: $199* ✉ *1715 S. Surf Rd.* ☎ *954/921–9666, 800/255–0595* 🌐 *www.mantarayinn.com* 🛏 *12 units* 🍽 *No meals.*

$$ HOTEL 🏨 **Seminole Hard Rock Hotel & Casino.** On the industrial flatlands of western Hollywood, the Seminole Hard Rock Hotel & Casino serves as a magnet for pulsating Vegas-style entertainment and folks looking for 24 hours of casino, clubbing, and hedonism. **Pros:** nonstop entertainment; plenty of activities; rooms renovated in 2012. **Cons:** in an unsavory

neighborhood; no tourist sights in close proximity; endless entertainment can be exhausting. Ⓢ *Rooms from: $259* ✉ *1 Seminole Way* ☎ *866/502–7529, 800/937–0010* ⊕ *www.seminolehardrockhollywood.com* ⟿ *395 rooms, 86 suites* ⦿ *No meals.*

$$$$
RESORT
FAMILY
Fodor's Choice
★

🖼 **The Westin Diplomat Resort & Spa.** This colossal 39-story, contemporary, triple-tower property effectively brings style, sophistication, and pizzazz to Hollywood Beach with its massive, 60-foot-high atrium, casual-chic guest rooms, a 120-foot bridged infinity pool (extending from lobby to oceanfront), one of South Florida's largest and most high-design spas, and a handful of excellent restaurants. **Pros:** heavenly beds for adults and kids; excellent gym; eye-popping architecture. **Cons:** large complex; numerous conventioneers. Ⓢ *Rooms from: $415* ✉ *3555 S. Ocean Dr.* ☎ *954/602–6000, 888/627–9057* ⊕ *www.diplomatresort.com* ⟿ *902 rooms, 96 suites* ⦿ *No meals.*

NIGHTLIFE

Fodor's Choice
★

Seminole Hard Rock Casino. The glitzy, Vegas-style Seminole Hard Rock Casino is the superlative gaming and entertainment complex in Florida. Though located in a somewhat downtrodden area of inland Hollywood, once inside the Hard Rock enclave, you'll be mesmerized by the excitement radiating from the 145,000-square-foot casino, the 5,500-seat arena (Hard Rock Live), a dozen restaurants, and near dozen bars and nightclubs. The casino has blackjack, baccarat, three-card poker, more than 2,500 gaming machines, and just under 100 tables. It's open 24/7 and is connected to a hotel tower and entertainment complex, including great nightlife options such as an Improv Comedy Club, an outpost of the famous European club Pangaea, a classic piano bar, and two other multilevel nightclubs. While weekends are guaranteed party-hard mayhem, not all clubs are open on weekdays so check Hard Rock's detailed, user-friendly website for schedules. ■ **TIP→** The Seminole Hard Rock is not to be confused with its neighbor, the smoky and seedy Seminole Casino of Hollywood. ✉ *1 Seminole Way* ☎ *866/502–7529* ⊕ *www.seminolehardrockhollywood.com.*

SPORTS AND THE OUTDOORS

FISHING

Sea Legs III. *Sea Legs III* goes out three times daily, fishing for wahoo, yellowtail, grouper, and kingfish. Two 4½-hour drift-fishing trips run during the day (one at 8 am, the other at 1:30 pm), and bottom-fishing trips run nightly from 7 to midnight. Day trips cost $38, night trips $40, both including rod rental. ✉ *5398 N. Ocean Dr.* ☎ *954/923–2109* ⊕ *www.deepseafishingsealegs.com.*

PALM BEACH AND THE TREASURE COAST

WELCOME TO PALM BEACH

TOP REASONS TO GO

★ **Exquisite resorts:** Two grandes dames, the Breakers and the Boca Raton Resort & Club, perpetually draw the rich, the famous, and anyone else who can afford the luxury. The Eau Palm Beach and Four Seasons sparkle with service fit for royalty.

★ **Beautiful beaches:** From Jupiter, where dogs run free, to Stuart's tubular waves, to the broad stretches of sand in Delray Beach and Boca Raton, swimmers, surfers, sunbathers—and sea turtles looking for a place to hatch their eggs—all find happiness.

★ **Top-notch golf:** The Champion Course and re-envisioned Fazio Course at PGA National Resort & Spa are world-renowned; pros sharpen up at PGA Village.

★ **Horse around:** Wellington, with its popular polo season, is often called the winter equestrian capital of the world.

★ **Excellent fishing:** The Atlantic Ocean, teeming with kingfish, sailfish, and wahoo, is a treasure chest for anglers.

1 Greater Palm Beach.
With Gatsby-era archi-
tecture, stone-and-stucco
estates, and extravagant
dining, Palm Beach is a
must-see for travelers to
the area. Plan to spend
time on Worth Avenue,
also known as the Mink
Mile, a collection of more
than 200 chic shops, and
Whitehall, the palatial
retreat for Palm Beach's
founder, Henry Flagler.
West Palm Beach and its
environs—Lake Worth, Palm
Beach Gardens, and Singer
Island—are bustling with
their own identities. Culture
fans have plenty to cheer
about with the Kravis Center
and Norton Museum of Art;
sports enthusiasts will have
a ball golfing or boating;
and kids love Lion Country
Safari.

2 Delray Beach. Its lively
downtown, with galleries,
independent boutiques,
and trendy restaurants right
by the water, is perfect for
strolling. To the west is the
unique Morikami Museum
and Japanese Gardens.

3 Boca Raton. An
abundance of modern
shopping plazas mix with
historic buildings from the
1920s, masterpieces by
renowned architect Addison
Mizner. Parks line much of
the oceanfront.

4 Treasure Coast. Northern Palm Beach County and
beyond remains blissfully
low-key, with fishing towns,
spring-training stadiums,
and ecotourism attractions
until you hit the cosmopolitan—yet understated—Vero
Beach.

GETTING ORIENTED

This diverse region extends
120 miles from laid-back
Sebastian to tony Boca
Raton. The area's glitzy epicenter, Palm Beach, attracts
socialites, the well-heeled,
and interested onlookers.
The northernmost cities are
only about 100 miles from
Orlando, making that area
an ideal choice for families
wanting some beach time
to go with their visit to
Mickey Mouse. Delightfully
funky Delray Beach is only
an hour north of Miami. The
Intracoastal Waterway runs
parallel to the ocean and
transforms from a canal to
a tidal lagoon separating
islands from the mainland,
starting with Palm Beach
and moving northward to
Singer Island (Palm Beach
Shores and Riviera Beach),
Jupiter Island, Hutchinson
Island (Stuart, Jensen
Beach, and Fort Pierce),
and Orchid Island (Vero
Beach and Sebastian).

6

Map labels:
- ATLANTIC OCEAN
- Jupiter Island
- Hobe Sound
- Tequesta
- Jupiter
- Juno Beach
- Singer Island
- Palm Beach Gardens
- Palm Beach Shores
- Riviera Beach
- Palm Beach
- Lake Worth
- South Palm Beach
- Manalapan
- Boynton Beach
- Gulf Stream
- Delray Beach
- Highland Beach
- Boca Raton

By Paul Rubio   A golden stretch of the Atlantic shore, the Palm Beach
area resists categorization, and for good reason: the territory stretching south to Boca Raton, appropriately coined
the Gold Coast, defines old-world glamour and new-age
sophistication.

To the north you'll uncover the comparatively undeveloped Treasure
Coast—liberally sprinkled with seaside gems and wide-open spaces
along the road awaiting your discovery. Speaking of discovery, its moni-
ker came from the 1715 sinking of a Spanish fleet that dumped gold,
jewels, and silver in the waters; today the *Urca de Lima,* one of the
original 11 ships and now an undersea "museum," can be explored
by scuba divers.

Altogether, there's a delightful disparity between Palm Beach, pulsing
with old-money wealth, and under-the-radar Hutchinson Island. Seductive as the gorgeous beaches, eclectic dining, and leisurely pursuits can
be, you should also take advantage of flourishing commitments to historic preservation and the arts, as town after town yields intriguing
museums, galleries, theaters, and gardens.

Palm Beach, proud of its status as America's first luxe resort destination
and still glimmering with its trademark Mediterranean-revival mansions, manicured hedges, and highbrow shops, can rule supreme as
the focal point for your sojourn any time of year. From there, head off
in one of two directions: south toward Delray Beach and Boca Raton
along an especially scenic estate-dotted route known as A1A, or back
north to the beautiful barrier islands of the Treasure Coast. For rustic
inland activities such as bass fishing and biking on the dike around Lake
Okeechobee, head west.

PLANNING

WHEN TO GO

The weather is optimal from November through May, but the trade-off is that roadways and hotels are more crowded and prices higher. If the scene is what you're after, try the early weeks of December when the "season" isn't yet in full swing. However, be warned that after Easter, the crowd relocates to the Hamptons, and Palm Beach feels like another universe. For some, that's a blessing—and a great time to take advantage of lower summer lodging rates (the Breakers runs promos at a fourth its regular cost). Hurricanes can show up from June to November, but there's always plenty of notice. More important, you'll need to bring your tolerance for heat, humidity, and afternoon downpours.

GETTING HERE AND AROUND

AIR TRAVEL

If you're flying into the area, the most convenient airport is Palm Beach International Airport in West Palm, but it's possible (and sometimes cheaper) to fly to Fort Lauderdale or Orlando. Try to rent a car if you plan on exploring. Interstate 95 runs north–south, linking West Palm Beach with Fort Lauderdale and Miami to the south and with Daytona, Jacksonville, and the rest of the Atlantic Coast to the north. Florida's Turnpike runs from Miami north through West Palm Beach before angling northwest to reach Orlando. U.S. 1 threads north–south along the coast, connecting most coastal communities, whereas the more scenic Route A1A, also called Ocean Boulevard or Ocean Drive, depending on where you are, ventures out onto the barrier islands. I–95 runs parallel to U.S. 1, but a few miles inland.

From the airport, call Southeastern Florida Transportation Group, a local hotline for cabs, airport shuttles, and private sedans.

Airport Palm Beach International Airport (*PBI*). ⊠ *1000 Turnage Blvd., West Palm Beach* 🖀 *561/471-7420* ⊕ *www.pbia.org.*

Airport Transfers Southeastern Florida Transportation Group 🖀 *561/777-7777* ⊕ *www.yellowcabflorida.com.*

BUS TRAVEL

The county's bus service, Palm Tran, runs two routes (nos. 44 and 40) that offer daily service connecting the airport, the Tri-Rail stop near it, and locations in central West Palm Beach. A network of 34 routes joins towns all across the area; it's $5 for a day pass. The free Downtown Trolley connects the West Palm Beach Amtrak station and the Tri-Rail stop in West Palm on its Green Line. Its Yellow Line makes continuous loops down Clematis Street, the city's main stretch of restaurants and watering holes interspersed with stores, and through CityPlace, a shopping-dining-theater district. Hop on and off at any of the seven stops. The trolley's Yellow Line runs Sunday to Wednesday 11–9 and Thursday to Saturday 11–11. The trolley's Green Line, which stretches farther east, west, and south, runs weekdays 7–6, Saturday 9–6, and Sunday 11–6.

Contacts **Downtown Trolley** ☎ 561/833–8873 ⊕ www.westpalmbeachdda. com/transportation. **Palm Tran** ☎ 561/841–4287 ⊕ www.pbcgov.com/palmtran.

TRAIN TRAVEL

Amtrak stops daily in West Palm Beach. The West Palm Beach station is at the same location as the Tri-Rail stop, so the same free shuttle, the Downtown Trolley (⊕ www. westpalmbeachdda.com/transportation), is available (via the trolley's Green Line).

Tri-Rail Commuter Service is a rail system with 18 stops altogether between West Palm Beach and Miami; tickets can be purchased at each stop, and a one-way trip from the first to the last point is $6.90 weekdays, $5 weekends. Three stations—West Palm Beach, Lake Worth, and Boca—have free shuttles to their downtowns, and taxis are on call at others.

Contacts **Amtrak** ☎ 800/872–7245 ⊕ www.amtrak.com. **Tri-Rail** ☎ 800/874–7245 ⊕ www.tri-rail.com.

HOTELS

Palm Beach has a number of smaller hotels in addition to the famous Breakers. Lower-priced hotels and bed-and-breakfasts can be found in West Palm Beach and Lake Worth. Heading south, the oceanside town of Manalapan has the Eau Palm Beach Resort & Spa. The Seagate Hotel & Spa sparkles in Delray Beach, and the posh Boca Beach Club lines the superlative swathe of shoreline in Boca Raton. In the opposite direction there's the PGA National Resort & Spa, and across from it by the water is the Marriott on Singer Island, a well-kept secret for spacious, sleek suites. Even farther north, Vero Beach has a collection of luxury boutique hotels, as well as more modest options along the Treasure Coast. To the west, towns close to Lake Okeechobee offer country-inn accommodations.

Hotel reviews have been shortened. For full information, visit Fodors. com.

RESTAURANTS

Numerous elegant establishments offer upscale American, Continental, and international cuisine, but the area also is chock-full of casual waterfront spots serving affordable burgers and fresh seafood feasts. Grouper, fried or blackened, is especially popular here, along with the ubiquitous shrimp. Happy hours and early-bird menus, Florida hallmarks, typically entice the budget-minded with several dinner entrées at reduced prices offered during certain hours, usually before 5 or 6.

WHAT IT COSTS				
	$	$$	$$$	$$$$
RESTAURANTS	under $16	$16–$20	$21–$30	over $30
HOTELS	under $201	$201–$300	$301–$400	over $400

Restaurant prices are the average cost of a main course at dinner or, if dinner is not served, at lunch. Hotel prices are the lowest cost of a standard double room in high season.

PALM BEACH

70 miles north of Miami, off I–95.

Long reigning as the place where the crème de la crème go to shake off winter's chill, Palm Beach, which is actually on a barrier island, continues to be a seasonal hotbed of platinum-grade consumption. The town celebrated its 100th birthday in 2011, and there's no competing with its historic social supremacy. It's been the winter address for heirs of the iconic Rockefeller, Vanderbilt, Colgate, Post, Kellogg, and Kennedy families. Even newer power brokers, with names like Kravis, Peltz, and Trump, are made to understand that strict laws govern everything from building to landscaping, and not so much as a pool awning gets added without a town council nod. Only three bridges allow entry, and huge tour buses are a no-no.

To learn "who's who" in Palm Beach, it helps to pick up a copy of the *Palm Beach Daily News*—locals call it the Shiny Sheet because its high-quality paper avoids smudging society hands or Pratesi linens—for, as it's said, to be mentioned in the Shiny Sheet is to be Palm Beach.

All this fabled ambience started with Henry Morrison Flagler, Florida's premier developer, and cofounder, along with John D. Rockefeller, of Standard Oil. No sooner did Flagler bring the railroad to Florida in the 1890s than he erected the famed Royal Poinciana and Breakers hotels. Rail access sent real-estate prices soaring, and ever since, princely sums have been forked over for personal stationery engraved with 33480, the zip code of Palm Beach (which didn't actually get its status as an independent municipality until 1911). Setting the tone in this town of unparalleled Florida opulence is the ornate architectural work of Addison Mizner, who began designing homes and public buildings here in the 1920s and whose Moorish-Gothic Mediterranean-revival style has influenced virtually all landmarks.

But the greater Palm Beach area is much larger and encompasses several communities on the mainland and to the north and south. To provide Palm Beach with servants and other workers, Flagler created an off-island community across the Intracoastal Waterway (also referred to as Lake Worth in these parts). West Palm Beach, now cosmopolitan and noteworthy in its own right, evolved into an economically vibrant business hub and a sprawling playground with some of the best nightlife and cultural attractions around, including the glittering Kravis Center for the Performing Arts, the region's principal entertainment venue. The mammoth Palm Beach County Judicial Center and Courthouse and the State Administrative Building underscore the breadth of the city's governmental and corporate activity.

The burgeoning equestrian development of Wellington, with its horse shows and polo matches, lies a little more than 10 miles west of downtown, and is the site of much of the county's growth.

Spreading southward from the Palm Beach/West Palm Beach nucleus set between the two bridges that flow from Royal Poinciana Way and Royal Palm Way into Flagler Drive on the mainland are small cities like Lake Worth, with its charming artsy center, Lantana, and Manalapan (home to the fabulous Eau resort, formerly the Ritz-Carlton Palm Beach). All three have turf that's technically on the same island as Palm Beach, and at its bottom edge across the inlet is Boynton Beach, a 20-minute drive from Worth Avenue.

Most visitors don't realize that West Palm Beach itself doesn't have any beaches, so locals and guests hop over to Palm Beach or any of the communities just mentioned—or they head 15 minutes north to the residential Singer Island towns of Palm Beach Shores and Riviera Beach, known for their marinas and laid-back vibe. Another option is Peanut Island, which sits in the Intracoastal between Palm Beach and Singer Island, and to Juno Beach. Suburban Palm Beach Gardens, a paradise for golfers and shoppers (malls abound), is inland from Singer Island and 15 minutes northwest of downtown West Palm Beach. Because of its upscale slant, it has a ton of restaurants and bars (both independents and chains).

GETTING HERE AND AROUND

Palm Beach is 70 miles north of Miami. To access Palm Beach off I–95, exit east at Southern Boulevard, Belvedere Road, or Okeechobee Boulevard. To drive from Palm Beach to Lake Worth, Lantana, Manalapan, and Boynton Beach, head south on Ocean Boulevard/Route A1A; Lake Worth is roughly 6 miles south, and Boynton is another 6. Similarly, to reach them from West Palm Beach, take U.S. 1 or I–95. To travel between Palm Beach and Singer Island, you must cross over to West Palm before returning to the beach. Once there, go north on U.S. 1 and then cut over on Blue Heron Boulevard/Route 708. If coming straight from the airport or somewhere farther west, take I–95 up to the same exit and proceed east. The main drag in Palm Beach Gardens is PGA Boulevard/Route 786, which is 4 miles north on U.S. 1 and I–95; A1A merges with it as it exits the top part of Singer Island. Continue on A1A to reach Juno Beach.

TOURS

FAMILY **DivaDuck Amphibious Tours.** Running 75 minutes, these duck tours go in and out of the water on USCG-inspected amphibious vessels around West Palm Beach and Palm Beach. The tours depart two or three times most days for $25 per person; there are big discounts for kids. ⊠ *City-Place, 600 S. Rosemary Ave., corner of Hibiscus St. and Rosemary Ave., West Palm Beach* ☎ *877/844–4188* ⊕ *www.divaduck.com.*

Island Living Tours. Book a private mansion-viewing excursion around Palm Beach, and hear the storied past of the island's upper crust. Owner Leslie Diver also hosts an Antique Row Tour and a Worth Avenue Shopping Tour. All vehicle tours are 3 hours and from $60 per person to $150 per person, depending on the vehicle used. Leslie also

Draped in European elegance, the Breakers in Palm Beach sits on 140 acres along the oceanfront.

runs 90-minute bicycle tours through Palm Beach ($35, not including bike rental). One bicycle tour explores the Estate Section and historic Worth Avenue; another explores the island's lesser-known North End. Call in advance for location and to reserve. ☎ 561/868–7944 ⊕ *www. islandlivingpb.com.*

EXPLORING

PALM BEACH
Most streets around major attractions and commercial zones have free parking as well as metered spaces. If you can stake out a place between a Rolls Royce and a Bentley, do so, but beware of the "Parking by Permit Only" signs, as a $25 ticket might take the shine off your spot. Better yet, if you plan to spend an entire afternoon strolling Worth Avenue, valet-park at the garage next to Saks Fifth Avenue that's a block in from Ocean Boulevard (if you've reached South County Road you've gone too far); some stores will validate your parking ticket.

TOP ATTRACTIONS
Bethesda-by-the-Sea. Donald Trump and his wife, Melania were married here in 2005, but this gothic-style Episcopal church had a claim to fame upon its creation in 1926: it was built by the first Protestant congregation in southeast Florida. Church lecture tours, covering Bethesda's history, architecture, and more, are offered at 12:15 on the second and fourth Sunday each month from September to May (excluding December) and at 11:15 on the fourth Sunday each month from June to August. Adjacent is the formal, ornamental Cluett Memorial

Garden. ⊠ *141 S. County Rd.* ☎ *561/655–4554* ⊕ *www.bbts.org* 🖼 *Free* ☉ *Church and gardens daily 9–5.*

Fodor'sChoice **The Breakers.** Built by Henry Flagler in 1896 and rebuilt by his descen-
★   dants after a 1925 fire, this magnificent Italian Renaissance–style resort
helped launch Florida tourism with its Gilded Age opulence, attracting influential wealthy Northerners to the state. The hotel, still owned
by Flagler's heirs, is a must-see even if you aren't staying here. Walk
through the 200-foot-long lobby, which has soaring arched ceilings
painted by 72 Italian artisans and hung with crystal chandeliers, and
the ornate Florentine Dining Room, decorated with 15th-century Flemish tapestries. ■TIP→ Book a pampering spa treatment or dine on top
of the Seafood Bar's whimsical aquarium counter, where leggy green
starfish prance below your plate, and the $20 parking is free. ⊠ *1 S.
County Rd.* ☎ *561/655–6611* ⊕ *www.thebreakers.com.*

Fodor'sChoice **Henry Morrison Flagler Museum.** The worldly sophistication of Florida's
★   Gilded Age lives on at Whitehall, the plush 55-room "marble palace"
Henry Flagler commissioned in 1901 for his third wife, Mary Lily
Kenan. Architects John Carrère and Thomas Hastings were instructed
to create the finest home imaginable—and they outdid themselves.
Whitehall rivals the grandeur of European palaces and has an entrance
hall with a baroque ceiling similar to Louis XIV's Versailles. Here you'll
see original furnishings; a hidden staircase Flagler used to sneak from
his bedroom to the billiards room; an art collection; a 1,200-pipe organ;
and Florida East Coast Railway exhibits, along with Flagler's personal
railcar, No. 91, showcased in an 8,000-square-foot beaux-arts-style
pavilion behind the mansion. Docent-led tours and audio tours are
included with admission. The museum's Café des Beaux-Arts, open
from Thanksgiving through mid-April, offers a Gilded Age–style early
afternoon tea for $40 (11:30–2:30); the price includes museum admis-
sion. ⊠ *1 Whitehall Way* ☎ *561/655–2833* ⊕ *www.flaglermuseum.us*
🖼 *$18* ☉ *Tues.–Sat. 10–5, Sun. noon–5.*

WORTH NOTING

El Solano. No Palm Beach mansion better represents the town's luminous
legacy than the Spanish-style home built by Addison Mizner as his own
residence in 1925. Mizner later sold El Solano to Harold Vanderbilt,
and the property was long a favorite among socialites for parties and
photo shoots. Vanderbilt held many a gala fund-raiser here. Beatle John
Lennon and his wife, Yoko Ono, bought it less than a year before Lennon's death. It's still privately owned and not open to the public, but
it's well worth a drive-by on any self-guided Palm Beach mansion tour.
⊠ *720 S. Ocean Blvd.*

Mar-a-Lago. Breakfast-food heiress Marjorie Merriweather Post com-
missioned a Hollywood set designer to create Ocean Boulevard's famed
Mar-a-Lago, a 114-room, 110,000-square-foot Mediterranean-revival
palace. Its 75-foot Italianate tower is visible from many areas of Palm
Beach and from across the Intracoastal Waterway in West Palm Beach.
Owner Donald Trump has turned it into a private membership club.
So you'll have to enjoy the view from the car window unless you have

Palm Beach and
West Palm Beach

The Mansions of Palm Beach

Whether you aspire to be a Kennedy, Donald Trump, or Rod Stewart—all onetime or current Palm Beach residents—no trip to the island is complete without gawking at the megamansions lining its perfectly manicured streets.

No one is more associated with how the island took shape than Addison Mizner, architect extraordinaire and society darling of the 1920s. But what people may not know is that a "fab four" was really the force behind the residential streets as they appear today: Mizner, of course, plus Maurice Fatio, Marion Sims Wyeth, and John Volk.

The four architects dabbled in different genres, some more so than others, but the unmissable style is Mediterranean revival, a Palm Beach hallmark mix of stucco walls, Spanish red-tile roofs, Italianate towers, Moorish-Gothic carvings, and the uniquely Floridian use of coquina, a grayish porous limestone made of coral rock with fossil-like imprints of shells. As for Mizner himself, he had quite the repertoire of signature elements, including using differently sized and shaped windows on one facade, blue tile work inside and out, and tiered roof lines (instead of one straight-sloping panel across, having several sections overlap like scales on a fish).

The majority of preserved estates are clustered in three sections: along Worth Avenue; the few blocks of South County Road after crossing Worth and the streets shooting off it; and the 5-mile stretch of South Ocean Boulevard from Barton Avenue to near Phipps Ocean Park, where the condos begin cropping up.

If 10 miles of riding on a bike while cars zip around you isn't intimidating, the two-wheeled trip may be the best way to fully take in the beauty of the mansions and surrounding scenery. Many hotels have bicycles for guest use. Another option is the dependable Palm Beach Bicycle Trail Shop (📞 561/659–4583 ⊕ www.palmbeach-bicycle.com). Otherwise, driving is a good alternative. Just be mindful that Ocean Boulevard is a one-lane road and the only route on the island to cities like Lake Worth and Manalapan, so you can't go too slowly, especially at peak travel times.

If gossip is more your speed, in-the-know concierges rely on Leslie Diver's "Island Living Tours" (📞 561/868–7944 ⊕ www.islandlivingpb.com); she's one of the town's leading experts on architecture *and* dish, both past and present.

Top 10 Self-Guided Stops: (1) Casa de Leoni, 450 Worth Avenue (Addison Mizner); (2) Villa des Cygnes, 456 Worth Avenue (Addison Mizner and Marion Sims Wyeth); (3) 17 Golfview Road (Marion Sims Wyeth); (4) 220 and 252 El Bravo Way (John Volk); (5) 126 South Ocean Boulevard (Marion Sims Wyeth); (6) El Solano, 720 South Ocean Boulevard (Addison Mizner); (7) Casa Nana, 780 South Ocean Boulevard (Addison Mizner); (8) 920 and 930 South Ocean Boulevard (Maurice Fatio); (9) Mar-a-Lago, 1100 South Ocean Boulevard (Joseph Urban); (10) Il Palmetto, 1500 South Ocean Boulevard (Maurice Fatio).

—Dorothea Hunter Sönne

The Armory Art Center in West Palm Beach helps students of all ages create works of art in various mediums.

a membership. ⊠ *1100 S. Ocean Blvd.* ☎ *561/832–2600* ⊕ *www. maralagoclub.com.*

WEST PALM BEACH

Long considered Palm Beach's less privileged stepsister, West Palm Beach has come into its own over the past 35 years, and just in this millennium the $30 million Centennial Square waterfront complex at the eastern end of Clematis Street, with piers, a pavilion, and an amphitheater, has transformed West Palm into an attractive, easy-to-walk downtown area—not to mention there's the Downtown Trolley that connects the shopping-and-entertainment mecca CityPlace with restaurant-and-lounge-lined Clematis Street. West Palm is especially well regarded for its arts scene, with unique museums and performance venues.

The city's outskirts, vast flat stretches with fast-food outlets and car dealerships, may not inspire, but are worth driving through to reach attractions scattered around the southern and western reaches. Several sites are especially rewarding for children and other animal and nature lovers.

TOP ATTRACTIONS

Ann Norton Sculpture Gardens. This landmarked complex is a testament to the creative genius of the late American sculptor Ann Weaver Norton (1905–1982), who was the second wife of the Norton Museum founder, industrialist Ralph H. Norton. A set of art galleries in the studio and main house where she lived is surrounded by two acres of gardens with 300 species of rare palm trees, eight brick megaliths, a monumental figure in Norwegian granite, and plantings designed to attract native birds. ✉ *253 Barcelona Rd.* ☎ *561/832–5328* ⊕ *www.ansg.org* 🖃 *$10* ⊙ *Wed.–Sun. 10–4.* ⊙ *Closed Aug.*

FAMILY **Lion Country Safari.** Drive your own vehicle along four miles of paved roads through a cageless zoo with free-roaming animals (chances are you'll have a giraffe nudging at your window) and then let loose in a 55-acre fun-land with camel rides, bird feedings, and a pontoon-boat cruise past islands with monkeys. A CD included with admission narrates the winding trek past white rhinos, zebras, and ostriches grouped into exhibits like Gir Forest that's modeled after a sanctuary in India and has native twisted-horned blackbuck antelope and water buffalo. (For obvious reasons, lions are fenced off, and no convertibles or pets are allowed.) Aside from dozens more up-close critter encounters after debarking, including a petting zoo, kids can go paddleboating, do a round of mini-golf, climb aboard carnival rides, or have a splash in a 4,000-square-foot aquatic playground (some extra fees apply). ✉ *2003 Lion Country Safari Rd., at Southern Blvd.* W ☎ *561/793–1084* ⊕ *www. lioncountrysafari.com* 🖃 *$29.95, $6 parking* ⊙ *Mid-Dec.–Aug., daily 9:30–5:30 (last entry at 4:30); Sept.–Dec., daily 10–5 (last entry at 4).*

Mounts Botanical Garden. The oldest public green space in the county is, unbelievably, across the road from the West Palm Beach airport; but the planes are the last thing you notice while walking around and relaxing amid the nearly 14 acres of exotic trees, rain-forest flora, and butterfly and water gardens. The gift shop contains a selection of rare gardening books on tropical climes. ✉ *531 N. Military Trail* ☎ *561/233–1757* ⊕ *www.mounts.org* 🖃 *$5 (suggested donation)* ⊙ *Mon.–Sat. 8:30–4, Sun. noon–4.*

National Croquet Center. The world's largest croquet complex, the 10-acre center is also the headquarters for the U.S. Croquet Association. Vast expanses of orderly lawns are the stage for fierce competitions. There's also a clubhouse with a pro shop and the Croquet Grille, with verandas for dining and viewing (armchair enthusiasts can enjoy the games for no charge). You don't have to be a member to try your hand out on the lawns, and on Saturday morning at 10 am, there's a free group lesson with an introduction to the game and open play; call in advance to reserve a spot. ✉ *700 Florida Mango Rd., at Summit Blvd.* ☎ *561/478–2300* ⊕ *www.croquetnational.com* 🖃 *Center free; full day of croquet $25* ⊙ *Tues.–Sun. 9–5.*

Fodor's Choice **Norton Museum of Art.** Constructed in 1941 by steel magnate Ralph H. ★ Norton and his wife, Elizabeth, it has grown to become one of the most impressive museums in South Florida with an extensive collection of 19th- and 20th-century American and European paintings—including works by Picasso, Monet, Matisse, Pollock, Cassatt, and O'Keeffe—plus Chinese art, earlier European art, and photography. There is a sublime outdoor sculpture garden, a glass ceiling by Dale Chihuly, a gift shop, and a schedule of lectures, programs, and concerts for adults and children. Galleries showcase traveling exhibits, too. ■**TIP**➜ One of the city's best-kept secrets is the gourmet restaurant Fratelli Lyon in the West Courtyard of the Museum. Lunch is served Tuesday–Sunday; an a la carte dinner menu is available on Thursday evenings. ✉ *1451 S.*

Olive Ave. 🕾 *561/832–5196* ⊕ *www.norton.org* 🖃 *$12* 🕙 *Tues.–Wed. and Fri.–Sat. 10–5, Thurs. 10–9, Sun. 11–5.*

WORTH NOTING

Richard and Pat Johnson Palm Beach County History Museum. A beautifully restored 1916 courthouse downtown opened its doors in 2008 as the permanent home of the Historical Society of Palm Beach County's collection of artifacts and records dating back before the town's start—a highlight is furniture and decorative objects from Mizner Industries (a real treat since many of his mansions are not open to the public). ⊠ *300 N. Dixie Hwy.* 🕾 *561/832–4164* ⊕ *www.historicalsocietypbc.org* 🖃 *Free* 🕙 *Tues.–Sat. 10–5.*

FAMILY **South Florida Science Museum.** Aside from permanent exhibits with outta-this-world finds like moon and Mars rocks and a 232-pound meteorite, there are fresh- and saltwater aquariums, daily planetarium shows, and even 9 holes of mini-golf. On the second Saturday of each month, the planetarium offers three separate laser shows (at 6:30, 7:30, and 8:30) incorporating music from the likes of Dave Matthews, Pink Floyd, and Michael Jackson. ⊠ *4801 Dreher Trail N* 🕾 *561/832–1988* ⊕ *www.sfsciencecenter.org* 🖃 *$15, laser show $10* 🕙 *Weekdays 10–5, weekends 10–6.*

LAKE WORTH

For years, tourists looked here mainly for inexpensive lodging and easy access to Palm Beach, since a bridge leads from the mainland to a barrier island with Lake Worth's beach. Now Lake Worth has several blocks of restaurants, nightclubs, shops, and art galleries, making this somewhat a worthy destination on its own.

Museum of Polo and Hall of Fame. Start here in Lake Worth for an introduction to polo. See memorabilia, art, and a film on the history of the sport. Then, treat yourself to a Sunday match; polo season runs January through April. ⊠ *9011 Lake Worth Rd.* 🕾 *561/969–3210* ⊕ *www.polomuseum.com* 🖃 *Free (donations accepted)* 🕙 *Jan.–Apr., weekdays 10–4, Sat. 10–2; May–Dec., weekdays 10–4.*

LANTANA

Lantana—just a bit farther south from Palm Beach than Lake Worth—has inexpensive lodging and a bridge connecting the town to its own beach on a barrier island. Tucked between Lantana and Boynton Beach is **Manalapan,** a tiny but posh residential community.

BOYNTON BEACH

In 1884, when fewer than 50 settlers lived in the area, Nathan Boynton, a Civil War veteran from Michigan, paid $25 for 500 acres with a mile-long stretch of beachfront thrown in. How things have changed, with today's population at about 118,000 and property values still on an upswing. Far enough from Palm Beach to remain low-key, Boynton Beach has two parts, the mainland and the barrier island—the town of Ocean Ridge—connected by two bridges.

FAMILY **Arthur R. Marshall Loxahatchee National Wildlife Refuge.** The most robust part of the northern Everglades, this 221-square-mile refuge is one of two huge water-retention areas accounting for much of the "River of

The posh Palm Beach area has its share of luxury villas on the water; many are Mediterranean in style.

Grass" outside the national park near Miami. Start at the visitor center, which has fantastic interactive exhibits and videos like *Night Sounds of the Everglades* and an airboat simulator. From there, you can take a marsh trail to a 20-foot-high observation tower, or stroll a ½-mile boardwalk lined with educational signage through a dense cypress swamp. There are also guided nature walks (including some specifically for bird-watching), and there's great bass fishing (bring your own poles and bait) and a 5½-mile canoe trail loop (a rental kiosk is by the fishing pier). ✉ *10216 Lee Rd., off U.S. 441, between rtes. 804 and 806* ☎ *561/734–8303* ⊕ *www.loxahatcheefriends.com* ✉ *$5 per vehicle; $1 per pedestrian* ☉ *Daily sunrise–sunset, visitor center daily 9–4.*

SINGER ISLAND
Across the inlet from the northern end of Palm Beach is Singer Island, which is actually a peninsula that's big enough to pass for a barrier island, rimmed with mom-and-pop motels and high-rises. Palm Beach Shores occupies its southern tip (where tiny Peanut Island is a stone's throw away); farther north are Riviera Beach and North Palm Beach, which also straddle the inlet and continue on the mainland.

Palm Beach Maritime Museum. Though the main building of the Palm Beach Maritime Museum is found in Currie Park in West Palm Beach, its main treasure—the restored "Kennedy Bunker," a bomb shelter built for President John F. Kennedy, and a historic Coast Guard station—is located on Peanut Island. You can take a guided tour of the bunker through the museum's Peanut Island outpost. The museum also has a nice little gift shop, an outdoor deck on the water, and a lawn where you can play games including horseshoes. To get there, catch a water taxi from Riviera Beach Municipal Marina (⊕ www.peanutislandwatertaxi. com), but call ahead as the boats won't run in choppy waters. ⊠ *Peanut Island, Riviera Beach* ☎ *561/848–2960* ⊕ *www.pbmm.org* ⊠ *$14 (not including water transportation)* ⊙ *Thurs.–Sun. 11–4.*

PALM BEACH GARDENS

About 15 minutes northwest of Palm Beach is this relaxed, upscale residential community known for its high-profile golf complex, the **PGA National Resort & Spa.** Although not on the beach, the town is less than a 15-minute drive from the ocean.

JUNO BEACH

This small town east of Palm Beach Gardens has 2 miles of shoreline that becomes home to thousands of sea turtle hatchlings each year, making it one of the world's densest nesting sites. A 990-foot-long pier lures fishermen and beachgoers seeking a spectacular sunrise.

Fodor'sChoice ★ **Loggerhead Park Marine Life Center of Juno Beach.** Located in a certified green building in Loggerhead Park—and established by Eleanor N. Fletcher, the "turtle lady of Juno Beach"—the center focuses on the conservation of sea turtles with three core competencies of education, research, and rehabilitation. The education center houses displays of coastal natural history, detailing Florida's marine ecosystems and the life and plight of the various species of sea turtles found on Florida's shores. You can visit recovering turtles in their tanks out back; volunteers are happy to tell you the turtles' heroic tales of survival. The center has regularly scheduled activities, such as Kid's Story Time and Junior Vet Lab, and most are free of charge. During nesting season, the center hosts night walks to experience turtle nesting in action. Given that the adjacent beach is part of the second biggest nesting ground for loggerhead turtles in the world, your chances of seeing this natural phenomenon is pretty high (over 13,000 loggerheads nested here in 2012). ⊠ *14200 U.S. 1* ☎ *561/627–8280* ⊕ *www.marinelife.org* ⊠ *Free* ⊙ *Mon.–Sat. 10–5, Sun. noon–4.*

OFF THE BEATEN PATH

Forty miles west of West Palm Beach, amid the farms and cattle pastures rimming the western edges of Palm Beach and Martin counties, is **Lake Okeechobee,** the second-largest freshwater lake completely within the United States. It's girdled by 120 miles of road yet remains shielded from sight for almost its entire circumference. Lake Okeechobee—the Seminole's Big Water and the gateway of the great Everglades watershed—measures 730 square miles, at its longest roughly 33 miles north–south and 30 miles east–west, with an average natural depth of only 10 feet (flood control brings the figure up to 12 feet and deeper). Six major lock systems and 32 separate water-control structures manage the water. Encircling the lake is a 34-foot-high grassy levee that locals call "the wall," and the Lake Okeechobee Scenic Trail, a segment of the Florida National Scenic Trail that's an easy, flat ride for bikers. Anglers have a field day here as well, with great bass and perch catches. ■TIP➔ **There's no shade, so wear a hat, sunscreen, and bug repellent. Be sure to bring lots of bottled water, too, because restaurants and stores are few and far between.**

BEACHES

PALM BEACH

Phipps Ocean Park. About 2 miles south of "Billionaire's Row" on Ocean Boulevard sits this public oceanside park, with two metered parking lots separated by a fire station. The north side is better for beachgoers and currently houses the sole entry point to the beach itself (the other three entry points are closed for repairs). At the southern entrance, there is a six-court tennis facility. The beach is narrow and has natural rock formations dotting the shoreline, making it ideal for snorkelers. There are picnic tables and grills on site, as well as the Little Red Schoolhouse, an 1886 landmark that hosts educational workshops for local kids. If a long walk floats your boat, venture north to see the megamansions, but don't go too far inland, because private property starts just a few feet from the surf. There's a 2-hour time limit for free parking. **Amenities:** parking (no fee); showers; toilets; lifeguards. **Best for:** walking; solitude. ⊠ *2201 S. Ocean Blvd.* ☏ *561/838–5400, 561/227–6450 for tennis reservations* ⊒ *Free* ☉ *Daily 8–8.*

Town of Palm Beach Municipal Beach. You know you're here if you see Palm Beach's younger generation frolicking on the sands and non-xenophobic locals setting up chairs as the sun reflects off their gleaming white veneers. The Worth Avenue clock tower is within sight, but the gateways to the sand are actually on Chilean Avenue, Brazilian Avenue, and Gulfstream Road. It's definitely the most central and longest lifeguarded strip open to everyone and a popular choice for hotel guests from the Colony and Chesterfield. Lifeguards are present from Brazilian Avenue down to Chilean Avenue. It's also BYOC (Bring Your Own Chair). You'll find no water-sport or food vendors here; however, casual eateries are a quick walk away. Metered spots line A1A. **Amenities:** lifeguards; showers. **Best for:** swimming; sunsets. ⊠ *S. Ocean Blvd. from Brazilian Ave. to Gulfstream Rd.* ☏ *561/838–5483 for beach patrol* ☉ *Daily 8–8.*

LAKE WORTH

FAMILY **Lake Worth Beach.** This public beach bustles with beachgoers of all ages thanks to the prolific family offerings. The waterfront retail promenade—the old fashioned non-gambling Lake Worth "casino"—has a Mulligan's Beach House Bar & Grill, a T-shirt store, a pizzeria, and a Kilwin's ice cream shop. The beach also has a municipal Olympic-size public swimming pool, a playground, a fishing pier—not to mention the pier's wildly popular daytime eatery, Benny's on the Beach. Omphoy and Four Seasons guests are steps away from the action. **Amenities:** food and drink; lifeguards; parking (no fee); showers; toilets; water sports. **Best for:** sunsets; swimming. ⊠ *10 S. Ocean Blvd., at Rte. A1A and Lake Ave.* ⊕ *www.lakeworth.org/visitors/casino-building-and-beach-complex* ⊒ *$1 to enter pier, $3 to enter and fish; $2 per hr for parking.*

LANTANA

Town of Lantana Public Beach. Ideal for quiet ambles, this sandy stretch is also noteworthy for a casual restaurant, the no-frills breezy Dune Deck Café, which is perched above the waterline and offers great views for an oceanfront breakfast or lunch. The beach's huge parking lot is directly adjacent to the Eau Palm Beach, and diagonally across the street is a sizeable strip mall with all sorts of conveniences, including more eateries. Note: the beach is very narrow and large rocks loom in the water. However, these are some of the clearest waters along the Florida coastline, and they make an idyllic background for long walks and great photos. Bring plenty of quarters for the old school parking meters. **Amenities:** food and drink; lifeguards; parking (fee); showers; toilets. **Best for:** walking. ✉ *100 E. Ocean Ave.* 🄿 *$1.50 per hr for parking.*

SINGER ISLAND

FAMILY
Fodor'sChoice
★

John D. MacArthur Beach State Park. If getting far from rowdy crowds is your goal, this spot on the north end of Singer Island is a good choice. Encompassing 2 miles of beach and a lush subtropical coastal habitat, inside you'll find a great place for kayaking, snorkeling at natural reefs, bird-watching, fishing, and hiking. You might even get to see a few manatees! A 4,000-square-foot nature center has aquariums and displays on local flora and fauna, and there's a long roster of monthly activities, such as surfing clinics, art lessons, and live bluegrass music. Guided sea turtle walks are available at night in season, and daily nature walks depart at 10 am. Check the website for times and costs of activities. **Amenities:** water sports; parking (fee); showers; toilets. **Best for:** swimming; walking; solitude; surfing. ✉ *10900 Jack Nicklaus Dr., North Palm Beach* ☎ *561/624–6952* ⊕ *www.macarthurbeach.org* 🄿 *Parking $5, bicyclists and pedestrians $2* ☉ *Park daily 8–sunset; nature center and gift shop daily 9–5.*

Peanut Island Park. Partiers, families, and overnight campers all have a place to go on the 79 acres here. The island, in a wide section of the Intracoastal between Palm Beach Island and Singer Island with an open channel to the sea, is accessible only by private boat or water taxi, two of which set sail regularly from the Riviera Beach Municipal Marina (www.peanutislandwatertaxi.com) and the Sailfish Marina (www.sailfishmarina.com/water_taxi). Fun-loving seafarers looking for an afternoon of Jimmy Buffett and brewskis pull up to the day docks or the huge sandbar on the north—float around in an inner tube, and it's spring-break déjà vu. Walk along the 20-foot-wide paved path encircling the island, and you'll hit a 170-foot fishing pier, a campground, the lifeguarded section to the south that is particularly popular with families because of its artificial reef, and last but not least, the Palm Beach Maritime Museum's "Kennedy Bunker" (a bomb shelter prepared for President John F. Kennedy that was restored and opened to the public in 1999). There are picnic tables and grills, but no concessions. ■ TIP➔ A new ordinance means alcohol possession and consumption is restricted to permit areas. **Amenities:** lifeguards (summer only); showers; toilets. **Best for:** partiers; walking; swimming; sunrise. ✉ *6500 Peanut Island Rd., Riviera Beach* ☎ *561/845–4445* ⊕ *www.pbcgov.com/ parks/peanutisland* 🄿 *Beach free, water taxi $10.*

JUNO BEACH

FAMILY **Juno Beach Ocean Park.** An angler's dream, this beach has a 990-foot pier that's open daily, like the beach, from sunrise to sunset. From November through February, pier gates open at 6 am and don't close until 10 pm on weeknights and midnight on weekends, making it an awesome place to catch a full sunrise and sunset (that is, if you don't mind paying the small admission fee). A concession stand on the pier sells fish food as well as such human favorites as burgers, sandwiches, and ice cream. Families adore this shoreline because of the amenities and vibrant atmosphere. There are plenty of kids building castles but also plenty of teens having socials and hanging out along the beach. **Amenities:** lifeguards; food and drink; parking (no fee); showers; toilets. **Best for:** sunrise; sunset; swimming. ✉ *14775 U.S. 1* ☎ *561/799–0185 for pier* 🌐 *www.pbcgov.com/parks/locations/junobeach.htm* 🎫 *$4 to fish, $1 to enter pier* 🕑 *Daily sunrise–sunset.*

WHERE TO EAT

PALM BEACH

$$$$ ECLECTIC Fodor's Choice ★

🍴 **bûccan.** Lanterns cast a soft glow as young bluebloods rocking D&G jeans slip into tightly packed copper-topped tables alongside groups of silver-haired oil scions. It's island casual in its trendiest, most boisterous yet still refined incarnation, with a menu to match. Chef-owner Clay Conley's small plates to share (wood-fired wild mushroom pizza with black truffle vinaigrette) with unfussy presentations (house-made squid-ink orecchiette stewed with sausage, conch, and chilies in a mini–Le Creuset cocotte) and inventive, sophisticated flavor combinations and textures (hamachi sashimi with yuzu and crisped lotus root) make this the place to see and be seen—and the best-tasting meal at a price more expected of the mainland. [$] *Average main: $32* ✉ *350 S. County Rd., Palm Beach* ☎ *561/833–3450* 🌐 *www.buccanpalmbeach.com* ✍ *Reservations essential* 🕑 *No lunch.*

$$$$ FRENCH Fodor's Choice ★

🍴 **Café Boulud.** Palm Beach socialites just can't get enough of this prized restaurant by celebrated chef Daniel Boulud. This posh French-American venue in the Brazilian Court hotel is casual yet elegant, with a palette of honey, gold, and citron. Plenty of natural light spills through arched glass doors opening to a lush courtyard that's just the place to be on a warm evening. Lunch and dinner entrées on the restaurant's signature four-section menu include classic French, seasonal, vegetarian, and a rotating roster of international dishes. The lounge, with its illuminated amber glass bar, is the perfect perch to take in the jet-set crowd that comes for a hint of the south of France in South Florida. [$] *Average main: $38* ✉ *The Brazilian Court Hotel & Beach Club, 301 Australian Ave., Palm Beach* ☎ *561/655–6060* 🌐 *www.cafeboulud.com* ✍ *Reservations essential.*

$$$$ FRENCH

🍴 **Chez Jean-Pierre.** With walls adorned with avant-garde Dalí- and Picasso-like art, this bistro is where the Palm Beach old guard likes to let down its hair, all the while partaking of sumptuous French cuisine and an impressive wine selection. Forget calorie or cholesterol concerns, and indulge in scrambled eggs with caviar or homemade foie gras, along with desserts like frozen hazelnut soufflé or profiteroles au chocolat. Jackets are not required, although many men wear them. The main entrance is through a courtyard in the back. [$] *Average main: $39* ✉ *132 N. County Rd., Palm Beach* ☎ *561/833–1171* 🌐 *www.chezjean-pierre.com* ✍ *Reservations essential* 🕑 *Closed Sun. No lunch.*

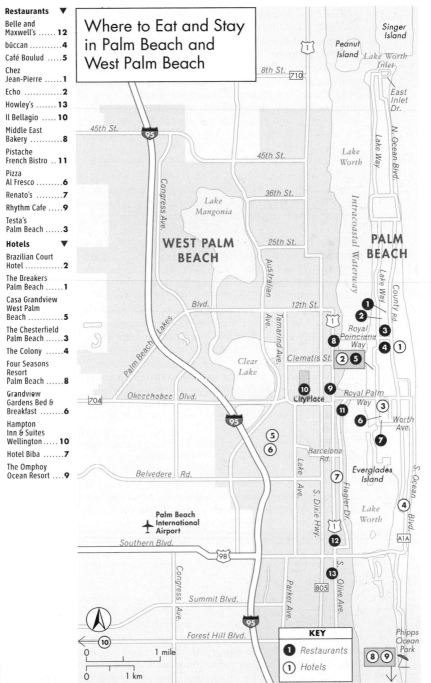

Where to Eat and Stay in Palm Beach and West Palm Beach

Restaurants ▼

Belle and
Maxwell's **12**

bûccan **4**

Café Boulud **5**

Chez
Jean-Pierre **1**

Echo **2**

Howley's **13**

Il Bellagio **10**

Middle East
Bakery **8**

Pistache
French Bistro .. **11**

Pizza
Al Fresco **6**

Renato's **7**

Rhythm Cafe **9**

Testa's
Palm Beach **3**

Hotels ▼

Brazilian Court
Hotel **2**

The Breakers
Palm Beach **1**

Casa Grandview
West Palm
Beach **5**

The Chesterfield
Palm Beach **3**

The Colony **4**

Four Seasons
Resort
Palm Beach **8**

Grandview
Gardens Bed &
Breakfast **6**

Hampton
Inn & Suites
Wellington **10**

Hotel Biba **7**

The Omphoy
Ocean Resort **9**

KEY

1 *Restaurants*

1 *Hotels*

$$$ ASIAN 🍴 **Echo.** Palm Beach's window on Asia has a sleek sushi bar and floor-to-ceiling glass doors separating the interior from the popular terrace dining area. Chinese, Japanese, Thai, and Vietnamese selections are neatly categorized: Wind (small plates starting your journey), Water (seafood mains), Fire (open-flame wok creations), Earth (meat dishes), and Flavor (desserts, sweets). Pick from dim sum to sashimi, pad thai to Szechuan beef, steamed sea bass to shrimp lo mein. On weekdays, come for the early shift (5–6:30 pm) for half-price sushi and cocktails in the restaurant's Dragonfly Lounge. [$] *Average main: $30* ✉ *230-A Sunrise Ave., Palm Beach* ☎ *561/802–4222* 🌐 *www.echopalmbeach.com* 🕒 *Closed Mon. No lunch.*

$$ PIZZA 🍴 **Pizza Al Fresco.** The secret-garden setting is the secret to the success of this European-style pizzeria, where you can dine under a canopy of century-old banyans in an intimate courtyard. Specialties are 12-inch hand-tossed brick-oven pizzas with such interesting toppings as prosciutto, arugula, and caviar. There's even a carbonara breakfast pizza (part of a small morning menu) and a Nutella dessert pizza. Piping-hot calzones, salads, and baked pastas round out the choices. Next to the patio, look for the grave markers of Addison Mizner's beloved pet monkey, Johnnie Brown, and Rose Sachs's dog, Laddie (she and husband Morton bought Mizner's villa and lived there 47 years). Delivery is available. This bistro is dog-friendly. [$] *Average main: $19* ✉ *14 Via Mizner, at Worth Ave., Palm Beach* ☎ *561/832–0032* 🌐 *www.pizzaalfresco.com.*

$$$$ ITALIAN 🍴 **Renato's.** Here, at one of the most romantic restaurants in Palm Beach, guests can dine in the beautiful courtyard under the stars and twinkling lights on the bougainvillea or in the intimate, low-lighted dining room flickering with candles and enhanced with fresh flowers and quiet classical music. Be sure to try the split-pea soup with small cubes of ham (a meal in itself) and the sautéed swordfish with white wine, lemon butter, and capers when it's offered. All are served on pretty, flowered porcelain plates atop crisp white-linen tablecloths. Although pricey, dinner here is worth every penny. Jackets are encouraged. [$] *Average main: $37* ✉ *87 Via Mizner, Palm Beach* ☎ *561/655–9752* 🌐 *www.renatospalmbeach.com* ✍ *Reservations essential* 🕒 *No lunch Sun.*

$$$ AMERICAN FAMILY 🍴 **Testa's Palm Beach.** Attracting a loyal clientele since 1921, this restaurant is still owned by the Testa family. Lunches range from burgers to crab salad, and dinner specialties include snapper Florentine and jumbo lump-crab cakes. You can dine inside in an intimate pine-paneled room with cozy bar, out back in a gazebo-style room for large groups, or outside at tables that are pet-friendly. Don't miss the signature strawberry pie made with fresh Florida berries. [$] *Average main: $27* ✉ *221 Royal Poinciana Way, Palm Beach* ☎ *561/832–0992* 🌐 *www.testasrestaurants.com.*

WEST PALM BEACH

$ AMERICAN 🍴 **Belle and Maxwell's.** Palm Beach's ladies who lunch gladly leave the island for an afternoon at Belle and Maxwell's. Hidden among the antique stores, every day looks like a storybook tea party at this quaint teahouse. Expect colorful luncheonette dresses and great soups, salads, and sandwiches at surprisingly affordable prices. People also frequent Belle and Maxwell's solely for its coffee and homemade desserts (including a $12 sweet sampler platter that gives you four different treats to taste). $ *Average main: $12* ⊠ *3700 S. Dixie Hwy., West Palm Beach* ☎ *561/832–4449* ⊕ *www.belleandmaxwells.netý* ⊙ *Closed Sun.*

$ ✕ **Howley's.** Since 1950 this diner's eat-in counter and "cooked in sight,

AMERICAN it must be right" motto have made it a congenial setting for meeting old friends and making new ones. Nowadays, Howley's prides itself on its kitsch factor and old-school eats like turkey potpie and a traditional Thanksgiving feast, as well as its retro-redux dishes like potato-and-brisket burrito. Forgo the counter for the retro tables or sit out on the covered patio. The café attracts a loyal clientele into the wee hours (it's open weekdays until 2 am and weekends until 5 am and has a full bar). $ *Average main: $13* ⊠ *4700 S. Dixie Hwy., West Palm Beach* ☎ *561/833–5691* ⊕ *www.sub-culture.org/howleys.*

$$$ ✕ **Il Bellagio.** In the heart of CityPlace, this European-style eatery offers

ITALIAN Italian specialties and a wide variety of fine wines. The menu includes

FAMILY classics like chicken parmigiana, risotto, and fettuccine alfredo. Pizzas from the wood-burning oven are especially good. Service is friendly and efficient, but the overall noise level tends to be high. Sit at the outdoor tables next to the main plaza's dancing fountains if you can. $ *Average main: $23* ⊠ *CityPlace, 600 S. Rosemary Ave., West Palm Beach* ☎ *561/659–6160* ⊕ *www.ilbellagiocityplace.com.*

$ ✕ **Middle East Bakery.** This hole-in-the-wall Middle Eastern bakery, deli,

MIDDLE EASTERN and market is packed at lunchtime with regulars who are on a first-name

Fodor's Choice basis with the gang behind the counter. From the nondescript parking

★ lot the place doesn't look like much, but inside, delicious hot and cold Mediterranean treats await. Choose from traditional gyro sandwiches and lamb salads with sides of grape leaves, tabbouleh, and couscous. There's a big take-out business, as seating is limited, and it closes shop at 6 pm (4:30 pm on Saturdays). $ *Average main: $10* ⊠ *327 5th St., West Palm Beach* ☎ *561/659–7322* ⊙ *Closed Sun.*

$$$ ✕ **Pistache French Bistro.** Although "the island" is no doubt a bastion

FRENCH of French cuisine, this cozy bistro across Lake Worth on the Clematis Street waterfront entices a lively crowd looking for a good meal with pretention checked at the door. The outdoor terrace can't be beat, and the fabulous modern French menu (revamped in early 2014), including roasted sliced duck with truffled polenta rather than the ubiquitous *à l'orange,* are a delight. Save room for dessert: the house-made pudding Breton, a fluffy, raisin-accented brioche bread pudding paired with Crème Anglaise, could be straight out of a Parisian café. $ *Average main: $27* ⊠ *101 N. Clematis St., West Palm Beach* ☎ *561/833–5090* ⊕ *www.pistachewpb.com.*

$$$ ✕ **Rhythm Cafe.** West Palm Beach's Rhythm Cafe is a true one-of-a-kind

MODERN and anything but Palm Beach formal (think décor like a feathered pink

AMERICAN flamingo perched on terrazzo floors). Fun, funky, cheesy, campy, and cool all at once, the former 1950's drugstore-cum-restaurant on West Palm Beach's Antique Row features an ever-changing creative menu of house-made items with Italian, Greek, American, and Creole influences. Favorites include "tapas-tizers" like the lemon-doused *saganaki* (flaming cheese) and the goat cheese pie; and main courses like the graham-cracker-crusted chicken in key lime sauce and fresh fish of the day prepared six totally different ways. The dessert menu features a variety of homemade ice creams. $ *Average main: $24 ⊠ 3800 S. Dixie Hwy., West Palm Beach* ☎ *561/833–3406* ⊕ *www.rhythmcafe.cc* ✆ *No lunch.*

LAKE WORTH

$ ✕**Benny's on the Beach.** Perched on the Lake Worth Pier, Benny's has a

AMERICAN walk-up bar, a take-out window, and a full-service, no-frills restaurant serving diner-style food that's cheap and filling. Eat-in diners come here for long afternoons of beer and cocktails, enjoying prolific alfresco seating and a spectacular view of the sun glistening on the water and the waves crashing directly below. ∎**TIP➔ Though officially open for just breakfast and lunch, on weekends Benny's usually serves until sunset.** $ *Average main: $12 ⊠ Lake Worth Beach, 10 S. Ocean Blvd., Lake Worth* ☎ *561/582–9001* ⊕ *www.bennysonthebeach.com* ✆ *No dinner.*

$$ ✕**Bizaare Ave Café.** Decorated with a mix of artwork and antiques,

ECLECTIC this cozy bistro housed in a circa-1926 building and inspired by TV's *Friends,* fits right into downtown Lake Worth's groovy, eclectic scene. Artwork and furnishings can be purchased. Daily specials are available on both the lunch and dinner menus, where crêpes, pizzas, pastas, and salads are the staples. A more formal dining space is now open on the second floor. $ *Average main: $18 ⊠ 921 Lake Ave., Lake Worth* ☎ *561/588–4488* ⊕ *www.bizaareavecafe.com.*

LANTANA

$$ ✕**Old Key Lime House.** An informal seafood spot covered by a chickee-

SEAFOOD hut roof built by Seminole Indians, it's perched on the Intracoastal

FAMILY Waterway and is open and airy, with observation decks that wrap around the back. In 1889, the Lyman family, some of the earliest settlers in Lantana, built this as their house, and it has grown over the years into the popular island-style eatery it is today. Kids love feeding the fish below. Of course, order the namesake key lime pie—the house specialty has been featured in *Bon Appétit.* $ *Average main: $20 ⊠ 300 E. Ocean Ave., Lantana* ☎ *561/582–1889* ⊕ *www.oldkeylimehouse.com.*

PALM BEACH GARDENS

$$$$ ✕**Café Chardonnay.** At the end of a strip mall, Café Chardonnay is sur-

AMERICAN prisingly elegant and has some of the most refined food in the suburban town of Palm Beach Gardens. Soft lighting, warm woods, white tablecloths, and cozy banquettes set the scene for a quiet lunch or romantic dinner. The place consistently receives praise for its innovative, continually changing menu and outstanding wine list. Starters can include wild-mushroom strudel and pancetta-wrapped diver scallops. Entrées might be grilled filet mignon or a pan-roasted veal chop with Parmesan risotto and brandy morel sauce. $ *Average main: $34 ⊠ The Gardens Square Shoppes, 4533 PGA Blvd., Palm Beach Gardens* ☎ *561/627–2662* ⊕ *www.cafechardonnay.com* ✆ *No lunch weekends.*

$$$$ ✕**Ironwood Steak & Seafood.** Located in the PGA National Resort &

STEAKHOUSE Spa, this eatery draws guests, locals, and tourists alike eager for a taste of its fired-up Vulcan steaks (Vulcan to meat-eaters is like Titelist to golfers—the best equipment around). The she-crab soup with sherry is a favorite from the sea, as are the raw bar items, like the jumbo shrimp cocktail and tuna tartare. Bright red banquettes, slate-tile walls, private rooms, and an impressive glass-walled wine cellar create a relaxed, contemporary setting that spills out onto the equally chic adjoining lobby bar, which becomes quite the scene on weekend nights when a DJ spins. [$] *Average main: $38* ✉ *PGA National Resort & Spa, 400 Ave. of the Champions, Palm Beach Gardens* ☎ *561/627–4852* 🌐 *www.pgaresort.com/restaurants/ironwood-grille.*

$$$ SEAFOOD 🍴 **Spoto's Oyster Bar.** If you love oysters and other raw bar nibbles, head here, where black-and-white photographs of oyster fisherman adorn the walls. The polished tables give the eatery a clubby look. Spoto's serves up a delightful bowl of New England clam chowder and a truly impressive variety of oysters and clams. The Caesar salad with crispy croutons and anchovies never disappoints. Sit outside on the patio to take advantage of the area's perfect weather. [$] *Average main: $26* ✉ *PGA Commons, 4560 PGA Blvd., Palm Beach Gardens* ☎ *561/776–9448* 🌐 *www.spotosoysterbar.com.*

WHERE TO STAY

PALM BEACH

$$$$ HOTEL Fodor's Choice ★ 🏨 **The Brazilian Court Hotel.** This posh boutique hotel, stomping ground of Florida's well-heeled, is full of historic touches and creature comforts—from its yellow facade with dramatic white-draped entry, to modern draws like the renowned spa and Daniel Boulud restaurant. **Pros:** Stylish and hip local crowd; charming courtyard; free beach shuttle; award-winning restaurant; plush spa. **Cons:** small fitness center; nondescript pool; 10-minute ride to ocean and suggested 24-hour advance reservation for shuttle. [$] *Rooms from: $409* ✉ *301 Australian Ave., Palm Beach* ☎ *561/655–7740* 🌐 *www.thebraziliancourt.com* 🛏 *80 rooms* 🍽 *No meals.*

$$$$ RESORT FAMILY Fodor's Choice ★ 🏨 **The Breakers Palm Beach.** More than an opulent hotel, the Breakers is a legendary 140-acre self-contained jewel of a resort built in an Italian Renaissance style and loaded with amenities, from a 20,000-square-foot luxury spa and grandiose beach club to 10 tennis courts and two 18-hole golf courses—not to mention Henry Flagler's heirs still run the place and invest $20 million a year to keep it at the cutting edge. **Pros:** impeccable attention to detail; fantastic service; beautiful room views; extensive activities for families. **Cons:** big price tag; short drive to reach off-property attractions. [$] *Rooms from: $579* ✉ *1 S. County Rd., Palm Beach* ☎ *561/655–6611, 888/273–2537* 🌐 *www.thebreakers.com* 🛏 *608 rooms* 🍽 *No meals.*

$$$ HOTEL 🏨 **The Chesterfield Palm Beach.** A distinctly upper-crust northern European feel pervades the peach stucco walls and elegant rooms here; the hotel sits just north of the western end of Worth Avenue, and high tea, a cigar parlor, and daily turndown service recall a bygone, more refined era. **Pros:** gracious, attentive staff; Leopard Lounge entertainment; free valet parking. **Cons:** long walk to beach; only one elevator; to some, can come off as a bit stuffy. [$] *Rooms from: $389* ✉ *363 Cocoanut Row, Palm Beach* ☎ *561/659–5800, 800/243–7871* 🌐 *www.chesterfieldpb.com* 🛏 *41 rooms, 11 suites* 🍽 *No meals.*

$$$$ HOTEL 🏨 **The Colony.** This legendary British colonial-style hotel has sunny rooms, suites, and villas with traditional furnishings and a slight Caribbean flair in a particularly convenient location, just one block from

Worth Avenue and one block from a pretty beach on the Atlantic Ocean. **Pros:** unbeatable location; famous polo bar; pillow-top mattresses; full English breakfast included. **Cons:** lobby is small; elevators are tight. [$] *Rooms from: $440* ✉ *155 Hammon Ave., Palm Beach* ☎ *561/655–5430, 800/521–5525* 🌐 *www.thecolonypalmbeach.com* 🛏 *83 rooms, 7 villas* 🍴 *Breakfast.*

$$$$ RESORT FAMILY Fodor's Choice ★ 🏨 **Four Seasons Resort Palm Beach.** Couples and families seeking relaxed seaside elegance in a ritzy yet understated setting will love this manicured 6-acre oceanfront escape at the south end of Palm Beach, with serene, bright, airy rooms in a cream-colored palette and spacious marble-lined baths. **Pros:** accommodating service; all rooms have balconies; outstanding complimentary kids' program. **Cons:** 10-minute drive to downtown Palm Beach (but can walk to Lake Worth); pricey. [$] *Rooms from: $499* ✉ *2800 S. Ocean Blvd., Palm Beach* ☎ *561/582–2800, 800/432–2335* 🌐 *www.fourseasons.com/palmbeach* 🛏 *210 rooms* 🍴 *No meals.*

$$$$ RESORT 🏨 **The Omphoy Ocean Resort.** From the monumental entrance and the lobby's exotic ebony pillars to a lounge with Balinese art and a pool table to the bronze-infused porcelain tile floors, this Zen-like boutique hotel has a sexy, sophisticated look and a loyal following with young, hip travelers. **Pros:** most rooms have beautiful views of the private beach; ultracontemporary vibe; luxury setting. **Cons:** a hike from shopping and nightlife; the infinity pool is across the driveway. [$] *Rooms from: $425* ✉ *2842 S. Ocean Blvd., Palm Beach* ☎ *561/540–6440, 888/344–4321* 🌐 *www.omphoy.com* 🛏 *144 rooms* 🍴 *No meals.*

WEST PALM BEACH

$$ B&B/INN 🏨 **Casa Grandview West Palm Beach.** In West Palm's charming Grandview Heights historic district—and just minutes away from both downtown and the beach—this warm and personalized B&B offers a wonderful respite from South Florida's big-hotel norm. **Pros:** daily dry cleaning of all linens; complimentary soft drinks, coffee, and snacks (and lots of them) in lobby; simple keyless entry (number code lock system). **Cons:** cottages and suites have seven-day minimum; free breakfast in B&B rooms only; art deco suites don't have air-conditioning; in a residential area. [$] *Rooms from: $225* ✉ *1410 Georgia Ave., West Palm Beach* ☎ *561/655–8932* 🌐 *www.casagrandview.com* 🛏 *17 rooms* 🍴 *Multiple meal plans.*

$$ B&B/INN 🏨 **Grandview Gardens Bed & Breakfast.** Defining the Florida B&B experience, this 1925 Mediterranean Revival home overlooks a serene courtyard pool and oozes loads of charm and personality, while the fabulous owners provide heavy doses of bespoke service. **Pros:** multilingual owners; outside private entrances to rooms; innkeepers offer historic city tours. **Cons:** not close to the beach; in a residential area; rental car needed. [$] *Rooms from: $219* ✉ *1608 Lake Ave., West Palm Beach* ☎ *561/833–9023* 🌐 *www.grandview-gardens.com* 🛏 *5 rooms, 2 cottages* 🍴 *Breakfast.*

$ HOTEL 🏨 **Hotel Biba.** In the El Cid historic district, this 1940s-era motel has gotten a fun stylish revamp from designer Barbara Hulanicki: each room has a vibrant mélange of colors, along with handcrafted mirrors, mosaic bathroom floors, and custom mahogany furnishings. **Pros:** cool, punchy design and luxe fixtures; popular wine bar; free continental breakfast with Cuban pastries. **Cons:** water pressure is weak; bathrooms are tiny; noisy when the bar is open late; not all rooms have central A/C. $ *Rooms from: $129* ✉ *320 Belvedere Rd., West Palm Beach* ☎ *561/832–0094* ⊕ *www.hotelbiba.com* ➹ *43 rooms* ⦿ *Breakfast.*

LAKE WORTH

$ ⌂ **Sabal Palm House.** Built in 1936, this romantic, two-story B&B is
B&B/INN a short walk from Lake Worth's downtown shops, eateries, and the Intracoastal Waterway, and each room is decorated with antiques and inspired by a different artist, including Renoir, Dalí, Norman Rockwell, and Chagall. **Pros:** on quiet street; hands-on owners; chairs and totes with towels provided for use at nearby beach. **Cons:** no pool; peak times require a two-night minimum stay; no parking lot. $ *Rooms from: $159* ✉ *109 N. Golfview Rd., Lake Worth* ☎ *561/582–1090, 888/722–2572* ⊕ *www.sabalpalmhouse.com* ➹ *5 rooms, 2 suites* ⦿ *Breakfast.*

SOUTH PALM BEACH AND MANALAPAN

$$$$ ⌂ **Eau Palm Beach.** In the coastal town of Manalapan (just south of
RESORT Palm Beach), this sublime, glamorous destination resort (formerly the
FAMILY Ritz-Carlton) showcases a newer, younger face of luxury, including a
Fodor's Choice 3,000-square-foot oceanfront terrace, two sleek pools, a huge fitness
★ center, a deluxe spa, and richly upholstered furnishings with contemporary, beachy patterns. **Pros:** magnificent aesthetic details throughout; indulgent pampering services; excellent on-site dining; kids love the cool cyber-lounge just for them. **Cons:** golf course is off property; 15-minute drive to Palm Beach. $ *Rooms from: $459* ✉ *100 S. Ocean Blvd., Manalapan* ☎ *561/533–6000, 800/241–3333* ⊕ *www.eaupalmbeach. com* ➹ *310 rooms* ⦿ *No meals.*

SINGER ISLAND

$$$ ⌂ **Palm Beach Marriott Singer Island Beach Resort & Spa.** Families with a
RESORT yen for the cosmopolitan but requiring the square footage and comforts
FAMILY of home revel in these spacious marble-tiled, granite-topped, Kitchen Aid–outfitted condos; couples wanting a private beach without the same level of sticker shock or bustle found 10 minutes to the south also appreciate the infinity pool and quiet sundeck. **Pros:** wide beach; genuinely warm service; plenty of kids' activities; sleek spa. **Cons:** no upscale dining or shopping nearby; unspectacular room views for an oceanside hotel. $ *Rooms from: $399* ✉ *3800 N. Ocean Dr., Singer Island, Riviera Beach* ☎ *561/340–1700, 877/239–5610* ⊕ *www.marriott.com* ➹ *202 suites* ⦿ *No meals.*

$ ⌂ **Sailfish Marina Resort.** A marina with deepwater slips—and prime
HOTEL location at the mouth to the Atlantic Ocean on the Intracoastal Waterway across from Peanut Island—lures boaters and anglers here to these rather basic rooms, studios, and efficiencies. **Pros:** inexpensive rates; great waterfront restaurant; has a water taxi; pretty grounds. **Cons:** no real lobby; not directly on beach; area attracts a party crowd and can be noisy; dated décor. $ *Rooms from: $90* ✉ *98 Lake Dr., Palm Beach Shores* ☎ *561/844–1724* ⊕ *www.sailfishmarina.com* ➹ *30 units* ⦿ *No meals.*

6

PALM BEACH GARDENS

$$ RESORT Fodor's Choice ★ 🏨 **PGA National Resort & Spa.** A soup-to-nuts renovation completed in 2012 elevated this golfer's paradise (five championship courses and the site of the yearly Honda Classic pro-tour tournament) from its *Caddyshack*-style beginnings to a sleek modern playground with a gorgeous zero-entry lagoon pool, seven different places to eat, and a full-service spa with unique mineral-salt therapy pools. **Pros:** dream golf facilities; affordable rates for top-notch amenities; close to shopping malls. **Cons:** no beach shuttle; difficult to get around if you don't have a car; long drive to Palm Beach proper. [$] *Rooms from: $279* ✉ *400 Ave. of the Champions, Palm Beach Gardens* ☎ *561/627–2000, 800/633–9150* 🌐 *www.pgaresort.com* 🛏 *280 rooms, 59 suites* 🍴 *No meals.*

NIGHTLIFE AND PERFORMING ARTS

PALM BEACH

NIGHTLIFE

Palm Beach is teeming with restaurants that turn into late-night hot spots, plus hotel lobby bars perfect for tête-à-têtes.

Fodor's Choice ★ **bûccan.** A hip Hamptons-esque scene with society darlings crowds the lounge, throwing back killer cocktails like the Basil Rathbone (gin, orange juice, mint, basil, strawberry) and Buccan T (vodka, black tea, cranberry, citrus, basil, and agave nectar). ✉ *350 S. County Rd., Palm Beach* ☎ *561/833–3450* 🌐 *www.buccanpalmbeach.com.*

Cucina Dell' Arte. Though this spot is popular for lunch and dinner, it's even more popular later in the night. The younger, trendier set comes late to dance and mingle and have a great time. ✉ *257 Royal Poinciana Way, Palm Beach* ☎ *561/655–0770* 🌐 *www.cucinadellarte.com/palmbeach.*

The Leopard Lounge. In the Chesterfield hotel, this enclave feels like an exclusive club. The trademark ceiling and spotted floors of the renovated lounge are a nod to this hotel's historic roots, but the rest of the décor is new age Palm Beach glam. Though it starts each evening as a restaurant, as the night progresses the Leopard is transformed into an old-fashioned club with live music for Palm Beach's old guard. ✉ *The Chesterfield Palm Beach, 363 Cocoanut Row, Palm Beach* ☎ *561/659–5800* 🌐 *www.chesterfieldpb.com.*

WEST PALM BEACH

NIGHTLIFE

West Palm is known for its exuberant nightlife—Clematis Street and CityPlace are the prime party destinations. In fact, downtown rocks every Thursday from 6 pm on with Clematis by Night (🌐 *www.wpb.org/clematis-by-night*), a celebration of music, dance, art, and food at Centennial Square.

Blue Martini. The CityPlace outpost of this South Florida hot spot for thirty, forty, and fiftysomething adults gone wild has a menu filled with tons of innovative martini creations (42 to be exact), and lots of cougars on the prowl, searching for a first, second, or even third husband. And the guys aren't complaining! The drinks are great and the scene is fun for everyone, even those who aren't single and looking to mingle. Expect DJs some nights, live music others. ⊠ *CityPlace, 550 S. Rosemary Ave. #244, West Palm Beach* ☎ *561/835–8601* ⊕ *www. bluemartinilounge.com.*

ER Bradley's Saloon. People of all ages congregate to hang out and socialize at this kitschy open-air restaurant and bar to gaze at the Intracoastal Waterway; the mechanical bull is a hit on Saturday. Live music's on tap five to seven nights a week. ⊠ *104 Clematis St., West Palm Beach* ☎ *561/833–3520* ⊕ *www.erbradleys.com.*

Fodor's Choice **Rocco's Tacos and Tequila Bar.** In the last few years, Rocco's has taken root
★ in numerous South Florida downtowns and become synonymous with wild nights of chips 'n' guac, margaritas, and intoxicating fun. This is more of a scene than just a restaurant. With pitchers of margaritas a-flowin', the middle-age crowd is boisterous and fun, recounting (and reliving) the days of spring break debauchery from their pre-professional years. Get your party started here with more than 220 choices of tequila. There's another branch at 5250 Town Center Circle in Boca Raton. ⊠ *224 Clematis St., West Palm Beach* ☎ *561/650–1001* ⊕ *www. roccostacos.com.*

PERFORMING ARTS

Palm Beach Dramaworks (pbd). Housed in an intimate venue with only 218 seats in downtown West Palm Beach, their modus operandi is "theater to think about" with plays by Pulitzer Prize winners on rotation. ⊠ *201 Clematis St., West Palm Beach* ☎ *561/514–4042* ⊕ *www. palmbeachdramaworks.org.*

Fodor's Choice **Raymond F. Kravis Center for the Performing Arts.** This is the crown jewel
★ amid a treasury of local arts attractions, and its marquee star is the 2,195-seat Dreyfoos Hall, a glass, copper, and marble showcase just steps from the restaurants and shops of CityPlace. The center also boasts the 289-seat Rinker Playhouse, 170-seat Persson Hall, and the Gosman Amphitheatre, which holds 1,400 total in seats and on the lawn. A packed year-round schedule features a blockbuster lineup of Broadway's biggest touring productions, concerts, dance, dramas, and musicals; Miami City Ballet and the Palm Beach Pops perform here. ⊠ *701 Okeechobee Blvd., West Palm Beach* ☎ *561/832–7469 for box office* ⊕ *www.kravis.org.*

SHOPPING

As is the case throughout Florida, many of the smaller boutiques in Palm Beach close in the summer, and most stores are closed on Sunday. Consignment stores in Palm Beach are definitely worth a look; you'll often find high-end designer clothing in impeccable condition.

PALM BEACH

SHOPPING AREAS

Royal Poinciana Way. Cute shops like resort-wear favorite Joy of Palm Beach (⊕ *www.joyofpalmbeach.com*) dot the north side of Royal Poinciana Way between Bradley Place and North County Road. Wind through the courtyards past upscale consignment stores to Sunset Avenue, then stroll down Sunrise Avenue: this is the place for specialty items like out-of-town newspapers, health foods, and rare books. ⊠ *Worth Ave., between Bradley Pl. and N. County Rd., Palm Beach.*

Fodor's Choice **Worth Avenue.** One of the world's premier showcases for high-quality
★ shopping runs half a mile from east to west across Palm Beach, from the beach to Lake Worth. The street has more than 200 shops (more than 40 of them sell jewelry), and many upscale chain stores (Gucci, Hermès, Pucci, Saks Fifth Avenue, Neiman Marcus, Louis Vuitton, Chanel, Cartier, Tiffany & Co., and Tourneau) are represented—their merchandise appealing to the discerning tastes of the Palm Beach clientele. Don't miss walking around the *vias*, little courtyards lined with smaller boutiques; historic tours are available each month during "season" from the Worth Avenue Association. ■TIP→ For those looking to go a little lighter on the pocket book, just north of Worth Avenue, the six blocks of South Country Road have interesting and somewhat less expensive stores. ⊠ *Worth Ave., between Cocoanut Row and S. Ocean Blvd., Palm Beach* ⊕ *www.worth-avenue.com.*

RECOMMENDED STORES

Betteridge at Greenleaf & Crosby. Jewelry is very important in Palm Beach, and for more than 119 years the diverse selection here has included investment pieces. Window shopping is allowed. ⊠ *236 Worth Ave., Palm Beach* ☎ *561/655–5850* ⊕ *www.betteridge.com.*

Calypso St. Barth. For those boutiques that are represented in the wealthiest cities across the country, having an outpost here on Via Encantada on Worth Avenue is almost obligatory. For its Palm Beach store (one of four Florida outposts—the others are in Bal Harbour, Naples, and Coral Gables), Calypso has curated a lively collection of resort wear like beautifully embroidered tunics and patterned bikinis as well as shoes, fragrances, and accessories for the pampered lady. ⊠ *247-B Worth Ave., Palm Beach* ☎ *561/832–5006* ⊕ *www.calypsostbarth.com.*

The Church Mouse. Many high-end resale boutique owners grab their merchandise at this thrift store run by the Episcopal Church of Bethesda-by-the-Sea, in business since 1970. The mouse accepts cheese from October to June, Monday–Saturday 10–4. You can feel good about your purchases here: proceeds go to regional nonprofits. ⊠ *378 S. County Rd., Palm Beach* ☎ *561/659–2154* ⊕ *www.bbts.org/churchmouse.*

Déjà Vu. There are so many gently used, top-quality pieces from Chanel here that this could be a resale house for the brand. There's no digging through piles here; clothes are in impeccable condition and are well organized. Sadly, Maxie Barley, owner of the store and Palm Beach legend, passed away in October 2013. ⊠ *Via Testa, 219 Royal Poinciana Way, Palm Beach* ☎ *561/833–6624.*

FAMILY **Spring Flowers.** Specializing in European labels, beautiful children's clothing starts with newborn gown sets by Petit Bateau and grows into fashions by Léon and Fleurisse. ⊠ *320 Worth Ave., Palm Beach* ☎ *561/832–0131* ⊕ *www.springflowerschildren.com.*

WEST PALM BEACH

Fodor's Choice ★ **Antique Row.** West Palm's U.S. 1, "South Dixie Highway," is the destination for those who are interested in interesting home décor. From thrift shops to the most exclusive stores, it is all here within 40 stores—museum-quality furniture, lighting, art, junk, fabric, frames, tile, and rugs. So if you're looking for an art deco, French provincial, or Mizner pièce de résistance, big or small, schedule a few hours for an Antique Row stroll. You'll find bargains during the off-season (May to November). Antique Row runs north–south from Belvedere Road to Forest Hill Boulevard, although most stores are bunched between Belvedere Road and Southern Boulevard. ⊠ *U.S. 1, between Belvedere Rd. and Forest Hill Blvd., West Palm Beach* ⊕ *www.westpalmbeachantiques.com.*

CityPlace. The 72-acre, four-block-by-four-block commercial and residential complex centered on Rosemary Avenue attracts people of all ages to with restaurants like Italian-inspired Il Bellagio, bars like Blue Martini, a 20-screen Muvico and IMAX, the Harriet Himmel Theater, and a 36,000-gallon water fountain and light show. The dining, shopping, and entertainment are all family-friendly; at night a lively crowd likes to hit the outdoor bars. Among CityPlace's stores are such popular national retailers as Macy's, H&M, Pottery Barn, Banana Republic, and Restoration Hardware. There are also shops unique to Florida: Behind the punchy, brightly colored clothing in the front window of C. Orrico (☎ 561/832–9203) are family fashions and accessories by Lily Pulitzer. ⊠ *700 S. Rosemary Ave., West Palm Beach* ☎ *561/366–1000* ⊕ *www.cityplace.com.*

FAMILY **Clematis Street.** If lunching is just as important as window-shopping, the renewed downtown West Palm around Clematis Street that runs west to east from South Rosemary Avenue to Flagler Drive is the spot for you. Centennial Park by the waterfront has an attractive design—and fountains where kids can cool off—which adds to the pleasure of browsing and resting at one of the many outdoor cafés. Hip national retailers such as Design Within Reach (⊕ *www.dwr.com*) mix with local boutiques, and both blend in with restaurants and bars. ⊠ *Clematis St., between S. Rosemary Ave. and Flagler Dr., West Palm Beach* ⊕ *www.westpalmbeach.com/clematis.*

PALM BEACH GARDENS

Downtown at The Gardens. This open-air pavilion down the street from The Gardens Mall has boutiques, chain stores, day spas, a 16-screen movie theater, and a lively restaurant and nighttime bar scene that includes the Dirty Martini and Cabo Flats, which both feature live music. ⊠ *11701 Lake Victoria Gardens Ave., Palm Beach Gardens* ☎ *561/340–1600* ⊕ *www.downtownatthegardens.com.*

Fodor's Choice ★ **The Gardens Mall.** One of the most refined big shopping malls in America, the 160-store Gardens Mall in northern Palm Beach County has stores like Burberry, Chanel, Gucci, Louis Vuitton, and David Yurman. There are also plenty of reasonably priced national retailers like H&M and Abercrombie & Fitch. This beautiful mall has prolific seating pavilions, making it a great place to spend a humid summer afternoon.

✉ *3101 PGA Blvd., Palm Beach Gardens* ☎ *561/775–7750* ⊕ *www. thegardensmall.com.*

SPORTS AND THE OUTDOORS

You can have a baseball bonanza while on vacation in the greater Palm Beach area by venturing up to the Treasure Coast's spring-training facilities, winter home to several major league teams and minor leagues the rest of the year. Northern towns like Palm Beach Gardens are only minutes away.

PALM BEACH

Palm Beach Island has two good golf courses—the Breakers and the Palm Beach Par 3 Golf Course, but only the latter is open to the public. Not to worry, there are more on the mainland, as well as myriad other outdoor sports opportunities.

BIKING

Bicycling is a great way to get a closer look at Palm Beach. Only 14 miles long, half a mile wide, flat as the top of a billiard table, and just as green, it's a perfect biking place.

Fodor'sChoice ★ **Palm Beach Bicycle Trail Shop.** Open daily year-round, the shop rents bikes by the hour or day, and it's about a block from the north Lake Trail entrance. The shop has maps to help you navigate your way around the island, or you can download the main map from the shop's website. They are experts on the nearby, palm-fringed 4-mile Lake Trail. ✉ *223 Sunrise Ave., Palm Beach* ☎ *561/659–4583* ⊕ *www. palmbeachbicycle.com.*

GOLF

Fodor'sChoice ★ **Palm Beach Par 3 Golf Course.** This course has been named the best par-3 golf course in the United States by *Golf Digest* magazine. The 18-hole course—originally designed by Dick Wilson and Joe Lee in 1961—was redesigned in 2009 by Hall of Famer Raymond Floyd. The par-3 course includes six holes directly on the Atlantic Ocean, with some holes over 200 yards. The grounds are exquisitely landscaped, as one would expect in Palm Beach. There's also a lavish clubhouse that houses Al Fresco, an Italian-inspired restaurant. Greens fees are $46; cart is an extra $25, but walking is encouraged. ✉ *2345 S. Ocean Blvd., Palm Beach* ☎ *561/547–0598* ⊕ *www.golfontheocean.com* 🍴 *$46 for 18 holes.* 🏌 *18 holes. 2458 yards. par 58.*

WEST PALM BEACH
POLO

Fodor'sChoice ★ **International Polo Club Palm Beach.** Attend matches and rub elbows with celebrities who make the pilgrimage out to Palm Beach polo country (the western suburb of Wellington) during the January-through-April season. The competition is not just among polo players. High society dresses in their best polo couture week after week, each outfit more fabulous than the next. An annual highlight at the polo club is the U.S. Open Polo Championship at the end of season. ■TIP→ One of the best ways to experience the polo scene is by enjoying a gourmet brunch on the veranda of the International Polo Club Pavilion; it'll cost

Worth Avenue is the place in Palm Beach for high-end shopping, from international boutiques to independent jewelers.

you from $100–$120 per person depending on the month, but it's well worth it. ✉ *3667 120th Ave. S, Wellington* ☎ *561/204–5687* ⊕ *www. internationalpoloclub.com.*

LAKE WORTH
GOLF

Palm Beach National Golf and Country Club. Despite the name, this classic 18-hole course resides in Lake Worth, not in Palm Beach. It is, however, in Palm Beach County and prides itself on being "the most fun and friendly golf course" in Palm Beach County. The championship layout was designed by Joe Lee in the 1970s and is famous for its 3rd and 18th holes. The 3rd: a par-3 island hole with a sand bunker. The 18th: a short par 4 of 358 yards sandwiched between a wildlife preserve and water. Due to the challenging nature of the course, it's more popular with seasoned golfers. The Steve Haggerty Golf Academy is also based here. ✉ *7500 St. Andrews Rd., Lake Worth* ☎ *561/965–0044* ⊕ *www. palmbeachnational.com* 🏌 *$89 for 18 holes* 🏌 *18 holes. 6734 yards. par 72.*

SINGER ISLAND
FISHING

Sailfish Marina. Book a full or half day of deep-sea fishing for up to six people with the seasoned captains and large fleet of 28- to 65-foot boats. ✉ *Sailfish Marina Resort, 98 Lake Dr., Palm Beach Shores* ☎ *561/844– 1724* ⊕ *www.sailfishmarina.com.*

PALM BEACH GARDENS

GOLF

Fodor's Choice **PGA National Resort & Spa.** If you're the kind of traveler who takes along
★ a set of clubs, you'll achieve nirvana on the greens of PGA National
Resort & Spa. The five championship courses are open only to hotel
guests and club members, which means you'll have to stay to play. The
Champion Course, redesigned by Jack Nicklaus and famous for its Bear
Trap holes, is the site of the yearly Honda Classic pro tournament. The
four other challenging courses are also legends in the golfing world: the
Palmer, named for its architect, the legendary Arnold Palmer; the Fazio
(formerly the "Haig," the resort's first course re-opened in November
2012 after a major renovation) and the Squire, both from Tom and
George Fazio; and the Karl Litten–designed Estates, the sole course
not on the property (it is located five miles west of the PGA resort).
Lessons are available at the David Leadbetter Golf Academy. ⊠ *PGA
National Resort & Spa, 1000 Ave. of the Champions, Palm Beach
Gardens* ☎ *561/627–1800* ⊕ *www.pgaresort.com/golf/pga-national-
golf* ⊠ *$347 for 18 holes for Champion Course, Fazio Course, and
Squire Course. $258 for 18 holes for Palmer Course and Estates Course.*
⚑ *Champion Course: 18 holes. 7048 yards. par 72. Palmer Course: 18
holes. 7079 yards. par 72. Fazio Course: 18 holes. 6806 yards. par 72.
Squire Course: 18 holes. 6465 yards. par 72. Estates Course: 18 holes.
6694 yards. par 72.*

DELRAY BEACH

15 miles south of West Palm Beach.

A onetime artists' retreat with a small settlement of Japanese farmers,
Delray has grown into a sophisticated beach town. Delray's current
popularity is caused in large part by the fact that it has the feel of an
organic city rather than a planned development or subdivision—and
it's completely walkable. Atlantic Avenue, the once-dilapidated main
drag, has evolved into a more-than-a-mile-long stretch of palm-dotted
sidewalks, lined with stores, art galleries, and dining establishments.
Running east–west and ending at the beach, it's a happening place for a
stroll, day or night. Another active pedestrian area, the Pineapple Grove
Arts District, begins at Atlantic and stretches northward on Northeast
2nd Avenue about half a mile, and yet another active pedestrian way
begins at the eastern edge of Atlantic Avenue and runs along the big,
broad swimming beach that extends north to George Bush Boulevard
and south to Casuarina Road.

GETTING HERE AND AROUND

To reach Delray Beach from Boynton Beach, drive 2 miles south on
I–95, U.S. 1, or Route A1A.

ESSENTIALS

VISITOR INFORMATION

Contacts Palm Beach County Convention and Visitors Bureau ⊠ *1555
Palm Beach Lakes Blvd., Ste. 800, West Palm Beach* ☎ *561/233–3000* ⊕ *www.
palmbeachfl.com.*

CLOSE UP

6

The Morikami: Essence of Japan in Florida

A magical 200-acre garden where the Far East meets the South lies just beyond Palm Beach's allure of sun, sea, and glittering resorts. It's called the Morikami Museum and Japanese Gardens and is a testament to one man's perseverance. One of the largest Japanese gardens outside of Japan, it's also a soothing destination for reflection, with a pine forest, trails, and lakes.

In 1904, Jo Sakai, a New York University graduate, returned to his homeland of Miyazu, Japan, to recruit hands for farming what is now northern Boca Raton. With help from Henry Flagler's East Coast Railroad subsidiary, they colonized as Yamato, an ancient name for Japan. When crops fell short, everyone left except for George Sukeji Morikami, who carried on cultivating local crops, eventually donating his land to memorialize the Yamato Colony in the mid-1970s to Palm Beach County. His dream took on a new dimension with the 1977 opening of the Morikami complex, a living monument bridging cultural

understanding between Morikami's two homelands.

The original Yamato-kan building chronicles the Yamato Colony, and a 32,000-square-foot main museum that opened in 1993 has rotating exhibits with 7,000 art objects and artifacts from the permanent collection, including 200 examples of textiles and a 500-piece collection of tea-ceremony items. No visit is complete without exploring the expansive Japanese gardens that have strolling paths, a tropical bonsai collection, and lakes teeming with koi. Enjoy a demonstration of *sado*, the Japanese tea ceremony, in the Seishin-an teahouse (check website for schedule), learn about Japanese history in the 5,000-book library, or register in advance for classes like calligraphy, bonsai, art, and intro to sushi making. The gift shop has some great finds for the whole family, and the Cornell Café has excellent pan-Asian fare and a relaxing terrace that overlooks the gardens.

EXPLORING

Colony Hotel. The chief landmark along Atlantic Avenue since 1926 is this sunny Mediterranean revival–style building, which is a member of the National Trust's Historic Hotels of America. Walk through the lobby to the parking lot where original garages still stand—relics of the days when hotel guests would arrive via chauffeured cars and stay there the whole season. ⊠ *525 E. Atlantic Ave.* ☎ *561/276–4123* ⊕ *www. thecolonyhotel.com.*

FAMILY **Delray Beach Center for the Arts at Old School Square.** Instrumental in the revitalization of Delray Beach circa 1995, this cluster of galleries and event spaces were established in restored school buildings dating from 1913 and 1925. The **Cornell Museum of Art & American Culture** offers ever-changing exhibits on fine arts, crafts, and pop culture, plus a hands-on children's gallery. From November to April, the 323-seat **Crest Theatre** showcases national-touring Broadway musicals, cabaret concerts, dance performances, and lectures. ⊠ *51 N. Swinton Ave.*

Morikami Museum and Japanese Gardens gives a taste of the Orient through its exhibits and tea ceremonies.

☎ *561/243–7922* ⊕ *www.oldschool.org* ✉ *$10 for museum* ☉ *Museum Tues.–Sat. 10:30–4:30, Sun. 1–4:30.*

FAMILY
Fodor's Choice
★

Morikami Museum and Japanese Gardens. The boonies west of Delray Beach seems an odd place to encounter one of the region's most important cultural centers, but this is exactly where you can find a 200-acre cultural and recreational facility heralding the Yamato Colony of Japanese farmers that settled here in the early 20th century. A permanent exhibit details their history, and all together the museum's collection has more than 7,000 artifacts and works of art on rotating display. Traditional tea ceremonies are conducted monthly from October to June, along with educational classes on topics like calligraphy and sushi-making (these require advance registration and come with a fee). The six main gardens are inspired by famous historic periods in Japanese garden design and have South Florida accents (think tropical bonsai), and the on-site Cornell Café serves light Asian fare at affordable prices and was recognized by the Food Network as being one of the country's best museum eateries. ✉ *4000 Morikami Park Rd.* ☎ *561/495–0233* ⊕ *www.morikami.org* ✉ *$14* ☉ *Tues.–Sun. 10–5.*

BEACHES

Fodor's Choice
★

Delray Municipal Beach. If you're looking for a place to see and be seen, head for this wide expanse of sand, the heart of which is where Atlantic Avenue meets A1A, close to restaurants, bars, and quick-serve eateries. Singles, families, and water-sports enthusiasts alike love it here. Lounge chairs and umbrellas can be rented every day, and lifeguards man stations half a mile out in each direction. The most popular section of beach is south of Atlantic Avenue on A1A, where the street parking is found. There are also two metered lots with restrooms across from A1A at Sandoway Park and Anchor Park (bring quarters if parking here!). On the beach by Anchor Park, north of Casuarina Road, are six volleyball nets and a kiosk that offers Hobie Wave rentals, surfing lessons, and snorkeling excursions to the 1903 SS *Inchulva* shipwreck half a mile offshore. The beach itself is open 24 hours, if you're at a nearby hotel and fancy a moonlight stroll. **Amenities:** water sports; food and drink; lifeguards; parking (fee); toilets; showers. **Best for:** windsurfing; partiers; swimming. ✉ *Rte. A1A and E. Atlantic Ave.* 🎫 *$1.50 per 1 hr parking* ⏲ *Daily 24 hrs.*

WHERE TO EAT

$$ BRITISH

🍴 **Blue Anchor.** Yes, this pub was actually shipped from England, where it had stood for 150 years in London's historic Chancery Lane. There it was a watering hole for famed Englishmen, including Winston Churchill. The Delray Beach incarnation has stuck to authentic British pub fare. Chow down on a ploughman's lunch (a chunk of Stilton cheese, a piece of bread, English pork pie, and pickled onions), fish-and-chips, and bangers and mash (sausages with mashed potatoes). This is a pub's pub—nothing fancy, very hearty. Don't be surprised to find a soccer game on TV. English beers and ales are available on tap and by the bottle. It's also a late-night place and has live music on weekends. [$] *Average main: $18* ✉ *804 E. Atlantic Ave.* ☎ *561/272–7272* 🌐 *www.theblueanchor.com.*

$$$ SEAFOOD Fodor's Choice ★

🍴 **City Oyster & Sushi Bar.** This trendy restaurant mingles the personalities and flavors of a New England oyster bar, a modern sushi eatery, an eclectic seafood grill, and an award-winning dessert bakery to create a can't-miss foodie haven in the heart of Delray's bustling Atlantic Avenue. With fruits of the sea delivered fresh daily and a winning culinary team, dishes like the New England clam chowder, New Orleans–style shrimp and crab gumbo, tuna crudo, and lobster fried rice are simply sublime. What's more? The restaurant's colossal bakery adds an unexpected element of carb bliss with a full roster of house-made breads and desserts, including the decadent, seasonal pies (ranging from chocolate–peanut butter to mixed berries) and the insanely divine pecan pie in a glass, smothered in salted caramel, pecan brittle, butter-pecan ice cream, and topped with whipped cream. Pastas are also made in-house. The wine list and craft beer menus are off the charts. [$] *Average main: $23* ✉ *213 E. Atlantic Ave.* ☎ *561/272–0220* 🌐 *www.cityoysterdelray.com.*

$$$ ITALIAN

🍴 **D'Angelo Trattoria.** One of South Florida's most renowned Italian chefs, Angelo Elia, continues to expand his empire with this lively trattoria off Atlantic Avenue in Delray Beach. In a refurbished and reinvented beach house, the restaurant delivers hefty portions of original Italian favorites—such as gnocchi *quattro formaggi* (four cheeses) and seafood risotto—as well as Italian-American delights, like jumbo-shrimp parmigiana over spicy linguini. The wood oven also commands a lot of attention for its excellent pizzas, from the more traditional margherita to the more avant-garde, like the Integrale made with whole-wheat flour and topped with mozzarella, brie, zucchini, and smoked salmon. Come hungry and prepare yourself for a major food hangover that's worth every bite. $ *Average main: $28* ⊠ *9 S.E. 7th Ave.* ☎ *561/330–1237* ⊕ *www.dangelotrattoria.com* ⊙ *No lunch.*

$$$
MODERN
AMERICAN
Fodor'sChoice
★

✕ **Max's Harvest.** A few blocks off Atlantic Avenue in the artsy Pineapple Grove neighborhood, a tree-shaded, fenced-in courtyard welcomes foodies eager to dig into its "farm-to-fork" offerings. The menu encourages people to experiment with "to share," "start small," and "think big" plates. An ideal sampling: organic deviled eggs with chives and truffle sea salt; tequila-cured salmon; ricotta gnocchi, boiled then sautéed with porcini mushrooms and truffle tremor (goat cheese with truffles); and a pork chop over mustard spaetzle. Sunday brunch is wildly popular and includes an unlimited interactive Bloody Mary bar and champagne cocktails. $ *Average main: $27* ⊠ *169 N.E. 2nd Ave.* ☎ *561/381–9970* ⊕ *www.maxsharvest.com* ⊙ *No lunch Mon.–Sat.*

$$$
AMERICAN
Fodor'sChoice
★

✕ **The Office.** Scenesters line the massive indoor-outdoor bar from noon 'til the wee hours at this cooler-than-thou retro library restaurant, but it's worth your time to stop here for the best burger in town. There's a whole selection, but the Prime CEO steals the show: Maytag bleu cheese and Gruyere with tomato-onion confit, arugula, and bacon. It's so juicy, you'll quickly forget the mess you're making. Other upscale renditions of comforting classics like nachos (a delicate puff of whipped crab per chip served with jicama slaw), fried green tomatoes (panko-and-cornmeal crusted with crisped bits of Serrano ham), and "naughty" alcoholic shakes are worth every indulgent calorie. $ *Average main: $24* ⊠ *201 E. Atlantic Ave.* ☎ *561/276–3600* ⊕ *www.theofficedelray.com.*

$$$$
AMERICAN
Fodor'sChoice
★

✕ **32 East.** Although restaurants come and go every year on Atlantic Avenue, 32 East remains one of the best—if not the best—in Delray Beach. An ever-changing daily menu defines modern American cuisine. Depending on what is fresh and plentiful, you might indulge in oak-fired organic dates and pears wrapped in bacon or perfectly prepared cumin-chili spiced cobia over black bean–tomato salad. Medium-tone wood accents and dim lighting make this brasserie seem cozy. There's a packed bar in front, an open kitchen in back, and patio seating on the sidewalk. ■TIP→ If you splurge on one dinner in Delray, make it 32 East. $ *Average main: $36* ⊠ *32 E. Atlantic Ave.* ☎ *561/276–7868* ⊕ *www.32east.com* ⚏ *Reservations essential* ⊙ *No lunch.*

WHERE TO STAY

$
HOTEL

▦ **Colony Hotel & Cabaña Club.** Not to be confused with the luxurious Colony in Palm Beach, this charming hotel in the heart of downtown Delray dates back to 1926; and although it's landlocked, it does have a cabana club 2 miles away for hotel guests only. **Pros:** pet-friendly; full breakfast buffet included with rooms; free use of cabanas, umbrellas, and hammocks. **Cons:** no pool at main hotel building; must walk to public beach for water sport rentals. $ *Rooms from: $195* ⊠ *525 E. Atlantic Ave.* ☎ *561/276–4123, 800/552–2363* ⊕ *www.thecolonyhotel.com* ⟿ *48 rooms, 22 suites* ⦿| *Breakfast.*

$$
HOTEL
FAMILY

▦ **Delray Beach Marriott.** By far the largest hotel in Delray Beach, the Marriott has two towers on a stellar plot of land at the east end of Atlantic Avenue—it's the only hotel that directly overlooks the water, yet it is still within walking distance of restaurants, shopping, and nightlife. **Pros:** fantastic ocean views; pampering spa; two pools. **Cons:** chain-hotel feel; charge for parking; must rent beach chairs. [$] *Rooms from: $279* ✉ *10 N. Ocean Blvd.* ☎ *561/274–3200* 🌐 *www.delraybeachmarriott.com* 🛏 *181 rooms, 88 suites* 🍴 *No meals.*

$$$ RESORT FAMILY Fodor's Choice ★ 🏨 **The Seagate Hotel & Spa.** Those who crave 21st-century luxury in its full glory (ultraswank tilework and fixtures, marble vanities, seamless shower doors) will love this LEED-certified hotel that offers a subtle Zen coastal motif throughout. **Pros:** two swimming pools; fabulous beach club; exceptionally knowledgeable concierge team. **Cons:** main building not directly on beach; daily resort fee; separate charge for parking. [$] *Rooms from: $369* ✉ *1000 E. Atlantic Ave.* ☎ *561/665–4800, 877/577–3242* 🌐 *www.theseagatehotel.com* 🛏 *154 rooms* 🍴 *No meals.*

$ B&B/INN Fodor's Choice ★ 🏨 **Sundy House.** Just about everything in this bungalow-style B&B is executed to perfection—especially its tropical, verdant grounds, which are actually a nonprofit botanical garden (something anyone can check out during free weekday tours) with a natural, freshwater swimming pool where your feet glide along limestone rocks and mingle with fish. **Pros:** charming eclectic décor; each room is unique; renowned restaurant with popular indoor-outdoor bar and free breakfast; in quiet area off Atlantic Avenue. **Cons:** need to walk through garden to reach rooms (i.e., no covered walkways); beach shuttle requires roughly half-hour advance notice; no private beach facilities. [$] *Rooms from: $199* ✉ *106 Swinton Ave.* ☎ *561/272–5678, 877/434–9601* 🌐 *www.sundyhouse.com* 🛏 *11 rooms* 🍴 *Breakfast.*

NIGHTLIFE

Boston's on the Beach. You'll find beer flowing and the ocean breeze blowing at this beach bar and eatery, a local watering hole since 1983. The walls are laden with paraphernalia from the Boston Bruins, New England Patriots, and Boston Red Sox, including a shrine to Ted Williams. Boston's can get loud and rowdy (or lively, depending on your taste) later at night. Groove to reggae on Monday, live blues music on Tuesday, and other live music from rock to country on Friday, Saturday, and Sunday. ✉ *40 S. Ocean Blvd.* ☎ *561/278–3364* 🌐 *www.bostonsonthebeach.com.*

Dada. Bands play in the living room of a historic house. It's a place where those who don't drink will also feel comfortable, and excellent gourmet nibbles are a huge bonus (a full dinner menu is available, too). ✉ *52 N. Swinton Ave.* ☎ *561/330–3232* 🌐 *www.sub-culture.org/dada.*

Jellies Bar at the Atlantic Grille. Within the Seagate Hotel, the fun and fabulous bar at the Atlantic Grille is known locally as Jellies Bar. The over-30 set consistently floats over to this stunning bar to shimmy to live music Tuesday to Saturday; the namesake jellyfish tank never fails to entertain as well. ✉ *The Seagate Hotel & Spa, 1000 E. Atlantic Ave.* ☎ *561/665–4900* 🌐 *www.theatlanticgrille.com.*

6

SHOPPING

Atlantic Avenue and Pineapple Grove, both charming neighborhoods for shoppers, have maintained Delray Beach's small-town integrity. Atlantic Avenue is the main drag, with art galleries, boutiques, restaurants, and bars lining it from just west of Swinton Avenue all the way east to the ocean. The up-and-coming Pineapple Grove Arts District is centered on the half-mile strip of Northeast 2nd Avenue that goes north from Atlantic.

Furst. This studio-shop gives you the chance to watch designer Flavie Furst or her pupils at work—and then purchase their fine, hand-crafted gold, gold-filled, and silver jewelry. ⊠ *123 N.E. 2nd Ave.* ☎ *561/272–6422* ⊕ *www.flaviefurst.com* ☽ *Closed Sun.*

Snappy Turtle. Jack Rogers sandals and Trina Turk dresses mingle with other fun resort fashions for the home and family at this family-run store. ⊠ *1100 E. Atlantic Ave.* ☎ *888/762–7798* ⊕ *www.snappy-turtle.com.*

SPORTS AND THE OUTDOORS

BIKING

There's a bicycle path in Barwick Park, but the most popular place to ride is up and down the special oceanfront bike lane along Route A1A. The city also has an illustrated and annotated map on key downtown sights available through the Palm Beach Convention and Visitors Bureau.

Richwagen's Bike & Sport. Rent bikes by the hour, day, or week (they come with locks, baskets, and helmets); Richwagen's also has copies of city maps on hand. A 7-Speed Cruiser rents for $55 per week. ⊠ *298 N.E. 6th Ave.* ☎ *561/276–4234* ⊕ *www.delraybeachbicycles.com.*

TENNIS

Delray Beach Tennis Center. Each year this complex hosts simultaneous professional tournaments where current stars like Andy Roddick and Juan Martin del Potro along with legends like Ivan Lendl and Michael Chang duke it out (⊕ *www.yellowtennisball.com*), as well as Chris Evert's Pro-Celebrity Tennis Classic charity event (⊕ *www.chrisevert. org*). The rest of the time, you can practice or learn on 14 clay courts and 7 hard courts; private lessons and clinics are available, and it's open from 7:30 am to 9 pm weekdays and until 6 pm weekends. Since most hotels in the area do not have courts, tennis players visiting Delray Beach often come here to play. ⊠ *201 W. Atlantic Ave.* ☎ *561/243–7360* ⊕ *www.delraytennis.com.*

BOCA RATON

6 miles south of Delray Beach.

Less than an hour south of Palm Beach and anchoring the county's south end, upscale Boca Raton has much in common with its fabled cousin. Both reflect the unmistakable architectural influence of Addison Mizner, their principal developer in the mid-1920s. The meaning of the name Boca Raton (pronounced boca rah-*tone*) often arouses curiosity, with many folks mistakenly assuming it means "rat's mouth." Historians say the probable origin is Boca Ratones, an ancient Spanish geographical term for an inlet filled with jagged rocks or coral. Miami's Biscayne Bay had such an inlet, and in 1823 a mapmaker copying Miami terrain confused the more northern inlet, thus mistakenly labeling this area Boca Ratones. No matter what, you'll know you've arrived in the heart of downtown when you spot the historic town hall's gold dome on the main street, Federal Highway. Much of the Boca landscape was heavily planned, and many of the bigger sights are clustered in the area around town hall and Lake Boca, a wide stretch of the Intracoastal Waterway between Palmetto Park Road and Camino Real (two main east–west streets at the southern end of town).

GETTING HERE AND AROUND

To get to Boca Raton from Delray Beach, drive south 6 miles on Interstate 95, Federal Highway (U.S. 1), or Route A1A.

ESSENTIALS

VISITOR INFORMATION

Contacts Palm Beach County Convention and Visitors Bureau ✉ *1555 Palm Beach Lakes Blvd., Ste. 800, West Palm Beach* ☎ *561/233–3000* ⊕ *www. palmbeachfl.com.*

6

EXPLORING

FAMILY **Boca Raton Museum of Art.** Changing-exhibition galleries on the first floor showcase internationally known artists—both past and present—at this museum in a spectacular building that's part of the Mizner Park shopping center; the permanent collection upstairs includes works by Picasso, Degas, Matisse, Klee, Modigliani, and Warhol, as well as notable African and pre-Columbian art. Daily tours are included with admission. In addition to the treasure hunts and sketchbooks you can pick up from the front desk, there's a roster of special programs that cater to kids, including studio workshops and gallery walks. Another fun feature is the cell phone audio guide—certain pieces of art have a corresponding number you dial to hear a detailed narration. ✉ *501 Plaza Real, Mizner Park* ☎ *561/392–2500* ⊕ *www.bocamuseum.org* 🎟 *$14* ⊙ *Tues., Thurs., and Fri. 10–5, Wed. 10–9, weekends noon–5.*

FAMILY **Gumbo Limbo Nature Center.** A big draw for kids, this stellar spot has four huge saltwater tanks brimming with sea life, from coral to stingrays to spiny lobsters, plus a sea turtle rehabilitation center. Nocturnal walks in spring and early summer, when staffers lead a quest to find nesting female turtles coming ashore to lay eggs, are popular; so are the hatching releases in August and September. Call to purchase tickets in advance as there are very limited spaces. Gumbo Limbo is one of only a handful of centers that offer the chance to observe the babies departing into the ocean. There is also a nature trail and butterfly garden, a ¼-mile boardwalk, and a 40-foot observation tower, where you're likely to see brown pelicans and osprey. ✉ *1801 N. Ocean Blvd.* ☎ *561/544–8605*

⊕ *www.gumbolimbo.org* ✉ *Free ($5 suggested donation), turtle walks $15* ⊙ *Mon.–Sat. 9–4, Sun. noon–4.*

Old Floresta. This residential area was developed by Addison Mizner starting in 1925 and is beautifully landscaped with palms and cycads. Its houses are mainly Mediterranean in style, many with balconies supported by exposed wood columns. Explore by driving northward on Paloma Avenue (Northwest 8th Avenue) from Palmetto Park Road, then weave in and out of the side streets. ✉ *Paloma Ave. north of W. Palmetto Park Rd.*

BEACHES

Boca's three city beaches (South Beach, Red Reef Park, and Spanish River Park, south to north, respectively) are beautiful and hugely popular; but unless you're a resident or enter via bicycle, parking can be very expensive. Save your receipt if you care to go in and out, or park hop—most guards at the front gate will honor a same-day ticket from another location if you ask nicely. Another option is the county-run South Inlet Park that's walking distance from the Boca Raton Bridge Hotel at the southern end of Lake Boca; it has a metered lot for a fraction of the cost, but not quite the same charm as the others.

FAMILY   **Red Reef Park.** The ocean with its namesake reef that you can wade up to is just one draw: a fishing zone on the Intracoastal Waterway across the street, a 9-hole golf course next door, and the Gumbo Limbo Environmental Education Center at the northern end of the park can easily make a day at the beach into so much more. But if pure old-fashioned fun-in-the-sun is your focus, to that end there are tons of picnic tables and grills, and two separate playgrounds. Pack snorkels and explore the reef at high tide when fish are most abundant. Swimmers, be warned: once lifeguards leave at 5, anglers flock to the shores and stay well past dark. **Amenities:** lifeguards; parking (fee); showers; toilets. **Best for:** snorkeling; swimming; walking. ✉ *1400 N. Rte. A1A* ☎ *561/393–7974, 561/393–7989 for beach conditions* ⊕ *www.ci.boca-raton.fl.us/rec/parks/redreef.shtm* ✉ *$16 parking (weekdays), $18 parking (weekends)* ⊙ *Daily 8 am–10 pm.*

South Beach Park. Perched high up on a dune, a large open-air pavilion at the east end of Palmetto Park Road offers a panoramic view of what's in store below on the sand that stretches up the coast. Serious beachgoers need to pull into the main lot ¼ mile north on the east side of A1A, but if a short-but-sweet visit is what you're after, the 15 or so one-hour spots with meters in the circle driveway will do (and not cost you the normal $15 parking fee). During the day, pretty young things blanket the shore, and windsurfers practice tricks in the waves. Quiet quarters are farther north. **Amenities:** lifeguards; parking (fee); showers; toilets. **Best for:** sunsets; windsurfing; walking; swimming. ✉ *400 N. Rte A1A* ⊕ *www.ci.boca-raton.fl.us/rec/parks/southbeach.shtm* ✉ *$15 parking (weekdays), $17 parking (weekends)* ⊙ *Daily 8–sunset.*

Spanish River Park. At 76 acres and including extensive nature trails, this is by far one of the largest ocean parks in the southern half of Palm Beach County and a great pick for people who want more space and fewer crowds. Big groups, including family reunions, favor it because of the number of covered picnic areas for rent, but anyone can snag a free table (there are plenty!) under the thick canopy of banyan trees. Even though the vast majority of the park is separated from the surf, you never actually have to cross A1A to reach the beach, because tunnels run under it at several locations. **Amenities:** lifeguards; parking (fee); showers; toilets. **Best for:** swimming; walking; solitude. ✉ *3001 N. Rte. A1A* ☎ *561/393-7815* 🌐 *www.ci.boca-raton.fl.us/rec/parks/spanishriver.shtm* 🎟 *$16 parking (weekdays), $18 parking (weekends)* ⏲ *Daily 8–sunset.*

WHERE TO EAT

$$$$ TUSCAN Fodor's Choice ★ 🍴 **Casa D'Angelo Ristorante.** The lines are deservedly long at Chef Angelo Elia's upscale Tuscan restaurant in tony Boca Raton. The third outpost of his renowned Casa D'Angelo chain impresses with an outstanding selection of antipasti, carpaccios, pastas, and specialties from the wood-burning oven. From staples like the antipasto *angelo* (grilled vegetables and buffalo mozzarella) and linguine with white-water clams and garlic, to the ever-changing gnocchi, risotto, veal scaloppine, and fish specials of the day, Angelo's dishes deliver pure perfection in every bite. The wine list is also exceptional with hundreds of Italian and American wines to choose from. [$] *Average main: $38* ✉ *171 E. Palmetto Park Rd.* ☎ *561/996–1234* 🌐 *www.casa-d-angelo.com* ✍ *Reservations essential* ⏲ *No lunch.*

$$$ AMERICAN 🍴 **Racks Downtown Eatery & Tavern.** Whimsical indoor–outdoor décor and comfort food with a twist help define this popular eatery in tony Mizner Park. Instead of dinner rolls, pretzel bread and mustard get things started. Share plates like bacon-wrapped shrimp and sea bass lettuce cups to promote convivial social dining. Move on to creative wood-fired pizzas and burgers; there's also a sushi menu. Happy hour at the bar is 4–7 and offers half-price drinks and appetizers. [$] *Average main: $23* ✉ *402 Plaza Real, Mizner Park* ☎ *561/395–1662* 🌐 *www.racksboca.com.*

$$$$ SEAFOOD Fodor's Choice ★ 🍴 **Truluck's.** This popular Florida and Texas seafood chain is so serious about its fruits of the sea that it supports its own fleet of 16 fishing boats. Stone crabs are the signature dish, and you can have all you can eat on Monday night from October to May. Other recommended dishes include salmon topped with blue crab and shrimp, hot-and-crunchy trout, crab cakes, and blackened Florida grouper. Portions are huge, so you might want to make a meal of appetizers. And don't miss the warm carrot cake—it's heaven on a plate! The place comes alive each night with its popular piano bar. [$] *Average main: $35* ✉ *351 Plaza Real, Mizner Park* ☎ *561/391–0755* 🌐 *www.trulucks.com.*

$$$ CHINESE 🍴 **Uncle Tai's.** The draw at this upscale eatery is some of the best Hunan cuisine on Florida's east coast. Specialties include sliced duck with snow peas and water chestnuts in a tangy plum sauce, and orange beef delight—flank steak stir-fried until crispy and then sautéed with pepper sauce, garlic, and orange peel. They'll go easy on the heat on request. The service is quietly efficient. The early-bird crowd will appreciate the very filling Sunset Dinner specials (5–6:15 pm), which come with a

6

starter, a dessert, and a main dish. $ *Average main: $21* ⊠ *5250 Town Center Circle* ☎ *561/368–8806* ⊕ *www.uncletais.com.*

WHERE TO STAY

$$$
RESORT
FAMILY
Fodor'sChoice
★

⛱ **Boca Beach Club.** Dotted with turquoise lounge chairs, ruffled umbrellas, and white-sand beaches, this newly reconceived and rebranded hotel is now part of the Waldorf-Astoria collection and looks as if it was carefully replicated from a retro-chic postcard. **Pros:** great location on the beach; kids' activity center. **Cons:** pricey; shuttle ride away from the main building. $ *Rooms from: $399* ⊠ *900 S. Ocean Blvd.* ☎ *888/564–1312* ⊕ *www.bocabeachclub.com* ⟿ *212 rooms* ⦿ *No meals.*

$$
RESORT
FAMILY
Fodor'sChoice
★

⛱ **Boca Raton Resort & Club.** Addison Mizner built this Mediterranean-style hotel in 1926, and additions over time have created a sprawling, sparkling resort, one of the most luxurious in all of South Florida and part of the Waldorf-Astoria collection. **Pros:** super-exclusive—grounds are closed to the public; décor strikes the right balance between historic roots and modern comforts; plenty of activities. **Cons:** daily resort charge; conventions often crowd common areas. $ *Rooms from: $249* ⊠ *501 E. Camino Real* ☎ *561/447–3000, 888/543–1277* ⊕ *www.bocaresort.com* ⟿ *635 rooms* ⦿ *No meals.*

NIGHTLIFE

Fodor'sChoice
★

Rustic Cellar. Warm and intimate, this dark cozy nook is modeled after a Napa Valley tasting room and is perhaps the best wine bar in Palm Beach County. More than 300 hand-selected vintages, most from top domestic and foreign vintners, are served—and nearly all are available by the glass. There's also an impressive collection of craft beers. ⊠ *Royal Palm Place, 409 S.E. Mizner Blvd.* ☎ *561/392–5237* ⊕ *www.rusticcellar.com.*

SHOPPING

Mizner Park. This distinctive 30-acre shopping center off Federal Highway, one block north of Palmetto Park Road, intersperses apartments and town houses among its gardenlike commercial areas. Some three dozen national and local retailers line the central axis that's peppered with fountains and green space, restaurants, galleries, a movie theater, the Boca Raton Museum of Art, and an amphitheater that hosts major concerts as well as community events. ⊠ *327 Plaza Real* ☎ *561/362–0606* ⊕ *www.miznerpark.com.*

Royal Palm Place. The retail enclave of Royal Palm is filled with independent boutiques selling fine jewelry and apparel. By day, stroll the walkable streets and have your pick of sidewalk cafés for lunch alongside Boca's ladies who lunch. Royal Palm Place assumes a different personality come nightfall, as its numerous restaurants and lounges attract throngs of patrons for great dining and fabulous libations. ⊠ *101 Plaza Real S* ☎ *561/392–8920* ⊕ *www.royalpalmplace.com.*

Town Center at Boca Raton. Over on the west side of Boca, this indoor megamall has over 220 stores, with anchor stores including Saks and

Neiman Marcus and just about every major high-end designer, including Bulgari and Anne Fontaine. But not every shop here requires deep pockets. The Town Center at Boca Raton is also firmly rooted with a variety of more affordable national brands like Gap and Guess. ✉ *6000 Glades Rd.* ☎ *561/368–6000* ⊕ *www.simon.com/mall/ town-center-at-boca-raton.*

SPORTS AND THE OUTDOORS

GOLF

Red Reef Park Executive Golf Course. This executive golf course offers 9 holes with varying views of the Intracoastal and the Atlantic Ocean. The Joe Palloka and Charles Ankrom designed course dates back to 1957. It was refreshed in 2001 through a multimillion-dollar renovation. The scenic holes are between 54 and 227 yards each—great for a quick round. The greens fees range from $16.25 to walk in the off-season to $25.75 with a cart in season. Park in the lot across the street from the main beach entrance, and put the greens-fees receipt on the dash; that covers parking. ✉ *1221 N. Ocean Blvd.* ☎ *561/391–5014* ⊕ *www. bocacitygolf.com* ✏ *$25.75 for 9 holes* ⛳ *9 holes. 1357 yards. par 32.*

SCUBA AND SNORKELING

Force-E. This company rents, sells, and repairs scuba and snorkeling equipment—and organizes about 80 dive trips a week throughout the region. The PADI-affiliated five-star center has instruction for all levels and offers private charters, too. They have two other outposts besides this Boca Raton location—one north in Riviera Beach and one south in Pompano Beach. ✉ *2181 N. Federal Hwy.* ☎ *561/368–0555, 866/307– 3483* ⊕ *www.force-e.com.*

TREASURE COAST

In contrast to the glitzy, überplanned Gold Coast that includes Greater Palm Beach and Boca Raton, the more bucolic Treasure Coast stretches from northernmost Palm Beach County into Martin, St. Lucie, and Indian River counties. Along the east are barrier islands all the way to Sebastian and beyond, starting with Jupiter Island, then Hutchinson Island, and finally Orchid Island—and reefs, too. Those reefs are responsible for the region's nickname: they've caused ships carrying riches dating back as far as 1715 to fall asunder and cast their treasures ashore. The Intracoastal Waterway here is called the Indian River starting at the St. Lucie Inlet in Stuart and morphs into a broad tidal lagoon with tiny uninhabited islands and wildlife galore. Inland, there's cattle ranching and tracts of pine and palmetto scrub, along with sugar and citrus production.

Despite a growing number of malls and beachfront condominiums, much of the Treasure Coast remains untouched, something not lost on ecotourists, game fishers, and people who want a break from the over-saturated digital age. Consequently, there are fewer lodging options in this region of Florida, but if 30 minutes in the car sounds like a breeze, culture vultures can live in the lap of luxury in Vero Beach and

6

detour south to Fort Pierce's galleries and botanical gardens. Likewise, families will revel in every amenity imaginable at the Hutchinson Island Marriott and be able to swing northwest to hit up the Mets spring-training stadium in Port St. Lucie or down to Jupiter for the Cardinals and the Marlins.

JUPITER AND VICINITY

12 miles north of West Palm Beach.

Jupiter is one of the few towns in the region not fronted by an island, and it's still quite close to the fantastic hotels, shopping, and dining of the Palm Beach area. The beaches here are on the mainland, and Route A1A runs for almost 4 miles along the beachfront dunes and beautiful homes.

Northeast across the Jupiter Inlet from Jupiter is the southern tip of Jupiter Island, which stretches about 15 miles to the St. Lucie Inlet. Here expansive and expensive estates often retreat from the road behind screens of vegetation, and the population dwindles the farther north you go. At the very north end, sea turtles come to nest. To the west, on the mainland, is the little community of Hobe Sound.

GETTING HERE AND AROUND

If you're coming from the airport in West Palm Beach, take I–95 to Route 706. Otherwise, Federal Highway (U.S. 1) and Route A1A are usually more convenient.

Contacts Palm Beach County Convention and Visitors Bureau ⊠ *1555 Palm Beach Lakes Blvd., Ste. 800, West Palm Beach* ☎ *561/233–3000* ⊕ *www. palmbeachfl.com.*

EXPLORING

Fodor's Choice
★

Blowing Rocks Preserve. Managed by the Nature Conservancy, this protected area on Jupiter Island is headlined by an almost otherworldly-looking limestone shelf that fringes South Florida's most turquoise waters. Also protected within its 73 acres are plants native to beachfront dunes, coastal strand (the landward side of the dunes), mangrove swamps, and tropical hardwood forests. There are two short walking trails on the Intracoastal side of the preserve, as well as an education center and a butterfly garden. The best time to come and seeing the "blowing rocks" is when a storm is brewing: If high tides and strong offshore winds coincide, the sea blows spectacularly through the holes in the eroded outcropping. During a calm summer day, you can swim in crystal clear waters on the mile-long beach and climb around the rock formations at low tide. Park in one of the two lots because police ticket cars on the road. ⊠ *574 S. Beach Rd., CR 707, Hobe Sound* ☎ *561/744–6668* ⊕ *www.nature.org/blowingrocks* ⊒ *$2* ⊙ *Daily 9–4:30.*

FAMILY
Fodor's Choice
★

Hobe Sound Nature Center. Though located in the Hobe Sound National Wildlife Refuge, this nature center is an independent organization. The exhibit hall houses live baby alligators, crocodiles, a scary looking tarantula, and more—and is a child's delight. ■TIP→ Among the center's more popular events are the annual nighttime sea turtle walks, held between May and June; reservations are accepted as early as April

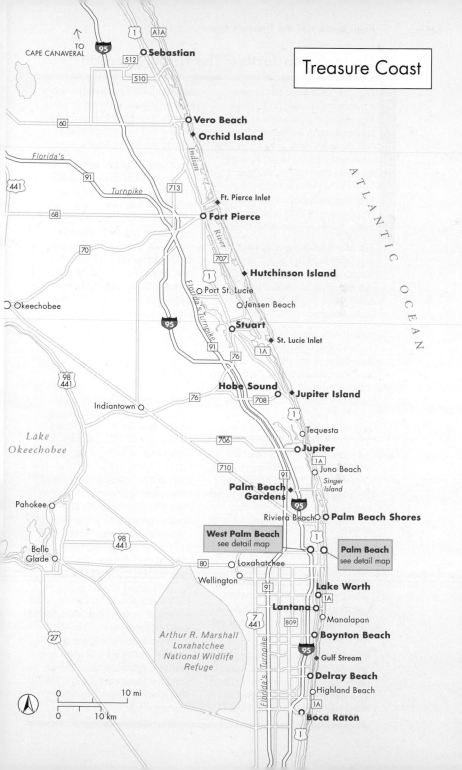

Treasure Coast

TO CAPE CANAVERAL

95
1 A1A
Sebastian
512
510

60
Vero Beach
Orchid Island

Florida's

441
91
Turnpike

713

68

Ft. Pierce Inlet
Fort Pierce

70

707

1
Hutchinson Island
Port St. Lucie
Jensen Beach

Florida's Turnpike

95
Stuart

Okeechobee

76
91
1A
St. Lucie Inlet

98
441

76

Hobe Sound
708
Jupiter Island

Indiantown

706
Tequesta

710
91
Jupiter
1A
Juno Beach
Singer Island

Palm Beach Gardens
95

Pahokee

Riviera Beach
Palm Beach Shores

Belle Glade

98
441

West Palm Beach
see detail map

1
Palm Beach
see detail map

80
Loxahatchee

Wellington

91
Lake Worth
1A

7
441
Lantana
809
Manalapan

27

Arthur R. Marshall
Loxahatchee
National Wildlife
Refuge

Boynton Beach

95
Gulf Stream

Delray Beach
Highland Beach
1A

Boca Raton
1

Lake Okeechobee

ATLANTIC OCEAN

Indian River

0   10 mi
0   10 km

Florida's Sea Turtles: The Nesting Season

From May to October, turtles nest all along the Florida coast. Female loggerhead, Kemp's ridley, and other species living in the Atlantic Ocean or Gulf of Mexico swim as much as 2,000 miles to the Florida shore. By night they drag their 100- to 400-pound bodies onto the beach to the dune line. Then each digs a hole with her flippers, drops in 100 or so eggs, covers them up, and returns to sea.

The babies hatch about 60 days later. Once they burst out of the sand, the hatchlings must get to sea rapidly or risk becoming dehydrated from the sun or being caught by crabs, birds, or other predators.

Instinctively, baby turtles head toward bright light, probably because for millions of years starlight or moonlight reflected on the waves was the brightest light around, serving to guide hatchlings to water. But now light from beach development can lead the babies in the wrong direction, toward the street rather than the water. To help, many coastal towns enforce light restrictions during nesting months. Florida homeowners are asked to dim their lights on behalf of baby sea turtles.

At night, volunteers walk the beaches, searching for signs of turtle nests. Upon finding telltale scratches in the sand, they cordon off the sites, so beachgoers will leave the spots undisturbed. Volunteers also keep watch over nests when babies are about to hatch, and assist if the hatchlings get disoriented.

It's a hazardous world for baby turtles. They can die after eating tar balls or plastic debris, or they can be gobbled by sharks or circling birds. Only about one in a thousand survives to adulthood. After reaching the water, the babies make their way to warm currents. East Coast hatchlings drift into the Gulf Stream, spending years floating around the Atlantic.

Males never return to land, but when females attain maturity, in 15–20 years, they return to shore to lay eggs. Remarkably, even after migrating hundreds and even thousands of miles out at sea, most return to the very beach where they were born to deposit their eggs. Each time they nest, they come back to the same stretch of beach. In fact, the more they nest, the more accurate they get, until eventually they return time and again to within a few feet of where they last laid their eggs. These incredible navigation skills remain for the most part a mystery despite intense scientific study.

Several local organizations offer nightly turtle walks during nesting season. Most are in June and July, starting around 8 pm and sometimes lasting until midnight. Expect a $10 to $15 fee. Call in advance to confirm times and to reserve a spot—places usually take reservations as early as April. If you're in southern Palm Beach County, contact Boca Raton's **Gumbo Limbo Nature Center** (☎ 561/338–1473 ⊕ www.gumbolimbo.org). The **John D. MacArthur Beach State Park** (☎ 561/624–6952 ⊕ www.macarthurbeach.org) is convenient for Palm Beach–area visitors at the northern end of Singer Island. **Hobe Sound Nature Center** (☎ 772/546–2067 ⊕ www.hobesoundnaturecenter.com) is farther up. Treasure Coasters in or near Vero Beach can go to **Sebastian Inlet State Park** (☎ 321/984–4852 ⊕ www.floridastateparks.org/sebastianinlet).

Away from developed shorelines, Blowing Rocks Preserve on Jupiter Island lets you wander the dunes.

1. Just off the center's entrance is a mile-long nature trail loop that snakes through three different kinds of habitats: coastal hammock, estuary beach, and sand pine scrub, which is one of Florida's most unusual and endangered plant communities and what composes much of the refuge's nearly 250 acres. ✉ *13640 S.E. U.S. 1, Hobe Sound* ☎ *772/546–2067* ⊕ *www.hobesoundnaturecenter.com* ✉ *Free (donation requested)* ⊗ *Mon.–Sat. 9–3.*

Jonathan Dickinson State Park. This serene state park provides a glimpse of pre-development "real" Florida. A beautiful showcase of Florida inland habitat, the park teems with endangered gopher tortoises and manatees. From Hobe Mountain, an ancient dune topped with a tower, you are treated to a panoramic view of this park's more than 11,000 acres of varied terrain and the Intracoastal Waterway. The Loxahatchee River, which cuts through the park, is home to plenty of charismatic manatees in winter and alligators year-round; two-hour boat tours of the river depart daily *(⇨ see Jonathan Dickinson State Park River Tours).* Kayak rentals are available, as is horseback riding (it was reintroduced after a 30-year absence). Among the amenities are a dozen newly redone cabins for rent, tent sites, bicycle and hiking trails, two established campgrounds and some primitive campgrounds, and a snack bar. Don't skip the Elsa Kimbell Environmental Education and Research Center, which has interactive displays, exhibits, and a short film on the natural history of the area. The park is also a fantastic birding location, with about 150 species to spot. ✉ *16450 S.E. U.S. 1, Hobe Sound* ☎ *772/546–2771* ⊕ *www.floridastateparks.org/jonathandickinson* ✉ *Vehicles $6,* *bicyclists and pedestrians $2 ☉ Daily 8–sunset, Elsa Kimbell Environmental Education and Research Center daily 9–5.*

Fodor's Choice ★ **Jupiter Inlet Lighthouse & Museum.** Designed by Civil War hero Lieutenant George Gordon Meade, this brick lighthouse has been under the Coast Guard's purview since 1860. Tours of the 108-foot-tall landmark are held approximately every half-hour and are included with admission. (Children must be at least 4 feet tall to go to the top.) The museum tells about efforts to restore this graceful spire to the way it looked from 1860 to 1918; its galleries and outdoor structures, including a pioneer home, also showcase local history dating back five thousand years. ⊠ *Lighthouse Park, 500 Capt. Armour's Way* 🕾 *561/747–8380* ⊕ *www.jupiterlighthouse.org* 🖼 *$9 ☉ Jan.–Apr., daily 10–5; May–Dec., Tues.–Sun. 10–5. Last tour at 4.*

BEACHES

Carlin Park. About ½ mile south of the Jupiter Beach Resort and Indiantown Road, the quiet beach here is just one draw; otherwise, the manicured park, which straddles A1A, is chock-full of activities and amenities. Two bocce ball courts, six lighted tennis courts, a baseball diamond, a wood-chip-lined running path, and an amphitheater that hosts free concerts and Shakespeare productions are just some of the highlights. Locals also swear by the Lazy Loggerhead Café that's right off the seaside parking lot for a great casual breakfast and lunch. **Amenities:** lifeguards; food and drink; parking (no fee); showers; toilets. **Best for:** swimming; walking. ⊠ *400 S. Rte. A1A* ⊕ *www.pbcgov.com/ parks/locations/carlin.htm.*

Hobe Sound National Wildlife Refuge. Nature lovers seeking to get as far as possible from the madding crowds will feel at peace at this refuge managed by the U.S. Fish & Wildlife service. It's a haven for people who want some quiet while they walk around and photograph the gorgeous coastal sand dunes, where turtle nests and shells often wash ashore. The beach has been severely eroded by high tides and strong winds (surprisingly, surfing is allowed and many do partake). You can't actually venture within most of the 735 protected acres, so if hiking piques your interest, head to the refuge's main entrance a few miles away on Hobe Sound (⊠ *13640 S.E. U.S. 1 in Hobe Sound*) for a mile-long trek close to the nature center, or to nearby Jonathan Dickinson State Park (⊠ *16450 S.E. U.S. 1 in Hobe Sound*). **Amenities:** parking (fee); toilets. **Best for:** solitude; surfing; walking. ⊠ *198 N. Beach Rd., at end of N. Beach Rd., Jupiter Island* 🕾 *772/546–6141* ⊕ *www.fws. gov/hobesound* 🖼 *$5.*

Fodor's Choice ★ **Jupiter Beach.** Famous throughout all of Florida for a unique pooch-loving stance, the town of Jupiter's beach welcomes Yorkies, Labs, pugs—you name it—along its 2½-mile oceanfront. Dogs can frolic unleashed or join you for a dip. Free parking spots line A1A in front of the sandy stretch, and there are multiple access points and continuously refilled dog-bag boxes (29 to be exact). The dog beach starts on Marcinski Road (Beach Marker #25) and continues north until Beach Marker #5. Before going, read through the guidelines posted on the Friends of Jupiter Beach website; the biggest things to note are be sure to clean up after your dog and to steer clear of lifeguarded areas to the north and south. **Amenities:** showers; toilets. **Best for:** walking. ✉ *2188 Marcinski Rd., across the street from the parking lot* ☎ *561/748–8140* 🌐 *www.friendsofjupiterbeach.com.*

WHERE TO EAT

$$ SEAFOOD 🍴 **Guanabanas.** Expect a wait for dinner, which is not necessarily a bad thing at this island paradise of a waterfront restaurant and bar. Take the wait time to explore the bridges and trails of the open-air tropical oasis and nibble on some conch fritters at the large tiki bar until your table is ready. Try the lemon-butter hogfish for dinner and stick around for the live music (a full concert calendar is on the website). Breakfast, offered only on weekends, is good, too. That said, it's more about the view than the food here. [$] *Average main: $18* ✉ *960 N. Rte. A1A* ☎ *561/747–8878* 🌐 *www.guanabanas.com* ✍ *Reservations not accepted.*

$$ SEAFOOD 🍴 **Little Moir's Food Shack.** This local favorite is not much to look at and a bit tricky to find, but well worth the search. The fried-food standards you might expect at such a casual place that uses plastic utensils are not found on the menu; instead there are fried tuna rolls with basil, and panko-crusted fried oysters with spicy fruit salad. A variety of beers are fun to pair with the creatively prepared seafood dishes that include wahoo, mahimahi, and snapper. [$] *Average main: $17* ✉ *103 S. U.S. 1* ☎ *561/741–3626* 🌐 *www.littlemoirs.com/food-shack* ✍ *Reservations not accepted* 🕓 *Closed Sun.*

$$$$ SEAFOOD 🍴 **Sinclair's Ocean Grill.** Remodeled in late 2012 to give it a slick, contemporary look, this upscale restaurant at the Jupiter Beach Resort & Spa is a favorite of locals in the know. The menu has a daily selection of fresh fish, such as Atlantic black grouper over lemon crab salad, sesame-seared tuna, and mahimahi with fruit salsa. There are also thick, juicy cuts of meat, including New York strip steak and beef tenderloin, as well as mouth-watering chicken and lamb dishes. The new Sinclair's Lounge is idyllic for a pre-dinner aperitif. For something more casual, dine outside on the terrace to hear the waves lapping and take in the beachscape. [$] *Average main: $31* ✉ *Jupiter Beach Resort, 5 N. Rte. A1A* ☎ *561/746–2511* 🌐 *www.jupiterbeachresort.com.*

$$ AMERICAN 🍴 **Taste Casual Dining.** Located in the center of historic Hobe Sound, this cozy dining spot with a pleasant, screened-in patio offers piano dinner music on Fridays. Locals like to hang out at the old, English-style wine bar; however, the food itself is the biggest draw here. Try a lobster roll and the signature Gorgonzola salad for lunch, and any fish dish for dinner. On weekend nights, order the excellent, slow-cooked prime rib, another specialty. [$] *Average main: $18* ✉ *11750 S.E. Dixie Hwy., Hobe Sound* ☎ *772/546–1129* 🌐 *www.tastehobesound.com* 🕓 *Closed Sun. May–Oct.*

WHERE TO STAY

$$$ RESORT FAMILY Fodor's Choice ★ 🏨 **Jupiter Beach Resort & Spa.** Families love this nine-story hotel filled with rich Caribbean-style rooms containing mahogany sleigh beds and armoires. All rooms have balconies, and many have stunning views of the ocean and local landmarks like the Jupiter Lighthouse and Juno Pier. **Pros:** fantastic beachside pool area with hammocks and a fire

6

pit; marble showers; great restaurant. **Cons:** $25 nightly resort fee; no covered parking; bathttubs only in suites. [$] *Rooms from: $360* ✉ *5 N. Rte. A1A* ☎ *561/746–2511, 800/228–8810* 🌐 *www.jupiterbeachresort.com* 🛏 *134 rooms, 34 suites* 🍴 *No meals.*

SPORTS AND THE OUTDOORS

BASEBALL

Roger Dean Stadium. It's a spring training doubleheader! Both the St. Louis Cardinals and the Miami Marlins call this 6,600-seat facility home base from February to April. The rest of the year two minor league teams (Jupiter Hammerheads and Palm Beach Cardinals) share its turf. In the Abacoa area of Jupiter, the grounds are surrounded by a mix of restaurants and sports bars for pre- and postgame action. ✉ *4751 Main St.* ☎ *561/775–1818* 🌐 *www.rogerdeanstadium.com.*

BOATING AND CANOEING

Fodor's Choice ★ **Canoe Outfitters of Florida.** See animals from otters to eagles along 8 miles of the Loxahatchee River in Riverbend County Park daily except Tuesday and Wednesday. Canoe and kayak rentals are $26.50 for four hours. Bike rentals are available, too. ✉ *Riverbend County Park, 9060 W. Indiantown Rd.* ☎ *561/746–7053* 🌐 *www.canoeoutfittersofflorida.com* 🕓 *Closed Tues. and Wed.*

FAMILY Fodor's Choice ★ **Jonathan Dickinson State Park River Tours.** Boat tours of the Loxahatchee River and guided horseback rides, along with canoe, kayak, bicycle, and boat rentals are offered daily. The popular Wilderness Guided Boat Tour leaves four times daily at 9, 11, 1, and 3 pm and costs $18.87 (for best wildlife photos take the 11 or 1 tour). The pontoon cruises up the Loxahatchee in search of manatees, herons, osprey, alligators, and more. The skipper details the region's natural and cultural history; and from Thursday to Monday the boat also stops at the Trapper Nelson Interpretive Site for a tour of the home of a local legend, the so-called "Wildman" of the Loxahatchee. ✉ *Jonathan Dickinson State Park, 16450 S.E. U.S. 1, Hobe Sound* ☎ *561/746–1466* 🌐 *www.floridaparktours.com.*

GOLF

Abacoa Golf Club. Built in 1999, the tag line for this Joe Lee–designed 18-hole course in Jupiter is "public golf at its finest." Most of the courses in this golfing community are private, but the range at Abacoa is on par with them and membership (nor deep pockets) *isn't* required. One of the course's more interesting features includes the several elevation changes throughout, which is a rarity in flat Florida. The course caters to golfers at all skill levels. The greens fees range from $30 to $99 (including cart), depending on time of year, time of day, and weekday versus weekend. ✉ *105 Barbados Dr.* ☎ *561/622–0036* 🌐 *www.abacoagolfclub.com* 🎫 *$89 for 18 holes* ⛳ *18 holes. 7200 yards. par 72.*

Golf Club of Jupiter. Locally owned and operated since 1981, this Lamar Smith–designed golf club features a public, championship golf course—the "Jupiter" course—with 18 holes of varying difficulty. It has a course rating of 69.9 and a slope rating of 117 on Bermuda grass. There's a full-time golf pro on staff and an on-site bar and restaurant. ✉ *1800 S.*

Central Blvd. ☎ *561/747–6262* ⊕ *www.golfclubofjupiter.com* ▭ *$70 for 18 holes.* 🏌 *18 holes. 6275 yards. par 70.*

STUART AND JENSEN BEACH

10 miles north of Hobe Sound.

The compact town of Stuart lies on a peninsula that juts out into the St. Lucie River off the Indian River and has a remarkable amount of shoreline for its size. It scores huge points for its charming historic district and is the self-described "Sailfish Capital of the World." On the southern end, you'll find Port Salerno and its waterfront area, the Manatee Pocket, which are a skip away from the St. Lucie Inlet.

Immediately north of Stuart is down-to-earth Jensen Beach. Both Stuart and Jensen Beach straddle the Indian River and occupy Hutchinson Island, the barrier island that continues into the town of Fort Pierce. Between late April and August, hundreds, even thousands, of turtles come here to nest along the Atlantic beaches. Residents have taken pains to curb the runaway development that has created commercial crowding to the north and south, although some high-rises have popped up along the shore.

GETTING HERE AND AROUND

To get to Stuart and Jensen Beach from Jupiter and Hobe Sound, drive north on Federal Highway (U.S. 1). Route A1A crosses through downtown Stuart and is the sole main road throughout Hutchinson Island. Route 707 runs parallel on the mainland directly across the tidal lagoon.

ESSENTIALS

Visitor Information Martin County Convention & Visitors Bureau
☎ *772/288–5451, 877/585–0085* ⊕ *www.discovermartin.com.*

EXPLORING

Strict architectural and zoning standards guide civic-renewal projects in the heart of Stuart. Antiques stores, restaurants, and more than 50 specialty shops are rooted within the two-block area of Flagler Avenue and Osceola Street north of where A1A cuts across the peninsula (visit ⊕ *www.stuartmainstreet.org* for more information). A self-guided walking-tour pamphlet is available at assorted locations to clue you in on this once-small fishing village's early days.

Elliott Museum. Opened in March 2013, the museum's glittering, green-certified 48,000-square-foot facility is double its previous size and houses a permanent collection along with traveling exhibits pertaining to art, history, and technology. The original museum was founded in 1961 in honor of Sterling Elliott, an inventor of an early automated-addressing machine, the egg crate, and a four-wheel bicycle, and it celebrates history, art, and technology, much of it viewed through the lens of the automobile's effect on American society. There's an impressive array of antique cars, plus paintings, historic artifacts, and nostalgic goods like vintage baseball cards and toys. ✉ *825 N.E. Ocean Blvd., Jensen Beach* ☎ *772/225–1961* ⊕ *www.elliottmuseumfl.org* ▭ *$12* ⊗ *Daily. 10–5.*

FAMILY **Florida Oceanographic Coastal Center.** This hydroland is the place to go for an interactive marine experience and to live the center's mission "to inspire environmental stewardship of Florida's coastal ecosystems through education and research." Petting and feeding stingrays can be done at various times; in the morning, a sea turtle program introduces you to three full-time residents. Make sure to catch the "feeding frenzy" when keepers toss food into the 750,000-gallon lagoon tank and sharks, tarpon, and snook swarm the surface. Join a 1-mile guided walk through the coastal hardwood hammock and mangrove swamp habitats, or explore the trails on your own—you may see a dolphin or manatee swim by. ✉ *890 N.E. Ocean Blvd.* ☎ *772/225–0505* 🌐 *www.floridaocean.org* 🎟 *$12* 🕒 *Mon.–Sat. 10–5, Sun. noon–4. Nature trails close at 4.*

Gilbert's House of Refuge Museum. Built in 1875 on Hutchinson Island, this is the only remaining example of ten such structures that were erected by the U.S. Life-Saving Service (a predecessor of the Coast Guard) to aid stranded sailors. The displays here include antique lifesaving equipment, maps, artifacts from nearby wrecks, and boatbuilding tools. The museum is affiliated with the nearby Elliott Museum. ✉ *301 S.E. MacArthur Blvd., Jensen Beach* ☎ *772/225–1875* 🌐 *www.houseofrefugefl.org* 🎟 *$8* 🕒 *Mon.–Sat. 10–4, Sun. 1–4.*

BEACHES

FAMILY **Stuart Beach.** When the waves robustly roll in, the surfers are rolling in, too. Beginning surfers are especially keen on Stuart Beach because of its ever-vigilant lifeguards, and pros to the sport like the challenges that the choppy waters here bring. Families enjoy the snack bar known for its chicken fingers, the basketball courts, the large canopy-covered playground, and the three walkways interspersed throughout the area for easy ocean access. **Amenities:** lifeguards; food and drink; parking (no fee); showers; toilets. **Best for:** surfing; swimming. ✉ *889 N.E. Ocean Blvd.* 🕒 *Daily 24 hrs.*

WHERE TO EAT

$$$ SEAFOOD 🍴 **Conchy Joe's.** Like a hermit crab sliding into a new shell, Conchy Joe's moved up from West Palm Beach in 1983 to its current home, a 1920s rustic stilt house on the Indian River. It's full of antique fish mounts, gator hides, and snakeskins and is a popular tourist spot—but the waterfront location, casual vibe, and delicious seafood lures locals, too. Grouper marsala (the house specialty), coconut shrimp, and fried Bahamian cracked conch are menu fixtures, and live reggae gets people out of their shells Thursday through Sunday. [$] *Average main: $27* ✉ *3945 N.E. Indian River Dr., Jensen Beach* ☎ *772/334–1130* 🌐 *www.conchyjoes.com.*

$$$ FRENCH 🍴 **Courtine's.** A husband-and-wife team oversees this quiet and hospitable restaurant under the Roosevelt Bridge. French and American influences are clear in the Swiss chef's dishes, from rack of lamb with Dijon mustard to grilled filet mignon stuffed with Roquefort and fresh spinach. The formal dining room has subtle, elegant touches, such as votive candlelight and white tablecloths. A more casual menu is available at

the bar. $ *Average main: $25* ✉ *514 N. Dixie Hwy.* ☎ *772/692–3662* ⊕ *www.courtines.com* ⊙ *Closed Sun. and Mon. No lunch.*

$$$$
ECLECTIC
✕ **11 Maple Street.** This cozy spot is as good as it gets on the Treasure Coast. Soft music and a friendly staff set the mood in the antiques-filled dining room, which holds only 21 tables. An extensive list of small plates can be ordered as starters or mains and include tasty treats like black-rice-and-calamari fritters with Thai sauce and Wagyu hanger steak with onion rings and salsa verde. The limited but superb selection of entrées include wood-grilled elk with roasted faro and Wagyu ribeye with port wine. All desserts are made from scratch and are also seductive, including white-chocolate custard with blackberry sauce. $ *Average main: $42* ✉ *3224 N.E. Maple Ave., Jensen Beach* ☎ *772/334–7714* ⊕ *www.elevenmaple.com* ⚏ *Reservations essential* ⊙ *Closed Sun. and Mon. No lunch.*

WHERE TO STAY

$
RESORT
FAMILY
🏨 **Hutchinson Island Marriott Beach Resort & Marina.** With a 77-slip marina, a full water sports program, a golf course, tons of tennis courts, and children's activities, this self-contained resort is excellent for families, most of whom prefer to stay in the tower directly on the ocean. **Pros:** attentive, warm staff; rooms are comfortable and casually chic; all rooms have balconies. **Cons:** only one sit-down indoor restaurant; common areas are a bit dated; no spa; extra charge for parking. $ *Rooms from: $189* ✉ *555 N.E. Ocean Blvd., Hutchinson Island* ☎ *772/225–3700, 800/775–5936* ⊕ *www.marriott.com* ↰ *204 rooms, 70 suites* ⍟ *No meals.*

$
RESORT
🏨 **Pirate's Cove Resort & Marina.** This cozy enclave on the banks of the Manatee Pocket with ocean access at the southern end of Stuart is the perfect place to set forth on a day at sea or wind down after one—it's relaxing and casual, and has amenities like a swimming pool courtyard, restaurant, and fitness center. **Pros:** spacious tropical-themed rooms; great for boaters, with a 50-slip full-service marina; each room has a balcony overlooking the water; free Wi-Fi and parking. **Cons:** lounge gets noisy at night; décor and furnishings are pretty but not luxurious; pool is on the small side. $ *Rooms from: $150* ✉ *4307 S.E. Bayview St., Port Salerno* ☎ *772/287–2500* ⊕ *www.piratescoveresort.com* ↰ *50 rooms* ⍟ *No meals.*

SHOPPING

More than 60 restaurants and shops with antiques, art, and fashion have opened downtown along Osceola Street.

B&A Flea Market. A short drive from downtown and operating for more than two decades, the oldest and largest flea market on the Treasure Coast has a street-bazaar feel, with shoppers happily scouting the 500 vendors for the practical and unusual. If you have an open mind and love to shop garage sales, you'll do just fine here. ✉ *2885 S.E. U.S. 1* ☎ *772/288–4915* ⊕ *www.bafleamarket.com* ▱ *Free* ⊙ *Weekends 8–3.*

6

SPORTS AND THE OUTDOORS
FISHING
Sailfish Marina of Stuart. Nab a deep-sea charter here, the closest public marina to the St. Lucie Inlet. ⊠ *3565 S.E. St. Lucie Blvd.* ☎ *772/283–1122* ⊕ *www.sailfishmarinastuart.com.*

FORT PIERCE AND PORT ST. LUCIE

11 miles north of Jensen Beach.

About an hour north of Palm Beach, Fort Pierce has a distinctive rural feel—but it has a surprising number of worthwhile attractions for a town of its size, including those easily seen while following Route 707 on the mainland (A1A on Hutchinson Island). A big draw is an inlet that offers fabulous fishing and excellent surfing. Nearby Port St. Lucie is largely landlocked southwest of Fort Pierce and is almost equidistant from there and Jensen Beach. It's not a big tourist area except for two sports facilities near I–95: the St. Lucie Mets' training grounds, Tradition Field, and the PGA Village. If you want a hotel directly on the sand or crave more than simple, motel-like accommodations, stay elsewhere and drive up for the day.

GETTING HERE AND AROUND
You can reach Fort Pierce from Jensen Beach by driving 11 miles north on Federal Highway (U.S. 1), Route 707, or Route A1A. To get to Port St. Lucie, continue north on U.S. 1 and take Prima Vista Boulevard west. From Fort Pierce, Route 709 goes diagonally southwest to Port St. Lucie, and I–95 is another choice.

ESSENTIALS
Visitor Information St. Lucie County Tourist Development Council ⊠ 2300 Virginia Ave. ☎ 800/344-8443 ⊕ www.visitstluciefla.com.

EXPLORING
Heathcote Botanical Gardens. Stroll through this 3½-acre green space, which includes a palm walk, a Japanese garden, and a collection of 100 bonsai trees. There is also a gift shop with whimsical and botanical knickknacks. Guided tours are available by appointment for an extra fee. ⊠ *210 Savannah Rd.* ☎ *772/464–0323* ⊕ *www. heathcotebotanicalgardens.org* ▨ *$6* ⊙ *Nov.–Apr., Tues.–Sat. 9–5; May–Oct., Tues.–Sat. 9–5, Sun. 1–5.*

National Navy UDT-SEAL Museum. Commemorating the more than 3,000 troops who trained on these shores during World War II when this elite military unit got its start, there are weapons, vehicles, and equipment on view. Exhibits honor all frogmen and underwater demolition teams and depict their history. The museum houses the lifeboat from which SEALs saved the *Maersk Alabama* captain from Somali pirates in 2009. ⊠ *3300 N. Rte. A1A* ☎ *772/595–5845* ⊕ *www.navysealmuseum.com* ▨ *$8* ⊙ *Tues.–Sat. 10–4, Sun. noon–4.*

FAMILY **Savannas Recreation Area.** Once a reservoir, the 550 acres have been returned to their natural wetlands state. Today the wilderness area has trails and a boat ramp, and the recreation area is open year-round. Canoe and kayak rentals are available Thursday through Monday.

✉ 1400 E. Midway Rd. ☎ 772/464–7855 🌐 www.stlucieco.gov/parks/savannas.htm 🎟 Free ⏲ Daily 6 am–7:30 pm.

BEACHES

Fort Pierce Inlet State Park. Across the inlet at the northern side of Hutchinson Island, a fishing oasis lures beachgoers who can't wait to reel in snook, flounder, and bluefish, among others. The park is also known as a prime wave-riding locale, thanks to a reef that lies just outside the jetty. Summer is the busiest season by a long shot, but don't be fooled: it's a laid-back place to sun and surf. There are covered picnic tables but no concessions; however, from where anglers perch, a bunch of casual restaurants can be spotted on the other side of the inlet that are a quick drive away. Note that the area of Jack Island Preserve has been closed indefinitely. **Amenities:** lifeguards (summer only); parking (fee); showers; toilets. **Best for:** surfing; walking; solitude. *✉ 905 Shorewinds Dr. ☎ 772/468–3985 🌐 www.floridastateparks.org/fortpierceinlet 🎟 Vehicle $6, bicyclists and pedestrians $2 ⏲ Daily 8–sunset.*

WHERE TO STAY

$ HOTEL 🏨 **Dockside Inn.** This hotel is the best of the lodgings lining the scenic Fort Pierce Inlet on Seaway Drive (and that's not saying much). It's a practical base for fishing enthusiasts with nice touches like two pools and a waterfront restaurant. **Pros:** good value; overnight boat docking available; reasonable rates at marina; parking included. **Cons:** basic décor; some steps to climb; grounds are nothing too fancy but have great views. *[$] Rooms from: $109 ✉ 1160 Seaway Dr. ☎ 772/468–3555, 800/286–1745 🌐 www.docksideinn.com 🛏 36 rooms 🍴 No meals.*

SPORTS AND THE OUTDOORS

BASEBALL

Tradition Field. Out west by I-95, this Port St. Lucie baseball stadium, formerly known as Digital Domain Park as well as Thomas J. White Stadium, is where the New York Mets train; it's also the home of the St. Lucie Mets minor league team. *✉ 525 N.W. Peacock Blvd., Port St. Lucie ☎ 772/871–2115 🌐 www.stluciemets.com.*

GOLF

PGA Village. Owned and operated by the PGA of America, the national association of teaching pros, PGA Village is the winter home to many northern instructors, along with permanent staff. The facility is a little off the beaten path and the clubhouse is basic, but serious golfers will appreciate the three championship courses by Pete Dye and Tom Fazio and the chance to sharpen their skills at the 35-acre PGA Center for Golf Learning and Performance, which has nine practice bunkers mimicking sands and slopes from around the globe. Between the Fazio-designed Wanamaker Course, the Ryder Course, and the Dye-designed Dye Course, there is a total of 54 holes of championship golf at PGA Village. Beginners can start out on the lesser-known (and easier) PGA Short Course and the Country Club Course. *✉ 1916 Perfect Dr., Port St. Lucie ☎ 772/467–1300, 800/800–4653 🌐 www.pgavillage.com 🎟 $119 for 18 holes ⛳ Wanamaker Course: 18 holes. 7123 yards. par 72. Ryder Course: 18 holes. 7037 yards. par 72. Dye Course: 18 holes. 7279 yards. par 72.*

SCUBA DIVING

The region's premier dive site is actually on the National Register of Historic Places. The *Urca de Lima* was part of the storied treasure fleet bound for Spain that was destroyed by a hurricane in 1715. It's now part of an underwater archaeological preserve about 200 yards from shore, just north of the National Navy UDT-SEAL Museum and under 10 to 15 feet of water. The remains contain a flat-bottom, round-bellied ship and cannons that can be visited on an organized dive trip.

Dive Odyssea. This full-service dive shop offers kayak rentals, tank rentals, and scuba lessons. Guided dive excursions (two-tank dive trips starting at $65) can be arranged to nearby reefs or the Urca de Lima Underwater Archaeological Preserve, a shipwreck from 1715 that's listed on the National Register of Historic Places. This shipwreck was part of the storied treasure fleet bound for Spain that was destroyed by a hurricane in 1715. It's about 200 yards from shore and under 10 to 15 feet of water; the remains contain a flat-bottom, round-bellied ship and cannons. ⊠ *Fort Pierce Inlet, 621 N. 2nd St.* ☎ *772/460–1771* ⊕ *www.diveodyssea.com.*

VERO BEACH AND SEBASTIAN

12 miles north of Fort Pierce.

Tranquil and picturesque, these Indian River County towns have a strong commitment to the environment and culture, particularly to the upscale yet low-key Vero Beach, which is home to eclectic galleries and even trendy restaurants. Sebastian, a coastal fishing village that feels as remote as possible between Jacksonville and Miami Beach, has plenty of outdoor activities—including those at the Sebastian Inlet State Park, one of Florida's biggest and best recreation areas (and a paradise for surfers). It's actually within the boundaries of the federal government's massive protected Archie Carr National Wildlife Refuge, which encompasses several smaller parks within its boundaries. Downtown Vero is centered on the historic district on 14th Avenue, but much of the fun takes place across the Indian River (aka the Intracoastal Waterway) around Orchid Island's beaches.

GETTING HERE AND AROUND

To get here, you have two basic options: Route A1A along the coast (not to be confused with Ocean Drive, an offshoot on Orchid Island), or either U.S. 1 or Route 605 (also called Old Dixie Highway) on the mainland. As you approach Vero on the latter, you pass through an ungussied-up landscape of small farms and residential areas. On the beach route, part of the drive bisects an unusually undeveloped section of the Florida coast. If flying in, consider Orlando International Airport, which is larger (more flights and lower prices) and a smidge closer than Palm Beach International Airport.

ESSENTIALS

Visitor Information Indian River County Chamber of Commerce ⊠ *1216 21st St.* ☎ *772/567–3491* ⊕ *www.indianriverchamber.com.* **Sebastian River Area Chamber of Commerce** ⊠ *700 Main St., Sebastian* ☎ *772/589–5969* ⊕ *www.sebastianchamber.com.*

EXPLORING

Environmental Learning Center. Off of Wabasso Beach Road, the 64 acres here are almost completely surrounded by water. In addition to a 600-foot boardwalk through the mangrove shoreline and a 1-mile canoe trail, there are aquariums filled with Indian River creatures. Boat and kayak trips to see the historic Pelican Island rookery are also on offer. Call or check the center's website for times. ⊠ *255 Live Oak Dr.* ☎ *772/589–5050* ⊕ *www.discoverelc.org* ⊠ *$5* ⊘ *Tues.–Fri. 10–4, Sat. 9–noon (until 4 in winter), Sun. 1–4.*

Fodor'sChoice ★ **McKee Botanical Garden.** On the National Register of Historic Places, the 18-acre plot is a tropical jungle garden—one of the most lush and serene around. This is *the* place to see spectacular water lilies, and the property's original 1932 Hall of Giants, a rustic wooden structure that has stained-glass and bronze bells, contains the world's largest single-plank mahogany table at 35 feet long. There's a Seminole bamboo pavilion, a gift shop, and café, which serves especially tasty snacks and sandwiches. ⊠ *350 U.S. 1* ☎ *772/794–0601* ⊕ *www.mckeegarden.org* ⊠ *$12* ⊘ *Tues.–Sat. 10–5, Sun. noon–5.*

McLarty Treasure Museum. On a National Historic Landmark site on the southern boundary of Sebastian Inlet State Park, this museum underscores the credo, "Wherever gold glitters or silver beckons, man will move mountains." It has displays of coins, weapons, and tools salvaged from the fleet of Spanish treasure ships that sank here in the 1715 storm, leaving some 1,500 survivors struggling to shore between Sebastian and Fort Pierce. The museum sits on the site of the survivors' camp. The museum's last video showing of *The Queen's Jewels and the 1715 Fleet* begins at 3:15. ⊠ *Sebastian Inlet State Park, 13180 Rte. A1A, Sebastian* ☎ *772/589–2147* ⊕ *www.floridastateparks.org/sebastianinlet/activities. cfm* ⊠ *$2* ⊘ *Daily 10–4.*

Mel Fisher's Treasure Museum. You'll really come upon hidden loot when you enter this place operated by the family of late treasure hunter Mel Fisher. See some of what he recovered in 1985 from the Spanish *Atocha* that sank in 1622 and dumped 100,000 gold coins, Colombian emeralds, and 1,000 silver bars into Florida's high seas—and what his team still salvages each year off the Treasure Coast. The museum certainly piques one's curiosity about what is still buried, and the website is all about the quest for more booty. ⊠ *1322 U.S. 1, Sebastian* ☎ *772/589–9875* ⊕ *www.melfisher.com* ⊠ *$6.50* ⊘ *Mon.–Sat. 10–5, Sun. noon–5* ⊘ *Closed Sept.*

Pelican Island National Wildlife Refuge. Founded in 1903 by President Theodore Roosevelt as the country's first national wildlife refuge, the park encompasses the historic Pelican Island rookery itself—a small island in the Indian River Lagoon and important nesting place for 16 species of birds such as endangered wood storks and, of course, brown pelicans—and the land surrounding it overlooking Sebastian. The rookery is a closed wilderness area, so there's no roaming alongside animal kingdom friends; however, there is an 18-foot observation tower across from it with direct views and more than 6 miles of nature trails in the refuge. Another way to explore is via guided kayak tours from the Florida Outdoor Center (⇨ *See listing below*). ⊠ *Rte. A1A, 1 mile north of Treasure Shores Park* ✛ *Take A1A and turn on Historic Jungle Trail* ☎ *772/581–5557* ⊕ *www.fws.gov/pelicanisland* ☑ *Free* ☉ *Daily 7:30–sunset*.

BEACHES

Most of the hotels in the Vero Beach area are clustered around South Beach Park or line Ocean Drive around Beachland Boulevard just north of Humiston Park. Both parks have lifeguards daily. South Beach, at the end of East Causeway Boulevard, is one of the widest, quietest shores on the island, and has plenty of hammock shade before the dunes to picnic in, plus volleyball nets on the beach. Humiston Park is smack-dab in the main commercial zone with restaurants galore, including the lauded Citrus Grillhouse at its southern tip.

Humiston Park. Just south of the Driftwood Resort on Ocean Drive sits Humiston Park, one of the best beaches in town. Parking is free and plentiful, as there's a large lot on Easter Lily Lane and there are spots all over the surrounding business district. The shore is somewhat narrow and there isn't much shade, but the vibrant scene and other amenities make it a great choice for people who crave lots of activity. With lifeguards on call daily, there's a children's playground, plus a ton of hotels, restaurants, bars, and shops within walking distance. **Amenities:** food and drink; lifeguards; showers; toilets, free parking. **Best for:** swimming; partiers; sunsets; walking. ⊠ *3000 Ocean Dr., at Easter Lily La.* ☎ *772/231–5790*.

FAMILY
Fodor'sChoice
★

Sebastian Inlet State Park. The 578-acre park, which spans from the tip of Orchid Island across the passage to the barrier island just north, is one of the Florida park system's biggest draws, especially because of the inlet's highly productive fishing waters. Views from either side of the tall bridge are spectacular, and a unique hallmark is that the gates never close—an amazing feature for die-hard anglers who know snook bite better at night. The park has two entrances, the entrance in Vero Beach and the main entrance in Melbourne (⊠ *9700 Rte. A1A*). Within its grounds, you'll discover a wonderful two-story restaurant that overlooks the ocean, a fish and surfing shop (by the way, this place has some of the best waves in the state, but there are also calmer zones for relaxing swims), two museums, guided sea turtle walks in season, 51 campsites with water and electricity, and a marina with powerboat, kayak, and canoe rentals. **Amenities:** food and drink; parking (fee); showers; toilets; water sports. **Best for:** surfing; sunrise; sunset; walking. ⊠ *14251 N. Rte. A1A* ☎ *321/984–4852* ⊕ *www.floridastateparks.org/ sebastianinlet* ☑ *$8 vehicles with up to 8 people, $4 single drivers, $2 bicyclists and pedestrians* ☉ *Daily 24 hrs (gates never close)*.

FAMILY
Wabasso Beach Park. A favorite for local surfboarding teens and the families at the nearby Disney's Vero Beach Resort, the park is nestled in a residential area at the end of Wabasso Road, about 8 miles up from the action on Ocean Drive and 8 miles below the Sebastian Inlet. Aside from regular amenities like picnic tables, restrooms, and a dedicated parking lot (which really is the "park" here—there's not much green space—and it's quite small, so arrive early), the Disney crowd walks there for its

lifeguards (the strip directly in front of the hotel is unguarded) and the local crowd appreciates its conveniences, like a pizzeria and a store that sells sundries, snacks, and beach supplies. **Amenities:** food and drink; lifeguards; parking (no fee); showers; toilets. **Best for:** swimming; surfing. ⊠ *1820 Wabasso Rd.* ⊙ *Daily 7–sunset.*

WHERE TO EAT

$$$

MODERN
AMERICAN

Fodor'sChoice

★

✕ **Citrus Grillhouse.** There are rooms with a view, and then there's this view: uninterrupted sea from a wraparound veranda at the southern end of Humiston Park. Even better, the food here is a straightforward, delicious celebration of fresh and fabulous. One such dish—the fire-roasted baby squid with grilled lemon, garlic, toasted crouton—is an exercise in restraint that you can't help but gobble up. Speaking of gobble-gobble, the herb-roasted breast of turkey sandwich with arugula, tomato, red onion, and red-wine vinaigrette on a toasted sesame roll is the idyllic light lunch on the beach. Sunset lovers (and bargain hunters) rejoice over the 3-course prix-fixe menu Monday through Thursday from 5 to 6:30 pm. Ⓢ *Average main: $24* ⊠ *Humiston Park, 1050 Easter Lily La.* ☎ *772/234–4114* ⊕ *www.citrusgrillhouse.com* ⊙ *No lunch Sun.*

$$

DINER
FAMILY

✕ **The Lemon Tree.** If Italy had old-school luncheonettes, this is what they'd look like: a storefront of yellow walls, dark-green booths, white linoleum tables, and cascading sconces of faux ivy leaves and hand-painted Tuscan serving pieces for artwork. It's self-described by the husband-and-wife owners (who are always at the front) as an "upscale diner," and locals swear by it for breakfast, lunch, and dinner (breakfast only on Sunday), so expect a short wait in season at peak hours. There's always a treat on the house—like a glass of sorbet to finish lunch—and don't miss the shrimp scampi: the sauce is so good, you'll want to dip every bit of the fresh focaccia in it. Ⓢ *Average main: $20* ⊠ *3125 Ocean Dr.* ⊕ *www.lemontreevero.com* ⊙ *No lunch or dinner Sun. No dinner June–Sept.*

$$$

ECLECTIC

Fodor'sChoice

★

✕ **The Tides.** A charming cottage restaurant west of Ocean Drive prepares some of the best food around—not just in Vero Beach, but all of South Florida. The chefs, classically trained, present a trip around the globe through food, but the setting, although effortlessly elegant (think pale blue coral-printed fabrics and a brick fireplace), is down-to-earth. Putting the crab in crab cake, an appetizer's two jumbo patties have scarcely anything but sweet, fresh flesh; the Southern-inspired corn-and-pepper sauce surrounding them is heavenly. For dinner, the inside-out chicken saltimbocca (rolled up, stuffed, and sliced) hits a high note, and the English pudding dessert is perfectly sticky and sweet. To boot, there's a notable wine list. Ⓢ *Average main: $27* ⊠ *3103 Cardinal Dr.* ☎ *772/234–3966* ⊕ *www.tidesofvero.com* ⌫ *Reservations essential* ⊙ *No lunch.*

WHERE TO STAY

$

HOTEL

⛵ **Capt Hiram's Resort.** Popular with boaters, this Key West–style inn on Sebastian's Riverfront has a lobby embellished with a classic surfboard collection and no-frills guestrooms, all of which have private balconies (and most, oak furnishings). **Pros:** great location for fishing; good price; plenty of amenities. **Cons:** eastern rooms can be noisy; simple décor. $ *Rooms from: $125 ⊠ 1580 U.S. 1, Sebastian* ☎ *772/388–8588* ⊕ *www.hirams.com* ⤳ *67 rooms* ⦿| *No meals.*

$$
RESORT
Fodor's Choice
★

⛱ **Costa d'Este Beach Resort.** This stylish, contemporary boutique hotel in the heart of Vero's bustling Ocean Drive area has a gorgeous infinity pool overlooking the ocean and a distinctly Miami Beach vibe—just like its famous owners, singer Gloria Estefan and producer Emilio Estefan, who bought the property in 2004. **Pros:** all rooms have balconies or secluded patios; huge Italian marble showers; complimentary signature mojitos on arrival. **Cons:** spa is on small side; rooms have only black-out shades; daily resort fee. $ *Rooms from: $239 ⊠ 3244 Ocean Dr.* ☎ *772/562–9919* ⊕ *www.costadeste.com* ⤳ *94 rooms* ⦿| *No meals.*

$
RESORT
FAMILY

⛱ **The Driftwood Resort.** On the National Register of Historic Places, the two original buildings of this 1935 inn were built entirely from ocean-washed timbers; over time more buildings were added, and all are now decorated with such artifacts as ship's bells, Spanish tiles, and a cannon from a 16th-century Spanish galleon, which create a quirky, utterly charming landscape. **Pros:** central location and right on the beach; free Wi-Fi; laundry facilities; weekly treasure hunt is a blast. **Cons:** older property; rooms can be musty; no-frills furnishings. $ *Rooms from: $150 ⊠ 3150 Ocean Dr.* ☎ *772/231–0550* ⊕ *www.verobeachdriftwood.com* ⤳ *100 rooms* ⦿| *No meals.*

$$
RESORT
FAMILY
Fodor's Choice
★

⛱ **Vero Beach Hotel & Spa.** With a sophisticated, relaxed British West Indies feel, this luxurious five-story beachfront hotel at the north end of Ocean Drive is an inviting getaway and, arguably, the best on the Treasure Coast. **Pros:** beautiful pool; daily complimentary wine hour with hors d'oeuvres. **Cons:** separate charge for valet parking; some rooms overlook parking lot. $ *Rooms from: $279 ⊠ 3500 Ocean Dr.* ☎ *772/231–5666* ⊕ *www.verobeachhotelandspa.com* ⤳ *102 rooms* ⦿| *No meals.*

SHOPPING

The place to go when in Vero Beach is **Ocean Drive.** Crossing over to Orchid Island from the mainland, the Merrill P. Barber Bridge turns into Beachland Boulevard; its intersection with Ocean Drive is the heart of a commercial zone with a lively mix of upscale clothing stores, specialty shops, restaurants, and art galleries.

Just under 3 miles north of that roughly eight-block stretch on A1A is a charming outdoor plaza, the **Village Shops.** It's a delight to stroll between the brightly painted cottages that have more unique, high-end offerings.

Back on the mainland, take 21st Street westward and you'll come across a small, modern shopping plaza with some independent shops and national chains. Keep going west on 21st Street, and then park around 14th Avenue to explore a collection of art galleries and eateries in the historic downtown.

SHOPPING CENTERS AND MALLS
Vero Beach Outlets. Need some retail therapy? Just west of I–95 off Route 60 is a discount shopping destination with 50 high-end brand-name stores, including Ann Taylor, Polo Ralph Lauren, Restoration Hardware, White House/Black Market, and Jones New York. ⊠ *1824 94th*

Dr. ✦ On Rte. 60, west of I–95 at Exit 147 ☎ *772/770–6097* ⊕ *www. verobeachoutlets.com.*

SPORTS AND THE OUTDOORS

BOATING AND FISHING

Most of the region's fishing outfitters are based at the Capt. Hiram's Resort marina in Sebastian.

Big Easy Fishing Charters. For over forty years, Big Easy has offered Sebastian off-shore fishing, including guided backwater and deep-sea excursions. ⊠ *Capt Hiram's Resort, 1606 N. Indian River Dr., Sebastian* ☎ *772/538–1072* ⊕ *www.bigeasyfishingcharter.com.*

Sebastian Watercraft Rentals. Based at Capt Hiram's Resort, this rental company has a fleet that ranges from 16-passenger pontoons to jet skis, and the company also organizes fishing charters on the Indian River. ⊠ *Capt Hiram's Resort, 1606 N. Indian River Dr., Sebastian* ☎ *772/589–5560* ⊕ *www.floridawatercraftrentals.com.*

Skipper Sportfishing Charters. Based at the marina at Capt Hiram's Resort, Captain Eric Olsen offers full- and half-day ocean and river fishing trips at $500 and $300, respectively. ⊠ *Capt Hiram's Resort, 1606 N. Indian River Dr., Sebastian* ☎ *772/589–8505* ⊕ *www.skipperfish.com.*

GOLF

Sandridge Golf Club. The Sandridge Golf Club features two public 18-hole courses designed by Ron Garl: the Dunes course, with six holes located on a sand ridge; and the Lakes course, named for—you guessed it—the ubiquitous lakes around the course. The Dunes course, opened in 1987, follows a history-steeped pathway once used during mining operations. The Lakes course, opened in 1992, is renowned for the very challenging, par-4 14th hole with an island green. There's a pro-shop on site offering lessons and clinics. ⊠ *5300 73rd St.* ☎ *772/770–5000* ⊕ *www. sandridgegc.com* 🖾 *$50 for 18 holes.* ⅃ *Dunes course: 18 holes. 6817 yards. par 72. Lakes course: 18 holes. 6181 yards. par 72.*

GUIDED TOURS

Florida Outdoor Center. Guided tours explore the area's natural wonders like the Pelican Island National Wildlife Refuge and begin at only $35 per person. Tours include: Adventure Walk, a Bird Biking Safari, or Wildlife Watching Paddling Excursion. The company is mobile and, therefore, flexible. ☎ *772/202–0220* ⊕ *www.floridaoutdoorcenter.com.*

TRAVEL SMART
SOUTH FLORIDA

GETTING HERE AND AROUND

■ AIR TRAVEL

Average flying times to Miami is about 3 hours from New York, 4 hours from Chicago, 2¾ hours from Dallas, 4½–5½ hours from Los Angeles, and 8–8½ hours from London.

AIRPORTS

Florida has 21 commercial airports, the busiest in South Florica being Miami International Airport (MIA) and Fort Lauderdale–Hollywood International Airport (FLL). Flying to alternative airports can save you both time and money. Fort Lauderdale is close to Miami. FLL is a 30-minute drive from MIA (and as close to certain neighborhoods of Miami).

■**TIP→** Flying to secondary airports can save you money—sometimes even when there are additional ground transportation costs—so price things out before booking. But sometimes one-way car rentals in Florida can be more cost-effective than shared van shuttles.

Airport Information Fort Lauderdale–Hollywood International Airport (FLL). ✉ Fort Lauderdale ☎ 866/435–9355 ⊕ www. broward.org/airport. **Key West International Airport** (EYW). ✉ Key West ☎ 305/809–5200 ⊕ www.eywairport.com. **Miami International Airport** (MIA). ✉ Miami ☎ 305/876–7000 ⊕ www.miami-airport.com. **Palm Beach International Airport** (PBI). ✉ West Palm Beach ☎ 561/471–7420 ⊕ www.pbia.org.

GROUND TRANSPORTATION

There's SuperShuttle service from Miami. That said, most airports have some type of shuttle service or another.

If you book a shuttle from your hotel to the airport, allow at least 24 hours, and expect to be picked up 2½ hours before your scheduled departure.

Cab fares from Florida's larger airports into town can be high. Note that in some cities airport cab fares are a single flat rate; in others, flat-rate fares vary by zone;

and in others still, the fare is determined by the meter. Private car service fares are usually more than taxi fares.

Shuttle Service SuperShuttle ☎ 800/258–3826 ⊕ www.supershuttle.com.

FLIGHTS

AirTran. Miami, Fort Lauderdale, Key West, and West Palm Beach. ☎ 800/247–8726 ⊕ www.airtran.com.

American Airlines. Fort Lauderdale, Key West, Miami, and West Palm Beach. ☎ 800/433–7300 ⊕ www.aa.com.

Delta. Fort Lauderdale, Key West, Miami, and West Palm Beach. ☎ 800/221–1212 for U.S. reservations, 800/241–4141 for international reservations ⊕ www.delta. com.

Frontier. Fort Lauderdale. Charges for a carry-on bag if you don't book on the airline's website. ☎ 800/432–1359 ⊕ www. frontierairlines.com.

JetBlue. Fort Lauderdale, West Palm Beach, and Key West. ☎ 800/538–2583 ⊕ www. jetblue.com.

Southwest. Fort Lauderdale, Key West, and West Palm Beach. ☎ 800/435–9792 ⊕ www.southwest.com.

Spirit Airlines. Fort Lauderdale and West Palm Beach. This is one of a few airlines that charges for a carry-on bag. ☎ 801/401–2200 ⊕ www.spirit.com.

United. Fort Lauderdale, Key West, Miami, and West Palm Beach. ☎ 800/864–8331 for U.S. reservations, 800/538–2929 for international reservations ⊕ www.united. com.

US Airways. Fort Lauderdale, Key West, Miami, and West Palm Beach. ☎ 800/428–4322 for U.S. and Canadian reservations, 800/622–1015 for international reservations ⊕ www.usairways.com.

▌CAR TRAVEL

Three major interstates lead to Florida. I–95 begins in Maine, runs south through the Mid-Atlantic states, and enters Florida just north of Jacksonville. It continues south past Daytona Beach, the Space Coast, Vero Beach, Palm Beach, and Fort Lauderdale, ending in Miami.

I–75 begins in Michigan at the Canadian border and runs south through Ohio, Kentucky, Tennessee, and Georgia, then moves south through the center of the state before veering west into Tampa. It follows the west coast south to Naples, then crosses the state through the northern section of the Everglades, and ends in Miami.

California and most Southern and Southwestern states are connected to Florida by I–10, which moves east from Los Angeles through Arizona, New Mexico, Texas, Louisiana, Mississippi, and Alabama. It enters Florida at Pensacola and runs straight across the northern part of the state, ending in Jacksonville.

RENTAL CARS

Unless you plan to plant yourself at a beach or theme-park resort, you really need a car to get around in most parts of Florida. Rental rates usually start at $35 a day/$160 a week, plus tax ($2 per day), though rates have been going up lately and can more than double during busy periods. In Florida you must be 21 to rent a car, and rates are higher if you're under 25.

ROAD CONDITIONS

Downtown areas of such major cities can be extremely congested during rush hours, usually 7–9 am and 3:30–6:30 pm on weekdays. ▌TIP→ Florida has a website (⊕ www.fl511.com) with real-time traffic information—including details on congestion owing to construction or accidents.

FROM–TO	MILES	HOURS +/-
Fort Lauderdale–Miami	30	0:30
Miami–Naples	125	2:15
Miami–Key Largo	65	1
Miami–Palm Beach	70	1:15
Key Largo–Key West	100	2

RULES OF THE ROAD

Speed limits are generally 60 mph on state highways, 30 mph within city limits and residential areas, and 70 mph on interstates and Florida's turnpike. Be alert for signs announcing exceptions. Children younger than four years old must be strapped into a separate carrier or child seat; children four through five can be secured in a separate carrier, an integrated child seat, or by a seat belt. The driver will be held responsible for passengers under the age of 18 who aren't wearing seat belts, and all front-seat passengers are required to wear seat belts.

Electronic tolls are becoming more common, and there's often no way of paying them in cash. Renting a toll pass may be a good idea in some areas. You can also buy a mini-window transponder for your personal vehicle (and add value to the account) online for $4.99, and this will allow you to get the best rates on tolls. A regular transponder costs $25 and can also be purchased and recharged online.

Florida's Alcohol/Controlled Substance DUI Law is one of the toughest in the United States. A blood-alcohol level of .08 or higher can have serious repercussions even for a first-time offender.

CAR RENTAL RESOURCES

Local Agencies

Continental (Fort Lauderdale and Orlando)	800/221-4085 or 954/332-1125	www.continentalcar.com
Sunshine Rent A Car (Fort Lauderdale)	888/786-7446 or 954/467-8100	www.sunshinerentacar.com

Major Agencies

Alamo	877/222-9075	www.alamo.com
Avis	800/331-1212	www.avis.com
Budget	800/218-7992	www.budget.com
Hertz	800/654-3131	www.hertz.com
National Car Rental	800/227-7368	www.nationalcar.com

▌FERRY TRAVEL

If you would like to avoid traffic to the Keys and make the trip less of a hassle, Key West Express ferries people from Fort Myers Beach on a daily basis (and Marco Island in season) to the historic seaport in Key West. The trip, just under four hours, is much cheaper than airfare, and doesn't require months-in-advance booking.

Contact Key West Express ☎ *888/539-2628* ⊕ *www.keywestexpress.us.*

ESSENTIALS

■ ACCOMMODATIONS

In general, the peak seasons are during the Christmas holidays and late January through Easter in the southern half of the state. Holiday weekends at any point during the year are packed; if you're considering home or condo rentals, minimum-stay requirements go up in these periods, too. Fall is the slowest season, with only a few exceptions (Key West is jam-packed for Fantasy Fest at Halloween). Rates are low and availability is high, but this is also the prime time for hurricanes.

Children are welcome generally everywhere in Florida, except for some Key West B&Bs and Inns; however, the buck stops at spring breakers. While most hotels allow them—and some even cater to them—almost all rental agencies won't lease units to anyone under 25 without a guardian present.

Pets, although allowed at hotels more and more often (one upscale chain, Kimpton, celebrates its pet-friendliness with treats in the lobby and doggie beds for rooms), often carry an extra flat-rate fee for cleaning and de-allergen treatments, and are not a sure thing. Inquire ahead if Fido is coming with you.

APARTMENT AND HOUSE RENTALS

The state's reputation for visiting snowbirds (Northerners who "flock" to Florida in the winter) has caused private home and condo rentals to be a booming business and at times a better option for vacationers, particularly families who want to have some extra space and cooking facilities. In some destinations, home and condo rentals are more readily available than hotels. Fort Myers, for example, doesn't have many luxury hotel properties downtown. Everything aside from beach towels is provided during a stay, but some things to consider are that sizable down payments must be made at booking (15%

to 50%), and the full balance is often due before arrival. Check for any cleaning fees (usually not more than $150). If being on the beach is of utmost importance, carefully screen properties that tout "water views," because they might actually be of bays, canals, or lakes rather than of the Gulf of Mexico or the Atlantic.

Finding a great rental agency can help you weed through the junk. Target offices that specialize in the area you want to visit, and have a personal conversation with a representative as soon as possible. Be honest about your budget and expectations. For example, let the rental agent know if having the living room couch pull double-duty as a bed is not OK. Although websites listing rentals directly from homeowners are growing in popularity, there's a higher chance of coming across Pinocchios advertising "gourmet" kitchens that have one or two nice gadgets but fixtures from 1982. To protect yourself, talk extensively with the owners in advance, see if there's a system in place for accountability should something go wrong, and make sure there's a 24-hour phone number for emergencies.

Contacts Endless Vacation Rentals. Unused time-share units from all major Florida cities and regions. ☎ 877/782-9387 ⊕ www.evrentals.com. **Florida Keys Rental Store.** Florida Keys ☎ 800/585-0584, 305/451-3879 ⊕ www.floridakeysrentalstore. com. **Freewheeler Vacations.** Florida Keys ☎ 866/664-2075, 305/664-2075 ⊕ www. freewheeler-realty.com. **Interhome.** Daytona Beach, Miami, Orlando, Sarasota, Florida Keys, Lower Gulf Coast, Tampa Bay Area ☎ 954/791-8282, 800/882-6864 ⊕ www. interhomeusa.com. **Villas International.** Miami, Orlando, Broward County, Florida Keys, Lower Gulf Coast, Palm Beach County, Tampa Bay Area ☎ 415/499-9490, 800/221-2260 ⊕ www.villasintl.com. **Wyndham Vacation Resorts.** Orlando, Daytona Beach, Broward

County, Panhandle ☎ *800/251–8736* ⊕ *www.
wyndhamvacationresorts.com.*

BED-AND-BREAKFASTS

Small inns and guesthouses in Florida
range from modest, cozy places with
home-style breakfasts and owners who
treat you like family, to elegantly furnished Victorian houses with four-course
breakfasts and rates to match. Since most
B&Bs are small, they rely on various agencies and organizations to get the word out
and to help coordinate reservations.

**Reservation Services BedandBreak-
fast.com** ☎ *512/322–2710, 800/462–2632*
⊕ *www.bedandbreakfast.com.* **Bed & Breakfast Inns Online** ☎ *800/215–7365* ⊕ *www.
bbonline.com.* **Florida Bed & Breakfast Inns**
☎ *561/223–9550* ⊕ *www.florida-inns.com.*

HOTELS AND RESORTS

Wherever you look in Florida, you'll find
lots of plain, inexpensive motels and luxurious resorts, independents alongside
national chains, and an ever-growing
number of modern properties as well as
quite a few classics. All hotels listed have a
private bath unless otherwise noted.

*Hotel reviews have been shortened. For
full reviews, visit Fodors.com.*

▌EATING OUT

Smoking is banned statewide in most
enclosed indoor workplaces, including
restaurants. Exemptions are permitted
for stand-alone bars where food takes a
backseat to the libations.

One caution: Raw oysters are a potential
problem for people with chronic illness of
the liver, stomach, or blood, or who have
immune disorders. All Florida restaurants
that serve raw oysters must post a notice
in plain view warning of the risks associated with consuming them.

FLORIBBEAN FOOD

A true marriage of Floridian, Caribbean,
and Latin cultures yields the homegrown
cuisine known as "Floribbean." (Think
freshly caught fish with tropical fruit

salsa.) A trip to the Tampa area or South
Florida, however, isn't complete without a taste of Cuban food. The cuisine is
heavy, including dishes like *lechon asado*
(roasted pork) that are served in garlic-
based sauces. The two most typical dishes
are *arroz con frijoles* (the staple side dish
of rice and black beans) and *arroz con
pollo* (chicken in sticky yellow rice).

Key West is famous for its key lime pie
(the best is found here) and conch fritters. Stone-crab claws, a South Florida
delicacy, can be savored from October
through May.

MEALS AND MEALTIMES

Unless otherwise noted, you can assume
that the restaurants we recommend are
open daily for lunch and dinner.

RESERVATIONS AND DRESS

We discuss reservations only when they're
essential (there's no other way you'll ever
get a table) or when they're not accepted.
It's always smart to make reservations
when you can, particularly if your party
is large or if it's high season. It's critical
to do so at popular restaurants (book as
far ahead as possible, often 30 days, and
reconfirm on arrival).

We mention dress only when men are
required to wear a jacket or a jacket and
tie. Expect places with dress codes to truly
adhere to them.

Contacts OpenTable ⊕ *www.opentable.com.*

▌HEALTH

Sunburn and heat prostration are concerns, even in winter. So hit the beach or play tennis, golf, or another outdoor sport before 10 am or after 3 pm. If you must be out at midday, limit exercise, drink plenty of nonalcoholic liquids, and wear a hat. If you feel faint, get out of the sun and sip water slowly.

Even on overcast days, ultraviolet rays shine through the haze, so use a sunscreen with an SPF of at least 15, and have children wear a waterproof SPF 30 or higher.

While you're frolicking on the beach, steer clear of what look like blue bubbles on the sand. These are Portuguese men-of-war, and their tentacles can cause an allergic reaction. Also be careful of other large jellyfish, some of which can sting.

If you walk across a grassy area on the way to the beach, you'll probably encounter the tiny, light-brown, incredibly prickly sand spurs. If you get stuck with one, just pull it out.

▌HOURS OF OPERATION

Many museums are closed Monday but have late hours on another weekday and are usually open on weekends. Some museums have a day when admission is free. Popular attractions are usually open every day but Thanksgiving and Christmas Day. Watch out for seasonal closures at smaller venues; we list opening hours for all sights we recommend, but these can change on short notice. If you're visiting during a transitional month (for example, May in the southern part of the state), it's always best to call before showing up.

▌MONEY

Prices here are given for adults. Substantially reduced fees are almost always available for children, students, and senior citizens.

WORD OF MOUTH

Did the food give you shivers of delight or leave you cold? Did the resort look as good in real life as it did in the photos? Did you sleep like a baby, or were the walls paper-thin? Was the service stellar or not up to snuff? Rate and review hotels and restaurants or start a discussion about your favorite (or not so favorite) places on ⊕ www.fodors.com. Your comments might even appear in our books. Yes, you, too, can be a correspondent!

CREDIT CARDS

We cite information about credit cards only if they aren't accepted at a restaurant or a hotel. Otherwise, assume that most major credit cards are acceptable.

Reporting Lost Cards American Express 📠 *800/528–4800* ⊕ *www.americanexpress. com.* **Discover** 📠 *800/347–2683* ⊕ *www. discovercard.com.* **MasterCard** 📠 *800/622– 7747* ⊕ *www.mastercard.com.* **Visa** 📠 *800/847–2911* ⊕ *www.visa.com.*

▌PACKING

Aside from an occasional winter cold spell (when the mercury drops to, say, 50), South Florida is usually warm year-round and extremely humid in summer. Be prepared for sudden storms all over in summer, and note that plastic raincoats are uncomfortable in the high humidity. Often storms are quick, usually in the afternoons, and the sun comes back in no time. (This also means that it's best to get in your beach time earlier in the day; if it's nice in the morning in August, go to the beach. Don't wait.)

Dress is casual throughout the state—sundresses, sandals, or walking shorts are appropriate. Palm Beach is more polos and pearls, Miami is designer jeans, and elsewhere the Tommy Bahama-esque look dominates. Even beach gear is OK at a lot of places, but just make sure you've got a proper outfit on (shirt, shorts, and shoes). A very small number of restaurants request that men wear jackets and ties, but most don't. Where there are dress codes, they tend to be fully adhered to. Funnily enough, the strictest places are golf and tennis clubs. Many ask that you wear whites or at least special sport shoes and attire. Be prepared for air-conditioning working in overdrive anywhere you go.

You can generally swim year-round in South Florida. Bring a sun hat and sunscreen.

▌ SAFETY

Stepped-up policing of thieves who prey on tourists in rental cars has helped address what was a serious issue in the early 1990s. Still, visitors should be wary when driving in strange neighborhoods and leaving the airport, especially in the Miami area. Don't assume that valuables are safe in your hotel room; use in-room safes or the hotel's safety-deposit boxes. Try to use ATMs only during the day or in brightly lighted, well-traveled locales. Don't leave valuables unattended while you walk the beach or go for a dip. And never leave anything of value in a car; thefts from parked cars are on the rise in Florida, and visitors have reported the loss of their belongings while stopped for lunch or dinner as they travel to or from the airport.

If you're visiting Florida during the June through November hurricane season and a hurricane is imminent, be sure to follow directions from local authorities.

▌ TAXES

Florida's sales tax varies by locality but is between 6% and 7.5%. Hotel taxes vary between 11% and 13%. There are also hefty taxes on car rentals of up to 25% of rental rates.

▌ TIME

South Florida is in the Eastern time zone.

▌ TIPPING

Tip airport valets or hotel bellhops $1 to $3 per bag (there is also usually a charge to check bags outside the terminal, but this isn't a tip). Maids should get $1 to $2 per night per guest, more at expensive resorts, left each morning since your cleaner could change from day to day. Room service waiters still receive a 15% tip despite hefty room-service charges and service fees, which don't usually go to the waiters. A doorman or parking valet should get $1 to $3. Waiters should get 15% to 20% (on the before tax amount). Bartenders get $1 or $2 per round of drinks. Golf caddies get 15% of the greens fee.

▌ VISITOR INFORMATION

There are Florida welcome centers on I–10 (near Pensacola), I–75 (near Jennings), I–95 (near Yulee, north of Jacksonville), and U.S. 231 (near Campbellton), and in the lobby of the New Capitol in Tallahassee.

Contact Visit Florida ☎ *850/488–5607, 866/972–5280* ⊕ *www.visitflorida.com.*

INDEX

PHOTO CREDITS

About Our Writers: All photos are courtesy of the writers except for the following: Lynne Helm, courtesy of John Rude.

NOTES

ABOUT OUR WRITERS

After being hired sight unseen by a South Florida newspaper, Fort Lauderdale–based freelance travel writer and editor Lynne Helm arrived from the Midwest anticipating a few years of palm-fringed fun. More than a quarter century later (after covering the state for several newspapers, consumer magazines, and trade publications), she's still enamored of Florida's sun-drenched charms. Lynne updated the Everglades chapter.

Updating the Florida Keys and much of the Lower Gulf Coast is Miami native, Jill Martin. As a freelance writer, she has blogged more than 1,000 articles for the state's tourism website, Visit Florida, and also writes for various travel sites and print magazines. She has appeared on numerous TV and radio shows as a Florida travel expert and is the creator of Sunshine Brain Games, a trivia card game all about Florida. She resides full time in the Redland and part time on Sanibel.

Paul Rubio's quest to discover the world has taken him to 107 countries and counting. Paul graduated from Harvard in 2002 with master's degrees in both Public Administration and Economics, but in 2008 he gave into his passion and became a full-time travel writer. He's won over a dozen national awards for his articles and guidebooks. The prolific writer is the travel editor of *Palm Beach Illustrated, Naples Illustrated,* and *Weddings Illustrated* and regularly contributes to *Ultratravel US, Robb Report, Private Clubs,* and the full family of Modern Luxury publications.